Microsoft Official Academic Course
MICROSOFT WORD 2013

WILEY

Editor	Bryan Gambrel
Executive Publisher	Don Fowley
Director of Sales	Mitchell Beaton
Technical Editor	Joyce Nielsen
Executive Marketing Manager	Chris Ruel
Assistant Marketing Manager	Debbie Martin
Microsoft Strategic Relationships Manager	Gene Longo of Microsoft Learning
Editorial Program Assistant	Allison Winkle
Project Coordinator	Ashley Barth
Senior Content Manager	Kevin Holm
Production Editor	Tim Lindner
Creative Director	Harry Nolan
Cover Designer	Tom Nery
Product Designer	Jennifer Welter
Content Editor	Wendy Ashenberg

This book was set in Garamond by Aptara®, Inc. and printed and bound by Courier/Kendallville. The covers were printed by Courier/Kendallville.

ISBN 978-0-470-13307-1

Printed in the United States of America

10 9 8 7 6 5 4 3 2 1

Foreword from the Publisher

Wiley's publishing vision for the Microsoft Official Academic Course series is to provide students and instructors with the skills and knowledge they need to use Microsoft technology effectively in all aspects of their personal and professional lives. Quality instruction is required to help both educators and students get the most from Microsoft's software tools and to become more productive. Thus our mission is to make our instructional programs trusted educational companions for life.

To accomplish this mission, Wiley and Microsoft have partnered to develop the highest quality educational programs for Information Workers, IT Professionals, and Developers. Materials created by this partnership carry the brand name "Microsoft Official Academic Course," assuring instructors and students alike that the content of these textbooks is fully endorsed by Microsoft, and that they provide the highest quality information and instruction on Microsoft products. The Microsoft Official Academic Course textbooks are "Official" in still one more way—they are the officially sanctioned courseware for Microsoft IT Academy members.

The Microsoft Official Academic Course series focuses on workforce development. These programs are aimed at those students seeking to enter the workforce, change jobs, or embark on new careers as information workers, IT professionals, and developers. Microsoft Official Academic Course programs address their needs by emphasizing authentic workplace scenarios with an abundance of projects, exercises, cases, and assessments.

The Microsoft Official Academic Courses are mapped to Microsoft's extensive research and job-task analysis, the same research and analysis used to create the Microsoft Office Specialist (MOS) exams. The textbooks focus on real skills for real jobs. As students work through the projects and exercises in the textbooks they enhance their level of knowledge and their ability to apply the latest Microsoft technology to everyday tasks. These students also gain resume-building credentials that can assist them in finding a job, keeping their current job, or in furthering their education.

The concept of life-long learning is today an utmost necessity. Job roles, and even whole job categories, are changing so quickly that none of us can stay competitive and productive without continuously updating our skills and capabilities. The Microsoft Official Academic Course offerings, and their focus on Microsoft certification exam preparation, provide a means for people to acquire and effectively update their skills and knowledge. Wiley supports students in this endeavor through the development and distribution of these courses as Microsoft's official academic publisher.

Joe Heider
Senior Vice President, Wiley Global Education

Illustrated Book Tour

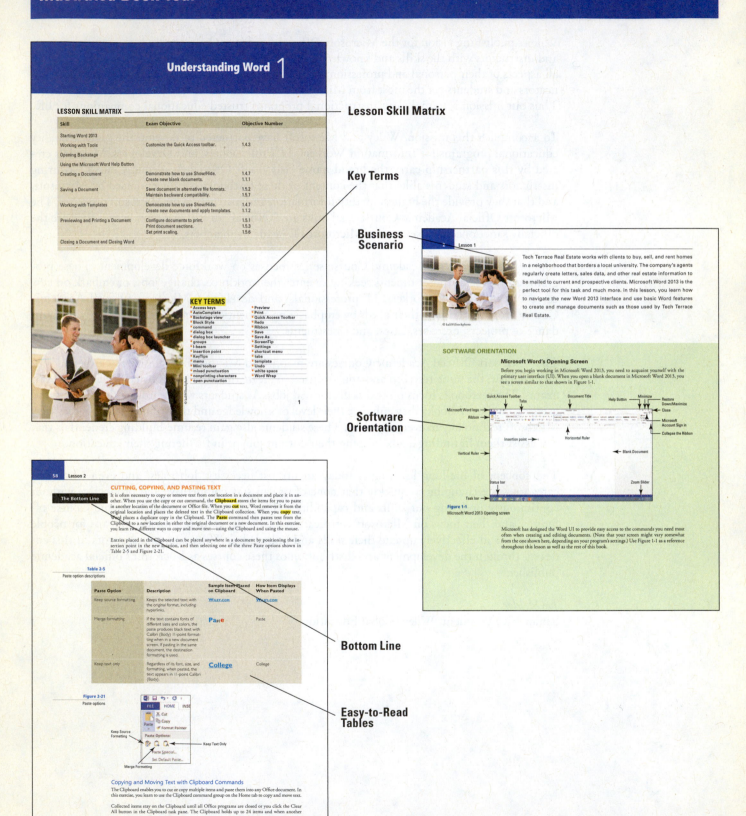

Lesson Skill Matrix

Key Terms

Business Scenario

Software Orientation

Bottom Line

Easy-to-Read Tables

Illustrated Book Tour

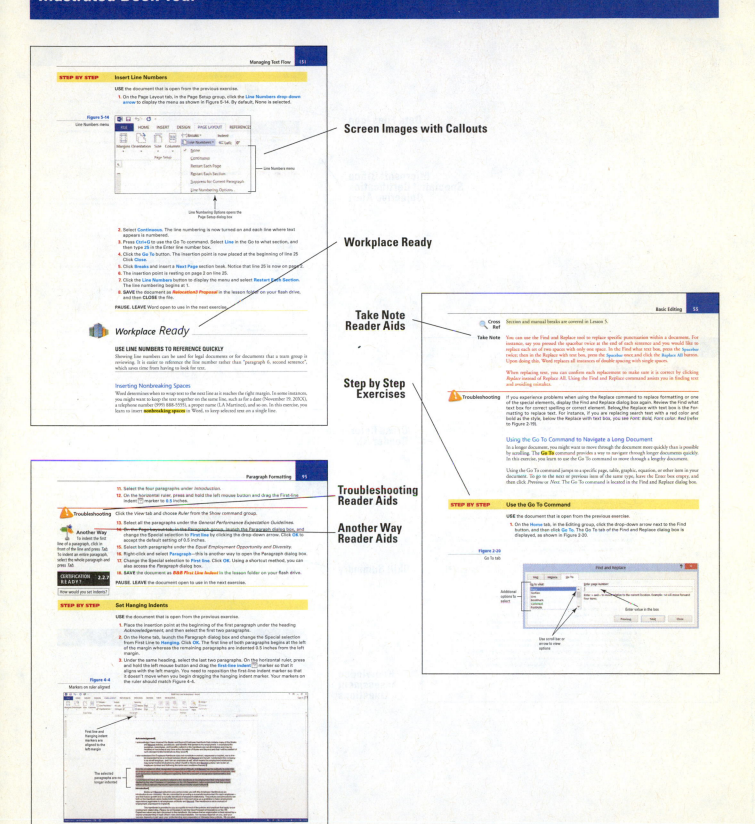

Screen Images with Callouts

Workplace Ready

Take Note Reader Aids

Step by Step Exercises

Troubleshooting Reader Aids

Another Way Reader Aids

Illustrated Book Tour

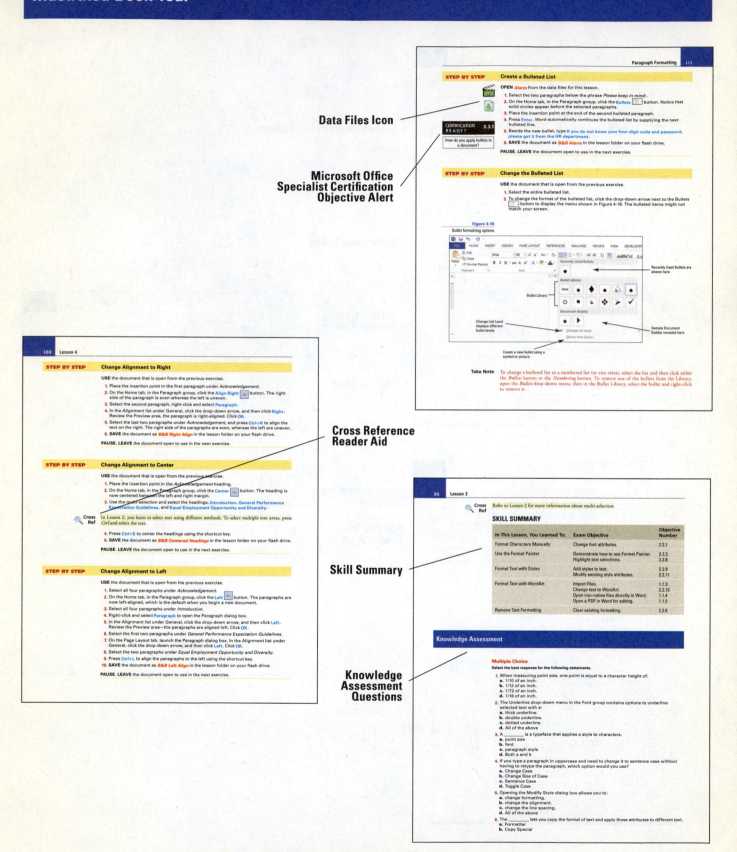

Data Files Icon

Microsoft Office Specialist Certification Objective Alert

Cross Reference Reader Aid

Skill Summary

Knowledge Assessment Questions

www.wiley.com/college/microsoft
or call the MOAC Toll-Free Number: 1+(888) 764-7001 (U.S. & Canada only)

Illustrated Book Tour

Competency Assessment

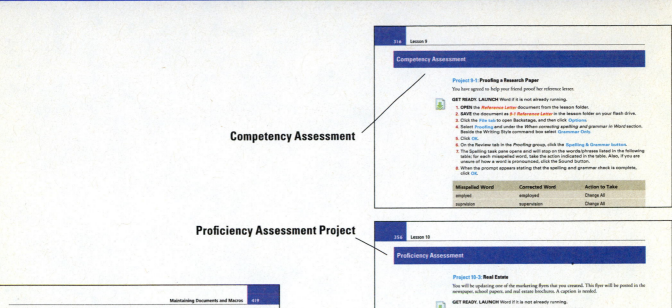

Proficiency Assessment Project

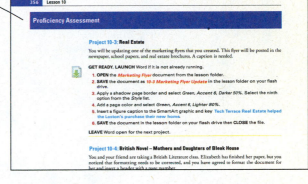

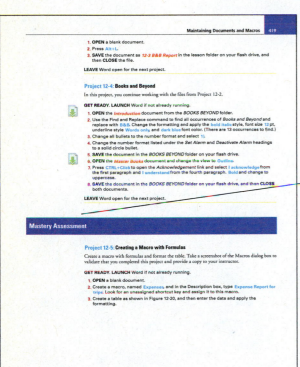

Mastery Assessment Projects

Circling Back Exercises

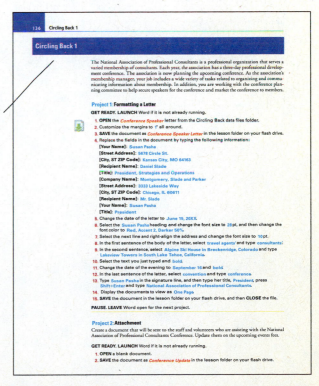

Preface

Welcome to the Microsoft Official Academic Course (MOAC) program for Microsoft Office 2013. MOAC represents the collaboration between Microsoft Learning and John Wiley & Sons, Inc. publishing company. Microsoft and Wiley teamed up to produce a series of textbooks that deliver compelling and innovative teaching solutions to instructors and superior learning experiences for students. Infused and informed by in-depth knowledge from the creators of Microsoft Office and Windows, and crafted by a publisher known worldwide for the pedagogical quality of its products, these textbooks maximize skills transfer in minimum time. Students are challenged to reach their potential by using their new technical skills as highly productive members of the workforce.

Because this knowledgebase comes directly from Microsoft, architect of the Office 2013 system and creator of the Microsoft Office Specialist (MOS) exams (www.microsoft.com/learning/mcp/mcts), you are sure to receive the topical coverage that is most relevant to students' personal and professional success. Microsoft's direct participation not only assures you that MOAC textbook content is accurate and current; it also means that students will receive the best instruction possible to enable their success on certification exams and in the workplace.

THE MICROSOFT OFFICIAL ACADEMIC COURSE PROGRAM

The Microsoft Official Academic Course series is a complete program for instructors and institutions to prepare and deliver great courses on Microsoft software technologies. With MOAC, we recognize that, because of the rapid pace of change in the technology and curriculum developed by Microsoft, there is an ongoing set of needs beyond classroom instruction tools for an instructor to be ready to teach the course. The MOAC program endeavors to provide solutions for all these needs in a systematic manner in order to ensure a successful and rewarding course experience for both instructor and student—technical and curriculum training for instructor readiness with new software releases; the software itself for student use at home for building hands-on skills, assessment, and validation of skill development; and a great set of tools for delivering instruction in the classroom and lab. All are important to the smooth delivery of an interesting course on Microsoft software, and all are provided with the MOAC program. We think about the model below as a gauge for ensuring that we completely support you in your goal of teaching a great course. As you evaluate your instructional materials options, you may wish to use the model for comparison purposes with available products.

PEDAGOGICAL FEATURES

The MOAC courseware for *Microsoft Office 2013 system* are designed to cover all the learning objectives for that MOS exam, which is referred to as its "objective domain." The Microsoft Office Specialist (MOS) exam objectives are highlighted throughout the textbooks. Many pedagogical features have been developed specifically for *Microsoft Official Academic Course* programs. Unique features of our task-based approach include a Lesson Skills Matrix that correlates skills taught in each lesson to the MOS objectives; Certification, and three levels of increasingly rigorous lesson-ending activities: Competency, Proficiency, and Mastery Assessment.

Presenting the extensive procedural information and technical concepts woven throughout the textbook raises challenges for the student and instructor alike. The Illustrated Book Tour that follows provides a guide to the rich features contributing to *Microsoft Official Academic Course* program's pedagogical plan. Following is a list of key features in each lesson designed to prepare students for success on the certification exams and in the workplace:

- Each lesson begins with a **Lesson Skill Matrix**. More than a standard list of learning objectives, the skill matrix correlates each software skill covered in the lesson to the specific MOS exam objective domain.

- Each lesson features a real-world **Business Case** scenario that places the software skills and knowledge to be acquired in a real-world setting.

- Every lesson opens with a **Software Orientation**. This feature provides an overview of the software features students will be working with in the lesson. The orientation will detail the general properties of the software or specific features, such as a ribbon or dialog box; and it includes a large, labeled screen image.

- Concise and frequent **Step-by-Step** instructions teach students new features and provide an opportunity for hands-on practice. Numbered steps give detailed, step-by-step instructions to help students learn software skills. The steps also show results and screen images to match what students should see on their computer screens.

- **Illustrations**: Screen images provide visual feedback as students work through the exercises. The images reinforce key concepts, provide visual clues about the steps, and allow students to check their progress.

- **Key Terms:** Important technical vocabulary is listed at the beginning of the lesson. When these terms are used later in the lesson, they appear in bold italic type with yellow highlighter and are defined. The Glossary contains all of the key terms and their definitions.

- Engaging point-of-use **Reader aids**, located throughout the lessons, tell students why this topic is relevant (*The Bottom Line*), provide students with helpful hints (*Take Note*), or show alternate ways to accomplish tasks (*Another Way*), or point out things to watch out for or avoid (*Troubleshooting*). Reader aids also provide additional relevant or background information that adds value to the lesson.

- **Certification Ready?** features throughout the text signal students where a specific certification objective is covered. They provide students with a chance to check their understanding of that particular MOS exam objective and, if necessary, review the section of the lesson where it is covered. MOAC provides complete preparation for MOS certification.

- **Workplace Ready.** These new features preview how the Microsoft Office 2013 system applications are used in real-world situations.

- Each lesson ends with a **Skill Summary** recapping the topics and MOS exam skills covered in the lesson.

- **Knowledge Assessment:** Provides a total of 20 questions from a mix of True/False, Fill-in-the-Blank, Matching or Multiple Choice testing students on concepts learned in the lesson.

- **Competency, Proficiency, and Mastery Assessment:** provide three progressively more challenging lesson-ending activities.

- **Circling Back:** These integrated projects provide students with an opportunity to renew and practice skills learned in previous lessons.

- **Online files:** The student companion website contains the data files needed for each lesson. These files are indicated by the file download icon in the margin of the textbook.

Conventions and Features Used in This Book

This book uses particular fonts, symbols, and heading conventions to highlight important information or to call your attention to special steps. For more information about the features in each lesson, refer to the Illustrated Book Tour section.

Convention	Meaning
Bottom Line	This feature provides a brief summary of the material to be covered in the section that follows.
CLOSE	Words in all capital letters indicate instructions for opening, saving, or closing files or programs. They also point out items you should check or actions you should take.
CERTIFICATION READY?	This feature signals the point in the text where a specific certification objective is covered. It provides you with a chance to check your understanding of that particular MOS objective and, if necessary, review the section of the lesson where it is covered.
Take Note	Reader aids appear in shaded boxes found in your text. Take Note provides helpful hints related to particular tasks or topics.
Another Way	Another Way provides an alternative procedure for accomplishing a particular task.
Cross Ref	These notes provide pointers to information discussed elsewhere in the textbook or describe interesting features that are not directly addressed in the current topic or exercise.
ALT + Tab	A plus sign (+) between two key names means that you must press both keys at the same time. Keys that you are instructed to press in an exercise will appear in the font shown here.
A **shared printer** can be used by many individuals on a network.	Key terms appear in bold italic.
Key **My Name is**	Any text you are asked to key appears in color.
Click **OK**	Any button on the screen you are supposed to click on or select will also appear in color.
	The names of data files will appear in bold, italic and red for easy identification. These data files are available for download from the Student Companion Site (www.Wiley.com/college/Microsoft).
	Step-by-step tutorial videos are available for many of the activities throughout this course. For information on how to access these videos, see the Student Companion Site (www.Wiley.com/college/Microsoft).
OPEN *BudgetWorksheet1*	The names of data files will appear in bold, italic and red for easy identification.

Instructor Support Program

The *Microsoft Official Academic Course* programs are accompanied by a rich array of resources that incorporate the extensive textbook visuals to form a pedagogically cohesive package. These resources provide all the materials instructors need to deploy and deliver their courses. Resources available online for download include:

- The **Instructor's Guide** contains Solutions to all the textbook exercises as well as chapter summaries and lecture notes. The Instructor's Guide and Syllabi for various term lengths are available from the Instructor's Book Companion site (www.wiley.com/college/microsoft).

- The **Solution Files** for all the projects in the book are available online from our Instructor's Book Companion site (www.wiley.com/college/microsoft).

- The **Test Bank** contains hundreds of questions organized by lesson in multiple-choice, true-false, short answer, and essay formats and is available to download from the Instructor's Book Companion site (www.wiley.com/college/microsoft). A complete answer key is provided.

  This title's test bank is available for use in Respondus' easy-to-use software. You can download the test bank for free using your Respondus, Respondus LE, or StudyMate Author software.

  Respondus is a powerful tool for creating and managing exams that can be printed to paper or published directly to Blackboard, WebCT, Desire2Learn, eCollege, ANGEL and other eLearning systems.

- **Test Bank Projects.** Two projects for each lesson are provided on the Instructor's Book Companion Site as well as solution files suitable for grading with OfficeGrader. These projects cover topics from within one specific lesson.

- **Comprehensive Projects:** Two comprehensive projects are provided on the Instructor's Book Companion Site for each Circling Back These projects cover topics from all lessons in the book up to that point. Solution files suitable for grading with OfficeGrader are also provided.

- **Capstone Projects:** Two capstone projects are provided with the final Circling Back on the Instructor's Book Companion Site. These projects are suitable for a final exam or final project for the course. These projects cover a range of topics from throughout the entire book. Solution files suitable for grading with OfficeGrader are also provided.

- **PowerPoint Presentations and Images**. A complete set of PowerPoint presentations is available on the Instructor's Book Companion site (www.wiley.com/college/microsoft) to enhance classroom presentations. Tailored to the text's topical coverage and Skills Matrix, these presentations are designed to convey key Microsoft .NET Framework concepts addressed in the text.

  All figures from the text are on the Instructor's Book Companion site (www.wiley.com/college/microsoft). You can incorporate them into your PowerPoint presentations, or create your own overhead transparencies and handouts.

  By using these visuals in class discussions, you can help focus students' attention on key elements of Windows Server and help them understand how to use it effectively in the workplace.

- **Office Grader** automated grading system allows you to easily grade student data files in Word, Excel, PowerPoint or Access format, against solution files. Save tens or hundreds of hours each semester with automated grading. More information on OfficeGrader is available from the Instructor's Book Companion site (www.wiley.com/college/microsoft).

- The **Student Data Files** are available online on both the Instructor's Book Companion Site and for students on the Student Book Companion Site.

- Wiley **Faculty Network:** When it comes to improving the classroom experience, there is no better source of ideas and inspiration than your fellow colleagues. The Wiley Faculty Network connects teachers with technology, facilitates the exchange of best practices, and helps to enhance instructional efficiency and effectiveness. Faculty Network activities include technology training and tutorials, virtual seminars, peer-to-peer exchanges of experiences and ideas, personal consulting, and sharing of resources. For details visit www.WhereFacultyConnect.com.

IMPORTANT WEB ADDRESSES AND PHONE NUMBERS

To locate the Wiley Higher Education Rep in your area, go to the following Web address and click on the "*Contact Us*" link at the top of the page.

www.wiley.com/college

Or Call the MOAC Toll Free Number: 1 + (888) 764-7001 (U.S. & Canada only).

To learn more about becoming a Microsoft Certified Professional and exam availability, visit **www.microsoft.com/learning/mcp.**

DREAMSPARK PREMIUM

Free 3-Year Membership available to Qualified Adopters

DreamSpark Premium is designed to provide the easiest and most inexpensive way for schools to make the latest Microsoft developer tools, products, and technologies available in labs, classrooms, and on student PCs. DreamSpark Premium is an annual membership program for departments teaching Science, Technology, Engineering, and Mathematics (STEM) courses. The membership provides a complete solution to keep academic labs, faculty, and students on the leading edge of technology.

Software available through the DreamSpark Premium program is provided at no charge to adopting departments through the Wiley and Microsoft publishing partnership.

Contact your Wiley rep for details.

For more information about the DreamSpark Premium program, go to www.microsoft.com

Student Support Program

BOOK COMPANION WEBSITE (WWW.WILEY.COM/COLLEGE/MICROSOFT)

The students' book companion site for the MOAC series includes any resources, exercise files, and web links that will be used in conjunction with this course.

WILEY E-TEXT: POWERED BY VITALSOURCE

When you choose a Wiley E-Text you not only save money; you benefit from being able to access course materials and content anytime, anywhere through a user experience that makes learning rewarding.

With the Wiley E-Text you will be able to easily:
• Search
• Take notes
• Highlight key materials
• Have all your work in one place for more efficient studying

In addition, the Wiley E-Text is fully portable. Students can access it online and download to their computer for off line access and access read and study on their device of preference—computer, tablet, or smartphone.

WHY MOS CERTIFICATION?

Microsoft Office Specialist (MOS) 2013 is a valuable credential that recognizes the desktop computing skills needed to use the full features and functionality of the Microsoft Office 2013 suite.

In the worldwide job market, Microsoft Office Specialist is the primary tool companies use to validate the proficiency of their employees in the latest productivity tools and technology, helping them select job candidates based on globally recognized standards for verifying skills. The results of an independent research study show that businesses with certified employees are more productive compared to non-certified employees and that certified employees bring immediate value to their jobs.

In academia, as in the business world, institutions upgrading to Office 2013 may seek ways to protect and maximize their technology investment. By offering certification, they validate that decision—because powerful Office 2013 applications such as Word, Excel and PowerPoint can be effectively used to demonstrate increases in academic preparedness and workforce readiness.

Individuals seek certification to increase their own personal sense of accomplishment and to create advancement opportunities by establishing a leadership position in their school or department, thereby differentiating their skill sets in a competitive college admissions and job market.

PREPARING TO TAKE THE MICROSOFT OFFICE SPECIALIST (MOS) EXAM

The Microsoft Office Specialist credential has been upgraded to validate skills with the Microsoft Office 2013 system. The MOS certifications target information workers and cover the most popular business applications such as Word 2013, Excel 2013, PowerPoint 2013, Outlook 2013 and Access 2013.

By becoming certified, you demonstrate to employers that you have achieved a predictable level of skill in the use of a particular Office application. Employers often require certification either as a condition of employment or as a condition of advancement within the company or other organization. The certification examinations are sponsored by Microsoft but administered through exam delivery partners like Certiport.

To learn more about becoming a Microsoft Office Specialist and exam availability, visit http://www.microsoft.com/learning/en/us/mos-certification.aspx.

Preparing to Take an Exam

Unless you are a very experienced user, you will need to use a test preparation course to prepare to complete the test correctly and within the time allowed. The *Microsoft Official Academic Course* series is designed to prepare you with a strong knowledge of all exam topics, and with some additional review and practice on your own. You should feel confident in your ability to pass the appropriate exam.

After you decide which exam to take, review the list of objectives for the exam. This list can be found in the MOS Objectives Appendix at the back of this book. You can also easily identify tasks that are included in the objective list by locating the Lesson Skill Matrix at the start of each lesson and the Certification Ready sidebars in the margin of the lessons in this book.

To take the MOS test, visit http://www.microsoft.com/learning/en/us/mos-certification.aspx to locate your nearest testing center. Then call the testing center directly to schedule your test. The amount of advance notice you should provide will vary for different testing centers, and it typically depends on the number of computers available at the testing center, the number of other testers who have already been scheduled for the day on which you want to take the test, and the number of times per week that the testing center offers MOS testing. In general, you should call to schedule your test at least two weeks prior to the date on which you want to take the test.

When you arrive at the testing center, you might be asked for proof of identity. A driver's license or passport is an acceptable form of identification. If you do not have either of these items of documentation, call your testing center and ask what alternative forms of identification will be accepted. If you are retaking a test, bring your MOS identification number, which will have been given to you when you previously took the test. If you have not prepaid or if your organization has not already arranged to make payment for you, you will need to pay the test-taking fee when you arrive.

Test Format

MOS exams are Exams are primarily performance-based and conducted in a "live," or simulated, environment. Exam candidates taking exams for MOS 2007 or 2010 are asked to perform a series of tasks to clearly demonstrate their skills. For example, a Word exam might ask a user to balance newspaper column lengths or keep text together in columns. The new MOS 2013 exam format presents a short project the candidate must complete, using the specifications provided. This creates a real-world testing experience for candidates. All MOS exams must be completed in 90 minutes or less.

Student Data Files

All of the practice files that you will use as you perform the exercises in the book are available for download on our student companion site. By using the practice files, you will not waste time creating the samples used in the lessons, and you can concentrate on learning how to use Microsoft Office 2013. With the files and the step-by-step instructions in the lessons, you will learn by doing, which is an easy and effective way to acquire and remember new skills.

COPYING THE PRACTICE FILES

Your instructor might already have copied the practice files before you arrive in class. However, your instructor might ask you to copy the practice files on your own at the start of class. Also, if you want to work through any of the exercises in this book on your own at home or at your place of business after class, you may want to copy the practice files.

1. OPEN Internet Explorer.
2. In Internet Explorer, go to the student companion site: **www.wiley.com**
3. Search for your book title in the upper right hand corner
4. On the Search Results page, locate your book and click on the **Visit the Companion Sites** link.
5. Select **Student Companion Site** from the pop-up box.
6. From the menu, select the **arrow** next to Browse By Resource and select **Student Data Files** from the menu.
7. A new screen will appear.
8. On the Student Data Files page, you can select to download files for just one lesson or for all lessons. Click on the file of your choice.
9. On the File Download dialog box, select **Save As** to save the data files to your external drive (often called a ZIP drive or a USB drive or a thumb drive) or a local drive.
10. In the Save As dialog box, select a local drive in the left-hand panel that you'd like to save your files to; again, this should be an external drive or a local drive. Remember the drive name that you saved it to.

Acknowledgments

We would like to thank the many instructors and reviewers who pored over the Microsoft Official Academic Course series design, outlines and manuscript, providing invaluable feedback in the service of quality instructional materials.

Erik Amerikaner, *Oak Park Unified*

Connie Aragon, *Seattle Central Community College*

Sue Bajt, *Harper College*

Gregory Ballinger, *Miami-Dade College*

Catherine Bradfield, *DeVry University*

DeAnnia Clements, *Wiregrass Georgia Technical College*

Mary Corcoran, *Bellevue College*

Andrea Cluff, *Freemont High School*

Caroline de Gruchy, *Conestoga College*

Janis DeHaven, *Central Community College*

Rob Durrance, *East Lee County High School*

Janet Flusche, *Frenship High School*

Greg Gardiner, *SIAST*

Debi Griggs, *Bellevue College*

Phil Hanney, *Orem Junior High School*

Portia Hatfield, *Tennessee Technology Center-Jacksboro*

Dee Hobson, *Richland College*

Terri Holly, *Indian River State College*

Kim Hopkins, *Weatherford College*

Sandra Jolley, *Tarrant County College*

Keith Hoell, *Briarcliffe College*

Joe LaMontagne, *Davenport University*

Tanya MacNeil, *American InterContinental University*

Donna Madsen, *Kirkwood Community College*

Lynn Mancini, *Delaware Technical Community College*

Edward Martin, *Kingsborough Community College-City University of New York*

Lisa Mears, *Palm Beach State College*

Denise Merrell, *Jefferson Community and Technical College*

Diane Mickey, *Northern Virginia Community College*

Robert Mike, *Alaska Career College*

Cynthia Miller, *Harper College*

Sandra Miller, *Wenatchee Valley College*

Mustafa Muflehi, *The Sheffield College*

Aditi Mukherjee, *University of Florida—Gainesville*

Linda Nutter, *Peninsula College*

Diana Pack, *Big Sandy Community & Technical College*

Bettye Parham, *Daytona State College*

Tatyana Pashnyak, *Bainbridge State College*

Kari Phillips, *Davis Applied Technical College*

www.wiley.com/college/microsoft
or call the MOAC Toll-Free Number: 1+(888) 764-7001 (U.S. & Canada only)

Michelle Poertner, *Northwestern Michigan College*

Barbara Purvis, *Centura College*

Dave Rotherham, *Sheffield Hallam University*

Theresa Savarese, *San Diego City College*

Janet Sebesy, *Cuyahoga Community College-Western*

Lourdes Sevilla, *Southwestern College*

Elizabeth Snow, *Southwest Florida College*

Denise Spence, *Dunbar High School*

Amy Stolte, *Lincoln Land Community College*

Linda Silva, *El Paso Community College*

Dorothy Weiner, *Manchester Community College*

We would also like to thank the team at Microsoft Learning Xperiences (LeX), including Alison Cunard, Tim Sneath, Zubair Murtaza, Keith Loeber, Rob Linsky, Anne Hamilton, Wendy Johnson, Gene Longo, Julia Stasio, and Josh Barnhill for their encouragement and support in making the Microsoft Official Academic Course programs the finest academic materials for mastering the newest Microsoft technologies for both students and instructors. Finally we would like to thank Jeff Riley and his team at Box Twelve Communications, Laura Town and her team at WilliamsTown Communications, Debbie Collins and Sandy DuBose for their editorial and technical assistance.

We would like to thank the following instructors for their contributions to particular titles in the series as well:

ACCESS 2013

Catherine Bradfield, *DeVry University*

Mary Corcoran, *Bellevue College*

Cynthia Miller, *Harper College*

Aditi Mukherjee, *University of Florida—Gainesville*

Elizabeth Snow, *Southwest Florida College*

EXCEL 2013

Catherine Bradfield, *DeVry University*

DeAnnia Clements, *Wiregrass Georgia Technical College*

Dee Hobson, *Richland College*

Sandra Jolley, *Tarrant County College*

Joe Lamontagne, *Davenport University*

Edward Martin, *Kingsborough Community College-City University of New York*

Aditi Mukherjee, *University of Florida—Gainesville*

Linda Nutter, *Peninsula College*

Dave Rotherham, *Sheffield Hallam University*

POWERPOINT 2013

Mary Corcoran, *Bellevue College*

Rob Durrance, *East Lee County High School*

Phil Hanney, *Orem Junior High School*

Terri Holly, *Indian River State College*

Kim Hopkins, *Weatherford College*
Tatyana Pashnyak, *Bainbridge State College*
Michelle Poertner, *Northwestern Michigan College*
Theresa Savarese, *San Diego City College*

WORD 2013

Erik Amerikaner, *Oak Park Unified*
Sue Bajt, *Harper College*
Gregory Ballinger, *Miami-Dade College*
Andrea Cluff, *Freemont High School*
Caroline de Gruchy, *Conestoga College*
Donna Madsen, *Kirkwood Community College*
Lynn Mancini, *Delaware Technical Community College*
Denise Merrell, *Jefferson Community and Technical College*
Diane Mickey, *Northern Virginia Community College*
Robert Mike, *Alaska Career College*
Bettye Parham, *Daytona State College*
Barbara Purvis, *Centura College*
Janet Sebesy, *Cuyahoga Community College-Western*
Dorothy Weiner, *Manchester Community College*

Author Credits

LINDA SILVA

Linda has been teaching for nineteen years and has been working at El Paso Community College for more than thirty-seven years. She is currently a full-time faculty member with the Business Management program—of which she was formerly the district-wide coordinator. El Paso Community College has five campuses to serve the educational needs of the community population; it has been recognized as the fastest-growing community college in Texas and the largest grantor of associate degrees to Hispanic students in the nation. Linda believes that EPCC is "the best place to start" and "the best place to continue."

The Business Management program has adopted textbooks from the MOAC series; the students enrolled in the program are highly encouraged to take Microsoft application software courses (Word, Excel, PowerPoint, Access, and Outlook), which prepare them for the Microsoft Office Specialist exams. Linda takes the exams ahead of her students and challenges them to beat her score. Linda enjoys the art of innovative teaching, and when she is not teaching enjoys taking on new and exciting challenges.

Her family continues to provide her support, especially when she was working on the Word 2010 and 2013 books. This book is dedicated to her mom, Miriam, and in memory her dad, Santiago, who provided her love and support in achieving her dreams. Special thank you to her sisters, Dorothy, Hazel, Josie, and brother Sonny; and son, David, who provided her with love, inspiration, and encouragement.

Brief Contents

Contents

Lesson 1: Understanding Word

© kali9/iStockphoto

Lesson 2: Basic Editing

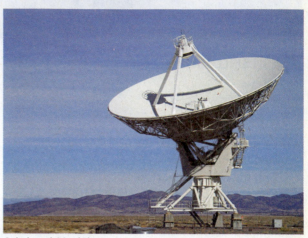

© duckycards/iStockphoto

Lesson 3: Character Formatting

© bowdenimages/iStockphoto

Lesson 4: Paragraph Formatting

© mbtphotos/iStockphoto

Lesson 5: Managing Text Flow

© Yuri_Arcurs/istockphoto

Lesson 6: Creating Tables

© NathanGleave/iStockphoto

www.wiley.com/college/microsoft
or call the MOAC Toll-Free Number: 1+(888) 764-7001 (U.S. & Canada only)

Lesson 7: Working with Themes, Style Sets, Backgrounds, Quick Parts, and Text Boxes

© nyul/iStockphoto

Lesson 8: Using Illustrations and Graphics

© majana/iStockphoto

Lesson 9: Proofing Documents

© spooh/iStockphoto

Lesson 10: Formatting a Research Paper

© Viorika/iStockphoto

Lesson 11: Performing Mail Merges

© kyoshino/iStockphoto

Lesson 12: Maintaining Documents and Macros

© Photomorphic/iStockphoto

Lesson 13: Protecting and Sharing Documents

© youngvet/iStockphoto

Lesson 14: Using Advanced Options

© GlobalStock/iStockphoto

LESSON SKILL MATRIX

Skill	Exam Objective	Objective Number
Starting Word 2013		
Working with Tools	Customize the Quick Access toolbar.	1.4.3
Opening Backstage		
Using the Microsoft Word Help Button		
Creating a Document	Demonstrate how to use Show/Hide. Create new blank documents.	1.4.7 1.1.1
Saving a Document	Save document in alternative file formats. Maintain backward compatibility.	1.5.2 1.5.7
Working with Templates	Demonstrate how to use Show/Hide. Create new documents and apply templates.	1.4.7 1.1.2
Previewing and Printing a Document	Configure documents to print. Print document sections. Set print scaling.	1.5.1 1.5.3 1.5.6
Closing a Document and Closing Word		

© kali9/iStockphoto

KEY TERMS

- Access keys
- AutoComplete
- Backstage view
- Block Style
- command
- dialog box
- dialog box launcher
- groups
- I-beam
- insertion point
- KeyTips
- menu
- Mini toolbar
- mixed punctuation
- nonprinting characters
- open punctuation
- Preview
- Print
- Quick Access Toolbar
- Redo
- Ribbon
- Save
- Save As
- ScreenTip
- Settings
- shortcut menu
- tabs
- template
- Undo
- white space
- Word Wrap

© kali9/iStockphoto

Tech Terrace Real Estate works with clients to buy, sell, and rent homes in a neighborhood that borders a local university. The company's agents regularly create letters, sales data, and other real estate information to be mailed to current and prospective clients. Microsoft Word 2013 is the perfect tool for this task and much more. In this lesson, you learn how to navigate the new Word 2013 interface and use basic Word features to create and manage documents such as those used by Tech Terrace Real Estate.

SOFTWARE ORIENTATION

Microsoft Word's Opening Screen

Before you begin working in Microsoft Word 2013, you need to acquaint yourself with the primary user interface (UI). When you open a blank document in Microsoft Word 2013, you see a screen similar to that shown in Figure 1-1.

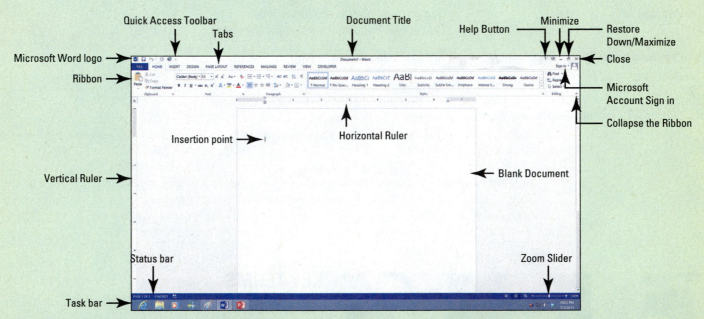

Figure 1-1
Microsoft Word 2013 Opening screen

Microsoft has designed the Word UI to provide easy access to the commands you need most often when creating and editing documents. (Note that your screen might vary somewhat from the one shown here, depending on your program's settings.) Use Figure 1-1 as a reference throughout this lesson as well as the rest of this book.

STARTING WORD 2013

Microsoft Word is a word processing tool for creating different types of documents that are used in the work and school environment. The appearance of Microsoft Word 2013 is similar to Word 2010 but with more enhanced features. It contains a new look for the Word ▇ icon, a customized Office Background that appears above the Ribbon, live access to your SkyDrive account, an option to work in Read Mode, tab text that appears blue when active, the status bar displays in a blue background, and many more exciting new features. When you first launch Word, it opens with the Recent screen displayed. This screen allows you to create a new document from either a blank document or from a template. And when you exit a document and later return, Word 2013 resumes where you left off.

Starting Word

In this exercise, you learn how to start Word using Windows 8 or Windows 7.

For instructional purposes, Windows 8 will be used to begin working in Word 2013. Microsoft Windows 8 is the latest operating system that interacts with your desktop, laptop, or touch-screen devices, such as a touch-screen monitor or tablet. Steps on using Windows 7 to start Word 2013 also are discussed.

When using Windows 8, the screen you see is called the *Windows Start screen* (see Figure 1-2). You can choose which application to begin by using your mouse or, if you have a touch-screen monitor, tap the application you want to begin. The Start screen provides access to mail, SkyDrive, Internet Explorer, photos, games, music, video, and of course the latest version of the Microsoft Office applications. Tablets with Windows RT and the Office 2013 applications installed can be customized the same way as your desktop.

If you don't have Office 2013 installed on your computing device, you can still create, view, and perform simple edits on Word documents using an online Word Web App. Office Web Apps are available for Word, Excel, PowerPoint, and OneNote. Office Web Apps are launched using a web browser, such as Internet Explorer. One of the differences between the Word Web App and the Word 2013 application installed on your computer is the number of features available. The Word Web App allows you to create, open, and edit documents with only the most basic commands. It is a wonderful way to create a simple document and share it. The main advantage of using the Word 2013 application installed on your computer is having full access to all the features to create a professional-looking document. If you use the Word Web App, you will not be able to complete all the exercises in this book, because it does not include all the features we cover.

Microsoft has an online storage space referred to as the *Cloud*. You are provided with 7 GB of free online storage space and are able to share and manage your documents with anyone. Before you can use this, you need to create a Microsoft account profile. Once you create your account, you will find it easy to share and manage your documents with others.

Windows 8 works seamlessly with Office 2013. In the upper-right corner of the Windows 8 screen, it displays your Microsoft account profile once your account is activated. If you are logged on to your Microsoft account, it appears in the same location in each of the Office 2013 applications. Microsoft has made it easier for you to continue working on your documents at any computer and reminds you where you left off.

To begin using Word 2013, locate the Word icon and click the left mouse button or, if you are using a touch-screen monitor, tap the icon.

If your school is operating on Windows 7, launch Word 2013 by double-clicking the Word program icon on your desktop or by choosing Microsoft Word 2013 from the Start menu.

When Word is launched, the program opens with the *new* Word 2013 screen (see Figure 1-3). On the left side of the screen under Recent, you see a list of documents that have been accessed recently. The right window pane displays a blank document page and several templates to create customized documents. To create a blank document, click the Blank document page and Word will open.

The blinking **insertion point** in the upper-left corner of this document is where you begin creating your text. When you place your cursor near it, the insertion point changes to a large "I," which is called the **I-beam**.

Take Note   The lessons in this book are created using the Windows 8 operating system. If your computer is running the Windows 7 operating system, some screenshots and steps might appear slightly different than those provided in this book.

STEP BY STEP   **Start Word**

GET READY. Before you begin these steps, be sure to turn on and/or log on to your computer.

1. From the Start screen of Windows 8 (see Figure 1-2), locate Word 2013 and click the icon . For Windows 7 users, locate the Windows task bar, click the **Start** button, and then click **All Programs**. A menu of installed programs appears. Click the **Microsoft Office** folder. Next click **Microsoft Word 2013**. The new Word 2013 screen opens.

Figure 1-2

New Start screen

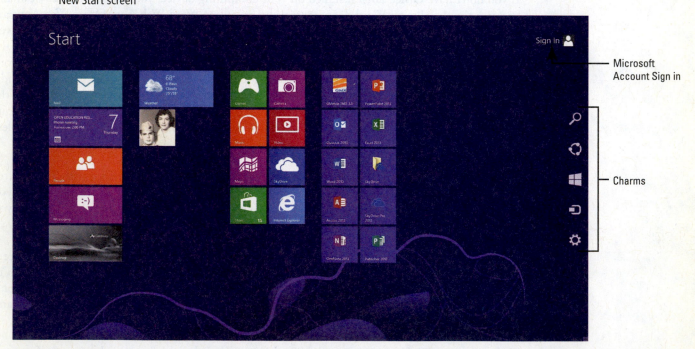

2. The new Word 2013 screen appears (see Figure 1-3). On the left side of the screen, you see the recent documents that have been accessed, and the right side displays the blank document page and templates.

Figure 1-3

Word 2013 window

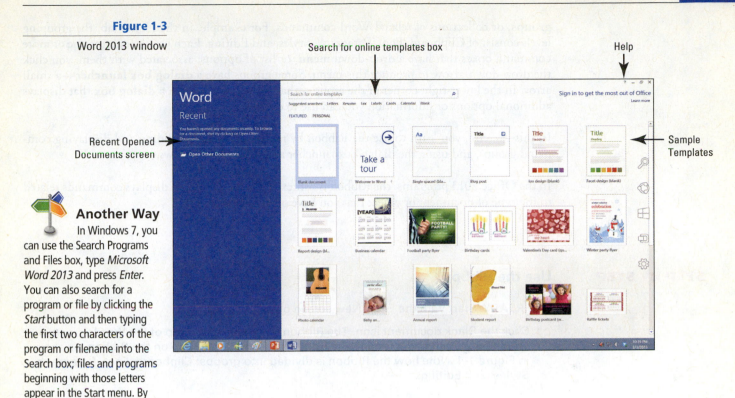

Search for online templates box

Help

Recent Opened Documents screen →

Sample Templates

Another Way

In Windows 7, you can use the Search Programs and Files box, type *Microsoft Word 2013* and press *Enter*. You can also search for a program or file by clicking the *Start* button and then typing the first two characters of the program or filename into the Search box; files and programs beginning with those letters appear in the Start menu. By right-clicking on the Word 2013 icon, you can pin Word 2013 to the Start menu and task bar, so that it is always visible.

PAUSE. LEAVE the Word 2013 screen open to use in the next exercise.

Take Note

Another Way

For Windows 7 users, when Office was installed on your computer, a shortcut icon might have been added to the Start menu or to your desktop. Double-click the shortcut icon on your desktop to start Word without having to go through the Start menu.

Windows 8 and Windows 7 are for PC users at home, work, and school. Both are powerful tools that control the user interface, storage devices, other softwares, peripheral devices, networks/security, system resources, and task scheduling. Windows 8 is the latest operating system standard for computers, laptops, and tablets. Windows 8 also comes in multiple versions, such as Windows 8 Pro and Windows RT to support your personal needs and how you use your device. Windows 8 is an improvement on Windows 7 that supports touch-capable devices in addition to traditional mouse and keyboard commands. You can get started with Windows 8 by practicing using the Narrator. On the keyboard, press the *Windows logo* key plus *Enter*. To Exit the Narrator, press *Caps Lock+ESC*.

The Bottom Line

WORKING WITH TOOLS

The Word 2013 window has many onscreen tools to help you create and edit documents quickly and efficiently. In this section, you learn how to locate and use the Ribbon, the Mini toolbar, and the Quick Access Toolbar to access Word commands. A **command** is an instruction based on the action that you give to Word by clicking a button or entering information into a command box. You also learn how to use **Access keys**, a tool that enhances the keyboard shortcuts and appears as small letters on the Ribbon. Access keys are also known as **KeyTips**.

Using the Ribbon

In Word 2013, the **Ribbon** contains multiple commands separated by **tabs**. Microsoft has represented each of its Office application with a color. Word is symbolized with the color blue and active tab text is blue—this is one of the new features in Word 2013. In turn, each tab contains several

groups, or collections of related Word commands. For example, in the Home tab, the grouping levels consist of Clipboard, Font, Paragraph, Styles, and Editing. Each group contains one or more command boxes that have a drop-down **menu**, or list of options, associated with them; you click the drop-down arrow to produce this menu. Some groups have a **dialog box launcher**—a small arrow in the lower-right corner of the group—that you click to launch a **dialog box** that displays additional options or information you can use to execute a command.

In this exercise, you learn to use the Ribbon by making tabs active, hiding and displaying command groups, and using the dialog box launcher and drop-down arrows.

In the Office 2013 programs, the Ribbon is contextual, which means it displays commands related to the type of document or object that you have open and onscreen.

STEP BY STEP   **Use the Ribbon**

GET READY. Start with the File > New screen open.

1. Click the Blank document icon. The Ribbon is located at the top of the Word screen. In your newly opened document, the Home tab is the default tab on the Ribbon, as shown in Figure 1-4. Note how the Ribbon is divided into groups: Clipboard, Font, Paragraph, Styles, and Editing.

Figure 1-4

The Ribbon

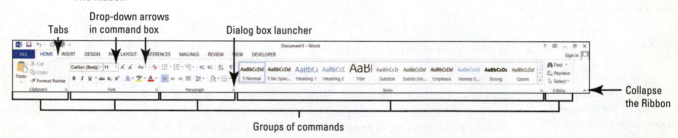

2. Review the other tabs on the Ribbon and review each group associated with the tab, and identify the arrows that launch a dialog box (if present).

3. Click the **Page Layout** tab to make it the active tab. Notice that the groups of commands change. The Page Layout tab contains three groups: Page Setup, Paragraph, and Arrange. Notice that in the Page Setup and Paragraph group a small arrow appears in the lower-right corner. Clicking on the arrow opens the dialog box with more options to select or complete a command.

4. Click the **Home** tab.

5. Click the **dialog box launcher** in the lower-right corner of the Font group. The Font dialog box, as shown in Figure 1-5, appears. The Font dialog box contains two tabs with the Font tab being the active tab. There are many options to select within the Font dialog box. Click **Cancel** to close the dialog box.

Figure 1-5

Font dialog box

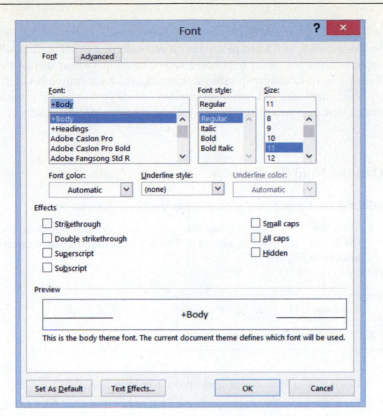

Another Way
Also you can locate a font quickly by typing the first three characters of the name in the Font command box.

6. Click the drop-down arrow on the Font command box in the Font group to produce a menu of available fonts, as shown in Figure 1-6.

Figure 1-6

Font menu

Clicking on the drop-down arrow produces available fonts to select

Use scroll bar or buttons to view additional fonts

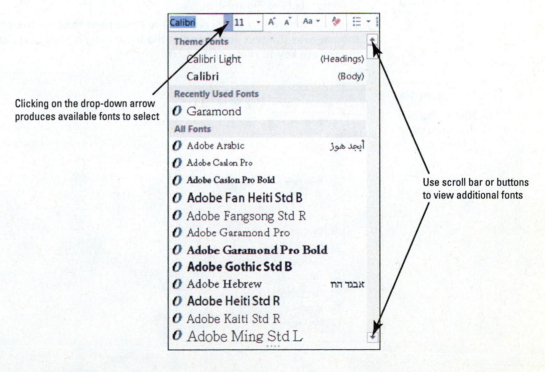

Another Way
To unclutter the screen, press the ^ key located above the vertical scroll bar in the right corner or press *Ctrl+F1*. Holding the Ctrl while pressing F1 is a toggle key, which hides the Ribbon and then displays the Ribbon.

7. Click the arrow again to close the menu.

8. Double-click the **Home** tab. Notice the command groups are hidden to give you more screen space to work on your document.

9. Double-click **Home** again to redisplay the groups.

PAUSE. LEAVE the document open to use in the next exercise.

Using the Mini Toolbar

In this exercise, you learn to use the <mark>**Mini toolbar**</mark>, a small toolbar with popular commands that appears when you point to selected text. The Mini toolbar displays after text has been selected. You also learn to display the <mark>**shortcut menu**</mark>, which contains a list of useful commands. To display the shortcut menu, right-click on selected text. If you are familiar with the Mini toolbar, you will notice that new commands have been added to the Mini toolbar.

STEP BY STEP **Use the Mini Toolbar**

USE the document that is open from the previous exercise.

1. Type the term **mini toolbar** into your blank document. Drag the mouse pointer over the word "toolbar" to select it. The Mini toolbar appears once the word is selected, as shown in Figure 1-7.

Figure 1-7

Mini toolbar

2. Point to the Font command on the Mini toolbar.

3. Click the drop-down arrow on the Font command box. A font menu appears. Press **Esc** once or click the drop-down arrow again to exit the command box. To close the Mini toolbar, click anywhere in a blank area within the document.

4. Now, position the insertion point on the selected text and right-click; the Mini toolbar appears, accompanied by a shortcut menu that displays a variety of commonly used commands (see Figure 1-8).

5. Click anywhere in a blank area of the document to close the Mini toolbar. Drag your mouse over the text you typed at the beginning of this exercise to select the text. Press the **Delete** key to remove the text.

Figure 1-8

Mini toolbar and shortcut menu

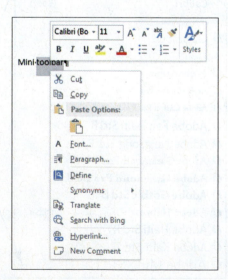

PAUSE. LEAVE the document open to use in the next exercise.

Using the Quick Access Toolbar

The **Quick Access Toolbar** is located above the Ribbon and contains commands that users' access most often, such as Save, Undo, and Redo—by default, the Save, Undo, and Redo commands display when you launch Word 2013. You can customize the contents of the Quick Access Toolbar by clicking the drop-down arrow on the right side of the toolbar and choosing options from the menu that appears. Microsoft has added the option Touch/Mouse Mode to the Quick Access Toolbar for Word 2013. If you have a touch-capable device, you can use Touch Mode. Touch Mode provides more space between buttons and icons to prevent you from accidently pressing one with your finger or stylus. In this exercise, you learn to customize the Quick Access Toolbar. You also learn to change its position in relation to the Ribbon.

Another Way
Press *Ctrl+Z* to use the Undo command. Press *Ctrl+Y* to repeat your last command.

Clicking the **Save** 💾 button in the Quick Access Toolbar for the first time opens the Save As screen. **Save As** also appears as a command listed in Backstage view when you click the File tab. When saving a document for the first time, you need to specify the filename and location where the document will be saved. You can save a document to your flash drive, SkyDrive, computer, or any other portable device. After you select a save location, such as your computer, the Save As dialog box lets you select a file format. The **Undo** ↩ command lets you cancel or undo your last command or action. You can click the Undo command as many times as necessary to undo previously executed commands. Also, if you click the arrow beside the Undo command, a history of actions you can undo appears. Clicking the **Redo** ↪ command repeats your last action. Note that commands on the Quick Access Toolbar are not available if their button is dimmed.

STEP BY STEP   **Use the Quick Access Toolbar**

USE the document that is open from the previous exercise.

1. Click the **Save** 💾 button on the Quick Access Toolbar.
2. If this is the first time you've attempted to save this document, the new Save As opens in Backstage. You have three options for where to save your work: SkyDrive, Computer, or +Add a Place. For now, you are just exploring the Save command on the Quick Access Toolbar. Later in the lesson, you learn to save a document using the Save As command.
3. Click the **Return to Document** icon, which is a circled left arrow ⬅ located in the upper-left corner or press the **Esc** key to return to the document screen.
4. Click the drop-down arrow on the right side of the Quick Access Toolbar. A menu appears as shown in Figure 1-9. Selecting one of the commands automatically places the command on the Quick Access Toolbar or moves the Quick Access Toolbar to a new location.

Figure 1-9

Customizing the Quick Access Toolbar

A check mark indicates the command appears on the Quick Access Toolbar

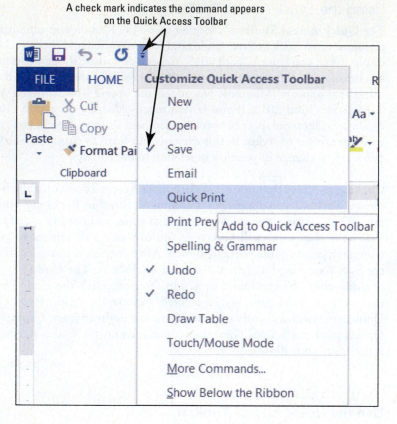

5. Click **Show Below the Ribbon**. Notice that the toolbar is moved below the Ribbon.

6. Click the drop-down arrow on the right side of the Quick Access Toolbar again. Click **Show Above the Ribbon** to return the toolbar to its original position.

PAUSE. LEAVE the document open to use in the next exercise.

CERTIFICATION READY?   1.4.3

How do you customize the Quick Access toolbar?

Cross Ref   In Lesson 14, you learn to further customize the toolbar by adding buttons for other commands you use often.

Using Access Keys

In Word 2013, Access keys allows you to launch a command with keystrokes. Access keys are also known as *KeyTips*. Every command on the Ribbon and the Quick Access Toolbar has an Access key. To display Access keys, press the *Alt* key; KeyTips appears in small black letters across the tab. The Quick Access Toolbar has numbers hovering over their associated commands. In this exercise, you learn to display KeyTips and use Access keys.

STEP BY STEP   **Use Access Keys**

USE the document that is open from the previous exercise.

1. If necessary, Click the **Home** tab. Press the **Alt** key. KeyTips appears on the Ribbon and Quick Access Toolbar to let you know which key to use to access specific commands or tabs (see Figure 1-10).

Figure 1-10

Access Keys

Press the ALT key on keyboard to activate. To turn off, press the ALT key again. Each letter is associated with the tab on the Ribbon

2. Press **H** to activate the Home tab.

3. Press **PG** to open the Paragraph dialog box, and then click **Cancel**.

4. Press the **Alt** key again to display the KeyTips.

5. Press **P** to activate the Page Layout tab.

6. Press **O** to display the options to change the page orientation.

7. Press the **Alt** key twice to display the KeyTips again, and then press the **Alt** key to turn them off.

PAUSE. LEAVE the document open to use in the next exercise.

Take Note   Shortcut keys are keys or are a combination of keys pressed together to perform a command. Shortcut keys provide a quick way to give commands without having to take your hands from the keyboard. Keyboard shortcuts from previous versions of Word that began with Ctrl have remained the same, such as Ctrl+C (copy) and Ctrl+V (paste). However, Office 2007 introduced Access keys, which begin by pressing the Alt key. Later in the lesson, you learn to use Help to learn more about keyboard shortcuts.

SOFTWARE ORIENTATION

Backstage Screen

Before you begin working in Backstage, you need to be familiar with Microsoft's Office new UI. When you first launch Microsoft Word 2013, open a document, and click the File tab, you should see a screen similar to that shown in Figure 1-11. This is what is known as *Backstage view*.

Return to Document icon

Backstage commands

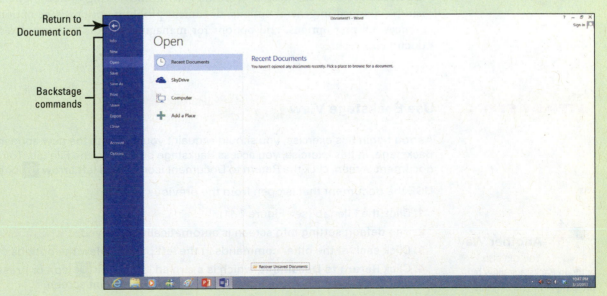

Figure 1-11

Backstage—The New Open screen

Use Figure 1-11 as a reference throughout this lesson as well as the rest of this book.

OPENING BACKSTAGE

Backstage view offers quick access to commands for performing many file management tasks—such as opening, closing, saving, printing, and sharing Word documents.

The new appearance for Backstage displays the command pane on the left side. These commands allow you to open, save, print, share, and export documents; to display accounts; and to customize options within Word 2013.

Here is a brief overview of the commands that appear in the Backstage of Word 2013:

- **Info:** The options in this group prepares and mark documents as final so that no changes can be made to them; protects documents with a password or restricted permissions; protects integrity of the document by adding a digital signature; checks the document for sensitive information; checks document accessibility and compatibility; and manages different versions of a document. The Document Properties can also be opened from this command.
- **New:** Creates a new document from a blank page or template.
- **Open:** Displays recently opened locations where documents were saved for quick access.
- **Save:** Saves the current document using the Word format and location you chose when you last used the Save As command.
- **Save As:** Enables you to save a document in multiple locations, such as your computer, flash drive, SkyDrive, or desktop area. This command also saves a document in a different file format (e.g., .pdf, .txt, .rtf, .htm, and so on).
- **Print:** Offers several sets of options—the **Print** options enable you to send documents straight to a default printer and choose the number of copies to be printed; the Printer options enable you to choose a printer and set printer properties; the **Settings** options enable you to change the settings for a page, and the **Preview** screen enables you to visually check your document for errors before printing.
- **Share:** Allows documents to be shared with family, friends, and colleagues by using SkyDrive, e-mail, presenting online, or publishing links on a blog post or social networking page.
- **Export:** Documents are saved in a PDF, XPS, or another type of format.
- **Close:** Closes an open document (the program remains open).
- **Account:** Displays how you can access your documents from any account and how information is shared via Flickr, Facebook, LinkedIn, and Twitter. Accounts must be activated to be viewed.
- **Options:** Includes the default Word document and setting options. The settings for Word can be changed in general options, document proofing options, save options, language preferences, editing options, and options for managing add-ins and templates and for keeping documents secure.

Use Backstage View

As you begin this exercise, you should acquaint yourself with the new appearance to Backstage. In this exercise, you access Backstage by clicking the File tab. To return to your document screen, click the Return to Document icon circled left arrow ⊙ or press the **Esc** key.

USE the document that is open from the previous exercise.

1. Click the **File** tab (see Figure 1-11).
2. The default setting Info screen is automatically displayed.
3. Click each of the other commands in the left pane to view the options of each one.
4. Click **Return to Document**, which is a circled left arrow ⊙ icon or press the **Esc** key to exit Backstage. This action returns you to the document screen.

PAUSE. LEAVE the document open to use in the next exercise.

Another Way
You can also activate Backstage view by pressing *Alt+ F.* Using this shortcut opens the Access keys in Backstage.

Cross Ref   You learn about Backstage options in Lesson 13.

USING THE MICROSOFT WORD HELP BUTTON

The Bottom Line

Microsoft Word 2013 has options for accessing the Help features by pressing *F1* or clicking the question mark ⟦ ? ⟧ in the upper-right corner of the screen. You can access help from Office.com or from your computer.

Take Note

When you hover over a command on the Ribbon, a **ScreenTip** appears displaying the name of the command and additional information about the command. You also can click the Help button ⟦ ? ⟧ to get more information and advice.

Using the Help Button

Microsoft Word Help works much like an Internet browser and has many of the same buttons, such as Back, Forward, Home, Print, and Use Large Text for easier reading. To access Help, press F1 or click the question mark located in the upper-right corner of the screen. A quick way to find Help information is to type a word or words into the search box and then click the *Search* button. Word displays a list of popular searches as links—to access that topic click the link. Under Getting Started are more links to videos, training, tips for tablets, and more. In this exercise, you learn to open Word Help and to use Help by typing in search words.

The Help screen displays content available online (you must be connected to the Internet to access this content, which is located on Office.com). The advantage of being connected to the Internet is that you will have access to the latest articles, videos, and training when using the Help command. You can print Help information within the Word Help main window by clicking the Print button and pin the information to the Help screen to refer back to it quickly.

STEP BY STEP   **Use the Help Button**

USE the document that is open from the previous exercise.

1. Make sure you are connected to the Internet.
2. Click the **Microsoft Word Help** ⟦ ? ⟧ button in the upper-right corner of the screen or press **F1**. The *Word Help* window appears, as shown in Figure 1-12.

Figure 1-12

Word Help window

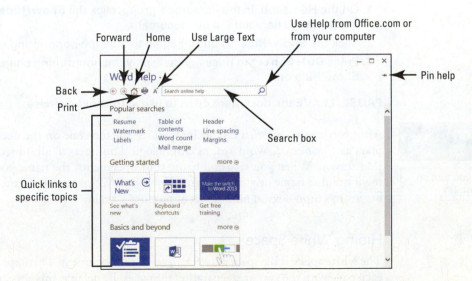

3. Under the section, "Getting started," click the tile **See what's new** and review the content. Then click the back arrow ⊙ to return to the Help menu.

4. Click the tile **Keyboard shortcuts**, and then click **+Show All** and review the information displayed.

5. Click the **Home** 🏠 button to return to the main Help screen.

6. Click the **Close** ✕ button to close Microsoft Word Help.

PAUSE. LEAVE the document open to use in the next exercise.

CREATING A DOCUMENT

The Bottom Line

You can create a document from a blank page or use a template that is already formatted. When you start typing text at the insertion point in a blank document, you have begun to create a Word document. As you type, Word inserts the text to the left of the insertion point and uses the program's defaults for margins and line spacing. Word also has a number of tools and automatic features to make creating a document easier, including nonprinting characters, AutoComplete, and Word Wrap.

When you begin typing text into a document, it is inserted to the left of the insertion point and the document is created using the Word defaults for margins and line spacing. The margin defaults are set to one-inch top, bottom, left, and right margins; the line spacing is set to 1.08; and the spacing after each paragraph is set to 8 points. Later you learn to begin a new document by selecting the single-spaced document with the margins set to one inch.

Displaying Nonprinting Characters

When documents are created, Word inserts **nonprinting characters**, which are symbols for certain formatting commands, such as paragraphs (¶), indents and tabs (→), and spaces (•) between words. These symbols can help you create and edit your document. By default, these symbols are hidden. To display them, click the Show/Hide (¶) button in the Paragraph group of the Home tab. When you print your document, these hidden symbols do not appear. In this exercise, you learn to display nonprinting characters in Word.

STEP BY STEP   **Display Nonprinting Characters**

USE the document that is open from the previous exercise.

1. On the Home tab, in the Paragraph group, click the **Show/Hide** (¶) button to display the nonprinting characters in the document.

2. Click the **Show/Hide** (¶) button again to hide the nonprinting characters.

3. Press **Ctrl+Shift+*** to once again display the nonprinting characters. This time, leave Show/Hide on.

PAUSE. LEAVE the document open to use in the next exercise.

CERTIFICATION READY?   **1.4.7**

How would you turn on Show/Hide?

After you create your first document, you see the filename on the document title bar, which displays as *Document1*. Word assigns chronological numbers to all subsequent files that you open in that session. When you save and name your documents, the name you assign replaces the document number name originally assigned by Word. When you close and reopen Word, the program begins its chronological numbering at number 1 again.

Hiding White Space

The **white space** is the space between pages of the document. This appears at the top and bottom of each page with the gray area separating the pages. By default, this appears in Print Layout view. You can change the view of the document to reduce the amount of gray appearing by double-clicking between the pages. In this exercise, you learn to hide and unhide the white space.

Hide White Space

USE the document open from the previous exercise.

1. Make sure your insertion point is at the beginning of the document. Place the mouse below the Ribbon until you see the ScreenTip *Double-click to hide white space* and then double-click. Notice the gray border line representing the white space becoming thinner.
2. Place the mouse over the gray border line until you see two arrows again and then double-click. This reveals the white space.

PAUSE. LEAVE the document open to use in the next exercise.

Using AutoComplete

The **AutoComplete** feature automatically completes the text of the current date, day of the week, and month. When you type the first four characters of the day of the week, a ScreenTip appears with a suggestion for the completed text; press Enter to accept the suggestion. AutoComplete reduces the amount of time spent typing content or phrases in a document. The AutoComplete feature is turned on by default and can be turned off in the Word Options settings. In this exercise, you learn to use Word's AutoComplete feature.

Use AutoComplete

USE the document open from the previous exercise.

1. Type the name of the current month; as you type the first four characters, a ScreenTip appears. Press **Enter** to accept the suggested text.
2. Press the **Spacebar** and the current day and year appears, and then press **Enter**.

PAUSE. LEAVE the document open to use in the next exercise.

Entering Document Text

Another Way
To use AutoComplete, you can also type the first four characters of the current day of the week, and then press *Enter* or *F3*.

Entering document text is easy in Word. Word sets default margins and line-spacing measurements for newly created documents, and **Word Wrap** automatically wraps text to the next line as it reaches the right margin. To separate paragraphs and create blank lines, press Enter. In this lesson, you create a letter using the Block Style format with mixed punctuation. Be sure to type the document text exactly as shown in the steps that follow—in a later lesson, you learn to format the document.

When sending professional correspondence to customers, it is good business practice to ensure the document is in an acceptable format and error free. The Block Style letter format has open or mixed punctuation and is common to many business documents. **Block Style** format aligns text along the left margin, including the date, inside address, salutation, body of the letter, closing, and signature. **Open punctuation** requires no punctuation after the salutation or the closing, whereas **mixed punctuation** requires a colon after the salutation and a comma after the closing.

Enter Document Text

USE the document that is open from the previous exercise.

1. The insertion point should be positioned at the end of the year. Press **Enter** twice.
2. Type the delivery address as shown:

   Ms. Miriam Lockhart (Press **Enter** once.)

   764 Crimson Avenue (Press **Enter** once.)

   Boston, MA 02136 (Press **Enter** twice.)

3. Type **Dear Ms. Lockhart:**

4. Press Enter once.

5. Type the following text and press **Enter** once after each paragraph.

   We are pleased that you have chosen to list your home with Tech Terrace Real Estate. Our office has bought, sold, renovated, appraised, leased, and managed more homes in the Tech Terrace neighborhood than anyone and now we will be putting that experience to work for you.

   Our goal is to sell your house quick for the best possible price.

   The enclosed packet contains a competitive market analysis, complete listing data, a copy of the contracts, and a customized house brochure. Your home has been input into the MLS listing and an Internet ad is on our website. We will be contacting you soon to determine the best time for an open house.

   We look forward to working with you to sell your home. Please do not hesitate to call if you have any questions.

6. Press **Enter** once.

7. Type **Sincerely,**

8. Press **Enter** twice.

9. Type **Steve Buckley**. Your document should appear as shown in Figure 1-13. This letter still needs to be formatted in an accepted mailable format and this is discussed in a later lesson.

Figure 1-13

Block Style format with mixed punctuation

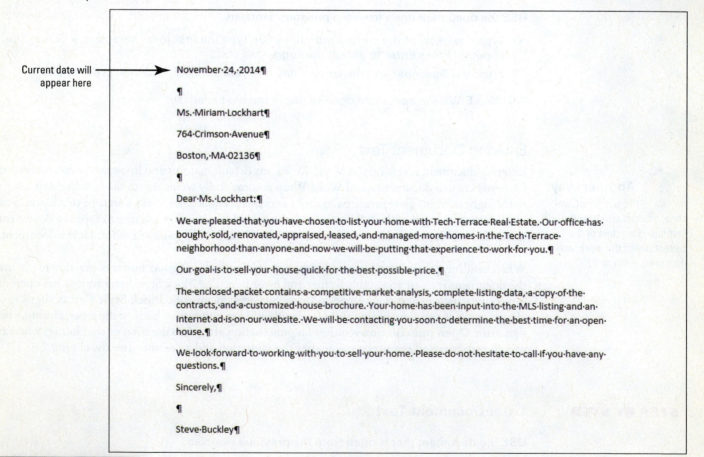

Current date will appear here →

November·24,·2014¶

¶

Ms.·Miriam·Lockhart¶

764·Crimson·Avenue¶

Boston,·MA·02136¶

¶

Dear·Ms.·Lockhart:¶

We·are·pleased·that·you·have·chosen·to·list·your·home·with·Tech·Terrace·Real·Estate.·Our·office·has· bought,·sold,·renovated,·appraised,·leased,·and·managed·more·homes·in·the·Tech·Terrace· neighborhood·than·anyone·and·now·we·will·be·putting·that·experience·to·work·for·you.¶

Our·goal·is·to·sell·your·house·quick·for·the·best·possible·price.¶

The·enclosed·packet·contains·a·competitive·market·analysis,·complete·listing·data,·a·copy·of·the· contracts,·and·a·customized·house·brochure.·Your·home·has·been·input·into·the·MLS·listing·and·an· Internet·ad·is·on·our·website.·We·will·be·contacting·you·soon·to·determine·the·best·time·for·an·open· house.¶

We·look·forward·to·working·with·you·to·sell·your·home.·Please·do·not·hesitate·to·call·if·you·have·any· questions.¶

Sincerely,¶

¶

Steve·Buckley¶

CERTIFICATION READY?   1.1.1

How do you create a new document?

PAUSE. LEAVE the document open to use in the next exercise.

Take Note   To create a new blank document, click the *File* tab and then click the *New* command. Select the first option, *Blank document*, and Word 2013 automatically opens a new document. You can also open a new blank document using the keyboard shortcut *Ctrl+ N*.

It is always important to save your document before closing the program. However, if you close the document or Word by accident, a prompt appears, asking whether you want to save your document. Choose *Yes* to save and close, *No* to close without saving, or *Cancel* to stop the Close command. The Spelling & Grammar commands are discussed in a later lesson.

SAVING A DOCUMENT

The Bottom Line   By default, newly created documents are saved with a specific filename closely related to the content of the document so that you can locate the file quickly. After editing an existing document, you can choose to save that document with a new filename, file format, or in another location. When saving a document to the Cloud, such as SkyDrive, you have access to your documents at any computer or tablet and can share them with others. In some cases, you might want to save the original and edited documents in the same place but with different filenames. Keeping the original document allows you to reference it at a future date on any computer.

Saving a Document for the First Time

When saving a document for the first time, you must specify a filename, the file type, and a place where you can access the document. The filename should help users find and identify the file, and the file location should be convenient for the file's future users. You can save files to portable storage devices such as a flash drive, to your computer's desktop or hard drive, to a network location, or to SkyDrive. Word 2013 enhanced the Save As command, which allows users to save their work to the cloud and access the document quickly from any computer or tablet. In Lesson 13, you learn to save documents to SkyDrive. In this exercise, you learn to save a document with a specific filename to your flash drive.

STEP BY STEP   **Save a Document for the First Time**

USE the document that is open from the previous exercise.

1. If necessary, connect your flash drive to one of the USB ports on your computer.
2. Click the **File** tab, and then click the **Save As** command. The new Save As screen is shown in Figure 1-14. There are three options available to save your document: SkyDrive, Computer, and +Add a Place. Click **Computer**. The right side of the screen changes and displays Recent Folders that have been opened.

Figure 1-14

The New Save As screen

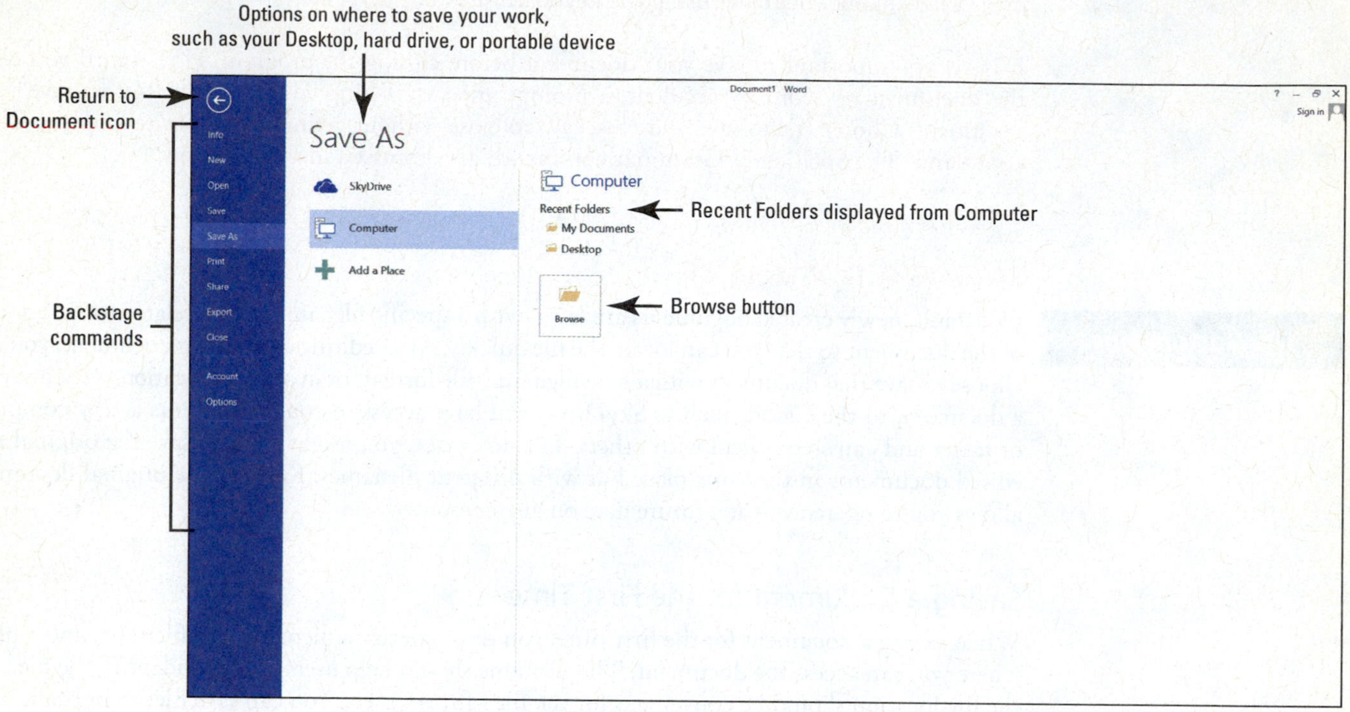

Options on where to save your work,
such as your Desktop, hard drive, or portable device

Return to → Document icon

Backstage commands

Save As

SkyDrive

Computer

Add a Place

Computer

Recent Folders ← Recent Folders displayed from Computer
My Documents
Desktop

Browse ← Browse button

Document1 — Word

Sign in

3. Click **Browse**. The *Save As* dialog box opens. In the Windows 8 environment, the Documents Library is the default location for saving new files. Change the location from the default to your flash drive by using the vertical scroll bar and scrolling down until you see your flash drive. Storage devices are given a specific letter identified by the operating system. For example, your flash drive might be labeled as *TravelDrive (I:)*.

4. Click the **flash drive** to open that location to save your document.

5. Type **Tech Terrace Letter** in the File name box and click **Save**. By default, the first few characters that you typed in your document appear in the File name box. Drag the mouse over the text and press **Delete** or begin typing over the highlighted text.

6. If a prompt appears to upgrade to the newest format click the **OK** button. This action allows you to use the new features in Word 2013.

PAUSE. LEAVE the document open to use in the next exercise.

Another Way
You can also save a document by clicking the *Save* button on the Quick Access Toolbar or by pressing *Ctrl+S*.

Cross Ref

It is a common business practice to send documents as an attachment through e-mail. When documents are opened as an attachment, they open in Protected view. Protected view is covered in greater depth in Lesson 13.

Saving a Document in a Folder

Folders help you organize the documents you create in Word. The documents that you open for Word 2013 are organized in folders by lesson. To help you manage documents for this lesson, you create a folder in your flash drive. You can also create a folder within a folder, and the new folder is called a *subfolder*. Always remember to check the full location path listed in the Save As address bar to be certain that you have identified the right location. In this exercise, you create a new folder on your flash drive and save the document in that folder with its original filename.

STEP BY STEP   **Save a Document in a Folder**

USE the document that is open from the previous exercise.

1. Click the **File** tab, and then click **Save As**.

2. Click **Computer**. Under the Computer heading, you should see your flash drive under Current Folders. Click your flash drive—the *Save As* dialog box opens.

3. Click **New folder** located below the address bar and type **Word 2013**. Press **Enter**.

4. In the main pane of the dialog box, double-click the **Word 2013** folder; notice the address bar displays your flash drive followed by *Word 2013*, as shown in Figure 1-15. Note also that the flash drive TravelDrive (I :) in Figure 1-15 might not appear on your screen; therefore, you need to check with your instructor for the correct path. *Tech Terrace Letter* should already appear in the File name box.

Figure 1-15

Save As dialog box in a
specific folder

Click to create new folder   Address bar displays location
                                              of flash drive and folder

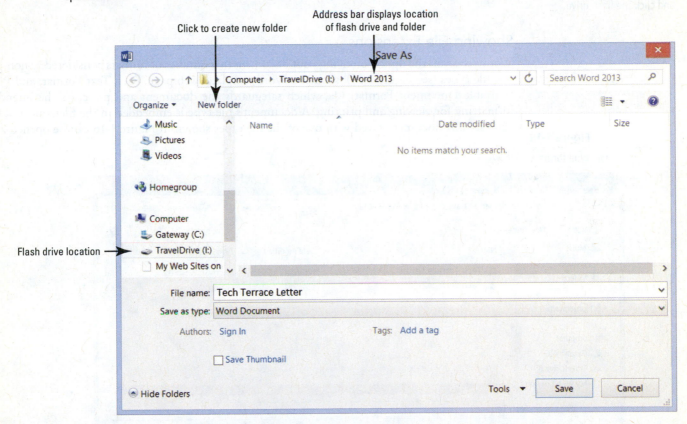

Flash drive location →

5. Click **Save** to close the dialog box.

PAUSE. LEAVE the document open to use in the next exercise.

 **Troubleshooting**   AutoRecover is a feature that automatically saves your data at scheduled intervals. Be default, Word 2013 saves your work every 10 minutes. This makes it possible to recover some of your work if a problem occurs. However, this useful option is not a substitute for frequently saving your documents as you work. You should always click the *Save* button regularly to avoid losing work in case of a power outage or computer crash.

Saving a Document with a Different Name

You can use the Save As command to save a copy of your document with a new filename, to save the document in a new location, or to save the document as a different file type. In this exercise, you learn to save an existing document with a new filename in the Word 2013 folder.

Save Document in a Folder with a Different Name

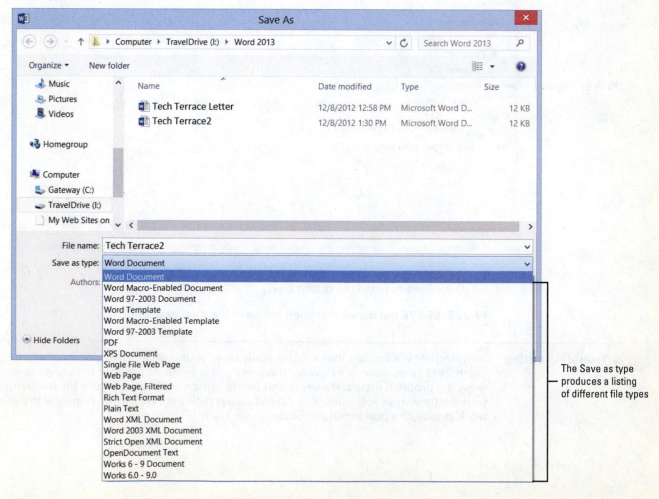

Another Way
The Save As dialog box can also be opened by pressing *F12*. To locate your flash drive, click the drop-down arrow beside the address bar at the top of the dialog box, and then scroll through the listings and click the flash drive.

USE the document that is open from the previous exercise.

1. Click the **File** tab, and then click the **Save As** command. On the right side of the screen under Current Folder, you should see the folder that you created.
2. Click **Word 2013** and the *Save As* dialog box opens.
3. Type *Tech Terrace2* in the File name box.
4. Click **Save**.

PAUSE. LEAVE the document open to use in the next exercise.

Showing File Extensions

Word gives you the option of saving your document in a number of formats considered as non-native file types (see Figure 1-16), such as a Word template, web page, Rich Text Format, and PDF (Portable Document Format) file, which safeguards the document and preserves the intended formatting for viewing and printing. A document's file type is embedded in the filename as a file extension. A document saved with one of the file types shown in Figure 1-16 can be opened and

Figure 1-16

File type formats

The Save as type produces a listing of different file types

edited in Word. File extensions are associated with certain programs. (The Save as type drop-down list shows the file type formats available in Windows 8 and Windows 7, and Table 1-1 provides a description for some of the file extensions.) In this exercise, you learn how to display file extensions in Windows 8 and in Windows 7.

Table 1-1

File Extensions

File Type	Description
Word Document (*.docx)	Used for Microsoft Word 2007, 2010, and 2013.
Word 97-2003 (*.doc)	Used for Microsoft Word 97-2003.
Word Template (*.dotx)	Template for Microsoft Word 2007, 2010, and 2013.
Word 97-2003 Template (*.dot)	Template for Microsoft Word 97-2003.
PDF (*.pdf)	Portable Document Format, which preserves the intended formatting of a file for later editing, viewing, and printing. PDF files open with Adobe Reader. In Word 2013, you can edit PDF documents.
XPS Document (*.xps)	XPS is a file format that preserves document formatting and enables file sharing.
Web Page (*.htm,*.html)	Both extensions denote HTML files, which is an acronym for the Hypertext Markup Language format. These type of documents open in a web browser.
Rich Text Format (*.rtf)	RTF documents are opened with text editor programs such as Notepad, WordPad, and Microsoft Word. Only limited formatting is allowed.
Plain Text (*.txt)	Plain text documents are associated with Notepad, WordPad, and Microsoft Word. The .txt extension does not permit formatting other than spaces and line breaks.
OpenDocument Text (*.odt)	Used by some word processing applications such as OpenOffice.org and Google. docs. Some Microsoft Word formatting might be lost when files are saved in the .odt format.

STEP BY STEP | **Show File Extensions in Windows 8**

USE the document that is open from the previous exercise.

1. Hover the mouse in the upper-right edge of the screen until the Windows 8 Charms appear on the right side of the screen (see Figure 1-17). Another way to display the Windows 8 Charms is to press the keyboard combination **Windows logo key +C**. The Windows logo key is located on the keyboard.

Figure 1-17

Windows 8 commands on the Charm Bar.

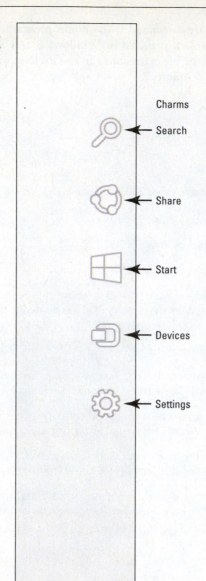

Charms

Search

Share

Start

Devices

Settings

2. Click the **Settings** ⚙ icon. A command pane appears on the right side.

3. Under Settings, click **Control Panel**. The Control Panel opens. The Control Panel contains a menu bar. (If the menu is not visible, press the ALT key to display the menu).

4. Click **Tools** on the menu bar.

5. Click **Folder options**. The *Folder Options* dialog box opens with the General tab as the active tab.

6. Make the **View** tab active by clicking on the tab.

7. Under the Files and Folders heading, locate **Hide extensions for known file types** and then click in the check box to remove the check mark. By default, the file extensions are hidden. When the check mark is removed, the file extensions will be displayed on the title bar each time you open a new document. Note, the document that is opened, needs to be closed and reopened to see the file extension associated with Word 2013.

8. Click **OK** to close the *Folder Options* dialog box, and then click the **Close** ⊠ button to close the Control Panel.

PAUSE. The Word program is still open from the previous exercise.

Another Way

In Windows 8, file extensions are off. If the file extensions on your computer are hidden, you can show them in Windows 8. Click the Windows 8 Search charm. Type *Control Panel*. Select *Control Panel > Tools > Folder options > View tab*. Clear the check box by Hide Extension for known file types.

Show File Extensions in Windows 7

USE the document that is open from the previous exercise.

Another Way
By default, file extensions are off. If the file extensions on your computer are hidden, you can show them in Windows 7 using two different methods. Either choose *Start* > *Control Panel* > *Appearance and Personalization* > *Folder Options* or choose *Start*, type *folder options* in the Search box, and press *Enter*.

1. Click **Start**. In the Search box, type **Show hidden files and folders**.
2. Click **Show hidden files and folders** under the Control Panel.
3. The *Folder Options* dialog box appears. Click the **View** tab, and then clear the **Hide extensions for known file types** check box. In some cases, the System Administrator who manages the lab environment might set up the computers in the lab so that each computer system displays the same. Check with your instructor to see whether the file extensions will display on your computer.
4. Click **OK** to close the dialog box.

PAUSE. The Word program is still open from the previous exercise.

Choosing a Different File Format

Some individuals and companies might have not upgraded their Office suite to the latest version of Office 2013 and might still be working in an earlier version, such as Word 2003. Changing the file format of a document allows those individuals and companies to open and edit your document without losing its text formatting. In this exercise, you learn to save a document in a format compatible with an earlier version of Word.

Choose a Different File Format

USE the document that is open from the previous exercise.

1. Click the **File** tab, and then click **Save As** to open the Save As screen.
2. Under Current Folder, click **Word 2013**. The folder you created earlier opens.
3. In the Save as type box, click the drop-down arrow and choose **Word 97-2003 Document (*.doc)**.
4. Type *Tech Terrace2 97-2003* in the File name box. Click **Save**. You should see the .doc extension in the File name box—the file extension is associated with a previous version of Word. On the title bar, the file extension appears along with Compatibility Mode. In the next exercise, you learn about Compatibility Mode.

CERTIFICATION READY? 1.5.2

How do you save a document in a different file format?

PAUSE. LEAVE document open for the next exercise.

Converting a Document

Compatibility Mode enables you to work in a document created in an earlier version of Word without saving the file in a different file format. In this exercise, you learn to use the Convert command to clear the compatibility options and convert a document to the Word 2013 file format.

Convert a Document

USE the document that is open from the previous exercise.

1. With the *Tech Terrace2 97-2003.doc* document open, click the **File** tab.
2. In the main pane of the Info command, click **Convert**, and then click **OK** to confirm the conversion, as shown in Figure 1-18. Converting the document clears the Compatibility Mode on the title bar and upgrades your document to Word 2013 format, which allows you to access Word's new features.

Figure 1-18

Convert prompt

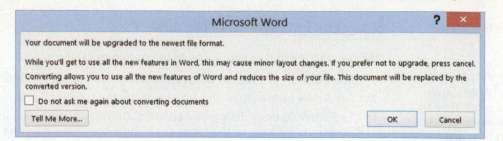

> **Microsoft Word**
>
> Your document will be upgraded to the newest file format.
>
> While you'll get to use all the new features in Word, this may cause minor layout changes. If you prefer not to upgrade, press cancel.
>
> Converting allows you to use all the new features of Word and reduces the size of your file. This document will be replaced by the converted version.
>
> ☐ Do not ask me again about converting documents
>
> Tell Me More...   OK   Cancel

CERTIFICATION READY? 1.5.7

How do you maintain backward compatibility by converting a document?

3. To save the document in the Word 2013 file format, click the **File** tab.

4. Click **Save As**, and then click the **Word 2013** folder. Then in the File name box, type *Tech Terrace Update*. Click **Save**. The filename displays the .docx extension in the title bar after the file name.

PAUSE. LEAVE the document open for the next exercise.

STEP BY STEP   **Export a Document to a PDF**

USE the document that is open from the previous exercise.

1. Now you export the document to a PDF file format. Click the **File** tab and click the **Export** command. The Export screen opens (see Figure 1-19). You use the Export command to share your documents with others. Publishing the document as a PDF file preserves the formatting. You can also select what you want to share before exporting. In Lesson 13, you learn to select what you want to share.

Figure 1-19

Export screen

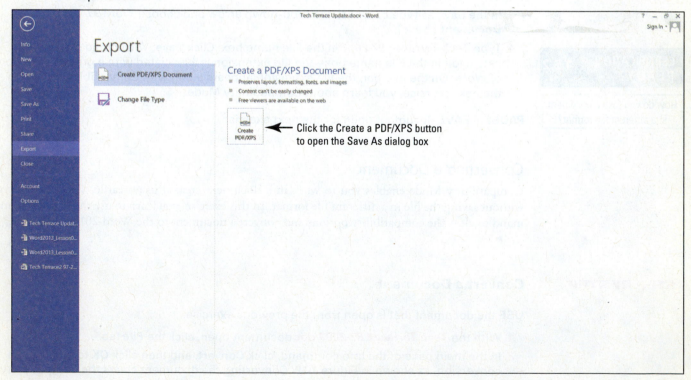

Export

Create PDF/XPS Document

Change File Type

Create a PDF/XPS Document
- Preserves layout, formatting, fonts, and images
- Content can't be easily changed
- Free viewers are available on the web

Create PDF/XPS ← Click the Create a PDF/XPS button to open the Save As dialog box

2. Click the **Create PDF/XPS** button. The *Publish as PDF or XPS* dialog box opens, and the Word 2013 folder automatically opens.

3. In the File name box, type *Tech Terrace 3*. In the Save as type box, notice that the PDF (*.pdf) is showing. The file extension is automatically selected when using the Export command.

4. Click **Publish**. By default, the document will not open after the file is published. To open the document in a reader format, enable the *Open file after Publishing* check box.

5. Click **File**, and then click **Close** to close the Word document.

PAUSE. LEAVE Word open for the next exercise.

Take Note   PDF is a popular Save As format for documents and preserves document formatting for viewing. Word 2013 now allows editing documents that are saved in a PDF format. In a later lesson, you learn to edit a PDF document. To edit in PDF format, you must download the appropriate add-in from microsoft.com.

SOFTWARE ORIENTATION

Template Options in Backstage

You can work more efficiently by basing many of your new documents on templates that Word provides—there are many choices available for working with different templates, as shown in Figure 1-20 (you will likely see a different selection of templates than shown in this figure).

Figure 1-20
New screen displaying templates

Using templates keeps you from having to recreate the layout and formatting of recurring documents such as interoffice memorandums, monthly newsletters that you share with employees, recordings of minutes from meetings, and more. The New command has many options to select a template of your choice. You can work with templates that are already installed or search for a template online.

WORKING WITH TEMPLATES

You can choose from many different categories of templates, such as letters, resumes, faxes, labels, cards, calendars, and more. Some templates are preinstalled with Word and there are more options available online. A **template** is a master document with predefined page layout, fonts, margins, and styles that is used to create new documents with the same basic formatting. Templates are reusable even if you saved the document with a different file name. In this exercise, you locate an installed template, enter information, and save the document as a template.

Locating a Template Installed on Your Computer

Microsoft continues to add new templates to its categories. If you are looking for a document that contains no formatting, single spaced, margins at one-inch top, bottom, left, and right, then the Single spaced (blank) document template will do just that. In this exercise, you select this template to create and save a Word document.

STEP BY STEP **Locate a Template Installed on Your Computer**

GET READY. OPEN Word if it is not already open.

1. Click the **File** tab, and then click **New**. The New screen displays the available templates as shown in Figure 1-20. Scroll down and review the accessible templates. First determine what type of document needs to be created. For this exercise, you select a blank template.

2. Click the **Single spaced (blank)** document, and then click the **Create** button.

3. Display the Show/Hide button (¶) to show paragraph marks.

PAUSE. LEAVE the document open to use in the next exercise.

Creating a Document Using a Template

STEP BY STEP **Create a Single-Spaced Document Using a Template**

GET READY. OPEN Word if it is not already open.

1. Click the **File** tab, and then click **Save As**. In the Save As screen, click **Computer**. Under Recent Folders, click the **Word 2013** folder to open that location. In the File name box, type Welcome Memo. Click **Save**.

2. Type the document as follows and press the **Tab** or **Enter** key as indicated. By pressing the **Tab** key twice, you are aligning the text at the one-inch marker on the ruler.

   Forest Hills Home Owner's Association [Press **Enter** three times.]

   To: [Press **Tab** twice.] **New Neighbor Welcoming Committee Members** [Press **Enter** twice.]

   From: [Press **Tab** twice.] **Committee Chair** [Press **Enter** twice.]

   Date: [Press **Tab** twice.] **December 15, 20XX** [Press **Enter** twice.]

   Subject: [Press **Tab** twice.] **Meeting and Refreshment Schedule** [Press **Enter** twice.]

   Thank you for volunteering to be on the New Neighbor Welcoming Committee. Enclosed please find the meeting and refreshment schedule for the next six months. See you in January!

3. **SAVE** the document leave open for the next exercise.

PAUSE. LEAVE the document open to use in the next exercise.

Finding Templates on the Internet

Microsoft offers numerous templates online and other templates are also available from third-party providers, as well as other users in the community. You can select from a category using the Office.com Templates section or search for a template using the Search bar and searching by keywords.

You can also use the Help feature and search for additional information on templates on your computer or online. You must be connected to the Internet to search for templates online. In this exercise, you select a template category and view a listing of templates online.

Find Templates on the Internet

GET READY. OPEN Word if it is not already open.

1. Click the **File** tab, and then click **New**.
2. In the Search for online templates box, type **forms**, and then click the **Start Searching** button. Additional templates are displayed as shown in Figure 1-21. You can also filter the templates by category to narrow your search. Preview by using the scroll bar and select any template. Click **Create**.

Figure 1-21

Online templates

Key a category in text box then click the magnifier to begin search

New

Home   forms

					Category	
					Form	133
					Business	102
					Industry	77
					Education	51
					Student	48
					Finance - Accounting	47
Project change au...	Donation pledge f...	Medical phone co...	Client travel plan...	Job description fo...	Teacher	44
					Design Sets	36
					Print	31
					Invoice	30
					Single page	30
					Evaluation	28
					Personal	26
					Small Business	25
					Employee	22
Travel permission...	Direct deposit aut...	Job applicant asse...	Field Trip Permissi...	Field trip permissi...	Basic	21
					Calculator	21
					Orientation	18
					Sales	18
					List	17
					Log	17
					Parent	17
					Human Resources	14
					Order	14
Web based trainin...	Patient registratio...	Yearly physical ex...	Absence request f...	Employee inform...	Sample	14

3. **CLOSE** the forms template and do not save.
4. As the assistant to the Tech Terrace Real Estate manager, you are in the beginning stages of gathering the materials together for the annual report. You decide to use one of the available templates in Word 2013. Click the **File** tab, and then select **New**.
5. In the Search for online templates box, type **Annual Report (Timeless design)**, and then click the **Start Searching** button. Select the template with the image, and then click **Create**. The template will download.
6. Complete the placeholders with the following text: type text inside the brackets, **[FY] [Year]**. Click the drop-down arrow by the year and select the current date—note the year displays in the placeholder. As you gather information for the report, you begin entering data into the document.
7. Click **File**, and then click **Save As**. In the *Save As* dialog box screen, click **Computer**. Under Current Folders, select the Word 2013 folder.

8. In the File name box, type **Annual Report**.

9. Change the file type by clicking the drop-down arrow and select **Word Template (*.dotx)**. Note that you might need to select your flash drive again because Word automatically saves templates to the Templates folder located on the computer.

10. Click **SAVE**.

PAUSE. LEAVE the document open for the next exercise.

Another Way
You can double-click on a template to open it.

Take Note   You must be connected to the Internet to view online templates.

Workplace *Ready*

USE TEMPLATES TO SAVE TIME AND MONEY

Templates are a great tool for helping create documents in the workplace. Companies can create professional-looking marketing plans, brochures, invoices, timesheets, and other common documents directly from the supplied templates. By using the supplied templates, companies can save time and money from creating complex documents from scratch.

Take Note   To find additional information on templates, use the Help feature by pressing the *F1* button or click the *Help* button.

PREVIEWING AND PRINTING A DOCUMENT

The Bottom Line

The Print command is located on the File tab in Backstage. There are three groups of printing options available, which are the printing properties and settings. The Preview pane gives you an opportunity to see what your printed document will look like so you can correct errors before printing.

Previewing in Backstage

Before printing your document, you need to preview its contents so you can correct any text or layout errors. In this exercise, you learn to use Backstage to preview your document.

The Print command feature includes three sets of options: Print, Printer, and Settings. Choosing the Print button automatically prints the document to the default printer using the default settings. Use the selection arrow to change the number of copies to be printed. The Printer options enable you to select a printer, print to file, or change printer properties. Use the Settings options to print only specific pages or selections of the document, collate the document, and so on. You also have access to Page Setup here, where additional settings can be changed on the document. You learn more about changing the document's layout in Lesson 5.

The Preview screen to the right of the Print options settings enables you to view your document as it will appear when it is printed, so you can make any necessary changes, such as changing the margins or orientation, before printing. The Preview screen lets you preview every page by clicking on the right and left arrows to page through multiple-page documents.

STEP BY STEP   **Use Print Preview**

OPEN the *Welcome Memo* document that you created earlier.

1. Click the **File** tab, and then click **Print**. The Print screen opens with the Print options on the left and the Print Preview on the right, as shown in Figure 1-22.

Figure 1-22

Print options and Print Preview screen

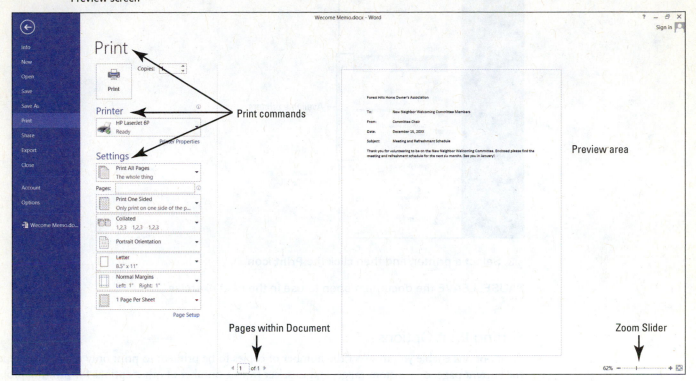

Print commands

Preview area

Pages within Document

Zoom Slider

2. Click the **plus symbol (+)** on the Zoom slider located on the bottom-right of your screen until the zoom level changes to **100%**.

3. Click the **Return to Document** icon or press the **Esc** key to close Backstage.

4. Click the **File** tab, and then click **Save**. Your document will be saved with the same filename on your flash drive.

PAUSE. LEAVE the document open to use in the next exercise.

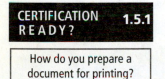

CERTIFICATION READY? **1.5.1**

How do you prepare a document for printing?

Cross Ref

You learn more about Page Setup in Lesson 5.

Choosing a Printer

If your computer is connected to multiple printers, you might need to choose a destination printer for your document. If your printer is already set up to print, as is the case in most classroom environments, you do not need to complete this exercise. Otherwise, follow this exercise to choose a printer.

Take Note Before printing your document, check with your instructor.

STEP BY STEP **Choose a Printer**

USE the document that is open from the previous exercise.

1. Click the **File** tab, and then click **Print**.

2. In the Printer selection area, click the **drop-down arrow** to produce a list of all printers connected to your computer (see Figure 1-23).

Figure 1-23

Available printers

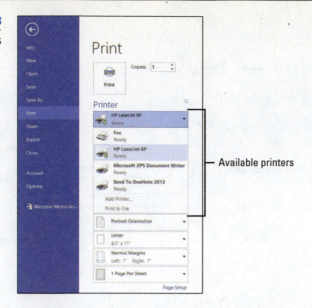

Available printers

3. Select a printer, and then click the **Print** icon.

PAUSE. LEAVE the document open to use in the next exercise.

Setting Print Options

Print options enable you to select the number of copies to be printed; to print only selected content, the current page, or a custom range; and to select from a number of other options for printing properties, collation, and page layout. Changes to Settings options apply to the current document. In this lesson, you learn how to change the Settings options before printing. (Check with your instructor before printing this exercise on a lab printer).

STEP BY STEP **Set Print Options**

USE the document that is open from the previous exercise.

1. Click the **File** tab, and then click **Print**. Click the drop-down arrow on Print All Pages to produce the menu shown in Figure 1-24.

Figure 1-24

Print settings

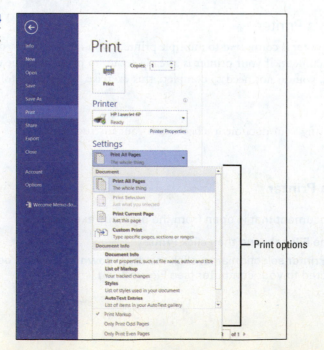

Print options

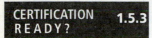

2. Select **Print Current Page**, and then click the **Print** icon. Selecting this option prints the current page.

3. Return to the Print screen area. In the Copies section of the Print options area, click the up arrow to select **2**, and then click the **Print** icon.

4. Place your insertion point at the beginning of the first paragraph, and then hold down the left mouse button and drag to the end of the paragraph to select it.

5. Click the **File** tab, and then click **Print**. Click the **Print Current Page** drop-down arrow, select **Print Selection**, and then change the number of copies from 2 to **1** by clicking the down arrow. Next, click the **Print** icon. The selected paragraph is printed.

6. Click the **File** tab, and then click **Close** to close the document.

7. The Annual Report document should still be open from a previous exercise. Click the **File** tab, and then click **Print**. Under Settings, click the drop-down arrow by 1 Page Per Sheet and select **2 Pages Per Sheet**, and then click the **Print** icon. This eight-page document is now printed on four pages with two pages per sheet.

PAUSE. LEAVE the document open to use in the next exercise.

Another Way
You can also print a document by pressing *Ctrl+P*.

CLOSING A DOCUMENT AND CLOSING WORD

The Bottom Line

Closing a document removes it from the screen. It is a good idea to close a document before exiting a program or turning off your computer. Saving your work before closing allows you to continue working on your document at a later date.

STEP BY STEP | **Close a Document and Close Word**

USE the document that is open from the previous exercise.

1. Click the **Close** ☒ button to close both the document and Microsoft Word.

STOP.

SKILL SUMMARY

In This Lesson, You Learned to:	Exam Objective	Objective Number
Start Word 2013		
Work with Tools	Customize the Quick Access toolbar.	1.4.3
Open Backstage		
Use the Microsoft Word Help Button		
Create a Document	Demonstrate how to use Show/Hide.	1.4.7
	Create new blank documents.	1.1.1
Save a Document	Save document in alternative file formats.	1.5.2
	Maintain backward compatibility.	1.5.7
Work with Templates	Demonstrate how to use Show/Hide.	1.4.7
	Create new documents and apply templates.	1.1.2
Preview and Print a Document	Configure documents to print.	1.5.1
	Print document sections.	1.5.3
	Set print scaling.	1.5.6
Close a Document and Close Word		

Multiple Choice

Select the best response for the following statements.

1. Assuming that you are using Windows 8, the first screen you see when you start your computer is called the:
   a. Word screen.
   b. Windows 7 screen.
   c. Start screen.
   d. Screen saver.

2. When text is selected, what automatically appears on the screen?
   a. I-beam
   b. Mini toolbar
   c. Insertion point
   d. All of the above

3. The ——————— contains the commands you use most often, such as Save, Undo, and Redo.
   a. Quick Access Screen
   b. Quick toolbar
   c. Quick Access Toolbar
   d. Quick command

4. Letters and numbers that appear on the Ribbon when you press the Alt key are called:
   a. key trips.
   b. KeyTips.
   c. Edit keys.
   d. key shortcut tips.

5. How would you search for templates online?
   a. Template search box
   b. Search for online templates box
   c. Open a blank template box
   d. Create your own template box

6. Which command would you use to save a document for the first time?
   a. Save
   b. Save As
   c. Save for the first time
   d. Either a or b

7. When you open new documents in Word, the program names them with a(n) ——————— determined by the number of files opened during that session.
   a. chronological number
   b. odd number
   c. even number
   d. decimal number

8. Which of the following options would you use when saving a document with a new filename?
   a. Save
   b. Save As
   c. Ctrl+S
   d. Either a or b

9. Which of the following is an acceptable format for a business letter?
   a. Block style with mixed punctuation
   b. Semi-block style
   c. All text keyed to the left of the margin
   d. Block style with open punctuation
   e. Both a and d

10. Which of the following allows you to access the Help command?
   a. F1
   b. [?]
   c. Some dialog boxes
   d. Both a and b

True/False

Circle "T" if the statement is true or "F" if the statement is false.

T F **1.** When you start Word, a new blank document appears.

T F **2.** The Undo button is on the Mini toolbar.

T F **3.** Quick-printing a document sends the document straight to the printer.

T F **4.** The File tab can be used to save and print files.

T F **5.** The Zoom slider is located in Backstage in the Info command.

T F **6.** You can hide the Ribbon by double-clicking the active tab.

T F **7.** Saving a document in a PDF format allows users to edit the document in Word 2013.

T F **8.** Previewing and printing can be completed by accessing Backstage.

T F **9.** You can close a document and begin working on a new document.

T F **10.** The Help command CANNOT be accessed in dialog boxes.

Competency Assessment

Project 1-1: Typing a Business Letter

You work for Proseware, Inc., and need to send a follow-up letter regarding price quotes. Create the following letter in block style with mixed punctuation.

GET READY. LAUNCH Word if it is not already running.

1. When Word 2013 opens, the Recent screen appears. Click **Single spaced (blank)** document. Click **Create**.

2. Click the **File** tab, and then click **Save As**. In the Save As screen, click **Computer**, and then click **Browse**. Use the vertical scroll bar to locate your flash drive. Open your Word 2013 folder and create a folder within this folder and name it **Lesson 1 Projects**. Double-click to open the folder.

3. In the File name box, type *1-1 Quotes*. Click **Save**.

4. Display the **Show/Hide** nonprinting characters. At the insertion point, type **January 10, 20XX**.

5. Press **Enter** four times to create blank lines.

6. Type the recipient's address as shown:

   Mr. David Pacheco (Press **Enter** once.)
   A Datum Corporation (Press **Enter** once.)
   2133 Montana (Press **Enter** once.)
   El Paso, TX 79938 (Press **Enter** twice.)

7. Type the salutation **Dear Mr. Pacheco:**

8. Press **Enter** twice.

9. Type the body of the letter:

   It was our pleasure meeting with you last week to discuss quotes for the components you requested. As agreed upon, the specifications discussed will be provided to you once we receive final approval from you.

10. Press **Enter** twice.
11. Type **At Proseware, Inc., we appreciate your business.**
12. Press **Enter** twice.
13. Type the closing **Sincerely,**.
14. Press the **Enter** key four times.
15. Type **Joe Villanueva**.
16. Proof your document carefully.
17. Click the **File** tab, and then click **Save**. The updated version of the letter will be saved with the same filename in the lesson folder on your flash drive.

PAUSE. LEAVE the document open for the next project.

Project 1-2: Printing a Document

After proofing the letter you just wrote, you are ready to print copies of the document.

GET READY. LAUNCH Word if it is not already running.

1. Use the *1-1 Quotes* document you created in Project 1-1.
2. Click the **File** tab, and then click **Print**. In the Copies section of the Print options area, click the **up arrow** to change the number of copies from 1 to **2**.
3. Click the **Print** icon.
4. Click **Save** on the Quick Access Toolbar.
5. Click the **File** tab, then click **Close**.

PAUSE. LEAVE Word open for the next project.

Proficiency Assessment

Project 1-3: Creating a Job Responsibilities Document

Your supervisor, Leonard Lachmann, has asked you to type your job duties and responsibilities into a new document.

GET READY. LAUNCH Word if it is not already running.

1. Click the **File** tab, and then click the **New** command and select **Blank document**.
2. Click the **File** tab, and then click **Save As**.
3. Click **Computer**, and then click the **Lesson 1 Projects** folder under Recent Folders.
4. In the File name box, type *1-3 Job Responsibilities*. Click **Save**.
5. Type **October 4, 20XX**. Press **Enter** twice.
6. Type **Duties & Responsibilities:** Press **Enter** once.
7. Type the following paragraphs and press **Enter** once after each paragraph:
   Manage a variety of user experience functions, including programming and promotions
   Manage the online customer experience by creating new site features and maintaining site usability
   Define the website's look and feel
   Partner with the Director of Technology on project planning
   Analyze site usage, feedback, and research

Improve website experience and performance

Manage a team of seven user-experience specialists, including graphic designers, information architects, copywriters, and developers

8. Proof your document carefully.

9. Click the **File** tab, and then click **Save**. The updated file will be saved with the same filename in the lesson folder on your flash drive.

PAUSE. LEAVE the document open for the next project.

Project 1-4: Saving in Different Formats

Now, you want to save your job responsibilities document in a different file format and export the document in a PDF file format.

GET READY. LAUNCH Word if it is not already running.

1. Use the *1-3 Job Responsibilities* document that is open from Project 1-3.

2. Click the **File** tab, and then click **Save As**. Save the document in the Lesson 1 Projects folder. Change the filename to *1-4 Job Responsibilities*. In the Save as type box, click the drop-down arrow and choose **Rich Text Format (*.rtf)**. Click **Save**.

3. Click the **File** tab, and then click **Export**. Click the **Create PDF/XPS** button. Click **Publish**. Close the Adobe Reader.

4. Click the **File** tab, and then **CLOSE** the document.

PAUSE. LEAVE Word open for the next project.

Mastery Assessment

Project 1-5: Saving a Word Document as a Web Page

Your coworker at the Grand Resort Restaurant has been working on a new menu for Thanksgiving. She asks you to look at the new templates that are available in Word 2013.

GET READY. LAUNCH Word if it is not already running.

1. Click the **File** tab, and then click **New**. In the Search for online templates box, search for **menus**. Locate the *Thanksgiving* menu and download the template.

2. **SAVE** the document *1-5 Thanksgiving Menu* as a template in the lesson folder on your flash drive.

3. Type the following under each heading:

Appetizer:	**Sweet and Spicy Cranberry Spread**
First Course:	**Pumpkin Soup Shooters**
Main Course:	**Herb Roasted Turkey Breast**
Sides:	**Apple Stuffing and Dressing**
	Bacon Roasted Potato Salad
	Granola Crunch Sweet Potato Casserole
Dessert:	**Pecan Pumpkin Cheesecake**
	Pecan Pie
	Pumpkin Mousse

4. **SAVE** the document with the same filename in the lesson folder and **CLOSE** the file.

PAUSE. LEAVE Word open for the next project.

Project 1-6: Creating an Invitation

You work for Tech Terrace Real Estate and have been assigned to help with the annual Christmas party. You decided to use one of the available templates on your computer.

GET READY. LAUNCH Word if it is not already running.

1. Locate and download the *Annual Holiday Party* invitation with ornaments and blue ribbon template.

2. **SAVE** the document *1-6 Annual Holiday Party* as a template in the lesson folder on your flash drive.

3. Change the company name to **Tech Terrace Real Estate**.

4. Change the date from December 13 to December **19**.

5. Replace Stephanie Bourne with **Miriam Loera**.

6. **SAVE** the document with the same filename in the lesson folder and **CLOSE** the file.

STOP. CLOSE Word.

LESSON SKILL MATRIX

Skill	Exam Objective	Objective Number
Changing and Organizing Document Views	Change document views.	1.4.1
	Customize the Ribbon.	1.4.4
	Demonstrate how to use Zoom.	1.4.2
	Split the window.	1.4.5
Navigating and Searching through a Document	Search for text within document.	1.2.1
	Find and replace text.	2.1.2
	Demonstrate how to use Find and Replace to format text.	2.2.2
	Demonstrate how to use Go To.	1.2.4
Selecting, Replacing, and Deleting Text		
Cutting, Copying, and Pasting Text	Copy and paste text.	2.1.3
Removing Blank Paragraphs	Remove blank paragraphs.	2.1.5
Changing Information in the Properties	Add values to document properties.	1.4.6

© duckycards/iStockphoto

KEY TERMS

- Clipboard
- copy
- cut
- document properties
- Go To
- gridlines
- multi-selection
- Navigation Pane
- Object Zoom
- paste
- Read Mode
- replace
- rulers
- scroll bars
- scroll box
- scroll buttons
- thumbnails
- wildcard

Star Bright Satellite Radio is the nation's leading satellite radio company. The company sells its subscription service to automobile owners, home listeners, and people on the go with portable satellite radios. The public relations department is responsible for promoting a favorable image of Star Bright Satellite Radio to the media, potential customers, and current customers. Microsoft Word 2013 is the perfect tool for viewing and searching through the department's many documents. In this lesson, you learn to navigate and view a document in Word.

© duckycards/iStockphoto

SOFTWARE ORIENTATION

The View Tab

Word offers several different ways to view a document, locate text or objects quickly, and manipulate windows. After opening a document, you can access related commands on the View tab, shown in Figure 2-1. Use this figure as a reference throughout this lesson as well as the rest of the book.

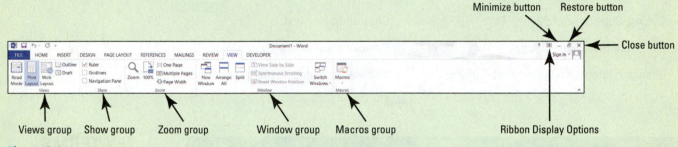

Figure 2-1
View tab

Word provides options to change a document's onscreen appearance by viewing the document in Read Mode, Print Layout, Web Layout, Outline, and Draft view. Adding horizontal and, vertical rulers, or gridlines; increasing or decreasing the view of the document; arranging the document windows; viewing the document side by side; or splitting the document can also change the view on the screen. In addition, the Navigation Pane provides options for browsing and conducting a search in a document.

CHANGING AND ORGANIZING DOCUMENT VIEWS

The Bottom Line

You can enable features to show gridlines, thumbnails, and rulers to help in navigating the document, or you can zoom in or out. Word also allows you to open and arrange multiple document windows. You learn about all these features in this section.

Opening an Existing Document

Word can open files that have been saved in Word format or many other popular formats, such as .RTF, .TXT, or .PDF. You can edit the documents in Word and save the document in the original file format or another file format. The Open button in the Open dialog box contains a drop-down arrow that displays options for opening a document in a different manner. See Table 2-1 for a listing of options. In this exercise, you learn to open a document using the Open dialog box.

Table 2-1

Options for displaying the Clipboard

List	Description
Open Read-Only	Opens the document as a read-only file—no changes can be made to the document.
Open as Copy	Opens a copy of the original document.
Open in Browser	Opens the document that was saved as a web page in a web browser.
Open with Transform	Opens documents that were saved with an XML file type.
Open in Protected View	Opens documents in protected view—to edit, click Enable Editing.
Open and Repair	Opens and repairs corruption to the document.

Clicking the Open command in the File tab produces the new Open screen. You can locate a file quickly in the Recent Documents where it displays the last 25 documents you accessed. From any computer, you can open documents that were saved to the Cloud using SkyDrive. Or, you can open documents that were saved to your local Computer. The Open dialog box opens when you click *Computer*, and then click *Browse*. You can open existing documents from locations such as a flash drive, hard drive, network location, desktop, or portable device. For the purpose of these exercises, the instructions assume that all data files are stored on your flash drive.

 Cross Ref   Saving documents in Compatibility Mode is covered in Lesson 1.

STEP BY STEP   **Open an Existing Document**

 GET READY. Before you begin these steps, be sure to turn on and/or log on to your computer and start Word 2013.

1. Connect your flash drive to one of the USB ports on your computer.
2. Click the **File** tab to open Backstage.
3. Click **Open**. The new Open screen is shown on the left side whereas the right side displays the recently opened documents.
4. Click **Computer**; notice the right side of the screen displays the current recent folders. (See Figure 2-2, but note that your screen will not be identical to the figure.)

Figure 2-2

The new Open screen

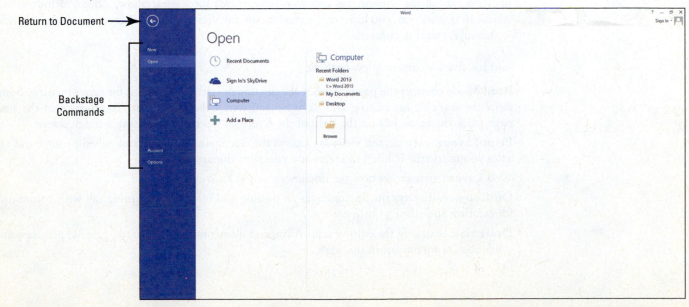

5. Click the **Browse** button. The *Open* dialog box appears.

6. Use the scroll bar and scroll down and locate the data files for this lesson on your flash drive. Double-click the **Lesson02** folder to open it.

7. Locate and click *Star Bright Satellite Proposal* once, as shown in Figure 2-3.

8. Click the **Open** button. The document appears.

Figure 2-3

Open dialog box with subfolder

File path location on flash drive

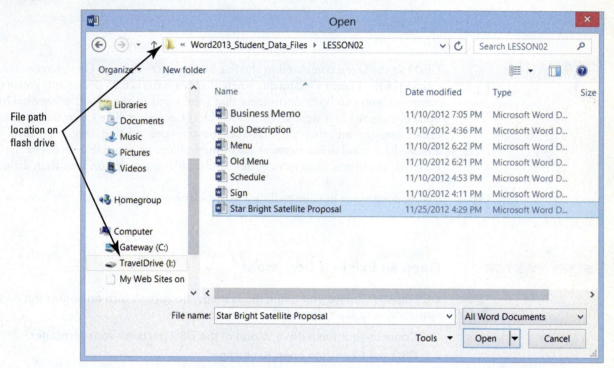

PAUSE. LEAVE the document open to use in the next exercise.

Another Way

To open a document quickly, double-click the filename.

Changing Document Views

The View tab on the Ribbon has groups of commands for Views, Show, Zoom, Window, and Macros. In this section, you learn to use the Document Views command group to change the way Word displays your document.

Word has five Document View options:

- **Read Mode** changes the page layout of the document with a larger font for easier reading. Some tools are available for editing and navigating through the document. To advance to the next page, click the arrow key on the right of the screen or tap if you are using a touch screen.

- **Print Layout** is the default view. It displays the document as it will look when printed and enables you to use the Ribbon to create and edit your document.

- **Web Layout** view shows how the document would look as a web page.

- **Outline** view displays the document as an outline and offers an Outlining tab with commands for creating and editing outlines.

- **Draft** view is strictly for editing text. Advanced elements such as charts, graphs, pictures, and other objects are hidden in this view.

STEP BY STEP   **Change Document Views**

USE the document that is open from the previous exercise.

<table>
<tr><td>CERTIFICATION READY?</td><td>1.4.1</td></tr>
</table>

How would you change the document views?

1. Click the **View** tab to see the command groups that are available.

2. In the Views group, click the **Read Mode** button to change the view of the document as shown in Figure 2-4. The document page layout changes with an increased font size for easier reading.

Figure 2-4

Read Mode view

Menu bar

Previous button

Next button

3. Click **Tools** on the menu in the upper-left corner of the screen to produce the Tools options menu, as shown in Figure 2-5. Four additional commands appear. Note that the first two options are active whereas Can't Undo and Can't Redo are inactive. The inactive commands change to active after an action has been performed.

Figure 2-5

Tools options menu

4. Click **View** on the menu to produce additional commands, such as Edit Document, Navigation Pane, Show Comments, Column Width, Page Color, and Layout.

5. Hover the mouse over each command to view a ScreenTip, and then click **Edit Document**. The screen changes to the Print Layout view for editing.

6. Click the **Read Mode** button again.

7. Click **View** on the menu, and then click **Navigation Pane**. The pane opens on the left side of the screen. This allows you to navigate your document quickly by selecting headings and pages, or by searching for text.

8. In the Navigation Pane, click **Option 3** and notice that your document jumps to that location. Option 3 is formatted with a heading style.

Cross Ref You learn more about styles in Lesson 3.

9. Click the **Pages** tab, and then click the first page. Page images are called *thumbnails*.

10. Click **Close (X)** on the Navigation Pane to close.

11. Press **Esc** to turn off Read Mode view and return to the Print Layout view.

12. Click the **Web Layout** button in the View tab. This view allows you to see the document as a web page.

13. Click the **Outline** button, and notice the Outlining tab and the groups of commands that appear for editing outlines.

14. Click the **Close Outline View** button.

15. Click the **View** tab, and then click the **Draft** view button. This view is typically used for editing text.

16. Click the **Print Layout** view button to return the view of the document back to its default setting.

17. Note that some of the View options buttons are also available on the status bar at the bottom right of your screen . Click each button and compare the resulting views with the views you accessed from the View tab.

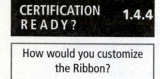

CERTIFICATION READY? 1.4.4

How would you customize the Ribbon?

18. You can also adjust your screen to change the way the Ribbon displays. In the upper-right corner, click the **Ribbon Display Options** button.

19. Select **Auto-hide Ribbon**. The Ribbon is hidden to provide more document workspace.

20. Click the **Ribbon Display Options** button, and then select **Show Tabs**—only the tabs are shown.

21. To return the screen to its original settings, click the **Ribbon Display Options** button and select **Show Tabs and Commands** (see Figure 2-6).

Figure 2-6

Ribbon Display Options menu

PAUSE. LEAVE the document open to use in the next exercise.

 Cross Ref Lesson 12 covers using Outline view in master documents.

Using Show Commands

The Show command group offers options for displaying various onscreen features that can help you create, edit, and navigate your document. In this exercise, you display the ruler and gridlines. You also use the Navigation Pane to browse by headings and by page and to search for text.

Rulers are measuring tools to align text, graphics, and other elements within a document. The horizontal ruler can be used to change a document's first-line indent, hanging indent, and left and right indents. The markers display on the ruler as first-line indent, hanging indent, left indent, and right indent. Manual tab settings can be set on the horizontal ruler without launching the Tabs dialog box.

Gridlines provide a grid of vertical and horizontal lines that help you align graphics and other objects in your documents. Gridlines are displayed only in Print Layout view and are non-printable objects.

Cross Ref   Tabs are discussed in greater detail in Lesson 4.

The **Navigation Pane** appears in the left side of the window when you select its check box in the Show group. The Navigation Pane has three tabs. The first tab, Headings, displays the structure of your document by levels based on the document's headings styles. The second tab, Pages, displays **thumbnails**—tiny images of your document pages. The third tab, Results, displays a list of search results when you have used the Navigation Pane's search tool (marked by a search box and magnifying glass icon) to look for particular text or objects in your document.

On the Results tab, the user can type text in the Search text box, and Word searches the document for every incident where the text occurs. Under the Results tab, a list appears with text or objects found in the document in the order those elements appear in the document. For example, the search results might indicate that the first instance of a word appears on page five, the next instance appears on page eight, and so on. The text in the document appears highlighted in a light yellow and the text is bolded in the Results tab.

You can also see the results of the search in other tabs. In the first tab, Headings, the section that has the found instance appears highlighted in yellow. In the Pages tab, the thumbnail instances found appear highlighted in a light yellow. To clear the search box, click the *X* in that box.

In this exercise, you learn to use Show commands. The Navigation Pane is discussed later in this lesson.

STEP BY STEP   **Use Show Commands**

USE the document that is open from the previous exercise.

1. In the Show command group, click the **Ruler** check box to insert a check mark and activate the command. The horizontal and vertical rulers appear.
2. Click the **Gridlines** check box. A grid appears behind text on the page, as shown in Figure 2-7.

Figure 2-7

Gridlines and rulers

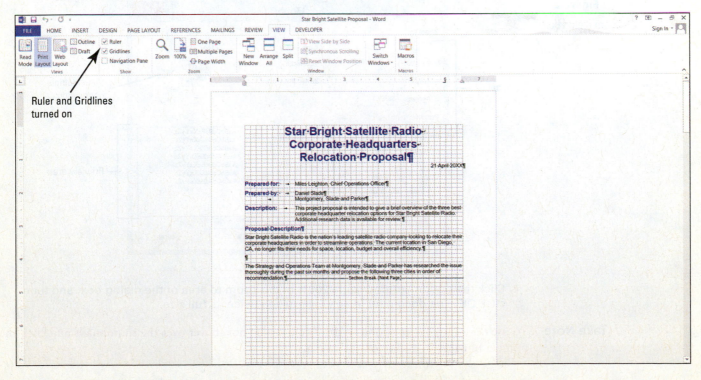

Ruler and Gridlines turned on

3. Click the **Gridlines** check box to remove the check mark.

PAUSE. LEAVE the document open to use in the next exercise.

Using Zoom

The Zoom group of commands lets you zoom in to get a closer view of a page or zoom out to see more of the document at a smaller size. These commands also enable you to determine how many document pages Word displays within a single screen. **Object Zoom** is new in Read Mode and allows you to zoom in on objects such as tables, charts, or images while in Read Mode. In Lesson 6, you practice using the Object Zoom. In this exercise, you use the Zoom commands to view one or two pages; you also use the Zoom slider in the status bar to increase or decrease the size of the displayed image.

Within the Zoom group, the Page Width button expands your document to fit the width of the window. The Zoom button launches the Zoom dialog box, where you have more options for zooming in and out. For instance, you can enter a specific number in the Percent box to modify the view or view multiple pages. Similarly, in the Zoom to section, you can expand the document by clicking a specific zoom amount up to 200%. The preview area shows how the document will appear on screen. The Zoom slider can also be used to zoom in and out; this slider is located in the bottom right of your screen on the status bar. The Zoom slider is also located in the Print screen of Backstage.

STEP BY STEP   **Use Zoom**

USE the document that is open from the previous exercise.

1. Click the **One Page** button in the Zoom command group to display one entire page on the screen.

2. Click the **Multiple Pages** button to switch to a display of multiple pages.

3. Click the **Zoom** 🔍 button. The Zoom dialog box appears, as shown in Figure 2-8.

Figure 2-8

Zoom dialog box

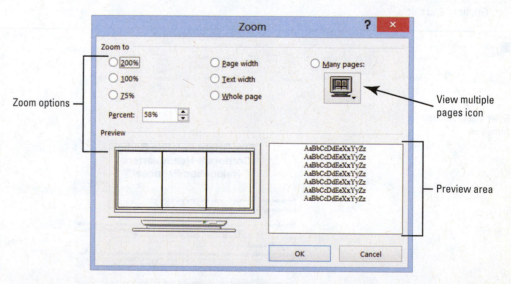

4. Click the option button beside 200% in the Zoom to area of the dialog box, and then click **OK**. The document image enlarges to twice its full size.

Take Note   To use the Many Pages option in the Zoom dialog box, hover over the thumbnails and click the number of pages to display on the screen.

5. Click the **Zoom Out** ▬ button on the Zoom slider, which is located at the right end of the status bar (see Figure 2-9). Each time you click the Zoom Out button, Word decreases the size of the displayed portion of your document by 10%. Click until the Zoom Out indicator displays **60%**.

6. Click the **Zoom In** ➕ button on the Zoom Slider, as shown in Figure 2-9. Zoom to **80%**.

Figure 2-9

The Zoom In and Zoom Out buttons on the Zoom slider

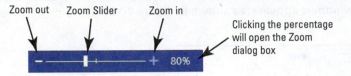

Zoom out   Zoom Slider   Zoom in

Clicking the percentage will open the Zoom dialog box

80%

7. Drag the Zoom slider all the way to the left; Word reduces the document to thumbnail size.

8. Now, in the Zoom command group on the View tab, click the **Page Width** button. The document display expands to the width of the window.

9. Click the **100%** button to return document to its normal size.

PAUSE. LEAVE the document open to use in the next exercise.

Another Way
You can also click the percentage displayed to the right of the Zoom slider to open the Zoom dialog box.

CERTIFICATION READY? 1.4.2

How would you use the Zoom command?

Changing Window Views

The commands in the Window command group enable you to open and arrange multiple document windows. In this exercise, you learn to manipulate your screen by creating a second document in a new window, arranging multiple open documents on one screen, splitting a single document to view different parts, viewing multiple documents side by side, resetting window positioning to divide the screen equally, and switching between windows.

The commands in the Window command group are as follows:

- The **New Window** button opens a new window displaying the current document; this window shows the document name in the title bar followed by the number 2. Each new window you open in the same document receives a chronologically numbered name. This feature allows you to work in different places in your document.

- The **Arrange All** button displays two or more windows on the screen at the same time. This is useful when comparing documents or when using information from multiple documents.

- The **Split** command divides one document window into two windows that scroll independently. This enables you to view two parts of a single document at the same time.

- The **View Side by Side** button allows you to view two documents next to each other. When you are viewing documents side by side, you can use the **Synchronous Scrolling** command to link the scrolling of the two documents so that you move through both at the same time.

- The **Reset Window Position** button is used with the View Side by Side button, and when viewing two documents side by side, the Reset Window Position button will position both documents equally on the screen.

- The **Switch Windows** button allows you to select which document will be the active document (the document that is ready for editing). The name of the active document appears on the title bar.

On occasion, you might need to move a window out of the way without exiting the associated application. This is where the three buttons in the upper-right corner of the Word screen come in handy. The Minimize button ▬ minimizes the window display—in other words, the window disappears and is replaced with an icon on the Status task bar Restore button ⧉ returns a document to its previous size by minimizing or maximizing its display. Finally, the Close button ☒ closes the window. If you have only one Word document open, the close button will also close Word.

Change Window Views

USE the document that is open from the previous exercise.

1. In the Window command group, click the **New Window** button. A new window with *Star Bright Satellite Proposal:2* in the document title bar appears and becomes the active document.

2. In the Window command group, click the **Switch Windows** button. A menu of open windows appears, as shown in Figure 2-10.

Figure 2-10

Switch Windows button and menu

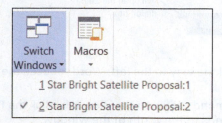

3. In the Switch Windows drop-down menu, click *Star Bright Satellite Proposal:1*. The original document becomes the active document.

4. Click the **Arrange All** button. Word displays the two windows, one above the other, on your screen, as shown in Figure 2-11.

Figure 2-11

Two windows displayed using the Arrange All command

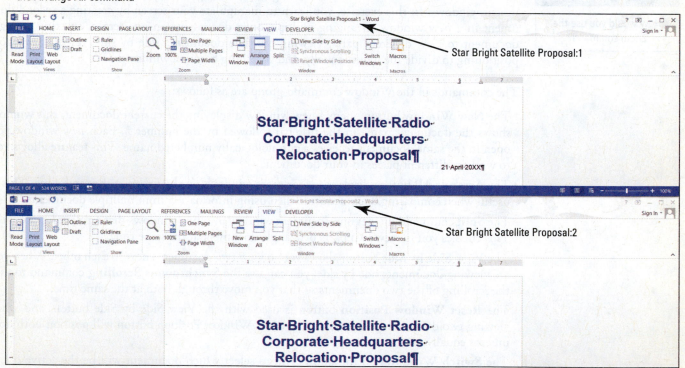

5. Click the **View Side by Side** button to arrange the windows beside each other on the screen.

6. Note that **Synchronous Scrolling** is on by default. Place your insertion point on the slider in the vertical scroll bar and press the left mouse button as you move the slider up and down to scroll through the documents; notice that both scroll simultaneously.

7. Click anywhere in the *Star Bright Satellite Proposal:2* document; this now becomes the active document.

8. Click the **Synchronous Scrolling** button to turn off that feature. Place your insertion point on the vertical scroll bar and scroll down; notice that the *Star Bright Satellite Proposal:2* document is now scrolling independently.

CERTIFICATION READY? 1.4.5

How would you split the window?

9. Click the **Close** ⊠ button to close the *Star Bright Satellite Proposal:2* document.
10. Click the **Maximize** button on the *Star Bright Satellite Proposal* document to fill the screen.
11. Click the **Split** button. Notice you now have a horizontal split bar. Drag the split bar below the text Relocation Proposal and release the mouse button. Splitting your document makes it easy to edit two different sections. The document window splits in two and the **Split** button changes to a **Remove Split** button (see Figure 2-12).

Figure 2-12

Split window and Remove Split button

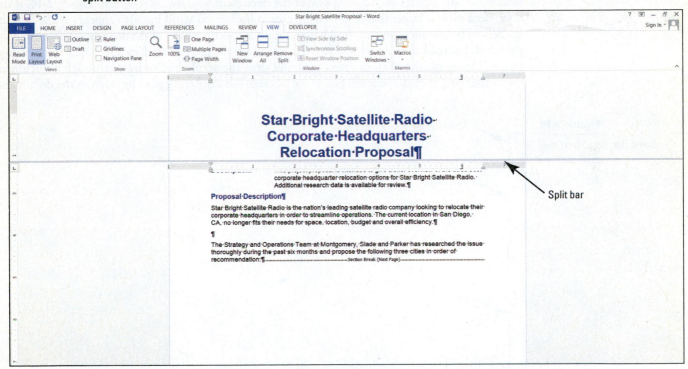

Split bar

12. Click **Remove Split**.
13. Click the **Minimize** ⊟ button. The document minimizes to become an icon in the Windows task bar at the bottom of the screen, and the desktop appears.
14. Hover your mouse over the Word icon in the task bar (as shown in Figure 2-13), and then click the *Star Bright Satellite Proposal* document's icon in the task bar to maximize the document on the screen.

Figure 2-13

Document minimized to task bar

PAUSE. LEAVE the document open to use in the next exercise.

NAVIGATING AND SEARCHING THROUGH A DOCUMENT

As you already learned, the Navigation Pane contains commands for moving and searching through a document. You also can use Find command options, the mouse, scroll bars, and various keystroke and keyboard shortcut commands to navigate through Word documents. In this section, you practice using the mouse and scroll bar, keystroke commands, the Navigation Pane, and a number of command group commands to move quickly through a document; search for specific text, graphics, or other document elements; and remove or replace those elements.

Scroll bars allow a user to move up or down or side to side within a document. In Word, a vertical scroll bar appears on the right side of the document window, as shown in Figure 2-14; if the document view is larger than the viewing area, a horizontal scroll bar also appears at the bottom of the window to allow you to scroll left and right across the width of the document. You can click the **scroll buttons** to move up or down one line at a time, or you can click and hold a scroll button to scroll more quickly. You can also click and drag the **scroll box** to move through a document even faster or just click the scroll box to see a ScreenTip displaying your position in the document.

Figure 2-14

Scroll bar, scroll box, and scroll buttons

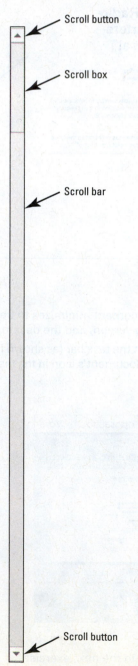

Scroll button

Scroll box

Scroll bar

Scroll button

Using the Mouse and Scroll Bar to Navigate

Using the mouse in combination with the scroll bar is a simple way to scroll through a document.

| STEP BY STEP | Use the Mouse and Scroll Bar to Navigate |

USE the document that is open from the previous exercise.

1. Click the **scroll down** button to scroll down one line at a time.
2. Click and hold the **scroll down** button until you scroll all the way to the end of the document.
3. Drag the **scroll box** all the way to the top of the scroll bar; the view quickly scrolls to the beginning of the document.
4. Position the mouse pointer on the **scroll box**. Click and hold to see a ScreenTip identifying your current location in the document (see Figure 2-15).

Figure 2-15

Scroll box ScreenTip

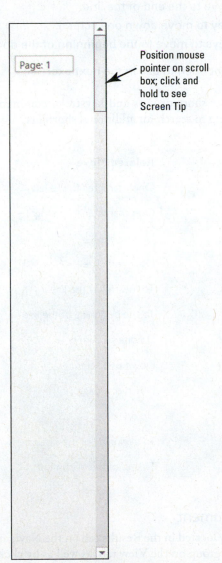

Position mouse pointer on scroll box; click and hold to see Screen Tip

Page: 1

PAUSE. LEAVE the document open to use in the next exercise.

Using Keystrokes to Navigate

The arrow keys and other keyboard commands can also help you move through a document.

Use Keystrokes to Navigate

USE the document that is open from the previous exercise.

1. In the first line of the body of the document, position the insertion point before the *S* in *Star*.
2. On the keyboard, press the **Right arrow** key to move the insertion point one character to the right.
3. Press the **Left arrow** key to move one character to the left.
4. Press the **Down arrow** key to move down one line.
5. Press the **End** key to move to the end of the line.
6. Press the **Page Down** key to move down one screen.
7. Press the **Ctrl+Home** keys to move to the beginning of the document.

PAUSE. LEAVE the document open to use in the next exercise.

Table 2-2 lists these and other shortcut keys and keystroke commands you can use to navigate through a document. Use Help to search for additional shortcuts.

Table 2-2

Keyboard shortcuts for navigating a document

Shortcut Key	Related Move
Left arrow	One character to the left
Right arrow	One character to the right
Up arrow	Up one line
Down arrow	Down one line
End	To the end of the line
Home	To the beginning of the line
Page up	Up one screen
Page down	Down one screen
Ctrl+Page down	Down one page
Ctrl+Page up	Up one page
Ctrl+Home	To beginning of the document
Ctrl+End	To end of the document

Searching within a Document

Word's Find command is now located in the Results tab on the Navigation Pane. You can open the Navigation Pane in the Show group on the View tab, as well as by clicking the Find button on the Home tab in the Editing group. By using the Navigation Pane, you can easily locate specific text, graphics, objects, and equations within a document. The document contains highlighted text, and the Results tab displays the results in bold. Word places the results in the order they appear in the document. In this exercise, you learn to use the Navigation Pane to search for every occurrence of a specific word within a document.

In the Home tab on the Editing group, the drop-down arrow by the Find button displays a menu that contains the Find, Advanced Find, and Go To commands. The Find command opens the

Navigation Pane with the Results tab active; the Advanced Find command opens the Find and Replace dialog box with Find as the active tab; and the Go To command opens the same dialog box with Go To as the active tab. In the Editing group, the Replace command opens the Find and Replace dialog box with Replace as the active tab. The Select command provides options in selecting text or objects.

To highlight every occurrence of a particular word or phrase in your document, you must activate Advanced Find. To do so, click the drop-down arrow by the Search text box, as shown in Figure 2-16, and then click *Advanced Find*. The Find and Replace dialog box opens. Within the Find what box, type your desired word or phrase, and then click the drop-down arrow on the Reading Highlight button and select *Highlight All*. When you close the Find and Replace dialog box, each instance of your desired word or phrase is highlighted in the document. To clear all occurrences of highlighted text, return to the Advanced Find options, click the *Reading Highlight* button, and then select *Clear Highlighting*.

Figure 2-16

Navigation Pane displaying additional options

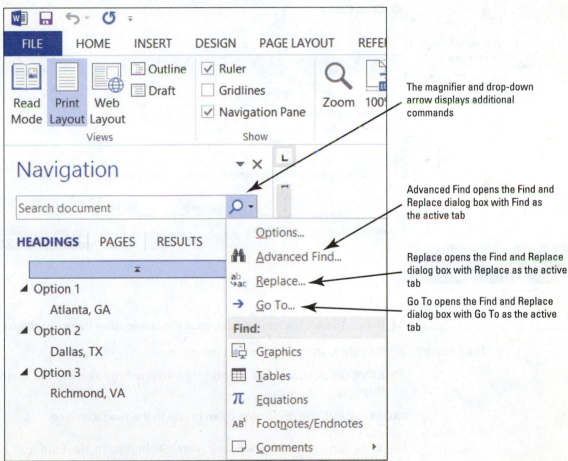

The magnifier and drop-down arrow displays additional commands

Advanced Find opens the Find and Replace dialog box with Find as the active tab

Replace opens the Find and Replace dialog box with Replace as the active tab

Go To opens the Find and Replace dialog box with Go To as the active tab

STEP BY STEP   **Use the Navigation Pane to Search for Text in a Document**

USE the document that is open from the previous exercise.

1. Click the **View** tab, and then in the Show command group, click the **Navigation Pane** check box. The Navigation Pane opens.

2. Type **relocation** in the Search text box; the text is highlighted in the document and results are shown in the Headings, Pages, and Results tabs of the Navigation Pane.

Another Way
To open the Navigation Pane using the keyboard, press *Ctrl+ F*, or you can click the Find drop-down arrow in the Editing group on the Home tab.

3. Click the third tab, **Results**. Note that the found text is bolded, and it appears in the order of its occurrence in the document.

4. Click the first tab, **Headings**, and note the headings of sections that contain the found text are highlighted.

5. Click the second tab, **Pages**, and note the highlighted found text in the thumbnails.

6. Click each **thumbnail** until you get to page 4.

7. Click the **X** in the Search text box to end your search. Word automatically returns to page one.

8. Click the **magnifying glass** icon on the right side of the Navigation Pane box to open a list of available Options.

9. From the Options list opened, click the **Advanced Find** command. The *Find and Replace* dialog box opens.

10. The word "relocation" should be in the Find what text box; click the **Find Next** button. Click **Yes** to return to the top of the document, if prompted.

11. Click the **Reading Highlight** button and select **Highlight All** to highlight all instances of this word. Review each page.

12. Before closing the Find and Replace dialog box, remove the highlight from the text by clicking the **Reading Highlight** button; and then **Clear Highlighting** (see Figure 2-17).

13. Click **Close**.

Figure 2-17

Reading Highlight

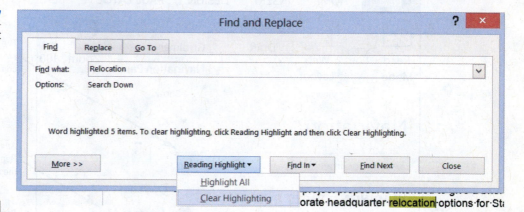

How would you search for text?

14. In the Show command group, click the **Navigation Pane** check box to turn off this pane.

Take Note   To end your search, click the *X* in the text box.

15. **SAVE** the document as *Star Bright Satellite Proposal 1* in the lesson folder of your flash drive.

PAUSE. LEAVE the document open to use in the next exercise.

For more search options, click the *More>>* button in the Find and Replace dialog box. In the Search Options area that appears, you can choose additional criteria to refine the search process—for example, you can choose to match case or whole words only. You can also use **wildcard** characters to find words or phrases that contain specific letters or combinations of letters. Simply type a question mark (?) to represent a single character—for example, typing **b?t** finds *bat*, *bet*, *bit*, and *but*. Similarly, type an asterisk (*) to represent a string of characters—for example, **m*t** finds *mat*, *moment*, or even *medium format*.

Within the Find and Replace dialog box, you can click the Format button to find text with specific formatting, such as a particular font, paragraph setting, or style. You can also click the *Special* button to find special elements in a document, such as fields, footnote marks, or section breaks.

Finding and Replacing Text in a Document

Located on the Home tab in the Editing group, the Replace command opens the Find and Replace dialog box. You can use the Replace command to replace one word or phrase with another. You can also use the Find and Replace command to search for and **replace** formatting—such as a specific font color, bolding, or italics. It is also possible to search for and replace special characters and document elements such as page breaks and tabs. In this exercise, you learn to search for and replace a word with a particular type of formatting.

| STEP BY STEP | Replace Text in a Document |

USE the document that is open from the previous exercise.

1. Place the insertion point at the beginning of the document by pressing **Ctrl+Home**.
2. Click the **Home** tab to make it active. In the Editing group, click the **Replace** button; the *Find and Replace* dialog box opens.
3. Click the **More>>** button to review the options, and then click the **<<Less** button to hide them.
4. In the Find what box, type **Montgomery, Slade, and Parker**. (If "relocation" appears in the Find what box, select it and press **Delete**, and then type in the new search string.)
5. In the Replace with box, type **Becker, Steele, and Castillo**.
6. Click **Find Next**. Word searches for the first occurrence of the phrase **Montgomery, Slade, and Parker** and highlights it. Note: If Word does not find any matches, check the spelling in the Find what text box.
7. Click **Replace All**. Word searches for all occurrences of the phrase *Montgomery, Slade, and Parker* and replaces them with *Becker, Steele, and Castillo*. Word then displays a message revealing how many replacements were made, as shown in Figure 2-18.

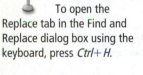

Another Way
To open the Replace tab in the Find and Replace dialog box using the keyboard, press *Ctrl+H*.

Figure 2-18

Find and Replace message

Microsoft Word

All done. We made 2 replacements.

OK

8. Click **OK**, and then click **Close**.
9. Position the insertion point at the beginning of the document.
10. Click the **View** tab; then, in the Show command group, click the **Navigation Pane** check box.
11. In the Navigation Pane, click the drop-down arrow or magnifier so that the ScreenTip displays Search for more things; then, click **Replace** to open the *Find and Replace* dialog box.
12. In this next step, you reverse the search order. In the Find what text box, type **Becker, Steele, and Castillo**; then, in the Replace with text box, type **Montgomery, Slade, and Parker**. Keep your insertion point in the Replace with text box.
13. Click the **More>>** button to expand the dialog box to include additional search and replace options (see Figure 2-19).
14. Click the **Format** button and select **Font** from the drop-down list; the Replace Font dialog box appears.
15. In the Font area, use the scroll bar to scroll to **Garamond**, and then click to select it.
16. In the Font Style area, select **Bold Italic**.
17. Select size **14**.
18. Click the **Font Color** drop-down arrow, and then select **Dark Red** in the Standard Colors and preview the results.

19. Click **OK**. Below the Replace with text box, you see the format selections—refer to Figure 2-19.

20. Click **Replace All**; two replacements will be completed.

21. Click **OK**, and then click **Close**. Inspect your document and notice that the replacements have been made with formatting changes.

Figure 2-19

Find and Replace dialog box with Search Options

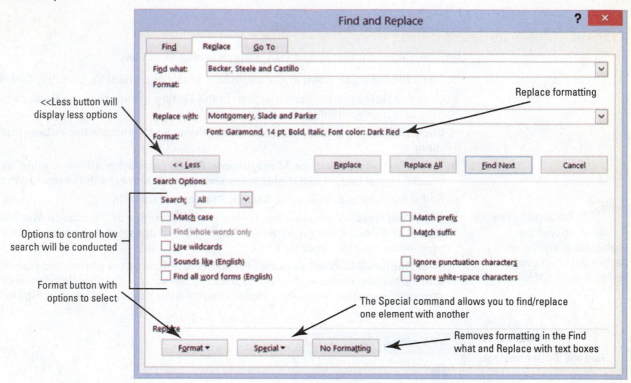

22. On the Navigation Pane, click the **X**, or on the Show command group, click the check box for Navigation Pane to close.

23. Click the Show/Hide button to display the nonprinting characters.

24. To use the Advanced Search feature, click the **Home** tab, and in the Editing group, click **Replace**.

25. Place the insertion point in the Find what text box, and select and delete any text in the box by pressing **Backspace** or **Delete**.

26. Place your insertion point in the Replace with text box, select and delete any text in that box by pressing **Backspace** or **Delete** and click the **No Formatting** button at the bottom of the screen—this removes all formatting in the Replace with text box.

27. Place your insertion point in the Find what text box, and then click the **Special** button. In the list of searchable elements that appears, click **Section Break**; Word places the characters **(^b)** in the text box.

28. Place your insertion point in the Replace with text box. Click the **Special** button.

29. Click **Manual Page Break**; **(^m)** appears in the text box.

30. Click **Find Next**, and notice that Word highlights the first occurrence. Click **Replace All**. Three replacements are made in the document and the document has Page Breaks instead of Section Breaks.

31. Click **OK**, and then click **Close** to close the *Find and Replace* dialog box.

32. Review the page breaks in the document and leave the Show/Hide button on.

33. **SAVE** the document on your flash drive as *Star Bright Satellite Proposal Update*.

PAUSE. LEAVE the document open to use in the next exercise.

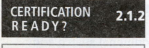

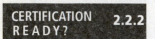

Cross Ref   Section and manual breaks are covered in Lesson 5.

Take Note   You can use the Find and Replace tool to replace specific punctuation within a document. For instance, say you pressed the spacebar twice at the end of each sentence and you would like to replace each set of two spaces with only one space. In the Find what text box, press the **Spacebar** twice; then in the Replace with text box, press the **Spacebar** once and click the **Replace All** button. Upon doing this, Word replaces all instances of double spacing with single spaces.

When replacing text, you can confirm each replacement to make sure it is correct by clicking *Replace* instead of Replace All. Using the Find and Replace command assists you in finding text and avoiding mistakes.

Troubleshooting   If you experience problems when using the Replace command to replace formatting or one of the special elements, display the Find and Replace dialog box again. Review the Find what text box for correct spelling or correct element. Below the Replace with text box is the Formatting to replace text. For instance, if you are replacing search text with a red color and bold as the style, below the Replace with text box, you see *Font: Bold, Font color: Red* (refer to Figure 2-19).

Using the Go To Command to Navigate a Long Document

In a longer document, you might want to move through the document more quickly than is possible by scrolling. The **Go To** command provides a way to navigate through longer documents quickly. In this exercise, you learn to use the Go To command to move through a lengthy document.

Using the Go To command jumps to a specific page, table, graphic, equation, or other item in your document. To go to the next or previous item of the same type, leave the Enter box empty, and then click *Previous* or *Next*. The Go To command is located in the Find and Replace dialog box.

 **STEP BY STEP**   **Use the Go To Command**

USE the document that is open from the previous exercise.

1. On the **Home** tab, in the Editing group, click the drop-down arrow next to the Find button, and then click **Go To**. The Go To tab of the Find and Replace dialog box is displayed, as shown in Figure 2-20.

Figure 2-20

Go To tab

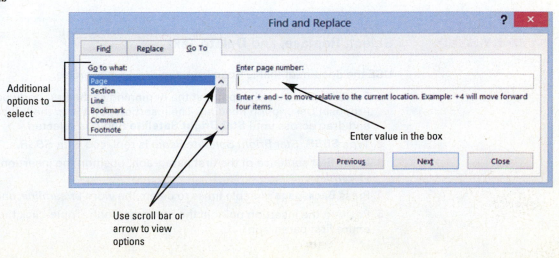

Another Way
To open the Go To tab in the Find and Replace dialog box using the keyboard, press *Ctrl+ G* or press *F5*.

CERTIFICATION READY? **1.2.4**

How would you Go To specific places in a document?

🔍 **Cross Ref**

Take Note

2. In the Go to what box, Page is selected by default. In the Enter page number box, type **4**, and then click **Go To**. The insertion point moves to page 4 of the document.

3. In the Go to what box, select **Line**. In the Enter line number box, type **10**, and then click **Go To**. The insertion point moves to line 10 in the document.

4. In the Go to what box, select **Bookmark**. In the Enter bookmark name box, Option_1 displays. Click **Go To**. The insertion point moves to the bookmark.

5. Click the drop-down arrow in the Enter bookmark name box and select **Top**, and then click **Go To**. The insertion point is placed at the beginning of the document.

6. Click **Close**.

PAUSE. LEAVE the document open to use in the next exercise.

Bookmarks and hyperlinks are described in Lesson 12. This is another way to navigate through a document quickly.

Word keeps track of where you typed or edited text. To go to a previous editing location in your document, press *Shift+ F5*. After saving your document in your computer, flash drive, or SkyDrive, Word 2013 will remember where you left off in your document.

SELECTING, REPLACING, AND DELETING TEXT

The Bottom Line

Word offers a number of tools for selecting, deleting, and replacing text. You also can apply formatting to selected text. In this exercise, you use the mouse and keyboard to select text and delete it or replace it with new text.

Selecting, Replacing, and Deleting Text

You can delete text in Word documents by pressing the *Backspace* key to delete characters to the left of the insertion point, pressing the *Delete* key to delete characters to the right of the insertion point, or selecting text and pressing either the *Delete* key or *Backspace* key. In this exercise, you learn to select and delete text and to type in replacement text. You also practice using the Undo and Redo buttons in the Quick Access Toolbar.

The **multi-selection** feature of Word enables you to select multiple text items that are not continuous. For example, to select every other line in a paragraph, select the first line, and then press and hold the *Ctrl* key as you select the other lines by clicking the left mouse button.

To replace text in a Word document, simply select the text you want to replace, and then type new text. To cancel a selection, click in any blank area of the document screen.

STEP BY STEP **Select, Replace, and Delete Text**

USE the document that is open from the previous exercise.

1. Position your insertion point at the beginning of the first body paragraph, under the Proposal Description heading. The insertion point is to the left of the *S* in *Star*. Click and drag across until **Star Bright Satellite Radio** is selected.

2. Type **SBSR**. *Star Bright Satellite Radio* is replaced with *SBSR*.

3. In the first sentence of the first paragraph, position the insertion point after the word *streamline*.

4. Press **Backspace** multiple times to delete the word *streamline*, and then type **restructure**.

5. Position the insertion point in the first paragraph. Triple-click the mouse to select the entire first paragraph.

6. Position the insertion point at the beginning of the first paragraph under Proposal Description. To select multiple text, press and hold the **Ctrl** key and double-click every other word on the first line beginning with *SBSR*. Every other word is now selected.

7. Click in a blank part of the page, such as the margin, to deselect the selected words.

8. Then place your insertion point at the beginning of the same paragraph, beginning with *SBSR is the nation's leading. . .* and click. Move the I-Beam pointer to the end of the sentence (*restructure operations*), press the **Ctrl** key, and click. The sentence is now selected.

9. Press **Backspace** or **Delete** to delete the sentence.

10. Click the **Undo** button in the Quick Access Toolbar to undo the action.

11. **SAVE** the document as *Star Bright Satellite Proposal Second Update* in the lesson folder on your flash drive.

PAUSE. LEAVE the document open to use in the next exercise.

When you position the mouse pointer to the left of the margin, it changes to a selection arrow that enables you to click to select the entire line to the right of the pointer. You then can drag down to continue selecting adjacent words, lines of text, or entire paragraphs. Table 2-3 lists this and other techniques for selecting text with the mouse.

Table 2-3

Selecting text with the mouse

To Select	Do This
Any amount of text	Click and drag across the text
A word	Double-click the word
A line	Click in the left margin with the mouse pointer
Multiple lines	Click and drag in the left margin
A sentence	Hold Ctrl and click anywhere in the sentence
A paragraph	Double-click in the left margin or triple-click in the paragraph
The entire document	Triple-click in the left margin

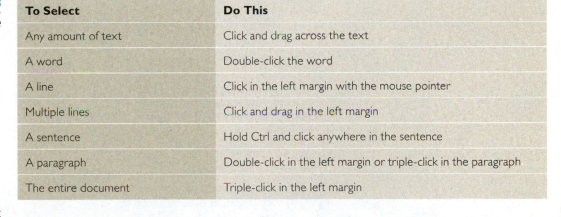

Another Way

The Select button in the Editing command group of the Home tab lets you select all text in a document, or select text with similar formatting.

You also can use keyboard commands to select text. Table 2-4 shows various keyboard shortcuts you can press to select text.

Table 2-4

Selecting text with the keyboard

To Select	Key This
One character to the right	Shift+Right Arrow
One character to the left	Shift+Left Arrow
To the end of a word	Ctrl+Shift+Right Arrow
To the beginning of a word	Ctrl+Shift+Left Arrow
To the end of a line	Shift+End
To the beginning of a line	Shift+Home
To the end of a document	Ctrl+Shift+End
To the beginning of a document	Ctrl+Shift+Home
The entire document	Ctrl+A
To the end of a paragraph	Ctrl+Shift+Down Arrow

CUTTING, COPYING, AND PASTING TEXT

It is often necessary to copy or remove text from one location in a document and place it in another. When you use the copy or cut command, the **Clipboard** stores the items for you to paste in another location of the document or Office file. When you **cut** text, Word removes it from the original location and places the deleted text in the Clipboard collection. When you **copy** text, Word places a duplicate copy in the Clipboard. The **Paste** command then pastes text from the Clipboard to a new location in either the original document or a new document. In this exercise, you learn two different ways to copy and move text—using the Clipboard and using the mouse.

Entries placed in the Clipboard can be placed anywhere in a document by positioning the insertion point in the new location, and then selecting one of the three Paste options shown in Table 2-5 and Figure 2-21.

Table 2-5

Paste option descriptions

Paste Option	Description	Sample Item Placed on Clipboard	How Item Displays When Pasted
Keep source formatting	Keeps the selected text with the original format, including hyperlinks.	**WILEY.COM**	**WILEY.COM**
Merge formatting	If the text contains fonts of different sizes and colors, the paste produces black text with Calibri (Body) 11-point formatting when in a new document screen. If pasting in the same document, the destination formatting is used.	**Pa**st**e**	Paste
Keep text only	Regardless of its font, size, and formatting, when pasted, the text appears in 11-point Calibri (Body).	**College**	College

Figure 2-21

Paste options

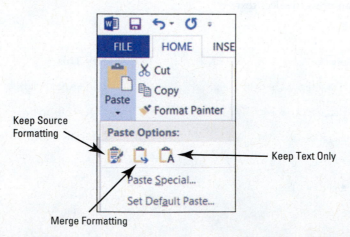

Keep Source Formatting

Merge Formatting

Keep Text Only

Copying and Moving Text with Clipboard Commands

The Clipboard enables you to cut or copy multiple items and paste them into any Office document. In this exercise, you learn to use the Clipboard command group on the Home tab to copy and move text.

Collected items stay on the Clipboard until all Office programs are closed or you click the Clear All button in the Clipboard task pane. The Clipboard holds up to 24 items and when another item is added, the first item is deleted from the Clipboard and the latest item is placed at the top of the list. Each entry in the Clipboard includes an icon representing the source Office program and a portion of copied text or a thumbnail of a copied graphic. By default, when text is selected, a message appears on the status bar showing how many words are selected and the total number of words in the document.

STEP BY STEP   **Use the Clipboard to Copy and Move Text**

USE the document that is open from the previous exercise.

1. Triple-click to select the **second paragraph** of the document under the Proposal Description heading.

2. On the **Home** tab, in the Clipboard group, click the **Cut** button. When using the Cut or Copy command, the item is automatically placed in the Clipboard.

3. Click to place the insertion point in front of the first character of the sentence that begins "*SBSR is the nation's leading . . .*"

4. Click the **Clipboard** command group dialog box launcher to display the Clipboard task pane.

5. In the list of cut and copied items, move your mouse pointer to the text you cut in step 2, and click the drop-down arrow to produce the menu shown in Figure 2-22.

Figure 2-22

Clipboard task pane options

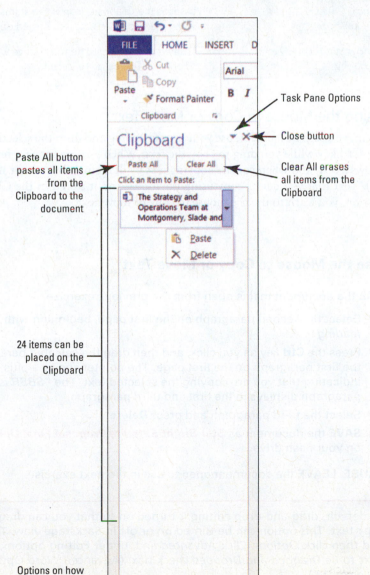

Task Pane Options

Close button

Paste All button pastes all items from the Clipboard to the document

Clear All erases all items from the Clipboard

24 items can be placed on the Clipboard

Options on how to display the Clipboard

Another Way
To copy an item to the Clipboard using the keyboard, select the item, and then press *Ctrl+C*. To cut a selected item using the keyboard, press *Ctrl+X*. To paste the item most recently collected on the Clipboard, click to locate the insertion point, and then press *Ctrl+V* on the keyboard. To produce a shortcut menu containing Cut, Copy, and Paste commands, right-click in the document.

6. Click **Paste** to insert the text into the document in the new location.

7. Click the **Close** button on the Clipboard task pane.

PAUSE. LEAVE the document open to use in the next exercise.

Take Note   Your Clipboard task pane might look different depending on how many items have been collected.

The Options drop-down arrow at the bottom of the Clipboard task pane offers multiple options for displaying the Clipboard. Table 2-6 describes these options.

Table 2-6

Options for displaying the Clipboard

Option	Description
Show Office Clipboard Automatically	Automatically displays the Clipboard when copying.
Show Office Clipboard When Ctrl+C Pressed Twice	Automatically displays the Clipboard when you press *Ctrl+C* twice.
Collect Without Showing Office Clipboard	The Clipboard is not displayed when copying or cutting text.
Show Office Clipboard Icon on Taskbar	Displays the Clipboard icon in the status area of the system task bar when the Clipboard is active. Turned on by default.
Show Status Near Taskbar When Copying	Displays the "collected item" message when copying items to the Clipboard. Turned on by default.

Using the Mouse to Copy or Move Text

To move a selection of text, use your mouse to drag and drop the selection in a new location. Hold the Ctrl key while you drag to copy the text. When you are moving text by dragging, the pointer shows a box, and when you are copying text by dragging, the pointer shows a box with a plus sign (+). Text that you cut or copy using the mouse is not stored in the Clipboard collection. In this section, you learn to use the mouse to copy or move text.

STEP BY STEP   **Use the Mouse to Copy or Move Text**

USE the document that is open from the previous exercise.

1. Select the second paragraph on the first page, beginning with *"SBSR is the nation's leading . . ."*

2. Press the **Ctrl** key as you click, and then drag the selected paragraph and drop it above the first paragraph on the first page. The pointer shows a plus sign (+) as you drag, indicating that you are copying the selected text. The *"SBSR is the nations' leading . . ."* paragraph displays in the first and third paragraph.

3. Select the third paragraph and press **Delete**.

4. **SAVE** the document as *Star Bright Satellite Proposal Final Update* in the lesson folder on your flash drive.

PAUSE. LEAVE the document open to use in the next exercise.

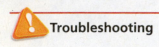

CERTIFICATION READY?   2.1.3

How would you use the copy and paste commands?

Troubleshooting   By default, drag-and-drop editing is turned on so that you can drag the pointer to move and copy text. This option can be turned on or off in Backstage view. To do so, click the *File* tab, and then click *Options*. Click *Advanced* and, under Editing options, select or clear the *Allow Text to Be Dragged and Dropped* check box. (Advanced Word Options are covered in depth in Lesson 14.)

Removing Blank Paragraphs

As you create a document or review an existing document, it is good practice to remove extra blank lines between paragraphs. In this section, you learn to remove blank paragraphs.

Remove Blank Paragraphs

USE the document that is open from the previous exercise.

1. If necessary, enable the Show/Hide (¶).
2. In the first page after the second paragraph, place the insertion point at the beginning of the paragraph mark and press **Delete**.
3. On page two, remove the extra paragraph marks in the body text under the heading *Atlanta, GA* by pressing **Delete**. Repeat these steps for page 3 to remove the extra paragraph marks under the heading *Dallas, TX* and on page 4 under the heading *Richmond, VA*.
4. **SAVE** the document with the same filename in the lesson folder on your flash drive.

PAUSE. LEAVE the document open to use in the next exercise.

CERTIFICATION READY? 2.1.5

How would you remove blank paragraphs?

CHANGING INFORMATION IN THE PROPERTIES

The Bottom Line

Backstage view enables you to access the properties to add information about the document, such as the author's name, subject, company, and much more. In this exercise, you learn two different ways to add information to the properties.

Document properties identify the creator of the document, date the document was created, subject, category, and keywords that can be used to search for the document.

The Document Properties panel is displayed on the document screen, by accessing Info in the Backstage, and then selecting *Show Document Panel*. The Show Document Panel displays the Document Properties below the Ribbon. You can access the Advanced Properties by clicking the drop-down arrow in the Document Properties, or you can open them through Backstage.

Change Information in the Properties

USE the document that is open from the previous exercise.

1. Click **File** to open Backstage, and then click the drop-down arrow on the right-side of Properties to view the options as shown in Figure 2-23.

Figure 2-23

Properties options

2. Click **Show Document Panel**. The Document Properties panel is displayed above the document.

3. Type the following information in the appropriate text box:

Author: [Your Name]

Title: Policies & Procedures

Subject: Handbook

4. Click the drop-down arrow in the Document Properties located in the upper-left side of the panel as shown in Figure 2-24.

Figure 2-24

Document Properties option to open Advanced Properties

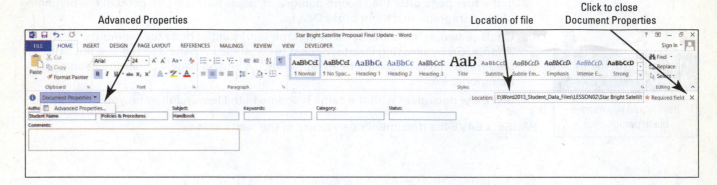

5. Click **Advanced Properties** to open the Properties dialog box, and then click the **Summary** tab to make it active.

6. Add the following information to the appropriate text box:

Manager: Aggie Becker

Company: Star Bright Satellite Radio

Keywords: policies, procedures, benefits (separate keywords with a comma)

7. Click **OK** to confirm the update made to the properties, and then close the Document Panel by clicking the **X**.

8. **SAVE** the document in the lesson folder on your flash drive then **CLOSE** the document.

CLOSE Word.

CERTIFICATION READY?   1.4.6

How would you add information to the document properties?

SKILL SUMMARY

In This Lesson, You Learned to:	Exam Objective	Objective Number
Change and Organize Document Views	Change document views.	1.4.1
	Customize the Ribbon.	1.4.4
	Demonstrate how to use Zoom.	1.4.2
	Split the window.	1.4.5
Navigate and Search through a Document	Search for text within document.	1.2.1
	Find and replace text.	2.1.2
	Demonstrate how to use Find and Replace to format text.	2.2.2
	Demonstrate how to use Go To.	1.2.4
Select, Replace, and Delete Text		
Cut, Copy, and Paste Text	Copy and paste text.	2.1.3
Remove Blank Paragraphs	Remove blank paragraphs.	2.1.5
Change Information in the Properties	Add values to document properties.	1.4.6

Knowledge Assessment

Multiple Choice

Select the best response for the following statements.

1. Which Word feature enables you to select multiple pieces of text that are not next to each other?
   a. Multi-selection feature
   b. Multi-task feature
   c. Multi-select all text feature
   d. Ctrl+A feature

2. _____ are reduced-size versions of images.
   a. Thumb drives
   b. Thumb documents
   c. Thumbnails
   d. Preview panes

3. The Advanced Properties allows you to add:
   a. keywords.
   b. category.
   c. author's name.
   d. All of the above

4. In what view is Synchronous Scrolling active?
   a. Split
   b. Arrange All
   c. New Window
   d. View Side by Side

5. When Heading Styles have been applied to a document, the user has the option to navigate through the document using which tab on the Navigation Pane?
   a. Headings
   b. Pages
   c. Results
   d. None of the above

6. Commands for replacing text with formatted text are located in the:
   a. Find and Replace dialog box.
   b. Advanced Find in the Navigation Pane.
   c. Dialog box that opens when you press Ctrl+H.
   d. All of the above

7. The keyboard shortcut for finding text is:
   a. Ctrl+H.
   b. Ctrl+F.
   c. Ctrl+G.
   d. Ctrl+5.

8. The Replace command can be opened using:
   a. the Find and Replace dialog box.
   b. Ctrl+H.
   c. Advanced Find in the Navigation Pane.
   d. All of the above

9. Which wildcard would you use to find a single character?
   a. ?
   b. *
   c. **
   d. ??

10. The Go To command allows you to navigate by page, text, graphics, equations, or tables by doing which of the following?
    a. F5 shortcut key
    b. Find and Replace dialog box
    c. Ctrl+G
    d. All of the above

True/False

Circle "T" if the statement is true or "F" if the statement is false.

T F   1. The New Window command launches a new window that contains the current document.

T F   2. By selecting text, the user has the ability to change the font or font size, bold, and delete text.

T F   3. Read Mode view displays the document as it will look when printed.

T F   4. The Zoom slider is located in the View tab.

T F   5. The Synchronous Scrolling button is used when viewing documents side by side.

T F   6. The Switch Windows command allows you to toggle between documents.

T F   7. Double-clicking a word in a document selects the word.

T F   8. When you type text in the search box while in the Navigation Pane, Word identifies this text by bolding the results in the document.

T F   9. The Arrange All command places all open documents in a separate window on the screen.

T F   10. You can use the Navigation Pane to search for words or phrases in a document.

Competency Assessment

Project 2-1: Updating a Sign

The Grand Street Coffee Shop places a sign on the door and near the order counter listing the featured coffees of the day. You need to update today's sign.

GET READY. LAUNCH Word if it is not already running.

1. Click **Open Other Documents** from the Recent screen.
2. Under the Open screen, click **Computer**, and then click **Browse**.
3. Click the location of the data files for this lesson.
4. Locate and open the *Sign* document.
5. Click the **File** tab, and then click **Save As**. In the File name box, type *2-1 New Sign*.
6. Click **Save**.
7. Position the I-beam before the *M* in *Morning Blend*. Drag over the words to select *Morning Blend*.
8. Type **Grand Street Blend**.
9. Click the **Home** tab. In the Editing group, click **Replace**.
10. Place the insertion point in the Find what text box and type **Kona Blend**.
11. Click in the **Replace with** text box and type **Hawaiian Blend**.
12. Click the **More >>** button.
13. Click the **Format** button and select **Font**.
14. In the Replace Font text box, click the scroll bar down arrow and select **Comic Sans MS**; for the Style, select **Bold Italic**; for the font size, select **26**; and for the font color, select **Dark Blue** in the Standard Colors.
15. Click **OK**, and then click the **<< Less** button.
16. Click **Find Next**, and then click the **Replace** button.
17. Click **OK**, and then click **Close**.

18. Position the I-beam before the *T* in *Try Me* and click to place the insertion point.
19. Type **$2** and press the **spacebar**.
20. In the next line, double-click the word **Mocha** to select it.
21. Type **White Chocolate**.
22. In the Zoom group, click **Page Width**.
23. Click **One Page**.
24. Click the **Save icon** in the Quick Access Toolbar.
25. Click the **File** tab. Click **Print**, and then click the **Print** button. (Check with your instructor before you print this document.)
26. Click the **File** tab and select **Close**.

PAUSE. LEAVE Word open for the next project.

Project 2-2: Editing a Job Description

Star Bright Satellite Radio is hiring. Edit the job description so that it can be sent to the human resources department for processing and posting.

GET READY. LAUNCH Word if it is not already running.

1. Click the **File** tab and choose **Open**.
2. Click **Computer**, and then click **Browse**.
3. Navigate to location of the data files for this lesson. Locate and click *Job Description* one time to select it.
4. Click **Open**.
5. Click the **File** tab, and then click **Save As**. In the File name box, type *2-2 Updated Job Description*.
6. In the second line of the document, position the I-beam before the *D* in *Date* and click to place the insertion point.
7. Beginning at the *D*, click and drag down and to the right until *Date Posted* and the line below it, *5/15/10*, is selected.
8. Press **Backspace** to delete both lines.
9. In the *Duties & Responsibilities* heading, position the insertion point before the *&*.
10. Press **Shift + Right arrow** to select **&**.
11. Type **and**. The & is replaced with the word *and*.
12. Position the mouse pointer in the left margin beside the line in the first bulleted list that reads *Define the web site's look and feel*. Click to select the line.
13. Press the **Delete** key to delete the line.
14. In the *Education and/or Experience* heading, position the I-beam to the right of the letter *r* in *or*.
15. Press **Backspace** three times to delete the *r*, *o*, and */*.
16. In the first line of the bulleted list that begins *College degree required. . .*, click to position the insertion point after *master's degree*.
17. Press the **spacebar** and type **preferred**.
18. Click the **View** tab. In the Zoom command group, click **Zoom**, click **75%**, and click **OK**.
19. On the Zoom command group, click **Page Width**, and then click **100%**.
20. **SAVE** the document in the lesson folder on your flash drive then **CLOSE** the file.

PAUSE. LEAVE Word open for the next project.

Proficiency Assessment

Project 2-3: Creating a Schedule

You are chair of the New Neighbor Welcoming Committee in your neighborhood. The group meets monthly at a committee member's house. A different committee member is responsible for bringing refreshments to each meeting. Use Word to create a schedule to share with members, and then view the document in different views.

GET READY. LAUNCH Word if it is not already running.

1. **OPEN** *Schedule* from the data files for this lesson.
2. **SAVE** the file as *2-3 Updated Schedule* in the lesson folder of your flash drive.
3. For the May 11 meeting details, beside *Meeting place*, type **D. Lorenzo, 7501 Oak, 8 p.m.** Beside *refreshments*, type **S. Wilson**.
4. The June 15 meeting details are **R. Mason, 7620 Oak, 8 p.m.**, and **J. Estes is bringing the refreshments**.
5. View the document in a **New Window**. Then click **Switch Windows** to display the window ending in ":1".
6. Click **Web Layout**, and then click **Draft** view.
7. Click the **Split** button, and reposition the split under the second title, *Meeting and Refreshment Schedule* and review. Click **Remove Split**.
8. Return the document to **Print Layout** view.
9. Remove the blank paragraph located above *January 7*.
10. **SAVE** the document in the lesson folder on your flash drive then **CLOSE** the file.

PAUSE. LEAVE Word open for the next project.

Project 2-4: Copying and Pasting Text

In this exercise, you work with a document that you created in Project 1-5 and apply the skills that you learned in this lesson. You also save the document in the Word 2013 format.

GET READY. LAUNCH Word if it is not already running.

1. **OPEN** *1-5 Thanksgiving Menu* from your Lesson 1 folder.
2. **SAVE** the document as *2-4 Thanksgiving Menu* in the lesson folder on your flash drive.
3. Follow the steps as listed under *Menu*, on the right side of the document.
4. **SAVE** the document in the lesson folder on your flash drive then **CLOSE** the file.

PAUSE. LEAVE Word open for the next project.

Mastery Assessment

Project 2-5: Fixing the Coffee Shop Menu

A co-worker at the Grand Street Coffee Shop has been working on a new menu for the coffee shop. She asks you to take a look at it before she sends it to a graphic designer. You find the old menu file and decide to compare the two.

GET READY. LAUNCH Word if it is not already running.

1. **OPEN** *Menu* from the data files for this lesson.
2. **OPEN** *Old Menu* from the data files for this lesson.
3. View the two files side by side to compare them.
4. Find and insert the two items that are missing from the new menu.
5. Find and change five pricing errors on the new menu.
6. Delete the blank paragraph in the document.
7. **SAVE** the corrected menu as *2-5 New Menu* in the lesson folder on your flash drive, and then **CLOSE** the file.
8. **CLOSE** the *Old Menu* file.

PAUSE. LEAVE Word open for the next project.

Project 2-6: Creating a New Memo

You open a new memo that was created using one of Word's template. In this project, you use the copy and paste commands.

GET READY. LAUNCH Word if it is not already running.

1. **OPEN** *Business Memo* from the data files for this lesson.
2. **SAVE** the file as a template and name it *2-6 Welcome Memo* in the lesson folder on your flash drive.
3. Select December 18, 20XX in the date placeholder.
4. Type the following information in the placeholders:

   To: Dorothy Martinez

   Ann Smith

   Dell Najera

   Patty James

   From: Sara Wilson

   Re: Planning Committee
5. Delete the CC placeholder.
6. **OPEN** the *Welcome Memo* document you created in Lesson 1.

7. Display both documents on your screen using the View Side by Side command. Beginning with *Thank you for volunteering* to the end of the paragraph, copy to the placeholder under *Comments*.
8. **CLOSE** the *Welcome Memo* document without saving.
9. **SAVE** the updated changes to the *2-6 Welcome Memo* document in the lesson folder on your flash drive, and then **CLOSE** the file.

STOP. CLOSE Word.

3 Character Formatting

LESSON SKILL MATRIX

Skill	Exam Objective	Objective Number
Formatting Characters Manually	Change font attributes.	2.2.1
Using the Format Painter	Demonstrate how to use Format Painter.	2.2.3
	Highlight text selections.	2.2.8
Formatting Text with Styles	Add styles to text.	2.2.9
	Modify existing style attributes.	2.2.11
Formatting Text with WordArt	Import Files.	1.1.3
	Change text to WordArt.	2.2.10
	Open non-native files directly in Word.	1.1.4
	Open a PDF in Word for editing.	1.1.5
Removing Text Formatting	Clear existing formatting.	2.2.6

KEY TERMS

- character
- character styles
- font
- live preview
- monospaced
- paragraph styles
- point size
- proportional space
- sans serif
- serif
- Text Effects
- WordArt

© bowdenimages/iStockphoto

© bowdenimages/iStockphoto

With more than 20 million members and 2,600 facilities, the YMCA ("the Y") is the largest community service organization in the United States. Health and fitness programs offered at the Y include group exercises for adults and youth, family time, sports and recreation, and group interests for senior citizens. The staff and volunteers at the Y need to create various types of documents for announcing and advertising programs throughout the year and for organizing and registering members for participation in these programs. Microsoft Word is a great tool for creating professional-looking documents that will capture attention. In this lesson, you learn how to use character formatting to create professional-looking documents.

SOFTWARE ORIENTATION

The Font Group

As you learn to format text, it is important to become familiar with the Font group of commands. The Font group, shown in Figure 3-1, is displayed in the Home tab of the Ribbon.

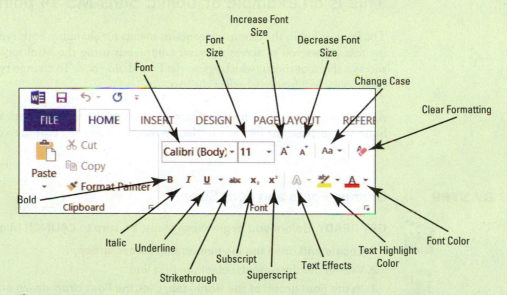

Figure 3-1

The Font group

The Font group contains commands for changing the appearance of text. Characters can have a specific font, font size, text color, text highlight, and shadow/glow. Refer to Figure 3-1 throughout this lesson as well as the rest of the book.

FORMATTING CHARACTERS MANUALLY

The Bottom Line

Formatting characters makes your text more noticeable and eye-catching and can visibly change the look of the document. Selecting the right font for your document is important because you want to make it readable.

Changing Fonts and Font Sizes

A **character** is any single letter, number, symbol, or punctuation mark. When formatting a character, you use a font to change the text appearance. A **font** is the same as a typeface that applies a style to characters. Each font has a unique name, such as Times New Roman, Garamond, or Arial. The default font for Word is Calibri. Microsoft Word has a variety of fonts and font sizes to help you communicate your intended message in a document. If you want your document to grab attention, select an appropriate font that makes the document readable. In this exercise, you use commands from the Font command group and the Mini toolbar to apply a specific font and font size to selected text.

Font sizes are measured in points. **Point size** refers to the height of characters, with one point equaling approximately 1/72 of an inch. Point sizes range from the very small 8-point size to 72 points or higher. Below are a few examples of fonts and sizes.

This is an example of Garamond 10 point.

This is an example of Arial 14 point.

This is an example of Comic Sans MS 14 point.

The Font group in the Home tab contains menus for changing both typeface and font size. Selecting text allows you to access the same commands using the Mini toolbar or by right-clicking to access a shortcut menu, which opens the Font dialog box. To change typeface or size using any of these tools, you first must select the text.

Another way to change the size of text is to select the text and click the *Increase Font Size* button to increase the font size or the *Decrease Font Size* button to decrease the size.

STEP BY STEP   **Change Fonts and Font Sizes**

GET READY. Before you begin these steps, be sure to **LAUNCH** Microsoft Word.

1. Locate and open the file named *Class Descriptions*.

2. Within the document, select the first line.

3. In the Font group of the Home tab, click the **Font drop-down arrow** to display the Font menu. The menu appears, as shown in Figure 3-2. The first line is formatted with the Theme Font, Calibri.

Figure 3-2

Font menu

The drop-down arrow
will produce Font menu

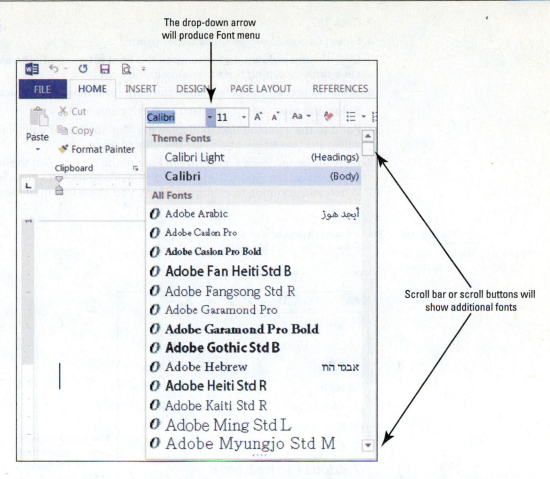

Scroll bar or scroll buttons will
show additional fonts

4. Scroll down the list and position the mouse pointer on **Century Gothic**. Notice that as you point to each font in the list, the selected text changes with a **live preview** of what it would look like in that font.

5. Click **Century Gothic**.

6. With the text still selected, click the **drop-down arrow** on the Font Size menu. The menu appears, as shown in Figure 3-3.

Figure 3-3

Font Size menu

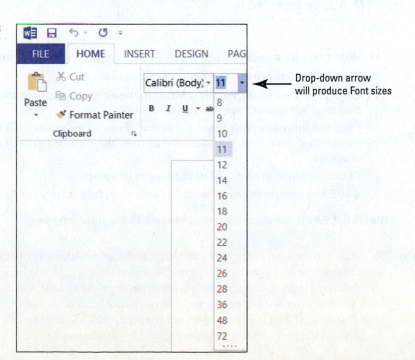

Drop-down arrow
will produce Font sizes

7. Click **18**.

8. Select **Group Exercise Class Descriptions**.

9. Click the **drop-down arrow** to open the Font menu, and then select **Gungsuh**. You can save time by typing the font name in the Font box.

10. With the text still selected, open the Font Size menu and select **16**.

11. Select the remainder of the text in the document.

12. Point to the selected text to display the Mini toolbar. If you accidently deselect the text, select the text again to display the Mini toolbar.

13. Click the **drop-down arrow** on the Font menu on the Mini toolbar and choose **Constantia** (see Figure 3-4). Word displays one font at a time in the Font text box. When you continue to change the font, you see a listing of recently used fonts.

Figure 3-4

Font menu on the Mini toolbar

The Font menu displays by clicking on the drop-down arrow on the Mini toolbar

Mini toolbar contains some commands from the Font, Paragraph, and Styles group

14. With text still selected, click the **Font Size** menu on the Mini toolbar and choose **12**.

15. Click in a blank area of the document to deselect.

16. Select **Preston Creek Family YMCA**. In the Font group, click the **Increase Font Size** button once to increase the size of the text.

17. Click the **Increase Font Size** button three more times until the point size is **26**. Notice that each time you click the button, the number in the Font Size text box changes.

18. Click in a blank area of the document to deselect.

19. **SAVE** the document as *Classes* in the lesson folder on your flash drive.

PAUSE. LEAVE the document open to use in the next exercise.

Another Way

Open the Font dialog box by clicking on the dialog box launcher on the Font group. You can also right-click the selected text, and press *Ctrl+Shift+F*, or *Ctrl+D*.

Take Note

Courier New is an example of a **monospaced** font, which means **proportional space** take up the same amount of horizontal space. Times New Roman is an example of a **proportional** font, because the horizontal spacing varies. There are two types of proportional fonts, serif and sans serif. **Serif** fonts have small lines at the beginning and end of characters and are usually used with large amounts of text. A **sans serif** font is one that does not have the small line extensions on its characters. Times New Roman and Courier New are examples of serif fonts, whereas Arial and Calibri are sans serif fonts.

Applying Character Attributes

In addition to changing the font and font size of text, you can change the appearance of characters to apply emphasis to text. In this exercise, you learn how to apply character attributes such as bolding, italics, underlining, font colors, and effects to selected text in Word documents.

The Font group in the Home tab includes the commands for applying bold, italic, and underline attributes to draw attention to words or phrases in your document. You can use these attributes one at a time, such as **Bold**, or together, such as **Bold Underline**. Select the text to apply one or more of the character attributes using the Font command group or the Mini toolbar. To open the Font dialog box use one of the keyboard shortcuts, such as Ctrl+D, or right-click the selection to access a shortcut menu.

Click the Font command group dialog box launcher to open the Font dialog box for more options to format characters. In this dialog box, you can specify a font color, underline style, and a variety of other effects, such as small caps, strikethrough, superscript, and shadow.

Text Effects A ⌄ add a distinctive appearance to selected text, such as outline, shadow, glow, and reflection. To add Text Effects to selected text, click the drop-down arrow on the Text Effects button, and then select from the available options on the menu. You can also access the Text Effects by opening the Font dialog box. At the end of the lesson, you learn to remove effects by selecting the affected text, and then clicking the Clear Formatting button on the Font group.

STEP BY STEP   **Apply Character Attributes**

USE the document that is open from the previous exercise.

Another Way
You also can select text, and then press the keyboard shortcut *Ctrl+B* to apply bolding.

Another Way
You also can use the keyboard shortcut *Ctrl+I* to apply italics to selected text.

Another Way
You can also use the keyboard shortcut *Ctrl+U* to apply underlining to selected text.

1. Select the title of the document, **Preston Creek Family YMCA**.

2. In the Font command group, click the **Bold** B button. Notice that the Bold button in the Font group is now selected.

3. Select the subtitle, **Group Exercise Class Descriptions**, and click the **Italic** I button. The Italics button appears highlighted.

4. Select **Active Older Adults** and click the **Bold** B button on the Mini toolbar.

5. With the text still selected, click the **Underline** U button on the Mini toolbar.

6. With the text still selected, click the **drop-down arrow** beside the Underline U button in the Font group. A menu of underlining choices appears, as shown in Figure 3-5.

7. Hover over each option to see how the selected text will appear, and then click **Thick Underline**, the third line down in the menu. Before you click, a ScreenTip displays Thick Underline.

Figure 3-5

Underline menu

Drop-down arrow produces
the Underline menu

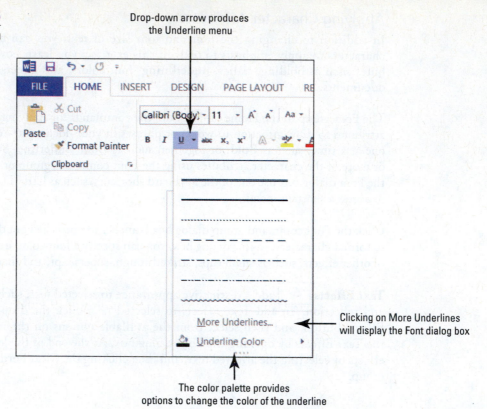

Clicking on More Underlines
will display the Font dialog box

The color palette provides
options to change the color of the underline

8. Select the title, **Preston Creek Family YMCA**. In the Font group, click the **dialog box launcher**. The *Font* dialog box appears, as shown in Figure 3-6.

Figure 3-6

Font dialog box

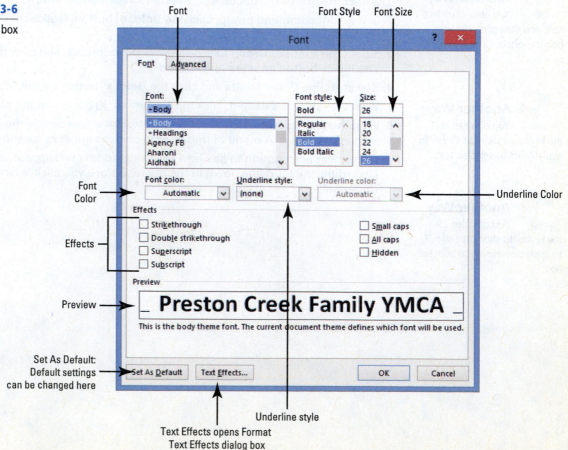

Font

Font Style   Font Size

Font
Color

Underline Color

Effects

Preview

Set As Default:
Default settings
can be changed here

Underline style

Text Effects opens Format
Text Effects dialog box

9. In the Effects section, click the **All Caps** check box to insert a check mark. Review the Preview area and notice how the text is now in all caps.

10. Click the **drop-down arrow** on the Font Color menu. A menu of colors appears.

11. A ScreenTip appears when you place your insertion point over the colors; click **Aqua, Accent 5, Darker 50%** from the Theme Colors section at the top.

12. Click **OK**.

13. With the text still selected, click the **Text Effects** drop-down arrow in the Font group.

14. Hover over each of the options, and then select **Fill – White, Outline - Accent 1, Shadow**, as shown in Figure 3-7. Applying the Text Effects to the selected text changes it back to the original capitalization.

Figure 3-7

Text Effects drop-down arrow

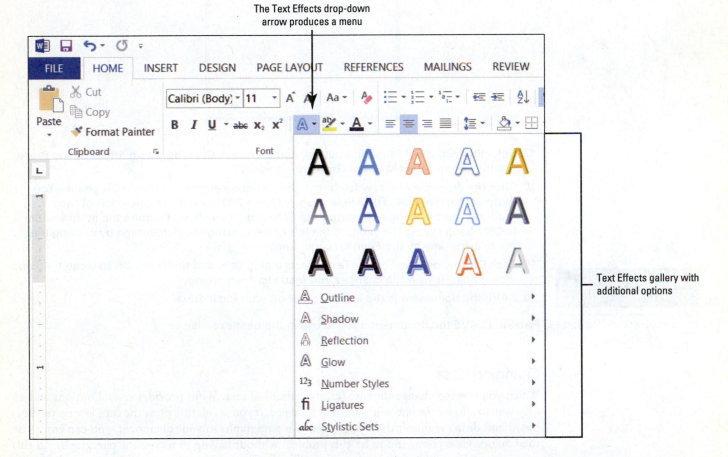

15. With the title text still selected, right-click to access the shortcut menu, and then select **Font**. Click the **Text Effects** button to open the Format Text Effects dialog box. Notice that you have two options to select: Text Fill & Outline ⬛ and Text Effects ⬛. You can access the command to display additional options by clicking on the icon or Expand ▷ button.

16. Click the **Expand** ▷ button by the Text Fill command (see Figure 3-8).

Figure 3-8

Format Text Effects dialog box

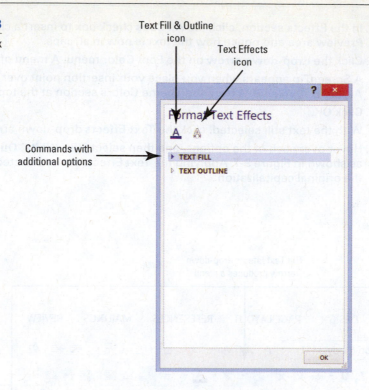

17. Select the **Gradient fill** option button, and then click the drop-down arrow by the Preset gradients and select **Medium Gradient – Accent 2**.

18. Click the **drop-down arrow** to change the *Direction* and select **Linear Diagonal – Top Right to Bottom Left**. The Angle changed from 270° to 135°. The position of the gradient can be changed by using the *Gradient stop*s slider. Position the middle slider to **26%** by dragging the slider to the left or decreasing the percentage by clicking the down arrow key by the *Position* command.

19. Click **OK** to close the *Format Text Effects* dialog box, and then click **OK** to close the *Font* dialog box. Review the changes you made to the heading.

20. **SAVE** the document in the lesson folder on your flash drive.

PAUSE. LEAVE the document open to use in the next exercise.

Changing Case

When you need to change the case (capitalization) of text, Word provides several options and an easy way to choose the one you want. For instance, if you accidently press the caps key on the keyboard and didn't realize it until you typed two paragraphs in your document, you can easily use the Change Case command to fix this problem without having to retype the paragraphs. In this exercise, you learn to use the commands in Word's Change Case menu to change capitalization.

The Change Case menu in the Font group has five options for changing the capitalization of text:

• **Sentence case:** Capitalizes the first word in each sentence

• **lowercase:** Changes all characters to lowercase

• **UPPERCASE:** Changes all characters to capital letters

• **Capitalize Each Word:** Capitalizes the first character of each word

• **tOGGLE cASE:** Changes each character to its opposite case

Change Case

USE the document that is open from the previous exercise.

1. Select the title, **Preston Creek Family YMCA**. In the Font group, click the **Change Case**
   Aa ▾ button. A menu of case options appears, as shown in Figure 3-9.

Figure 3-9

Change Case menu

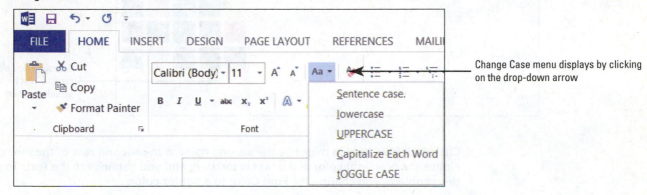

Change Case menu displays by clicking on the drop-down arrow

2. Click **UPPERCASE**. All letters are capitalized.
3. With the text still selected, click the **Change Case** button again and select **lowercase**.
4. With the text still selected, click the **Change Case** button again, and then click **Capitalize Each Word**.
5. Select **YMCA**. Click the **Change Case** button again and choose **UPPERCASE**.
6. Click in a blank area of the document to deselect the text.
7. **SAVE** the document in the lesson folder on your flash drive.

PAUSE. LEAVE the document open to use in the next exercise.

Highlighting Text

The Highlighting tool in the Font group enables you to apply a highlighting color across text to stress the importance of that text and draw attention to it quickly. For example, you mark your textbook with a yellow highlighter marker to mark its importance in the book. In this exercise, you learn to use the Text Highlighting feature in Word 2013 to add highlighting color to selected text.

To highlight text, first select the text you want to emphasize, click the *Text Highlight Color* button in the Font group, and select the color of your choice. To remove highlighting, select the highlighted text and choose *No Color* from the Text Highlight Color menu.

Highlight Text

USE the document that is open from the previous exercise.

1. Under the *Core Express* heading in your document, select the last sentence, *"This new class is open to all fitness levels!"*
2. In the Font group, click the **Text Highlight Color** ▾ button. The text automatically is highlighted in the default color yellow.
3. Select the text you highlighted in step 1.
4. Click the **drop-down arrow** beside the Text Highlight Color ▾ button. A menu of colors appears, as shown in Figure 3-10.

Figure 3-10

Text Highlight Color menu

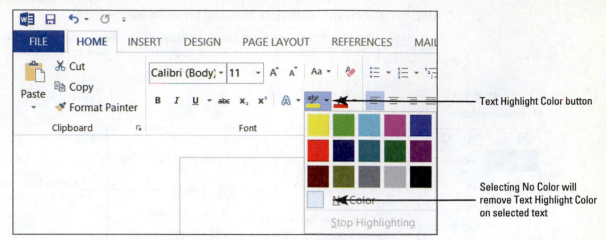

Text Highlight Color button

Selecting No Color will remove Text Highlight Color on selected text

5. Click **dark blue** (which might be the second color in the second row of the menu). Notice the highlight color in the text is too dark and you cannot see the text. To solve this problem, you change the Font Color to a lighter color.

6. Select the text again. Click the **Text Highlight Color** button again. To remove the highlight color, select **No Color**.

7. Select the text again and apply the yellow highlight color.

8. **SAVE** the document with the same filename in the lesson folder on your flash drive.

PAUSE. LEAVE the document open to use in the next exercise.

<table>
<tr><td>CERTIFICATION READY?</td><td>2.2.8</td></tr>
</table>

How would you highlight text?

 Cross Ref In Lesson 2, you learned to select text using different methods. To select multiple areas of text, press Ctrl and select the text.

USING THE FORMAT PAINTER

The Bottom Line

To format your text so that it has the look and feel you want, you might need to copy existing formatting. The Format Painter helps you copy formats to use in other areas of the document without having to repeat the same steps.

Using the Format Painter

The Format Painter command is located in the Clipboard group on the Home tab. It is used to copy attributes and other formatting from one block of text and apply them to other selected text within the document. When you activate Format Painter, the mouse pointer becomes a paintbrush. Clicking once on the Format Painter button enables you to copy and apply the format once; double-clicking allows you to apply the copied format to as many locations as you want. In this exercise, you learn to use the Format Painter to copy and apply formatting to selected text.

STEP BY STEP   **Use the Format Painter**

USE the document that is open from the previous exercise.

1. Select the **Active Older Adults** heading.

2. On the Home tab, in the Clipboard group, click the **Format Painter** button once; Format Painter copies the formatting from your selected text, and the pointer changes to a paintbrush icon when you point to text.

3. Use the paintbrush pointer to select the next heading, **Boot Camp**. The copied format is applied, and the Format Painter is turned off.

Another Way

The Format Painter button is also available on the Mini toolbar.

4. With *Boot Camp* still selected, double-click the **Format Painter** button. Notice the status bar message "Select content to apply the copied formatting, or press Esc to cancel." Notice also that the mouse pointer becomes a paintbrush icon when you place it over text. You will now be able to apply the same formatting to several items in the document.

5. Select the next heading, **Cardio Combo**. The copied format is applied.

6. Select the next heading, **Cardio Kickboxing**. The copied format is applied again.

7. Select the remaining headings using the method you learned to select multiple text by pressing **Ctrl** and then click the text to apply the copied format.

8. When you are finished with the last heading, click the **Format Painter** button to turn it off or press the **ESC** key.

9. **SAVE** the document in the lesson folder on your flash drive.

PAUSE. LEAVE the document open to use in the next exercise.

FORMATTING TEXT WITH STYLES

The Bottom Line

Word provides predefined styles for formatting documents instantly with a number of characters and paragraphs attributes. Modifications can be made to existing styles, or new styles can be created and placed in the Styles gallery, current document, or template. In this exercise, you learn to apply a style and to modify an existing style.

The Styles pane lists the same Styles displayed in the Styles gallery. When you point to a style in the list, a ScreenTip displays the style's properties.

There are two types of styles: paragraph styles and character styles. Styles created for paragraphs are marked in the Styles pane by a paragraph mark to the right of the style name. When you choose **paragraph styles**, the formats are applied instantly to all text in the paragraph where the insertion point is located, whether or not that text is selected. In the Styles group, the paragraph mark is visible by the style name.

Character styles are applied to individual characters or words that you select. Character styles have a lowercase letter *a* beside them. You can see the lowercase letter *a* in the Styles gallery by launching the dialog box or by pressing *Alt+Ctrl+Shift+S*.

Sometimes, a style can be used for either selected paragraphs or characters. These linked styles have a paragraph symbol as well as a lowercase *a* beside them. Select the text to which you want to apply a linked style.

In Lesson 2, you learn to view a document with the Navigation Pane using one of the three tabs. When you apply a style to a document, such as in headings, you are able to search through your document quickly.

Applying Styles

In this exercise, you learn to use Word's Styles to apply paragraph styles and character styles to selected text and paragraphs to create a uniform and polished look within your document.

STEP BY STEP **Apply a Style**

USE the document that is open from the previous exercise.

1. Select the **Active Older Adults** heading. In the Styles command group on the Home tab, click **Heading 1**. The style is applied to the heading.

2. Use multi-selection to select all the headings, and then click **Heading 1**. The Heading 1 style is applied to all the remaining headings.

3. In the second sentence of the *Active Older Adults* description, select **low-impact**. In the Styles group, click the **dialog box launcher**. The Styles pane appears, as shown in Figure 3-11.

Figure 3-11

Styles pane

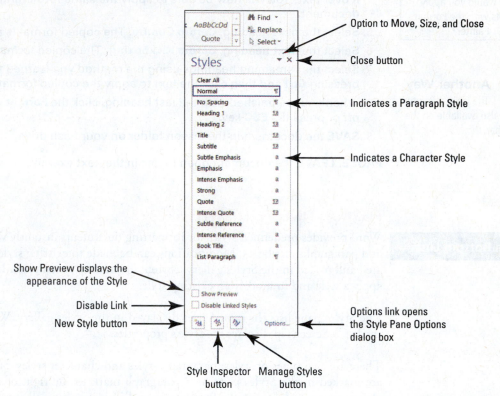

Option to Move, Size, and Close

Close button

Indicates a Paragraph Style

Indicates a Character Style

Show Preview displays the appearance of the Style

Disable Link

New Style button

Style Inspector button   Manage Styles button

Options link opens the Style Pane Options dialog box

4. Point to **Subtle Emphasis** in the Styles list. Notice a ScreenTip appears with the defaults for this style. Click **Subtle Emphasis**. The style is applied to the selected text.

5. In the *Boot Camp* description, select **challenging** and click **Subtle Emphasis** in the Styles pane.

6. In the *Core Express* description, select **strengthen** and click **Subtle Emphasis** in the Styles pane.

7. In the *Indoor Cycling* description, select **high-energy** and click **Subtle Emphasis** in the Styles pane.

8. In the *Yoga* description, select **breathing** and **relaxation** and click **Subtle Emphasis** in the Styles pane. Deselect the text. Click the **X** to close the Styles pane.

9. Open the Navigation Pane and practice browsing through the document using the Headings tab. Then, close the Navigation Pane.

10. **SAVE** the document in the lesson folder on your flash drive.

PAUSE. LEAVE the document open to use in the next exercise.

Modifying Styles

You can make modifications to an existing style using the Modify Style dialog box. Word also gives you the option of where to place changes made to styles, such as adding them to the Styles gallery, current document, or applying them to new documents based on a template. In this exercise, you learn to use the Modify Style options to modify styles in Word.

To change an existing style, right-click the style's name in the Style gallery or the Style window, and then click *Modify*. The Modify Style dialog box is opened, as shown in Figure 3-13. Character attributes can be applied to a style by clicking on the *Bold* B button, *Italics* I button, and the *Underline* U button. Similarly, clicking the drop-down arrow for Font and Font Size allows you to adjust both of these settings.

The Modify Style dialog box has options for where to place the new modified style. The modified style can be placed on the Style gallery so you can access it quickly. Selecting the option to save the style *Only in this document* affects only the current document. Selecting the option for *New documents based on this template* ensures that the same style is applied. For instance, say you are writing a group research paper and would like uniformity for the paper. Providing everyone within the group with a copy of the template ensures consistency in the formatting of the paper, and all styles within the document update automatically.

STEP BY STEP   **Modify Styles**

USE the document that is open from the previous exercise.

1. In the Styles group, click the **dialog box launcher** to display the Styles pane.

2. Right-click **Subtle Emphasis** to display the Subtle Emphasis menu or click the **drop-down arrow**, as shown in Figure 3-12.

Figure 3-12

Subtle Emphasis menu

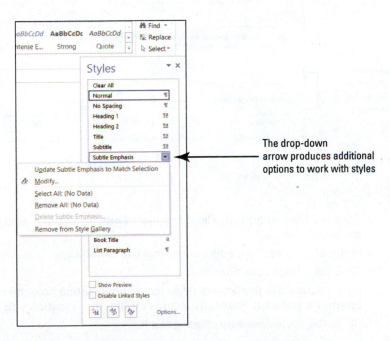

The drop-down arrow produces additional options to work with styles

3. Click **Modify**. The *Modify Style* dialog box appears, as shown in Figure 3-13.

4. Click the **Bold** button.

5. Click the Font Color **drop-down arrow**, and then select **Dark Red** in the Standard Colors section. Notice the preview in the dialog box changes.

6. Click the **Add to the Styles gallery** check box to clear it. The modifications you just made apply to this document and will not appear on the Style list.

Figure 3-13

Modify Style dialog box
displaying Subtle Emphasis

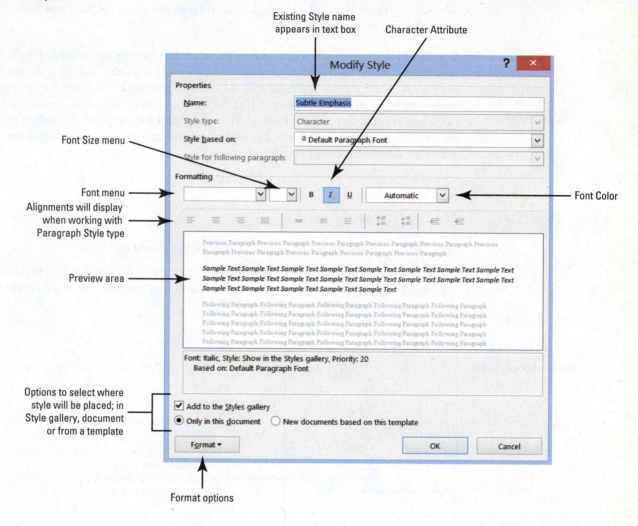

Existing Style name
appears in text box

Character Attribute

Font Size menu

Font menu

Alignments will display
when working with
Paragraph Style type

Preview area

Options to select where
style will be placed; in
Style gallery, document
or from a template

Font Color

Format options

7. Click the **Format** button, and then select **Font**. The *Font* dialog box opens to give you more options.

8. In the Effects section, add a check mark to **Small caps**.

9. Click **OK** to close the *Font* dialog box.

10. Click **OK** to close the *Modify Style* dialog box. Notice how the text with the Subtle Emphasis style automatically changes to the modification you just completed.

11. Close the Styles pane by clicking the **X**.

12. In the Styles group, right-click **Heading 1** from the gallery to display the Heading 1 menu, and then click **Modify**.

13. In the Modify Style dialog box, click the Font Color **drop-down arrow** and choose **Red, Accent 2, Darker 50%**.

14. Click the Font Size **drop-down arrow** and select **18**.

15. Click the **Add to the Styles gallery** check box to clear the check mark. The modifications made apply to this document and will not appear on the Style list.

16. Click **OK**. All the headings with the Heading 1 style update automatically to the new color and size.

17. **SAVE** the document in the lesson folder on your flash drive.

PAUSE. LEAVE the document open to use in the next exercise.

CERTIFICATION READY? 2.2.11

How would you modify an existing style attribute?

FORMATTING TEXT WITH WORDART

The Bottom Line

Word provides attractive and enhancing effects to text. WordArt has special effects that you can apply to your text to make it noticeable.

Formatting Text with WordArt

WordArt is a feature that creates decorative effects with text. For instance, you can apply effects to the text by adding shadow, reflection, glow, soft edges, bevel, or 3-D rotation. As you begin working with WordArt, the Drawing Tools Format tab appears and allows you to format the WordArt by adding special effects.

Inserting WordArt

WordArt has been enhanced for Word 2013 with more vibrant colors and shapes and a gallery of text styles. When you insert a WordArt object, the Drawing Tools Format tab opens. In this exercise, you learn to insert WordArt in a document.

STEP BY STEP   **Insert WordArt**

USE the document that is open from the previous exercise.

1. Select **Preston Creek Family YMCA**.
2. Click the **Insert** tab and, in the Text group, click the **WordArt** button to display the menu as shown in Figure 3-14.

Figure 3-14

WordArt menu

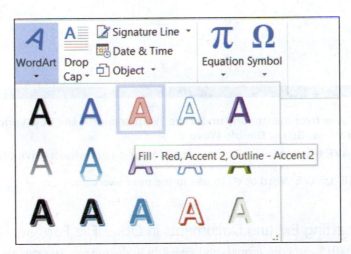

3. In the WordArt gallery, select **Fill – Red, Accent 2, Outline – Accent 2**. The text is now formatted as WordArt and the Drawing Tools Format tab opens.
4. A box appears around the WordArt; select the heading and change the font size to **28 pt** on the Home tab. Notice the word *Group* moved up one line.
5. Place your insertion point along the box outline until it changes to the move command—four arrows. Press the **left mouse button** to select the box, and drag the box to the horizontal center until the word *Group* moves to the second line. As you resize or move a heading, the text that surrounds the box automatically moves.
6. Select the heading text again. In the WordArt Styles group on the Drawing Tools tab, select the **drop-down arrow** by Text Outline and select **No Outline**. This action Format removes the outline in the text.
7. Click the **Text Fill** drop-down arrow and select **Red, Accent 2**.
8. Select **Text Effects**, and then click **Transform**. Refer to Figure 3-15.

Figure 3-15

Transform Options

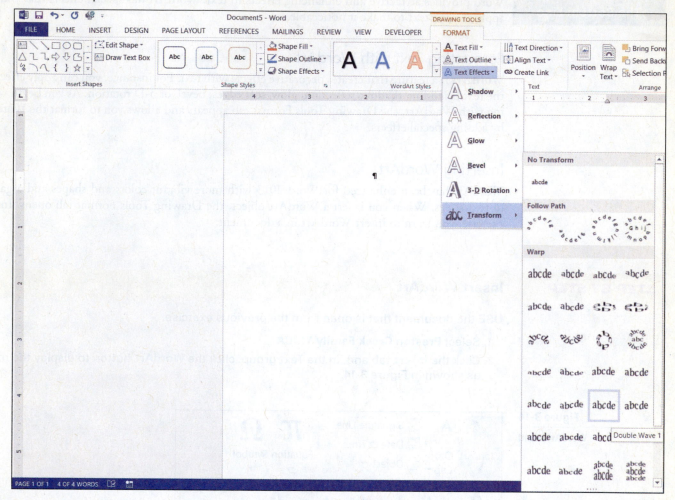

9. Hover over the options under the Warp section—see how your text changes with live preview. Select **Double Wave 1**.

10. **SAVE** the document in the lesson folder on your flash drive then **CLOSE** the file.

PAUSE. LEAVE Word open to use in the next exercise.

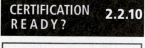

CERTIFICATION READY?   2.2.10

How would you apply WordArt to text?

CERTIFICATION READY?   1.1.3

How do you import a PDF file?

Formatting Existing Documents in Other File Formats

Word 2013 can edit, format, and save a PDF document. You can also open, edit, and save documents that were saved in another type of file format, such as RTF and TXT. Each document contains properties, and you can determine what to share—more about sharing and excluding content is discussed in Lesson 13. In Lesson 1 you learned to export a document as a PDF document. In this exercise, you learn to import a PDF file, apply formatting, and save as a PDF file.

Take Note   Importing documents that were saved in other file formats, such as PDF, enables you to edit the document and save it as a PDF or in Word 2013 format.

STEP BY STEP   **Import a PDF File and Apply Formatting**

GET READY. OPEN Word if it is not already running.

1. From within Word, **OPEN** the *Tech Terrace 3.pdf* file from the data files for this lesson. A prompt appears stating, *"Word will now convert your PDF to an editable document."* Refer to Figure 3-16.

2. Click **OK**. By opening the PDF document, you have imported the document into Word. The Ribbon is now active and you can begin applying formatting to the document.

Figure 3-16

Convert PDF file prompt

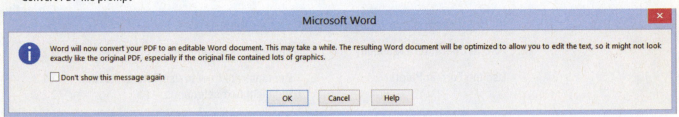

> **Microsoft Word**   ✕
>
> ℹ Word will now convert your PDF to an editable Word document. This may take a while. The resulting Word document will be optimized to allow you to edit the text, so it might not look exactly like the original PDF, especially if the original file contained lots of graphics.
>
> ☐ Don't show this message again
>
> [OK]   [Cancel]   [Help]

3. Select the whole document by pressing **Ctrl A**, and then change the Font to **Times New Roman** and Size to **12** pt. You can also select text from the Editing group on the Home tab.
4. In the first paragraph, select **Tech Terrace Real Estate**, and then format the text with **Bold**, **Italics**, **Dark Red text color**, and **Small caps**.
5. In the first paragraph, select **sold**, **renovated**, **appraised**, **leased**, and **managed** and format by italicizing and bolding and changing the color to **Blue-Gray, Text 2**.
6. Save As a PDF file in your flash drive and change the filename to *Tech Terrace Update.pdf*. The new document opens in a new window. Notice the file contains the updated formatting changes.
7. To close the window, press **ALT + F4**. Click to return to the Word screen.
8. **CLOSE** the file. If a prompt appears to confirm saving the changes to the *Tech Terrace 3.docx* file, click **Don't Save**.

PAUSE. LEAVE Word open for the next exercise.

Cross Ref   Refer to Lesson 13 for more information about PDF document properties.

REMOVING TEXT FORMATTING

The Bottom Line   When you are formatting documents, sometimes you need to try a few different options before you get the appearance you want. Clearing unwanted formatting is easy using Word's Clear Formatting button.

Using the Clear Formatting Button

The Clear Formatting button is located in the Font group and the Styles gallery. In this exercise, you learn to use the Clear Formatting button.

STEP BY STEP   **Use the Clear Formatting Button**

OPEN the *Classes* document from the lesson folder. Remember that this is a file you saved earlier.

1. Select **Active Older Adults**. In the Font group, click **Clear Formatting** 🧹 . The formatting is removed and the text returns to the default font, Calibri.
2. Select **Boot Camp**. In the Styles group, click the More **drop-down arrow**, and then click **Clear Formatting**. The formatting is removed.
3. Press and hold **Ctrl** and select **Cardio Combo**; continue to hold the **Ctrl** key to select the remaining headings, and then click the **Clear Formatting** button in the Font group. (By holding the **Ctrl** key, you can use multi-selection to select noncontiguous text.) Deselect all text.
4. **SAVE** the document as *Classes 2* in the lesson folder on your flash drive.

CLOSE Word.

Cross Ref   Refer to Lesson 2 for more information about multi-selection.

SKILL SUMMARY

In This Lesson, You Learned To:	Exam Objective	Objective Number
Format Characters Manually	Change font attributes.	2.2.1
Use the Format Painter	Demonstrate how to use Format Painter.	2.2.3
	Highlight text selections.	2.2.8
Format Text with Styles	Add styles to text.	2.2.9
	Modify existing style attributes.	2.2.11
Format Text with WordArt	Import Files.	1.1.3
	Change text to WordArt.	2.2.10
	Open non-native files directly in Word.	1.1.4
	Open a PDF in Word for editing.	1.1.5
Remove Text Formatting	Clear existing formatting.	2.2.6

Knowledge Assessment

Multiple Choice

Select the best response for the following statements.

1. When measuring point size, one point is equal to a character height of:
   a. 1/10 of an inch.
   b. 1/12 of an inch.
   c. 1/72 of an inch.
   d. 1/18 of an inch.

2. The Underline drop-down menu in the Font group contains options to underline selected text with a:
   a. thick underline.
   b. double underline.
   c. dotted underline.
   d. All of the above

3. A _____ is a typeface that applies a style to characters.
   a. point size
   b. font
   c. paragraph style
   d. Both a and b

4. If you type a paragraph in uppercase and need to change it to sentence case without having to retype the paragraph, which option would you use?
   a. Change Case
   b. Change Size of Case
   c. Sentence Case
   d. Toggle Case

5. Opening the Modify Style dialog box allows you to:
   a. change formatting.
   b. change the alignment.
   c. change the line spacing.
   d. All of the above

6. The _____ lets you copy the format of text and apply those attributes to different text.
   a. Formatter
   b. Copy Special

    c. Format Painter

    d. Both a and b

7. The _____ feature removes all formatting from the selected text.

    a. Formatting Cleared

    b. Erase Formatting

    c. Remove Formatting

    d. Clear Formatting

8. Tiny lines at the ends of characters are known as:

    a. serifs.

    b. sans serifs.

    c. monospaces.

    d. proportional lines.

9. To increase the point size of selected text, click the:

    a. Increase Font button.

    b. Increase Font Size button.

    c. Enlarge Font button.

    d. Enhance Font button.

10. Changing the font and font size of selected text can be completed using:

    a. the Font dialog box.

    b. the Mini toolbar.

    c. the Font group of the Home tab.

    d. All of the above

True/False

Circle T if the statement is true or F if the statement is false.

T F 1. Toggle Case changes each character to its opposite case.

T F 2. Applying bold to text gives it special emphasis.

T F 3. The Format Painter is found on the Mini toolbar.

T F 4. The default color for Text Highlighting is pink.

T F 5. The Decrease Font Size button increases point size.

T F 6. The Clear Formatting button clears text from one location and lets you apply it in another location.

T F 7. PDF files can be edited using Word 2013.

T F 8. The Font dialog box has an option to display the underline drop-down menu.

T F 9. To apply a style to selected text, click the style from the Styles group.

T F 10. Styles cannot be modified.

Competency Assessment

Project 3-1: Formatting a Sales Letter

Star Bright Satellite Radio will be sending sales letters to people who have just purchased new vehicles equipped with their radios. Add some finishing formatting touches to this letter.

GET READY. LAUNCH Word if it is not already running.

1. OPEN the *Letter* document from the data files for this lesson.

2. SAVE the document as *3-1 Sales Letter* in the lesson folder on your flash drive.

3. Select the title of the company, **STAR BRIGHT SATELLITE RADIO**.

4. Apply the **Title** style and reduce the font size to **24** pt.

5. In the second paragraph of the body of the letter, select the first sentence, **Star Bright Satellite...**.

6. In the Font group on the Home tab, click the **Bold** button.

7. In the second paragraph, select the fifth sentence, **Star Bright also broadcasts....**
8. In the Font group, click the **Italic** button.
9. In the fourth paragraph, select the first sentence, **Star Bright is only $10.95 a month**.
10. On the Mini toolbar, click the **Bold** button.
11. In the third sentence of the fourth paragraph, select **Subscribe**.
12. In the Font group, click the Change Case **drop-down arrow**, and then click **UPPERCASE**.
13. With the word still selected, click **Bold**, and then deselect the text.
14. Change the view of the document to **100%**, if necessary.
15. **SAVE** the document in the lesson folder on your flash drive, then **CLOSE** the file.

PAUSE. LEAVE Word open for the next project.

Project 3-2: Formatting a Flyer

You've been recruited to help find coaches for the local youth sports organization. Create a flyer that will attract attention.

GET READY. LAUNCH Word if it is not already running.

1. **OPEN** *Volunteer Coaches* from the data files for this lesson.
2. **SAVE** the document as *3-2 Volunteers* in the lesson folder on your flash drive.
3. Select **We Need You!**
4. Click the **drop-down arrow** in the Font menu, and then click **Arial Black**.
5. Click the **drop-down arrow** in the Font Size menu, and then click **48**.
6. Select **Volunteer Coaches Needed For Youth Sports**.
7. Click the **drop-down arrow** in the Font menu, and then click **Arial Black**.
8. Click the **drop-down arrow** in the Font Size menu, and then click **18**.
9. Select **Sports include** and the four lines below it.
10. Click the **drop-down arrow** in the Font menu, and then click **Calibri**.
11. Click the **drop-down arrow** in the Font Size menu, and then click **18**.
12. Select the four sports listed, and then click the **Italic** button.
13. Select the three lines of contact information, beginning with *Contact Patrick Edelstein...*
14. Click the **drop-down arrow** in the Font menu, and then click **Arial Black**.
15. Click the **drop-down arrow** in the Font Size menu, and then click **11**.
16. Select **YMCA**. Click the **drop-down arrow** in the Font Color button, and then choose **red** from the Standard Colors section.
17. With the text still selected, click the **Bold** button.
18. Click the **drop-down arrow** in the Font menu, and then click **Arial Black**.
19. Click the **drop-down menu** in the Font Size menu, and then click **36**. Deselect the text.
20. **SAVE** the document in the lesson folder on your flash drive, then **CLOSE** the file.

LEAVE Word open for the next project.

Proficiency Assessment

Project 3-3: Creating a Flyer

The Grand Street Coffee Shop has decided to install a wireless Internet service for customers. To announce the news, create a flyer for distribution in the coffee shop.

GET READY. LAUNCH Word if it is not already running.

1. **OPEN** *Wireless* from the data files for this lesson.
2. **SAVE** the document as *3-3 WiFi at Coffee Shop* in the lesson folder on your flash drive.
3. Select the first four paragraphs and change the Font to **Franklin Gothic Heavy**, size **48** pt., and change to **uppercase**.
4. Change the color for each of the four headings as follows:
   - SIP, **Dark Blue, Text 2**
   - SURF, **Aqua, Accent 5, Darker 50%**
   - WORK, **Dark Blue, Text 2, Darker 25%**
   - WIFI IS HERE, **Blue**
5. Select the paragraph beginning with *The Grand Street Coffee Shop...* and change the Font to **Franklin Gothic Book**, size **20**. Then select **Grand Street Coffee Shop**, set as **Bold**, and change the color to **Dark Blue, Text 2**.
6. Select the next paragraph and change the Font to **Franklin Gothic Book**, size **14** pt.
7. Select the last paragraph and change the Font to **Franklin Gothic Book**, size **16** pt. and **Bold**.
8. Change the document view to **One Page**.
9. **SAVE** the document in the lesson folder on your flash drive, then **CLOSE** the file.

LEAVE Word open for the next project.

Project 3-4: Formatting Nutritional Information

Customers of the Grand Street Coffee Shop have asked about the nutritional makeup of some of the blended coffee items on the menu. Format a document you can post or make available for customers to take with them.

GET READY. LAUNCH Word if it is not already running.

1. **OPEN** *Nutrition Info* from the data files for this lesson.
2. **SAVE** the document as *3-4 Nutrition* in the lesson folder on your flash drive.
3. Change the view of the document to **100%**.
4. Select **Grand Street Coffee Shop**.
5. Click the **Font Color** menu and select **Purple, Accent 4, Darker 50%**, **bold**, and font size to **48**.
6. Click the **Insert** tab, and in the Text group, select **WordArt Fill-Purple, Accent 4, Soft Bevel**.
7. Select **Nutritional Information** without selecting the paragraph mark.
8. In the Font group, click the **dialog box launcher**. In the Effects section, click the **Small caps** box, change the font size to **16**, font color to **Purple**, **Underline words only**, and **Bold Italic**. Click **OK**.
9. Select **Brewed Coffee, Caffé Latte, Caffé Mocha, Cappuccino,** and **White Chocolate Mocha**, and then click the **Font dialog box launcher**.
10. Click the **All caps** box, change the font size to **14**, make the text both **Bold** and **Italic**, and change the font color to **Purple**. Click **OK**.
11. Select the three lines of text under the *Brewed Coffee* heading. Click **Italic** on the Font group.
12. Use the Format Painter to copy the format from the text under *Brewed Coffee* to the text under each heading.
13. **SAVE** the document in the lesson folder on your flash drive, then **CLOSE** the file.

LEAVE Word open for the next project.

Mastery Assessment

Project 3-5: Formatting a Resume

Your friend Mike asks you to help him with his resume. Format the resume so that it looks professional.

GET READY. LAUNCH Word if it is not already running.

1. **OPEN** *Resume* from the data files for this lesson.
2. **SAVE** the document as *3-5 MZ Resume* in the lesson folder on your flash drive.
3. Format the resume to the following specifications:
   - Format Mike's name with **Cambria**, **24** pt., **bold**.
   - Change his address, phone, and e-mail information to **Times New Roman 9** pt.
   - Change the main headings by bolding and italicizing; change the font to **Cambria** and the font size to **16**.
   - For job titles, apply **Times New Roman**, **12** pt., **Small caps**, and **bold**.
   - Italicize the sentence or sentences before the bulleted lists.
   - For places and years of employment, as well as the college name, apply **Times New Roman**, **12** pt., and **Small caps**.
4. In the Editing group of the Home tab, click **Select**, and then click **Select All**.
5. Click the **Clear All Formatting** button in the Font group.
6. Click **Undo**.
7. **SAVE** the document with the same filename in the lesson folder, then **CLOSE** the file.

LEAVE Word open for the next project.

Project 3-6: Formatting References

Your friend Mike liked your work on his resume so much that he asks you to format his reference list with the same design as his resume.

GET READY. LAUNCH Word if it is not already running.

1. **OPEN** *References* from the data files for this lesson.
2. **SAVE** the document as *3-6 MZ References* in the lesson folder on your flash drive.
3. **OPEN** *3-5 MZ Resume* from the data files for this lesson.
4. View the documents side by side and compare the fonts, styles, sizes, and attributes of both. Review the document carefully.
5. Update the *3-6 MZ References* document by changing the font, styles, size, and attributes to match those in the *3-5 MZ Resume* document.
6. **SAVE** the document in the lesson folder on your flash drive, then **CLOSE** both files.

CLOSE Word.

LESSON SKILL MATRIX

Skill	Exam Objective	Objective Number
Formatting Paragraphs	Set indentation.	2.2.7
Setting Line Spacing in Text and Between Paragraphs	Set line spacing. Modify line spacing. Set paragraph spacing.	2.2.5 3.3.4 2.2.4
Creating and Formatting a Bulleted List	Add numbering or bullets. Create custom bullets. Modify list indentation. Increase and decrease list levels.	3.3.1 3.3.2 3.3.3 3.3.5
Creating and Formatting a Numbered List	Add numbering or bullets. Modify numbering.	3.3.1 3.3.6
Creating and Modifying a Multilevel List		
Setting and Modifying Tabs		

© mbtphotos/iStockphoto

KEY TERMS

- alignment
- first-line indent
- hanging indent
- horizontal alignment
- indent
- leaders
- line spacing
- negative indent
- vertical alignment

© mbtphotos/iStockphoto

You are employed at Books and Beyond, an independent used bookstore. Your job responsibilities include receiving and assessing used books, issuing trade credit, stocking the bookshelves, and placing special orders. Because you have good computer skills, you are also responsible for creating and modifying documents as needed. Currently, you are working on the store's employee handbook. In this lesson, you learn how to use Word's formatting features to change the appearance of paragraphs. In particular, you learn to set indents; change alignment and line spacing; create numbered, bulleted, and multilevel lists; and set tabs.

SOFTWARE ORIENTATION

The Indents and Spacing Tab in the Paragraph Dialog Box

The Paragraph dialog box contains Word's commands for changing paragraph alignment, indentation, and spacing. The Indents and Spacing tab of the Paragraph dialog box is shown in Figure 4-1. Use this figure as a reference throughout this lesson as well as the rest of this book.

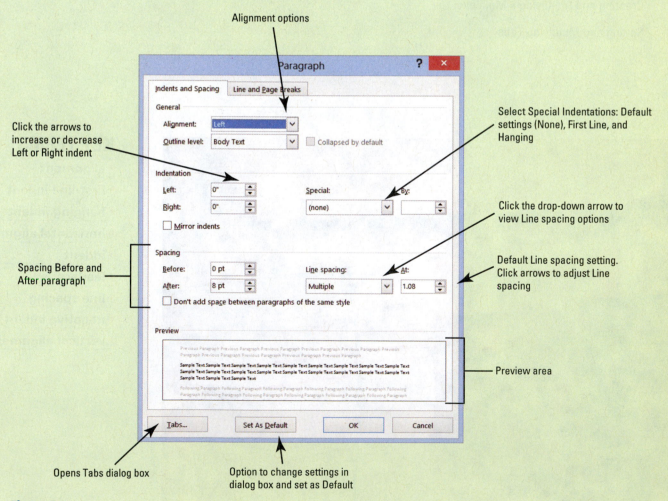

Figure 4-1

Indents and Spacing tab of the Paragraph dialog box

FORMATTING PARAGRAPHS

The Bottom Line

Paragraph formatting is an essential part of creating effective, professional-looking documents in Word. When a document is formatted properly and text is spaced and positioned, the reader can focus on the content. Word's paragraph formatting feature enables you to determine paragraph alignment, indentation, and spacing between paragraphs. Word's formatting features also enable you to remove paragraph formatting altogether.

Setting Indents

Indents can be used to set paragraphs off from other text in your documents. Word documents can include first-line indents, hanging indents, and negative indents. The commands for indenting paragraphs are available in the Paragraph command group on the Home tab, as well as in the Paragraph command group of the Page Layout tab. Both command groups have dialog box launchers that give you access to additional commands. In this exercise, you learn to set indents using the dialog box and the ruler.

An **indent** is a blank space inserted between text and the left or right margin. A **first-line indent** inserts blank space between the left margin and the first line of the paragraph (one-half inch is the default setting for this indent). A **hanging indent**, common in legal documents and in a bibliography page, begins the first full line of text in a paragraph at the left margin; all the remaining lines in the paragraph are then indented from the left margin. A **negative indent** extends paragraph text into the left margin. You can indent paragraphs from the left margin, the right margin, or both, and you can set the sizes of indents using Word's paragraph-formatting tools. You can also drag the markers on the ruler to set indents. Table 4-1 shows the various indent markers as they appear on the ruler.

Table 4-1

Types of indents on the Ruler

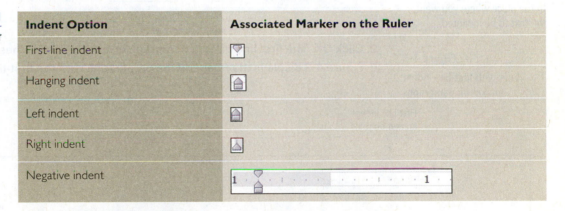

Indent Option	Associated Marker on the Ruler
First-line indent	
Hanging indent	
Left indent	
Right indent	
Negative indent	

STEP BY STEP

Set First-Line Indents

GET READY. Before you begin these steps, be sure to launch Microsoft Word.

1. Connect your flash drive to one of the USB ports on your computer.
2. Click the **File** tab, and then click **Computer**.
3. Click the **Browse** button. Use the vertical scroll bar to scroll down and locate the data files for this lesson on your flash drive. Double-click the lesson folder to open it.
4. Locate and **OPEN** the file named *Books Beyond*.

5. Click the **View** tab. Then, in the Show group, click the check box that displays the Ruler.
6. Select the four paragraphs under *Acknowledgement*.
7. On the Home tab, in the Paragraph group, click the dialog box launcher located in the bottom right corner of the group. Verify that the Indents and Spacing tab is the active tab.
8. In the Indentation section of this tab, change the Special selection by clicking the drop-down arrow and selecting **First line**. The By box lists 0.5 inches by default, as shown in Figure 4-2.

Figure 4-2

Paragraph dialog box

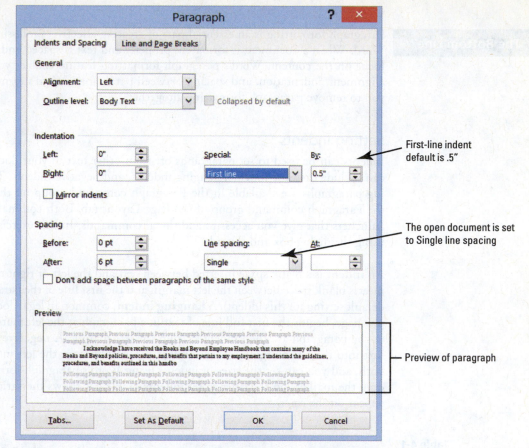

First-line indent default is .5"

The open document is set to Single line spacing

Preview of paragraph

Another Way

You can also click to place the insertion point anywhere within the paragraph to set the indent, and then drag the first-line indent marker on the ruler (see Figure 4-3) to the place where you want the text to be indented.

9. Click **OK**. The first line of each paragraph is indented 0.5 inches from the left margin.

10. Figure 4-3 displays the ruler and the paragraphs with the first-line indent you just set.

Figure 4-3

Ruler with first-line indent marker on paragraphs

First line indent marker on ruler

Acknowledgement¶

I acknowledge I have received the Books and Beyond Employee Handbook that contains many of the Books and Beyond policies, procedures, and benefits that pertain to my employment. I understand the guidelines, procedures, and benefits outlined in this handbook are not all-inclusive and may be modified or rescinded at any time at the discretion of Books and Beyond and that I will be notified of such changes to the handbook as they occur.¶

I also understand the Employee Handbook does not constitute a contract, expressed or implied, nor is it to be interpreted to be a contract between Books and Beyond and myself. I understand the company is an at-will employer, and I am an employee-at-will, which means the employment relationship may be terminated at anytime by either myself or Books and Beyond (unless I am under an employee contract and following the terms and conditions therein).¶

Only the president or other designated representative of Books and Beyond has the authority to enter into an employment agreement or agreement regarding benefits with any current or prospective employee. Any such agreement must be in writing and signed by both the president or designated representative and myself.¶

I understand if I have any questions related to this handbook or my employment that I may have them clarified by the Vice President of Operations or the HR Department. I also understand that this current edition of the Employee Handbook supersedes all previously issued editions.¶

11. Select the four paragraphs under *Introduction*.

12. On the horizontal ruler, press and hold the left mouse button and drag the First-line indent ▽ marker to **0.5** inches.

Troubleshooting   Click the *View* tab and choose *Ruler* from the Show command group.

Another Way
To indent the first line of a paragraph, click in front of the line and press *Tab*. To indent an entire paragraph, select the whole paragraph and press *Tab*.

13. Select all the paragraphs under the *General Performance Expectation Guidelines*.

14. On the Page Layout tab, in the Paragraph group, launch the Paragraph dialog box, and change the Special selection to **First line** by clicking the drop-down arrow. Click **OK** to accept the default setting of 0.5 inches.

15. Select both paragraphs under the *Equal Employment Opportunity and Diversity*.

16. Right-click and select **Paragraph**—this is another way to open the Paragraph dialog box.

17. Change the Special selection to **First line**. Click **OK**. Using a shortcut method, you can also access the *Paragraph* dialog box.

18. **SAVE** the document as *B&B First Line Indent* in the lesson folder on your flash drive.

PAUSE. LEAVE the document open to use in the next exercise.

CERTIFICATION READY?   2.2.7

How would you set indents?

STEP BY STEP   **Set Hanging Indents**

USE the document that is open from the previous exercise.

1. Place the insertion point at the beginning of the first paragraph under the heading *Acknowledgement*, and then select the first two paragraphs.

2. On the Home tab, launch the Paragraph dialog box and change the Special selection from First Line to **Hanging**. Click **OK**. The first line of both paragraphs begins at the left of the margin whereas the remaining paragraphs are indented 0.5 inches from the left margin.

3. Under the same heading, select the last two paragraphs. On the horizontal ruler, press and hold the left mouse button and drag the **first-line indent** ▽ marker so that it aligns with the left margin. You need to reposition the first-line indent marker so that it doesn't move when you begin dragging the hanging indent marker. Your markers on the ruler should match Figure 4-4.

Figure 4-4

Markers on ruler aligned

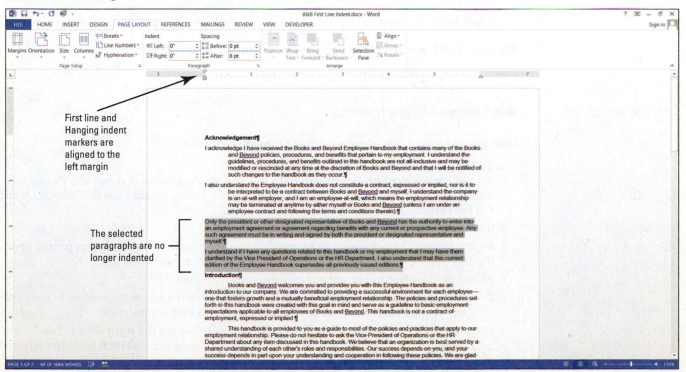

First line and Hanging indent markers are aligned to the left margin

The selected paragraphs are no longer indented

4. Press and hold the left mouse button and drag the **hanging indent** ⌂ marker to **0.5** inches. You have now repositioned the marker using the ruler, and both paragraphs are indented. Your document should look similar to the one shown in Figure 4-5.

Figure 4-5

Sample document with hanging indent

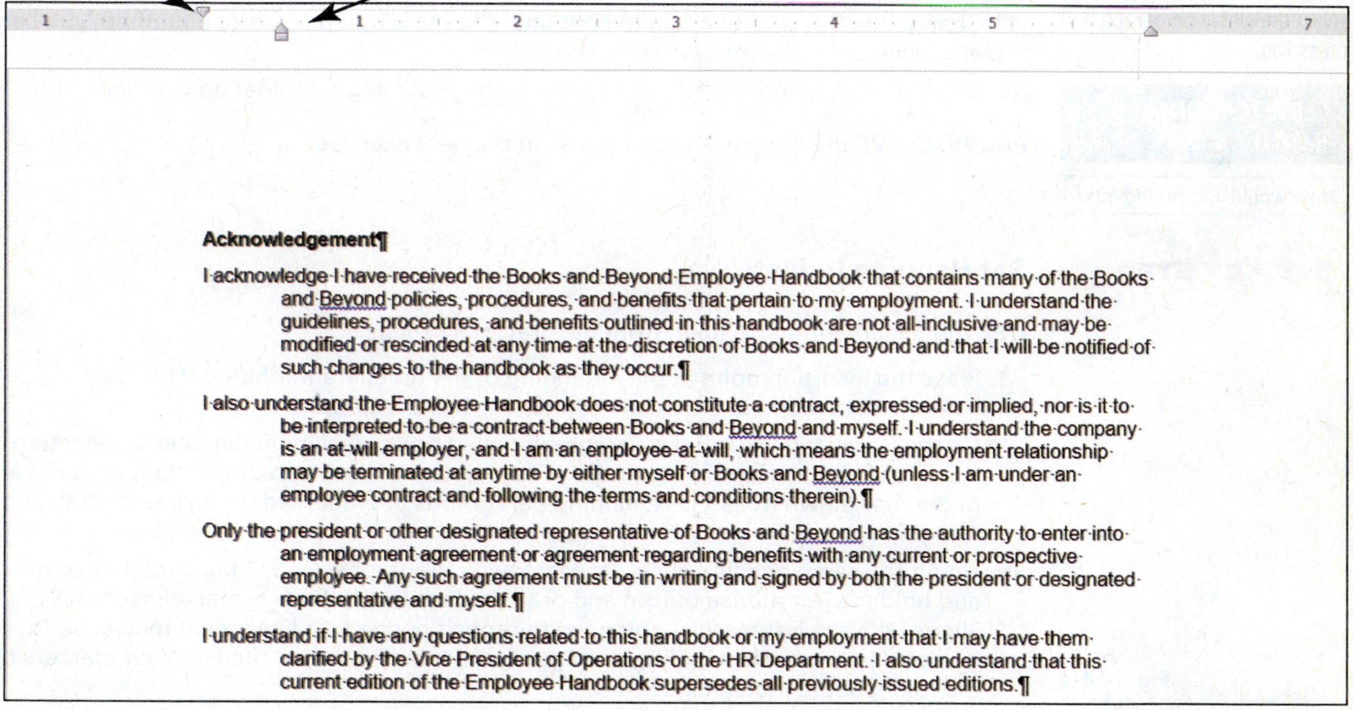

First line indent marker is positioned on left margin

Hanging indent marker is positioned 0.5" from the left margin

Acknowledgement¶

I acknowledge I have received the Books and Beyond Employee Handbook that contains many of the Books and Beyond policies, procedures, and benefits that pertain to my employment. I understand the guidelines, procedures, and benefits outlined in this handbook are not all-inclusive and may be modified or rescinded at any time at the discretion of Books and Beyond and that I will be notified of such changes to the handbook as they occur.¶

I also understand the Employee Handbook does not constitute a contract, expressed or implied, nor is it to be interpreted to be a contract between Books and Beyond and myself. I understand the company is an at-will employer, and I am an employee-at-will, which means the employment relationship may be terminated at anytime by either myself or Books and Beyond (unless I am under an employee contract and following the terms and conditions therein).¶

Only the president or other designated representative of Books and Beyond has the authority to enter into an employment agreement or agreement regarding benefits with any current or prospective employee. Any such agreement must be in writing and signed by both the president or designated representative and myself.¶

I understand if I have any questions related to this handbook or my employment that I may have them clarified by the Vice President of Operations or the HR Department. I also understand that this current edition of the Employee Handbook supersedes all previously issued editions.¶

5. **SAVE** the document as *B&B Hanging Indent* in the lesson folder on your flash drive.

PAUSE. LEAVE the document open to use in the next exercise.

STEP BY STEP   **Set Left and Right Indents**

USE the document that is open from the previous exercise.

1. Select the paragraphs under *Introduction*.
2. You will move the first-line indent back to the default settings. Launch the Paragraph dialog box from the Home tab. Under the Special group, select **(none)**. Click **OK**. Notice the paragraphs are left aligned.
3. Select the first two paragraphs under *Introduction*.
4. Right-click and click **Paragraph** to open the dialog box. In the Indentation group, **change the left and right indents to 1 inch** by clicking the up arrow. Click **OK**.
5. Select the last two paragraphs under the same heading.
6. On the Page Layout tab, in the Paragraph group, click the up arrow next to **Indent Left** ⊒ Left: to indent the left side of the paragraph to **1** inch on the ruler.
7. Click the up arrow next to **Indent Right** ⊒ Right: to indent the right side of the paragraph to **1** inch on the ruler. Notice that paragraphs are one inch from the left and right margins (see Figure 4-6).

Figure 4-6

Sample document displaying
left and right indents

Left indent marker is
one-inch from the
margin

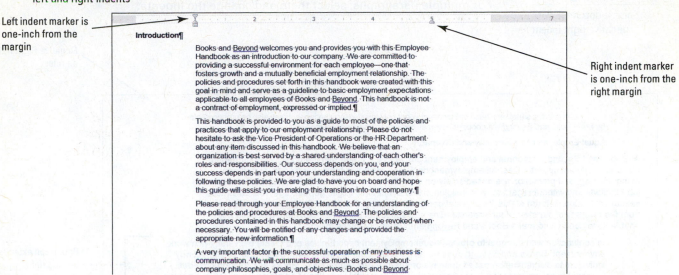

Right indent marker
is one-inch from the
right margin

8. **SAVE** the document as *B&B Left&Right Indent* in the lesson folder on your flash drive.

PAUSE. LEAVE the document open to use in the next exercise.

STEP BY STEP   **Set Negative Indents**

USE the document that is open from the previous exercise.

1. Under the *Equal Employment Opportunity and Diversity* heading, select both paragraphs.

2. Launch the Paragraph dialog box from the Home tab. Under the Special group, select **(none)**. Click **OK**.

3. Select the first paragraph under the heading.

4. Click the Page Layout tab, in the Paragraph group, click the down arrow next to **Indent Left** **Left:** to indent the left side of the paragraph to **−0.5** inch on the ruler as shown in Figure 4-7.

Figure 4-7

Sample document with
negative left indent

Negative left
indent on ruler

Paragraph
extends into
left margin

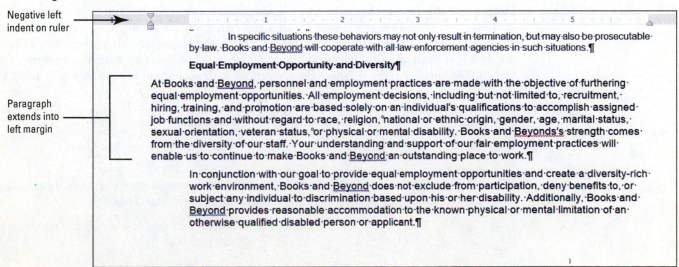

5. Position your insertion point anywhere in the last paragraph, and then launch the Paragraph dialog box from the Page Layout tab.

6. Under the Indentation group, click the down arrow next to **Right** to indent the right side of the paragraph to **−0.5** inch (see Figure 4-8). Click **OK**. When repositioning the indentations, you can select or place the insertion point anywhere in the paragraph. For multiple paragraphs, select them and change the indents.

Figure 4-8

Sample document with negative right indent

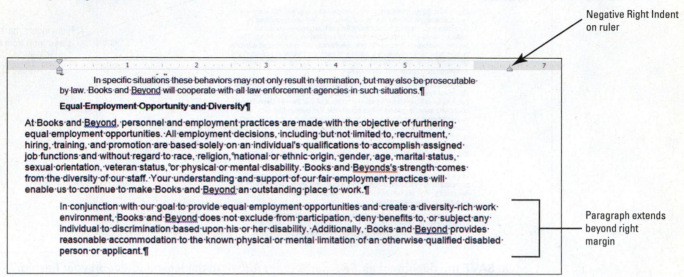

Negative Right Indent on ruler

In specific situations these behaviors may not only result in termination, but may also be prosecutable by law. Books and Beyond will cooperate with all law enforcement agencies in such situations.¶

Equal Employment Opportunity and Diversity¶

At Books and Beyond, personnel and employment practices are made with the objective of furthering equal employment opportunities. All employment decisions, including but not limited to, recruitment, hiring, training, and promotion are based solely on an individual's qualifications to accomplish assigned job functions and without regard to race, religion, national or ethnic origin, gender, age, marital status, sexual orientation, veteran status, or physical or mental disability. Books and Beyonds's strength comes from the diversity of our staff. Your understanding and support of our fair employment practices will enable us to continue to make Books and Beyond an outstanding place to work.¶

In conjunction with our goal to provide equal employment opportunities and create a diversity-rich work environment, Books and Beyond does not exclude from participation, deny benefits to, or subject any individual to discrimination based upon his or her disability. Additionally, Books and Beyond provides reasonable accommodation to the known physical or mental limitation of an otherwise qualified disabled person or applicant.¶

Paragraph extends beyond right margin

7. SAVE the document as **B&B Negative Indent** in the lesson folder on your flash drive, and then **CLOSE** the file.

PAUSE. LEAVE Word open for the next exercise.

Take Note Changing paragraph indents can be completed by using the Ruler or launching the Paragraph dialog box found on the Home or Page Layout tabs.

Changing Alignment

Another Way
To access the Paragraph dialog box using the shortcut method, place the insertion point in the paragraph, and then right-click and select *Paragraph* from the menu that appears.

Paragraph **alignment** refers to how text is positioned between a document's margins. By default, text is left-aligned at the top of the page. However, as you continue to format a document, you might need to change your text's horizontal or vertical alignment. In this exercise, you learn to align text left, center, right, and justify and to vertically center text in the document.

Horizontal alignment refers to how text is positioned between the left and right margins. There are four types of horizontal alignments: left align, center align, right align, or justify. Horizontal alignment can be changed in the Paragraph group on the Home tab. Also, when the Paragraph dialog box is open and the Indents and Spacing tab is active, you can change alignment in the General section of the tab. Alternatively, you can use various shortcut keys, as shown in Table 4-2.

Table 4-2

Horizontal alignment options

Option	Button	Shortcut Keys	Description
Align left		Ctrl+L	Lines up text flush with the left margin, leaving a ragged right edge
Center		Ctrl+E	Centers text between the left and right margins, leaving ragged edges on both sides
Align right		Ctrl+R	Lines up text flush with the right margin, leaving a ragged left edge
Justify		Ctrl+J	Lines up text flush on both the left and right margins, adding extra space between words as necessary for a clean look

Vertical alignment refers to how text is positioned between the top and bottom margins of the page. Text can be aligned vertically at the top margin, at the center of the page, or at the bottom of the page, or it can be justified. Top-of-the-page vertical alignment is the default when launching Word. Centered vertical alignment places the text evenly between the top and bottom margins. Bottom vertical alignment places text next to the bottom margin of the document. Finally, justified vertical alignment aligns text evenly among the top, bottom, left, and right margins (see Table 4-3).

Table 4-3

Vertical alignment options

Option	Description
Top vertical alignment	Aligns text at the top margin
Centered vertical alignment	Aligns text between the top and bottom margins
Bottom vertical alignment	Aligns text at the bottom margin
Justified vertical alignment	Aligns text equally among the top, bottom, left, and right margins

There are two ways to set vertical alignment.

- From the Page Layout tab, in the Page Setup group, launch the Page Setup dialog box. From the Layout tab, under the Page group, you will find the Vertical Alignment pull-down menu.
- From the File tab, select Print then Page Setup. This launches the Page Setup dialog box also. From the Layout tab, under the Page group, you will find the Vertical Alignment pull-down menu.

STEP BY STEP   **Change Alignment to Justify**

OPEN *Books Beyond* from the data files from this lesson.

1. Select all four paragraphs under *Acknowledgement*.
2. On the Home tab, in the Paragraph group, click the **Justify** button. The paragraphs are justified between the left and right margins. Notice that the Justify button is highlighted.
3. Select all four paragraphs under *Introduction*.
4. On the Home tab, in the Paragraph group, click the arrow in the lower-right corner of the group to launch the Paragraph dialog box. The Indents and Spacing tab should be selected.
5. In the Alignment list under General, click the drop-down arrow, and then click **Justified**. Click **OK**.
6. Select the first two paragraphs under *General Performance Expectation Guidelines*. Avoid selecting the numbered list.
7. Press **Ctrl+J** to justify the paragraphs. Using the keyboard shortcut is a quick way to change the alignment in a paragraph.
8. Select the two paragraphs under *Equal Employment Opportunity and Diversity* and justify the paragraph using one of the methods.
9. **SAVE** the document as *B&B Justify* in the lesson folder on your flash drive.

PAUSE. LEAVE the document open to use in the next exercise.

STEP BY STEP **Change Alignment to Right**

USE the document that is open from the previous exercise.

1. Place the insertion point in the first paragraph under *Acknowledgement*.
2. On the Home tab, in the Paragraph group, click the **Align Right** button. The right side of the paragraph is even whereas the left is uneven.
3. Select the second paragraph, right-click and select **Paragraph**.
4. In the Alignment list under General, click the drop-down arrow, and then click **Right**. Review the Preview area, the paragraph is right-aligned. Click **OK**.
5. Select the last two paragraphs under *Acknowledgement*, and press **Ctrl+R** to align the text on the right. The right side of the paragraphs are even, whereas the left are uneven.
6. **SAVE** the document as *B&B Right Align* in the lesson folder on your flash drive.

PAUSE. **LEAVE** the document open to use in the next exercise.

STEP BY STEP **Change Alignment to Center**

USE the document that is open from the previous exercise.

1. Place the insertion point in the *Acknowledgement* heading.
2. On the Home tab, in the Paragraph group, click the **Center** button. The heading is now centered between the left and right margin.
3. Use the multi-selection and select the headings, **Introduction**, **General Performance Expectation Guidelines**, and **Equal Employment Opportunity and Diversity**.

 Cross Ref In Lesson 2, you learn to select text using different methods. To select multiple text areas, press *Ctrl* and select the text.

4. Press **Ctrl+E** to center the headings using the shortcut key.
5. **SAVE** the document as *B&B Centered Headings* in the lesson folder on your flash drive.

PAUSE. **LEAVE** the document open to use in the next exercise.

STEP BY STEP **Change Alignment to Left**

USE the document that is open from the previous exercise.

1. Select all four paragraphs under *Acknowledgement*.
2. On the Home tab, in the Paragraph group, click the **Left** button. The paragraphs are now left-aligned, which is the default when you begin a new document.
3. Select all four paragraphs under *Introduction*.
4. Right-click and select **Paragraph** to open the Paragraph dialog box.
5. In the Alignment list under General, click the drop-down arrow, and then click **Left**. Review the Preview area—the paragraphs are aligned left. Click **OK**.
6. Select the first two paragraphs under *General Performance Expectation Guidelines*.
7. On the Page Layout tab, launch the Paragraph dialog box. In the Alignment list under General, click the drop-down arrow, and then click **Left**. Click **OK**.
8. Select the two paragraphs under *Equal Employment Opportunity and Diversity*.
9. Press **Ctrl+L** to align the paragraphs to the left using the shortcut key.
10. **SAVE** the document as *B&B Left Align* in the lesson folder on your flash drive.

PAUSE. **LEAVE** the document open to use in the next exercise.

Change Alignment to Vertical

USE the document that is open from the previous exercise.

1. Select the text beginning with the heading *Introduction...* to the end of the document and press **Delete**.

2. Press **Ctrl+Home** to position the insertion point at the beginning of the document.

3. On the Page Layout tab, in the Page Setup group, click the arrow in the lower-right corner of the group to open the *Page Setup* dialog box.

4. Select the **Layout** tab.

5. In the Vertical alignment list under Page, click the drop-down arrow and select **Center**.

6. In the Apply to list under Preview, Whole document is selected as the default, as shown in Figure 4-9.

Figure 4-9

Page Setup dialog box

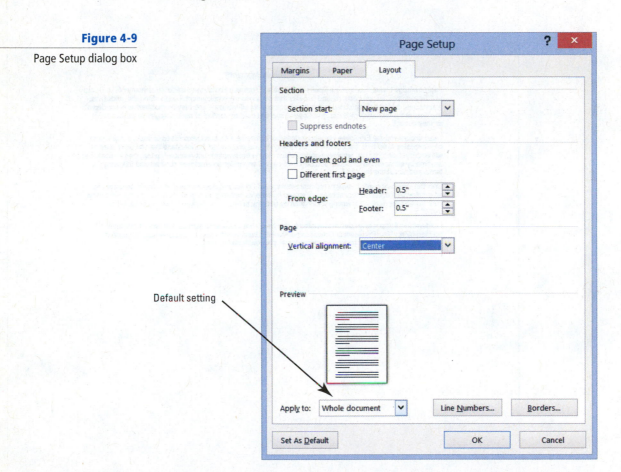

7. Click **OK**. The text is centered between the top and bottom margins, as shown in Figure 4-10.

Figure 4-10

Horizontal and vertical alignments

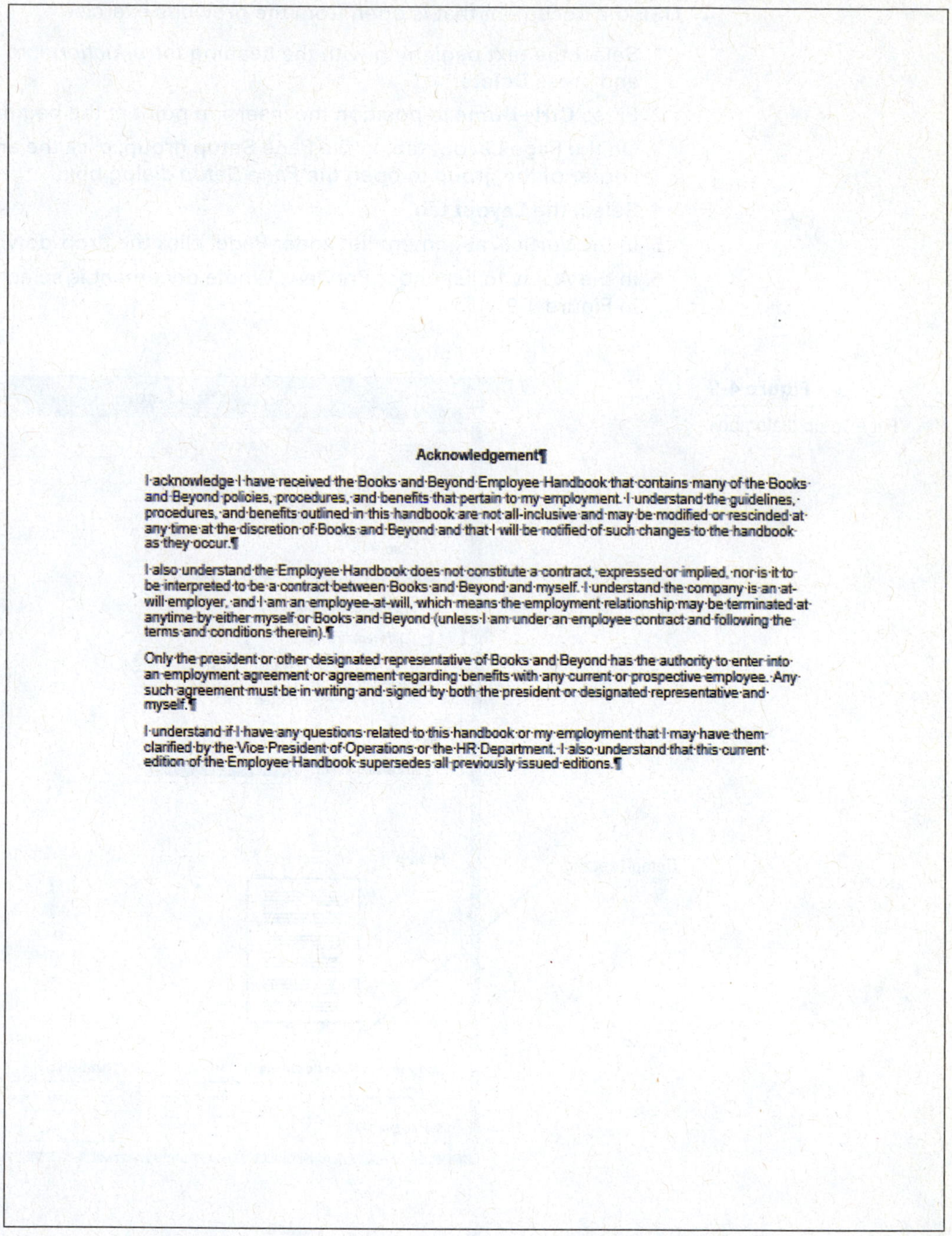

Acknowledgement¶

I·acknowledge·I·have·received·the·Books·and·Beyond·Employee·Handbook·that·contains·many·of·the·Books·and·Beyond·policies,·procedures,·and·benefits·that·pertain·to·my·employment.·I·understand·the·guidelines,·procedures,·and·benefits·outlined·in·this·handbook·are·not·all-inclusive·and·may·be·modified·or·rescinded·at·any·time·at·the·discretion·of·Books·and·Beyond·and·that·I·will·be·notified·of·such·changes·to·the·handbook·as·they·occur.¶

I·also·understand·the·Employee·Handbook·does·not·constitute·a·contract,·expressed·or·implied,·nor·is·it·to·be·interpreted·to·be·a·contract·between·Books·and·Beyond·and·myself.·I·understand·the·company·is·an·at-will·employer,·and·I·am·an·employee-at-will,·which·means·the·employment·relationship·may·be·terminated·at·anytime·by·either·myself·or·Books·and·Beyond·(unless·I·am·under·an·employee·contract·and·following·the·terms·and·conditions·therein).¶

Only·the·president·or·other·designated·representative·of·Books·and·Beyond·has·the·authority·to·enter·into·an·employment·agreement·or·agreement·regarding·benefits·with·any·current·or·prospective·employee.·Any·such·agreement·must·be·in·writing·and·signed·by·both·the·president·or·designated·representative·and·myself.¶

I·understand·if·I·have·any·questions·related·to·this·handbook·or·my·employment·that·I·may·have·them·clarified·by·the·Vice·President·of·Operations·or·the·HR·Department.·I·also·understand·that·this·current·edition·of·the·Employee·Handbook·supersedes·all·previously·issued·editions.¶

8. SAVE the document as ***B&B Vertical Alignment*** in the lesson folder on your flash drive.

PAUSE. LEAVE the document open to use in the next exercise.

Shading a Paragraph

In this exercise, you learn to use Word's Shading feature to color the background behind selected text or paragraphs.

To apply shading to a paragraph, click the *Shading* button in the Paragraph group on the Home tab. To choose another color, click the drop-down arrow next to the Shading button, and choose a color in the current theme or a standard color from the Shading menu (place your insertion point over a color to see a ScreenTip with the color's precise name). To remove shading, click *No Color*.

Click *More Colors* to open the Colors dialog box, where additional options are available. You can choose standard colors on the Standard tab, or you can create a custom color from the Custom tab.

STEP BY STEP   **Shade a Paragraph**

USE the document that is open from the previous exercise.

1. Select the first paragraph under the heading.

2. On the Home tab, in the Paragraph group, click the drop-down arrow next to the Shading button to display the menu shown in Figure 4-11.

Figure 4-11

Shading menu

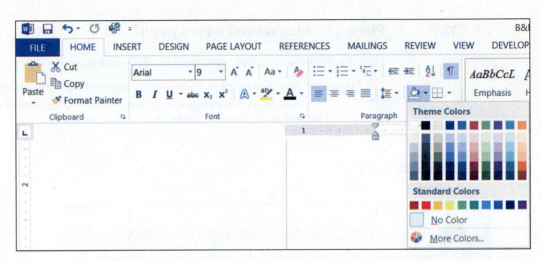

3. In the Theme Colors palette, locate and select **Orange, Accent 6, Lighter 40%** as shown in Figure 4-12.

Figure 4-12

Selecting the color

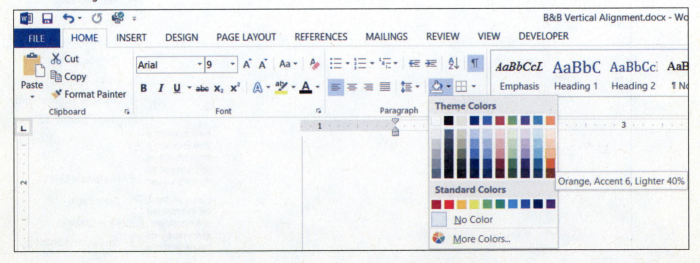

4. **SAVE** the document as *B&B Shaded Paragraph* in the lesson folder on your flash drive.

PAUSE. LEAVE the document open to use in the next exercise.

Placing a Border around a Paragraph or Text

Like shading, borders can add interest and emphasis to paragraphs or text. Borders can be formatted with a variety of styles, colors, and widths. In this exercise, you use Word's Borders options to apply a border to a paragraph in your document.

You can apply a border to a paragraph by clicking the *Borders* button in the Paragraph group on the Home tab. To change the border style, click the drop-down arrow next to the Borders button.

For additional options, click the *Borders and Shading* option on the Borders menu to open the Borders tab of the Borders and Shading dialog box. You can choose a number of border colors and styles in this dialog box, or you can remove a border completely. This dialog box also contains tabs for page border options and shading.

STEP BY STEP   **Place a Border around a Paragraph**

USE the document that is open from the previous exercise.

1. Place the insertion point in the second paragraph beginning with "*I also understand…*"
2. On the Home tab, in the Paragraph group, click the drop-down arrow next to the Borders button to display the menu shown in Figure 4-13.

Figure 4-13

Border menu

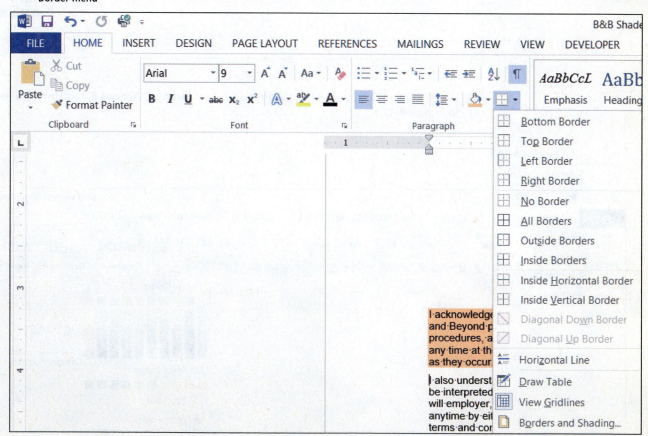

3. Select **Outside Borders** on the menu. Your document should look similar to Figure 4-14.

Figure 4-14

Shading and border

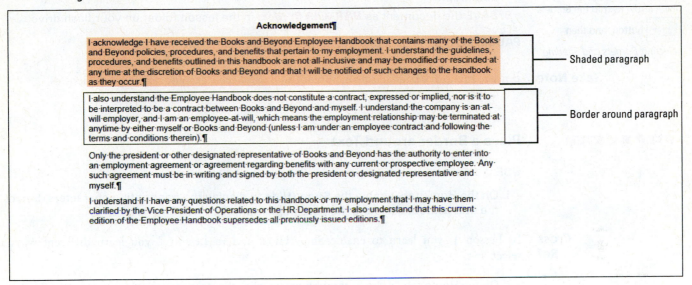

Acknowledgement¶

I acknowledge I have received the Books and Beyond Employee Handbook that contains many of the Books and Beyond policies, procedures, and benefits that pertain to my employment. I understand the guidelines, procedures, and benefits outlined in this handbook are not all-inclusive and may be modified or rescinded at any time at the discretion of Books and Beyond and that I will be notified of such changes to the handbook as they occur.¶ — Shaded paragraph

I also understand the Employee Handbook does not constitute a contract, expressed or implied, nor is it to be interpreted to be a contract between Books and Beyond and myself. I understand the company is an at-will employer, and I am an employee-at-will, which means the employment relationship may be terminated at anytime by either myself or Books and Beyond (unless I am under an employee contract and following the terms and conditions therein).¶ — Border around paragraph

Only the president or other designated representative of Books and Beyond has the authority to enter into an employment agreement or agreement regarding benefits with any current or prospective employee. Any such agreement must be in writing and signed by both the president or designated representative and myself.¶

I understand if I have any questions related to this handbook or my employment that I may have them clarified by the Vice President of Operations or the HR Department. I also understand that this current edition of the Employee Handbook supersedes all previously issued editions.¶

4. Place the insertion point in the third paragraph.

5. On the Design tab, in the Page Background group, click **Page Borders** to open the Borders and Shading dialog box, and then click the **Borders** tab to make it active (see Figure 4-15). The Design tab on the Ribbon is a new tab for Word 2013 and contains many additional features to format a document. In Lesson 7, you learn more about the Design tab.

Figure 4-15

Borders and Shading dialog box

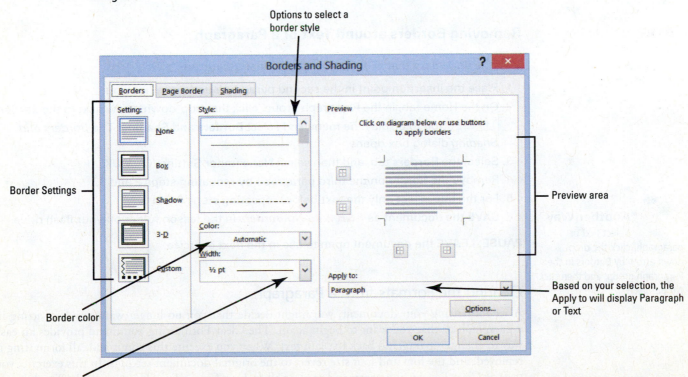

Options to select a border style

Border Settings

Border color

Width selector

Preview area

Based on your selection, the Apply to will display Paragraph or Text

Another Way
The Borders and Shading dialog box can be accessed by clicking the drop-down arrow next to the Borders button, and then selecting *Borders and Shading*.

6. Select **Shadow** under the Settings.

7. Select the **ninth** option under Style. Select **Dark Blue, Text 2** for color, and change the width to **2 ¼ pt.**

8. Review the Preview area before you click **OK**. Note that the border is applied to the paragraph.

9. **SAVE** the document as *B&B with Borders* in the lesson folder on your flash drive.

PAUSE. LEAVE the document open to use in the next exercise.

Take Note   Borders can also be added to pages, sections, tables, cells, graphic objects, and pictures.

STEP BY STEP   **Place a Border around Text**

USE the document that is open from the previous exercise.

1. On the Home tab, enable the **Show/Hide** to display the nonprinting characters. Select the title without selecting the paragraph mark (¶).

Cross Ref   In Lesson 1, you learn to enable Show/Hide, and in Lesson 2 you learn different ways to select text.

2. On the Home tab, in the Paragraph group, click the drop-down arrow next to the Borders button to display the menu and select **Borders and Shading** to open the dialog box.

3. Click the **Borders** tab to make it active. Notice the title appears in the Preview area and in the Apply to section, Text is displayed. Not selecting the paragraph mark (¶) allows you to place a border around text only.

4. Select **Box** under Setting and change the width to **1 ½ pt.** Click **OK**. Notice that the border wraps around the text.

5. **SAVE** the document with the same filename in the lesson folder on your flash drive.

PAUSE. LEAVE the document open to use in the next exercise.

STEP BY STEP   **Removing Borders around Text or a Paragraph**

USE the document that is open from the previous exercise.

1. Place the insertion point in the second paragraph under the heading.

2. On the Home tab, in the Paragraph group, click the drop-down arrow next to the Borders button to display the menu and select **Borders and Shading**. The *Borders and Shading* dialog box opens.

3. Select the **Borders** tab, and then select **None** under Setting. Click **OK**.

4. Remove the border on the third paragraph by repeating steps 2 and 3.

5. For the title select only the text before repeating steps 2 and 3.

6. **SAVE** the document as *B&B with No Borders* in the lesson folder on your flash drive.

PAUSE. LEAVE the document open to use in the next exercise.

Another Way
Select text or paragraph, click the drop-down arrow by Borders in the Paragraph group, and then click *No Border*.

Clearing the Formats from a Paragraph

After formatting your document, you might decide that you no longer want any formatting in a paragraph or that you want to begin again. The Clear Formatting command provides an easy way to change a paragraph back to plain text. When you execute this command, all formatting is removed, and the font and font size revert to the original document settings. In this exercise, you use the Clear Formatting command to clear all formats from selected paragraphs in Word.

STEP BY STEP   **Clear Paragraph Formats**

USE the document that is open from the previous exercise.

1. Select the whole document.
2. On the Home tab, in the Font group, click the **Clear Formatting** button.

🔍 **Cross Ref**   You can also clear formatting in the Styles group by clicking the *More* button. For more information, see Lesson 3.

3. **SAVE** the document as *B&B No Formatting* in the lesson folder on your flash drive, and then **CLOSE** the file.

PAUSE. LEAVE Word open for the next exercise.

SETTING LINE SPACING IN TEXT AND BETWEEN PARAGRAPHS

The Bottom Line   In Word, you can determine how much space separates lines of text, and you also can set the spacing between paragraphs. By default, Word sets line spacing (the space between each line of text) to 1.08. Line spacing is paragraph based and can be customized by specifying a point size. Paragraph spacing, which affects the space above and below paragraphs, is set to 8 points after each paragraph by default. The higher the point size is, the greater the space between paragraphs. In this exercise, you learn to set both line and paragraph spacing.

Setting Line Spacing

Line spacing is the amount of space between the lines of text in a paragraph. In this exercise, you learn to set line spacing using a number of Word paragraph formatting tools.

Line spacing options are available in the Home and Page Layout tabs within the Paragraph group by using the Line and Paragraph Spacing button. The line spacing options can also be accessed through the Indents and Spacing tab of the Paragraph dialog box. New in Word 2013 is the Design tab, which includes Paragraph Spacing settings. Table 4-4 provides additional information regarding line spacing options and descriptions.

Table 4-4

Line spacing options

Option	Keyboard Shortcut	Description
Single	Ctrl+1	Accommodates the largest letter in a line, plus a small amount of extra space.
1.5	Ctrl+5	One-and-one-half times the amount of space used in single spacing.
Double	Ctrl+2	Twice the amount of space used in single spacing.
At least		Sets the spacing at the minimum amount needed to fit the largest font on the line.
Exactly		Sets the spacing at a fixed amount that Word does not adjust.
Multiple		Sets the spacing at an amount that is increased or decreased from single spacing by a percentage that you specify. Setting the line spacing to 1.3, for example, increases the space by 30%.
No Paragraph Spacing		The Built-in Before and After spacing is set to 0 pt. and the line spacing is set to 1.
Compact		The Built-in Before spacing is set to 0 pt., After is set to 4 pt., and the line space is set to 1.
Tight		The Built-in Before spacing is set to 0 pt., After to 6 pt., and line spacing 1.15.
Open		The Built-in Before spacing is set to 0 pt., After to 10 pt., and line spacing 1.15.
Relaxed		The Built-in Before spacing is set to 0 pt., After to 6 pt., and line spacing to 1.5.
Double		The Built-in Before spacing is set to 0 pt., After 8 pt., and line spacing 2.

Set Line Spacing in a Paragraph

OPEN the *Books Beyond* document from the lesson folder.

1. Place the insertion point in the first paragraph under the *Acknowledgement* heading.

2. On the Home tab, in the Paragraph group, click the **Line and Paragraph Spacing** button to display the Line Spacing menu and options to add and remove spacing before and after paragraphs (see Figure 4-16).

Figure 4-16

Line Spacing menu

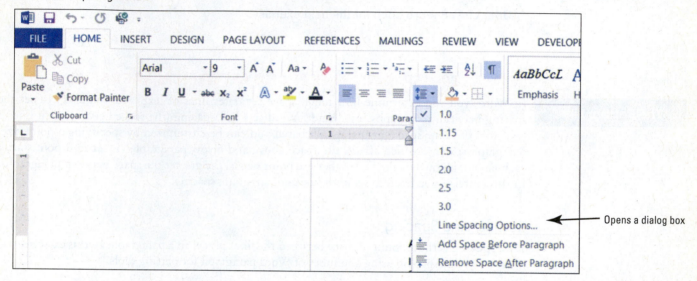

Opens a dialog box

3. Select **2.0** to double-space the text.

4. Place the insertion point in the second paragraph.

5. In the Paragraph group, launch the dialog box.

6. In the Spacing group, change the Line spacing by clicking the drop-down arrow and selecting **Double**. Click **OK**. The paragraph is now double-spaced.

7. Place the insertion point in the third paragraph.

8. Press **Ctrl+2** to double-space the paragraph.

9. Click the **Design** tab and in the Document Formatting group, click the **Paragraph Spacing** button to display the menu as shown in Figure 4-17.

Figure 4-17

Paragraph Spacing menu

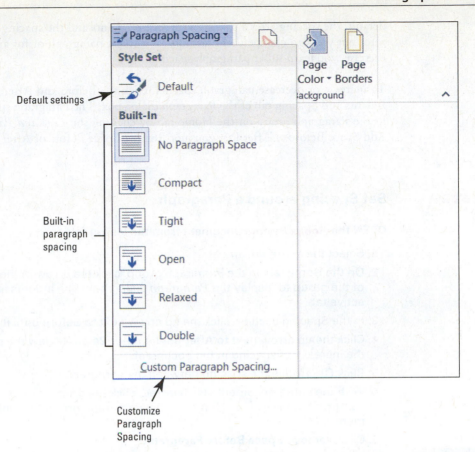

Default settings

Built-in paragraph spacing

Customize Paragraph Spacing

10. Select **Double**. Notice that the remaining document is double-spaced. This new feature in Word 2013 changes spacing for the entire document to include new paragraphs.

Take Note   When using the Document Formatting group to apply paragraph spacing, the document does not need to be selected when using one of the built-in formatting commands.

11. **SAVE** the document as **B&B Double Spacing** in the lesson folder on your flash drive.

PAUSE. LEAVE the document open to use in the next exercise.

CERTIFICATION READY?   2.2.5

How would you set line spacing in a paragraph?

STEP BY STEP   **Modify Line Spacing in a Paragraph**

USE the document that is open from the previous exercise.

1. Select the four paragraphs under *Acknowledgement*.
2. Return to the **Line and Paragraph Spacing** drop-down menu in the Paragraph group on the Home tab. To set more precise spacing measurements, click **Line Spacing Options** to display the Indents and Spacing tab of the Paragraph dialog box.
3. In the Spacing section, click the drop-down arrow and select **Exactly** in the Line spacing list. In the At list, click the up arrow until it reads **22** pt. The line spacing is increased.
4. Click **OK**.
5. **SAVE** the document as **B&B Exact Spacing** in the lesson folder on your flash drive, and then **CLOSE** the file.

PAUSE. LEAVE Word open for the next exercise.

CERTIFICATION READY?   3.3.4

How would you modify line spacing in a paragraph?

Setting Paragraph Spacing

Paragraphs are usually separated by a blank line in Word documents. When you press the Enter key at the end of a paragraph, Word adds the designated space above or below the paragraph. By default, the spacing after a paragraph is set to 8 points and the spacing before paragraphs is set to zero, but you can change these settings for a single paragraph or for an entire document. In this exercise, you learn to set paragraph spacing.

To increase or decrease paragraph spacing, click the Before and After up or down arrows in the Indents and Spacing tab of the Paragraph dialog box. The Paragraph spacing can also be changed in the Paragraph group on the Home tab by clicking the *Line and Paragraph Spacing* button to Add Space Before or After Paragraph or Remove Space Before or After Paragraph.

STEP BY STEP   ### Set Spacing around a Paragraph

OPEN the *Books Beyond* document from the lesson folder.

1. Select the entire document.

2. On the Home tab, in the Paragraph group, click the arrow in the lower-right corner of the group to display the *Paragraph* dialog box. The Indents and Spacing tab is the active tab.

3. In the Spacing section, click the up arrow next to Before until it reads **24** pt.

4. Click the up arrow next to After until it reads **24** pt. Review the preview area and notice the increase of spacing in the document.

5. Click **OK**. Notice the spacing between the paragraphs.

6. With the entire document still selected, click the drop-down arrow next to the Line and Paragraph Spacing [icon] button in the Paragraph group to display the Line Spacing menu.

7. Click **Remove Space Before Paragraph**.

8. Repeat step 6, and then click **Remove Space After Paragraph**. The spacing before and after have been removed from the document.

9. Place the insertion point in the heading, *Acknowledgement*.

10. Click the Page Layout tab, and then in the Paragraph group, click the up arrow and increase the Spacing After [After:] to **12** pt.

11. Use the Format Painter and repeat step 10 for each heading, *Introduction*, *General Performance Expectation Guidelines*, and *Equal Employment Opportunity and Diversity*.

12. Use multi-selection to select the paragraphs under each heading and change the Spacing After to **6** pt.

13. **SAVE** the document as *B&B Spacing Before&After* in the lesson folder on your flash drive, and then **CLOSE** the file.

PAUSE. LEAVE Word open for the next exercise.

CERTIFICATION READY?   2.2.4

How would you apply paragraph spacing?

Another Way
You also can right-click to open the Paragraph dialog box.

The Bottom Line

CREATING AND FORMATTING A BULLETED LIST

Bulleted lists are an effective way to format lists of items that don't have to appear in any specific order. (Use numbered lists for items in a set order.) Items in a bulleted list are marked by small icons—dots, diamonds, and so on. In Word, you can create bulleted lists from scratch, change existing lines of text into a bulleted list, choose from a number of bullet styles, create levels within a bulleted list, and insert a symbol or picture as a bullet.

Creating a Bulleted List

By creating and formatting a bulleted list, you can draw attention to major points in a document. In this exercise, you learn to create, format, and modify such a list.

| STEP BY STEP | Create a Bulleted List |

OPEN **Alarm** from the data files for this lesson.

1. Select the two paragraphs below the phrase *Please keep in mind:*.
2. On the Home tab, in the Paragraph group, click the **Bullets** button. Notice that solid circles appear before the selected paragraphs.
3. Place the insertion point at the end of the second bulleted paragraph.
4. Press **Enter**. Word automatically continues the bulleted list by supplying the next bulleted line.
5. Beside the new bullet, type **If you do not know your four-digit code and password, please get it from the HR department**.
6. **SAVE** the document as **B&B Alarm** in the lesson folder on your flash drive.

PAUSE. LEAVE the document open to use in the next exercise.

CERTIFICATION READY?   **3.3.1**

How do you apply bullets in a document?

| STEP BY STEP | Change the Bulleted List |

USE the document that is open from the previous exercise.

1. Select the entire bulleted list.
2. To change the format of the bulleted list, click the drop-down arrow next to the Bullets button to display the menu shown in Figure 4-18. The bulleted items might not match your screen.

Figure 4-18

Bullet formatting options

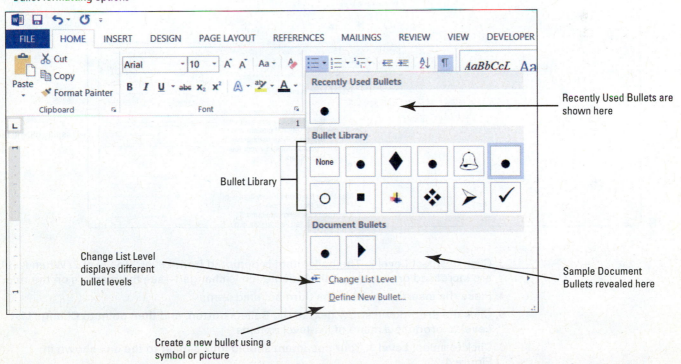

Take Note   To change a bulleted list to a numbered list (or vice versa), select the list and then click either the *Bullets* button or the *Numbering* button. To remove one of the bullets from the Library, open the *Bullets* drop-down menu; then in the Bullet Library, select the bullet and right-click to remove it.

3. Click the hollow circle in the Bullet Library.

4. **SAVE** the document as *B&B Alarm with Hollow Bullets* in the lesson folder on your flash drive.

PAUSE. LEAVE the document open to use in the next exercise.

Change the Bullet List Level

Adding an unordered list such as bullets appears with no rank over the others. Changing the bullet list level can change the appearance of the bullet and indentation.

USE the document that is open from the previous exercise.

1. Place the insertion point in the second bulleted item.

2. Click the drop-down arrow next to the Bullets [icon] button, point to **Change List Level**, and note the levels that appear (see Figure 4-19). When you point to the list level, a ScreenTip appears displaying the level.

Figure 4-19

Change List Level

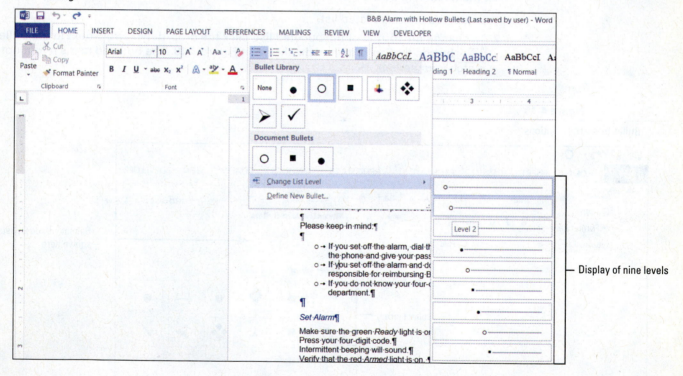

— Display of nine levels

3. Click to select **Level 2**. The bullet item is demoted from Level 1 to Level 2. When levels are increased or decreased, the indentation is changed—see the markers on the rulers.

4. Place the insertion point in the third bulleted item.

5. Click the drop-down arrow next to the Bullets button, and then point to **Change List Level** to produce a menu of list-level options.

6. Click to select **Level 3**. Your document should look similar to the one shown in Figure 4-20.

Figure 4-20

Sample document with
bullet levels

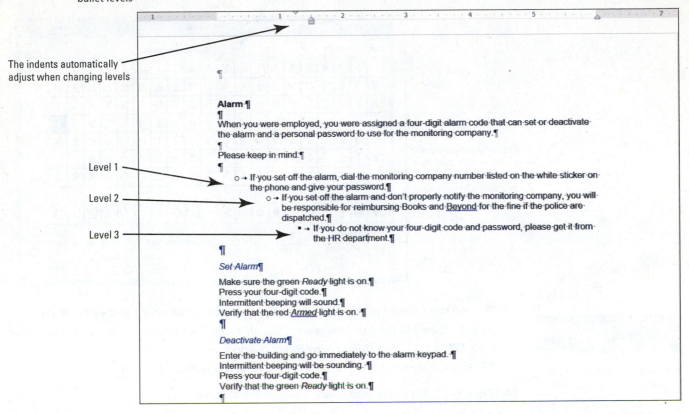

The indents automatically
adjust when changing levels

Level 1

Level 2

Level 3

7. **SAVE** the document as ***B&B Alarm with Bullet Levels*** in the lesson folder on your flash drive.

8. Select the second and third bulleted items and click the drop-down arrow next to the Bullets button. Point to **Change List Level** and promote the selected bullets to **Level 1**. The two selected items now match the first bulleted item.

9. Click **Undo** to return the bulleted items to second and third level.

10. **SAVE** the document with the same filename in the lesson folder on your flash drive.

PAUSE. LEAVE the document open to use in the next exercise.

How do you increase or
decrease the list level?

STEP BY STEP   **Insert Special Character Symbols**

The Define New Bullet dialog box provides options to change the alignment and add bullet characters, such as a symbol or a picture. When you click on either option, a new dialog box opens.

USE the document that is open from the previous exercise.

1. Select the second and third bulleted items and Promote to the first level, and then select all three bulleted items.

2. Click the drop-down arrow next to the Bullets button, and then click **Define New Bullet**.

3. Click the **Symbol** button in the Define New Bullet dialog box. The *Symbol* dialog box opens, as shown in Figure 4-21.

Figure 4-21

Symbol dialog box

Change the font by clicking the drop-down arrow

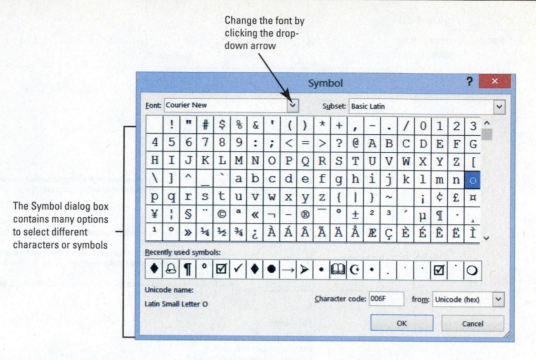

The Symbol dialog box contains many options to select different characters or symbols

CERTIFICATION READY?   3.3.2

How do you create a bullet using special characters?

4. Change the Font by clicking the drop-down arrow. Scroll down and select **Wingdings**.

5. Select the bell in the first row, sixth column. Click **OK** to close the *Symbol* dialog box.

6. Click **OK** to close the *Define New Bullet* dialog box.

7. **SAVE** the document as ***B&B Alarm Update*** in the lesson folder on your flash drive.

PAUSE. LEAVE the document open to use in the next exercise.

STEP BY STEP   **Insert a Picture Bullet**

USE the document that is open from the previous exercise.

1. The three bulleted items are still selected. Click the drop-down arrow next to the Bullets ⋮≡ button, and then click **Define New Bullet**.

2. Click the **Picture** button in the *Define New Bullet* dialog box. The Insert Pictures location box opens, as shown in Figure 4-22. Microsoft has provided a new insert picture location screen where you have the option to locate a picture from the Office.com location, Bing, SkyDrive, or in your computer or network.

Figure 4-22

Insert Pictures location

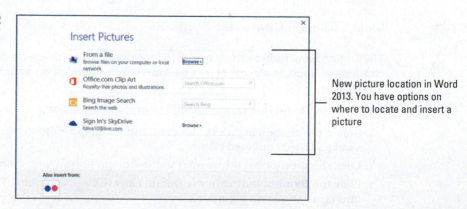

New picture location in Word 2013. You have options on where to locate and insert a picture

3. Type **alarms** in the Office.com Clip Art search box, and then click the magnifier to begin search.

4. Select the **Close-up Hand configuring alarm system** image as shown in Figure 4-23. The image is surrounded by a border. Your search results may look different than those shown in the figure.

Figure 4-23

Office.com Clip Art

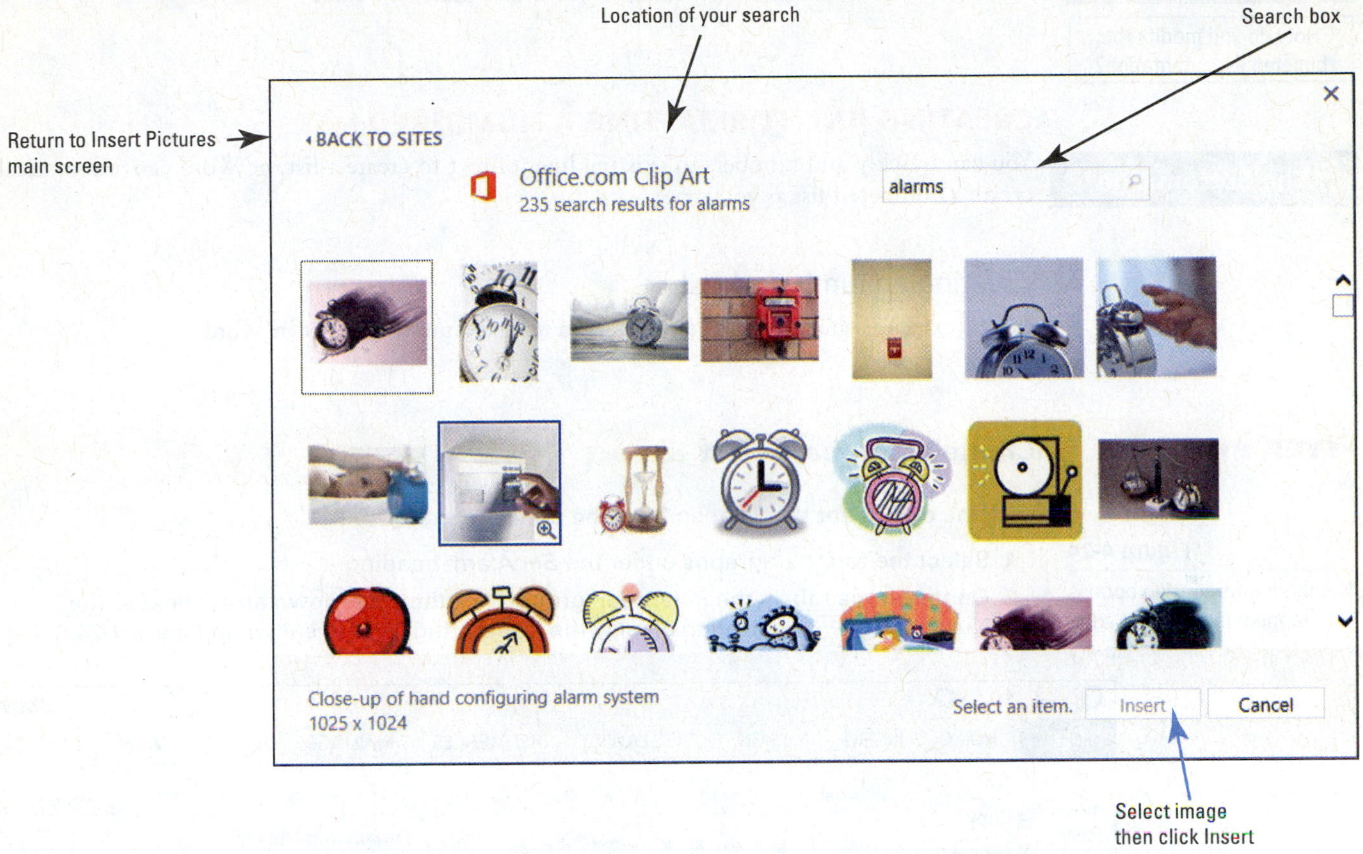

Location of your search

Search box

Return to Insert Pictures main screen

‹ BACK TO SITES

Office.com Clip Art
235 search results for alarms

alarms

Close-up of hand configuring alarm system
1025 x 1024

Select an item. Insert Cancel

Select image
then click Insert

5. Click **Insert** to begin downloading the image to your document.

6. Click **OK** to close the *Define New Bullet* dialog box.

7. After the image is downloaded, it displays on your document in a small font size. Select the first image—notice the other two images are also selected. Increase the font size to **28** pt.

8. **SAVE** the document as ***B&B Alarm Update1*** in the lesson folder on your flash drive.

PAUSE. LEAVE the document open to use in the next exercise.

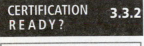

CERTIFICATION READY? **3.3.2**

How do you create a picture bullet?

STEP BY STEP **Change the Alignment in Bullets**

In the previous exercises, you learn to create bullets using the Bullet Library, create a bullet using symbols, and insert pictures as bullets from the web. You also changed the levels of the bullets by promoting or demoting the list levels. In this exercise, you learn to adjust the alignment to any type of bullet.

USE the document that is open from the previous exercise.

1. In the bulleted list, notice the distance between the image and text. Adding a custom bullet allows you to change the alignment.

2. Select the three bullets items.

3. Click the drop-down arrow next to the Bullets button, and then click **Define New Bullet**.

4. Under the Alignment group, click the drop-down arrow and select **Right**. Notice the space between the image and text in the Preview area.

5. Click **OK**.

CERTIFICATION
READY? 3.3.3

How do you modify the
bulleted list indentation?

6. SAVE the document with the same filename in the lesson folder on your flash drive.

PAUSE. LEAVE the document open to use in the next exercise.

CREATING AND FORMATTING A NUMBERED LIST

The Bottom Line

You can quickly add numbers to existing lines of text to create a list, or Word can automatically create a numbered list as you type.

Creating a Numbered List

In this exercise, you learn how to create and format a numbered list in Word.

STEP BY STEP **Create a Numbered List**

USE the document that is open from the previous exercise.

Figure 4-24

Numbering formatting options appear in the Numbering Library

1. Select the four paragraphs under the *Set Alarm* heading.
2. On the Home tab, in the Paragraph group, click the drop-down arrow next to the Numbering button to display the Numbering Library shown in Figure 4-24.

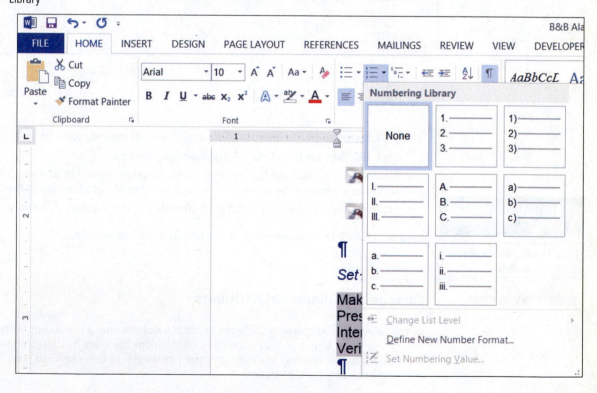

3. Select the option, **1.**, **2.**, **3.** The paragraphs are now listed as an ordered list.
4. Place the insertion point at the end of item number four and press **Enter**. Notice that Word automatically numbers the next line sequentially.
5. In the new numbered line, type **Leave the premises immediately**.
6. Select the four paragraphs under the *Deactivate Alarm* heading.

CERTIFICATION
READY? 3.3.1

How do you create a
numbered list?

7. On the Home tab, in the Paragraph group, click the drop-down arrow next to the Numbering button.
8. Select the option, **a.**, **b.**, **c.**, The four paragraphs are numbered and aligned left.
9. **SAVE** the document as ***B&B Numbered Alarm List*** in the lesson folder on your flash drive.

PAUSE. LEAVE the document open to use in the next exercise.

Modify a Numbered List

USE the document that is open from the previous exercise.

1. Select the numbered list under the *Set Alarm* heading.

2. To change the format of the numbered list, click the drop-down arrow next to the Numbering ⊟▾ button, and then click **Define New Number Format**. The *Define New Number Format* dialog box appears.

3. Click the **Number style** drop-down arrow and select **uppercase roman numerals** (see Figure 4-25). The format for the selected text changed to uppercase roman numerals. The default alignment is left and can also be changed to center or right.

Figure 4-25

Define New Number Format
dialog box

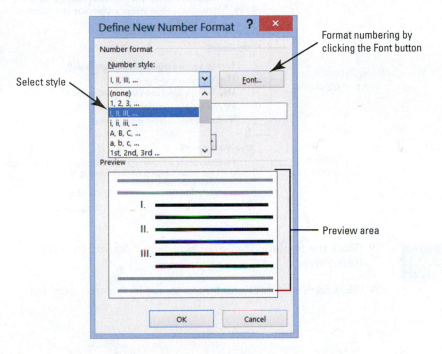

Select style

Format numbering by
clicking the Font button

Preview area

4. Click the **Font** button and select **Arial Black**, size **12** pt. Review the preview area to see how the numbering will appear. Click **OK** to close the *Font* dialog box.

5. Click **OK** to close the *Define New Number Format* dialog box.

Take Note   To change the formatting of list numbers, click any number to select the entire list. If you select the text as well, the formatting of both the text and the numbering change.

6. Select the numbered list under the *Deactivate Alarm* heading.

7. In this next step you renumber an existing list using the lowercase letters. Click the drop-down arrow next to the Numbering button, and then click **Set Numbering Value**. The *Set Numbering Value* dialog box appears as shown in Figure 4-26.

Figure 4-26

Set Numbering Value
dialog box

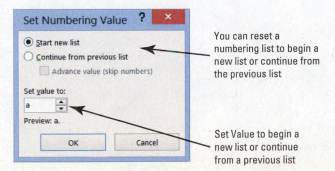

You can reset a
numbering list to begin a
new list or continue from
the previous list

Set Value to begin a
new list or continue
from a previous list

8. The Start new list option button is already selected. In the Set value to section, click the up-arrow to **f**. Click **OK**. Your document should match Figure 4-27.

Figure 4-27

Sample document with different modified numbering list

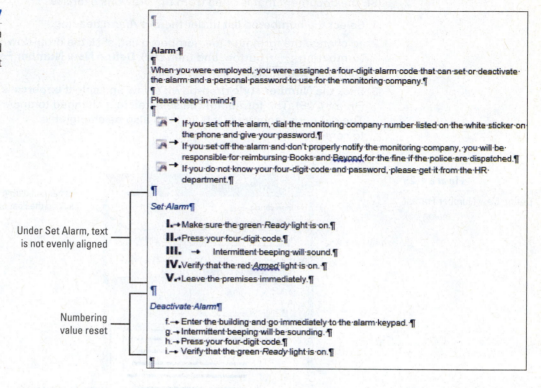

Under Set Alarm, text is not evenly aligned

Numbering value reset

9. **SAVE** the document as *B&B Numbered Alarm List 1* in the lesson folder on your flash drive.

PAUSE. LEAVE the document open to use in the next exercise.

STEP BY STEP   **Change the Alignment of a Numbered List**

USE the document that is open from the previous exercise.

1. Select the numbered list under the *Set Alarm* heading.

2. To change the alignment format of the numbered list, click the drop-down arrow next to the Numbering button, and then click **Define New Number Format**. The *Define New Number Format* dialog box appears.

3. In the Alignment group, click the drop-down arrow and select **Right** to change the alignment of the numbering list.

4. Click **OK**. Notice how nicely the list is aligned (see Figure 4-28).

Figure 4-28

Sample document with modified alignment

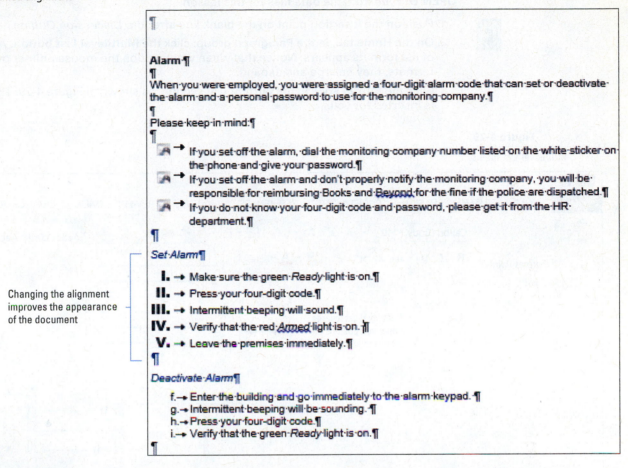

Changing the alignment improves the appearance of the document

¶

Alarm¶
¶
When·you·were·employed,·you·were·assigned·a·four-digit·alarm·code·that·can·set·or·deactivate· the·alarm·and·a·personal·password·to·use·for·the·monitoring·company.¶
¶
Please·keep·in·mind:¶
¶
If·you·set·off·the·alarm,·dial·the·monitoring·company·number·listed·on·the·white·sticker·on· the·phone·and·give·your·password.¶
If·you·set·off·the·alarm·and·don't·properly·notify·the·monitoring·company,·you·will·be· responsible·for·reimbursing·Books·and·Beyond·for·the·fine·if·the·police·are·dispatched.¶
If·you·do·not·know·your·four-digit·code·and·password,·please·get·it·from·the·HR· department.¶
¶

Set·Alarm¶

I. → Make·sure·the·green·*Ready*·light·is·on.¶
II. → Press·your·four-digit·code.¶
III. → Intermittent·beeping·will·sound.¶
IV. → Verify·that·the·red·*Armed*·light·is·on.¶
V. → Leave·the·premises·immediately.¶
¶

Deactivate·Alarm¶

f. → Enter·the·building·and·go·immediately·to·the·alarm·keypad.·¶
g. → Intermittent·beeping·will·be·sounding.·¶
h. → Press·your·four-digit·code.¶
i. → Verify·that·the·green·*Ready*·light·is·on.¶
¶

5. SAVE the document as ***B&B Numbered Alarm List Final*** in the lesson folder on your flash drive, and then **CLOSE** the file.

PAUSE. LEAVE Word open to use in the next exercise.

Take Note The same process used in Backstage for turning automatic bulleting on and off in Word's Auto-Format feature is applied the same way for the Automatic Numbered List. In Lesson 14, you learn about using the Advanced Options in Word.

CREATING AND MODIFYING A MULTILEVEL LIST

The Bottom Line Word provides a multilevel feature that is used for outlines and other documents that require many levels—these levels can be a combination of letters and numbers.

Creating a Multilevel List

Multilevel lists are typically used in documents where subsets of information are needed within the list, such as preparing an agenda, outline, or exam questions. As an example, you can use the multilevel list for outlining your research paper. In this exercise, you learn how to create and format a multilevel list in Word.

Create a Multilevel Outline List

OPEN *Outline* from the data files for this lesson.

1. Position the insertion point on the blank line after the *Discussion Outline* heading.

2. On the Home tab, in the Paragraph group, click the **Multilevel List** button. A menu of list formats appears. Notice that when you position the mouse pointer over the formats, they enlarge and expand.

3. Click the **format style** in the Current List section, as shown in Figure 4-29. The number 1. is inserted for you.

Figure 4-29

Multilevel List menu

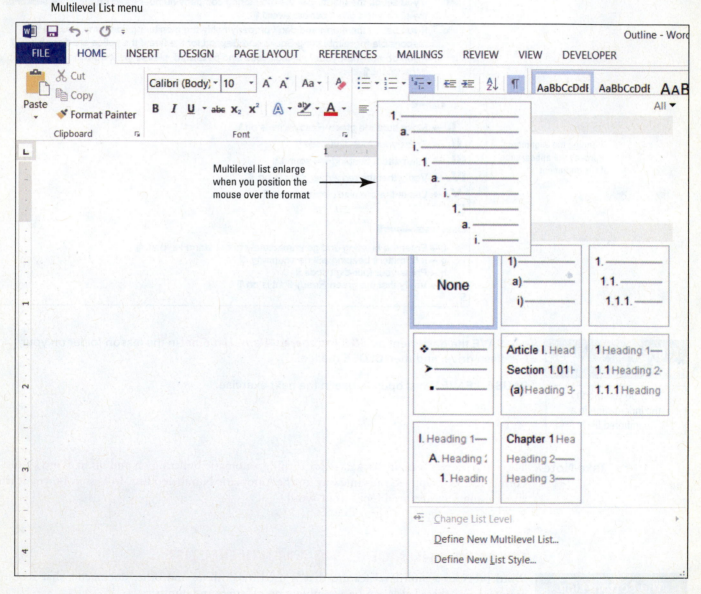

Take Note   Use the *Tab* key or *Shift + Tab* to move to different levels.

4. Type **Experience**, and then press the **Enter** key. When you press Enter, the number 2. is inserted.

5. Type **Communication with Client** and press the **Enter** key.

6. Press the **Tab** key and type **Initial Meeting**. Pressing the Tab key advances to the next level with a lowercase *a*. Press the **Enter** key.

7. Press the **Tab** key and type **Identify Position**. Notice that Word inserts a lowercase roman numeral as the next level. Press the **Enter** key.

8. Press the **Tab** key and type **Qualifications**. Another level is inserted beginning with the number 1. Press the **Enter** key.

9. Type **Compensation Package** and press the **Enter** key.

10. Type **Time Frame** and press the **Enter** key.

11. Press **Shift+Tab** once to move back one level. Type **Progress Reporting** and press the **Enter** key.

12. Press **Shift+Tab** to move back one more level. Type **Methods for Finding Candidates** and press the **Enter** key.

13. Press the **Tab** key. Type **Database** and press the **Enter** key.

14. Type **Contacts** and press the **Enter** key.

15. Type **Networking**. Your document should resemble Figure 4-30.

Figure 4-30

Sample document using multilevel list

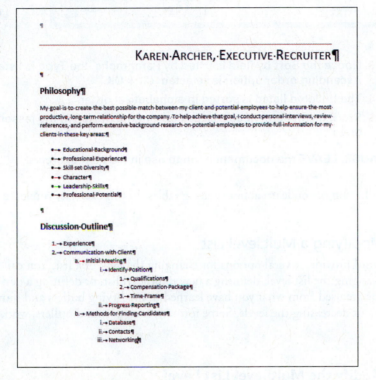

16. **SAVE** the document as *Discussion Outline* in the lesson folder on your flash drive.

PAUSE. LEAVE the document open for use in the next exercise.

Sorting a List's Contents

You can sort a single-level list in much the same way that you sort a column in a table.

STEP BY STEP **Sort a List's Contents**

USE the document that is open from the previous exercise.

1. Select the bulleted list under the *Philosophy* section.

2. On the Home tab, in the Paragraph group, click the **Sort** button. The *Sort Text* dialog box appears as shown in Figure 4-31.

Figure 4-31

Sort Text dialog box

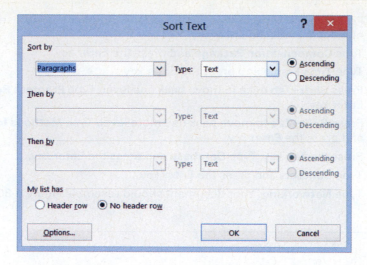

3. Notice the Sort by field is listed by Paragraphs, the Type is listed by Text, and the Ascending order option is selected. Click **OK**.

4. The bulleted listed is sorted in alphabetical order.

5. **SAVE** the document as *Discussion Outline Sorted* in the lesson folder on your flash drive.

PAUSE. LEAVE the document open to use in the next exercise.

Cross Ref   In Lesson 6, you learn about creating tables. In this exercise, you learn to sort a list.

Modifying a Multilevel List

Word provides several options for changing the look of a list. You can change a multilevel list by changing the list level, defining a new multilevel list, or defining a new list style. The same methods are used from what you have learned in modifying bullets and numbering lists when increasing or decreasing the levels. Some formats, such as round bullets, work well for most documents.

STEP BY STEP   **Modify the Multilevel List Level**

USE the document that is open from the previous exercise.

1. Select the bulleted list.

2. On the Home tab, in the Paragraph group, click the **drop-down arrow** on the Bullets button. Previously in this lesson, you learned to change bullets—the same process is used here.

3. Click the **square bullet format** in the Bullet Library.

4. Select the multilevel list you typed previously.

5. On the Home tab, in the Paragraph group, click the **drop-down arrow** on the Multilevel List button. A menu appears.

6. Under List Library, click the third column in the top row. Notice the difference in the numbering and alignment level.

7. **SAVE** the document as *Discussion Outline Modified* in the lesson folder on your flash drive, and then **CLOSE** the file.

PAUSE. LEAVE Word open for the next exercise.

SOFTWARE ORIENTATION

Tab Dialog Box

Tabs in Word insert blank spaces before or within text and paragraphs. You use the Tabs dialog box, shown in Figure 4-32, to set and clear tabs in Word. Use this figure as a reference throughout the remainder of this lesson as well as the rest of the book.

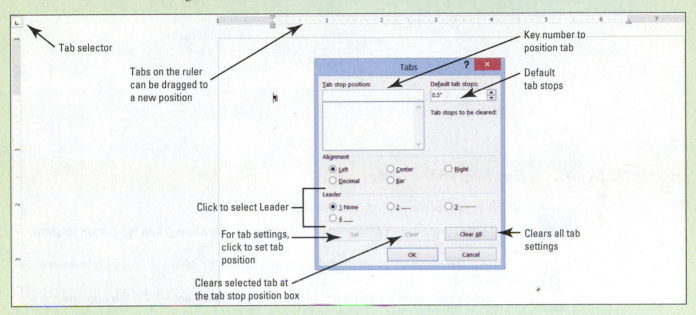

Figure 4-32

Tabs selector and dialog box

SETTING AND MODIFYING TABS

The Bottom Line

Tabs are used to align text or numbers nicely in your document. The ruler can be used to set tabs or for a more exact setting, use the Tabs dialog box. As you apply custom tabs to selected text, tabs are applied to paragraphs. When the Enter key is pressed, the tab settings are carried forward into the next paragraph.

Take Note   To view tabs as they are being set, display nonprinting characters, as discussed in Lesson 1.

Setting Tabs on the Ruler

By default, left-aligned tab stops are set every half-inch on the ruler. To set a tab at a different position on the ruler, you can click the tab selector at the left end of the ruler and a ScreenTip will appear showing the type of tabs at the tab selector. Tabs are part of a paragraph formatting—the selected text is affected by the tab setting or when modified. In this exercise, you learn to set tabs on Word's ruler.

Table 4-5 lists the types of tabs available in Word and their descriptions. To view tabs on the ruler, place your insertion point in the paragraph.

After tabs are set, press the *Tab* key; the insertion point moves to the position set. To move a tab stop to a different position on the ruler, click and drag the tab left or right to a new position.

Table 4-5

Tab stops on the ruler

Name	Button	Description
Left tab	L	Left-aligns text at the tab place indicated on the horizontal ruler
Center tab	⊥	Centers text at the place indicated on the horizontal ruler
Right tab	⌐	Right-aligns text at the place indicated on the horizontal ruler
Decimal tab	⊥⋅	Aligns numbers around a decimal point at the place indicated on the horizontal ruler
Bar tab	⏐	Inserts a vertical bar line at the place indicated on the horizontal ruler

---

STEP BY STEP   **Set Tabs on the Ruler**

OPEN *Per Diem* from the data files for this lesson.

1. On the Home tab in the Paragraph group, click the **Show/Hide (¶)** button to show nonprinting characters.

2. Place the insertion point on the blank line below the *Meals & Incidentals Breakdown* heading.

3. Click the tab selector at the left of the ruler until the Center ⊥ tab appears. The horizontal ruler is shown in Figure 4-33, displaying the different types of tabs.

Figure 4-33

The horizontal ruler with tab sets

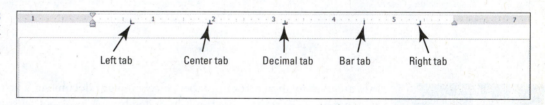

> Left tab   Center tab   Decimal tab   Bar tab   Right tab

⚠ **Troubleshooting**   If the horizontal ruler is not visible, click the *View* tab, and then add a check mark by Ruler.

4. Click the ruler at the **2.5-inch** mark to set a Center ⊥ tab. The Center tab appears as an inverted *T*.

5. Click the ruler at the **4-inch** mark to set a Center tab. The ruler shows two tab settings.

6. Press **Tab** and type **Chicago**.

7. Press **Tab** and type **New York**.

8. Select the list of words starting with *Breakfast* and ending with *Totals*. When setting tabs, tabs are part of the paragraph formatting—the selected text will be affected by the tab settings after the Tab key is pressed.

9. Click the tab selector until the **Right** ⌐ tab appears—displays as an inverted *L*.

10. Click the ruler at the **1-inch** mark to set a Right tab.

11. Deselect the list, and place the insertion point in front of each word in the list, and then press **Tab** to align it at the Right tab. When setting a Right tab, press the **Tab** key with existing text or press the **Tab** key, and then type the new text. The text characters are aligned at the right and move to the left. Your document should look similar to the one shown in Figure 4-34.

Figure 4-34

Right tab formatting

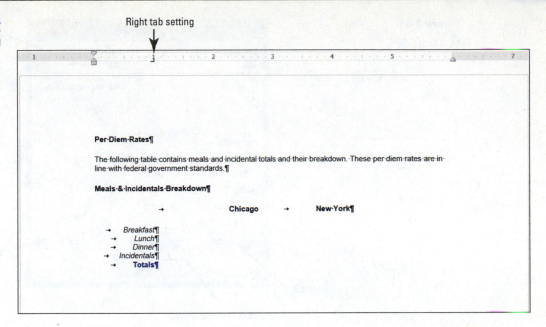

12. **SAVE** the document as *Per Diem First Draft* in the lesson folder on your flash drive.

PAUSE. LEAVE the document open to use in the next exercise.

Using the Tabs Dialog Box

The Tabs dialog box is useful for setting tabs at precise locations on the ruler, clearing all tabs, and setting tab leaders. Tab **leaders** are symbols such as dotted, dashed, or solid lines that fill the space before a tab (see Figure 4-35). In this exercise, you practice setting tabs and leaders using the Tabs dialog box.

STEP BY STEP   **Use the Tabs Dialog Box**

USE the document that is open from the previous exercise.

1. Select the list of words starting with *Breakfast* and continuing to the end of the document.

2. On the Home tab, in the Paragraph group, click the dialog box launcher to launch the *Paragraph* dialog box.

3. Click the **Tabs** button on the bottom left of the Paragraph dialog box to display the *Tabs* dialog box. In the *Tabs* dialog box, you should see the 1" Right tab setting that you set in the previous exercise.

4. In the Tab stop position box, type **2.6**. In the Alignment section, select **Decimal**. In the Leader section, select **2**, and then click **Set**. After setting individuals tabs, you must click **Set** to position the tab setting.

5. In the Tab stop position box, type **4.1**. In the Alignment section, select **Decimal**. In the Leader section, select **2**, and then click **Set**. Setting a leader provides a guide to the next tab setting. Refer to Figure 4-35 and compare with your screen.

Figure 4-35

Tabs dialog box

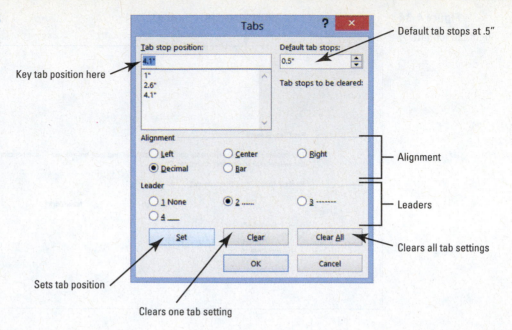

Key tab position here

Default tab stops at .5"

Sets tab position

Clears one tab setting

Alignment

Leaders

Clears all tab settings

6. **OK** to close the *Tabs* dialog box. Notice that nothing happens yet.

7. Place the insertion point after the word *Breakfast* and press **Tab**.

8. Type **$10.98** and press **Tab**.

9. Type **$12.50**. Repeat this process for each line, typing the numbers shown in Figure 4-36. Notice how the decimals align properly.

Figure 4-36

Tabs and tab leaders formatting

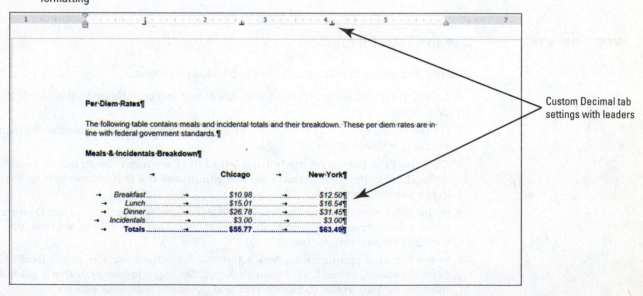

Custom Decimal tab settings with leaders

10. **SAVE** the document with the same filename in the lesson folder on your flash drive.

PAUSE. LEAVE the document open to use in the next exercise.

Cross Ref

Another Way
To open the Tabs dialog box, double-click any tab stop on the ruler. The Paragraph dialog box can also be accessed in the Page Layout tab. Also, you can right-click on selected text.

In Lesson 1, you created the *Welcome Memo* and aligned text manually by pressing *Tab* twice. Open the document from your Lesson 2 folder, delete the tabs, and set a left tab at the one-inch marker using the ruler or dialog box.

Moving Tabs

Tabs can be repositioned using your mouse pointer by dragging to a new position on the ruler or opening the Tabs dialog box.

STEP BY STEP **Move Tabs**

USE the document that is open from the previous exercise.

1. Select the block of text beginning with *Breakfast...* and ending with *...$63.49.* Include the non-printing character (¶) in your selection.

2. Position the mouse pointer at **4.1"** on the ruler until you see the Decimal Tab ScreenTip.

3. Press and hold the left mouse button and drag on the ruler to **5"**. Release the left mouse button. Notice the Decimal Tab setting for the five lines is positioned at 5" on the ruler.

4. With the text still selected, position the mouse pointer at **2.6"** on the ruler until you see the Decimal Tab ScreenTip.

5. Press and hold the left mouse button and drag on the ruler to **3"**. Release the left mouse button. Notice the Decimal Tab setting for the five lines is positioned at 3" on the ruler.

6. Select **Chicago**. Drag the center tab setting and position it at **3"** on the ruler. Double-click the center tab on the ruler to open the *Tabs* dialog box—check the positioning of the tab. *Chicago* should align nicely above the amounts.

7. Select **New York**. Drag the center tab setting and position it at **5"** on the ruler. Double-click the center tab on the ruler to open the *Tabs* dialog box—check the positioning of the tab. *New York* should align nicely above the amounts.

8. **SAVE** the document as ***Per Diem Final*** in the lesson folder on your flash drive.

PAUSE. LEAVE the document open to use in the next exercise.

Clearing Tabs

Tabs can be removed by dragging them off the ruler, or you can use the Tabs dialog box to clear one or all tabs. To remove a tab stop from the ruler, click and drag it off the ruler. When you release the mouse button, the tab stop disappears. Or, open the Tabs dialog box, where you can choose to clear one tab or all tabs. In this exercise, you practice clearing tabs from your document.

STEP BY STEP **Clear Tabs**

USE the document that is open from the previous exercise.

1. Place the insertion point on the last line (**Totals**).

2. Move your mouse pointer to the tab stop at **5"** on the ruler. Wait for the ScreenTip to appear.

3. Press and hold the mouse button and drag it off the ruler. Release the mouse button to remove the tab stop. The New York amount moves to the left.

4. On the Home tab, in the Paragraph group, click the dialog box launcher to launch the *Paragraph* dialog box.

5. Click the **Tabs** button on the bottom left of the dialog box to display the *Tabs* dialog box.

6. In the Tab stop position list, click **3"**, and then click **Clear** to clear that tab.

7. Click the **Clear All** button to clear all tabs on that line.

8. Click **OK** to close the *Tabs* dialog box.

9. Select all the text on the *Totals* line and press the **Delete** button to delete it.

10. **SAVE** the document with the same filename, and then **CLOSE** the file.

PAUSE. **LEAVE** Word open for the next exercise.

Setting Tab Stops

Tab stops can be reset from the default of 0.5 inch. Each time you press the tab key, the tab moves half an inch on the ruler. Thus, by pressing the tab key twice, for example, the insertion point moves to one inch on the ruler. In this exercise, you practice setting default tab stops.

STEP BY STEP	Set Tab Stops

Another Way
Press *Ctrl+N* to use the shortcut key to open a new, blank document.

1. **OPEN** a new blank document.

2. Press the **Tab** key once.

3. Press the **Tab** key two more times; the insertion point is now positioned at 1½ inches on the ruler.

4. Press the **Tab** key three times; the insertion point moves to the 3-inch mark on the ruler. Each time you press the Tab key, it advances half an inch on the ruler. By default, the tab stops are set at half an inch.

5. Press **Enter.**

6. On the Home tab, in the Paragraph group, click the dialog box launcher.

7. In the Paragraph dialog box, click the **Tabs** button to open the Tabs dialog box.

8. Click the up arrow below Default Tab Stops until it stops at **1** inch. Click **OK**.

9. Press the **Tab** key three times and notice the insertion point on the ruler now stops at every 1 inch.

STOP. CLOSE Word without saving the changes.

Take Note   Many of the predesigned document layout options in Word 2013 make it possible to create documents, such as an index or table of contents, without setting any tabs manually.

SKILL SUMMARY

In This Lesson, You Learned To:	Exam Objective	Objective Number
Format Paragraphs	Set indentation.	2.2.7
Set Line Spacing in Text and Between Paragraphs	Set line spacing. Modify line spacing. Set paragraph spacing.	2.2.5 3.3.4 2.2.4
Create and Format a Bulleted List	Add numbering or bullets. Create custom bullets. Modify list indentation. Increase and decrease list levels.	3.3.1 3.3.2 3.3.3 3.3.5
Create and Format a Numbered List	Add numbering or bullets. Modify numbering.	3.3.1 3.3.6
Create and Modify a Multilevel List		
Set and Modify Tabs		

Knowledge Assessment

Multiple Choice

Select the best response for the following statements.

1. Which of the following is NOT a type of indent?
   a. Hanging
   b. Negative
   c. Positive
   d. First-line

2. Which word(s) refers to how text is positioned between the top and bottom margins of the page?
   a. Horizontal alignment
   b. Vertical alignment
   c. Justified
   d. Line spacing

3. Which line spacing command sets the spacing at a fixed amount that Word does not adjust?
   a. Exactly
   b. Double
   c. Multiple
   d. At least

4. Where is the View Ruler button located?
   a. In the Tabs dialog box
   b. At the top of the vertical scroll bar
   c. In the Paragraph group
   d. It does not exist

5. What does dragging a tab off the ruler do?
   a. Moves it to another position
   b. Turns it into a left-aligned tab
   c. Clears it
   d. Hides it from view

6. Bullets can be defined by adding a:
   a. symbol.
   b. box.
   c. picture.
   d. all of the above.

7. Which property of borders can be changed in the Borders tab of the Borders and Shading dialog box?
   a. Color
   b. Width
   c. Style
   d. All of the above

8. The inverted *L* sets which tab on the ruler?
   a. Left
   b. Right
   c. Center
   d. Decimal

9. Which tab setting do you use to align a list of currency values?
   a. Decimal
   b. Center
   c. Right
   d. Decimal with leaders

10. You can define a New Number format by selecting which of the following styles?
    a. I, II, III
    b. 1), 2), 3)
    c. 1., 2., 3.
    d. All of the above

True/False

Circle T if the statement is true or F if the statement is false.

T F 1. Pressing the Enter key indents the first line of a paragraph.

T F 2. An indent is the space between a paragraph and the document's left and/or right margin.

T F 3. You can use the ruler to set tabs.

T F 4. A bar tab inserts a vertical bar line at the place indicated on the vertical ruler.

T F 5. Tab leaders are dotted, dashed, or solid lines that fill the space before a tab.

T F 6. The Clear Formatting command clears only the fonts applied to the selected text.

T F 7. Horizontal alignment refers to the position of text with regard to the top and bottom margins of a document.

T F 8. Centered vertical alignment aligns text between the top and bottom margin.

T F 9. Indents can be changed using the markers on the ruler.

T F 10. The shortcut to double-space a paragraph is Ctrl+2.

Competency Assessment

Project 4-1: Creating an Expense Report for Blue Yonder Airlines

You are employed in the financial department at Blue Yonder Airlines and have been asked to create a document to show expenses for fiscal years 2009–2012.

GET READY. LAUNCH Word if it is not already running.

1. **OPEN** a blank document.
2. **SAVE** the document as *4-1 Expense Report* in the lesson folder on your flash drive.
3. Type **BLUE YONDER AIRLINES**, and press **Enter**.
4. Type **Expense Report**, and press **Enter**.
5. Set a center tab using the ruler at the **2"**, **3"**, **4"**, and **5"** marks. Then at the left margin, press the **Tab** key.
6. Type the following text: at the 2", type **2009**, and press **Tab**; at the 3", type **2010**, and press **Tab**; at the 4", type **2011**, and press **Tab**; and at 5", type **2012**, and press **Enter**.
7. Remove the center tab settings by dragging them off the ruler.
8. Select the paragraph mark, and then change the tab selector to **Decimal**. Set decimal tabs at the **2"**, **3"**, **4"**, and **5"** marks.
9. Type the following text and values:

Corporate Contracts, press **Tab**	**$316.00** press **Tab**	**$396.00** press **Tab**	**$368.00** press **Tab**	**$393.00** press **Enter**
Sky Diving, press **Tab**	**$17.00** press **Tab**	**$17.00** press **Tab**	**$16.00** press **Tab**	**$65.00** press **Enter**
Charter Flights, press **Tab**	**$22.00** press **Tab**	**$24.00** press **Tab**	**$24.00** press **Tab**	**$27.00** press **Enter**
Flight School, press **Tab**	**$63.00** press **Tab**	**$61.00** press **Tab**	**$59.00** press **Tab**	**$55.00**

10. Center the title, *BLUE YONDER AIRLINES*. Change the font size for the title to **26** pt., **bold**, and apply the font color **Blue-Gray**, **Text 2, Darker 50%**.

11. Center the subtitle, *Expense Report*. Change the font size for the subtitle to **18** pt., **bold**, and apply the font color **Black**, **Text 1**.

12. Select the years beginning with *2009 . . .2012*, **bold**, and **underline only words**.

13. Use the multi-selection to select *Corporate Contracts, Sky Diving, Charter Flights,* and *Flight School*, and **bold**.

14. Select the **Page Setup** dialog box launcher from the Page Layout tab, and then click the **Layout** tab. In the Page group, change the vertical alignment to **Center**.

15. **SAVE** the document with the same filename in the lesson folder and **CLOSE** the file.

LEAVE Word open for the next project.

Project 4-2: General Performance Expectation Guidelines

In your job at Books and Beyond, you continue to work on documents that will be part of the employee handbook.

GET READY. LAUNCH Word if it is not already running.

1. **OPEN** *Guidelines* from the data files for this lesson.

2. **SAVE** the document as *4-2 Handbook Guidelines* in the lesson folder on your flash drive.

3. In the third paragraph, select the two lines that begin *Verbal discussion . . .* and *Written warning . . . .*

4. On the Home tab, in the Paragraph group, click the drop-down arrow next to the Bullets button and select the solid circle.

5. Place the insertion point after the second item in the bulleted list and press **Enter**.

6. Type **Termination** as the third bulleted item.

7. Select the five double-spaced paragraphs beginning with *abuse, misuse . . .* and ending with *falsification, misinterpretation . . . .*

8. Click the drop-down arrow next to the Bullets button and click **Define New Bullet**.

9. Click the **Symbol** button, and then click the drop-down arrow in the Font box and select **Wingdings**.

10. Scroll to the top of the Wingdings menu and select the solid diamond (character code 116).

11. Click **OK** to close the *Symbol* dialog box, and then click **OK** to close the *Define New Bullet* dialog box.

12. Select the remaining paragraphs beginning with *insubordination, willful disregard . . .* and ending with *engaging in conduct . . . .*

13. Click the drop-down arrow next to the Bullets button and click **Define New Bullet**.

14. Click the **Picture** button, and then type **handbook** in the Search box for Office.com.

15. Select the first picture and then click **Insert**; click **OK** to close the *Define New Bullet* dialog box.

16. Select the image and change the font size to **20** pt.

17. Select the first, second, third, and last paragraph in the document. Avoid selecting the bulleted lists.

18. On the Home tab, in the Paragraph group, click the **Justify** button.

19. With the paragraphs still selected, apply the first-line indent by launching the *Paragraph* dialog box.

20. Under Special, select the drop-down arrow and select **First Line**.

21. Click **OK** to close the *Paragraph* dialog box.

22. **SAVE** the document with the same filename in the lesson folder and **CLOSE** the file.

LEAVE Word open for the next project.

Proficiency Assessment

Project 4-3: Blue Yonder Expense Report

You are now ready to format the expense report that you created in Project 4-1.

GET READY. LAUNCH Word if it is not already running.

1. **OPEN** *4-1 Expense Report* from the data files for this lesson.
2. **SAVE** the document as *4-3 Expense Report Updated* in the lesson folder on your flash drive.
3. Select the heading **Expense Report**, and increase the Spacing After to **24** pt.
4. Select the four lines of text beginning with *Corporate Contracts* and ending with *$55.00,* and sort text in ascending order.
5. With the text still selected, apply the **Blue-Gray, Text 2, Lighter 80%** shading.
6. **SAVE** the document with the same filename in the lesson folder and **CLOSE** the file.

LEAVE Word open for the next project.

Project 4-4: Phone List

Open a partially completed list of committee members. Your task is to type the phone numbers by the committee members' names, sort in ascending order, format using tabs, and save as a Word document.

GET READY. LAUNCH Word if it is not already running.

1. **OPEN** *Phone List* from the data files for this lesson.
2. **SAVE** the document as *4-4 Committee Phone List* in the lesson folder on your flash drive.
3. Select the whole document and create a **Right** tab setting at **6.5"** with **dot leaders**, and then type the phone number beside each name. The phone numbers should align evenly between the left and right margins. Maintain a balanced look for your document.
4. Type the following phone numbers next to each committee member:

Ted Bremer	555-9999
Hao Chen	555-8888
Alice Ciccu	555-7777
Josie Camacho	555-1111
Gioff Grisso	555-4444
Jose Lugo	555-3333
Naomi Solis	555-5555

5. Change the spacing after to **12** pt, font to **Times New Roman**, and font size to **12** pt to the whole document.
6. Sort on the first column by text.
7. **SAVE** the document with the same filename in the lesson folder and **CLOSE** the file.

LEAVE Word open for the next project.

Project 4-5: Developer Job Description

You are a content specialist at a software development company. Your supervisor asks you to format the job description for the developer position.

GET READY. LAUNCH Word if it is not already running.

1. **OPEN** *Developer* from the data files for this lesson.

2. **SAVE** the document as *4-5 Developer Description* in the lesson folder on your flash drive.

3. Use the skills you learned in this lesson—such as alignment, line spacing, shading, borders, tabs, and bulleted lists—to format the document as shown in Figure 4-37. Be sure to follow these guidelines:

   a. Display the **Show/Hide**.

   b. Delete all of the paragraph marks (¶) in the document where a blank line appears.

   c. For the title, apply the shading: **Orange, Accent 6, Lighter 40%** and set the paragraph Spacing After to **24** pts.

   d. Select the headings: **Position Title**, **Position Objective**, and **Reports To** and apply the shading **Orange, Accent 6, Lighter 80%**.

   e. Select the headings, **Principle Accountabilities and Essential Duties of the Job** and **Qualifications** and apply a paragraph border with the **Shadow setting**; Width: **2¼"**; Color: **Orange, Accent 6, Darker 50%**.

   f. Set the paragraph Spacing After to **12** pts. after the paragraph headings: *Position Title* and *Position Objective*.

   g. For the *Reports To* heading, set the paragraph Spacing After to **24** pts. after *Director of Development*.

Figure 4-37

Developer job description

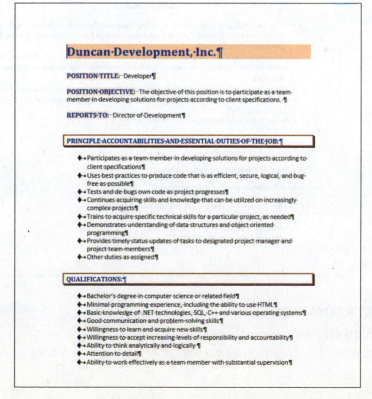

h. Under the headings, *Principle Accountabilities and Essential Duties of the Job* and *Qualifications*, apply the solid diamond bullets to the paragraphs.

i. At the beginning of the first bulleted item under *Principle Accountabilities and Essential Duties of the Job* and *Qualifications,* set the paragraph Spacing Before to **12** pts.

j. After the last bulleted item under *Principle Accountabilities and Essential Duties of the Job*, set the Spacing After to **18** pts.

4. SAVE the document with the same filename in the lesson folder and **CLOSE** the file.

LEAVE Word open for the next project.

Project 4-6: Rabbit Show

You are a volunteer at the annual Falls Village Fair, and you have been assigned to work on a document about one of the exhibits. The person who created the document was not as familiar with line spacing, tabs, and lists as you are, so you need to format the document as shown in Figure 4-38.

Figure 4-38

Rabbit Show

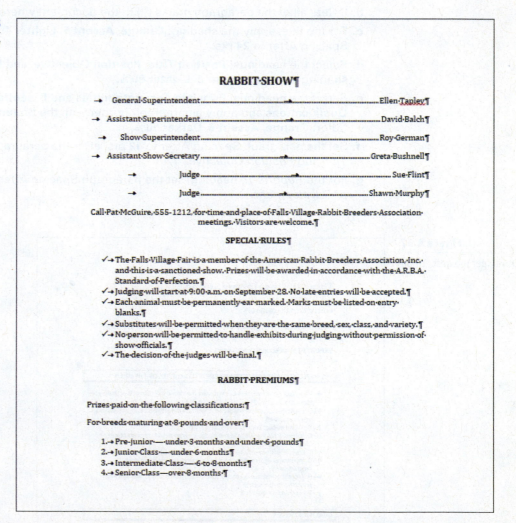

GET READY. LAUNCH Word if it is not already running.

1. **OPEN** *Rabbit* from the data files for this lesson.

2. **SAVE** the document as *4-6 Rabbit Show* in the lesson folder on your flash drive.

3. Make any adjustments necessary to format the tabs, line spacing, and lists as shown in Figure 4-38, following these guidelines:

   a. On the title, remove the first-line indent and make sure the alignment is set to center.

   b. Select the first six lines under the heading, remove the first-line indent, and then remove all existing tab settings and reset the tab settings to a right tab at **2"** and **6"** with leaders.

   c. Remove extra paragraph marks before and after *Call Pat . . .* and center.

   d. Apply a bullet using a check mark under the heading *Special Rules*.

   e. Remove the paragraph mark before the heading *RABBIT PREMIUMS*. Change the paragraph spacing by setting the Spacing Before/After to **18** pts.

   f. Select the items under *RABBIT PREMIUMS* and clear formatting. Beginning with *Pre-Junior* and ending with *Senior Class . . .* apply the numbering list **1., 2., 3., 4.**.

4. **SAVE** the document with the same filename in the lesson folder and **CLOSE** the file.

CLOSE Word.

Circling Back 1

The National Association of Professional Consultants is a professional organization that serves a varied membership of consultants. Each year, the association has a three-day professional development conference. The association is now planning the upcoming conference. As the association's membership manager, your job includes a wide variety of tasks related to organizing and communicating information about membership. In addition, you are working with the conference planning committee to help secure speakers for the conference and market the conference to members.

Project 1: Formatting a Letter

GET READY. LAUNCH Word if it is not already running.

1. **OPEN** the *Conference Speaker* letter from the Circling Back data files folder.
2. Customize the margins to **1"** all around.
3. **SAVE** the document as *Conference Speaker Letter* in the lesson folder on your flash drive.
4. Replace the fields in the document by typing the following information:

   [Your Name]: **Susan Pasha**

   [Street Address]: **5678 Circle Street**

   [City, ST ZIP Code]: **Kansas City, MO 64163**

   [Recipient Name]: **Daniel Slade**

   [Title]: **President, Strategies and Operations**

   [Company Name]: **Montgomery, Slade and Parker**

   [Street Address]: **3333 Lakeside Way**

   [City, ST ZIP Code]: **Chicago, IL 60611**

   [Recipient Name]: **Mr. Slade**
5. Change the date of the letter to **June 15, 20XX**.
6. Select the **Susan Pasha** heading and change the font size to **28** pt, and then change the font color to **Red, Accent 2, Darker 50%**.
7. Select the next line and right-align the address and change the font size to **10** pt.
8. In the first sentence of the body of the letter, select **travel agents'** and type **consultants'**.
9. In the second sentence, select **Alpine Ski House in Breckenridge, Colorado** and type **Lakeview Towers in South Lake Tahoe, California**.
10. Select the text you just typed and **bold**.
11. Change the date of the evening to **September 16** and **bold**.
12. In the last sentence of the letter, select **convention** and type **conference**.
13. Type **Susan Pasha** in the signature line, and then type her title, **President**, press **Shift+Enter** and type **National Association of Professional Consultants**.
14. Display the documents to view as **One Page**.
15. **SAVE** the document in the lesson folder on your flash drive, and then **CLOSE** the file.

PAUSE. LEAVE Word open for the next project.

Project 2: Attachment

Create a document that will be sent to the staff and volunteers who are assisting with the National Association of Professional Consultants Conference. Update them on the upcoming events fees.

GET READY. LAUNCH Word if it is not already running.

1. **OPEN** a blank document.
2. **SAVE** the document as *Conference Update* in the lesson folder on your flash drive.
3. Type **Update on Fees**, and press **Enter**.

4. Set **center** tabs on the second line at **3.88**" and **4.88**".

5. Type the following titles on the second line:

    Press **Tab**, **Early Bird**, and press **Tab**.

    Regular, and press **Enter**.

6. Set two tab settings on the third line with a right tab and with dot leaders at **4**" and **5**". Remove the previously set tabs.

7. Type the following:

    Conference Registration, and press **Tab**.

    $500, and press **Tab**.

    $600, and press **Enter**.

    Hotel Accommodations (per night), and press **Tab**.

    $195, and press **Tab**.

    $250, and press **Enter**.

    Exhibitor's Fee, and press **Tab**.

    $250, and press **Tab**.

    $350, and press **Enter**.

8. Adjust the tab stops and move them as follows:

    Move the *Center* tab for the headings from *3.88*" to **4.88**" and *4.88*" to **6.38**".

    Move the *Right* tab settings from *4*" to **5**" and *5*" to **6.5**".

9. Remove the tab settings in the paragraph below *Exhibitor's Fee*.

10. Select the title and apply a **Heading 1** style and **center**.

11. Apply a paragraph border with a **3D** setting, **Blue-Gray, Text 2, Darker 50%**, with a width of **3 pt**.

12. **SAVE** the document in the lesson folder in your flash drive, and then **CLOSE** the file.

PAUSE. LEAVE Word open for the next project.

Project 3: Finding and Replacing Text

You will work on a document and remove all formatting from the whole document, and use the Find and Replace commands. You will apply styles to specific text and apply the paragraph spacing after to the heading.

GET READY. LAUNCH Word if it is not already running.

1. **OPEN** the *Group Info* document from the lesson folder.

2. **SAVE** the document as *Group Update* in the lesson folder on your flash drive.

3. Remove all formatting in the document.

4. Select **Lakeville.NET User's Group** and paste the phrase into both the *Find what* and *Replace with* boxes of the *Find and Replace* dialog box.

5. In the *Replace with* box, replace the formatting with the following changes.

6. Select the **Format** button, select **Font**, select **Bold**, size **14**, change the font color to **Dark Blue, Text 2, Darker 50%**, and then select **All caps**. Click **OK** and then click **Replace All**. Three occurrences are replaced.

7. Apply the **Heading 2** style to *FAQ*. Change the font size to **22 pt**, and then **Bold**.

8. Apply the **Intense Reference** style to *How do I join your group?*, *When is the next meeting?*, *How do I sponsor a meeting?*, *How do I receive the newsletter?*, and *Locations and Directions*.

9. Set the spacing after on the first line heading to **6** point. **Center** the heading. Change the font size to the text *About* to match the remaining heading.

10. Apply a first line indent to the first paragraph.

11. **SAVE** the document with the updated changes and close the file.

PAUSE. CLOSE Word.

LESSON SKILL MATRIX

Skill	Exam Objective	Objective Number
Setting Page Layout	Modify page setup.	1.3.1
Working with Breaks	Force page breaks.	2.3.5
	Insert breaks to create sections.	2.3.2
Controlling Pagination	Prevent paragraph orphans.	2.3.1
Setting Up Columns	Create multiple columns within sections.	2.3.3
	Add titles to sections.	2.3.4
Inserting a Blank Page into a Document		

KEY TERMS

- columns
- hyphenation
- landscape orientation
- line break
- margins
- nonbreaking spaces
- orphan
- page break
- portrait orientation
- section break
- widow

© Yuri_Arcurs/iStockphoto

Health Resources is a Fortune 500 company looking to relocate its corporate headquarters. As a strategic associate for USA Health Resources, you are involved in the logistics for its relocation project. In particular, you are responsible for creating a proposal and exploring the different options that Word has. In this lesson, you learn to work with page layout, control paragraph behavior, work with section and page breaks, reference lines quickly, create and format columns, and insert a blank page.

© Yuri_Arcurs/iStockphoto

SOFTWARE ORIENTATION

The Page Layout Tab

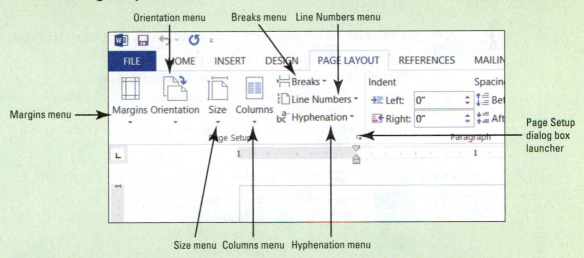

Figure 5-1

Page Layout

The Page Layout tab contains groups of commands that produce a formatted document's layout for the entire document or sections of the document. Commands in the Page Setup group (see figure 5-1) allow you to set margins, change the document's orientation, and adjust the paper size for the entire document or sections in the document. Columns allow you to split your document into two or more columns. Inserting section breaks into the document enables you to change the page setup for an existing section in the document without affecting the other pages in the document. The Show Line Numbers commands allow you to reference specific lines in your document. The Hyphenation command provides options to hyphenate words in a document automatically or manually and the non-breaking space wraps text to the next line to avoid awkward breaks at the right margin.

In the Paragraph group, Word contains features that control how a paragraph breaks within the document and pages. You control the pagination in the document by preventing widow and orphan lines of text to break in the document, or keeping text together, keeping lines together, and determining where page breaks will occur in the document.

You can also manage the text flow in the document by creating multiple columns in a document, customizing the column settings, and inserting column breaks in the Page Setup group.

Although most of the commands you will use to control the layout of your document are found on the Page Layout tab, there are a few other commands you might find helpful on the Insert tab in the Pages group.

SETTING PAGE LAYOUT

The Bottom Line

The layout of a page helps communicate your message. Although the content of your document is obviously important, having appropriate margins, page orientation, and paper size all contribute to the document's readability and appearance.

Setting Margins

Margins are the white space that borders the top, bottom, and sides of a document. You can change margins from Word's default size of one inch using commands in the Page Set on group in the Page Layout tab. You can choose preset options from a gallery or set Comize Margins in the Page Setup dialog box. In the Page Setup group, click the *Margins* menu, and a set of predefined margin settings are available for selection. Click the setting of your choice and the whole document will reflect the changes. Click the *Custom Margins* command to display the Page Setup dialog box, where you can specify custom margin sizes. In this exercise, you customize a document's margins.

STEP BY STEP   **Set Margins**

GET READY. Before you begin these steps, be sure to launch Microsoft Word.

1. **OPEN** the *Proposal* file for this lesson.
2. Delete the extra blank lines above *USA Health Resources*.
3. On the Page Layout tab, in the Page Setup group, click the **drop-down arrow** to display the Margins menu.
4. Choose **Narrow**, as shown in Figure 5-2. The margins are set to 0.5″ from top, bottom, left, and right.

Figure 5-2

Margins menu

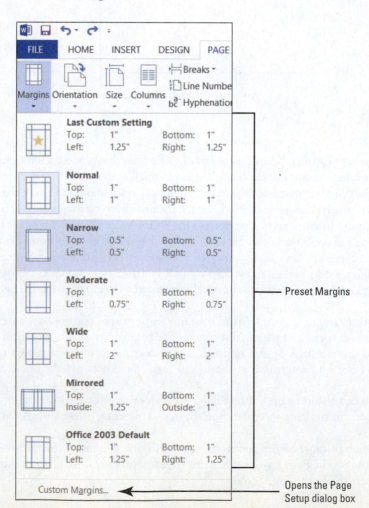

Preset Margins

Opens the Page
Setup dialog box

5. In the Page Setup group, click the **drop-down arrow** to display the Margins menu.

6. Click **Custom Margins** to open the *Page Setup* dialog box shown in Figure 5-3.

Figure 5-3

Page Setup dialog box

Margins can be customized in the Page Setup dialog box

The orientation of a document. Portrait is the default.

Preview area

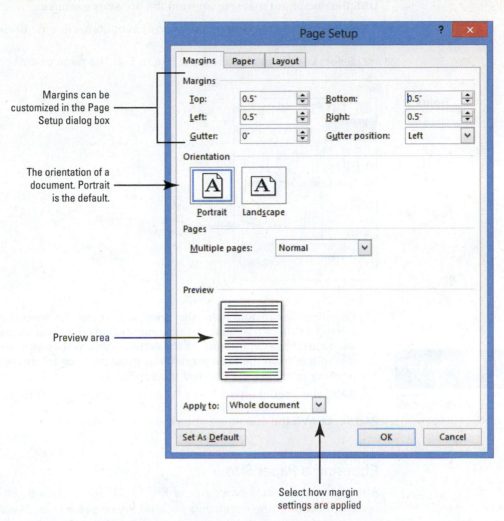

Select how margin settings are applied

7. Change the bottom, left, and right margins to **1"** and the top margin to **2"**. Changing the margins affects all pages within the document. Click **OK**.

8. **SAVE** the document as *Draft Proposal* in the lesson folder on your flash drive.

PAUSE. LEAVE the document open to use in the next exercise.

Selecting a Page Orientation

Another Way
The Page Setup dialog box can also be accessed through Backstage by clicking *File*, *Print*, and *Page Setup.*.

A document's orientation determines what direction the text extends across the page. A letter size document in portrait orientation is 8 ½" by 11" and the text extends across the shorter width of the document, whereas a letter size document in landscape orientation is 11" × 8½" and orients the text extending across the longer dimensions of the page. As you plan and format a document, you must choose its page orientation. In **portrait orientation**, which is commonly used for business documents, text extends across the shorter length of the document. **Landscape orientation**, which is commonly used for brochures, graphics, tables, and so on, orients text across the longer dimension of the page. In this exercise, you change a document's orientation from portrait (the default) to landscape.

Select a Page Orientation

USE the document that is open from the previous exercise.

1. In the Page Setup group of the Page Layout tab, click the **drop-down arrow** to display the Orientation menu.

2. Select **Landscape**, as shown in Figure 5-4. The page orientation changes to Landscape.

Figure 5-4

Orientation menu

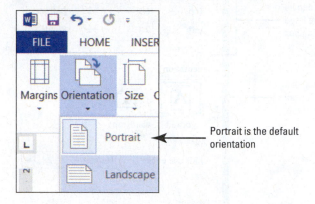

Portrait is the default orientation

3. Click the **File** tab, and then click **Print**, to preview the document in Backstage view. On the right side of the pane, the document displays in landscape and under Settings, you see Landscape Orientation as the setting. Also, notice you can access the Page Setup dialog box from the Print screen. It is good practice to preview your document before printing to ensure the text will print correctly.

4. **SAVE** the document as **Draft1 Proposal** in the lesson folder on your flash drive.

PAUSE. LEAVE the document open to use in the next exercise.

CERTIFICATION READY? 1.3.1

How would you change the orientation in a document?

Choosing a Paper Size

Although the standard paper size of 8½″ × 11″ is the default setting, Word provides several options for formatting documents for a variety of paper sizes. Word provides preset document sizes or you can customize the paper size by clicking the *More Paper Sizes* command. For instance, invitations, postcards, legal documents, or reports all require a different paper size. Many printers provide options for printing on different sizes of paper, and in some cases, you might need to change or customize the paper size in Word as you format your document. Legal documents, for example, must be formatted for 8½″ × 14″ paper. In this exercise, you change the size of paper from the default.

Choose a Paper Size

USE the document that is open from the previous exercise.

1. In the Page Setup group of the Page Layout tab, click the **drop-down arrow** to display the Orientation menu, and then select **Portrait**. The orientation is changed back to portrait from the previous exercise.

2. From the Page Setup group of the Page Layout tab, click the **drop-down arrow** to display the Size menu, and then select **Legal**, as shown in Figure 5-5.

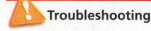 **Troubleshooting** If your printer cannot print on legal size paper, you won't see *legal size* as an option here. You should select another paper size instead.

Figure 5-5

Figure 5-5

Size menu

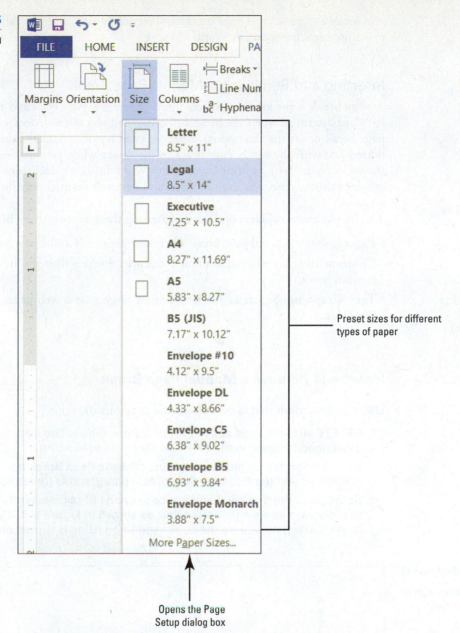

Preset sizes for different
types of paper

Opens the Page
Setup dialog box

3. On the File tab, click **Print** to preview your document in Backstage view. On the right side of the pane, the document displays in portrait orientation and legal size.

Cross Ref

In Lesson 1, you learn to use the Quick Access Toolbar. To customize the Quick Access Toolbar, click the down arrow and select *Print Preview* and *Print*.

4. Return to the document by clicking on the **Return to Document** button.
5. Click the **Page Layout** tab, and then click the **drop-down arrow** to display the Size menu; next, select **Letter**.
6. **SAVE** the document as ***Draft2 Proposal*** in the lesson folder on your flash drive.

PAUSE. LEAVE the document open to use in the next exercise.

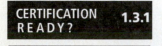

CERTIFICATION READY? 1.3.1

How would you change the paper size in a document?

WORKING WITH BREAKS

The Bottom Line

Word automatically starts a new page in long documents when the text reaches the bottom of the page. There might be times, however, when you will work with documents that contain various objects or special layouts that require you to control where a page or section breaks. You can insert and remove these manual page breaks and section breaks, and you can control word hyphenation or set nonbreaking spaces in Word.

Inserting and Removing a Manual Page Break

A **page break** is the location in a document where one page ends and a new page begins. You can let Word determine where the break will occur, and you can also decide where to insert the manual page break or set specific options for those page breaks. Manual page breaks display as a single dotted line with the words *Page Break* in the center when you enable the Show/Hide button (as shown in Figure 5-6). In Print Layout view, Word displays a document page by page, one after the other. In this exercise, you learn to insert and remove a manual page break.

The Breaks menu contains options for inserting three types of Page Breaks:

- **Page:** Inserts a manual page break where one page ends and a new page begins.
- **Column:** Inserts a manual column break where text will begin in the next column after the column break.
- **Text Wrapping:** Separates the text around objects on a web page, such as caption text from body text.

STEP BY STEP   **Insert and Remove a Manual Page Break**

USE the document that is open from the previous exercise.

1. **DELETE** all blank lines above *Proposal Description*. The insertion point should be positioned before *P* in the *Proposal Description* heading.

2. On the Insert tab, in the Pages group, click the **Page Break** button. A manual page break is inserted and the *Proposal Description* paragraph is forced to the next page.

3. Scroll up to the first page and notice the page break marker that has been inserted and that displays as a single dotted line, as shown in Figure 5-6. If you cannot see the page break marker, make sure the command Show/Hide is turned on.

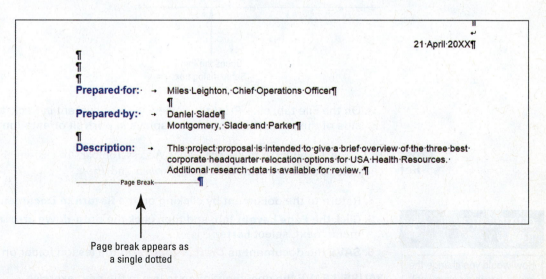

Figure 5-6

Page Break in Print Layout view

Page break appears as a single dotted

4. Scroll down and position the insertion point before the *O* in the *Option 1* heading.

5. On the Page Layout tab, in the Page Setup group, click the **drop-down arrow** to display the **Breaks** menu. The Breaks menu appears, as shown in Figure 5-7.

Figure 5-7

Breaks menu

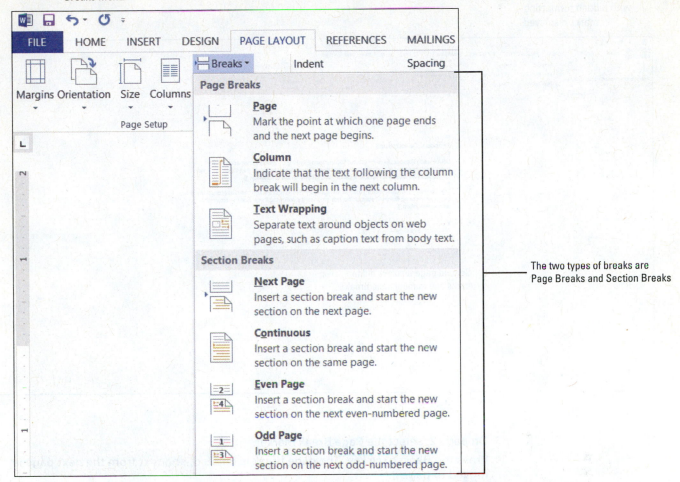

The two types of breaks are
Page Breaks and Section Breaks

6. Select **Page** from the menu and a manual page break is inserted, and text is forced to the next page.

7. Position the insertion point before the *O* in the *Option 2* heading and repeat steps 5 and 6.

8. Position the insertion point before the *O* in the *Option 3* heading and press **Ctrl+Enter** to enter a manual page break using the keyboard shortcut.

9. **SAVE** the document as *Draft3 Proposal* in the lesson folder on your flash drive.

10. Click the **View** tab, change the view to **Draft**, and review the page breaks in your document.

11. Return to the **Print Layout** view.

12. Scroll to the second page and notice the manual page break marker, shown in Figure 5-8.

Figure 5-8

Manual page break
with hidden formatting
marks displayed

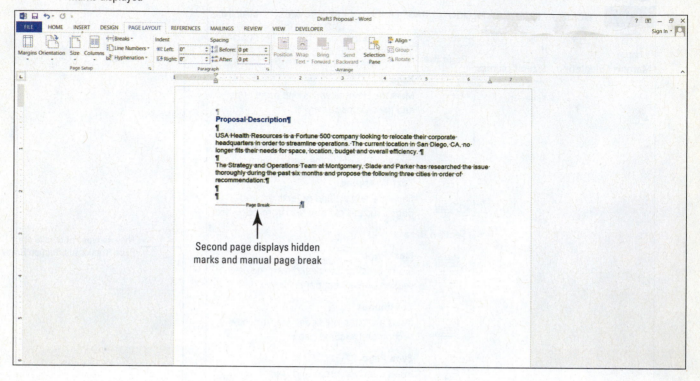

Second page displays hidden
marks and manual page break

13. On page 2, select the **Page Break** marker.

14. Press the **Backspace** key. The page break is deleted, and text from the next page is moved to page 2.

15. Scroll up to page 1, select the **Page Break** marker below the last paragraph in *Description*, and press the **Backspace** key. The *Proposal Description* heading is moved to page 1.

16. Select the remaining **Page Break** markers and press **Delete**.

17. Keep the document open without saving the changes made in the last three steps.

PAUSE. LEAVE the document open to use in the next exercise.

Take Note   Click the *Show/Hide* ¶ button to view page breaks and section breaks for editing purposes.

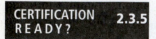

CERTIFICATION READY? 2.3.5

How would you insert a manual page break?

Inserting Section Breaks

A **section break** is used to create multiple sections in the same document. You can even create different sections on the same page. Each section can have its own layout or formatting. You can use section breaks to create a section in your document that contains a page with margins and orientation that is different from the remainder of the document. A section breaks appears with a dotted double line, labeled *Section Break*. You can select and delete section breaks just as you can remove page breaks. In this exercise, you insert a continuous section break and then change the margins for that section.

There are four available options for creating Section Breaks in Word, as shown in Table 5-1.

Table 5-1

Types of Section Breaks

Type	Description
Next Page	Inserts a section break and starts the new section on the next page
Continuous	Inserts a section break and starts the new section on the same page
Even Page	Inserts a section break and starts the new section on the next even-numbered page
Odd Page	Inserts a section break and starts the new section on the next odd-numbered page

STEP BY STEP   **Insert a Section Break**

USE the document that is open from the previous exercise.

1. Press **Ctrl+Home** to move to page 1 and position the insertion point after *Relocation Proposal*.

2. On the Page Layout tab, in the Page Setup group, click the **Breaks** button.

3. Under Section Breaks, select **Continuous**. A Continuous Section Break is inserted, which begins a new section on the same page.

4. Position the insertion point on the blank line before *P* in *Prepared for...*

5. On the Page Layout tab, in the Page Setup group, click the **Breaks** button.

6. In the Section Breaks section of the menu, select **Next Page**. A next page section break is inserted in your document, as shown in Figure 5-9. Inserting a section break allows you to format the page without affecting the other pages in the document.

Figure 5-9

Section breaks

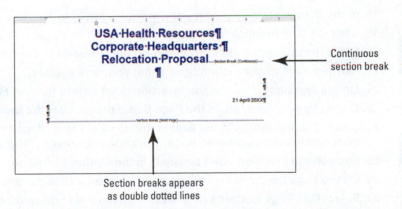

Continuous section break

Section breaks appears as double dotted lines

7. Position the insertion point before the *O* in the *Option 1* heading.

8. On the Page Layout tab, in the Page Setup group, click the **Breaks** button.

9. Under Section Breaks, select **Next Page**. The Next Page break begins a new section on the following page.

10. Place the insertion point on page 1 and select the three line headings to include the blank line below.

11. Click the **dialog box launcher** in the Page Setup group to display the *Page Setup* dialog box.

12. In the Margins tab using Custom Margins, change the top margin from 2″ to **1**″. In the lower-left corner of the dialog box, notice the Apply to section displays as Selected sections.

13. Click the **Layout** tab and under the Page section, Vertical alignment, select **Center**, and then click **OK**. The changes made in the Layout tab are applied to this section.

14. Click the **File** tab, and then click **Print** to preview your document in Backstage view. The first page is vertically centered, as shown in Figure 5-10; whereas the remaining pages are vertically aligned at the top with a 2" margin. Use the **Next Page** ▶ button in Backstage to go to the next page. Then use the **Previous Page** ◀ button to return to page 1.

Figure 5-10

Document with section break and vertical centering

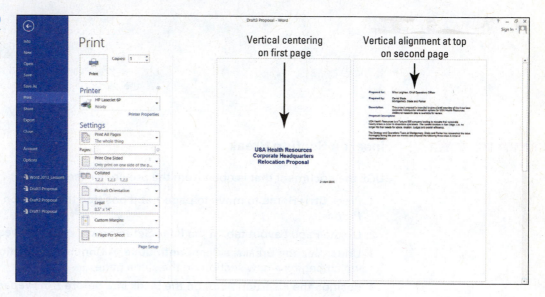

15. Click the **Return to Document** button.

16. Position the insertion point anywhere on page 3.

17. In the Page Setup group, click the **dialog box launcher** to display the *Page Setup* dialog box.

18. In the Margins tab, change the top margin from 2" to **1"**.

19. Click **OK**. The margins for pages 3 and 4 are set to 1".

20. SAVE the document as ***Draft4 Proposal*** in the lesson folder on your flash drive.

21. Remove each of the section breaks that you have applied.

22. On the first page, position the insertion point before the *P* in *Prepared for*.

23. On the Page Layout tab, in the Page Setup group, click the **Breaks** button.

24. Under Section Breaks in the Breaks menu, select **Even Page** to start a new section on the next even-numbered page. The status bar reads *PAGE 2 of 3*.

25. Position the insertion point before *O* in the *Option 1* heading.

26. On the Page Layout tab, in the Page Setup group, click the **Breaks** button.

27. Select **Odd Page** to start a new section on the next odd-numbered page. The status bar reads *PAGE 3 of 4*. Section breaks have been inserted for both even and odd pages.

28. SAVE the document as ***Draft5 Proposal*** in the lesson folder on your flash drive, and then **CLOSE** the file.

PAUSE. LEAVE Word open to use in the next exercise.

CERTIFICATION READY? 2.3.2

How would you insert a continuous break?

CERTIFICATION READY? 2.3.2

How would you insert a next page break?

CERTIFICATION READY? 2.3.2

How would you insert an even-numbered page break?

CERTIFICATION READY? 2.3.2

How would you insert an odd-numbered page break?

Section breaks can be used to change types of formatting for:

• Columns

• Footnotes and endnotes

• Headers and footers

• Line numbering

• Margins

• Page borders

- Page numbering
- Paper size or orientation
- Paper source for a printer
- Vertical alignment of text on a page

Take Note Remember that when you delete a section break, you remove the section formatting as well.

Using Hyphenation

Hyphens, shown as the punctuation mark - , are used to join words and separate syllables of a single word. When a word has a hyphen, the different parts of the word can appear on different lines. By default, **hyphenation** is off in Word; all words appear on a single line, rather than hyphenated and split between lines. As you format a document, however, you might need to determine when to apply a hyphen. In this exercise, you practice using Word's hyphenation feature.

Note the differences here between a document with hyphenation and one without hyphenation.

Without hyphenation:

```
As a strategic associate for USA Health Resources, you are
involved in the logistics for their relocation project.
```

With hyphenation:

```
As a strategic associate for USA Health Resources, you are in-
volved in the logistics for their relocation project.
```

STEP BY STEP **Insert Hyphens in a Document**

OPEN *Relocation Proposal* from the data files for this lesson.

1. On the Page Layout tab, in the Page Setup group, click the **Hyphenation drop-down arrow**.
2. Select **Automatic**; review your document.
3. Click the **drop-down arrow** to display the Hyphenation menu and select **None**, as shown in Figure 5-11.

Figure 5-11

Hyphenation menu

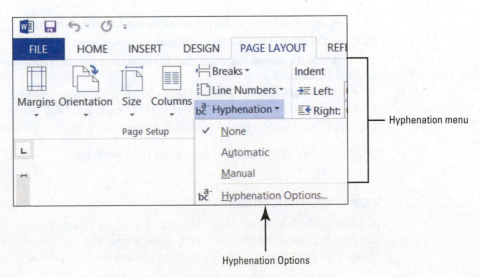

4. Click the **Hyphenation drop-down arrow** again, and select **Manual**. The *Manual Hyphenation* dialog box stops at the first suggested text for hyphenation (*headquarter*), as shown in Figure 5-12.

Figure 5-12

Manual Hyphenation
dialog box

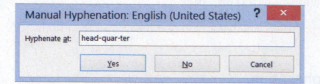

5. Click **Yes**. Manual Hyphenation allows you to determine where to hyphenate the word by clicking **Yes**, **No**, or **Cancel**, and you can decide where to position the insertion point.

6. Click **No** to *review*.

7. Click **Yes** to *headquarters*.

8. Click **No** to *issue, seeking,* and *ample*.

9. Click **Yes** to *technology* and *location*.

10. When Word stops at *transportation,* move the insertion point to the third hyphen (after "*ta*") and click **Yes**.

11. Click **No** to *proximity* and **Yes** to *business*.

12. A message box appears when Word has completed the process of searching for words to hyphenate within the document. Click **OK**.

13. **SAVE** the document as ***Relocation1 Proposal*** in the lesson folder on your flash drive.

14. Click the **Hyphenation drop-down arrow** and select **Hyphenation Options** to open the *Hyphenation* dialog box, as shown in Figure 5-13.

Figure 5-13

Hyphenation dialog box

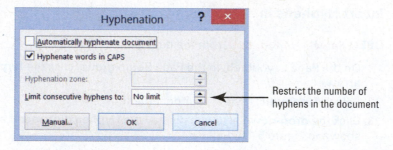

Restrict the number of
hyphens in the document

15. Click the check box to **Automatically hyphenate document**.

16. Click **OK**. The document is automatically hyphenated.

17. Click the **Hyphenation drop-down arrow** and select **Hyphenation Options** to open the *Hyphenation* dialog box.

18. Click the **up arrow** to set the Limit Consecutive Hyphens to **2**. Click **OK**. The number of hyphens in the document is restricted once the default is changed from No Limit.

19. **SAVE** the document as ***Relocation2 Proposal*** in the lesson folder on your flash drive.

PAUSE. LEAVE Word open to use in the next exercise.

Inserting Line Numbers

Displaying the line numbering makes it easy to reference specific places in the document. Line numbering places a number to the left of each line. You can start a new number by page or section or suppress line numbers. In this exercise, you enable the line numbering.

STEP BY STEP   **Insert Line Numbers**

USE the document that is open from the previous exercise.

1. On the Page Layout tab, in the Page Setup group, click the **Line Numbers drop-down arrow** to display the menu as shown in Figure 5-14. By default, None is selected.

Figure 5-14

Line Numbers menu

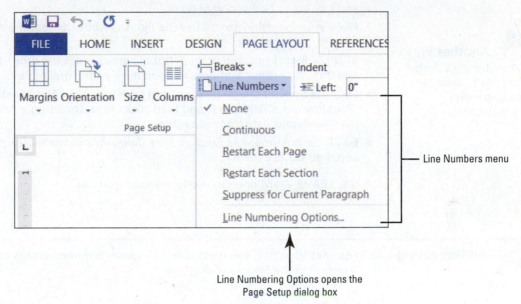

Line Numbers menu

Line Numbering Options opens the
Page Setup dialog box

2. Select **Continuous**. The line numbering is now turned on and each line where text appears is numbered.

3. Press **Ctrl+G** to use the Go To command. Select **Line** in the Go to what section, and then type **25** in the Enter line number box.

4. Click the **Go To** button. The insertion point is now placed at the beginning of line 25 Click **Close**.

5. Click **Breaks** and insert a **Next Page** section beak. Notice that line 25 is now on page 2.

6. The insertion point is resting on page 2 on line 25.

7. Click the **Line Numbers** button to display the menu and select **Restart Each Section**. The line numbering begins at 1.

8. **SAVE** the document as *Relocation3 Proposal* in the lesson folder on your flash drive, and then **CLOSE** the file.

PAUSE. LEAVE Word open to use in the next exercise.

 Workplace Ready

USE LINE NUMBERS TO REFERENCE QUICKLY

Showing line numbers can be used for legal documents or for documents that a team group is reviewing. It is easier to reference the line number rather than "paragraph 6, second sentence", which saves time from having to look for text.

Inserting Nonbreaking Spaces

Word determines when to wrap text to the next line as it reaches the right margin. In some instances, you might want to keep the text together on the same line, such as for a date (November 19, 20XX), a telephone number (999) 888-5555), a proper name (LA Martinez), and so on. In this exercise, you learn to insert **nonbreaking spaces** in Word, to keep selected text on a single line.

| STEP BY STEP | Insert a Nonbreaking Space |

OPEN the document *Employment Offer Letter* from the lesson folder.

1. On the Home tab, in the Paragraph group, click the **Show/Hide** button to display hidden marks on the page.

2. In the first paragraph of the body of the letter at the end of the second line, the month and day are in two separate lines.

3. Place your insertion point after the *r* in *November*. Select the nonprinting space mark between *"November"* and *"3"*.

4. Click the **Insert** tab, and in the Symbols group, click the **drop-down arrow** on Symbol, and then click **More Symbols** to open the *Symbol* dialog box.

5. Click the **Special Characters** tab, and then select the **Nonbreaking Space** option in the Character list. Click **Insert**, and then click **Close**. Inserting a nonbreaking space prevents the month and date from separating.

6. **SAVE** the document as *Employment Confirmed* in the lesson folder on your flash drive, and then **CLOSE** the file.

PAUSE. LEAVE Word open to use in the next exercise.

Another Way
Using the shortcut keys *Ctrl+Shift+Space bar* is a quick way to insert a nonbreaking space.

⚠️ **Troubleshooting**   To keep text together, you must select all spaces between words and insert the nonbreaking space option in the Symbol dialog box.

Inserting Line Breaks

Using the line break instead of beginning a new paragraph keeps text together when changing the alignment in a document. For instance, if you create a title page that contains three headings separated with line breaks, there is no need to select text when changing the alignment. Because all three headings are still part of the same paragraph, placing the insertion point anywhere in one of the headings lets the lines move together when changing the alignment to center, align right, or align left. A nonprinting curved left arrow appears in the document showing that you have used the line break command. In this exercise, you learn to insert a **line break** in Word, to align text together.

| STEP BY STEP | Insert a Line Break |

1. **OPEN** a blank document and turn on the Show/Hide.

2. Type **USA Health Resources**.

3. Press **Shift+Enter** to insert a line break. Notice the left arrow appears at the end of the line instead of the paragraph mark, and the insertion point is moved to the next line.

4. Type **Corporate Headquarters**.

5. Press **Shift+Enter** to insert a line break.

6. Type **Relocation Proposal**.

7. Press **Enter**. Notice a paragraph mark appears at the end of this line indicating the start of a new paragraph.

8. Place the insertion point in the second heading, and then click **Center**. Notice how all lines move together. Change the alignment to align right then to align left, then center.

9. **SAVE** the document as *Title with Line Breaks* in the lesson folder on your flash drive, and then **CLOSE** the file.

PAUSE. LEAVE Word open to use in the next exercise.

CONTROLLING PAGINATION

A well-organized and formatted document captures and maintains the reader's attention. Microsoft Word allows you to control how your text flows onto different pages.

Controlling Widows and Orphans

To maintain an appealing appearance and readable content, you might need to keep the first or last line of a paragraph from appearing alone on the page. Word provides options for keeping text lines together and avoiding single lines of text at the top or bottom of a page. By default, the Widow and Orphan control is enabled. In this exercise, you manage Word's Widow/Orphan control.

A **widow** is the last line of a paragraph that appears as a single line of text at the top of a page as shown in Figure 5-15.

Figure 5-15

A widow at the top of a page

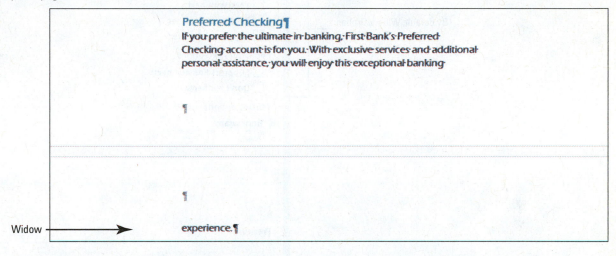

Widow ⟶ experience.¶

An **orphan** is the first line of a paragraph that appears alone at the bottom of a page as shown in Figure 5-16.

Figure 5-16

An orphan at the bottom of a page

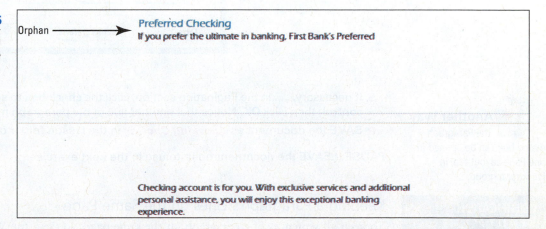

Orphan ⟶

Turn on Widow/Orphan Control

OPEN the ***Checking*** document from the data files for this lesson.

1. Scroll to the top of page 2 and notice the widow *experience . . .* at the top of the page.
2. On page 1 of the document, place the insertion point anywhere in the paragraph under *Preferred Checking*.
3. On the Home tab, in the Paragraph group, click the **dialog box launcher**. The *Paragraph* dialog box appears.
4. Click the **Line and Page Breaks** tab, as shown in Figure 5-17.

Figure 5-17

Paragraph dialog box

By default, Widow/Orphan Control is on

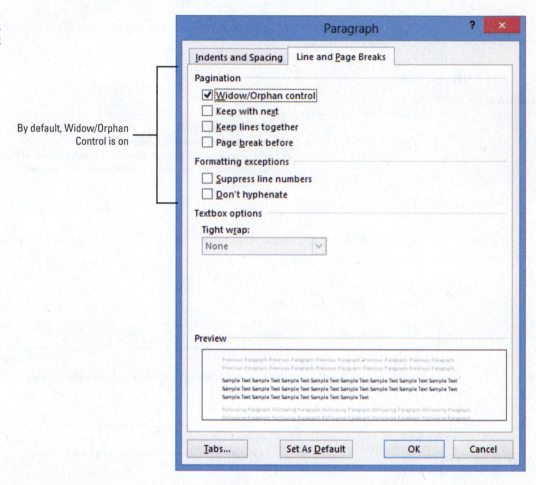

5. If necessary, . . . In the Pagination section, click the **check box** to select **Widow/Orphan control**; then click **OK**. Notice that another line of the paragraph moves to the second page.
6. **SAVE** the document as ***Checking Choices*** in the lesson folder on your flash drive.

PAUSE. LEAVE the document open to use in the next exercise.

Another Way

The Paragraph dialog box can be opened in one Page Layout tab, in Paragraph group.

CERTIFICATION READY?   2.3.1

How do you prevent an orphan from occurring in a document?

Keeping a Paragraph's Lines on the Same Page

To keep all sentences of a paragraph on the same page, you can use Word's Keep lines together command. By default, the Keep Lines Together feature in Word is off. To keep the lines of a paragraph together, select the paragraph; then open the Paragraph dialog box and click to select the *Keep lines together* check box from the Line and Page Breaks tab. In this exercise, you practice keeping lines together on the selected paragraph.

Keep Lines Together

USE the document that is open from the previous exercise.

1. Place the insertion point anywhere in the two lines under *Preferred Checking*.
2. On the Home tab, in the Paragraph group, click the **dialog box launcher**. The *Paragraph* dialog box appears.
3. On the Line and Page Breaks tab, in the Pagination section, click to select the **Keep lines together** check box; then click **OK**. Notice that the two lines that were at the bottom of page 1 moved to page 2.
4. SAVE the document with the same filename in the lesson folder on your flash drive.

PAUSE. LEAVE the document open to use in the next exercise.

Keeping Two Paragraphs on the Same Page

Word considers any line of text followed by a paragraph mark to be a paragraph. For instance, when you press Enter after typing a heading, the heading becomes a paragraph. To keep two paragraphs on the same page, you select both paragraphs, and then in the Line and Page Breaks tab of the Paragraph dialog box, click to select the *Keep with next* check box. In this exercise, you practice keeping two paragraphs together on the same page, such as a heading and the text below it, using Word's Keep with next command.

Keep Two Paragraphs on the Same Page

USE the document that is open from the previous exercise.

1. Place the insertion point in the *Preferred Checking* heading.
2. Launch the **Paragraph** dialog box. The *Paragraph* dialog box appears.
3. On the Line and Page Breaks tab, in the Pagination section, click to select the **Keep with next** check box; then click **OK**. Notice that the two paragraphs (the heading and paragraph that follows) are together and have moved to page 2.
4. SAVE the document with the same filename in the lesson folder on your flash drive.

PAUSE. LEAVE the document open to use in the next exercise.

Forcing a Paragraph to the Top of a Page

Automatic page breaks usually occur at acceptable places in a Word document, but there might be times when you need to force a paragraph to the top of a page. When you use this type of page break in your document, a nonprinting character (■) appears beside the text. In the previous exercise, you should also see this nonprinting character mark. This lets you know that a formatting change has been made in the document. To remove this type of page break, you need to change the paragraph formatting. In this exercise, you practice inserting a page break before a paragraph, to force the paragraph to the top of the next page.

Force a Paragraph to the Top of a Page

USE the document that is open from the previous exercise.

1. Position the insertion point before the *S* in the *Senior Preferred Checking* heading.
2. On the Home tab, in the Paragraph group, click the **dialog box launcher**. The *Paragraph* dialog box appears.

3. On the Line and Page Breaks tab, click to select the **Page break before** check box; then click **OK**. Using this command forces text to the top of a new page. Notice that you cannot actually see a page break in the document.

4. **SAVE** the document with the same filename in the lesson folder on your flash drive.

PAUSE. LEAVE the document open to use in the next exercise.

SETTING UP COLUMNS

The Bottom Line

Columns are vertical blocks of text in which text flows from the bottom of one column to the top of the next. Newspapers, magazines, and newsletters are formatted in columns to add interest and improve readability. Text formatted into columns produce shorter lines and a white space between columns. By default, Word documents are formatted as single columns, but you can change that formatting to display multiple columns or columns of varying widths. When adjusting column formatting, column breaks are used to move text to the next column. Also, a document can be formatted with many different column configurations within the same document.

Creating Columns

In this exercise, you practice creating columns within an existing Word document.

STEP BY STEP   **Create Columns**

USE the document that is open from the previous exercise.

1. Change the left and right margins to **1"**.

2. Place the insertion point in front of *F* in *Free Checking* on page 1.

3. On the Page Layout tab, in the Page Setup group, click the **drop-down arrow** to display the Columns menu. The Columns menu appears, as shown in Figure 5-18.

Figure 5-18

Columns menu

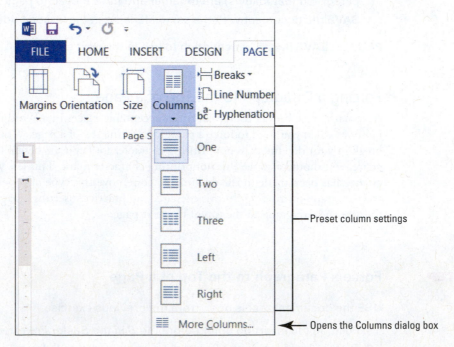

Preset column settings

Opens the Columns dialog box

4. Select Two. The text in the document is formatted into two columns. Notice that *Senior Preferred Checking* starts at the top of a new page because it is still formatted with a page break before.

5. **SAVE** the document as ***Checking Draft*** in the lesson folder on your flash drive.

PAUSE. LEAVE the document open to use in the next exercise.

 **Troubleshooting**   When formatting existing text into columns, avoid selecting the document's title heading if you want to keep it as a single column.

Formatting Columns

In addition to Word's common column formats, you can customize column formats to fit the text and the purpose of your document. By default, when you click the Columns button and select from the Columns menu options, the whole document is formatted as columns. Using the Columns dialog box, you can apply column formatting to the whole document or a selected part of the document only. You also can change a document formatted in multiple columns back to a single-column document. In this exercise, you learn to format multiple columns in Word.

On the Page Layout tab, in the Page Setup group, the Columns menu lists these options for creating common column formats:

- **One:** Formats the text into a single column
- **Two:** Formats the text into two even columns
- **Three:** Formats the text into three even columns
- **Left:** Formats the text into two uneven columns—a narrow one on the left and a wide one on the right
- **Right:** Formats the text into two uneven columns—a narrow one on the right and a wide one on the left
- **More Columns:** Contains options for customizing columns

Click the *Line Between* box in the Columns dialog box to insert a vertical line between columns.

STEP BY STEP   **Format Columns**

USE the document that is open from the previous exercise.

1. The insertion point should be positioned in front of *Free Checking*.
2. On the Page Layout tab, in the Page Setup group, click the **drop-down arrow** to display the Columns menu.
3. Select **More Columns**. The *Columns* dialog box appears, as shown in Figure 5-19.

Figure 5-19

Columns dialog box

Change the number of columns →

Column width can be automatically set or adjusted manually →

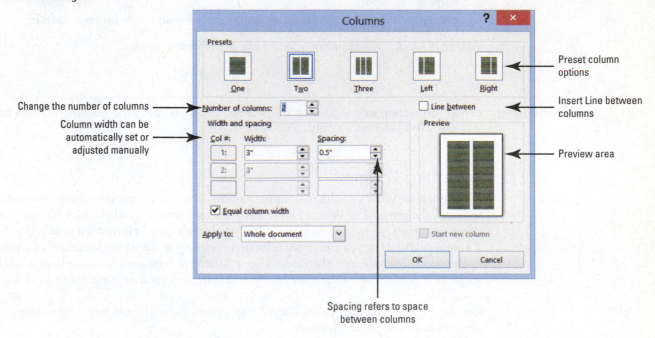

Preset column options

Insert Line between columns

Preview area

Spacing refers to space between columns

4. In the Number of columns box, type **3** or click the up arrow once. By changing the number of columns, the width automatically changes.

5. Click the **Line between** check box to add a check mark. This option places a vertical line between the columns.

6. Click **OK**. Notice that the document is now formatted in three columns.

7. Position the insertion point before the *S* in the *Senior Preferred* heading. The page break before that was added previously in this lesson will be removed in the next step.

8. Open the **Paragraph** dialog box. In the Line and Page Breaks tab of the dialog box, click to deselect the **Page break before** box and click **OK**. The Page break before command is removed from the document and the text moves to the previous page.

9. On the Page Layout tab, change the Orientation option to **Landscape**.

10. Change the paper size to **Legal** (if your printer can print legal documents).

11. Click **Margins**, and then click **Custom Margins** to open the *Page Setup* dialog box. Change the **Top** and **Bottom** margin settings to **0.5"**, and in the Apply To selection box at the bottom of the Margins tab, notice that this affects the Whole Document.

12. Click **OK**. The document now fits to one page.

13. Place the insertion point in front of the *V* in *Value Checking*. Click the **drop-down arrow** to display the Breaks menu; then select **Column** to insert a column break. *Value Checking* and the text below move to the second column.

14. Place the insertion point in front of the *P* in *Preferred Checking* and click the **drop-down arrow** to display the Breaks menu, and then select **Column** break. *Preferred Checking* and the text below move to the third column.

15. Place the insertion point in front of the *S* in *Senior Preferred Checking* and click the **drop-down arrow** to display the Breaks menu, and then select **Column**. The text is moved to the top of the next page.

16. Select the two headings beginning with *First Bank . . . Personal Checking Choices*.

17. Click the **drop-down arrow** in Columns and select **One**. The first two headings are now single columns.

18. Press the **Enter** key after the *s* in *Choices*. Notice the Continuous Section Break separating the heading in one column and the text formatted in three columns (as shown in Figure 5-20).

CERTIFICATION READY? 2.3.3

How would you create multiple columns within a document?

CERTIFICATION READY? 2.3.4

How would you add a heading to an existing document?

Figure 5-20

Formatted document
with columns

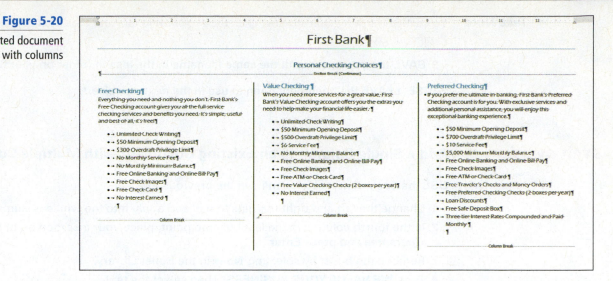

19. Click **Undo**.

20. Select the two headings and on the Home tab, and in the Paragraph group, click the **Center** ☰ button. Applying the Center feature does not affect the text in the columns.

21. **SAVE** the document with the same filename in the lesson folder on your flash drive.

PAUSE. LEAVE the document open to use in the next exercise.

Changing Column Widths

Column widths can be even or you can specify varying column widths. Word provides an option to keep the columns the same by selecting the Equal Column Width option. Column width and spacing settings are displayed in the Columns dialog box for the first column only and can be set to a specific width. When the settings are changed for the width, all columns will be affected with the changes. In this exercise, you learn to change column widths in Word documents.

STEP BY STEP   **Change Column Widths**

USE the document that is open from the previous exercise.

1. Place your insertion point anywhere in the first column.

2. On the Page Layout tab, in the Page Setup group, click the **drop-down arrow** to display the Columns menu.

3. Select **More Columns**. The *Columns* dialog box appears.

4. Type **4** in the Number of columns box or click the **up arrow**. Changing the columns automatically changes the width of the column. This two-page document is now a one-page document.

5. Select the text in the **Width** box and type **3**.

6. Press the **Tab** key to move to the Spacing box. Notice that the spacing adjusted automatically to .33″.

7. Click **OK**. The Apply to section affects only the columns.

8. Review the document in Backstage using the Print screen. Notice the heading, *Free Checking*, is not aligned vertically with the other headings. To correct this, decrease the Spacing Before to **zero**. Review the document again, and notice the headings are aligned evenly to create a balanced appearance in the document.

Take Note To change the paragraph spacing, click the *Page Layout* tab, and then change the spacing in the Paragraph group.

9. **SAVE** the document with the same filename in the lesson folder on your flash drive.

PAUSE. LEAVE the document open to use in the next exercise.

STEP BY STEP   **Add a Single Column to an Existing Document with Multiple Columns**

USE the document that is open from the previous exercise.

1. Change the left and right margins to **0.5**″ and apply it to the whole document.
2. In the fourth column, in the last bulleted point, place your insertion point after *e* in *Guarantee* and press **Enter**.
3. Remove the bullet by selecting **None** in the Bullet Library.
4. Type **WE VALUE YOUR BUSINESS!** Then select the text.
5. In the Paragraph group of the Page Layout tab, change the Left indent to **0**″.
6. Change the Spacing After to **0** pt to reduce the spacing.
7. In the Page Setup group, click the **drop-down arrow** to display the Columns menu and select **One**.
8. **Center**, **bold**, increase the font size to **22** pt and change the font color to **dark blue**. The final document should remain on one page.
9. **SAVE** the document as ***Checking Final*** in the lesson folder on your flash drive.

PAUSE. LEAVE the document open to use in the next exercise.

CERTIFICATION READY?   2.3.3

How would you create multiple columns within a document?

INSERTING A BLANK PAGE INTO A DOCUMENT

The Bottom Line

When creating or editing a document, you might need to insert a blank page to add more text, graphics, or a table. Rather than pressing the Enter key enough times to insert a blank page, Word provides a Blank Page command.

Inserting a Blank Page

You can insert a blank page at any point within a document—the beginning, middle, or end. To insert a blank page, position the insertion point and click the Blank Page command in the Pages group on the Insert tab. To delete a blank page, use the *Show/Hide* (¶) button to display hidden characters, and then select and delete the page break. In this exercise, you practice inserting a blank page in the middle of the document.

STEP BY STEP   **Insert a Blank Page**

USE the document that is open from the previous exercise.

1. Position the insertion point before the *F* in *Free Checking*.
2. On the Insert tab, in the Pages group, click **Blank Page** (see Figure 5-21). Page 2 is a blank page. The headings are left on page 1. Page 2 is a blank page and the text is moved to page 3. Notice that Word inserted two page breaks to create the blank page.

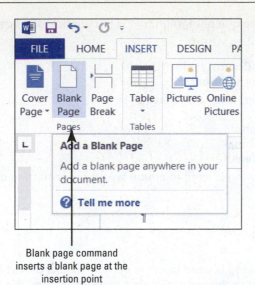

Figure 5-21

Blank page

Blank page command
inserts a blank page at the
insertion point

3. Click the **Undo** ↶ button on the Quick Access Toolbar.
4. **SAVE** the document with the same filename in the lesson folder on your flash drive, and then **CLOSE** the file.

STOP. CLOSE Word.

SKILL SUMMARY

In This Lesson, You Learned To:	Exam Objective	Objective Number
Set Page Layout	Modify page setup.	1.3.1
Work with Breaks	Force page breaks.	2.3.5
	Insert breaks to create sections.	2.3.2
Control Pagination	Prevent paragraph orphans.	2.3.1
Set Up Columns	Create multiple columns within sections.	2.3.3
	Add titles to sections.	2.3.4
Insert a Blank Page into a Document		

Knowledge Assessment

Multiple Choice

Select the best response for the following statements.

1. What is the term for the last line of a paragraph when it is left alone at the top of a page?
   a. Orphan
   b. Widow
   c. Widow/Orphan Control
   d. Keep Lines Together

2. What is the first line of a paragraph that is left alone at the bottom of a page called?
a. Widow
b. Orphan
c. Widow/Orphan Control
d. Keep Paragraphs Together

3. Pressing **Ctrl+Enter** produces what?
a. A section break
b. A tight paragraph
c. A manual page break
d. A continuous break

4. Which of the following is used to create layout or formatting changes in a portion of a document?
a. Section break
b. Page break
c. Next Page break
d. Text wrapping

5. Which of the following is used to move vertical blocks of text from the bottom of one block of text to the top of the next block of text (on the same page)?
a. Column breaks
b. Section breaks
c. Two columns
d. Three columns

6. Which of the following inserts an empty page at the insertion point?
a. Alt+Enter
b. Blank Page command
c. Page Break command
d. Both b and c

7. Which of the following displays the Columns dialog box?
a. The Insert tab
b. More Columns command
c. Right-click
d. All of the above

8. Which of the following is used to keep two adjacent words on the same line?
a. Keep lines together
b. Keep paragraphs together
c. Nonbreaking space
d. Nonbreaking hyphen

9. Hyphens are used to:
a. join words.
b. separate syllables.
c. break single words into two parts.
d. All of the above

10. Which of the following is true of the Manual Hyphenation command?
a. It automatically stops at a word and asks you to decide where to hyphenate.
b. It hyphenates words automatically.
c. It does not allow hyphenating on any words.
d. None of the above.

True/False

Circle T if the statement is true or F if the statement is false.

T F 1. A page height that is larger than the page width is characteristic of portrait orientation.

T F 2. In Word, the default margin size is 1.5 inches for the top, bottom, left, and right margins.

T F 3. Columns are blank spaces on the sides, top, and bottom of a document.

T F 4. Paper size refers to landscape or portrait orientation.

T F 5. Widow/Orphan Control is on by default.

T F 6. A column break moves text from one column to the next.

T F **7.** Use Widow/Orphan Control to keep all lines of a paragraph together on the same page.

T F **8.** When you insert a next page break, you CANNOT go back and delete it.

T F **9.** A Continuous section break starts the new section on the next page.

T F **10.** A page break is the location in a document where one page ends and a new page begins.

Competency Assessment

Project 5-1: Formatting the YMCA Newsletter

Format some data for the YMCA into a two-column newsletter.

GET READY. LAUNCH Word if it is not already running.

1. **OPEN** *Y News* from the data files for this lesson.

2. **SAVE** the document as *5-1 YMCA Newsletter* in the lesson folder on your flash drive.

3. Click the **Show/Hide** ¶ button to enable.

4. Position the insertion point before the *M* in the heading, *Mother's Day Out . . . .*

5. On the Page Layout tab, in the Page Setup group, click the **Breaks button** and select **Continuous** from the menu.

6. In the Page Setup group, click the **Columns button** and select **Two**. Notice that all the text under the section break is now in two columns.

7. Position the insertion point before the *F* in the *Fall Soccer . . .* heading.

8. Click the **Breaks button** and select **Column**. The heading and text move to the next column.

9. Click the **Columns button** and select **More Columns**.

10. In the Columns dialog box, click the **up arrow** on the Width box to change to **2.8**. The number in the Spacing box should adjust to .9".

11. Click the **Line between box** and click **OK**. The column width is increased and a vertical line is placed between the columns.

12. Place the insertion point on the second paragraph mark under the box at the end of the document and type **The Get Movin' Challenge!**

13. Select the text, and then click the **Columns button** from the Page Setup group and select **One**. With the text still selected, **center**, **bold**, increase the font size to **20** pt, and change the color to **dark red**. The document should fit on one page.

14. Click the **Show/Hide** ¶ button to turn off.

15. **SAVE** the document in the lesson folder on your flash drive, and then **CLOSE** the file.

PAUSE. LEAVE Word open for the next project.

Project 5-2: Computer Use Policy

You are updating First Bank's computer use policy and you need to adjust the flow of text on the page.

GET READY. LAUNCH Word if it is not already running.

1. **OPEN** *Books Beyond* from the data files for this lesson.

2. **SAVE** the document as *5-2 Books Beyond* in the lesson folder on your flash drive.

3. On the Home tab, in the Paragraph group, click the **dialog box launcher**. On the Line and Page Breaks tab, click to select the **Widow/Orphan control box** and click **OK**. Turning on the Widow/Orphan control affects the whole document.

4. On the Page Layout tab, in the Page Setup group, click the **drop-down arrow** by Line Numbers and select **Continuous**.

5. Select lines **30** through **38**.

6. Open the **Paragraph** dialog box. On the Line and Page Breaks tab, click the **Keep with next** and **Keep lines together** check boxes, and then click **OK**. The paragraph is no longer split between pages, and the heading, *Introduction*, appears on the same page as the following paragraph.

7. Position the insertion point before the *G* in the *General Performance Expectation Guidelines* heading. You should be on line 56.

8. On the Home tab, in the Paragraph group, click the **dialog box launcher**. On the Line and Page Breaks tab, click the **Page break before check box** and click **OK**. The paragraph moves to the next page.

9. Press **Ctrl+Home** to move the insertion point to the beginning of the document.

10. Click the **Page Layout tab** and in the Page Setup group, click the **Hyphenation button**, and then click **Hyphenation Options**. Click to select the **Automatically hyphenate document check box**, with a consecutive hyphens limit of **3**.

11. Click **OK**.

12. Position the insertion point anywhere on the second page.

13. In the Page Setup group, click the **Line Numbers** button and select **Restart Each Page**.

14. Position the insertion point at the beginning of the *General Performance Expectation Guidelines* heading. In the Page Setup group, click the **Line Numbers** button and select **Suppress for Current Paragraph**.

15. **SAVE** the document in the lesson folder on your flash drive then **CLOSE** the file.

PAUSE. LEAVE Word open for the next project.

Proficiency Assessment

Project 5-3: Coffee Shop Brochure

Your supervisor at the Grand Street Coffee Shop asks you to format the information in its coffee menu as a brochure.

GET READY. LAUNCH Word if it is not already running.

1. **OPEN** *Coffee Menu* from the data files for this lesson.

2. **SAVE** the document as *5-3 Coffee Shop Brochure* in the lesson folder on your flash drive.

3. Change the page orientation to **Landscape**.

4. Position the insertion point before the *M* in the *Menu* heading and insert a **Continuous** section break.

5. Position the insertion point in front of *Coffee* and select text to the end of the document. Create an uneven, two-column format using the **Left** column setting. Notice a section break is created before the word *Coffee*.

6. Position the insertion point before the *N* in the *Nutritional Information* heading and insert a **Column** break.

7. Increase the amount of space between columns to **.7**″. The document should fit to one page.

8. **SAVE** the document in the lesson folder on your flash drive, and then **CLOSE** the file.

PAUSE. LEAVE Word open for the next project.

Project 5-4: Mom's Favorite Recipes

Your mom asks you to help her create a small cookbook filled with her favorite recipes that she can share with family and friends. She has e-mailed you a Word document containing a few recipes to help you get started with creating a format.

GET READY. LAUNCH Word if it is not already running.

1. **OPEN** *Recipes* from the data files for this lesson.
2. **SAVE** the document as *5-4 Favorite Recipes* in the lesson folder on your flash drive.
3. Position the insertion point before the *C* in the *Chicken Pot Pie* heading and insert a **Continuous** section break.
4. Position the insertion point before the *B* in the *Breads* heading and insert a **Next Page** section break.
5. Position the insertion point before the *B* in the *Banana Nut Bread/Chocolate Chip Muffins* headings and insert a **Continuous** section break.
6. Position the insertion point anywhere within the *Chicken Pot Pie* recipe.
7. Format this and the other recipes in the *Main Dishes* section into two even columns with *.9″* spacing between columns and a line between.
8. Position the insertion point before the *R* in the *Ranch Chicken* heading and insert a **Column** break.
9. Position the insertion point anywhere within the *Banana Nut Bread/Chocolate Chip Muffins* heading.
10. Format this section into two even columns with *.9″* spacing between columns and a line between.
11. Insert a **Column** break before *E* in the *Easy Pumpkin Bread/Muffins* and *C* in the *Chocolate Zucchini Bread* headings.
12. Position the insertion point under *Very Blueberry Coffee Cake/Muffins*, and select the hidden space mark between the words *cream* and *cheese* for the second ingredient ½ (8 oz) package of . . . and add a nonbreaking space.
13. Delete the two nonprinting paragraph marks above the *Very Blueberry Coffee Cake/Muffins* heading.
14. In the ninth ingredient, select the hidden space mark between the words *or* and *huckleberries*, and add a nonbreaking space.
15. Click the **Show/Hide** button to hide formatting marks.
16. **SAVE** the document in the lesson folder on your flash drive, and then **CLOSE** the file.

PAUSE. LEAVE Word open for the next project.

Mastery Assessment

Project 5-5: Threefold Bank Brochure

The Checking Choices document needs to be formatted to accommodate the whole document on one page. Your task is to use the features learned in this lesson and apply them to this document as shown in Figure 5-22.

GET READY. LAUNCH Word if it is not already running.

1. **OPEN** *Checking Acct Choices* from the data files for this lesson.
2. **SAVE** the document as *5-5 Checking Brochure* in the lesson folder on your flash drive.

3. Reformat the document using a page size of 8½ x 14 with landscape orientation. Create the brochure to look like the one shown in Figure 5-22. Hint: You need to select the entire document or you will change only the page size and orientation of the first section.

Figure 5-22

Checking brochure

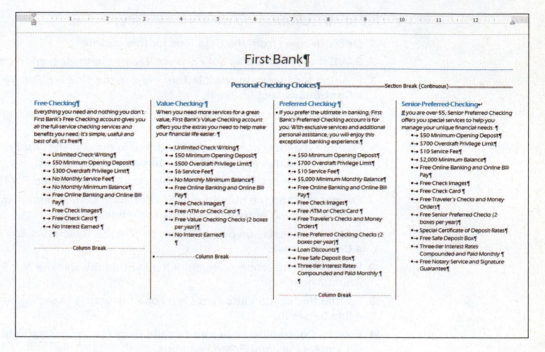

4. Change the columns to **four** columns.
5. Add column breaks before each column heading.
6. After *Personal Checking Choices*, apply a Spacing After to **18** pt.
7. After *Free Checking*, decrease the Spacing Before to **zero**.
8. **SAVE** the document in the lesson folder on your flash drive, and then **CLOSE** the file.

PAUSE. LEAVE Word open for the next project.

Project 5-6: Reformat the YMCA Newsletter

As an alternative to the layout you created previously, reformat the YMCA newsletter with two uneven columns.

GET READY. LAUNCH Word if it is not already running.

1. **OPEN** *Y Newsletter* from the data files for this lesson.
2. **SAVE** the document as *5-6 Right YMCA Newsletter* in the lesson folder on your flash drive.
3. Reformat the newsletter with two uneven columns using the Right column setting.
4. Format the document on one page. (Hint: Delete the column break in the first column and add a column break in front of *Volunteer Coaches . . . .*)
5. **SAVE** the document in the lesson folder on your flash drive, then **CLOSE** the file.

STOP. CLOSE Word.

LESSON SKILL MATRIX

Skill	Exam Objective	Objective Number
Creating a Table	Define table dimensions.	3.1.3
	Demonstrate how to use Quick Tables.	3.1.5
Formatting a Table	Apply styles to tables.	3.2.1
	Modify fonts within tables.	3.2.2
Managing Tables	Set AutoFit options.	3.1.4
	Modify table dimensions.	3.2.6
	Sort table data.	3.2.3
	Merge cells.	3.2.7
	Configure cell margins.	3.2.4
	Set a table title.	3.1.6
	Convert text to tables.	3.1.1
	Convert tables to text.	3.1.2
Using Formulas in a Table	Demonstrate how to apply formulas to a table.	3.2.5
Using Object Zoom		

KEY TERMS

- ascending
- cells
- cell range
- descending
- field code
- formulas
- header row
- merge cells
- Object Zoom
- Quick Tables
- sort
- split cells
- table

© NathanGleave/iStockphoto

Karen Archer is an executive recruiter. Many large companies hire her to find professional talent to fill communications and marketing executive positions within their firms. You were recently hired as her assistant; and although the business is small, you are expected to display a high degree of professionalism, confidentiality, and integrity. Because it is a small business, you are asked to perform many different duties. One of your main duties is to assist Ms. Archer with the constant updating of tables that contain data related to current clients, potential clients, and potential candidates for placement. Microsoft Word has table tools that can help you successfully manage this information. In this lesson, you learn to format lists as well as create, format, and manage tables, and use formulas within a table.

© NathanGleave/iStockphoto

CREATING A TABLE

The Bottom Line

A **table**, such as the one shown in Figure 6-1, is an arrangement of data made up of horizontal rows and vertical columns. **Cells** are the rectangles that are formed when rows and columns intersect. Tables are ideal for organizing information in an orderly manner. Calendars, invoices, adding formulas to tables, and contact lists are all examples of how tables are used every day. Word provides several options for creating tables, including the dragging method, the Insert Table dialog box, table drawing tools, and the Quick Table method.

Figure 6-1

A table created in Word

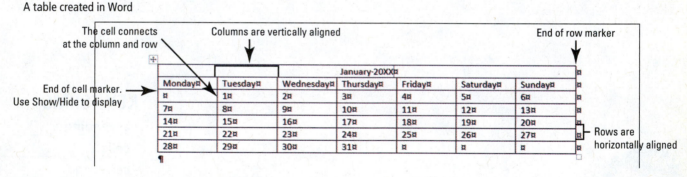

Inserting a Table by Dragging

In this exercise, you learn how easily and quickly you can create a table from the Table menu by dragging the mouse pointer to specify the number of rows and columns. Using this method, you can create a new empty table with up to eight rows and ten columns.

STEP BY STEP   **Insert a Table by Dragging**

GET READY. Before you begin these steps, **LAUNCH** Microsoft Word and **OPEN** a new blank Word document.

1. On the Insert tab, in the Tables group, click the **Table** button. The Insert Table menu appears.

2. Point to the cell in the fifth column, second row. The menu title should read *5x2 Table*, as shown in Figure 6-2. Click the mouse button to create the table. Once the table is inserted in the document, you are ready to begin entering text. Later in this lesson, you enter data into the table.

Figure 6-2

Insert Table menu

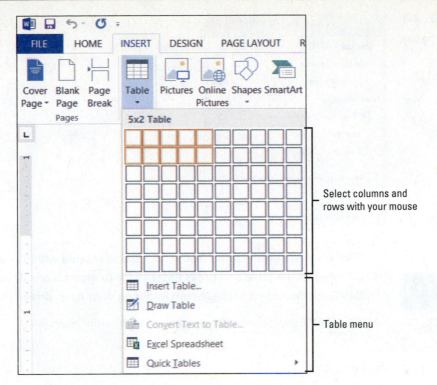

Select columns and
rows with your mouse

Table menu

3. Click below the table and press **Enter** twice to insert blank lines. When you insert more than one table in a document, you should separate them with a blank line to avoid joining the tables.

4. **SAVE** the document as *Tables* in the lesson folder on your flash drive.

PAUSE. LEAVE the document open to use in the next exercise.

Using the Insert Table Dialog Box

The Insert Table dialog box lets you create large tables by specifying up to 63 columns and thousands of rows. Note that in the Insert Table dialog box, you can click the up and down arrows or type in the number of columns and rows needed in a table. In this exercise, you use the Insert Table dialog box to insert a table.

STEP BY STEP   **Use the Insert Table Dialog Box**

USE the document that is open from the previous exercise.

1. On the Insert tab, in the Tables group, click the **Table button** to open the Insert Table menu.

2. On the menu, just below the rows and columns, select **Insert Table**. The *Insert Table* dialog box appears.

3. In the Number of columns box, click the **up arrow** until **9** is displayed.

4. In the Number of rows box, click the **up arrow** until **3** is displayed, as shown in Figure 6-3. The AutoFit behavior is shown in the dialog box and is discussed later in the lesson.

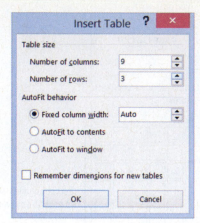

5. Click **OK** to insert the table. You inserted a new table with 9 columns and 3 rows.

6. Click below the table and press **Enter** twice to insert blank lines.

7. **SAVE** the document in the lesson folder on your flash drive.

PAUSE. LEAVE the document open to use in the next exercise.

CERTIFICATION READY?   3.1.3

How do you create a table using the Insert Table dialog box?

Drawing a Table

Word provides the option to draw complex tables using the Draw Table command, which lets you draw a table as you would with a pencil and piece of paper. The Draw Table command transforms the mouse pointer into a pencil tool, which you can use to draw the outline of the table, and then draw rows and columns exactly where you need them. In this exercise, you use the Draw Table command from the Table menu.

STEP BY STEP   **Draw a Table**

USE the document that is open from the previous exercise.

1. If your ruler is not displayed, on the View tab, in the Show group, click the **check box** to display the Ruler.

2. Make sure your insertion point is at the bottom of the document; then use the scroll bar to scroll down, so the insertion point is at the top of the screen.

3. On the Insert tab, in the Tables group, click the **Table button** to open the Insert Table menu.

4. On the menu, just below the rows and columns, select **Draw Table** from the menu. The pointer becomes a pencil tool.

5. To begin drawing the table shown in Figure 6-4, click at the **blinking insertion point** and drag down and to the right until you draw a rectangle that is approximately **3** inches high and **6** inches wide. Notice that the Table Tools contextual Design and Layout tabs automatically appears with the Layout tab active.

Figure 6-4

Draw a table

Use the horizontal and vertical
rulers as a guide to draw a table

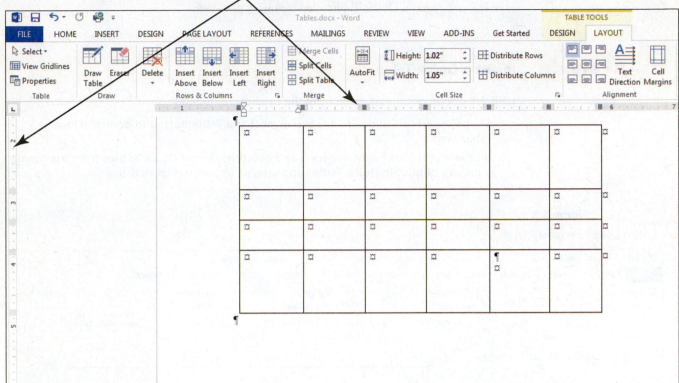

6. Starting at about 1 inch down from the top border, click and drag the pencil from the left border to the right border to draw a horizontal line. Use your ruler as your guide.

7. Draw two more horizontal lines about 0.5 apart.

8. Starting at about 1 inch from the left border, click and drag the pencil from the top of the table to the bottom of the table to create a column.

9. Move over about 1 inch and draw a line from the top of the table to the bottom. If you drew a line in the wrong position, click the **Eraser** button in the Draw group and begin again. The Draw group is located on the Layout tab.

10. Draw three more vertical lines about 1 inch apart from the first horizontal line to the bottom of the table to create a total of six columns. Your table should look similar to Figure 6-4.

11. Click the **Draw Table** button in the Draw group to turn the pencil tool off.

12. Click below the table and press **Enter** twice to create blank lines. If necessary, place your insertion point outside the last cell, and then press **Enter**.

13. **SAVE** the document in the lesson folder on your flash drive.

PAUSE. LEAVE the document open to use in the next exercise.

> **CERTIFICATION READY?** 3.1.3
>
> How do you create a customized table?

Take Note   You have now seen three ways to insert a blank table. Text separated by commas, tabs, paragraphs, or another character can also be converted to a table with the *Convert Text to Table* command on the Table menu.

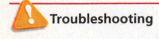 **Troubleshooting**   When drawing tables with the pencil tool, note that this tool will draw squares and rectangles as well as lines. If you are trying to draw a straight line and you move the pencil off your straight path, Word might think you are trying to draw a rectangle and insert one for you. If this happens, just click the Undo button on the Quick Access Toolbar and try again. It might take a bit of practice to master the difference between drawing straight lines and drawing rectangles.

Inserting a Quick Table

Quick Tables are built-in preformatted tables, such as calendars and tabular lists to insert and use in your documents. Word provides a variety of Quick Tables that you can insert into your documents. The Quick Table calendar can be edited to reflect the current month and year. In this exercise, you insert a Quick Table calendar into a document.

STEP BY STEP   **Insert a Quick Table**

USE the document that is open from the previous exercise.

1. On the Insert tab, in the Tables group, click the **Table** button to open the Insert Table menu.

2. On the menu, just below the rows and columns, select **Quick Tables** from the menu. A gallery of built-in Quick Tables appears, as shown in Figure 6-5.

Figure 6-5

Built-In Quick Table gallery

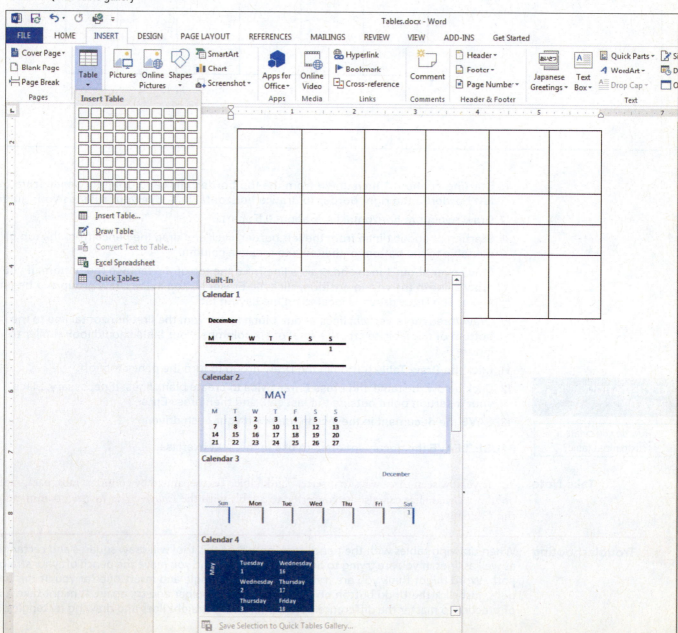

CERTIFICATION READY?   3.1.5

How do you create a table using Quick Tables?

3. Select **Calendar 2**. The data in the calendar can be edited to display the current month and year.

4. **SAVE** the document in the lesson folder on your flash drive.

PAUSE. LEAVE the document open to use in the next exercise.

Take Note   A table can be moved to a new page or a new document by clicking the Move handle to select the table and then using the Cut and Paste commands. You can also use the Copy command to leave a copy of the table in the original location.

Inserting Text in a Table

To add text to a table, your insertion point must be placed in the table where the data will be added. To move to the next cell, press the *Tab* key and to move to the previous cell, press *Shift+Tab*. In this exercise, you learn to add text and move from cell to cell in a table.

STEP BY STEP   **Insert Text in a Table**

USE the document that is open from the previous exercise.

1. Place your insertion point in the first cell of the first table that you created previously in the lesson.

2. Type **Inserting Tables** in the first cell.

3. Press the **Tab** key to move to the second column in the first row.

4. Type **Using the Insert Table dialog box** in the second column. Notice how the text wraps around the cell.

5. Press the **Tab** key to move to the third column in the first row.

6. Type **Drawing Tables** in the third column.

7. Press the **Tab** key to move to the fourth column in the first row.

8. Type **Quick Tables** in the fourth column.

9. You have now entered data in a table and advanced to the next cell by pressing the **Tab** key. Press **Shift+Tab** three times to move to the previous cell until you are positioned at the first cell. Using the keyboard command allows you to move through the table quickly. Note, you can also use your mouse to point and click in the cell to enter text.

10. Place your insertion point in the Calendar 2 Quick Table that you inserted previously.

11. Select **May** and replace with **June 20XX**. Inserting a table using Quick Tables also provides you an option to replace text.

12. **SAVE** the document in the lesson folder on your flash drive, and then **CLOSE** the file.

PAUSE. LEAVE Word open to use in the next exercise.

SOFTWARE ORIENTATION

Design Tab on the Table Tools Ribbon

After inserting a table, Word displays Table Tools in the Ribbon, as shown in Figure 6-6. It is important to become familiar with the commands available on the Design tab under Table Tools. Use this figure as a reference throughout this lesson as well as the rest of this book.

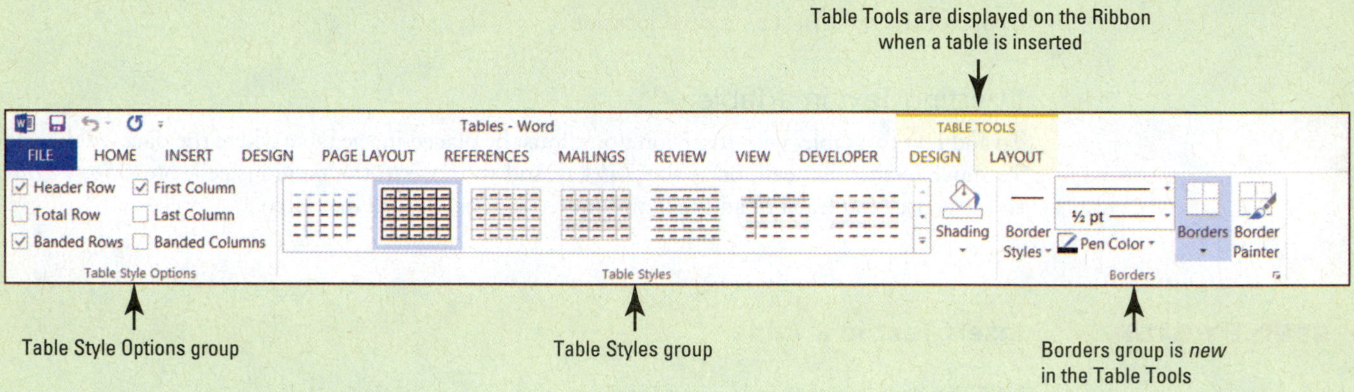

Table Tools are displayed on the Ribbon
when a table is inserted

Table Style Options group   Table Styles group   Borders group is *new*
in the Table Tools

Figure 6-6

Design Tab on the Table Tools Ribbon

FORMATTING A TABLE

The Bottom Line

Once a table is inserted into a document, a preformatted style can be applied using the Table Styles gallery. These styles add a professional appearance to the tables in your documents with a variety of selections to choose from. In the Design tab, Borders group, you can manually format a table's borders. The Borders group is new to the Table Tools and allows you to draw and apply styles to the table.

Applying a Style to a Table

With Table Styles, it is easy to quickly change a table's formatting. You can apply styles to tables in much the same way you learned to apply styles to text in previous lessons, by positioning the insertion point in the table before selecting a style from the Table Styles gallery. You can preview the style before applying it and change the style as many times as needed. You can modify an existing Table Style or create a New Table Style and add it to the gallery, and then modify or delete it, as appropriate. In this exercise, you apply a Table Style to a table in your Word document.

STEP BY STEP   **Apply a Style to a Table**

OPEN *Clients* from the data files for this lesson.

1. Position the insertion point anywhere in the table.

2. On the Design tab, in the Table Styles group, click the **More** ▼ button to view a gallery of Table Styles. There are three options available: Plain Tables, Grid Tables, and List Tables.

3. Scroll through the available styles. Notice that as you point to a style, Word displays a live preview, showing you what your table will look like if you choose that style.

4. Scroll down to the third row under the Grid Tables and select the **Grid Table 3 – Accent 3** style, as shown in Figure 6-7.

Figure 6-7

Table Styles gallery

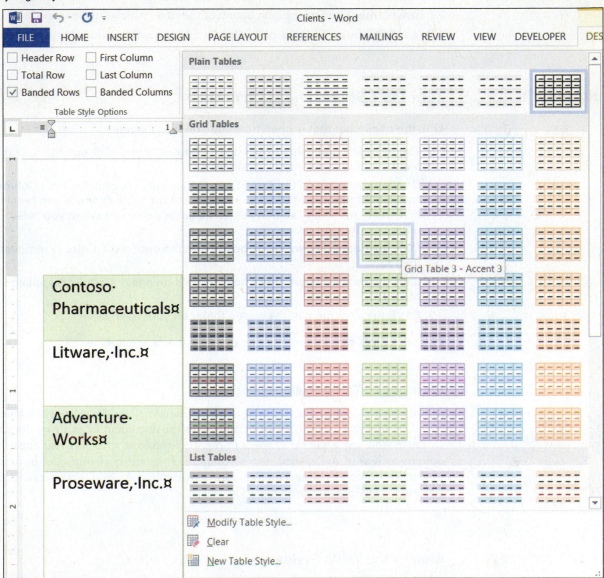

5. SAVE the document as *Clients Table* in the lesson folder on your flash drive.

PAUSE. LEAVE the document open to use in the next exercise.

Turning Table Style Options On or Off

Table Style Options enable you to change the appearance of the preformatted styles you apply to your tables. Table Style Options are linked to the Table Style you have selected and will be applied globally throughout the table. For example, if you select the Banded Columns option, all even-numbered columns in the table will be formatted differently than the odd-numbered columns. In this exercise, you learn to turn Table Style Options on or off by clicking each option's check box.

Examples of Table Style Options include the following:

- **Header Row:** Formats the top row of the table to provide a descriptive name.
- **Total Row:** Formats the last row, which usually contains column totals.

- **Banded Rows:** Formats even rows differently than odd rows to improve readability.
- **First Column:** Formats the first column of the table, which usually contains the row headings.
- **Last Column:** Formats the last column of the table, which often contains row totals.
- **Banded Columns:** Formats even columns differently than odd columns to improve readability.

STEP BY STEP   **Turn Table Style Options On or Off**

USE the document that is open from the previous exercise.

1. The insertion point should still be in the table. If you click outside the table, the Design and Layout tabs will not be available.
2. On the Design tab, in the Table Style Options group, click the **First Column** check box. Notice that the format of the first column of the table changes and text is right-aligned in the cell. Also, the Table Styles in the gallery changes when you select one of the options within the group.
3. Click the **Banded Rows check box** to turn the option off. Color is removed from the rows.
4. Click the **Banded Rows check box** to turn it on again. Color is reapplied to every other row.
5. **SAVE** the document in the lesson folder on your flash drive.

PAUSE. LEAVE the document open to use in the next exercise.

Changes to Table Styles

Modifying styles in a table is similar to what you have already learned when modifying styles for text. Changes to a table style can be applied to the document or as a new document based on a template. You can apply the changes to the whole table or specifically to one of the Table Styles options such as in the banded rows or columns. Formatting changes can be applied to the table properties, borders/shading, banding, font, paragraphs, tabs, and text effects. In this exercise, you learn to modify the font in a table style.

STEP BY STEP   **Modify the Table Styles**

USE the document that is open from the previous exercise.

1. The insertion point should still be in the table. If you click outside the table, the Design and Layout tabs will not be available.
2. In the Table Styles group, click the **More ⬇ button**.
3. Click **Modify Table Style** to open the *Modify Style* dialog box (see Figure 6-8). Notice that in the Name box, Grid Table 3 – Accent 3 is applied from a previous exercise.

Figure 6-8

Modify Style dialog box

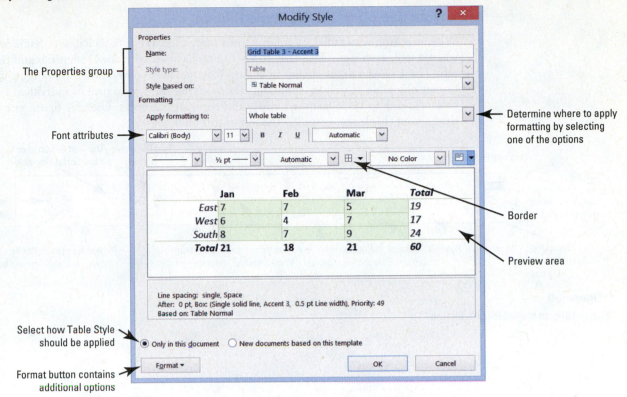

4. In the Apply formatting to box, click the **drop-down arrow** and select **First column**. For this exercise, you apply changes only to the first column.

5. Click the **Format button** in the *Modify Styles* dialog box and select **Font** to open the *Font* dialog box. The Format button displays the menu of available options. Each menu opens its own dialog box.

 Cross Ref In Lesson 3, you learn different ways to apply fonts and styles to text. You also learn how to modify a style to be applied only to that document.

6. With the Font dialog box open, type **Garamond** in the font box. Notice that when you type the first three characters, Word displays available fonts. Select **Garamond**.

7. In the Font style group, select **Bold Italic**, **12** pt for Size, and **Olive Green, Accent 3, Darker 50%** for Font color.

8. Click **OK** to close the *Font* dialog box. Changing the attributes affect only the first column. You should be able to preview the changes before accepting.

9. Click **OK** to close the *Modify Style* dialog box.

10. **SAVE** the document in the lesson folder on your flash drive.

PAUSE. LEAVE the document open to use in the next exercise.

CERTIFICATION READY? 3.2.2

How would you modify the font in a table style?

SOFTWARE ORIENTATION

Layout Tab on the Table Tools Ribbon

When working with tables, Word displays a contextual Table Tools Ribbon that is only visible when a table is in use. The Table Tools Ribbon has two tabs: the Design tab and the Layout tab. The Layout tab, as shown in Figure 6-9, includes commands for changing the entire format of a table as well as commands for changing the appearance of individual table components, such as cells, columns, rows, and applying formulas. Use this figure as a reference throughout this lesson as well as the rest of this book.

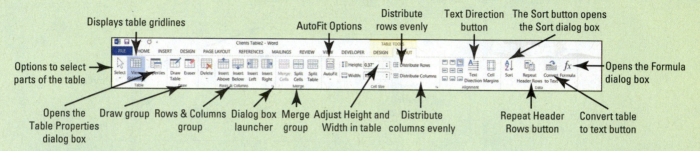

Figure 6-9

Layout Tab on the Table Tools Ribbon

MANAGING TABLES

The Bottom Line

As with any document that you edit, some adjustments are always necessary when you work with tables. After you create a table, you can resize and move its columns; insert columns and rows; change the alignment or direction of its text; set a header row to repeat on several pages; organize data by sorting the text, number, or date; convert text and tables; merge and split cells; add formulas in a table; and work with the table's properties.

Using AutoFit

The AutoFit command enables you to adjust column widths to fit the size of table contents, the window, or to fit all content to a fixed column width. You can AutoFit a column a couple of ways, using the mouse or using the command on the Ribbon. You can use commands in the Cell Size group on the Layout tab, and then select the AutoFit command. In this exercise, you practice using AutoFit in a Word table.

STEP BY STEP　**Use AutoFit**

USE the document that is open from the previous exercise.

1. On the Table Tools Layout tab, in the Table group, click the **View Gridlines button** to hide the gridlines. The gridlines are no longer displayed.

2. Click the **View Gridlines** button again to display gridlines and enable more precise editing.

3. On the Layout tab, in the Cell Size group, click the **AutoFit** button to open the drop-down menu, as shown in Figure 6-10. On the drop-down menu, click **AutoFit Contents**. Each column width changes to fit the data in the column.

Figure 6-10

AutoFit button and menu

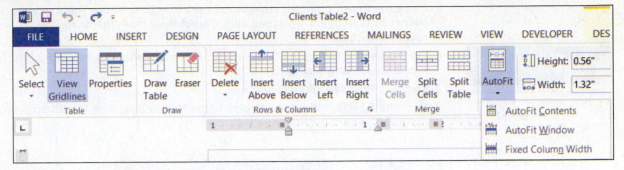

4. **SAVE** the document in the lesson folder on your flash drive.

PAUSE. LEAVE the document open to use in the next exercise.

Resizing a Row or Column

Word offers a number of tools for resizing rows or columns. You can resize a column or row using the mouse or using the commands on the Ribbon. You can use commands in the Cell Size group on the Layout tab to adjust height and width; or use the ruler to adjust the column width. In addition, the Table Properties dialog box allows you to set the measurements at a precise height for rows or ideal width for columns, cells, and tables. In this exercise, you practice using these techniques to resize rows and columns in a Word table.

USE the document that is open from the previous exercise.

1. Click in the first column and position the mouse pointer over the horizontal ruler on the first column marker (see Figure 6-11). The pointer changes to a double-headed arrow along with the ScreenTip *Move Table Column*.

Figure 6-11

Horizontal Ruler on the first column marker

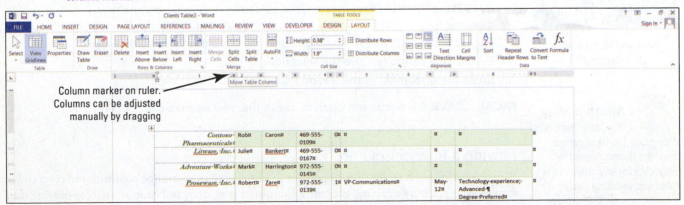

Column marker on ruler. Columns can be adjusted manually by dragging

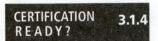

Another Way

Position the pointer outside the table, above the column containing the phone numbers. The pointer changes to a down selection arrow. Click to select the column.

2. Click and drag the column marker to the right until the contents in the cell extend in a single line along the top of the cell. On the Table Tools Layout tab, in the Cell Size group, the width automatically adjusts to 2.19". As the column is manually extended so is the width. Just as columns can be adjusted manually, so can rows—the vertical ruler is used to adjust the row markers.

3. Position the insertion point in the phone number column of the table. On the Layout tab, in the Table group, click the **Select button**, and choose **Select Column** from the drop-down menu.

4. On the Layout tab, in the Cell Size group, click the **up arrow** in the Width box until it reads **1.1"** and the column width changes. The phone numbers now fit on a single line.

5. Place the insertion point anywhere in the first row. In the Table group, click the **Select button** again, and then click **Select Row** from the drop-down menu. The first row is selected.

6. On the Layout tab, in the Cell Size group, click the **dialog box launcher**. The *Table Properties* dialog box appears.

7. Click the **Row tab** in the dialog box.

8. Click the **Specify height check box**. In the Height box, click the up arrow until the box reads **0.5"**, as shown in Figure 6-12.

Figure 6-12

Table Properties dialog box

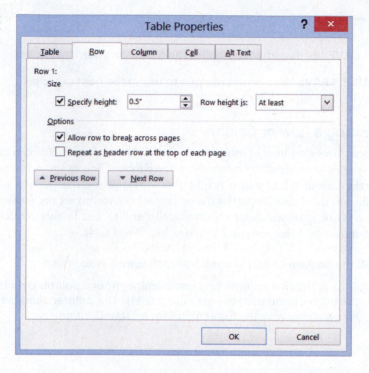

9. Click the **Next Row button** and notice that the changes are applied only to the first row. By clicking the **Next Row button**, the selection moves down one row.

10. Click **OK**. In the Cell Size group, notice that the height for row 2 is at .19" and row 1 is at 0.5". You can also adjust the height of a row individually or by selection.

11. Click in any cell to remove the selection.

12. **SAVE** the document in the lesson folder on your flash drive.

PAUSE. LEAVE the document open to use in the next exercise.

Another Way

The Table Properties dialog box can be accessed from the shortcut menu by right-clicking anywhere in the table and selecting *Table Properties* or click *Properties* in the Table group.

Moving a Row or Column

When working with tables, it is important to know how to rearrange columns and rows to better display your data. By selecting the entire column or row, drag and drop is used for moving data to a new area in the table. The mouse pointer changes and resembles an empty rectangle underneath with dotted lines. In this lesson, you practice moving rows and columns.

Cross Ref

In Lesson 2, you learn to use the Cut and Paste commands with text. The same process can be used with tables by selecting the column or row.

Move a Row or Column

USE the document that is open from the previous exercise.

1. In the table, select the fourth row of data, which contains the information for *Proseware, Inc.*

2. With the mouse over the selected text, hold down the **mouse button** and move the mouse. Notice the mouse pointer changes to a move pointer with a rectangular-shaped insertion point.

3. Drag the rectangular-shaped insertion point down and position it before the *W* in *Wingtip Toys.*

4. Release the mouse button and click in the table to deselect. The row is moved to above the *Wingtip Toys* row.

5. Place the insertion point in the second column of the table, which contains first names. Click the **Select button**, in the Table group, and then **Select Column** from the drop-down menu.

6. Position the pointer inside the selected cells and **right-click** to display the shortcut menu.

7. Select **Cut** to delete that column of text and move the remaining columns to the left.

8. Place the insertion point on the phone numbers column.

9. **Right-click** to display the shortcut menu under the Paste Options section. A new Paste Options menu is displayed with the options Insert as New Column, Nest Table, Insert as New Rows, and Keep Text Only.

10. Select the first option, **Insert as New Column**; the first name column is pasted to the left of the phone number column.

11. Click anywhere in the table to deselect.

12. **SAVE** the document in the lesson folder on your flash drive.

PAUSE. LEAVE the document open to use in the next exercise.

Take Note   Instead of using the shortcut menu, you can also use the Cut and Paste commands in the Clipboard group on the Home tab to cut and move rows and columns.

Setting a Table's Horizontal Alignment

Tables inserted into a report should align with the document to maintain the flow of the report. The horizontal alignment for a table can be set to the left or right margins or centered between the margins. In this exercise, you practice using the Table Properties dialog box to set a table's horizontal alignment.

Set a Table's Horizontal Alignment

USE the document that is open from the previous exercise.

1. Position the insertion point anywhere inside the table.

2. On the Layout tab, in the Table group, click the **Select button**, and then click **Select Table**.

3. On the Layout tab, in the Table group, click the **Properties button**. The *Table Properties* dialog box appears.

4. Click the **Table tab** to make it the active tab.

5. In the Alignment section, click **Center**, as shown in Figure 6-13.

Figure 6-13

Table Properties dialog box

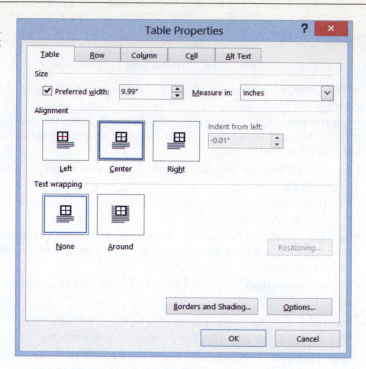

6. Click **OK**. The table is centered horizontally on the page.

7. Click anywhere within the table to deselect.

8. **SAVE** the document in the lesson folder on your flash drive.

PAUSE. LEAVE the document open to use in the next exercise.

Creating a Header Row

Column headings are usually placed in the header row. A **header row** is the first row of the table that contains information that helps identify the content of a particular column. It is usually formatted differently and should be repeated at the beginning of each new page for tables that extend beyond one page. When you specify a header row in the Table Style Options group, the row is distinguished from the entire table. In this exercise, you practice repeating header rows for lengthy tables.

STEP BY STEP   **Create a Header Row**

USE the document that is open from the previous exercise.

1. Position the insertion point anywhere inside the table. On the Layout tab, in the Table group, click the **Select button**, and then click **Select Table**.

2. Change the font size to **14** pt. By changing the font size in the table, the data extends to the next page.

3. Place the insertion point on the first row of the table.

4. On the Layout tab, in the Rows & Columns group, click **Insert Above**. A new blank row is inserted.

5. On the Design tab, in the Table Style Options group, click the **Header Row check box** to apply a distinctive format to the header row.

6. Type headings in each cell within the first row of the table, as shown in Figure 6-14.

Figure 6-14

Header row

Company Name	Contact Person	¤	Phone Numbers¤	Number of Current Open Positions¤	Position Title¤	Date Posted¤	Notes¤
Contoso Pharmaceuticals¤	Caron¤	Rob¤	469-555-0109¤	0¤	¤	¤	¤
Litware, Inc.¤	Bankert¤	Julie¤	469-555-0167¤	0¤	¤	¤	¤

7. On the Table group of the Layout tab, click the **Select button** and **Select Row**.

8. On the Layout tab, in the Data group, click the **Repeat Header Rows button**. Scroll down and view the headings on the second page.

9. Click anywhere in the table to deselect.

10. Position the insertion point anywhere inside the table. On the Layout tab, in the Table group, click the **Select button**, and then click **Select Table**.

11. Change the font size to **12** pt. As long as the content extends to a new page, the headings will appear regardless of the font size.

12. **SAVE** the document in the lesson folder on your flash drive.

PAUSE. LEAVE the document open to use in the next exercise.

Take Note   Repeating rows are only visible in Print Layout view, Backstage view, or on a printed document.

Sorting a Table's Contents

To **sort** data means to arrange it alphabetically, numerically, or chronologically. Sorting displays data in order so that it can be located more quickly. Text, numbers, or dates can be sorted in ascending or descending order. **Ascending** order sorts text from beginning to end, such as from A to Z, 1 to 10, and January to December. **Descending** order sorts text from the end to the beginning, such as from Z to A, 10 to 1, and December to January. In this exercise, you practice sorting data in a Word table using the Sort dialog box, which you access through the Sort command on the Layout tab in the Data group.

Take Note   You can sort by up to three columns of data in the Sort dialog box. Before beginning the sort process, you must select the column (or columns) to be sorted.

STEP BY STEP   **Sort a Table's Contents**

USE the document that is open from the previous exercise.

1. Place the insertion point on the first column to select the **Company Name** column. On the Table group of the Layout tab, click the **Select button** and **Select Column**.

2. On the Layout tab, in the Data group, click the **Sort button**. The *Sort* dialog box appears, as shown in Figure 6-15. Because you selected the *Company Name* column, the Company Name data is listed in the Sort by text box, with Ascending order selected by default. The column contains text; therefore, the type was listed as Text. The other options under type are Number and Date.

Figure 6-15

Sort dialog box

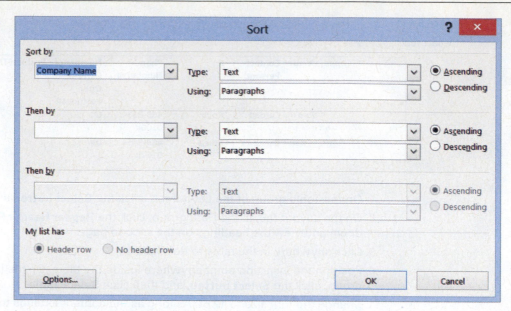

3. Click **OK**. Note that the table now appears sorted in ascending order by company name.

4. **SAVE** the document in the lesson folder on your flash drive.

PAUSE. LEAVE the document open to use in the next exercise.

**CERTIFICATION
READY?** **3.2.3**

How would you sort the
data in a table?

Merging and Splitting Table Cells

The ability to merge and split table cells provides flexibility in customizing tables. To **merge cells** means to combine two or more cells into one. Merging cells is useful for headings that extend over several columns. To **split cells** means to divide one cell into two or more cells. Cells might be split when more than one type of data needs to be placed in one cell. The Split Cells dialog box enables you to split a cell into columns or rows. In this lesson, you practice using commands in the Merge group on the Layout tab to merge and split cells.

STEP BY STEP   **Merge and Split Table Cells**

USE the document that is open from the previous exercise.

1. Position the insertion point on the header row located on page 1. Select the cell that contains the *Contact Person* heading and the empty cell to the right of it.

2. On the Table Tools Layout tab, in the Merge group, click the **Merge Cells button**. The selected cells merge into one cell.

3. In the Position Title column, on the Lucerne Publishing row, select the cell that contains the text *Director Marketing VP Public Relations*.

4. On the Table Tools Layout tab, in the Merge group, click the **Split Cells button** to open the *Split Cells* dialog box as shown in Figure 6-16.

Figure 6-16

Split Cells dialog box

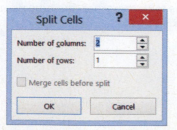

5. Click **OK** to accept the settings as they are. A new column is inserted within the cell.

6. Select the text *VP Public Relations* and drag and drop text to the new column.

7. In the *Company Name* column, select the *Woodgrove Bank* cell.

8. Click the **Split Cells button**. The default setting for the Number of columns is 2, whereas the Number of rows is 1. The Merge cells before split check box is checked. The single cell will be split into two columns.

9. Change the Number of columns setting to **1** and the Number of rows setting to **2** to split the cell into a single column containing two rows, as shown in Figure 6-17. Click **OK**.

Figure 6-17

Cell split into two rows

Company Name¤	Contact Person¤		Phone Numbers¤	Number of Current Open Positions¤	Position Title¤	Date Posted¤	Notes¤	¤
Trey Research¤	Tiano¤	Mike¤	469-555-0182¤	0¤	¤	¤	¤	¤
Wide World Importers¤	Culp¤	Scott¤	469-555-0141¤	0¤	¤	¤	¤	¤
Wingtip Toys¤	Baker¤	Mary¤	972-555-0167¤	1¤	VP Direct Marketing¤	June 1¤	50% Travel required¤	¤
Woodgrove Bank¤	Nash¤	Mike¤	972-555-0189¤	0¤	¤	¤	¤	¤
¤								¤

¶

Another Way
You can access the Merge Cells command on the shortcut menu. The Merge Cells command is visible only when you have multiple cells selected in a table.

10. Place the insertion point in front of *Woodgrove Bank*. Press and hold the **mouse button** to select the two rows within the column. **Right-click**, and then select **Merge Cells**. The cell is now a single row.

11. Click the **Undo**  **button**.

12. **SAVE** the document in the lesson folder on your flash drive.

PAUSE. LEAVE the document open to use in the next exercise.

CERTIFICATION READY? 3.2.7

How do you merge cells?

Changing Cell Margins

Word provides an option to change the cell margins and spacing between cells—you can set the margins for an individual cell or for selected cells. When changes are made in the cell, the appearance of the cell in the table also changes. In this lesson, you practice changing the cell margins and adding spacing between the cells.

STEP BY STEP **Change Cell Margins**

USE the document that is open from the previous exercise.

1. Position the insertion point in the *Phone Numbers* column. In the Table group, click the **Select button**, and click **Select Column**.

2. In the Alignment group, click the **Cell Margins**  **button**. The *Table Options* dialog box opens as shown in Figure 6-18.

Figure 6-18

Table Options dialog box

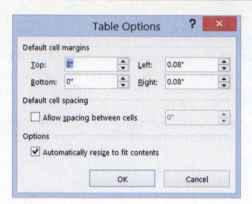

3. Change the top and bottom margins to **0.03**″ by clicking the **up arrow** to change the dimensions.

4. Click **OK**. The phone numbers no longer fit on one line.

5. With the *Phone Numbers* column still selected, click the **Cell Margins** 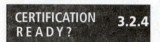 button.

6. Change the left and right margins to **0.03**″ by clicking the **down arrow**.

7. Click **OK**. By Changing the left and right margins automatically adjusted the phone numbers, and now they fit on one line.

8. With the *Phone Numbers* column still selected, click the **Cell Margins** button.

9. Click the **Allow spacing between cells check box** and increase the cell spacing to **0.09**″. You have changed the default cell spacing.

10. Click **OK**. Notice the difference in the spacing between the cells. By default the Automatically resize to fit contents option is turned on.

11. **SAVE** the document in the lesson folder on your flash drive.

PAUSE. LEAVE the document open to use in the next exercise.

CERTIFICATION READY? 3.2.4

How do you change the margins in a cell?

CERTIFICATION READY? 3.2.4

How do you increase the spacing between the cells?

Changing the Position of Text in a Cell

Word provides you with nine options for aligning text in a cell. These options enable you to control the horizontal and vertical alignment of cell text, such as Top Left, Top Center, and Top Right. To change cell text alignment, select the cell or cells you want to align, and click one of the nine alignment buttons in the Alignment group on the Layout tab. In this exercise, you practice changing the text alignment within a cell.

STEP BY STEP   **Change the Position of Text in a Cell**

USE the document that is open from the previous exercise.

1. Select the table's header row on page 1. On the Layout tab in the Table group, click the **Select button**, and then click **Select Row**.

2. In the Alignment group, click the **Align Center** button. The header row is centered horizontally and vertically within the cells.

3. **SAVE** the document in the lesson folder on your flash drive.

PAUSE. LEAVE the document open to use in the next exercise.

Changing the Direction of Text in a Cell

Rotating text in a cell provides additional options for creating interesting and effective tables. Changing the direction of text in a heading can be especially helpful. To change the direction of text in a cell, click the button three times to cycle through the three available directions. In this exercise, you practice changing the direction of text in a cell.

STEP BY STEP	Change the Direction of Text in a Cell

USE the document that is open from the previous exercise.

1. Select the cell that contains the *Company Name* heading.
2. On the Layout tab, in the Alignment group, click the **Text Direction button** three times to rotate the text direction to align to the right cell border, the left cell border, and then back to the top cell border. As you click the **Text Direction button**, the button face rotates to match the rotation of the text direction in the selected cell.
3. **SAVE** the document in the lesson folder on your flash drive.

PAUSE. LEAVE Word open to use in the next exercise.

Splitting a Table

Previously, you learned to split cells where you divided one cell into two or more cells. Splitting a table is dividing one table into two separate tables. In this exercise, you practice separating the table into two tables.

STEP BY STEP	Split Table Cells

USE the document that is open from the previous exercise.

1. Position the insertion point on page 2, and locate *The Phone Company*.
2. On the Layout tab, in the Merge group, click the **Split Table button**. The table is now split and remains in the current page.
3. **SAVE** the document in the lesson folder on your flash drive.

PAUSE. LEAVE Word open to use in the next exercise.

Adding Alternative Text to a Table

Alternative text is a useful interpretation for tables, diagrams, images, and other objects. Alternative text is also used by web browsers—when you hover over the object, text appears describing the object. The title and description that is added can be read to the individual with a disability. In this exercise, you learn to add alternative text to a table.

STEP BY STEP	Add Alternative Text to a Table

USE the document that is open from the previous exercise.

1. Place the insertion point anywhere in the table on page one. On the Tables Tools Layout tab, in the Table group, click **Select**, and then click **Select Table**.
2. Click the **Properties button** in the Tables group.
3. Click the **Alt Text tab** and in the Title box, type **Listing by Company**. In the Description box, type **Contact listing of individuals by company. The listing includes phone numbers, current positions that are open and titles for the contact person**. Click **OK**.
4. **SAVE** the document as *Clients Table Final* in the lesson folder on your flash drive, and then **CLOSE** the file.

PAUSE. LEAVE Word open for the next exercise.

CERTIFICATION READY?   3.1.6

How would you add a title and description as an alternative text?

Converting Text to Table or Table to Text

Text separated by a paragraph mark, tab, comma, or other character can be converted from text to a table or from a table to text. To convert text to a table, first select the text, click the *Insert tab*, click the *Table* button, and finally select *Convert Text to Table*. The Convert Text to Table dialog box appears, and Word determines the number of rows and columns needed based on how the text is separated. After text is converted to a table, the Convert to Text button will be available in the Layout tab in the Table Tools Ribbon. In this exercise, you practice using this technique to convert Word text into a table.

STEP BY STEP   **Convert Text to Table**

OPEN the *Part Numbers* document in your lesson folder.

1. Select the whole document.
2. On the Insert tab, in the Tables group, click the **Table button**. The Table menu appears.
3. Click **Convert Text to Table**. The *Convert Text to Table* dialog box opens. Word recognizes the number of columns and rows and places the number 10 in the Number of rows box—notice that it is shaded gray, making it unavailable to change (see Figure 6-19). Keep the default settings.

Figure 6-19

Convert Text to Table dialog box

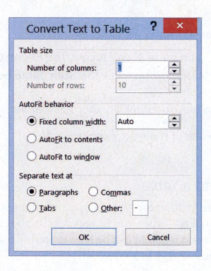

4. Click **OK**. The selected text was separated by paragraph marks, and by selecting the default of **one column**, Word converts the text to a table as shown in Figure 6-20. The Table Tools automatically opens.

Figure 6-20

Document converted from text
to a table

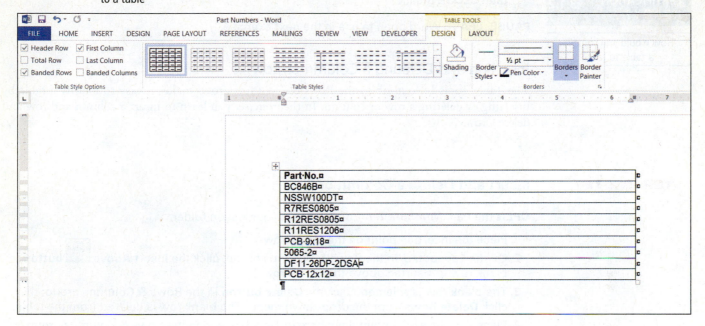

5. In the Table group, select the **Table**. Then in the Cell Size group, click the **AutoFit button** and select **AutoFit Contents**.

6. On the Layout tab, click the **Properties button** in the Table group, and then select the **Table tab**. Center the table. Click **OK**.

7. **SAVE** the document as *Part Numbers Table* in the lesson folder on your flash drive.

PAUSE. LEAVE the document open to use in the next exercise.

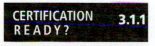

CERTIFICATION READY?   3.1.1

How would you convert text
to a table?

STEP BY STEP   **Convert Table to Text**

USE the document that is open from the previous exercise.

1. Position the insertion point anywhere in the table and click the **Layout tab**.

2. In the Table group, click the **Select button**, and then click **Select Table** to select the entire table.

3. In the Data group, click **Convert to Text**. The *Convert Table to Text* dialog box opens. The default setting in the *Convert Table to Text* dialog box is Paragraph marks. A table can be converted to text and separated by paragraph marks, tabs, commas, and other characters (see Figure 6-21).

Figure 6-21

Convert Table to Text
dialog box

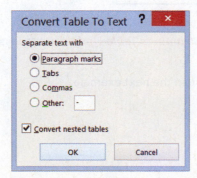

4. Click **OK**. The document is converted to text separated by paragraph marks.

5. **SAVE** the document as *Part Numbers Text* in the lesson folder on your flash drive, and then **CLOSE** the file.

PAUSE. LEAVE Word open to use in the next exercise.

CERTIFICATION READY?   **3.1.2**

How would you convert a table to text?

Inserting and Deleting a Column or Row

The Table Tools Layout tab in the Rows & Columns group makes it easy to modify a table by inserting or deleting a row or column. In the exercise, you learn to insert a column and row and delete a row.

STEP BY STEP   **Insert and Delete a Column or Row**

OPEN the *Part Numbers Table* document in your lesson folder.

1. Place the insertion point on the fourth row.

2. On the Layout tab, in the Rows & Columns group, click the **Insert Above** button; a blank row is inserted above the fourth row.

3. The blank row is selected. Click the **Delete button** in the Rows & Columns group; then click **Delete Rows** from the drop-down menu. The blank row is deleted from the table.

4. Place your insertion point anywhere in the table, and in the Rows & Columns group, click the **Insert Right** button. A new column is inserted to the right.

5. With the column still selected, move the insertion point to the right along the top border of the table to the plus symbol.

6. Click the **plus ⊕ symbol** to insert a new column between the two original columns. This is a *new* table feature for Word 2013. The plus symbol also appears if you need to insert a new row.

7. **Right-click** on the selected column and click **Delete Columns**.

8. Type the text as shown in Figure 6-22.

Figure 6-22

Sample of table document

Part·No.¤	Cost·Per·Unit¤
BC846B¤	12.50¤
NSSW100DT¤	84.00¤
R7RES0805¤	46.00¤
R12RES0805¤	78.00¤
R11RES1206¤	15.00¤
PCB·9x18¤	65.00¤
5065-2¤	45.00¤
DF11-26DP-2DSA¤	102.00¤
PCB·12x12¤	23.00¤

9. **SAVE** the document as *Part Numbers Table Update* in the lesson folder on your flash drive.

PAUSE. LEAVE Word open to use in the next exercise.

Using Formulas in a Table

As you learned previously, you can create tables in Word that contain data and numbers. Word provides options to use **formulas** to calculate a total, calculate an average, determine the highest/lowest number, and count values. These are simple functions that are used in Excel and can also be used in Word. Just like in Excel, formulas begin with an equal symbol followed by the function that you want to perform, such as SUM, AVERAGE, MAX, MIN, and COUNT. You can also use the math operators to perform addition, subtraction, division, and multiplication by the **cell range**. A cell range is identified by two or more cells within the table. The same rules that you learned in your math class also apply here when using formulas in your table. If you want to perform a certain action first, set the order of operation.

Formulas in a table can also be written by cell address location. For instance, columns are identified by letters beginning with *A* and rows are identified with numbers beginning with *1*. See the sample table with column and row headings in Table 6-1. To begin a formula, you first place your insertion point in the cell location where you want the formula to appear. In Table 6-1, the first formula begins in a blank cell, E1, and the formula is written by cell address location where the values appear =B1+C1+D1. The SUM function can be used to obtain the same result, and it is displayed as =SUM(LEFT). Two different approaches can be used to add the values in the cell range and get the same result. See Table 6-2 for descriptions of types of formulas and functions.

A number format can be applied to a selected cell. The available format options consists of a pound symbol (#), zero decimal places, a comma, a currency system ($), two-decimal places, percentage symbol (%), and parentheses ( ). Selecting any one of these changes the format of the number for that cell.

Sometimes it is necessary to edit a value and update the field with the new total, average, or another function that was applied. To update a field, select the field, right-click, and then select *Update Field*.

A **field code** is a placeholder where the function appears—it appears as {=SUM(ABOVE)}. When applying functions, only the result appears—by default, the field codes are not displayed. The field codes can be turned on in Backstage, Options, and then select *Advanced*; in the Show document content section, click the check box by Show field codes instead of their values. There are three options on how a field code appears in the table: Never, Always, and When Selected. Note that the function is enclosed with curly brackets.

Table 6-2 describes each of the functions. Word provides many more functions—not all functions are listed. In the exercise, you learn to apply a simple function to calculate values, apply a number format, and display the field codes.

Table 6-1

Sample of table columns and rows

	A	B	C	D	E
1	Dresses	123	87	456	
2	Pants	456	659	456	
3	Skirts	987	456	78	

Table 6-2

Formula Functions

File Type	Description
=SUM(ABOVE)	Adds the values in the range above cell.
=SUM(LEFT)	Adds the values in the range to the left of the cell.
=A1+A2+A3+A4	Adds values by cell address location.
=SUM(A1:A4)	Adds the value by using the range arguments. The cell address to the left of the colon is the beginning of the range, and the cell address to the right of the colon is the last cell in the range.
=AVERAGE(ABOVE)	Averages values in the range above the cell.
=AVERAGE(LEFT)	Averages values in the range to the left of the cell.
=MAX(ABOVE)	Displays the highest value in the range above the cell.
=MAX(LEFT)	Displays the highest value in the range to the left of the cell.
=MIN(ABOVE)	Displays the lowest value in the range above the cell.
=MIN(LEFT)	Displays the lowest value in the rage to the left of the cell.
=COUNT(ABOVE)	Counts values above the cell.
=COUNT(LEFT)	Counts values to the left of the cell.

STEP BY STEP   Use Formulas in a Table

USE the document that is open from the previous exercise.

1. Place the insertion point on the last row.
2. In the Rows & Columns group, click **Insert Below**. A new row is inserted below the last row.
3. Type **Total Cost** in the first column, last row. Bold the text and align right.
4. Position the insertion point in the second column, last row. You will calculate the total using the *Formula* dialog box.
5. On the Table Tools Layout tab, in the Data group, click the **Formula** fx **button**. The *Formula* dialog box opens (see Figure 6-23). If you are familiar with Excel, then you will notice the similarities in the Formula button. Refer to Table 6-2 for the formula functions.

Figure 6-23

Formula dialog box

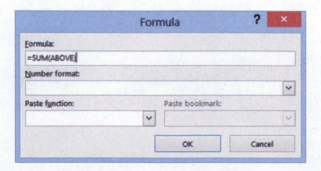

6. By default, the =SUM(Above) formula displays. This function totals the values listed previously in the second column. Word automatically detects values in a table when using the Formula button.

7. Click **OK** to accept the default and close the *Formula* dialog box.
8. **SAVE** the document as ***Part Numbers Update*** in the lesson folder on your flash drive.

PAUSE. LEAVE the document open to use in the next exercise.

STEP BY STEP | **Apply a Number Format**

USE the document that is open from the previous exercise.

1. Place the insertion point in the *470.5* value. By default, the cell value is shaded in gray. This value appears with one decimal place. To change the formatting of the decimal places, open the **Formula** dialog box again by clicking on the **Formula button**.

2. Click the drop-down arrow in the Number format section and select the third option, **$#,##0.00;($#,##0.00)** as shown in Figure 6-24.

Figure 6-24

Number format options

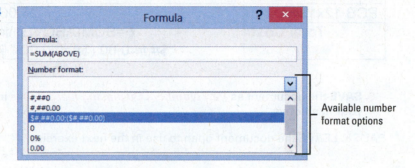

Available number format options

3. Click **OK**. This option inserts a currency symbol, a comma (the thousand place separator), and two decimal places.

4. Select all values in the second column and select **Align Center Right** from the Alignment group on the Layout tab.

5. **SAVE** the document as *Part Numbers First Update* in the lesson folder on your flash drive.

PAUSE. LEAVE the document open to use in the next exercise.

STEP BY STEP | **Update Fields**

USE the document that is open from the previous exercise.

1. Select the **12.50** value and change the value to **15.40**.

2. Place the insertion point in the *$470.50* value, **right-click**, and then click **Update Field**. Notice that the total cost value has been updated.

3. **SAVE** the document as *Part Numbers Final* in the lesson folder on your flash drive.

PAUSE. LEAVE the document open to use in the next exercise.

STEP BY STEP | **Display Field Codes**

USE the document that is open from the previous exercise.

1. Click the **File tab**, and then click **Options**.

2. Click **Advanced**.

3. Under the section, *Show document content*, click the **check box** by *Show field codes instead of their values*. By the Field shading area, *When selected* is showing—leave the default settings. The other options available are Never and Always.

4. Click **OK** to close the dialog box and accept the settings.

5. Your insertion point should be in the second column. In the Table group, click **Select**, and then click **Select Column**. Change the width to **2.7"** in the Cell Size group (see Figure 6-25).

Figure 6-25

Display of field codes in table

Part·No.¤	Cost·Per·Unit¤	¤
BC846B¤		15.40¤¤
NSSW100DT¤		84.00¤¤
R7RES0805¤		46.00¤¤
R12RES0805¤		78.00¤¤
R11RES1206¤		15.00¤¤
PCB·9x18¤		65.00¤¤
5065-2¤		45.00¤¤
DF11-26DP-2DSA¤		102.00¤¤
PCB·12x12¤		23.00¤¤
Total·Cost¤	{ ·=SUM(ABOVE)·\#·¤ "$#,##0.00;($#,##0.00)"·}¤	

6. SAVE the document as *Part Numbers Displaying Field Codes* in the lesson folder on your flash drive.

PAUSE. LEAVE the document open to use in the next exercise.

STEP BY STEP   **Disable Field Codes**

USE the document that is open from the previous exercise.

1. Click the **File tab**, and then click **Options**.
2. Click **Advanced**.
3. Under the section, *Show document content*, click the **check box** by *Show field codes instead of their values* to remove the check mark.
4. Click **OK** to close the dialog box. When disabling field codes in a table, the value where the formula was entered appears.

PAUSE. LEAVE the document open to use in the next exercise.

Using Object Zoom

In Lesson 2, you learn about the Zoom group and the new Read Mode view. Microsoft has enhanced reading documents using the Object Zoom. **Object Zoom** is *new* in Read Mode and allows you to zoom in on objects such as tables, charts, and images. In this exercise, you practice using the Object Zoom in Read Mode.

STEP BY STEP   **Use Object Zoom**

USE the document that is open from the previous exercise.

1. Click the **View tab** and select **Read Mode** to change the page layout of the document.
2. **Double-click** the table to zoom in on the table. The table appears with a magnifier beside it and a shadow background of the document appears behind the table.
3. Click the **magnifier button** to zoom in to the table. The table fills the screen, which makes it easier for reading.
4. Click the **magnifier button** again to zoom out.
5. Click anywhere outside of the table to exit the object zoom feature and return to the document in Read Mode.

Another Way
You can also exit from the object zoom feature by pressing the *Esc* key once, and exiting the Read Mode by pressing the *Esc* key again.

6. Click **View** on the menu, and then select **Edit Document** to return to the document screen.

7. **SAVE** the document with the same filename in the lesson folder on your flash drive.

CLOSE Word.

SKILL SUMMARY

In This Lesson, You Learned To:	Exam Objective	Objective Number
Create a Table	Define table dimensions.	3.1.3
	Demonstrate how to use Quick Tables.	3.1.5
Format a Table	Apply styles to tables.	3.2.1
	Modify fonts within tables.	3.2.2
Manage Tables	Set AutoFit options.	3.1.4
	Modify table dimensions.	3.2.6
	Sort table data.	3.2.3
	Merge cells.	3.2.7
	Configure cell margins	3.2.4
	Set a table title.	3.1.6
	Convert text to tables.	3.1.1
	Convert tables to text.	3.1.2
Use Formulas in a Table	Demonstrate how to apply formulas to a table.	3.2.5
Use Object Zoom		

Knowledge Assessment

Multiple Choice

Select the best response for the following statements.

1. Using the Sort feature in a table sorts selected content in what order?
   a. Ascending
   b. Descending
   c. Alphabetical order
   d. All of the above

2. Combining two or more cells into one cell uses a Word feature called:
   a. Split Cells.
   b. Merge Cells.
   c. Merge All Cells.
   d. Merge Selected Cells.

3. An arrangement of data made up of horizontal rows and vertical columns is called a:
   a. menu.
   b. heading.
   c. table.
   d. merge.

4. Built-in preformatted tables that can be inserted and used in your documents are called:
   a. Table Style Options.
   b. Tables.
   c. Quick Tables.
   d. Insert Tables.

5. The rectangles that are formed when rows and columns intersect are known as:
   a. cells.
   b. merged cells.

   c. split cells.

   d. tables.

6. Which sort order sorts text from the end to the beginning?
   a. Descending
   b. Ascending
   c. Plunging
   d. Downward

7. Sorted data can consist of:
   a. text.
   b. numbers.
   c. dates.
   d. All of the above

8. Which option would you choose to arrange data alphabetically, numerically, or chronologically?
   a. Filter
   b. Group
   c. Sort
   d. Category dialog box

9. When you create a table in Word, two new Ribbon tabs appear. Which of the following is in the Table Tools tab?
   a. Page Layout
   b. Design
   c. Insert
   d. Merge Cells

10. The first row of a table that is formatted differently than the rest of the table and contains information to identify the data in the column is called a:
    a. total row.
    b. banded column.
    c. header column.
    d. header row.

True/False

Circle T if the statement is true or F if the statement is false.

T F **1.** When you know how many rows and columns you need in a table, the quickest way to create the table is by dragging over the grid in the Table menu.

T F **2.** A formula can be applied by using only the functions that are available in Word.

T F **3.** When Word converts text to tables, it uses paragraph marks, tabs, and commas to determine how to organize the data within the table.

T F **4.** You can move a column or row using Cut and Paste.

T F **5.** Sorting can only sort one column of data at a time.

T F **6.** If a hyphen exists within a section of text, and you are converting that text to a table, the hyphen will create a new column.

T F **7.** Text can be aligned both horizontally and vertically in a cell.

T F **8.** Word provides four options for changing the direction of text in a cell.

T F **9.** You can sort single-level lists, such as bulleted or numbered lists in a table.

T F **10.** The Repeat Header Rows button is used for tables that extend to multiple pages.

Competency Assessment

Project 6-1: Creating a Placements Table

Ms. Archer, the executive recruiter, asks you to start working on a placements table that will list the candidates that have been placed, the companies that hired them, and the date of hire.

GET READY. LAUNCH Word if it is not already running.

1. **OPEN** *Placements* from the data files for this lesson.
2. **SAVE** the document as *6-1 Placements Table* in the lesson folder on your flash drive.
3. Place the insertion point in the last column. On the Layout tab, in the Table group, click the **Select button** and **Select Column**.
4. On the Layout tab, in the Cell Size group, click the **up arrow** in the Width box until it reads **1.3″**.
5. Select the first column in the table.
6. On the Layout tab, in the Cell Size group, click the **down arrow** in the Width box until it reads **.9″**.
7. Select the **Company column** and change the width to **1.5″**.
8. On the Design tab, in the Table Style Options group, click the **Header Row check box** and **Banded Rows check box** to enable. Place your insertion point within the table.
9. On the Design tab, in the Table Styles group, select the **Grid Table 4 – Accent 4 style**.
10. Select the last column in the table.
11. On the Layout tab, in the Data group, click the **Sort button** to open the *Sort* dialog box.
12. Under the *My list has* section, make sure the **Header row option button** is selected. Click **OK**. This sorts the column by date.
13. With the table selected, on the Layout tab, in the Table group, click the **Properties button**.
14. In the *Table Properties* dialog box, click **Center alignment** in the Table tab.
15. Click the **Alt Text tab** and in the Title box, type **Employee Placements**. In the Description box, type **Employees date of employment**. Click **OK**.
16. Select the header row.
17. On the Layout tab, in the Alignment group, click **Align Center**.
18. **SAVE** the document in the lesson folder on your flash drive, and then **CLOSE** the file.

LEAVE Word open for the next project.

Project 6-2: Quarterly Sales Data

Create a table showing the quarterly sales for Coho Vineyard.

GET READY. LAUNCH Word if it is not already running.

1. Create a new blank document.
2. **SAVE** the document as *6-2 Quarterly Sales* in the lesson folder on your flash drive.
3. On the Insert tab, in the Tables group, click the **Table button**. Drag to create a table that has 5 columns and 6 rows.
4. Enter the following data in the table as shown: Note: Press **Shift+Enter** to insert a line break after typing *Vineyard*.

Coho Vineyard 20XX				
	First Quarter	Second Quarter	Third Quarter	Fourth Quarter
Mark Hanson	19,098	25,890	39,088	28,789
Terry Adams	21,890	19,567	32,811	31,562
Max Benson	39,400	35,021	19,789	21,349
Cathan Cook	34,319	27,437	28,936	19,034

5. Select the first row. On the Layout tab, in the Merge group, click the **Merge Cells button**.

6. With the row still selected, center the title by clicking the **Align Center button** in the Alignment group on the Layout tab.

7. On the Design tab, in the Table Style Options group, click the **Last Column check box** to enable. The Header Row, First Column, and Banded Rows options should be turned on already.

8. On the Design tab, in the Table Styles gallery, click the **More button** to display the gallery. Under the List Table group, select **List Table 1 Light - Accent 6**.

9. Insert a column after *Fourth Quarter* by placing the insertion point above the end of row markers, and then clicking the **plus ⊕ symbol**.

10. Merge the last column with the title by selecting the first row, right-click, and select **Merge Cells**.

11. Type **Total** in last column. In the Alignment group, select **Align Center**.

12. Position the insertion point in the blank cell below *Total*. In the Data group, select **Formula**. The Formula box displays =SUM(LEFT); this totals the values to the left.

13. In the Number format box, click the **drop-down arrow** and select the third option **$#,##0.00;($#,##0.00)**.

14. Click **OK**.

15. Position the insertion point in the next blank cell and in the Data group, select **Formula**. Edit the formula by double-clicking on the text **ABOVE** and typing **LEFT**. Make sure you type the function inside the parentheses.

16. Apply the same number format that you selected in step 13. Click **OK**.

17. Position the insertion point in the next blank cell and in the Data group, and select **Formula**.

18. In the Formula box, delete **SUM(ABOVE)**—do not delete the equal sign.

19. In the Paste function box, click the **drop-down arrow** and select **SUM**. Place the insertion point inside the parentheses and type **LEFT**.

20. Apply the same number format that you completed in step 13.

21. Click **OK**.

22. Position the insertion point in the last blank cell and in the Data group, select **Formula**.

23. Edit the formula by **double-clicking** on the text **ABOVE** and typing **LEFT**.

24. Apply the same number format that you completed in step 13.

25. Click **OK**.

26. **SAVE** the document with the same filename in the lesson folder on your flash drive.

27. On the Layout tab, click the **Select button** in the Table group, and then choose **Select Table** from the drop-down menu.

28. In the Data group, select **Convert to Text**, and then select **Tabs**. Click **OK**.

29. **SAVE** the document as *6-2 Quarterly Sales2* in the lesson folder on your flash drive, and then **CLOSE** the file.

LEAVE Word open for the next project.

Proficiency Assessment

Project 6-3: Sales Table

Ms. Archer asks you to create a sales table including data from the past two years. She can use this table to set goals and project future income.

GET READY. LAUNCH Word if it is not already running.

1. **OPEN** *Sales* from the data files for this lesson.

2. **SAVE** the document as *6-3 Sales Table* in the lesson folder on your flash drive.

3. Select the column headings containing the months and change the text direction for all the months so that they begin at the bottom of the column and extend to the top.

4. Increase the row height of the row containing the months to **0.9** inches so that the text all fits on one line.

5. Use the **AutoFit Contents** for the selected months.

6. Make sure the **Header Row**, **Banded Rows**, and **First Column** Table Style Options are the only ones turned on.

7. Merge all the cells in the first row and align center the heading.

8. Increase the row height to **0.6**.

9. Merge all the cells in the second row and align center the subheading.

10. Choose the **Grid Table 4 - Accent 2 Table Style format**.

11. If necessary, select the heading in the top row and align center again.

12. Center the table horizontally in the *Table Properties* dialog box.

13. Select all values including the blank cells. Increase the Cell Margins to **0.08**″ for the top and bottom of the cells.

14. Increase the spacing between cells to **0.04**″.

15. **SAVE** the document in the lesson folder on your flash drive.

PAUSE. LEAVE the document open for the next exercise.

Project 6-4: Client Contact Table

Ms. Archer would like you to include the average projection in the project that you completed in Project 6-3. After you save the document with the field codes being displayed, return to Backstage and disable.

GET READY. LAUNCH Word if it is not already running.

1. **SAVE** the document as *6-4 Sales Table* in the lesson folder on your flash drive.

2. Replace the column heading *Totals* and type **Average**. Notice the column width automatically adjusts because it has been resized to fit content.

3. Press **Tab** to move the insertion point to the next blank cell.

4. Open the Formula dialog box and edit the formula in the Formula box, by deleting **SUM** and typing **AVERAGE**. Complete the same step for the remaining months.

5. **SAVE** the document in the lesson folder on your flash drive.

6. If necessary, display the field codes. Click **Advanced**, and then under the section *Show document content*, click the check box by Show field codes instead of their values. Leave the Field shading as the default. Click **OK**.

7. Select the table and change the page orientation to **Landscape**, font size **9** pt, alignment **left** from the Paragraph group, and **AutoFit Window**.

8. **SAVE** the document as *6-4 Field Codes in Table* in the lesson folder on your flash drive, and then **CLOSE** the file.

LEAVE Word open for the next project.

Mastery Assessment

Project 6-5: Quarterly Sales Table Update

The Coho Winery's Quarterly Sales Table includes some formatting mistakes. Find and correct the four problems within this document.

 GET READY. LAUNCH Word if it is not already running.

1. **OPEN** *Problem* from the data files for this lesson.

2. **SAVE** the document as *6-5 Fixed Quarterly Sales* in the lesson folder on your flash drive.

3. Find and correct four errors in the table.

4. Apply **AutoFit Contents** and center the table horizontally on the page.

5. Change the Table Styles and select **Grid Table 5 Dark**.

6. Insert a row after *Cathan Cook*.

7. Type **Highest Sales** in the first column, last row.

8. Use the MAX function to calculate the highest sale for each quarter and apply the number format by selecting the second option.

9. **SAVE** the document as *6-5 Fixed Quarterly Sales with Field Codes* in the lesson folder on your flash drive.

10. Turn the field codes off.

11. **SAVE** the document as *6-5 Fixed Quarterly Sales* in the lesson folder on your flash drive, and then **CLOSE** the file.

LEAVE Word open for the next project.

Project 6-6: Soccer Team Roster

As coach of your child's soccer team, you need to distribute a roster to all your players with contact information, uniform numbers, and assigned snack responsibilities. You received a rough list from the league, and you would like to convert it to table form. You haven't converted text to a table before, but you're confident you can do it.

 GET READY. LAUNCH Word if it is not already running.

1. **OPEN** *Soccer Team* from the data files for this lesson.

2. **SAVE** the document as *6-6 Soccer Roster* in the lesson folder on your flash drive

3. Select all the text.

4. Select **Convert Text to Table** from the menu in the Tables group.

5. In the *Convert Text to Table* dialog box, type **4** in the Number of columns box. Click the **Commas** button under the Separate text at section and click **OK**.

6. Use what you learned in this lesson to format the table as shown in Figure 6-26. Start by removing extra words, adjusting column widths for the last column to **1.82**", and aligning text. Sort the table by snack date in ascending order, insert a header row with the following headings for each column (**Name**, **Uniform Number**, **Telephone Numbers**, **Snacks**) and choose the **List Table 6 Colorful – Accent 3** Table Style. Change the header row height to **0.5**".

Figure 6-26

Soccer team roster

Name¤	Uniform·Number¤	Telephone·Numbers¤	Snacks¤	¤
Annette·Hill¤	#·4¤	806-555-0110¤	9/9¤	¤
Brian·Groth¤	#·3¤	806-555-0134¤	9/16¤	¤
Maria·Hammond¤	#2¤	806-555-0175¤	9/23¤	¤
Russell·King¤	#7¤	806-555-0161¤	9/30¤	¤
Lee·Oliver¤	#8¤	806-555-0154¤	10/7¤	¤
Chris·Preston¤	#6¤	806-555-0182¤	10/14¤	¤
Garrett·Young¤	#9¤	806-555-0192¤	10/28¤	¤
Dylan·Miller¤	#1¤	806-555-0149¤	11/4¤	¤
Eric·Parkinson¤	#5¤	806-555-0170¤	11/11¤	¤

7. **SAVE** the document in the lesson folder on your flash drive, and then **CLOSE** the file.

STOP. CLOSE Word.

LESSON SKILL MATRIX

Skill	Exam Objective	Objective Number
Formatting, Creating, and Customizing a Theme	Change document themes.	1.3.2
Formatting a Document Using Style Sets	Change document Style Sets.	1.3.3
Formatting a Document's Background	Insert watermarks.	1.3.5
Using Quick Parts in a Document	Insert Quick Parts.	5.1.1
	Append text to a document.	2.1.1
	Insert Built-in Fields.	2.1.6
Applying and Manipulating Text Boxes	Insert text boxes.	5.1.2
Making Text Graphically Appealing and Inserting a Special Character	Insert special characters (©, ™, £).	2.1.7

© nyul/iStockphoto

KEY TERMS

- AutoText
- building blocks
- document theme
- drop cap
- field
- pull quote
- Style Set
- text box
- Unicode
- watermarks

© nyul/iStockphoto

You are a content manager for Flatland Hosting Company, a position in which you are responsible for writing and editing all client material, such as hosting guidelines and agreements. When creating and revising documents, several Word commands can help you work more efficiently. In this lesson, you learn to apply a theme to a document, and add content to a document using Quick Parts, and insert page numbers, headers, and footers.

SOFTWARE ORIENTATION

The Design Tab

The Design tab is *new* in Word 2013 and it offers several different ways to format a document using Themes or selecting from the Document Formatting gallery. Changing the appearance of the document can capture the attention of your audience. After opening a document, you can access the commands on the Design tab, shown in Figure 7-1. Use this figure as a reference throughout this lesson as well as the rest of the book.

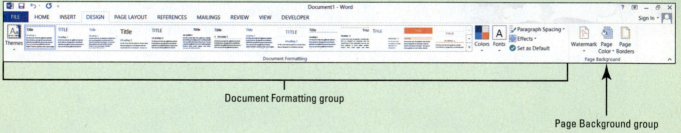

Document Formatting group

Page Background group

Figure 7-1

Design tab

Word provides options to change the appearance of a document with preset, built-in formatting Style Sets using themes or selecting from the Document Formatting gallery. Once a theme or document formatting is applied, the colors, fonts, and effects can be changed or customized. You also have the option to set the formatting as your default without having to reset each time you work on a new document. Another new feature in Word 2013 is Paragraph Spacing—the line and paragraph spacing is quickly changed to predefined values. Changing the appearance of a document's background will definitely grab someone's attention.

FORMATTING, CREATING, AND CUSTOMIZING A THEME

The Bottom Line

Word provides features such as Themes to produce creative and professional documents. In this lesson, you learn to change the appearance of a document using an existing theme, and then create and customize the theme.

Formatting a Document with a Theme

Predefined formatting preferences allow you to change the overall appearance of the document by selecting and applying a theme. A **document theme** is a set of predefined formatting options that includes theme colors, fonts, and effects. In this exercise, you learn how to apply a document theme in Word.

Theme colors contain four text and background colors, six accent colors, and two hyperlink colors. Click the *Colors* button to change the colors for the current theme as shown in Figure 7-2.

Figure 7-2

Colors menu

Theme fonts contain a heading font and a body text font. Click the *Fonts* button to change the fonts for the current theme, as shown in Figure 7-3.

Figure 7-3

Fonts menu

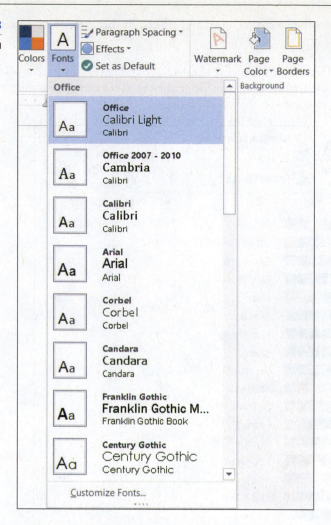

Theme effects are sets of lines and fill effects. Click the *Effects* button to change the effects for the current theme, as shown in Figure 7-4.

Figure 7-4

Effects menu

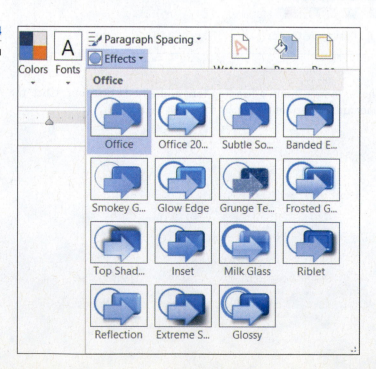

STEP BY STEP   **Format a Document with a Theme**

OPEN the *Hosting* document from the data files for this lesson.

1. On the Design tab, in the Document Formatting group, click **Themes**; the Themes menu opens, as shown in Figure 7-5.

   This document has already been preformatted with styles.

Cross Ref   In Lesson 3, you learn to format text using styles.

Figure 7-5

Document Themes

2. Place your mouse pointer over any built-in theme and notice that the document changes to display a live preview of the theme.

Take Note   Applying a theme changes the overall design of the entire document.

3. Click the **View theme** and the elements are applied to the document. Scroll down and view the changes in the document.

4. SAVE the document as *Hosting Term* in the lesson folder on your flash drive.

PAUSE. LEAVE the document open to use in the next exercise.

CERTIFICATION READY?   1.3.2

How do you change a document's theme?

Creating and Customizing a Document Theme

In a business environment, the company might want to show consistency by customizing a theme to be used for reports throughout the organization. In this exercise, you create, customize, and apply a new theme to a document.

STEP BY STEP   **Create and Customize a Document Color**

USE the document that is open from the previous exercise.

1. In the Document Formatting group, click the **Colors button** to open the Colors menu (refer to Figure 7-2). The Colors menu contains predefined formatting colors with four text and background colors, six accent colors, and two hyperlink colors. These colors can be customized and saved with a new name.

2. At the bottom of the Colors menu, click **Customize Colors**; the *Create New Theme Colors* dialog box opens (see Figure 7-6).

Figure 7-6

Create New Theme Colors dialog box

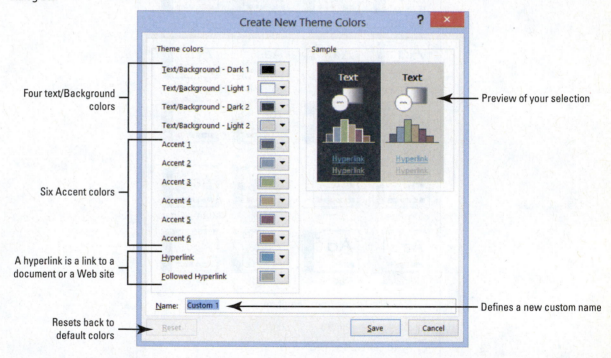

Four text/Background colors

Six Accent colors

A hyperlink is a link to a document or a Web site

Resets back to default colors

Preview of your selection

Defines a new custom name

Take Note   Throughout this chapter, you see information that appears within brackets, such as [your e-mail address]. The information contained in the brackets is intended to be directions for you rather than something you actually type word for word. It instructs you to perform an action or substitute text. Do *not* type the actual text that appears within brackets.

3. In the Name box, replace *Custom 1* by typing **Corporate [your initials]**.

4. Click **Save**; the dialog box closes and you have defined a new custom theme color name based on default colors.

Another Way

You can edit the Colors and Fonts in the Styles group, under Styles or use the shortcut keys, *ALT+CTRL+SHIFT+S*.

5. Click **Colors** and under the Custom section, place your insertion point over **Corporate [your initials]**. **Right-click** the theme name, and then click **Edit** from the shortcut menu that appears. The *Edit Theme Colors* dialog box appears.

6. In the list of theme colors, click the **Accent 2 drop-down arrow** to produce a menu of colors for this element.

CERTIFICATION
READY? **1.3.2**

How would you create a customized color and apply it to a document?

7. Select **Tan, Text 2, Darker 50%**.

8. Click **Save**. You changed the default color to a specific color and created your own custom theme colors for your document.

9. **SAVE** the document in the lesson folder on your flash drive.

PAUSE. LEAVE the document open to use in the next exercise.

STEP BY STEP | **Create and Customize a Document Font**

USE the document that is open from the previous exercise.

1. Click the **Fonts button** to produce the Fonts menu (refer to Figure 7-3). In the menu, click **Customize Fonts**; the *Create New Theme Fonts* dialog box opens.

2. In the Name box, replace *Custom 1* by typing **Corporate Fonts [your initials]**.

3. Change the Heading Font and Body Font to **Arial**.

   Notice the preview of your font choices that appears in the Sample pane of the dialog box.

4. Click **Save** to close the dialog box and apply your font choices to the document.

5. **SAVE** the document in the lesson folder on your flash drive.

PAUSE. LEAVE the document open to use in the next exercise.

CERTIFICATION
READY? **1.3.2**

How would you create a customized font and apply it to a document?

Take Note | A quick way to change fonts is by typing the font name in the Font box.

STEP BY STEP | **Create and Customize Document Effects**

USE the document that is open from the previous exercise.

1. Position the insertion point anywhere in the document.

2. Click the **Effects button** and select **Glossy** from the menu that appears (refer to Figure 7-4).

   When applying shapes to your document, such as a bevel shape, the shape displays based on the effect you selected. Notice the change in the bevel shape on page 1 next to the second paragraph under the heading *Introduction* (see Figure 7-7).

Figure 7-7

Sample bevel shape with effects

Applying one of the Effects produces a different effect on the bevel shape →

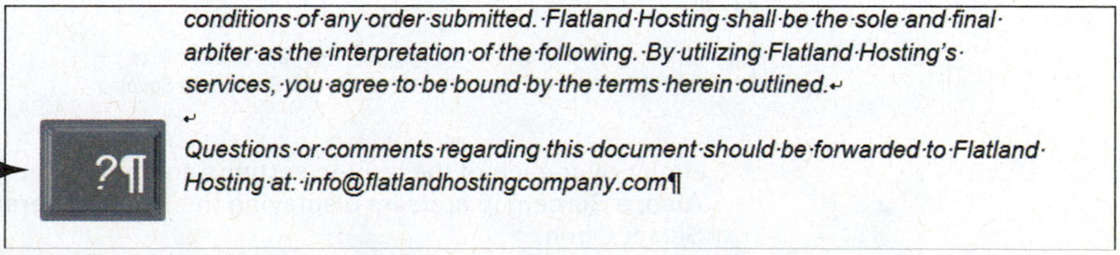

conditions·of·any·order·submitted.·Flatland·Hosting·shall·be·the·sole·and·final·arbiter·as·the·interpretation·of·the·following.·By·utilizing·Flatland·Hosting's·services,·you·agree·to·be·bound·by·the·terms·herein·outlined.↵

Questions·or·comments·regarding·this·document·should·be·forwarded·to·Flatland·Hosting·at:·info@flatlandhostingcompany.com¶

3. **SAVE** the document as *Hosting Term1* in your flash drive in the lesson folder.

PAUSE. LEAVE the document open to use in the next exercise.

CERTIFICATION
READY? **1.3.2**

How would you create a customized effect and apply it to a document?

Take Note Document formatting is the same throughout all Office programs, and documents can share the same appearance.

Applying Paragraph Spacing

Applying the paragraph spacing changes the line and paragraph spacing for the entire document. You can apply one of the predefined options or customize your own. When you customize paragraph spacing, the Manage Styles dialog box opens and you have the option to create a new style, edit styles, and restrict styles. Note that the Manage Styles feature will not be covered in this lesson because it is an advanced command. You also have an option to return the document back to the default settings.

STEP BY STEP	**Apply Paragraph Spacing**

USE the document that is open from the previous exercise.

1. Position the insertion point anywhere in the first paragraph. In the Document Formatting group, click the **Paragraph Spacing** button. The built-in menu appears (see Figure 7-8).

Figure 7-8

Paragraph Spacing Style Set

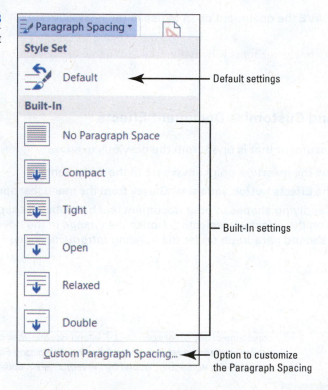

2. Hover over each of the built-in settings and notice the changes on the whole document. Also, a ScreenTip appears displaying the line and paragraph setting for that option. Select **Open**.

3. **SAVE** the document as *Hosting Term2* in your flash drive in the lesson folder.

PAUSE. LEAVE the document open to use in the next exercise.

FORMATTING A DOCUMENT USING STYLE SETS

The Bottom Line	Word 2013 has a *new* group called *Document Formatting* on the Design tab. The Document Formatting group contains many different Style Sets that change the appearance of the whole document.

Applying a Style Set to a Document

In Lesson 3, you learn to apply styles to text using the gallery of styles, and in this section you apply Style Sets that will affect the whole document. These **Style Sets** are predefined styles with fonts and paragraph spacing defined. You have an option to reset the document back to its default or save a new Style Set. In this exercise, you learn to apply a Style Set.

STEP BY STEP	**Apply a Style Set to a Document**

USE the document that is open from the previous exercise.

1. Hover the mouse over a few of the built-in Style Sets in the Document Formatting group and watch how the appearance of the document changes. Note, before applying Style Sets, the document must contain styles.

 Cross Ref In Lesson 3, you learn to apply styles to text and modify styles.

2. Click the **More** ☐ **button** and select **Lines (Distinctive)** as shown in Figure 7-9.

Figure 7-9

Document Formatting Style Sets

3. **SAVE** the document as *Hosting Term3* in your flash drive in the lesson folder, and then **CLOSE** the file.

PAUSE. LEAVE the document open to use in the next exercise.

CERTIFICATION READY? 1.3.3

How would you change a document's style?

FORMATTING A DOCUMENT'S BACKGROUND

The Bottom Line

Word's enhanced features allow the user to produce a creatively formatted document by changing the background color, inserting a watermark, and adding a border to the document.

Inserting a Page Color

Adding a background color to the title page of a report conveys originality. For example, you might want to distinguish your research paper from others by adding a background color to the first page. It is important to use background colors in moderation and to choose a page color that will not interfere with the text. If text is dark, for example, the background color should be light. If text is light, a dark background would improve the document's readability. Word also lets you add interesting Fill Effects for the Page Background, such as gradients, textures, patterns, and pictures. In this exercise, you learn to insert a page color in a document.

STEP BY STEP   **Insert a Page Color**

OPEN the *Hosting* document from the data files for this lesson.

1. Click the **Design tab**.
2. In the Page Background group, click the **Page Color button** to open the color menu and gallery, as shown in Figure 7-10.

Figure 7-10

Page Color menu

3. Click to select **White, Background 1, Darker 5%**; the page color is applied.
4. **SAVE** the document as *Hosting Term4* in your flash drive in the lesson folder.

PAUSE. LEAVE the document open to use in the next exercise.

Formatting the Page Color Background

You can apply formatting to a page color background with one color or with a fill effect, such as gradient, texture, pattern, or a picture. A gradient fill is a shape fill that changes from one color to another based on the shading style selected or applied with one of the preset colors. The layout of the page colors provides emphasis to the document. In this exercise, you learn to format the page background using two colors and changing the shading style.

STEP BY STEP   **Format the Page Color Background**

USE the document that is open from the previous exercise.

1. With the Design tab active, click the **Page Color button**, to display the menu.
2. Click **Fill Effects**. The *Fill Effects* dialog box opens with the Gradient tab active.
3. Under the Colors section, select **Preset**.
4. Click the Preset colors **drop-down arrow** to view available background colors in the Sample area.

5. In the Gradient tab under the Colors section, change your selection to **Two colors**. Two options appear, Color 1 and Color 2.

6. Under Color 2, click the **drop-down arrow** to produce the color palette. Select **Black, Text 1, Lighter 50%**. The selected color appears in the box under Color 2 (see Figure 7-11).

Figure 7-11

Fill Effects dialog box

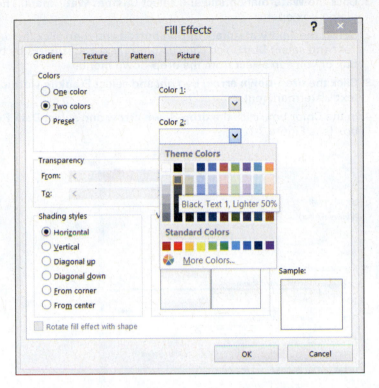

7. Under the Variants section, samples of the two colors are displayed. Under the Shading Styles section, you have choices on how the style should appear in the document. Select **From Center**. Notice the lower-right corner produces the Color 1 in the Center and Color 2 outside. Click **OK**.

8. **SAVE** the document as *Hosting Term5* in the lesson folder on your flash drive.

PAUSE. LEAVE the document open to use in the next exercise.

Inserting a Watermark

In business, some documents might contain sensitive information, and the nature of a document's status should be clearly conveyed on its pages. Word provides built-in text called ==watermarks== that display lightly behind text as words, such as *confidential*, *draft*, or *urgent*. Watermarks can be customized to include text or images, including company logos. In this exercise, you learn to insert a watermark using text, an image, and a custom watermark.

Insert a Watermark

USE the document that is open from the previous exercise.

1. In the Page Background group of the Design tab, click the **Watermark menu** and select **Confidential 1**.

   The watermark is placed behind the text and is semitransparent.

CERTIFICATION READY?   **1.3.5**

How do you insert a watermark?

2. **SAVE** the document with the same filename in the lesson folder on your flash drive.

PAUSE. LEAVE the document open to use in the next exercise.

STEP BY STEP   **Insert a Custom Watermark**

USE the document that is open from the previous exercise.

1. Click the **Watermark menu** and select **Custom Watermark**. The *Printed Watermark* dialog box opens.

2. Select the **Text watermark option button** and then click the **drop-down arrow** next to *Text* and select **Draft**. You can customize text watermarks by typing content in the text box or you can select from the drop-down menu.

3. Click the **drop-down arrow** by *Font* and select **Franklin Gothic Book**. This changes the text watermark font.

4. In the Color box, click the **drop-down arrow** and select **Dark Red** in the Standard Colors box (see Figure 7-12).

Figure 7-12

Printed Watermark dialog box

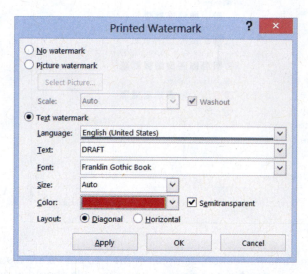

5. Click **OK**. The watermark is inserted on all pages. If you click **Apply**, the dialog box remains open and you can view your watermark in the document. When you click **OK**, the dialog box closes and you're back in the document screen.

6. **SAVE** the document as *Hosting Draft* in the lesson folder on your flash drive.

PAUSE. LEAVE the document open to use in the next exercise.

CERTIFICATION READY?   1.3.5

How do you insert a custom watermark?

STEP BY STEP   **Insert an Image Watermark**

USE the document that is open from the previous exercise.

1. Remove the Page Color background, by clicking the **Page Color button**, and then selecting **No Color**. The background is removed.

2. Click the **Watermark menu** and select **Custom Watermark**. The *Printed Watermark* dialog box opens.

3. Select the **Picture watermark option button** and then click the **Select Picture button**.

4. Click the **Browse button** next to From a file, and then locate your lesson folder and select *Internet Search*.

5. Click **Insert** to insert the image in the document, and then click **OK** to close the *Printed Watermark* dialog box.

6. **SAVE** the document as *Hosting with Image* in the lesson folder on your flash drive.

PAUSE. LEAVE the document open to use in the next exercise.

CERTIFICATION READY?   1.3.5

How do you insert a picture watermark?

STEP BY STEP   **Remove a Watermark**

USE the document that is open from the previous exercise.

1. Open the **Watermark menu** and select **Remove Watermark**. The watermark is removed from the document.

2. Click the **Undo** **button**.

3. **SAVE** the document in the lesson folder on your flash drive, and then **CLOSE** the file.

PAUSE. LEAVE Word open for the next exercise.

🔍 **Cross Ref**   Later in this lesson, you learn to insert a watermark using the Building Blocks Organizer.

Adding a Page Border

The Page Borders command allows you to insert a border around a document's page. Adding a border improves the appearance of the document. Applying elements by changing the color, width, and style adds emphasis to the page. In this lesson, you learn to add elements to a page border and insert them into a document.

STEP BY STEP   **Add a Page Border**

1. **OPEN** the *Hosting Term5* document you created earlier.

2. In the Page Background group of the Design tab, click the **Page Borders button**. The *Borders and Shading* dialog box appears with Page Border as the active tab.

3. In the Setting section, click the **Shadow option**. Notice the Preview area displays a shadow effect on the bottom and right border.

4. Click the **drop-down arrow** on the Color menu and choose **Black, Text 1, Lighter 5%**. You apply a specific color to the border.

5. Click the **drop-down arrow** on the **Width menu** and choose **2 1/4 pt**. The width of the border is increased to provide emphasis.

6. Click the **drop-down arrow** on the **Apply to menu** and click **This section–First page only** as shown in Figure 7-13. The page border is applied only to the first page of this section.

Figure 7-13

Borders and Shading
dialog box

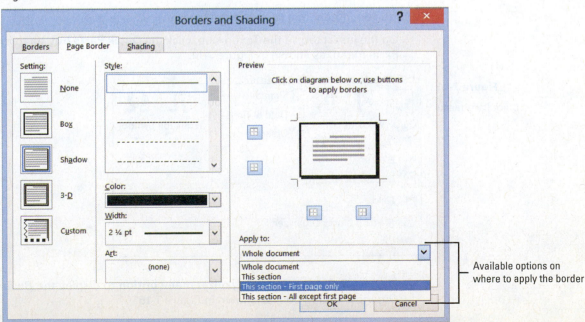

7. Click **OK**.

Scroll and review your document, and notice that the border does not appear on other pages.

8. Select the bevel shape on page 1 and press **Delete**. Hint: you need to see a solid border to delete the shape.

9. **SAVE** the document as *Hosting Term6* in the lesson folder on your flash drive.

PAUSE. LEAVE the document open to use in the next exercise.

 Cross Ref   In Lesson 4, you learn to place a border around text and paragraphs using the Borders and Shading dialog box.

USING QUICK PARTS IN A DOCUMENT

The Bottom Line   **Building blocks** contain built-in reusable content such as text, graphics, and objects. Building blocks are easily managed and inserted in a document for a quick format. Building blocks are organized in galleries and sorted by category. In the Building Blocks gallery, you can insert cover pages, headers, footers, page numbers, text boxes, and watermarks. In this exercise, you learn to use built-in building blocks and insert fields in a document.

Using Built-In Building Blocks

Another term for *building blocks* is *AutoText*, and both features are used the same way. Word provides a number of predefined building blocks or you can create or customize your own building blocks to be used in other documents. The Building Blocks Organizer provides a way to manage building blocks by editing, deleting, and/or inserting them. In the left pane of the dialog box, the built-in building blocks are listed by name; the Gallery column indicates the gallery that contains each building block, and the Category column indicates each element's general type, whereas the Template column indicates within which template the element is stored. You can use the buttons at the bottom of the dialog box to delete and edit selected building blocks. The right pane previews your selections (see Figure 7-15).

In this exercise, you learn to use built-in building blocks and insert fields in a document.

STEP BY STEP   **Use Built-In Building Blocks**

USE the document that is open from the previous exercise.

1. On the Insert tab, in the Text group, click the **Quick Parts button** to display the Quick Parts menu, as shown in Figure 7-14.

Figure 7-14

Quick Parts menu

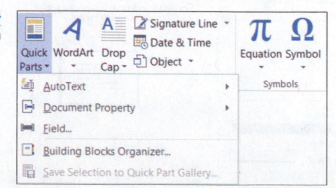

2. Click the **Building Blocks Organizer menu option** to display the *Building Blocks Organizer* dialog box, as shown in Figure 7-15.

Figure 7-15

Building Blocks Organizer

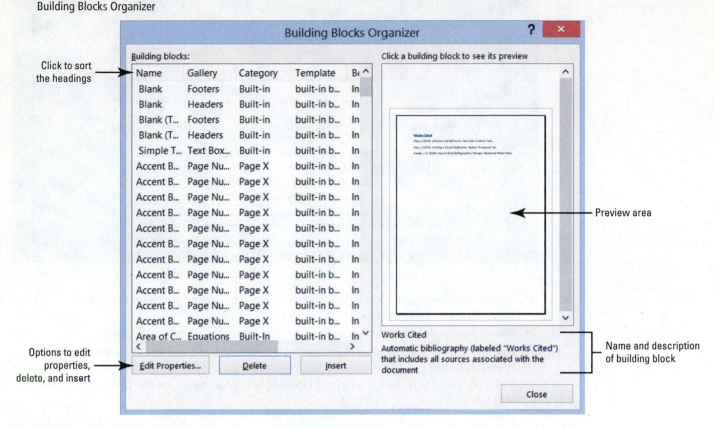

Figure 7-15

Building Blocks Organizer

Click to sort the headings

Options to edit properties, delete, and insert

Preview area

Name and description of building block

3. Click the **Name** heading to sort the building blocks by name.

4. Scroll down the list and select **Confidential 1 Watermark**.

 Troubleshooting You can adjust the Name column by dragging the resize bar to the right to change the width.

5. Click the **Insert button**. The Confidential watermark appears behind the text on every page.

6. Position the insertion point at the beginning of the first paragraph under *Introduction*.

7. Display the **Building Blocks Organizer dialog box**.

8. Click the **Gallery heading** to sort the building blocks by gallery.

9. Scroll down and select **Austin Quote** from the Text Box gallery. Click **Insert** and a pull quote is inserted in the document as shown in Figure 7-16. You can type text in the placeholders or drag and drop text in the area.

CERTIFICATION READY? 5.1.1

How would you insert a watermark using a Quick Part?

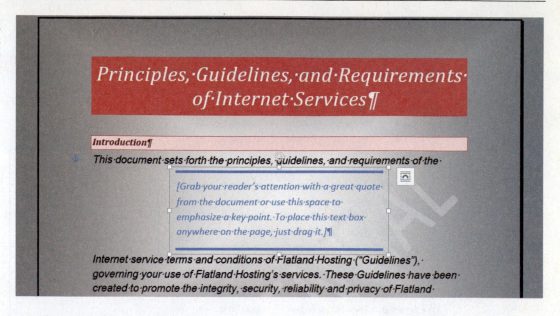

Principles, Guidelines, and Requirements of Internet Services¶

Introduction¶

This document sets forth the principles, guidelines, and requirements of the

[Grab your reader's attention with a great quote from the document or use this space to emphasize a key point. To place this text box anywhere on the page, just drag it.]¶

Internet service terms and conditions of Flatland Hosting ("Guidelines"), governing your use of Flatland Hosting's services. These Guidelines have been created to promote the integrity, security, reliability and privacy of Flatland

10. Under the heading, *Introduction*, select the second paragraph beginning with *Questions or comments . . . .*

11. Move the selected text inside the quote area by dragging and dropping.

12. Use the **Show/Hide Editing Marks button** to delete both line breaks after the first paragraph under *Introduction*.

13. Select the text box, and the Layout Options button appears on the right side of the text box.

14. Click the **Layout Options** button to open the menu. Options are available on laying out the text box in the document.

15. Click the **See more ... link** to open the *Layout* dialog box.

16. Click the **Text Wrapping tab** and select **Square**.

17. Click the **Left only option button** under the Wrap text section (see Figure 7-17). Click **OK**.

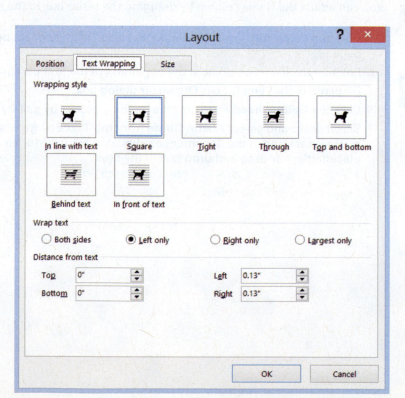

18. Place your pointer on the text box border—the pointer changes to four arrows to allow you to drag and drop. Drag the quote to the end of the first paragraph until the last seven lines of the paragraph wrap around it (see Figure 7-18).

Figure 7-18

Document with Text Box Pull Quote wrapped around paragraph

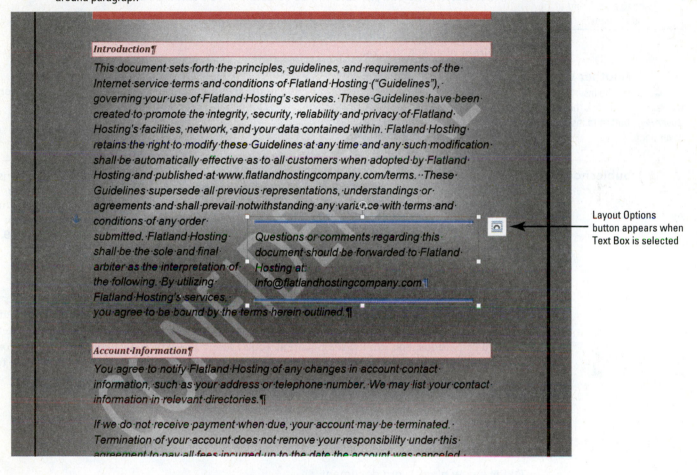

Layout Options button appears when Text Box is selected

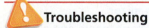 **Troubleshooting**   Deselect the text box and select again to see the border around the text box.

19. Press **Ctrl+End** to move the insertion point to the end of the document.

20. Display the **Building Blocks Organizer dialog box**.

21. Scroll down and select **Motion Sidebar** from the Text Box gallery.

22. Click **Insert**. The text box is inserted at the end of the document and positioned on the left side of the document. Your next step is to insert text into the text box.

23. Select the paragraph above *Refusal of Service* beginning with *You and Flatland Hosting further agree . . .* When selecting the paragraph, do not select the paragraph mark, because this will avoid displaying the horizontal line in the Text Box twice.

24. Change the font color to white so that the text will be visible on the sidebar.

25. Drag and drop the selection in the text box.

26. At the top of the text box, delete the **[Sidebar Title]** placeholder and blank line to move the text up one line.

27. **SAVE** the document as *Hosting Term7* in the lesson folder on your flash drive.

PAUSE. LEAVE Word open to use in the next exercise.

Insert a Cover Page Using the Built-In Building Blocks

USE the document that is open from the previous exercise.

1. Click the **Building Blocks Organizer** to display the dialog box and select **Whisp** in the Cover Pages gallery.
2. Click **Insert**. The cover page is inserted as page 1.
3. Type the following information in the placeholders:

   Year: **20XX** (The current date can be selected or you can type the year.)

   Document Title: **Flatland Hosting Company**

   Document Subtitle: **Guidelines & Agreements**

   Author Name: **A. Becker**
4. Remove the placeholders for the Company Name.
5. **SAVE** the document as *Hosting Term8* in the lesson folder on your flash drive, and then **CLOSE** the file.

PAUSE. LEAVE Word open to use in the next exercise.

CERTIFICATION READY? 2.1.1

How do you append a cover page to an existing document?

Another Way
On the Insert tab, in the Pages group, click the *Cover Page* button to insert a cover page.

⚠️ **Troubleshooting** | If you experience problems in saving the author's name, complete one of the following actions: (1) Right-click next to the placeholder and click *Remove Content Control*; (2) Change the author's name in Properties—located in Backstage; (3) Click the *File* tab, and then click *Options*. In the General category, under the Personalize your copy of Microsoft Office section, type the author's name next to the User name box and initials. Changing the user name is discussed in Lesson 9.

Inserting an Equation

Microsoft Word 2013 has built-in equations, which can be inserted from the Quick Parts gallery or by using the Equation command. When you create a table that contains values, you can calculate your answer by inserting an equation. The same rules that you learned in Math apply when inserting equations. You can use the Equation Tools Design tab, which displays when an equation is inserted in a document, to edit or construct your own equation. In this exercise, you learn to insert equations in a document.

Insert an Equation

OPEN a new blank Word document.

1. Open the **Quick Parts menu**, and then click **Building Blocks Organizer**.
2. In the *Building Blocks Organizer* dialog box, in the Equations gallery, locate and click the **Expansion of a Sum equation**.
3. Click **Insert**. The Expansion of a Sum equation is inserted in the document.
4. Position the insertion point after the equation placeholder, and then press the **Enter key** twice to place a blank line below the placeholder.
5. Open the *Building Blocks Organizer* dialog box, locate and click the **Area of Circle equation**, and then click **Insert**.
6. Position the insertion point after the equation placeholder, and then press the **Enter key** twice to place a blank line below the placeholder.
7. Open the *Building Blocks Organizer* dialog box, then locate and click the **Binomial Theorem equation**.
8. Click **Insert**.
9. Click after the equation placeholder, and press the **Enter key** twice.
10. **SAVE** the document as *Equations* in the lesson folder on your flash drive, and then **CLOSE** the file.

PAUSE. LEAVE Word open to use in the next exercise.

CERTIFICATION READY? 2.1.1

How do you append an equation to an existing document?

Another Way
In the Insert tab, in the Symbols group, click the *Equation* button, and select an equation from the built-in menu.

Inserting a Field from Quick Parts

A **field** is a placeholder where Word inserts content in a document. Word automatically uses fields when specific commands are activated, such as those for inserting dates, formulas, page numbers, and a table of contents. When you insert a date field in a document, the date is updated automatically each time the document is opened. In this exercise, you learn to insert a field in a document.

Fields, also called *field codes*, appear between curly brackets ({ }) when displayed. Field codes are turned off by default. To display field codes in a document, press *Alt+F9*. You can toggle back and forth to display text and field codes by pressing *Alt+F9*. To edit a field, place the insertion point within the field, right-click, and then click *Edit Field*.

STEP BY STEP   **Insert the Date and Time**

OPEN the *Billing Table* document from the lesson folder.

1. Position the insertion point on the last cell of the table in the second column.
2. Press **Tab** to insert a new row. Pressing the **Tab** key advances the insertion point to the next cell. If you are in the last cell of the table, it inserts a row quickly without having to access the Ribbon.
3. Position the insertion point in the first column, fifth row. Type **Total** and align center right.
4. Press **Tab**. This time, the next cell is selected.
5. On the Insert tab, in the Text group, click the **Quick Parts button** to open the menu.
6. Click **Field** on the menu. The *Field* dialog box appears (see Figure 7-19).

Figure 7-19

Field dialog box

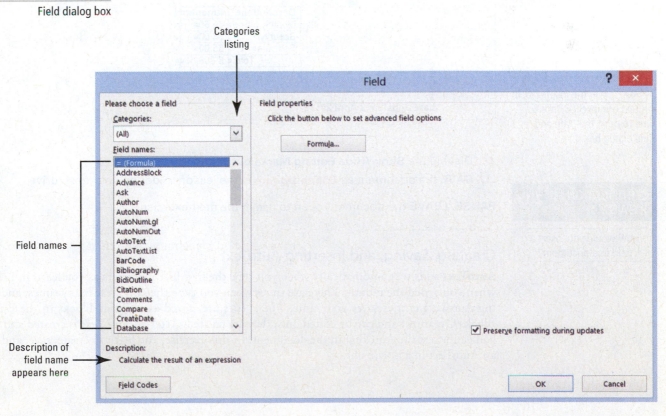

7. The default = (Formula) is selected in the Field names box. Click the **Formula**
 button. The *Formula* dialog box opens. This is the same dialog box that
is opened from the Table Tools Layout tab. Word automatically reads the values listed
above the formula, and =SUM(ABOVE) appears in the formula box.

8. Change the Number Format by selecting the third option. Click **OK**.

 Cross Ref   In Lesson 6, you learn to turn the field codes on and display them in the document.

9. Place the insertion point on the blank line below the table and press **Enter** three times.

10. Type **Last Updated:** in bold and press the **spacebar** once after the colon.

11. On the Insert tab, in the Text group, click the **Quick Parts button** and click **Field** on
the menu.

12. From the Categories drop-down list, click **Date and Time**.

Troubleshooting   If the Field is shaded in gray, double-click the text in the cell.

13. In the Field Names list, click **Date**.

14. In the Date Formats list, select the ninth option with the **Day Month Year format**.
d MMMM yyyy appears in the Date Formats box. These symbols represent how the
date will look in your document.

15. Click **OK** to close the dialog box and insert the date and time field in your document.

The document should look similar to the one shown in Figure 7-20, with the exception
that the current date will appear.

Figure 7-20

Document with Formula and
Date field inserted

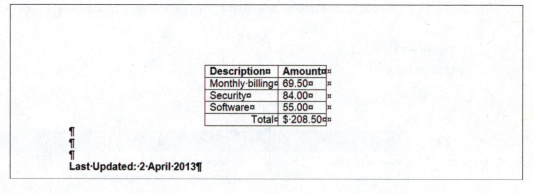

Description¤	Amount¤	¤
Monthly·billing¤	69.50¤	¤
Security¤	84.00¤	¤
Software¤	55.00¤	¤
Total¤	$·208.50¤	¤

Last·Updated:··2·April·2013¶

 **Another Way**
On the Insert tab, in
the Text group, click Date &
Time to open the Date and
Time dialog box.

16. Disable the **Show/Hide Editing Marks button**.

17. **SAVE** the document as *Billing Update* in the lesson folder on your flash drive.

PAUSE. LEAVE the document open to use in the next exercise.

CERTIFICATION READY?   **2.1.6**

How would you insert a
field in a document?

Creating, Saving, and Inserting AutoText

AutoText adds text automatically when you type the first few characters as you learn in Lesson 1
when you typed the month. There are times when you type the same text many times, and creating AutoText entries saves your time. The entries are stored as building blocks in the Building
Blocks Organizer and can be edited once they are created. After an AutoText is created and saved,
you can insert the AutoText in the document. In this exercise, you learn to create, save, and insert
an AutoText in a document.

Create an AutoText

USE the document that is open from the previous exercise.

1. Position the insertion point on the blank line above the date and type **Reviewed by Hazel Loera**.

2. Select **Reviewed by Hazel Loera**. To add text to the AutoText, you must first select text. Be careful not to select the paragraph mark.

3. On the Insert tab, in the Text group, click the **Quick Parts button** and click **AutoText** on the menu. As shown in Figure 7-21, the Save Selection to AutoText Gallery is active.

Figure 7-21

Save Selection to
AutoText Gallery

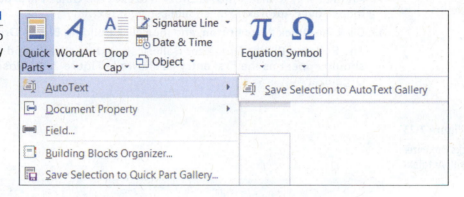

4. Click **Save Selection to AutoText Gallery**. The *Create New Building Block* dialog box opens (see Figure 7-22).

Figure 7-22

Create New Building Block
dialog box

5. Type the following information into the dialog box:

   Name: **Reviewed by Hazel Loera**

   Gallery: Select **AutoText**.

   Category: Select **General category** or you can create a new category.

6. Type the following text into the dialog box:

   Description: **The reviewer is the last individual to review all billings before mailing.**

   A description of the building block—this description—appears in the Building Blocks Organizer.

7. Under *Save In:* Select **Normal**.

   This is the template listing of where you would select to save the AutoText. If the extension *.dotm* appears after Normal, then the extension for known types is enabled allowing you to see the extension in the document title or dialog boxes. The default to save the AutoText is in the Normal format, which is a Macro-Enabled Template. In Lesson 12, you learn more about macros.

8. Under *Options:* Select **Insert content only**.

There are three options to choose from: *Insert content in its own page*—building block will be placed on separate page with page breaks inserted, *Insert content in its own paragraph*—the content will be placed in its own paragraph, even if the user's insertion point is in the middle of a paragraph, and *Insert content only*—the content will be inserted inline.

9. Click **OK**.

10. Delete the selected text, *Reviewed by Hazel Loera*.

11. Type the first four characters, and a ScreenTip appears displaying the AutoText. Press **Enter**. The AutoText is inserted into your document.

12. Another way to insert the AutoText is to click the **Quick Parts button** and hover the mouse over AutoText. You should see your text.

13. Click the **Quick Parts button**, and then click **Building Blocks Organizer**.

The Building Blocks Organizer Gallery should be sorted, and the new AutoText should appear as the first entry as shown in Figure 7-23. Close the Building Blocks Organizer.

Figure 7-23

Building Blocks Organizer
dialog box with AutoText

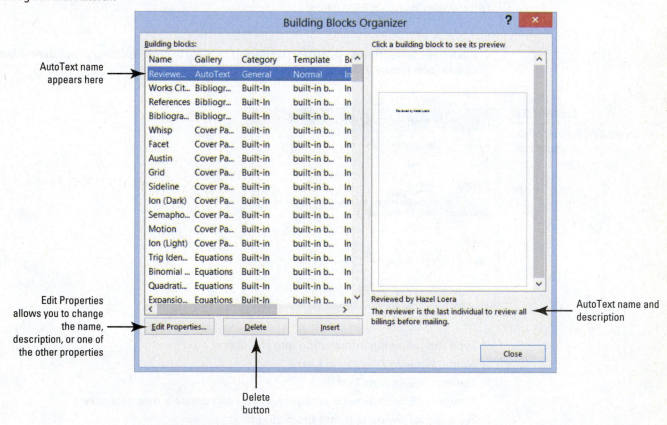

14. **SAVE** the document as *Billing Final* in the lesson folder on your flash drive, and then **CLOSE** the file.

PAUSE. LEAVE Word open for the next exercise.

 Cross Ref   In Lesson 1, you learn to show file extensions.

STEP BY STEP   **Delete a Building Block**

OPEN a blank document.

1. Open the **Building Blocks Organizer**.
2. Highlight **Reviewed by Hazel Loera**.

   At the bottom of the *Building Blocks Organizer* dialog box is the Delete button.

3. Click the **Delete button**.

   A prompt appears asking "Are you sure you want to delete the selected building block?"

4. Click **Yes** to close the Building Blocks Organizer.
5. **CLOSE** the document and do not save.

PAUSE. LEAVE Word open for the next exercise.

SOFTWARE ORIENTATION

Text Box Tools in the Ribbon

Before you begin working with text boxes, it is a good idea to become familiar with the new tools available in the Ribbon. When you insert a text box, the Drawing Tools FORMAT tab appears in the Ribbon, as shown in Figure 7-24.

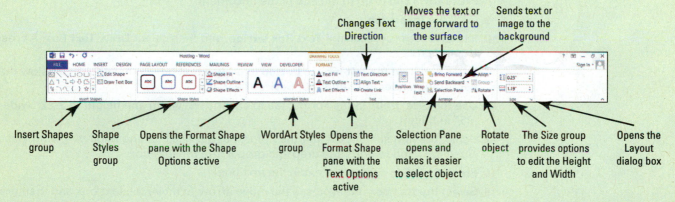

Figure 7-24

The Drawing Tools FORMAT tab

The Drawing Tools FORMAT tab provides commands for editing text boxes. Use this figure as a reference throughout this lesson as well as the rest of this book.

APPLYING AND MANIPULATING TEXT BOXES

The Bottom Line   A **text box** is a, formatted box in which you can insert and position text and/or graphic objects. Text boxes can be used for a variety of purposes. Most often, they are used to insert text within other document text or to lay out text for specific emphasis or visual interest. After you insert a text box, you can format the box using the Drawing Tools. You can also format the text in the box using the Font formats. A **pull quote** is a small selection of text that is pulled out or quoted from a larger selection of text. It is displayed within a box on the page that is formatted for emphasis, and it is often used along with drop caps in newsletters, advertisements, and magazines.

Inserting a Text Box

Word provides a gallery of built-in text boxes with pull quotes and sidebars that you can insert in a document. When you need a different kind of text box, you can draw and insert your own empty, unformatted text box. When drawing a text box, the Layout Options provide an option to wrap text around the object. In this exercise, you insert a preformatted text box and draw a text box.

STEP BY STEP	**Insert a Text Box**

OPEN the *Hosting* document from the data files for this lesson.

1. Position the insertion point after the first paragraph after the *Introduction* heading.
2. On the Insert tab, in the Text group, click the **Text Box button**. A menu of built-in quote and sidebar text box styles appears.
3. Click the **Simple Text Box option**. The text box, containing placeholder text, is inserted in the first paragraph.
4. Select the second paragraph beginning with *Questions or comments....com* and drag and drop in the text box.

   The Layout Options button appears to the right of the text box.
5. Click the **Layout Options button** to open the Layout Options menu.
6. In the With Text Wrapping section, select **Tight**.

   The text box wraps tightly around the paragraph. You also have the option to type text in the text box.
7. Delete one of the line breaks after the first paragraph.
8. Press **Ctrl+End** to go to the end of the document.
9. Click the **Insert tab**.
10. In the Text group, click the **Text Box button**, and then select **Draw Text Box**. A crosshair (+) appears.
11. Press and hold the **left mouse button** to draw a text box in the blank line below the last paragraph under the *Refusal of Service* heading.
12. Use the Size group in the Format tab to change the width and height to **2.22"** wide and **.95"** in height.
13. Select the first sentence under the *Refusal of Service* heading beginning with *Flatland Hosting . . . no refunds* and drag and drop it into the text box.
14. Press **Ctrl+E** to center the text in the text box.
15. Select the text box until you see the move arrow to move the text box and then drag the text box to the right to horizontally center—use the ruler as your guide. Your document should resemble Figure 7-25.

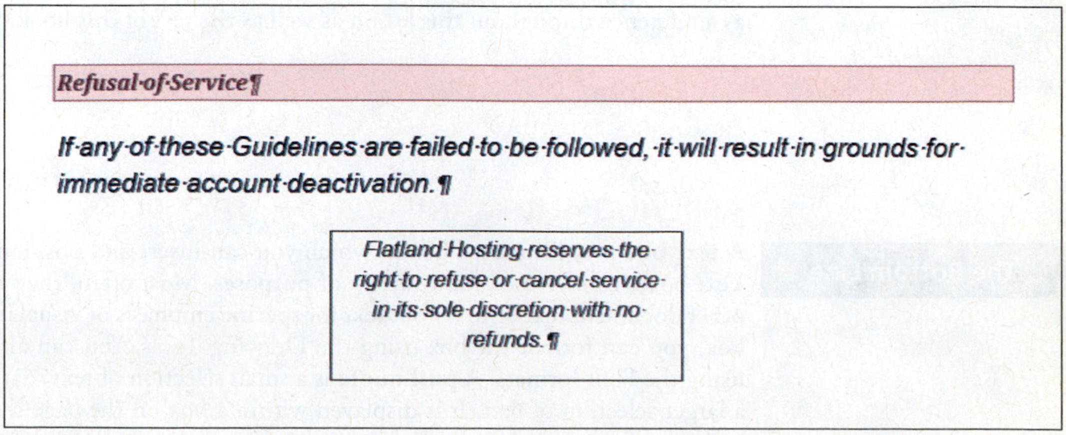

Figure 7-25

Document with text box horizontally centered

Refusal·of·Service¶

If·any·of·these·Guidelines·are·failed·to·be·followed,·it·will·result·in·grounds·for· immediate·account·deactivation.¶

Flatland·Hosting·reserves·the· right·to·refuse·or·cancel·service· in·its·sole·discretion·with·no· refunds.¶

16. **SAVE** the document as *Hosting Term9* in the lesson folder on your flash drive.

PAUSE. LEAVE the document open to use in the next exercise.

Formatting a Text Box

When a text box is selected, the Drawing Tools Format tab appears. In this exercise, you practice using these tools to format a text box.

STEP BY STEP **Format a Text Box**

USE the document that is open from the previous exercise.

1. Select the text box on page 7.

2. Click the **Format tab**.

3. In the Arrange group, click the **Position button** to open the menu, and select **Position in Middle Right with Square Text Wrapping** from the drop-down menu that appears. The text box is moved slightly down to the right of the document as shown in Figure 7-26.

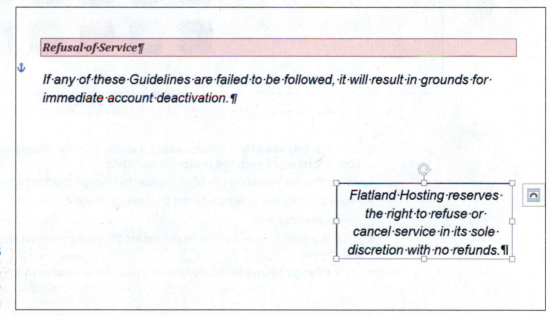

Refusal·of·Service¶

If·any·of·these·Guidelines·are·failed·to·be·followed,·it·will·result·in·grounds·for·
immediate·account·deactivation.¶

Flatland·Hosting·reserves·
the·right·to·refuse·or·
cancel·service·in·its·sole·
discretion·with·no·refunds.¶

Figure 7-26

Text box Position in Middle
Right with Square
Text Wrapping

4. The text box should still be selected. On the Format tab, in the Shape Styles group, click the **More button** to display the gallery of styles (see Figure 7-27).

Figure 7-27

Shape Styles gallery

5. Click the **Intense Effect – Red Accent 2 style** from the Shape Styles gallery. The text box is formatted with the preformatted style.
6. Select the text and use the Mini toolbar to change the font color to white.
7. Press **Ctrl+Home** to return to the beginning of the document.
8. Select the text box.
9. Click the **Edit Shape button** in the Insert Shapes group on the Format tab to display the menu.
10. Click **Change Shape** to display the Shapes menu as shown in Figure 7-28.

Figure 7-28

Change Shape menu

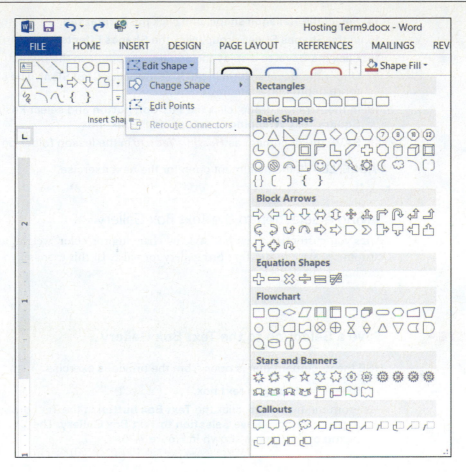

Figure 7-28

Change Shape menu

11. Under the Basic Shapes section, select the **Hexagon shape** in the first row, eighth option. The text box shape takes on a hexagon shape.

12. With the text box still selected, in the Size group, change the height to **.8"** and width to **4"**.

13. Change the font size to **9 pt**. Your document should match Figure 7-29. You might need to reposition the text box back toward the middle.

Figure 7-29

Text box with new shape

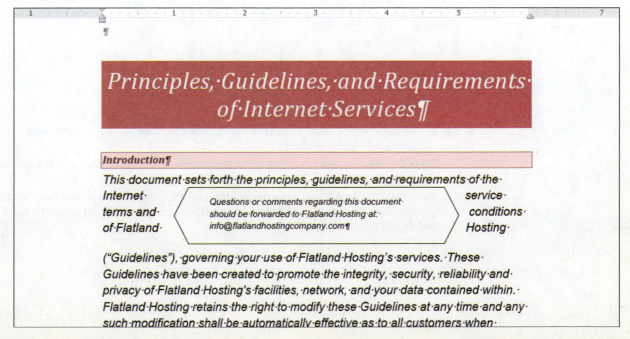

> # Principles, Guidelines, and Requirements of Internet Services¶
>
> **Introduction**¶
>
> This document sets forth the principles, guidelines, and requirements of the Internet terms and of Flatland
>
> Questions or comments regarding this document should be forwarded to Flatland Hosting at: info@flatlandhostingcompany.com¶
>
> service conditions Hosting
>
> ("Guidelines"), governing your use of Flatland Hosting's services. These Guidelines have been created to promote the integrity, security, reliability and privacy of Flatland Hosting's facilities, network, and your data contained within. Flatland Hosting retains the right to modify these Guidelines at any time and any such modification shall be automatically effective as to all customers when

14. Select the **Hexagon shape**, and click the **Format tab**.

15. In the Shapes Styles group, click the **Shapes Effects button** to display the menu.

16. Click the **Bevel** to display the additional options in the menu.

17. Under the Bevel section in the first row, click **Cool Slant**. The shape object acquires more depth and a shadow effect.

18. In the Arrange group, click the **Position button** and select **Position in Middle Left with Square Text Wrapping** to reposition the text box.

19. **SAVE** the document as *Hosting Term10* in the lesson folder on your flash drive.

PAUSE. LEAVE the document open for the next exercise.

Saving a Selection to the Text Box Gallery

After you customize a text box style by changing the color, weight, and so on, you can save the customized style to the Text Box gallery for reuse. In this exercise, you learn to save the hexagon text box in the gallery.

STEP BY STEP	**Save a Selection to the Text Box Gallery**

USE the document that is open from the previous exercise.

1. Select the **Hexagon text box**.

2. From the **Insert tab**, click the **Text Box button** in the Text group. From the menu that appears, choose **Save Selection to Text Box Gallery**. The *Create New Building Block* dialog box opens as shown in Figure 7-30.

Figure 7-30

Create New Building Block dialog box

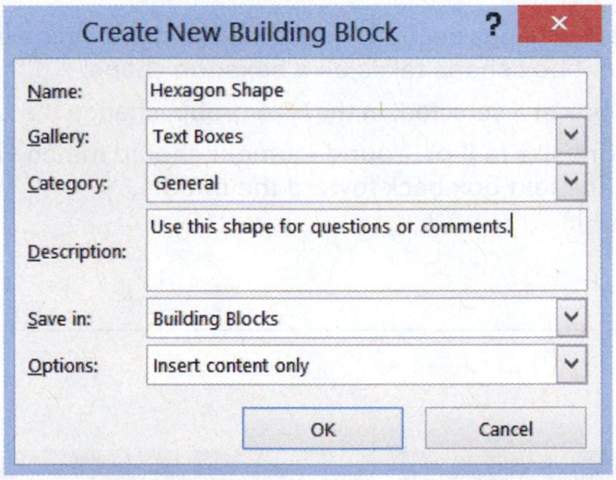

3. In the Name box, type **Hexagon Shape**.

4. In the Description box, type **Use this shape for questions or comments**. Keep the remaining defaults as listed.

5. Click **OK**. The saved selection for the Hexagon text box is saved in the gallery under the General category.

6. To view, click in a blank area of the document to deselect the text box. In the Text group, click the **Text Box button**. In the Built-in section, scroll down to the end of the list as shown in Figure 7-31.

Figure 7-31

Text Box gallery

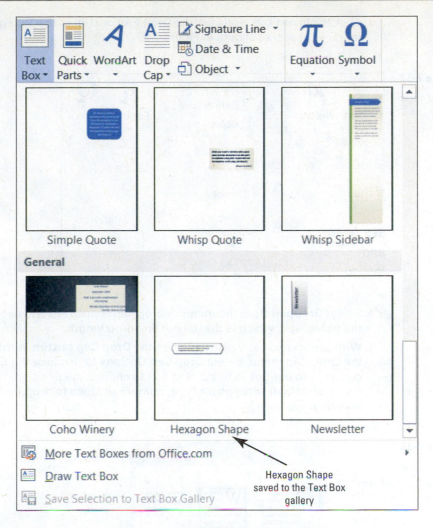

7. **SAVE** the document as *Hosting Final* in the lesson folder on your flash drive.

PAUSE. LEAVE the document open to use in the next exercise.

MAKING TEXT GRAPHICALLY APPEALING AND INSERTING A SPECIAL CHARACTER

The Bottom Line

The Text group in Word lets you insert professionally formatted text elements such as pull quotes and drop caps quickly. A **drop cap** is a large initial letter that drops down two or more lines at the beginning of a paragraph to indicate that a new block of information is beginning and to give interest to newsletters, magazine articles, and other documents.

Creating a Drop Cap

Drop caps are used to add visual interest to newsletters or magazine articles. In this exercise, you learn to add a drop cap to a Word document.

STEP BY STEP   **Create a Drop Cap**

USE the document that is open from the previous exercise.

1. Click the **View tab** and click the **Navigation Pane** check box to open the Navigation Pane.

2. Under the Headings tab, click **Account Information**, and then select the **Y** that begins the sentence *You agree to notify...*

3. Click the **Insert tab**, and click the **Drop Cap button** in the Text group. The Drop Cap menu appears, as shown in Figure 7-32.

Figure 7-32

Drop Cap menu

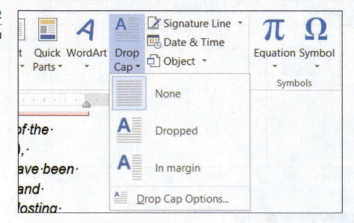

4. Select **Dropped** from the menu. A drop cap is inserted and extends down three lines in the paragraph, which is the default line drop length.

5. With the text box still selected, click the **Drop Cap button** in the Text group to display the Drop Cap menu. Select **Drop Cap Options** to produce the *Drop Cap* dialog box. You can use the options in this dialog box to change the position, font, and size of the drop cap. The default settings for Font, number of Lines to drop, and Distance from text are shown in Figure 7-33.

Figure 7-33

Drop Cap dialog box

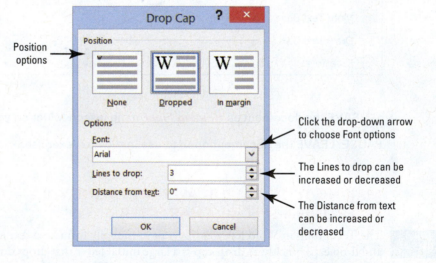

6. Click the **Font drop-down arrow** and change the font to **Bookman Old Style**.

7. Click **OK** to apply your changes and close the dialog box.

8. Click outside the drop cap to deselect it. The drop cap font is set to Bookman Old Style, whereas the remaining text is unaffected.

9. To provide more emphasis to the Drop Cap, select the **Y** and change the font color to dark red.

10. **SAVE** your document in the lesson folder on your flash drive.

PAUSE. LEAVE the document open to use in the next exercise.

Inserting Special Characters

Special characters include recognizable symbols used by individuals or businesses to differentiate their product or service to a specific target population. Copyright © symbols are used to protect books, songs, and other original work from authors or artists. Trademark™ is an unregistered trademark and is used to promote the company's goods. Other symbols used are fractions ½, em dash (—), and much more. Depending on the font that you select, you can insert international monetary symbols such as the pound sign, £, or yen sign, ¥. These symbols are represented by **Unicode**, which is a character code. Unicode enables most of the languages in the world to be symbolized with a special character identification. These special characters can be inserted using the Symbol command on the Ribbon, the Symbol dialog box, or keyboard shortcuts. In this exercise, you insert a special character in a document.

STEP BY STEP   **Insert Special Characters**

USE the document that is open from the previous exercise.

1. Press **Ctrl+End** to move to the end of the document.
2. Press **Enter** once after the last paragraph under the heading, *Refusal of Service*.
3. Type **Copyright Flatland Hosting 2013. All Rights Reserved.**
4. Place the insertion point after the *t* in *Copyright* and press the **Spacebar** once.
5. On the Insert tab in the Symbols group, click the **Symbol button**, and then click **More Symbols**.
6. Click the **Special Characters tab** to make it available. The *Symbol* dialog box is shown in Figure 7-34.

Figure 7-34

Symbol dialog box

Additional symbols are available in the Symbols tab

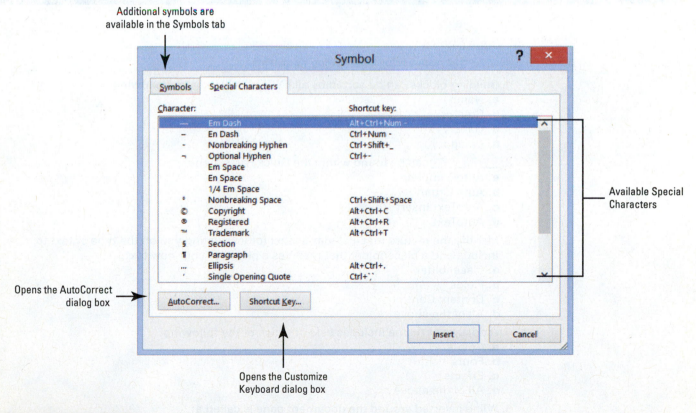

Available Special Characters

Opens the AutoCorrect dialog box

Opens the Customize Keyboard dialog box

CERTIFICATION READY?   2.1.7

How would you insert a special character in a document?

7. Select Copyright from the list and click **Insert**.
8. Click **Close**. The copyright symbol is inserted in front of the company name followed by the year this document was created.
9. **SAVE** your document in the lesson folder on your flash drive, and then **CLOSE** the file.

As you close Word, a prompt appears stating, *You have modified styles, building blocks (such as cover pages or headers), or other content that is stored in "Building Blocks." Do you want to save changes to "Building Blocks"?*

Another Way
A quick way to insert the copyright symbol is using the assigned keyboard shortcut *Alt+Ctrl+C.*

10. Click **SAVE**. This allows you to continue using the customized text box that you saved.

CLOSE Microsoft Word.

SKILL SUMMARY

In this lesson, you learned to:	Exam Objective	Objective Number
Format, Create, and Customize a Theme	Change document themes.	1.3.2
Format a Document Using Style Sets	Change document Style Sets.	1.3.3
Format a Document's Background	Insert watermarks.	1.3.5
Use Quick Parts in a Document	Insert Quick Parts. Append text to a document. Insert Built-in Fields.	5.1.1 2.1.1 2.1.6
Apply and Manipulate Text Boxes	Insert text boxes.	5.1.2
Make Text Graphically Appealing and Insert Special Characters	Insert special characters (©, ™, £).	2.1.7

Knowledge Assessment

Multiple Choice

Select the best response for the following statements.

1. Building blocks can be sorted by all EXCEPT which of the following?
   a. Name
   b. Creator
   c. Gallery
   d. Category

2. _____ can be found within the Quick Parts menu.
   a. AutoComplete
   b. Auto Organizer
   c. AutoText Insert
   d. AutoText

3. Identify the feature that includes a label for instructing you on the type of text to include and a placeholder that reserves a place for your new text.
   a. Placeholder
   b. Fields
   c. Content Control
   d. All of the above

4. A document theme includes sets of which of the following?
   a. Colors
   b. Fonts
   c. Effects
   d. All of the above

5. A line inserted around the document page is called a:
   a. Document page border.
   b. Page layout border.
   c. Page border.
   d. None of the above.

6. To preview a style or a theme, you must do which of the following?
   a. Place your mouse pointer over the choice
   b. Print the document

c. Set up the document properties

d. It is not possible to preview a style or theme

7. The _____ provides a way to manage building blocks by editing, deleting, and/or inserting them.

a. Quick Organizer

b. Cover Page

c. Text box

d. Building Blocks Organizer

8. A _____ is a placeholder that tells Word to insert changeable data into a document.

a. field name

b. field

c. data field

d. data source

9. A customized company logo applied to a page background behind a document's text is called a(n):

a. MarkArt.

b. Insert Picture refer to.

c. watermark.

d. SmartArt.

10. In the _____ dialog box, you can specify to insert a page border on only the first page of a document.

a. Page Border

b. Borders and Shading

c. Page Border tab dialog box

d. Line Border

True/False

Circle T if the statement is true or F if the statement is false.

T F   1. A watermark is text or a graphic printed behind text.

T F   2. When a Style Set has been inserted in a document, the spacing of the Style Set can be easily changed.

T F   3. Inserting special characters in a document can be completed using the Ribbon or a keyboard shortcut.

T F   4. AutoText can be inserted using the Building Blocks Organizer.

T F   5. If you make any changes to the colors, fonts, or effects of the current theme, you can save it as a custom theme and apply it to future documents.

T F   6. A picture can be inserted as a page background.

T F   7. You can customize a building block.

T F   8. Formulas can be inserted using only the Equation button.

T F   9. Page colors refer to the background color of a page.

T F 10. After a text box has been inserted, the text box can be moved to another location in the document.

Competency Assessment

Project 7-1: Creating Elevator Communications

Montgomery, Slade & Parker uses elevator communications for in-house announcements, invitations, and other employee-relations documents. In each elevator, a durable 8½″ × 14″ clear plastic frame has been installed in which announcements can be inserted and changed on a regular basis. Create a draft document for approval that recognizes employee award winners and invites employees to a reception to honor these award winners.

GET READY. LAUNCH Word if it is not already running.

1. **OPEN** *Congratulations* from the data files for this lesson.
2. **SAVE** the document as *7-1 Congratulations Reception* in the lesson folder on your flash drive.
3. On the Design tab, in the Page Background group, click the **Page Color menu**. In the Theme Colors section, select **Olive Green, Accent 3, Lighter 80%**.
4. Click the **Page Borders button**. In the *Borders and Shading* dialog box, click **Shadow** in the Setting section. Click the **Width menu** and choose **3 pt**. In the Color section, select **Olive Green, Accent 3, Darker 50%**. Click **OK** to apply the changes to the whole document.
5. On the Page Layout tab, in the Page Setup group, click the **Size menu** and select **Legal**. The legal option may not be included in the menu if you don't have a printer that uses legal sized paper; if not, just skip this step.
6. Launch the **Page Setup dialog box** and click the **Layout tab** to change the Vertical Alignment to **Center**.
7. Select **Congratulations!** Change the font color to **Olive Green, Accent 3, Darker 50%** to match the page border.
8. Click the **Watermark button** in the Page Background group on the Insert tab and select **Custom Watermark**. The *Printed Watermark* dialog box opens.
9. Select the **Text watermark option** and then click the **drop-down arrow** next to *Text*. Select **Draft**.
10. Customize the watermark by changing the color to dark red.
11. **SAVE** the document in the lesson folder on your flash drive, and then **CLOSE** the file.

LEAVE Word open for the next project.

Project 7-2: Creating a Reference Letter

A former employee at Flatland Hosting Company has asked for a reference letter.

GET READY. LAUNCH Word if it is not already running.

1. **OPEN** *Reference Letter* from the data files for this lesson.
2. **SAVE** the document as *7-2 Jasmine Reference* in the lesson folder on your flash drive.
3. On the Design tab, in the Document Formatting group, select **Basic (Simple)** from the Style Set gallery.
4. Click the **Fonts button** to produce the Fonts menu. In the menu, click **Customize Fonts**. The *Create New Theme Fonts* dialog box opens.
5. In the Name box, replace *Custom 1* by typing **Reference Letter Fonts [your initials]**.
6. Change the Heading and Body Font to **Times New Roman**.
7. Click **Save** to close the dialog box and apply your font choices to the document.
8. **SAVE** the document in the lesson folder on your flash drive, and then **CLOSE** the file.

LEAVE Word open for the next project.

Proficiency Assessment

Project 7-3: Creating Letterhead

Create a new letterhead for the Flatland Hosting Company.

GET READY. LAUNCH Word if it is not already running.

1. **OPEN** a new blank document.
2. **SAVE** the document as *7-3 FHC Letterhead* in the lesson folder on your flash drive.

3. On the Insert tab, in the Text group, open the **Building Blocks Organizer dialog box** and insert the **Sideline built-in header**.

4. In the [Document title] placeholder, type the document title as **Flatland Hosting Company**. Bold the text and change the size to **22 pt**.

5. The Header & Footer Tools Design tab is active. From the Insert group, click the **Quick Parts button**, and then open the **Building Blocks Organizer dialog box**.

6. Insert the **Sideline built-in footer** and select the page number and press **Delete**. Hint: Do *not* select the ¶ mark.

7. Type the company address along with inserting the solid diamond symbol as **1234 Grand Street ♦ Forest Grove, OR 97116** and center. In the Insert tab, in the Symbols group, click the **Symbol button** and select **More Symbols**. In the *Symbol* dialog box, change the font to **Wingdings** and select symbol **116**.

8. Click close Header and Footer in the Ribbon.

9. Change the view to one page.

10. **SAVE** the document in the lesson folder on your flash drive, and then **CLOSE** the file.

LEAVE Word open for the next project.

Project 7-4: Formatting a Two-Page Resume

Your friend Mike has revised and added some information to his resume, and it is now two pages long. Update the formatting to include a header and footer.

GET READY. LAUNCH Word if it is not already running.

1. **OPEN** *MZ Resume2* from the data files for this lesson.

2. **SAVE** the document as *7-4 MZ Resume2 Update* in the lesson folder on your flash drive.

3. Open the **Page Setup dialog box**, and change the top, bottom, left, and right margins to **1.25"**. Click **OK**.

4. Click the **Insert tab**, in the Text group, open the **Building Blocks Organizer**, and insert the **Austin header**.

5. In the header document title, type **Resume of Michael J. Zuberi** and right-align.

6. In the Options group, click the **Different First Page box**. Notice the text is no longer on the first page.

7. Close the Header and Footer.

8. On the Design tab, in the Document Formatting group, select **Black & White (Classic)**.

9. If necessary, enable the **Show/Hide Editing Marks button** and remove all blank lines.

10. Select **LONNCO, LTD—PLANO, TEXAS 1998 TO 2002 and STAFF ACCOUNTANT** and apply the **Keep with Next command**.

11. Change the view to **100%**.

12. **SAVE** the document in your flash drive in the lesson folder, and then **CLOSE** the file.

LEAVE Word open for the next project.

Mastery Assessment

Project 7-5: Customizing a Postcard

It's soccer season again, and the YMCA is sending out postcards to all participants who played last season.

GET READY. LAUNCH Word if it is not already running.

1. **OPEN** *Soccer* from the data files for this lesson.
2. **SAVE** the document as *7-5 Soccer Post Card* in the lesson folder on your flash drive.
3. Customize the page size to **4" x 6"**, the orientation to **Landscape**, and the margins to **Narrow**.
4. Insert a page border and add a **Dark Blue, Text 2** double-line page border with a box setting and set the width to **3/4 pt**.
5. In the *Page Color, Fill Effects* dialog box, select **Two Colors**. In the Color 2 section, and select **Blue, Accent 1, Lighter 80%**. In the Shading styles section, select **Diagonal down**. Under Variants, click the sample pattern in the lower-right corner.
6. Insert the soccer ball image from the data files as a picture watermark.
7. **SAVE** the document in your flash drive in the lesson folder, and then **CLOSE** the file.

LEAVE Word open for the next project.

Project 7-6: Creating a Thank-You Card

Create thank-you note cards that match the style of Mike's new two-page resume.

GET READY. LAUNCH Word if it is not already running.

1. Create a new blank document.
2. **SAVE** the document as *7-6 Thank You* in the lesson folder on your flash drive.

3. Customize the page size to **3.9" x 3.5"**, leave the orientation at the default, and change the margins to **Narrow**.
4. Refer to the built-in header used in the *MZ Resume2 Updated* document and insert the same format to be used as a footer in your current document.
5. In the footer, replace *pg 1* with **Michael J. Juberi** and right-align.
6. Insert the *Thank You* image as a picture watermark.
7. **SAVE** the document in your flash drive in the lesson folder, and then **CLOSE** the file.

CLOSE Word.

LESSON SKILL MATRIX

Skill	Exam Objective	Objective Number
Inserting and Formatting Pictures in a Document	Insert images	5.3.1
	Modify image properties	5.3.4
	Add Quick Styles to images	5.3.5
	Apply picture effects	5.3.3
	Insert simple shapes	5.2.1
	Modify SmartArt Properties	5.2.3
	Position shapes	5.2.5
	Apply artistic effects	5.3.2
	Wrap text around images	5.3.6
	Position images	5.3.7
Inserting and Formatting Shapes, WordArt, and SmartArt	Insert simple shapes	5.2.1
	Position shapes	5.2.5
	Wrap text around shapes	5.2.4
	Change text to WordArt	2.2.10
	Insert SmartArt	5.2.2
Inserting and Formatting Clip Art from Office.com	Insert images	5.3.1
	Modify image properties	5.3.4
	Add Quick Styles to images	5.3.5
Resetting and Compressing Images		
Inserting and Formatting a Chart		

© majana/iStockphoto

KEY TERMS

- caption
- cell
- clip art
- compress
- crop
- drawing canvas
- embedded object
- floating object
- inline object
- label
- linked object
- resetting
- scale
- Screen Clippings
- screenshot
- shapes
- SmartArt graphics
- WordArt

© majana/iStockphoto

Margie's Travel is a full-service travel agency that specializes in providing services associated with tours, cruises, adventure activities, group travel, and vacation packages all geared toward seniors. Agents at Margie's Travel frequently need to enhance a document with graphics, pictures, or drawings. *Word* provides eye-catching information, signs, brochures, and flyers using SmartArt, online <mark>clip art</mark> from Office.com, charts, and shapes. As you begin inserting objects, the Picture Tools will open. You will use this tool to enhance the objects. In this lesson, you learn how to insert SmartArt graphics, online pictures, pictures from files, <mark>screenshots</mark>, shapes, apply artistic art in a document, and much more.

SOFTWARE ORIENTATION

Insert Tab and Picture Tools

The Insert tab (see Figure 8-1) contains a group of features that you can use to add graphics to your document in Word 2013. Commands in the Illustrations group enable you to add several types of graphics to enhance your Word documents, including pictures from your computer, clip art from Office.com, shapes, SmartArt, charts, and screenshots.

The Picture Tools tab (see Figure 8-2) is a contextual command tab that appears after you have added a picture to the Word document. Formatting options on the Picture Tools tab enable you to make changes to the graphic object, including removing its background; applying corrections to improve brightness, sharpness, and contrast to the picture; applying color; adding artistic effects; adding borders; enhancing the image with picture effects; and <mark>cropping</mark>, resizing, and positioning the picture in the document.

Inserts Online pictures   Inserts SmartArt graphics

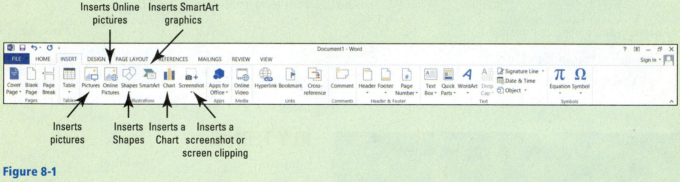

Inserts pictures   Inserts Shapes   Inserts a Chart   Inserts a screenshot or screen clipping

Figure 8-1

Insert tab

Removes Background or unwanted portions of selected image   Compress Pictures reduces picture size   Change Picture allows you to select another picture   Picture Effects   Picture Border   Positions picture as an inline object   Wrap Text changes picture to a floating object   Aligns object on page   Size by height and width

Corrections enhances brightness, contrast, & sharpness of the picture   Color changes and enhances color quality   Resets picture by removing formatting   More button displays Picture Styles Gallery   Picture Layout   Selection Pane makes it easier to select object   Rotate object   Crops unwanted edges of image   Launches the Layout dialog box

Figure 8-2

Picture Tools tab

Use these figures as a reference throughout this lesson, as well as the rest of the book.

INSERTING AND FORMATTING PICTURES IN A DOCUMENT

The Bottom Line

Word offers a number of tools to help you capture your readers' attention with illustrations that include pictures, shapes, SmartArt, charts, and screenshots. You can modify images in a number of ways, including: converting them to SmartArt, adding **captions**, resizing, cropping what you don't need, rotating, applying styles and colors, creating artistic effects, and positioning images within the document. Word also enables you to insert a screenshot, use a screen clipping, and to compress and reset the pictures that you have added to your documents.

Inserting Pictures

When you insert a picture into a document, Word marks it as an **embedded object** by default—which means it becomes part of the document and is no longer connected to the original image. Inserting a picture is very similar to opening a document file—the Pictures button from the Insert tab in the Illustrations group is used to open images instead of opening Backstage. In this exercise, you learn to insert a picture.

STEP BY STEP   **Insert Pictures**

GET READY. Before you begin, be sure to **LAUNCH** Microsoft Word.

1. On a blank page, key **Vacationing with Family**.
2. Select the text then right-click to display the Mini toolbar.
3. Change the font of the title to **Cambria**, and the font size to **28** pt and **bold**.
4. Center horizontally; then deselect the text.

 Cross Ref

In Lesson 3, you learned to change fonts and font sizes, and alignments were covered in Lesson 4.

5. Press **Enter**.
6. Click the **Insert** tab then click the **Pictures** button in the *Illustrations* group. The *Insert Picture* dialog box appears.
7. Locate your lesson folder on your flash drive and select the image *Family Traveling by Airplane* (see Figure 8-3).

Figure 8-3

Insert Picture dialog box

View Pane changes how files and images are viewed in the Insert Picture dialog box

Preview Pane allows you to view image before selecting

Option to select what is displayed by the format of the object or file

File name appears in box after you select

Insert button

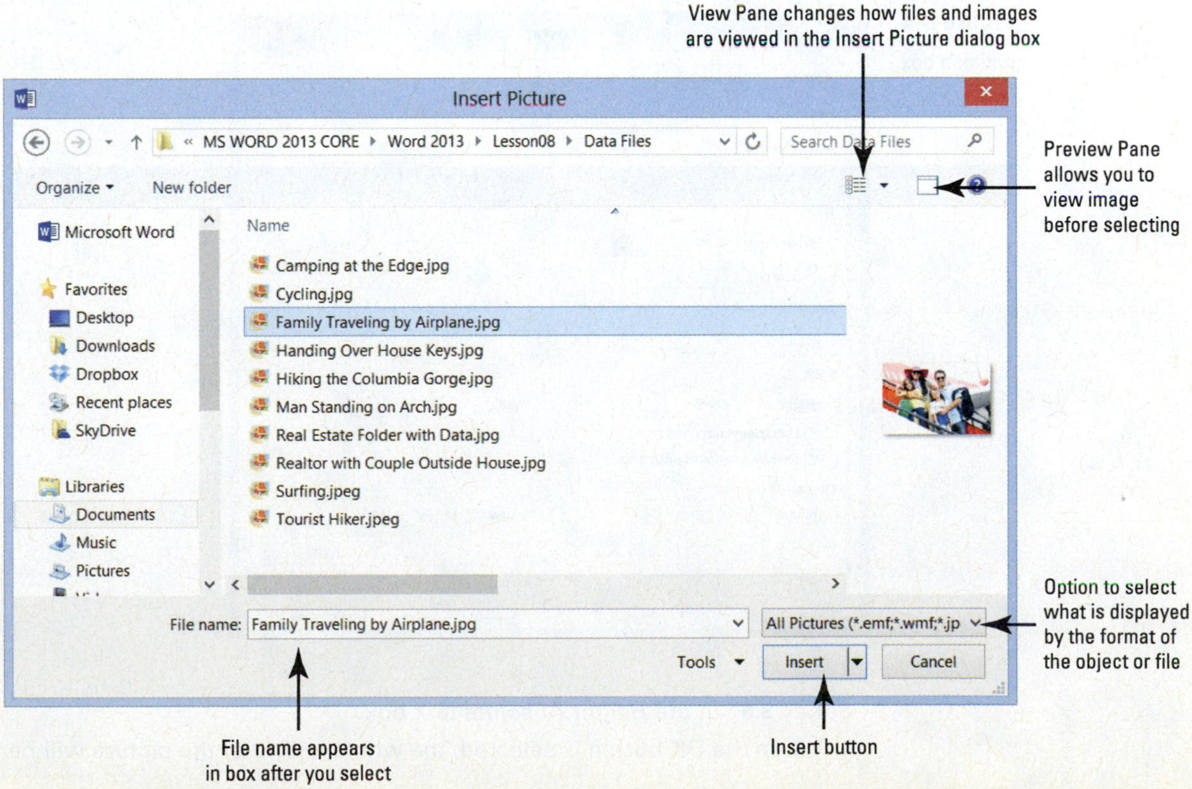

©Andresr/iStockphoto

8. Click **Insert**.

The picture appears in the document at the cursor location, and the *Format* tab opens with the *Picture Tools* command groups.

9. **SAVE** the document as *Family Vacation* in the lesson folder on your flash drive.

PAUSE. LEAVE the document open to use in the next exercise.

Take Note   Another option is to insert a picture as a <mark>linked object</mark>, which creates a connection between the document and picture, but doesn't combine them in the same file. Using linked objects can help minimize the file size of your final document, while still including pictures, photographs, and other objects that can eat up file space. However, this option is not recommended when creating a document that will be shared with other users because they may be unable to access the pictures.

Formatting Pictures

The Formatting tab with Picture Tools appears whenever you insert a picture into a document or select an existing picture within the document. The Picture Tools provide many options, such as cropping, resizing, scaling, and rotating. When you <mark>crop</mark> a picture, you trim the horizontal or vertical edges to remove unwanted areas. <mark>Scale</mark> increases or decreases the original picture's height and width by percentage. In this exercise, you will crop, resize, scale, and rotate a picture within a document.

STEP BY STEP   ### Crop, Resize, Scale, and Rotate a Picture

USE the document you left open from the previous exercise.

1. Select the picture if necessary and in the *Size* group, adjust the height  by using the arrow keys. Change to **4.9**".

As you increased the height, by default the Lock aspect ratio option is selected, so the width of the image also changes to accommodate the new dimensions.

2. In the *Size* group, launch the dialog box launcher to display the *Layout* dialog box, as shown in Figure 8-4.

In the *Layout* dialog box, you can resize a picture by changing the exact measurements of the height and width or rescale it by changing the height and width percentages.

Figure 8-4

Layout dialog box

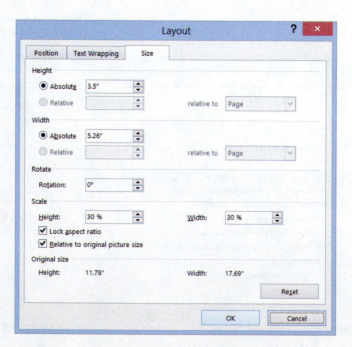

3. Key **3.5**" in the *Height Absolute* text box.

When the OK button is selected, the whole height of the picture will be altered.

In the *Scale* section, both the *Lock aspect ratio* and *Relative to original picture size* check boxes should be selected. When the *Lock aspect ratio* box is selected, you will be able to scale the picture in proportion by height and width by the same percentage. When the *Relative to original picture size* box is selected, the scaling Height and Width are comparative to the original size. The original size of the picture is under the *Original size* section.

4. Under the Scale section, for the *Height* key **25%** then press the **Tab** key.

   The scale width of the active picture automatically changes to 25% because *Lock aspect ratio* is selected. The *Absolute Height* dimension also changes to 2.92", to accommodate the new size compared to the original.

5. In the *Rotate* section, key **350** in the text box so that the position of the picture will rotate 350 degrees.

6. Press the **Tab** key to move to the next tab order in the dialog box.

7. Click **OK** to apply your changes and close the dialog box. Deselect the picture. Your image should resemble Figure 8-5.

Figure 8-5

Document with image

©Andresr/iStockphoto

8. **SAVE** the document in the lesson folder on your flash drive.

9. Select the picture. In the Size group, click the **Crop** button.

   The insertion point becomes a cropping tool, and cropping handles appear on the edges of the picture as shown in Figure 8-6.

Figure 8-6

Cropping handles on picture

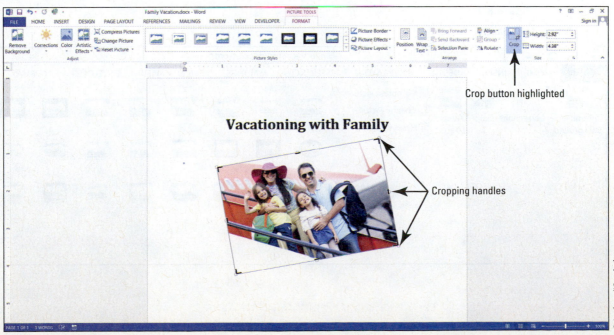

Crop button highlighted

Cropping handles

©Andresr/iStockphoto

10. Position the cropping tool over the top cropping handle. Then drag down until it is slightly above the pink hat.

11. Position the mouse in the lower left corner and drag up until it is close to the child's arm that is waving.

12. Release the mouse button, and then click the **Crop** button again to remove the cropping handles.

    The trimmed image has removed the unwanted area and displays only the cropped area.

13. Resize the image for precise measurements to **2.51"** for the height. The width will adjust automatically.

CERTIFICATION READY?   **5.3.4**

How do you resize a picture?

Take Note   In cropping you remove unwanted portions of the picture, and in scaling the original picture is increased or decreased in size to fit in the document.

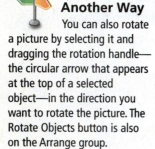

Another Way
You can also rotate a picture by selecting it and dragging the rotation handle— the circular arrow that appears at the top of a selected object—in the direction you want to rotate the picture. The Rotate Objects button is also on the Arrange group.

14. **SAVE** the document as **Family Vacation1** in the lesson folder on your flash drive.

PAUSE. LEAVE the document open to use in the next exercise.

Applying a Picture Style to a Picture

Applying a Picture Style to a picture allows you to select from various designs to give the picture an added appeal. Choosing from the available options from the Picture Styles group allows you to select from the Quick Styles, Picture Border, and Picture Effects, which adds interest to your picture. **Captions** consist of few descriptive words and are used for figures, tables, and equations. Adding a caption to a picture provides readers with information regarding the image. Formatting a picture using the Picture Layout enables you to use one of the built-in SmartArt graphics with captions placeholder. SmartArt graphics is covered later in this lesson. In this exercise, you learn to apply a quick style, insert a border, add effects, and add a caption by applying a Picture Style to an image.

STEP BY STEP   **Apply a Picture Style to a Picture**

USE the document that is open from the previous exercise.

1. To display the *Picture Tools*, select the picture so that the *Format* tab becomes available.

2. In the *Picture Styles* group, click the **More** button to display the *Picture Styles* gallery, shown in Figure 8-7.

Figure 8-7

Picture Styles Gallery

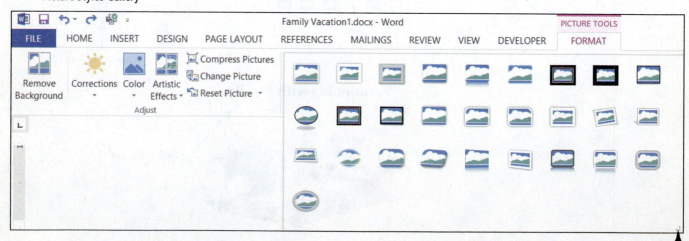

More button displays Picture Styles gallery

3. Hover over a few styles in the gallery and watch how the picture takes on a new look. Click **Bevel Rectangle** to apply that style to the image.

4. In the *Picture Styles* group, click the **Picture Border** button to display the menu shown in Figure 8-8.

5. Click the **Weight** submenu then select **2¼**.

   The border weight is increased, making it more noticeable.

6. Click the **Picture Border** button again.

7. Under the Theme Colors section, select **Blue-Gray**, **Text 2**, **Darker 50%**.

   The picture is now surrounded by a colored border.

CERTIFICATION READY?   **5.3.5**

How do you apply a style to a picture?

Figure 8-8

Picture Border menu

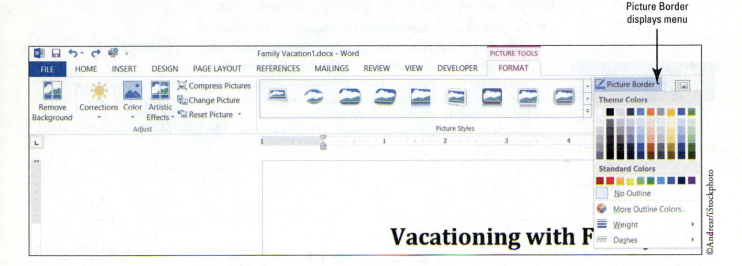

8. In the *Picture Styles* group, click the **Picture Effects** button to display the menu shown in Figure 8-9.

Figure 8-9

Picture Effects menu

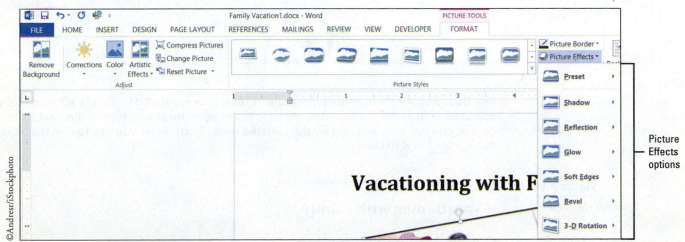

Scroll through each *Effects* option to view the available options.

9. Click the **Shadow** effect option. From the pop-up menu that appears, under the *Outer* heading, select **Offset Top** to apply that shadow effect to your image.

   The picture displays with a shadow on the upper portion of the image.

10. SAVE the document as *Family Vacation2* in the lesson folder on your flash drive.

PAUSE. LEAVE the document open for the next exercise.

Changing a Picture to a SmartArt Graphic

SmartArt graphics have preformatted designs with placeholders that allow you to enter text as a caption. In this exercise, you learn to apply a picture to a SmartArt graphic with a caption.

STEP BY STEP | **Change a Picture to a SmartArt Graphic**

USE the document that is open from the previous exercise.

1. The picture should be selected to display the *Picture Tools*.
2. In the *Pictures Styles* group, click the **Picture Layout** button to open the gallery.
3. Select the **Alternating Picture Circles** (see Figure 8-10).

The preset layout appears—each layout enables you to apply a picture with text. You can add a caption in the text area by adding a short description to your picture. The *Picture Layout* button automatically converts the picture to a SmartArt graphic and the picture is resized to accommodate a circled caption. The SmartArt Tools Design tab is activated.

Figure 8-10

Picture Layout gallery

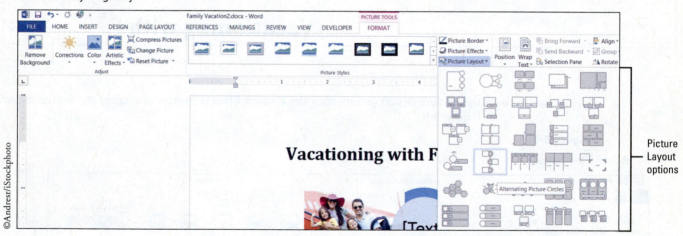

©Andresr/iStockphoto

Picture Layout options

4. Key **Boarding Airplane** in the placeholder [Text] (see Figure 8-11). Text is automatically adjusted to fit in the placeholder, which is the caption for the picture. If the *Text Pane* opens, you can also add text by the bulleted item [Text]. After you key text in the *Text Pane*, click the X to close.

Figure 8-11

SmartArt with caption

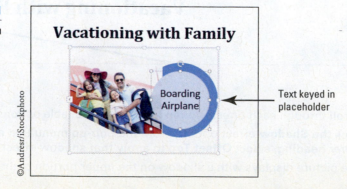

©Andresr/iStockphoto

Text keyed in placeholder

5. Click outside of the graphic to deselect.

CERTIFICATION READY? 5.2.3

How do I apply a new color to a SmartArt graphic?

6. **SAVE** the document as *Family Vacation3* in the lesson folder on your flash drive.

7. Select the image to continue applying changes to this document.

8. In the SmartArt Tools, select the **Design** tab, click the **Change Colors** button to produce a menu of options. Under the *Accent 6* group, select the **Colored Fill – Accent 6**. The SmartArt graphic color changes to the new color.

9. Select the **circle** containing the text, *Boarding Airplane* then click the **SmartArt Tools**, *Format* tab to change the format of the graphic. In the *Shape Styles* group, click the **More ▾** button and select the **Intense Effect – Gold, Accent 4**. The inner circle color is changed to the new style.

CERTIFICATION READY? 5.2.3

How do I change the shape of a SmartArt graphic?

10. Select the circle containing the text, and then click the **Shape Effects** button, select **Bevel** then apply **Art Deco**. The inner circle has taken on a different shape and is more eye-catching.

11. Select the outside circle then press the **Shift** key to select the inner circle.

12. Change the width by increasing it to **2.02**". Make sure you see the selection handles handles around the inner circle before changing the width.

CERTIFICATION READY? 5.2.3

How do I change the size of a SmartArt graphic?

13. **SAVE** the document as *Family Vacation3 Update* in the lesson folder on your flash drive then **CLOSE** the file.

PAUSE. LEAVE Word open to use in the next exercise.

Adjusting a Picture's Brightness, Contrast, and Color and Adding Artistic Effects

Although *Word* does not have all the advanced features of a stand-alone photo-editing program, it does offer many ways for you to adjust pictures using the *Picture Tools Format tab*—including correcting a picture's brightness, contrast, and color, and adding an artistic effect (see Table 8-1 for a list of options). The *Artistic Effects* feature can give the picture the appearance of a drawing, sketch, or painting. In this exercise, you will adjust the picture's brightness, contrast, and color, and apply an artistic effect.

STEP BY STEP   **Adjust a Picture's Brightness, Contrast, and Color and Add Artistic Effects**

Table 8-1

Adjust Group—provides options to enhance or return your picture to its original form

Type	Purpose
Remove Background	Removes unwanted portions of a background.
Corrections	Sharpen and Soften adjusts picture by highlighting the pixel colors. Brightness and Contrast alters the adjustment between the brightness and darkness of a picture.
Color	Color Saturation can be an intense deep color or a dim color. Color Tone adjusts the color cast of a picture that contains a dominance of one color by adjusting the color temperature to enhance the details. Recolor adjusts the image by changing the color to a gray scale, sepia tone, or another color for an added impact.
Artistic Effects	Applies distinct changes to an image to give it the appearance of a pencil drawing, line drawing, blur, watercolor sponge, film grain, photocopy, texturizer, and more.
Compress Pictures	Reduces the file size of an object.
Change Picture	Changes the image while maintaining the size of the current image.
Reset Picture	Removes all formatting from the picture and resets picture and size back to its original size.

OPEN the *Family Vacation* document from the lesson folder.

1. Select the picture to display the *Picture Tools* then click the **Format** tab.
2. Click the **Corrections** button in the *Adjust* group, to display the menu (see Figure 8-12).

Figure 8-12

Corrections gallery

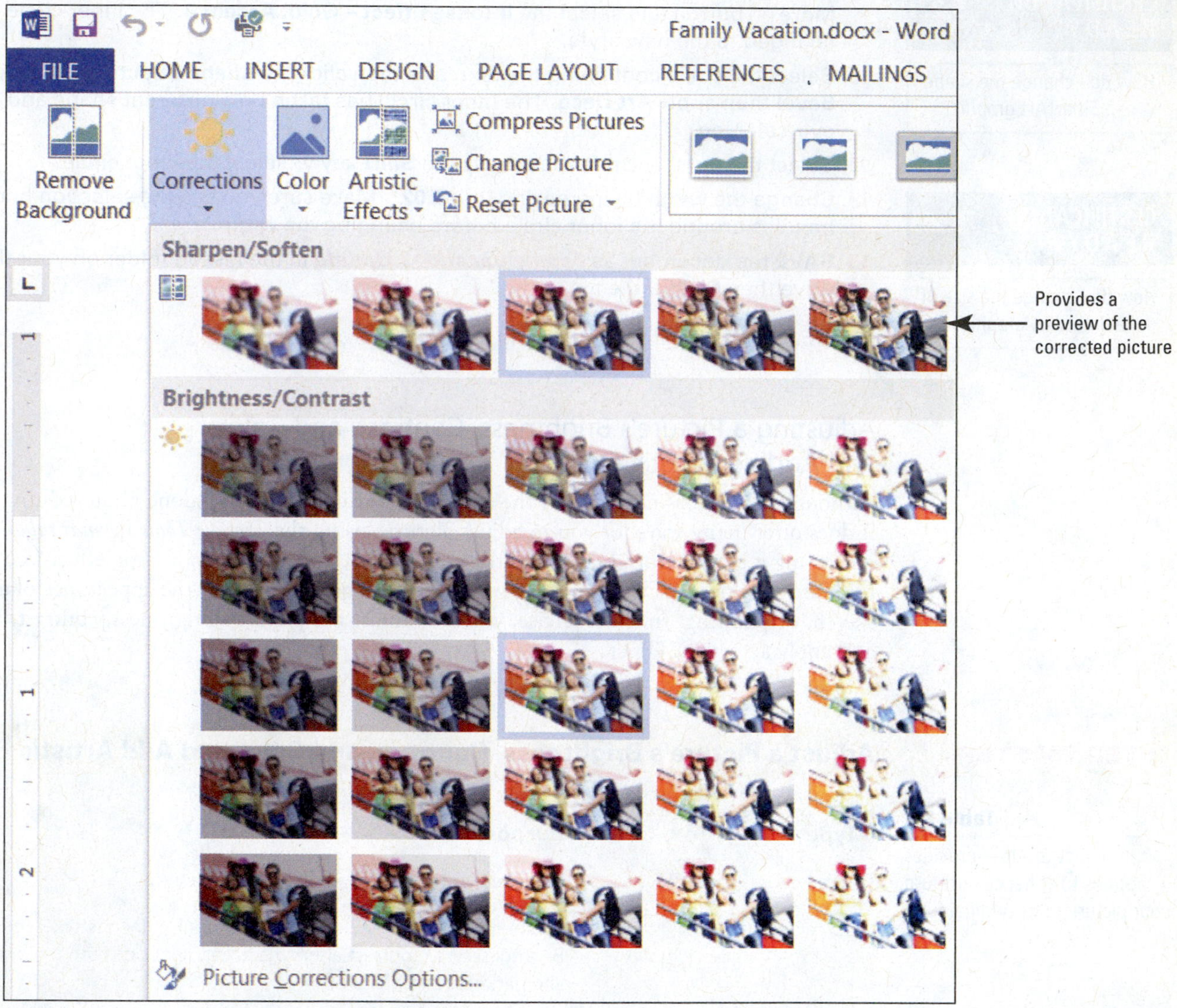

Provides a preview of the corrected picture

©Andresr/iStockphoto

3. In the *Brightness and Contrast* section, select **Brightness: +20% Contrast: +20%** (which might appear as the fourth option in the fourth row) to increase the brightness and contrast of your image by 20 percent. Notice the difference in the picture with an increased brightness and contrast.

4. Click the **Color** button in the *Adjust* group to display the menu (see Figure 8-13).

Figure 8-13

Color gallery

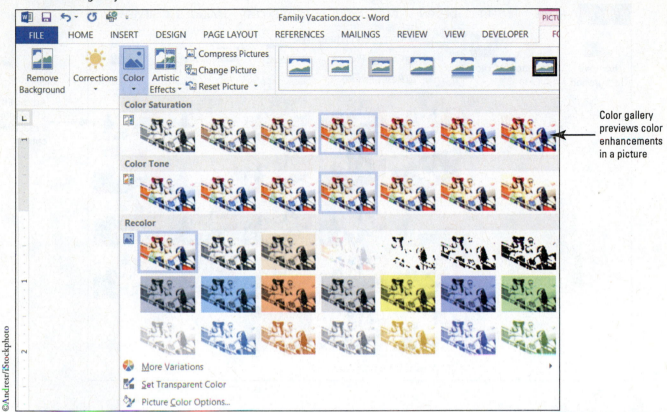

Color gallery previews color enhancements in a picture

5. Scroll through the options and notice how your picture changes. In the *Color Saturation* section, select **Saturation 200%**. The higher the saturation percentage, the more vibrant the colors appear in the picture, consequently making the plane's color in the picture more noticeable.

6. Click the **Color** button again to display the menu. In the *Color Tone* section, select **Temperature 5300 K**. The lower temperature tone creates a picture with a slight blue tint, while the higher temperature makes the picture appear with an orange tint.

7. Click the **Color** button again to display the menu. Under *Recolor*, No Recolor is selected by default. Hover over the Recolor options and you can see the changes in live preview. Keep the selection on No Color.

8. **SAVE** the document as *Family Vacation4* in the lesson folder on your flash drive.

9. Click the **Artistic Effects** button, to display the menu (see Figure 8-14).

CERTIFICATION READY?   **5.3.4**

How do I change the color of a picture?

Figure 8-14

Artistic Effects gallery

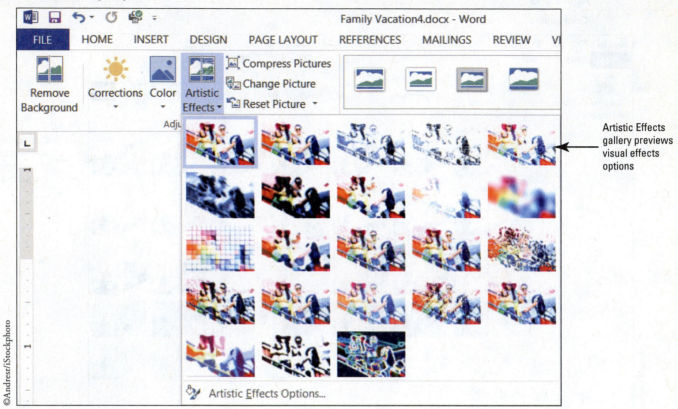

©Andresr/iStockphoto

CERTIFICATION
READY?   5.3.2

How do I apply artistic
effects to a picture?

10. Select the **Crisscross Etching** option from the *Artistic Effects* gallery. The impression of
    the picture is now of an etching sketch. Deselect the picture.

11. **SAVE** the document as ***Family Vacation5*** in the lesson folder on your flash drive.

PAUSE. LEAVE the Word document open to use in the next exercise.

Removing Backgrounds

Remove Background is a feature that removes portions of images you have inserted into documents.
You can use the Remove Background options either to automatically remove the image back-
ground or to mark and remove specific portions of the image. In this exercise, you learn to use the
Remove Background features.

STEP BY STEP   **Remove Background**

USE the document that is open from the previous exercise.

1. Select the picture to display the *Picture Tools;* then select the **Format** tab.

2. Click the **Remove Background** button. The *Background Removal* tab opens, as shown
   in Figure 8-15, and the picture is surrounded by a color selection marquee. A magenta
   color overlays the image, marking everything that is to be removed from the image.

Figure 8-15

Background Removal

3. To change the area of the picture that will be kept, resize the marquee by dragging the upper-left handle up until it meets the top of the lady's hat.

4. Drag the right middle-handle towards the bag until it reaches the man's elbow. Everything outside these boundaries will be removed from the image.

Take Note   Removing a background may take practice; therefore, you may need to use the Undo button to begin again.

5. In the *Close* group, click **Keep Changes** to remove the designated area of the image. Your edited image should be similar to the one shown in Figure 8-16. Removing the background of a picture is similar to cropping except that the background removal focuses on the picture you wish to point out. In this exercise, the background of the plane was removed.

Figure 8-16

Document without picture background

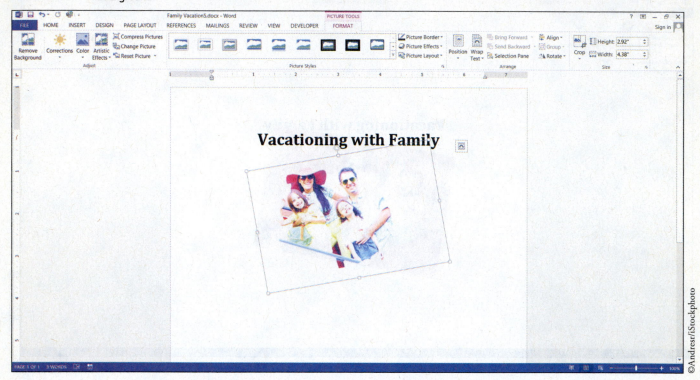

6. **SAVE** the document as *Family Vacation6* in the lesson folder on your flash drive.

7. Click the **Remove Background** button again.

8. If you cannot see the hand of the little girl who is waving, click the **Mark Areas to Keep** button in the *Refine* group. Press and hold the left mouse button, and draw around the little girl's hand. As you mark the area to keep, a circle with a plus symbol marks an area to keep.

9. Once you have completed, click the **Keep Changes** button. The little girl's hand appears as faded but can still be seen. Your document should match Figure 8-17.

Figure 8-17

Document showing little girl waving

10. **SAVE** the document as *Family Vacation7* in the lesson folder on your flash drive then **CLOSE** the file.

PAUSE. LEAVE the Word document open to use in the next exercise.

Arranging Text around a Picture

Arranging pictures and text together on the page is simple using Word's Positioning and Text Wrap commands. The Positioning command automatically positions the object in the location you select on the page. The Wrap Text command determines the way text wraps around the picture or other objects on the page, depending on the option you select. To configure the picture as an <mark>inline object</mark> that moves along with the text that surrounds it, select the In Line with Text option. If you choose to format the picture as a <mark>floating object</mark>, Word positions the image precisely on the page, and allows the text to wrap around it in one of several available formats. In this exercise, you learn to position text around a picture as you learned in Lesson 3.

STEP BY STEP   ### Arrange Text around a Picture

OPEN the *Family Vacation2* document completed earlier in the lesson.

1. If necessary, enable **Show/Hide** on the Home tab.
2. Place the insertion point by the paragraph mark by the SmartArt and press **Enter**. Key the following text:

   If you are looking for adventure with lots of activities that you can do as a family; then call Margie's Travel Agency. They will book all tours and outside activities, such as, bike riding, rafting, or zipping. They planned our last vacation, and we had a WONDERFUL time together as a family. Press **Enter** twice.

   Don't wait call!
3. Select the text and change the font size to **16** pt. Deselect the text.
4. Select the picture, in the *Arrange* group on the Picture Tools Format tab, click the **Position** button to display the menu (see Figure 8-18).

Figure 8-18

Position menu

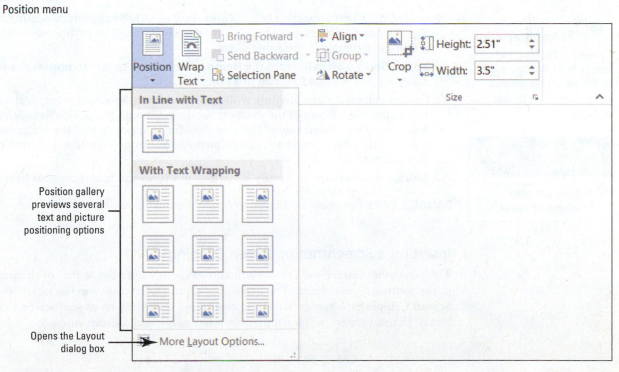

Position gallery previews several text and picture positioning options

Opens the Layout dialog box

5. Select **Position in Top Right with Square Text Wrapping**.
6. Delete the extra blank line below the heading.

CERTIFICATION
READY? **5.3.7**

How do you position the
picture in a document?

7. Place your insertion point anywhere in the paragraph you keyed in step 2, and press **Ctrl+L** to align text left. The title is centered to the left of the image and text is positioned at left of the margin and the picture is at the top right.

8. Select the picture again and the *Layout Options* button appears beside it. Microsoft has added this new feature to make it easy to wrap objects, such as pictures, drawings, SmartArt, and charts around text.

9. Click the **Layout Options** button to open the menu (see Figure 8-19).

Figure 8-19

Layout Options menu

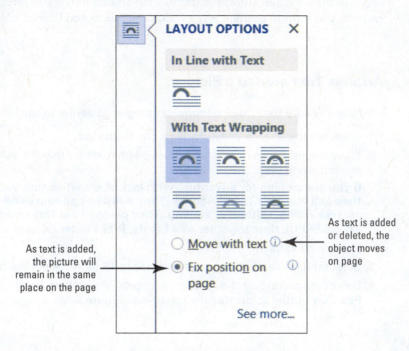

As text is added, the picture will remain in the same place on the page

As text is added or deleted, the object moves on page

10. Under *With Text Wrapping* select **Tight**. Text automatically wraps around the picture. The *Fix position on page* option is already selected and as additional text is added, the picture will remain in the same place.

Another Way
The Wrap Text feature in the Arrange group on the Format Tab provides additional options for text wrapping.

11. Select **Don't wait call!** From the **Home** tab, change the text to **uppercase** without rekeying and change font size to **36 pt**.

12. Editing can take place anytime while you're working in a document, and now you want to change the content of the existing heading. Change the title to **Family Vacation** by selecting the title and keying the new title. Did you notice that the picture stayed in place? That's because The *Fix position on page* option was selected from the *Layout Options* menu.

CERTIFICATION
READY? **5.3.6**

How do you wrap text
around a picture?

13. **SAVE** the document as *Family Vacation8* in the lesson folder on your flash drive.

PAUSE. LEAVE the document open to use in the next exercise.

Inserting a Screenshot or Screen Clipping

The Screenshot feature will capture a picture of the whole screen or part of the screen and save it in the format of your choice. The Screenshot captures an entire window of an open application. **Screen Clippings**, however, are image captures of only the part of your screen that you have selected. In this exercise, you learn to insert a screenshot and a screen clipping.

Insert a Screenshot

USE the document that is open from the previous exercise.

1. On the *View* tab click the **One Page** button in the *Zoom* group so that the entire page is displayed on your screen. Do not minimize the display, or the screenshot will not capture the image of this document.

2. Press **Ctrl+N** to open a new blank document.

3. On the *Insert* tab click the **Screenshot** button in the *Illustrations* group. The *Available Windows* gallery displays the image of the document (see Figure 8-20). If you have more than one window open, you will see images from all open documents on the *Available Windows* area.

Figure 8-20

Screenshot displaying Available Windows

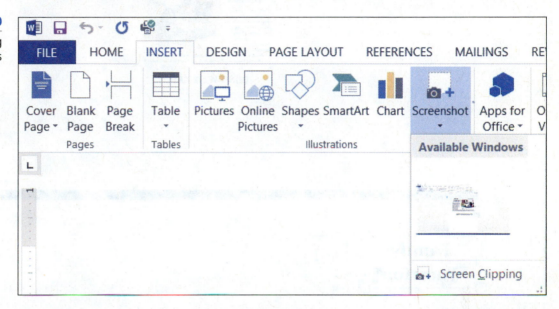

4. Under the *Available Windows* area, click the screenshot of the Family Vacation8 document to insert in the blank document.

5. **SAVE** the document as ***Family Vacation Screenshot*** in the lesson folder on your flash drive.

PAUSE. LEAVE the document open to use in the next exercise.

Insert a Screen Clipping

USE the document that is open from the previous exercise.

1. Deselect the image then press the **Enter** key twice.

2. Click the **Screenshot** button; then select **Screen Clipping** from the menu. The active document fades away, the ***Family Vacation8*** document appears in a faded gray and the mouse pointer changes to a crosshair (+).

3. Drag the mouse pointer over the heading, *Family Vacation*. When you release the mouse button, the heading is placed in the *Family Vacation Screenshot* document as shown in Figure 8-21. Deselect the heading.

Figure 8-21

Document with
Screen Clipping

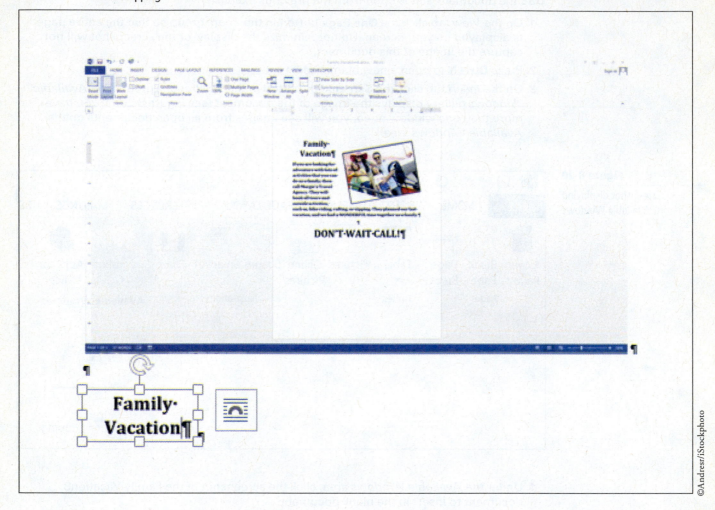

4. **SAVE** the document as *Family Vacation Screen Clipping* in lesson folder on your flash then **CLOSE** the file.

5. **CLOSE** the *Family Vacation8* document.

PAUSE. LEAVE Word open to use in the next exercise.

INSERTING AND FORMATTING SHAPES, WORDART, AND SMARTART

The Bottom Line

Word provides illustrations to enhance your document with different preset shapes, SmartArt, and WordArt. **Shapes** are figures such as lines, rectangles, block arrows, equation shapes, flowcharts, stars, banners, and callouts. You may also insert a **drawing canvas** which will serve as a guide. The Drawing Tools make it possible for you to change the shape, add text, apply styles, fill with theme or standard colors, gradient, texture colors, and apply preset effects. **SmartArt graphics** are graphical illustrations available from a list of various categories, including List diagrams, Process diagrams, Cycle diagrams, Hierarchy diagrams, Relationship diagrams, Matrix diagrams, and Pyramid diagrams. The SmartArt Tools enable you to manipulate the SmartArt by adding shapes, bullets, and text; changing the layout and colors; and applying special effects using styles. **WordArt** is a feature that creates decorative effects with text. The Drawing Tools allow you to format the WordArt by adding special effects to the text or outline, applying preset effects, and transforming the shape using one of the set styles.

SOFTWARE ORIENTATION

Shapes Menu and Drawing Tools

When you click the Shapes button in the Illustrations group of the Insert tab, the Shapes menu is displayed (see Figure 8-22). After you insert a shape into a Word document, the *Drawing Tools Format* tab opens (see Figure 8-23). You use these tools to format a shape's style, fill, color, outline, and many other attributes. Shapes can be overlapping where one object can be placed in front of other objects or sent behind another object. When you group objects together, it makes it easy to format and move them around in a document.

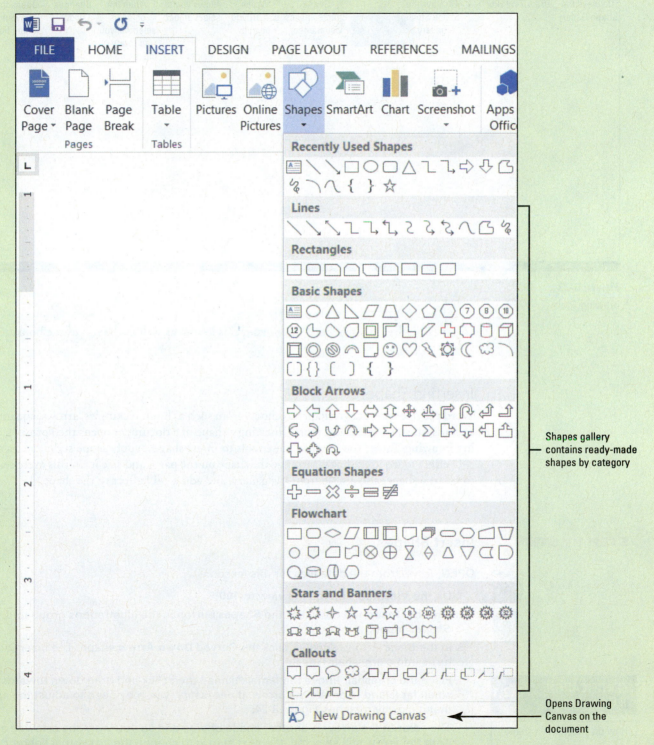

Shapes gallery contains ready-made shapes by category

Opens Drawing Canvas on the document

Figure 8-22

Shapes menu

Edit Shape points in the direction it can be reshaped | Shape Styles group | Adds color within shape | Format the object outline shape | Align object on page | Position object where you want it to appear | Brings the object forward | Sends object backward | Changes height

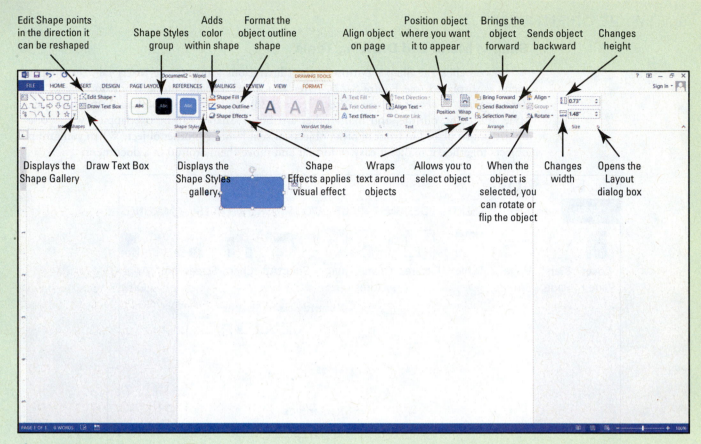

Displays the Shape Gallery | Draw Text Box | Displays the Shape Styles gallery | Shape Effects applies visual effect | Wraps text around objects | Allows you to select object | When the object is selected, you can rotate or flip the object | Changes width | Opens the Layout dialog box

Figure 8-23
Drawing Tools

Use these figures as a reference throughout this lesson, as well as the rest of the book.

Inserting Shapes

Word provides pre-drawn shapes to choose from such as lines, rectangles, arrows, equation shapes, callouts, stars, banners, and more. Inserting a shape in a document opens the Format tab containing Drawing Tools. You can use these tools to insert shapes, apply shape styles, add a shadow or 3-D effect to inserted shapes, arrange the shape on the page, and size it. In this exercise, you learn to insert a shape, add a style from the gallery, and add a 3-D effect to the shape.

| STEP BY STEP | Insert Shapes |

OPEN *Travel* from the data files for this lesson.

1. On the **View** tab, change the view to **100%**.

2. Click the **Insert** tab then click the **Shapes** button in the Illustrations group to display the *Shapes* menu.

3. In the *Block Arrows* section, click the **Curved Down Arrow** shape. The insertion point turns into a crosshair (+).

4. Place the crosshair above the female's head then click and drag down towards the small far island to create the arrow. If necessary, you may need to adjust the arrow so that it closely matches Figure 8-24.

The color of the arrow is another shade of blue and so you want the arrow to stand out. With the arrow still selected, the next step is to change the arrow to a lighter color to make it more visible.

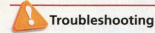 **Troubleshooting** If the shape you are drawing does not turn out the right size the first time, you can adjust the shape by selecting it and then dragging one of the sizing handles.

5. Click the **Shape Fill** button to open the menu then select *yellow*. The yellow fill is a good choice.

6. Resize the height to **0.6"** and width to **1.82"**. You can resize from the *Size* group or open the *Layout* dialog box. Some adjustment may be needed to move the arrow.

   Another change that you would like to make is increasing the weight of the outline and adding color to the outline.

7. Click the *Shape Outline* **drop down arrow** to open the menu.

   Select *Weight* then change the weight of the shape to **1 1/2**.

8. Click the *Shape Outline* **drop down arrow** again. Change the color to *Light Green* in the Standard Colors. Your document should match Figure 8-24.

Figure 8-24

Block arrow shape inserted in object

Picture Yourself Here

©4FR/iStockphoto

9. **SAVE** the document as *Travel Outing* in the lesson folder on your flash drive and then **CLOSE** the file.

PAUSE. LEAVE Word open to use in the next exercise.

Grouping Shapes into a Single Drawing

The Shapes menu contains a number of ready-made shapes that can be drawn in your document into a Drawing Canvas. A drawing can be a single object or multiple objects grouped together and can include any of the shapes. In this exercise, you learn to use the Drawing Canvas and place shapes within the canvas.

Take Note A **drawing canvas** is a frame-like boundary that keeps multiple drawing objects together. By default, the drawing canvas is off, but you can display it easily by clicking the Shapes button on the Insert tab, and then choosing the New Drawing Canvas option from the Shapes menu that appears.

STEP BY STEP **Insert Drawing Canvas and Shapes**

 OPEN a blank document.

1. At the top of the document, key **Margie's Travel Agency** press **Shift+Enter** to insert a line break. Then key **Exciting Places to See**.

2. Select *Margie's Travel Agency* and change the font to **Cambria** and font size to **36 pt**.

3. Select *Exciting Places to See* then change the font size to **24 pt** and *center*. By using the line break, both headings moved to the center.

4. Deselect the text and press **Enter** twice.

5. On the Insert tab, click the **Shapes** button then click **New Drawing Canvas** located at the bottom of the menu. The *New Drawing Canvas* frame appears on the document. You also see the *Drawing Tools Format* tab (see Figure 8-25).

Figure 8-25

New Drawing Canvas

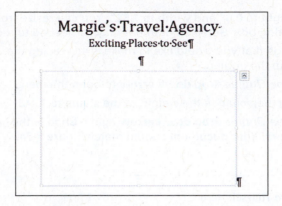

Margie's·Travel·Agency·
Exciting·Places·to·See¶

¶

6. Click the **More** button in the *Insert Shapes* group to open the Shapes menu; then select *Oval*.

7. Place the crosshair in the upper left part of the frame of the canvas and draw a **1"** shape in height and **1.5"** wide. When you finish drawing, you can resize the object in the *Size* group.

8. Click the **More** button then select *Trapezoid* from the *Basic Shapes* group, and draw the shape below the oval. The dimension for the height is **1.96"** and the width is **1.96"**.

9. In the same group in the Shapes menu, select *Regular Pentagon*. Place the cursor on the upper right side of the canvas next to the circle. Begin drawing with the dimensions of **1.14"** in height and **1.83"** wide.

10. Select the *Cube* shape from the same group in the Shapes menu, and place below the *Regular Pentagon* with the height being positioned at **1.59"** and width at **1.61"**.

11. **SAVE** the document as *Margie's Excursions* in the lesson folder on your flash drive.

Take Note   Anytime you add shapes to a document, you can group them so that when you move them, they move together. Formatting grouped objects works the same way—when you format grouped objects, they will be formatted with the same colors, text size, etc.

12. Select both the *Oval* and *Regular Pentagon* objects. Don't forget to hold the **Shift** key down when selecting the second object. When objects are selected, the *Group* command in the *Arrange* group becomes activated.

13. Click the **drop down arrow** by *Group*; then select Group. The objects are now placed in a border indicating these two are grouped together. Group the remaining two objects.

14. Now move the selected group so that it lays over the top of the other group. Notice that both shapes in the group move together.

15. In the *Arrange* group, there are two more commands that you will use for these objects, these are the *Bring Forward* and *Send Backward* commands.

16. Let's format the objects with different colors before using the next command. With the *Trapezoid* and *Cube* group selected, click **Shape Fill** then select **Blue, Accent 5, Darker 50%**. The objects now have a darker fill color and you think it would look better if the darker color was in the back instead of the front.

17. With the objects still selected, select *Send Backward* in the *Arrange* group. The lighter objects are both placed in front of the darker objects.

18. **SAVE** the document as *Margie's Excursions Objects* in the lesson folder on your flash drive then **CLOSE** the file.

PAUSE. LEAVE Word open to use in the next exercise.

Adding Text and a Caption to a Shape

You can add, edit, and format text in shapes, just as you do in any part of the Word document. Adding text to a flowchart, symbol, or other object opens the Drawing Tools Format tab. In this exercise, you will add text and a caption to the shapes.

Add Text and a Caption to a Shape

OPEN the *Margie's Excursions* document completed earlier in the lesson.

1. Select the object then begin typing or use the *Selection Pane* to select the object. **Cycling** (*Oval*); **Exploring the City** (*Trapezoid*); **Surfing** (*Regular Pentagon*); and **National Park** (*Cube*).

   After adding shapes, you can key text directly on the shape and begin formatting by adding a font color, changing the font size, and alignment. Try to match your document to Figure 8-26.

Figure 8-26

Shapes with text

2. Select all objects and change the font size to the contents in the object to **16 pt** and font color to **Blue-Gray, Text 2, Darker 50%**.

3. Click the **References** tab then click **Insert Caption** button of the *Captions* group to open the Caption dialog box (see Figure 8-27). The insertion point is located to the right of *Figure 1*.

Figure 8-27

Caption dialog box

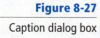

Captions are automatically labeled and numbered by Word

4. Press the **spacebar** key once.

5. Key **Types of Excursions**. Word automatically adds a label and will number each caption automatically. By default the caption will appear *Below selected item* but can be changed to *Above selected item*.

6. Click **OK**. The caption along with the short description appears below the objects. Compare your document with Figure 8-28.

Figure 8-28

Document with text and caption

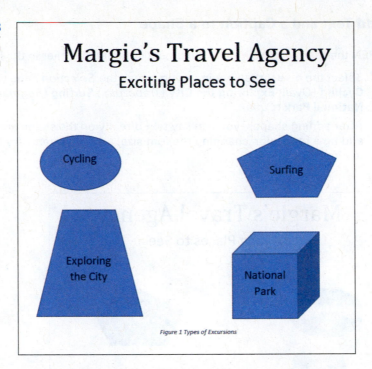

7. **SAVE** the document as **Margie's Excursions1** in the lesson folder on your flash drive.

PAUSE. LEAVE the Word document open to use in the next exercise.

Take Note   A shape cannot be converted to a SmartArt graphic like a picture because it is not an image. Adding a caption to a shape would require you to add the caption using the References tab.

Formatting Shapes

The Drawing Tools include a number of options for changing the appearance of shapes and positioning and wrapping text around shapes. In this exercise, you learn to use the shape styles, resize shapes, position shapes, and wrap text around shapes.

STEP BY STEP   **Format Shapes**

USE the document that is open from the previous exercise.

1. Select the *oval* object then click the **More** button in the *Shape Styles* group to display the gallery of preformatted styles available for the selected shape (see Figure 8-29).

Figure 8-29

Shape Styles gallery

2. Select **Intense Effect – Blue Accent 5** to apply to the *oval* object.

3. Select the **Trapezoid** object then select **Moderate Effect – Gray-50%, Accent 3**.

4. Select the **Regular Pentagon** object; then format with **Subtle Effect – Gold, Accent 4**.

5. Select the **Cube** object; then select **Colored Fill – Orange, Accent 2**.

   Each of the objects now have a different shape and fill color applied to it. Additional changes can be applied to give the object a more intense shape.

6. Select the **Cube** object; then click the **Shape Outline** button. In the Theme Colors section, select **Blue-Gray, Text 2, Darker 50%**. The outline of the border becomes darker.

7. Click the **Shape Outline** button again, and change the **Weight** for the cube to **3 pt** to change the thickness of the box's border.

8. Click the **Shape Effects** button and select **Shadow**. Then in the *Outer* group, select the **Offset Diagonal Top Right**. In the top right of the object, you should see a shadow background.

9. Click the **Shape Effects** button again and in the *3-D Rotation* of the *Perspective* group select **Perspective Contrasting Left**. The object has rotated to the left.

   You have formatted each of the shapes with a different style (color), but only the cube got an outline and effect.

10. **SAVE** the document as ***Margie's Excursions2*** in your flash drive in the lesson folder.

    Now let's reposition the shapes so that you determine where the shapes will appear. As you add text to the document the shapes will remain in place on the document.

11. Select the Drawing Canvas.

12. In the *Arrange* group on the Drawing Tools Format tab, click the **Position** button and select **Position in Middle Left with Square Text Wrapping**. The caption moves above the shapes.

13. For this step, **OPEN** the *Family Vacation8* document completed earlier in the lesson. Select the paragraph beginning with "*If you are . . . as a family*" then copy and return to the previous document. [Hint: To avoid selecting the picture, do not select the paragraph mark.]

14. Place the insertion point above the caption then click **Paste**. Did you notice that the shapes remained in their position when text was inserted in the document?

15. Reposition the objects so that the document appears better arranged. Select the Drawing Canvas, select the **Position** button then select **Position in Bottom Right with Square Text Wrapping**.

16. Change the document's view to one page. The shapes are at the bottom of the page while the text is at the top.

17. **SAVE** the document as *Margie's Excursions3* in your flash drive in the lesson folder.

18. **CLOSE** the *Family Vacation8* file.

19. The *Margie's Excursions3* file should still opened. On the **View** tab, change the view to **100%**. **Delete** all shapes by selecting the Drawing Canvas and the caption at the top of the page.

20. Position the insertion point at the beginning of the paragraph and insert the **smiley face** shape. Draw the shape with the height at **1.28"** by **1.24"** wide.

21. Apply a shape style and select **Light 1 Outline, Colored Fill – Gold, Accent 4** to give the smiley face a new look.

22. In the *Arrange* group, click the **Wrap Text** button and select **Tight**. The text wraps around the shape.

23. **SAVE** the document as *Margie's Excursions4* in your flash drive in the lesson folder then **CLOSE** the file.

PAUSE. LEAVE Word open to use in the next exercise.

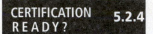

CERTIFICATION READY?   5.2.5

How do you position a shape in a document that contains content?

Another Way
By removing the Drawing Canvas first, all objects will also be deleted.

CERTIFICATION READY?   5.2.4

How do you wrap text around a shape?

Inserting WordArt

As you learned in Lesson 3, WordArt enhances text with more vibrant colors and shapes. In this exercise, you learn to insert WordArt in a document.

STEP BY STEP   **Insert WordArt**

OPEN the *Margie's Excursions2* document completed earlier in the lesson.

1. Select the text **Margie's Travel Agency**.

2. On the *Insert* tab click the **WordArt** button to display the menu.

3. Select **Fill – Gray-25%**, **Background 2**, **Inner Shadow**. The lettering for the *Margie's Travel Agency* heading takes on a new appearance and style.

4. Remove the line break to move the paragraph mark by the heading.

5. Select the WordArt, and click the **Text Effects** button then select *Transform*. Under the *Warp* group select **Wave 1**. This changes the WordArt to a wavy text.

6. With the WordArt still selected click the Text Fills **drop down arrow** and in the *Standard Colors,* select *Purple* to change the color to give it a more vibrant look. If the *Show/Hide* is enabled, disable it. The document should match Figure 8-30.

Figure 8-30

Formatted Document
with WordArt

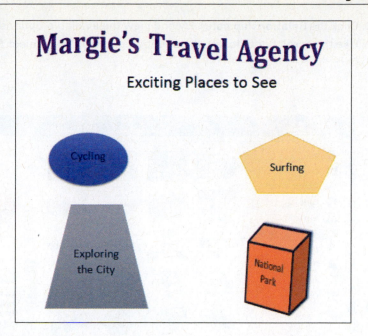

CERTIFICATION
READY?   **2.2.10**

How would you change text
to WordArt?

7. SAVE the document as *Margie's Excursions5* in the lesson folder on your flash drive then **CLOSE** the file.

PAUSE. LEAVE Word open to use in the next exercise.

Using SmartArt Graphics

SmartArt graphics are visual representations of information that can help communicate your message or ideas more effectively. SmartArt graphics and designer-quality illustrations can contribute to eye-catching documents that draw the attention of the target audience. Table 8-2 gives some examples of the type of information you can display with each category of SmartArt graphics. Earlier in this lesson, you learned to convert pictures to SmartArt with captions. In this exercise, you learn to insert SmartArt graphics into Word documents and add text to the graphics.

Table 8-2

SmartArt graphic categories

Type	Purpose
List	Show nonsequential or grouped blocks of information
Process	Show a progression of steps in a process, timeline, task, or workflow
Cycle	Show a continuing sequence of stages, tasks, or events in a circular flow
Hierarchy	Show a decision tree or create an organization chart
Relationship	Illustrate connections or interlocking ideas; show related or contrasting concepts
Matrix	Show how parts relate to a whole
Pyramid	Show proportional, foundation-based, containment, overlapping, or interconnected relationships
Picture	Show a central idea through a series of pictures, with little or no text

STEP BY STEP   **Use SmartArt Graphics**

OPEN a new, blank document.

1. In the *Illustrations* group on the *Insert* tab click the **SmartArt** button to open the *Choose a SmartArt Graphic* dialog box.

2. Click the **Relationship** category and view the available options.

3. Use the scroll bar to locate the equation graphic. Then select *Equation* as shown in Figure 8-31.

Figure 8-31

Choose a SmartArt Graphic dialog box

Several categories of SmartArt are available with preview option

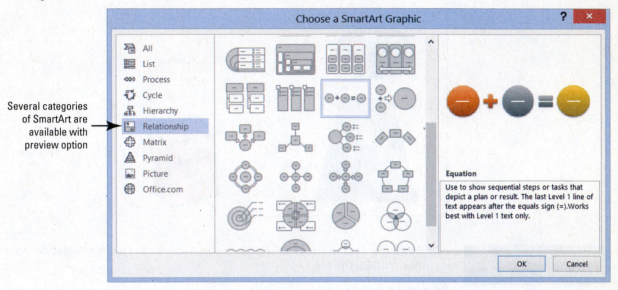

4. Click **OK** to insert the *Equation SmartArt* graphic into your document. The placeholders are placed in the graphic and ready for you to key information. Text can be keyed in the placeholders or in the Text Pane.

5. Click the **Text Pane** button in the *Create Graphic* group on the Ribbon to enable the Text Pane. The Text appears and you are ready to begin keying text in each element of the graphic equation. The first placeholder is selected by default and ready for you to key text (see Figure 8-32).

Another Way
Select the SmartArt graphic and double-click to insert.

Figure 8-32

SmartArt graphic with Text Pane open

Enable or disable Text Pane button

Text Pane makes entering text easy

Description of SmartArt graphic

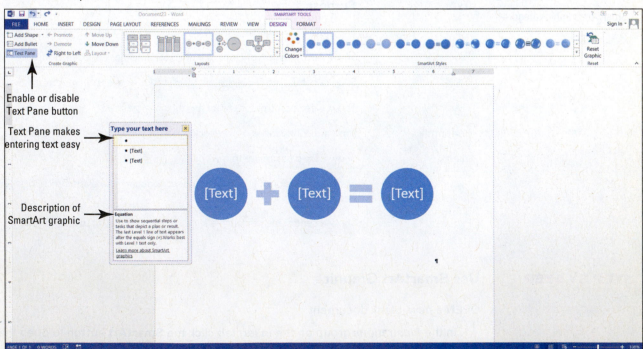

6. Key the information as displayed in Figure 8-33.

7. Click the **[Text]** placeholder to move to the next elements, and key the remaining text. As you key text, Word automatically adjusts the text to fit in the graphic. If you press the **Enter** key, another element is added to the equation.

8. Click the **Close** button in the *Text Pane* or click the *Text Pane* button to close it.

Figure 8-33

Text added to SmartArt graphic

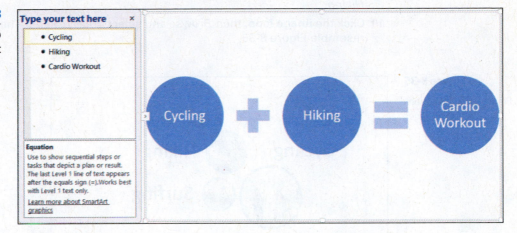

9. In the *Layouts* group on the SmartArt Tools Design tab, click the **drop down arrow** at the *More* button to produce the *Layouts* gallery.

10. Select **More Layouts**. The *Choose a SmartArt Graphic* dialog box appears.

11. Select the **Picture** category; then select **Bubble Picture List**.

12. Click **OK**. The Equation's graphic is replaced with the *Bubble Picture List*, and text is carried over to the new layout as captions. In the middle of each circle, an image icon appears—this is where you will insert a picture.

13. To add an image click the first image icon for **Cycling**; the *Insert Pictures* dialog box opens as shown in Figure 8-34.

14. Click the **Browse** button next to *From a file*; then locate your lesson folder.

15. Click to select the *Cycling* image, then click **Insert** or *double-click* on the image. The image is inserted in the first bubble and is automatically resized and adjusted. When you use the option to select images from Office.com; you will need to first save the image to a location on your computer or flash drive.

Figure 8-34

Insert Pictures dialog box

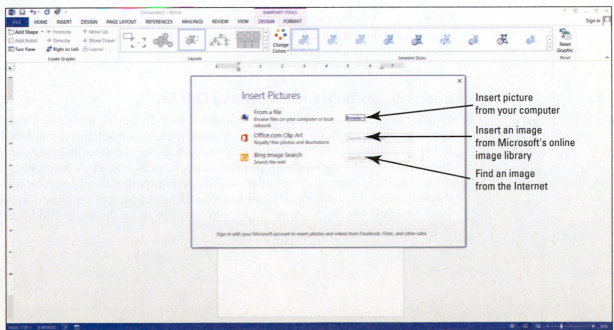

16. Text can be easily replaced by keying in the placeholder. Replace *Hiking* with *Surfing.*

17. Click the image icon by *Surfing.* The *Insert Pictures* dialog box opens. Click *Browse* and select the **Surfing** picture. Double-click to open. The *surfing* image is inserted in the bubble by the caption, *Surfing.*

18. Before you add the final image, edit the caption *"Cardio Workout"* and replace with *Hiking.*

19. Click the **image icon**, then *Browse* and select **Tourist Hiker**. The document should resemble Figure 8-35.

Figure 8-35

SmartArt with captions and images

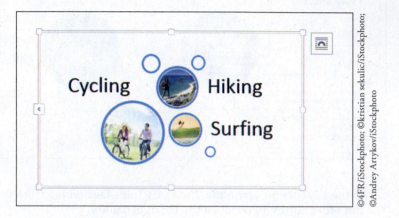

©4FR/iStockphoto; ©kristian sekulic/iStockphoto; ©Andrey Artykov/iStockphoto

20. **SAVE** the document as **Places to See** in the lesson folder on your flash drive then **CLOSE** the file.

PAUSE. LEAVE Word open to use in the next exercise.

INSERTING AND FORMATTING CLIP ART FROM OFFICE.COM

The Bottom Line

As you have seen so far, the Insert Pictures dialog box opens each time you click the Pictures icon. Online Pictures is a *new* button in the Illustrations group. You have more options on where to get your image. You can search for an image using Office.com, Bing, or other online sources. Or, you can scan or use your camera then save the picture to a location and retrieve it later.

Clip art is a collection of media files available for you to insert from Office.com. These include pictures and illustrations. After inserting a clip art object into your document, you can format it using many of the tools available.

Inserting, Resizing, and Formatting Clip Art

Clip art refers to picture files that are inserted in a document using the Office.com Clip Art option in the Insert Pictures dialog box. If you choose to copy pictures from a Web page, you do so by right-clicking, copying, saving on your flash drive, and then inserting the picture in your document. Just like working with pictures, clip art can be resized for better management within the document so that you can position it correctly. Formatting the clip art object is easy using the shortcut menu. The tools make it easy to format different parts of the object. In this exercise, you learn how to insert clip art from Office.com and then resize the image and format various parts of the object in the clip art.

STEP BY STEP   **Insert and Resize Clip Art**

OPEN a blank document.

1. Key **Explore the World** and change the font to **Cambria**, font size to **36 pt**, and **center** then deselect.

2. Press **Enter** to move the insertion point below the new heading.

3. In the *Illustrations* group on the *Insert* tab, click the **Online Pictures** button. The *Insert Pictures* dialog box appears (see Figure 8-34).

Take Note   This is the place where you decide where to get pictures. As mentioned earlier, you can look for a picture from your computer, Web page, or online sources. There are several online sources that contain royalty-free photos and illustrations and are used for corporations, personal use, or in this case, classroom instruction.

CERTIFICATION READY?   **5.3.1**

How do you insert an image?

4. In the *Search box* next to Office.com Clip Art, key **travel** and begin the search by pressing **Enter**. Pictures, illustrations, and clip art appears in the box below with many options to select from. Select the image highlighted in Figure 8-36 (or one similar, if you don't see that particular image). A border is placed around the selected clip art to show that it is the selected item.

Figure 8-36

Office.com Clip Art

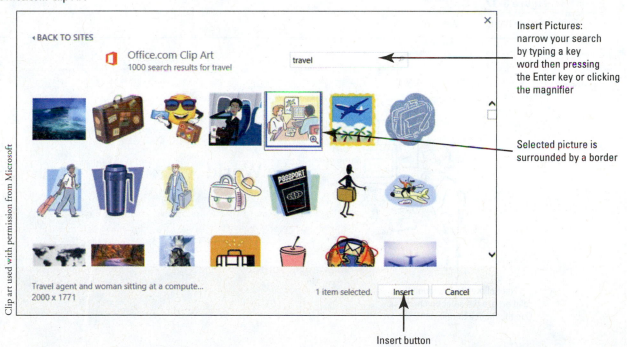

Clip art used with permission from Microsoft

Insert Pictures: narrow your search by typing a key word then pressing the Enter key or clicking the magnifier

Selected picture is surrounded by a border

Insert button

5. Click **Insert** to begin downloading.

 Cross Ref   Earlier in this lesson, the Picture Tools were introduced for pictures. They are used the same way for clip art.

6. Resize the clip art using the *Size* group and change the height to **3.12"** and width to.

Take Note   As you learned earlier, you can get precise measurements using the Layout dialog box.

CERTIFICATION READY?   **5.3.4**

7. **SAVE** the document as *Travel Plans* in the lesson folder on your flash drive.

PAUSE. LEAVE the document open to use in the next exercise.

How do you resize a clip art image?

Formatting Clip Art

The Picture Tools Format tab provides a number of commands for enhancing your document's appearance. You can use these tools to apply corrections, color, and picture styles to format the object. In this exercise, you learn to format different parts of the object and reposition the clip art in the document.

Format Clip Art

USE the document that is open from the previous exercise.

1. Select the clip art image you inserted into the document during the preceding exercise to display the *Picture Tools Format* tab.

2. Right-click the image, then select **Edit Picture** from the shortcut menu. Word automatically moves the clip art to the upper-left corner of the document to begin formatting.

3. Click just above the man's head in the yellow area to select the background area; then right-click. Above the shortcut menu, a new menu with three options appears to allow changes to the Style, Fill, and Outline, along with the shortcut menu (see Figure 8-37). When you select parts of an object, selection handles appears around it, and you are ready to begin formatting.

Figure 8-37

Format Shape menu

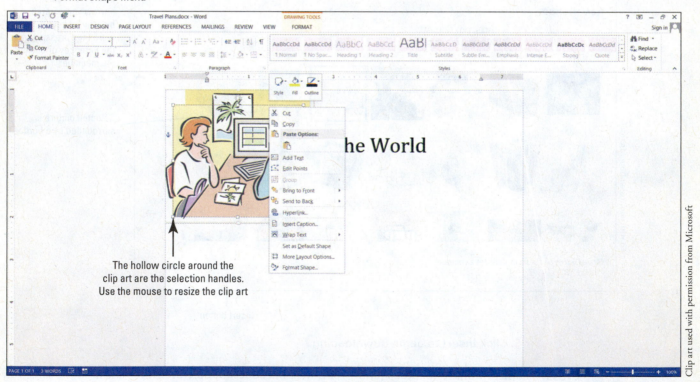

The hollow circle around the clip art are the selection handles. Use the mouse to resize the clip art

Clip art used with permission from Microsoft

4. Click the **Fill** button to produce the color palette and select **Blue-Gray, Text 2, Lighter 80%** to change the background color.

5. Select the palm tree within the frame to change the color of the palms to a darker green. The selection handles surround the palms. Right-click, and then apply **Green, Accent 6, Darker 50%** from the *Fill* menu.

6. Select the female's head to change her hair color to *yellow* using the *Fill* menu. Make sure the selection handles surround the area of her head. Now that you have made changes, let's apply the other formatting options available.

7. Position the insertion point in the background area located in the upper-right of the clip art; right-click then click the **Style** button to produce the style gallery. Select **Colored Fill–Black, Dark 1** to apply this background color behind the wall of the clip art.

8. Select the computer screen (the dark gray area) then click the **Outline** button and change the weight to **3 pt**.

9. Click the **Outline** button again and change the color to **Green, Accent 6, Darker 25%**. This action changes the inside frame of the computer.

10. Select the table to change the **Fill** color to **Orange, Accent 2, Darker 50%**. The table color changes to a darker color.

Now that you have completed formatting the clip art, it is time to format the text and position the object within the document.

11. Click the lower part of the clip art to select the whole object and to display the *Layout Options* icon (see Figure 8-38). The Layout Options were introduced earlier in this lesson.

Figure 8-38

Layout Options displays with formatted clip art

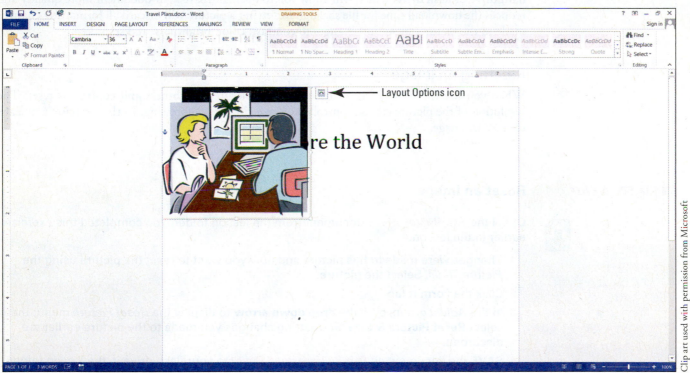

Layout Options icon

re the World

Clip art used with permission from Microsoft

12. Open the **Layout Options**.

13. Select the option button by **Fix position on page** then click **Top and Bottom** in the *With Text Wrapping* section. The text, "*Explore the World*" moves below the image.

14. Close the Layout Options menu.

15. Select the text without the paragraph mark. If the paragraph mark is selected so is the object.

16. Apply **WordArt** and select **Fill – Black, Text 1, Shadow**.

17. Adjust the WordArt and drag to the right of the image keeping it centered between the image and the margin. Disable Show/Hide.

18. **SAVE** the document as **_Formatted Clip Art_** in the lesson folder on your flash drive then **CLOSE** the file.

PAUSE. LEAVE Word open for the next exercise.

Workplace *Ready*

DOWNLOADING IMAGES

In today's world, you can download images from Web pages and from other online sources and insert them into documents, brochures, social pages, etc. Some of these online sources may contain royalty-free photos and illustrations that you can use. However, it is important to remember that permission is needed to use some images because of copyrights. A good example would be a company's logo. Before you start downloading any image, make sure it is royalty-free.

RESETTING AND COMPRESSING IMAGES

When you **compress** an image, it reduces the file size by reducing the resolution and making the document more manageable to share. Larger images may take up space on your flash drive leaving no room to save additional work. When an image is compressed, it occupies less space on your hard drive or flash drive, which will allow you to open and save your document more quickly and reduces the download time for file sharing. **Resetting** a picture will discard all formatting changes made to the picture, including changes to contrast, color, brightness, and style.

Resetting an Image

When you use the Reset Picture command, the picture's brightness and contrast is reset. The resolution of the picture can be controlled by resetting or compressing. In this exercise, you learn to reset an image.

STEP BY STEP   **Reset an Image**

OPEN the *Family Vacation5* document from the lesson folder. You completed this exercise earlier in the lesson.

1. Changes were made to this picture and now you want to reset the picture using the *Picture Tools*. Select the **picture**.

2. Click the **Format** tab.

3. In the *Adjust* group, click the **drop down arrow** to display the *Reset Picture* menu; then select **Reset Picture & Size**. Formatting changes you made to the picture earlier are discarded.

4. **SAVE** the document as *Family Vacation5 Reset* to your flash drive in the lesson folder.

PAUSE. LEAVE the document open to use in the next exercise.

Compressing Images

Some documents may contain images that you want to share by email. Images are set to various sizes and depending on the size of the image; you should also consider the download time it takes to send by email. Compressing images reduces the size but it will also decrease the resolution and the quality of the picture; and an uncompressed picture creates a very large file. Advanced options are available in Backstage and more discussion on using Options will be discussed in Lesson 14. In this exercise, you learn to compress and reset an image in preparation for sharing by email.

<table>
<tr><td>**STEP BY STEP**</td><td>**Compress Images**</td></tr>
</table>

USE the document that is open from the previous exercise.

1. To display the *Picture Tools*, select the picture then click the **Format** tab.
2. In the *Adjust* group, click the **Compress Pictures** button to display the Compress Pictures dialog box (see Figure 8-39).

Figure 8-39

Compress Pictures dialog box

Identify your target output and Word will recommend an ideal compression size →

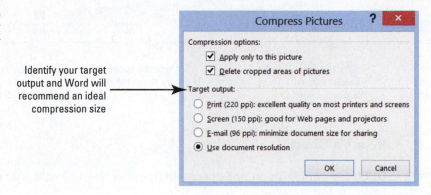

3. In the Compression Options section, check marks indicate which features are activated—in this case, both are turned on.
4. In the Target Output section, select the option button by **E-mail (96 ppi): minimize document size for sharing**. By selecting this option button, the picture file size will be compressed to make the document ready for sharing via email. The other options available are to compress the picture at a quality still acceptable for printing correctly on printers and to ensure screen quality when viewing on web pages and projectors.
5. Click **OK**.
6. **SAVE** the document as *Family Vacation5 Compress* in the lesson folder on your flash drive then **CLOSE** the file.

PAUSE. LEAVE Word open to use in the next exercise.

 Troubleshooting   You will not see the compression take place. To verify that the file is smaller after compressing pictures, you can compare the document's properties before and after performing the Compress Pictures command. Keep in mind that if your picture is already smaller than the compression option chosen, no compression will occur.

INSERTING AND FORMATTING CHARTS

The Bottom Line

There are two ways to insert a chart in Word—one is to use Word to create the chart, the other is to insert a chart from Excel. When inserting a chart in a document, a small spreadsheet and chart opens along with the Chart Tools tab. Chart Tools is a contextual command tab that appears after you insert the chart. Data is typed directly into the spreadsheet. Data consist of labels and values. A **label** is a descriptive name that can be easily identified when inputting data into the worksheet. A **cell** is an intersection between the column and row. Once data is typed into the spreadsheet, the chart begins to change in the document. The second way is to use Excel to create the chart and link to your Word document so that the values in the Word chart are always updated when the Excel file is changed. For this situation, you would use the Paste Special, or Paste Link command.

Inserting a Chart

For this lesson, you have been working on the family vacation documents, so your job is to track the anticipated expenses and create a chart. In this exercise, you learn to insert and format a chart and replace the default values with your own (see Figure 8-40).

Figure 8-40

Chart Tools Design tab

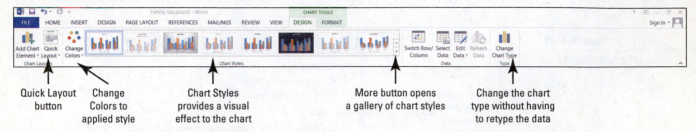

Quick Layout button

Change Colors to applied style

Chart Styles provides a visual effect to the chart

More button opens a gallery of chart styles

Change the chart type without having to retype the data

STEP BY STEP   **Insert a Chart**

OPEN the *Family Vacation5* document from the lesson folder. You completed this exercise earlier in the lesson.

1. Place the insertion point at the end of the document, and press the **Enter** key.

2. On the Insert tab, in the *Illustrations* group click the **Chart** button. The *Insert Chart* dialog box opens (see Figure 8-41). The left pane displays the various categories of charts that you can select with additional options on the type of chart. For instance, if you select the *Column* category and want to use the *3-D Clustered Column* chart type, then you would select *3-D Clustered Column* from above the preview area. Wait for the ScreenTip to appear to show the chart type.

Figure 8-41

Insert Chart dialog box

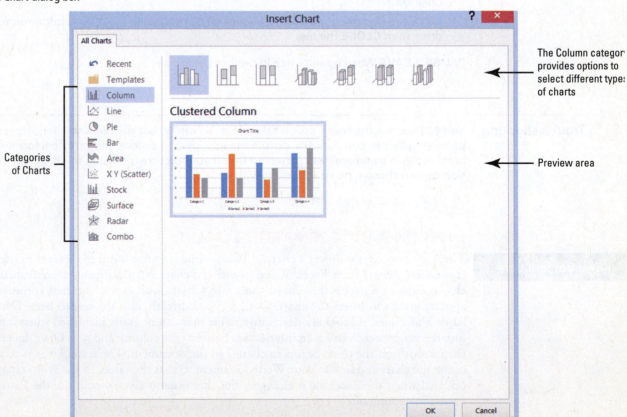

Categories of Charts

The Column category provides options to select different types of charts

Preview area

3. Click the **3-D Clustered Column**. In the preview area, the *3-D Clustered Column* chart type appears.

4. Hover over the chart, and watch how it increases in size.

5. Click **OK**.

6. The *Chart in Microsoft Word* spreadsheet opens along with the column chart below. The chart resembles a smaller version of an Excel worksheet. Where the labels appear, *Category 1 . . . Category 4* and *Series 1 . . . Series 3*, is where you will enter descriptive names. You will replace the numbers that appear with your values. As you enter the labels and values, the chart will display the changes right away. Key the information (see Figure 8-42).

Figure 8-42

Chart in Microsoft Word
with data

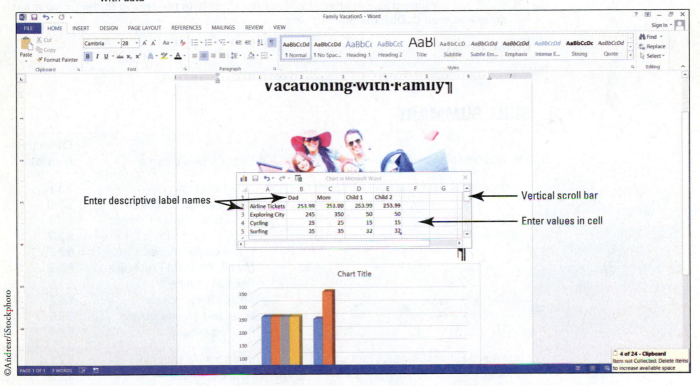

©Andresr/iStockphoto

7. Column A needs to be adjusted so that you can see the full label name. Place your insertion point between columns A and B, wait until you see a double-sided arrow, and then double click to quickly adjust. Now that you've entered the data, click the Close button to close the *Chart in Microsoft Word*.

8. Use the vertical scroll bar to view the chart, if necessary.

9. **SAVE** the document as **Expenses for Vacation** in the lesson folder on your flash drive.

PAUSE. LEAVE the document open for the next exercise.

STEP BY STEP   **Formatting a Chart**

USE the document that is open from the previous exercise.

1. Click inside the chart to activate the *Chart Tools*. Once The *Design* and *Format* tabs become visible then click the **Design** tab. The *Design* tab provides many options on formatting the chart such as applying a layout, styles, changing the chart type, and more. For this exercise, basic formatting will be applied.

2. In the *Chart Layouts* group select the *Quick Layout* button to display the gallery, and hover over each item to preview.

3. You determine that *Layout 10* will work best for you. Select that layout.

4. In the *Chart Styles*, select *Style 4*. More options are available when you click the *More* button.

5. Select the text where *Chart Title* appears and key **Vacation Expenses**. For now, this is the only formatting that will be done to this chart.

6. **SAVE** the document as **Expenses for Vacation Update** in the lesson folder on your flash drive and then **CLOSE** the file.

CLOSE Word.

SKILL SUMMARY

In this lesson you learned to:	Exam Objective	Objective Number
Insert and Format Pictures in a Document	Insert images	5.3.1
	Modify image properties	5.3.4
	Add Quick Styles to images	5.3.5
	Apply picture effects	5.3.3
	Insert simple shapes	5.2.1
	Modify SmartArt Properties	5.2.3
	Position shapes	5.2.5
	Apply artistic effects	5.3.2
	Wrap text around images	5.3.6
	Position images	5.3.7
Insert and Format Shapes, WordArt, and SmartArt	Insert simple shapes	5.2.1
	Position shapes	5.2.5
	Wrap text around shapes	5.2.4
	Change text to WordArt	2.2.10
	Insert SmartArt	5.2.2
Insert and Format Clip Art from Office.com	Insert images	5.3.1
	Modify image properties	5.3.4
	Add Quick Styles to images	5.3.5
Reset and Compress Images		
Insert and Format a Chart		

Knowledge Assessment

Multiple Choice

Select the best response for the following statements.

1. Clip Art can be accessed by clicking on which button?
   a. Illustrations
   b. Pictures
   c. Online Pictures
   d. Online Video

2. Decreasing the size of a picture file by reducing the resolution is called _____
   a. compressing.
   b. rotating.
   c. cropping.
   d. resizing.

3. Lines, block arrows, stars, and banners are examples of what?
   a. Diagrams
   b. Shapes
   c. Flowcharts
   d. Quick Styles

4. Which tools provide options for formatting shapes?
   a. Drawing
   b. Picture
   c. Text
   d. Effects

5. The _____ will capture a picture of the whole application window.
   a. Copy button
   b. Print Screen button
   c. Screenshot button
   d. None of the above

6. Which command enables you to remove unwanted parts from a picture?
   a. SmartArt
   b. Contrast
   c. Rotate
   d. Crop

7. The Artistic Effects command is available on which tool?
   a. Picture Tools
   b. Drawing Tools
   c. Recolor
   d. Corrections

8. What element can you use to provide a short descriptive label for an image in a newsletter or magazine?
   a. Caption
   b. Text
   c. Drop cap
   d. All of the above

9. Which command allows you to change the appearance of an inserted image without the use of photo editing programs?
   a. Artistic Effects
   b. Corrections
   c. Color
   d. All of the above

10. Which command would you use to discard all the formatting changes made to a picture?
    a. Original
    b. Undo
    c. Reset
    d. Discard

True/False

Circle T if the statement is true or F if the statement is false.

T F 1. Layout Options will appear next to objects, such as pictures, charts, shapes and SmartArt.

T F 2. Images shared by email should be compressed to avoid a long download time.

T F 3. Charts cannot be added to a Word document.

T F 4. In a document, images can be converted to SmartArt with captions.

T F 5. Positioning images in a document will move the object as text is added.

T F 6. Wrapping text around a shape cannot be completed in Word.

T F 7. Selecting a shape will open the Drawing Tools Format tab.

T F 8. You can use the Remove Background tool to select what areas of an inserted image to keep and discard.

T F 9. Resetting a picture will remove formatting that you have applied to it.

T F 10. WordArt is decorative text that enhances the document's appearance.

Competency Assessment

Project 8-1: House for Sale

In your position at Tech Terrace Real Estate, you were asked by the new home owners if a picture could be taken of them with their new home. The picture turned out so well that you asked them if Tech Terrace Real Estate could use this picture in a flyer for an advertisement. Your task is to create a new flyer that will be used for marketing.

GET READY. LAUNCH Word if it is not already running.

1. **OPEN** a blank document.
2. **SAVE** the document as *8-1 Marketing Flyer* in the lesson folder on your flash drive.
3. Key the following information and change the font size to **18** pt.
4. **Look at who just purchased their new dream home. Tech Terrace Real Estate agents can assist you in finding your next home or dream home. We'll take care of all the necessary details for you and show you quality homes just like we did for our last clients.**
5. Press **Enter** twice.

6. Click the **Pictures** button from the Illustrations group on the Insert tab.
7. Locate the lesson folder and insert the *Realtor with Couple outside House* image; then click **Insert**.
8. Resize the image height to **3.4"**.
9. In the *Picture Styles* group, convert the picture to the SmartArt graphic *Picture Accent Process*. In the placeholder, key **We love our new home!**
10. Click the **More** button in the *SmartArt Styles* group and select **Metallic Scene** from the *3-D* group.
11. In the SmartArt Styles group, click the **Change Colors** button then select **Colored Fill – Accent 6** from the Accent 6 group.
12. Center the document vertically on the page.
13. **SAVE** the document in the lesson folder on your flash drive then **CLOSE** the file.

PAUSE. LEAVE Word open for the next project.

Project 8-2: CD Case Insert

You have returned from a two-week fun vacation with friends. You took a lot of pictures, and you want to surprise your friends with a copy of the pictures on a CD. Create an insert for the front of the CD case.

GET READY. LAUNCH Word if it is not already running.

1. **OPEN** a blank document.

2. **SAVE** the document as *8-2 CD Insert* in your flash drive in the lesson folder.

3. In the *Page Layout* tab select the **Size** button. Change the paper size to **5"** for both the width and height. Click **OK**.

4. Change the *Margins* to **Narrow**.

5. Select the **Text Box** button from the *Text* group on the Insert tab and draw a text box. Draw a square box **4" × 4"** centered on the page leaving approximately half an inch of margin space on all sides.

6. With the box selected, in the *Arrange* group of the *Format* tab, click the **Position** button and select **Position in Middle Center with Square Text Wrapping**.

7. On the Insert tab, in the *Illustrations* group, click the **Pictures** button and locate the image from the lesson folder. Insert the *Hiking the Columbia Gorge* image and *insert*.

8. Use the selection handles and adjust the image size so that it fits closely in the box.

9. Select the text box then click the **Shape Fill** button and select the color, **Green, Accent 6, Darker 50%**.

10. Deselect the box and insert a *WordArt* and select **Fill – Gray-50%, Accent 3, Sharp Bevel**. Key **Vacation to Columbia**.

11. Decrease the text size to **26** pt. Apply a text fill color and select **Gray-25%, Background 2, Darker 90%**.

12. Disable the **Show/Hide** command.

13. **SAVE** the document in the lesson folder on your flash drive then **CLOSE** the file.

PAUSE. LEAVE Word open for the next project.

Proficiency Assessment

Project 8-3: House for Sale Flyer

You need to make some additional changes to the flyer completed in Project 8-1.

GET READY. LAUNCH Word if it is not already running.

1. **OPEN** the *8-1 Marketing Flyer* you completed for Project 8-1.

2. **SAVE** the document as *8-3 House Keys* in the lesson folder on your flash drive.

3. Under the first paragraph, add a new paragraph and key **Are you ready for us to hand over the keys to your new home?**

4. Select the SmartArt graphic, and replace it with a new image, *Handing Over House Keys*.

5. Select the **Reflected Bevel, Black** style from the *Picture Styles* group to apply a style to the image.

6. Change the border and apply the **Orange, Accent 2, Darker 25%**.

7. Change the Picture Effects and select **Slope** from the *Bevel* group. Adjust the height to **2.7"**.

8. Apply the **Square** style to wrap text only to the *right*.
9. **SAVE** the document in the lesson folder on your flash drive then **CLOSE** the file.

PAUSE. LEAVE Word open for the next project.

Project 8-4: Creating a Chart

In this exercise, you will create a 3-D pie chart to reflect quarterly sales.

GET READY. LAUNCH Word if it is not already running.

1. **OPEN** a blank document.
2. **SAVE** the document as *8-4 Expense Report* in the lesson folder on your flash drive.
3. Insert the Pie chart from Figure 8-43 into your document and format as shown.
4. Enter the data (see Figure 8-43).

Figure 8-43

Sales Report Chart

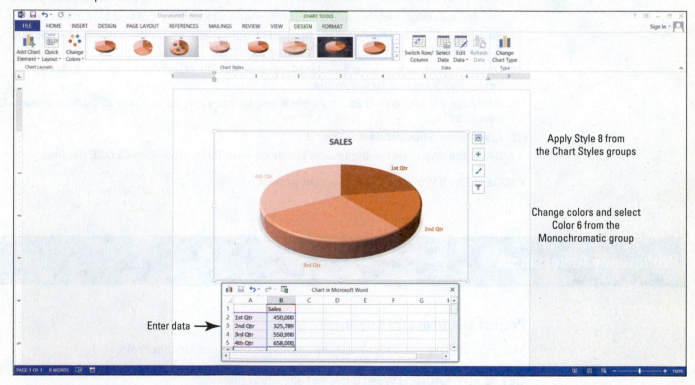

Apply Style 8 from the Chart Styles groups

Change colors and select Color 6 from the Monochromatic group

Enter data →

5. Insert a custom watermark and apply the image, *Real Estate Folder with Data*.
6. **SAVE** the document in the lesson folder on your flash drive then **CLOSE** the file.

PAUSE. LEAVE Word open for the next project.

Mastery Assessment

Project 8-5: Formatting a Flyer

Use the skills that you have learned in this lesson, and remove the background from an image.

GET READY. LAUNCH Word if it is not already running.

1. **OPEN** a blank document.
2. Insert the *Man Standing on Arch* image from the data files for this lesson.
3. **SAVE** the document as *8-5 Arch* in the lesson folder on your flash drive.
4. Use the skills learned in this lesson to remove the background including the man so that only the arch appears.
5. **SAVE** the document in the lesson folder on your flash then **CLOSE** the file.

PAUSE. LEAVE Word open for the next project.

Project 8-6: Creating Shapes

With your improved Word skills, create a newsletter for the YMCA newsletter.

GET READY. LAUNCH Word if it is not already running.

1. **OPEN** a blank document.
2. **SAVE** the document as *8-6 Working with Shapes* in the lesson folder on your flash drive.
3. Create the document (see Figure 8-44). Insert the *WordArt* at the beginning of the document, select **Fill – Black, Text 1, Shadow** and apply the text fill color, **Green, Accent 6, Darker 50%**. Then apply the Gradient Dark Variation **From Top Right Corner**. Format the shape using the **Transform Inflate Bottom**. Stretch the image across the page.

Figure 8-44

Working with Shapes

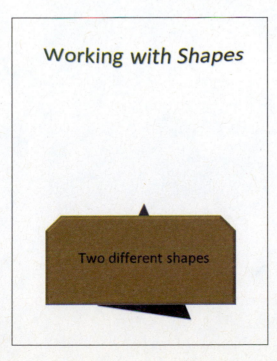

4. Insert the **Snip Same Side Corner Rectangle** shape. Change the size of the shape to **2.9"** in height and **6.15"** wide. Apply the fill color, **Gold, Accent 4, Darker 50%**. Apply the **Bevel** effect with the **Art Deco**.

5. Insert the **Isosceles Triangle** shape with the dimensions of **3.73"** in height and **3.39"** wide. Apply the **Intense Effect – Black, Dark 1** style then apply the 3-D rotation with the **Off Axis 2 Left**. Place this shape behind the first one.

6. Add WordArt to the shape and select the **Fill – Black, Text 1, Shadow** and key text as it appears in Figure 8-44. Place horizontally and vertically within shape.

7. Group all objects together then position in **Bottom Center with Square Text Wrapping**.

8. **SAVE** the document in the lesson folder on your flash drive then **CLOSE** the file.

CLOSE Word.

Circling Back 2

Create a postcard to announce the date of the conference to members and to solicit early registrations.

Project 1: Creating a Postcard

GET READY. LAUNCH Word if it is not already running.

1. Create a new blank document.

2. Create a custom document with a size height of **5.50**" by **4.25**" wide.

3. Change the document setup to **landscape** orientation with **narrow** margins.

4. **SAVE** the document as *NAPC Postcard* in the lesson folder on your flash drive.

5. Insert a header from *Office.com* and select **Element**.

6. Select the Title placeholder text and type **NAPC PROFESSIONAL CONFERENCE**. Change the font size and style to 14 pt **bold**.

7. Double-click the body of the postcard, and then type the following text:

   September 14–16

   Lakeview Towers in South Lake Tahoe, California

   Early Bird Registration $329; Regular Rate $389

   Admission to all keynotes, seminars, and breakout sessions

   Ticket to Saturday night banquet

   All meals included

   Early Bird Deadline is August 1, 20XX

   Register online at www.napc20XX.com or call 800-555-5678

8. Do *not* press Enter after the last line of typed text.

9. Select **September 14–16**, change the font size and style to **20** pt, **bold**, and **center**.

10. Select the **Lakeview Towers** line of text, and then change the font size to **14** pt and **center** the text.

11. Insert a first line indent of **0.25**" before the *E* in **Early Bird Registration**.

12. Select the three lines of text under the registration costs information and format them as a bulleted list by selecting the solid circle.

13. Select **$329**. Change the font color and style to **Blue, Accent 1, Darker 50%**, and then **bold**. Change the font size to **13**.

14. Use the Format Painter to copy the format of **$329** and apply it to **$389, August 1, 20XX, www.napc20XX.com**, and **800-555-5678**.

15. Select the last two lines and **center**.

16. Insert a 1½ pt wide box page border, using the color **Dark Blue**.

17. Adjust the header by dragging it below the page border. Make sure it fits on one page.

18. Create a custom diagonal watermark with the text **SAVE THE DATE** using the **Times New Roman** font, and then select the **Blue-Gray, Text 2, Darker 25%** color.

19. **SAVE** the document as *NAPC Postcard Draft* in the lesson folder on your flash drive.

20. Apply a page color and select **Gray-50%, Accent 3, Lighter 80%**.

21. Adjust the watermark and change the size to **30**.

22. Your document should look similar to Figure 1. Make any necessary adjustments.

Figure 1

NAPC Postcard

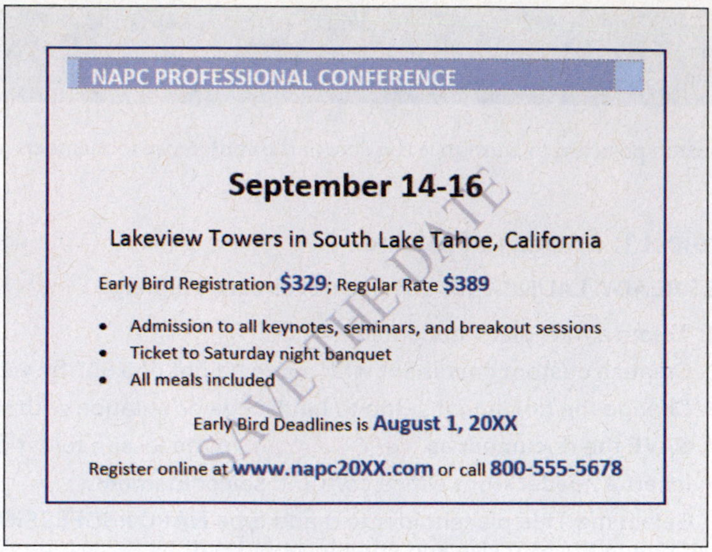

23. SAVE the document as *NAPC Postcard Final* in the lesson folder on your flash drive, and then **CLOSE** the file.

PAUSE. LEAVE Word for the next project.

Project 2: Creating a Letterhead Logo

As the scheduling manager for Consolidated Messenger, a full-service conference and retreat center, you use Word to create and revise all documents and forms used when coordinating the facility's events.

In recent years, the conference center has expanded and changed its focus. The owner needs your help in creating a new logo for all the business' documents.

GET READY. LAUNCH Word if it is not already running.

1. **OPEN** a new, blank document and type **Consolidated Messenger**.
2. **SAVE** the document as *Consolidated Letterhead* in the lesson folder on your USB flash drive.
3. Insert the **Fill-Gray-50%, Accent 3, Sharp Bevel** WordArt applied to the text in step 1.
4. Extend the WordArt to **6.5**" on the ruler, and then decrease the font size to **28** pt. Adjust the WordArt to **.5**" above the top margin.
5. Apply a text fill color and select **Gray-25%, Background 2, Darker 90%**. Then transform the WordArt and select the **Chevron Down**.
6. Insert a blank footer, and then type **Conference and Retreat Center** in the footer. Add a line break, and then type **555 Circling Road, South Lake Tahoe, CA 96150**.
7. Change the font of the footer text, *Conference and Retreat Center*, to **Bookman Old Style**, the font size to **20** pt, the font color to **Black, Text 1, Lighter 5%**, and then **center**. Change the font to Bookman Old Style for the address.
8. **SAVE** the document in the lesson folder on your flash drive.

PAUSE. LEAVE the document open for the next project.

Project 3: Editing a Document

You are working on a promotional piece for the conference center, but you need to make some changes and add the logo.

USE the document that is open from the previous project.

1. **OPEN** *Consolidated Intro* from the data files for this lesson.

2. Remove all blank lines in the document.

3. Select the whole document, and copy and paste to the *Consolidated Letterhead* document. Before pasting in the document, create three blank lines.

4. In the Replace tab, search for all occurrences of the word *Gallery* and replace them with the word **Theatre**.

5. Select all paragraphs and change the spacing after to **8** pt, single space. Then combine paragraph 4 and 5.

6. Locate and insert the *Old Theater* image (found in the data files for this lesson).

7. Position the image in the document with **Position in Bottom Center with Square Text Wrapping**, and then resize the image height to **2.53**".

8. Apply a picture style and select the **Center Shadow Rectangle**.

9. Change the Color Tone to **Temperature: 11200K**.

10. Apply the **Artistic Effects** and select **Crisscross Etching**. The document should match Figure 2.

Figure 2

Consolidated Promotion

Consolidated Messenger

Consolidated Messenger Conference and Retreat Center is perfectly suited to serve the needs of conferences, seminars, receptions, and meetings.

This state-of-the-art facility sets new and higher standards for excellence for the conference and training events of association, business, and government groups. We offer a comfortable and stimulating environment, an eager staff, and the latest communications and multi-media technology.

The Great Hall Theatre on the grounds is a restored 1930's vintage movie house. Technologically, however, the facility is all 21st Century. Equipped with a state-of-the-art presentation system, superb lighting and sound, full-size screen and projection unit, the Theatre makes an excellent gathering point for keynote addresses, plenary sessions, and, of course, entertainment.

Upstairs, the renovated Conference Center can be configured as four break-out rooms to accommodate simultaneous sessions - or opened fully to serve up to 250 participants. This space also houses an expansive catering kitchen and technological amenities amidst art deco styling. The conference area is ADA compliant and easily accessible by elevator from the lobby of the Theatre.

Another great reason for choosing the Consolidated Messenger Conference and Retreat Center for your next meeting or conference is its convenient location in Truman. Only 20 miles from Interstate 101, the city is a junction for US highways 315and 95. A 24-hour general aviation airport serves corporate jets and other private aircraft. Regional airports in Grand Junction and Vail, served by commuter flights from Denver, are just over an hour's drive.

Conference and Retreat Center
555 Circling Road, South Lake Tahoe, CA 96150

11. **SAVE** the document as *Consolidated Promotion* in the lesson folder on your flash drive.

12. Apply the **Casual** style from the Document Formatting group.

13. Remove the image and insert the same image as a watermark.

14. Format paragraphs with a first line indent.

15. **SAVE** the document as *Consolidated Promotion Update* in the lesson folder on your flash drive, and then **CLOSE** all open files.

PAUSE. LEAVE Word open to use in the next project.

Project 4: Audio-Visual Equipment Table

Create a table that contains a list of the audio and visual equipment available for rent at the conference center.

 OPEN the *Consolidated Letterhead* document from the lesson folder.

1. Place the insertion point below the letterhead logo. Make sure you have three blank lines below the letterhead logo.

2. Type the heading, **Audio Visual Equipment Rental**, change the font to **Cambria, 24** pt, and center the text.

3. Create a table that has three columns and eight rows.

4. Type the information shown in Figure 3 into the table.

Figure 3

Consolidated Equipment

Consolidated·Messenger¶

Audio·Visual·Equipment·Rental¶

¤	¤	¤
LCD¤	High-resolution·LCD·data·projector¤	$325¤¤
VID¤	Low-resolution·video·projector·with·VCR·and·monitor¤	$120¤¤
CAM¤	Mini·DVD·camcorder·with·tripod¤	$95¤¤
FSM¤	Color·42"·flat-screen·monitor·mounted·on·the·front·wall¤	$90¤¤
KEY¤	Full-size·electronic·keyboard·with·stool¤	$75¤¤
OHP¤	Overhead·projector¤	$35¤¤
CDP¤	Stereo·CD·player·with·cassette·deck·and·radio¤	$25¤¤

5. **Merge and center** the first row, and then drag and drop the heading to that row.

6. Apply the **Grid Table 5 Dark – Accent 6** style.

7. Sort the third column in ascending order.

8. Select the first row of the table and adjust the height to **0.8**" Center the text both horizontally and vertically.

9. Select all values in the third column, and then center both horizontally and vertically.

10. Insert a row below the last entry and merge the first two columns. Type **Total**. Increase the font size to **14** pt then right-align.

    Total the values above by writing a formula. Apply the third option for the number format.

11. **SAVE** the document as *Consolidated Equipment* in the lesson folder on your flash drive, and then **CLOSE** the file.

PAUSE. LEAVE Word open for the next project.

Project 5: Formatting a Document

You began creating a document to serve as a guide for introducing guests to the conference center. Open and format the document.

GET READY. LAUNCH Word if it is not already running.

1. **OPEN** *Consolidated Guests* from the data files for this lesson.

2. Use what you learned in this unit to complete the following tasks. You do not have to complete them in this order, but your goal is to make the document look similar to Figure 4.

   a. Create a drop cap for the first sentence, and then adjust manually to match Figure 4.

   b. Apply the **Facet Sidebar (Left)** text box. Then use the copy and paste commands to match Figure 4.

   c. Use the font color **Dark Blue, Text 2** to the text added to the text box.

   d. Remove the existing image and apply a watermark using the *Hiking* image. Your document should look similar to Figure 4.

Figure 4

Consolidated Guide

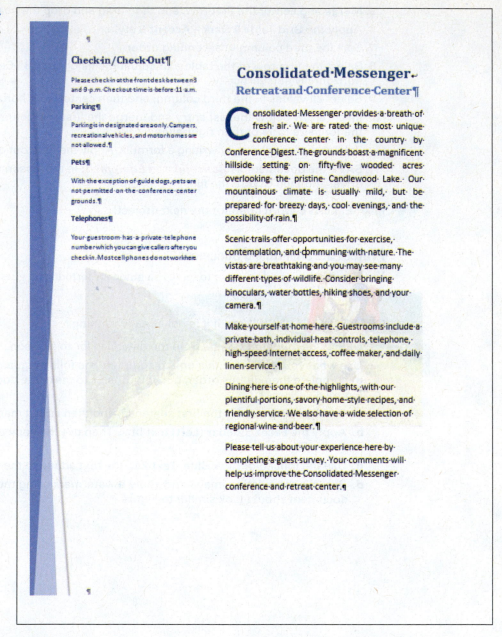

3. **SAVE** the document as *Consolidated Guide* in the lesson folder on your flash drive, and then **CLOSE** the file.

STOP. CLOSE Word.

LESSON SKILL MATRIX

Skill	Exam Objective	Objective Number
Validating Content by Using Spelling and Grammar Checking Options		
Configuring AutoCorrect Settings	Insert special characters (©, ™, £).	2.1.7
Inserting and Modifying Comments in a Document		
Viewing Comments		
Tracking Changes in a Document		

KEY TERMS

- **All Markup**
- antonym
- **AutoCorrect**
- **balloons**
- **inline**
- **Lock Tracking**
- markup
- **No Markup**
- **Original**
- **Person Card**
- **Simple Markup**
- synonym

287

© spooh/iStockphoto

Blue Yonder Airlines is a large company with hundreds of employees. In your job as a human resources specialist, you are involved in hiring, employee benefit programs, and employee communications. Many of the documents you work with relate to employee issues, and you need to ensure that these documents are error free. In this lesson, you learn to use the Spelling and Grammar feature, to find the meaning of a word, to use the Thesaurus, to review the statistics of words and paragraphs used in a document, to insert comments, to change the AutoCorrect settings, and to track changes.

SOFTWARE ORIENTATION

The Bottom Line

The Proofing group on the Review tab contains commands for launching Word's Spelling and Grammar functions, searching through references, using the Thesaurus, and counting words by characters, paragraphs, and lines. The Language group contains commands for translating words or paragraphs and an option to select a language. These and other commands for reviewing and editing Word documents are located on the Review tab, shown in Figure 9-1.

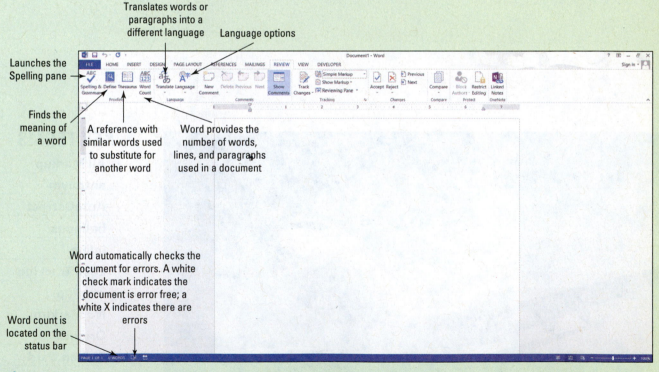

Translates words or paragraphs into a different language

Language options

Launches the Spelling pane

Finds the meaning of a word

A reference with similar words used to substitute for another word

Word provides the number of words, lines, and paragraphs used in a document

Word automatically checks the document for errors. A white check mark indicates the document is error free; a white X indicates there are errors

Word count is located on the status bar

Figure 9-1

Proofing and Language groups

Use this figure as a reference throughout this lesson and the rest of this book.

VALIDATING CONTENT BY USING SPELLING AND GRAMMAR CHECKING OPTIONS

The Bottom Line

It is a good business practice to proof a document to ensure it is error free before sharing or printing it. Word provides proofing tools such as a Spelling and Grammar checking function, the Define button, the Thesaurus button, and the Word Count tracker. All these tools and commands are located on the Ribbon on the Review tab. The status bar also contains Word Count and Proofing Error buttons that give you quick access to some proofing features. On the status bar, Word automatically displays the document's word count.

Checking the Spelling and Grammar Feature

Microsoft Word's Spelling and Grammar feature is automatically on by default and checks the spelling and grammar in a document. Word underlines misspelled words with a wavy red line and underlines grammatical errors with a wavy green line. Proper nouns are usually not found in the dictionary, so they will often be underlined with a wavy red line even if the word is spelled correctly. If there is a word that you use often that is not found in the dictionary, you might want to add it to your dictionary. Adding words to the dictionary is not covered in this lesson. Word can often detect whether words are used inappropriately and it underlines the word with a wavy blue line. In other words, if a word is underlined in blue, the word is in the dictionary but not used correctly in the context. In this exercise, you learn to use Word's automatic Spelling and Grammar feature and its options to proof and correct your document.

STEP BY STEP   **Check Spelling and Grammar**

GET READY. Before you begin these steps, launch Microsoft Word.

1. **OPEN** the *Employ Offer* document from the lesson folder.

2. Click the **Review tab**, and then click the **Spelling & Grammar** ⎘ button in the Proofing group. The Spelling pane opens—this is a new appearance for this feature (see Figure 9-2).

Figure 9-2

Spelling task pane

Misspelled word highlighted in document and placed in the Spelling pane

Ignores all occurrences in the document

Words can be added to the dictionary

Ignores the selected instance and stops at the next occurrence

Changes the misspelled word

Word provides suggested corrections

Changes all occurrences of the misspelled word throughout the document

Option to change dictionary

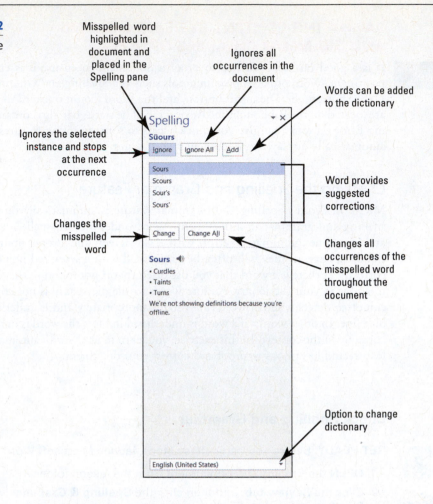

The first word appearing in the Spelling task pane is *Süours*, a proper noun not contained in the tool's dictionary. The Spelling task pane provides a listing of suggested words as shown in Figure 9-2.

3. Click the **Ignore All button** to ignore all occurrences within the document, because *Süours* is not in the main dictionary and it's spelled correctly.

   The word *cofim* is misspelled. The correct spelling is the second option.

4. Select the *confirm* suggestion and then click the **Change All button** to change all occurrences.

5. The next misspelled word is *employmnt*. The correct spelling is highlighted. Click the **Change All button**.

6. The next misspelled word is *beginning*; the correct spelling is highlighted in the Suggestions pane. Click the **Change All button**.

7. The next misspelled word is *asistance*. Click the **Change All button**.

8. A grammar error of *in the amount of* appears in the task pane. Click **Ignore**. This is covered later in the lesson.

9. The next misspelled word is another proper noun, *Sheila*. Some proper nouns are added in the main dictionary. The correct spelling is highlighted. Click the **Change All button**.

10. A prompt appears when the Spelling and Grammar check is complete. Click **OK**.

    Notice how the icon on the status bar changes from an *X* to a check mark.

11. **SAVE** the document as ***Employment Offer*** in the lesson folder on your flash drive.

PAUSE. LEAVE the document open to use in the next exercise.

Take Note   Ignore Once ignores the occurrence once and stops at the next occurrence.

Rechecking the Spelling and Grammar

Word has the option for users to ignore misspelled words. In this case, the previous user ignored misspellings. Once you ignore a misspelled word, it will no longer be marked with a wavy red line until you recheck the document. You will recheck the document to ensure you have captured all errors.

STEP BY STEP   **Recheck Spelling and Grammar**

USE the document that is open from the previous exercise.

1. Click the **File tab**, and then click **Options** to open the *Word Options* dialog box in Backstage.

2. Select **Proofing** in the left pane and review the section *When correcting spelling and grammar in Word* (see Figure 9-3). The check marks indicate that the feature is enabled. You also have the option to hide the spelling and grammar errors in the document.

Figure 9-3

Word Options dialog box

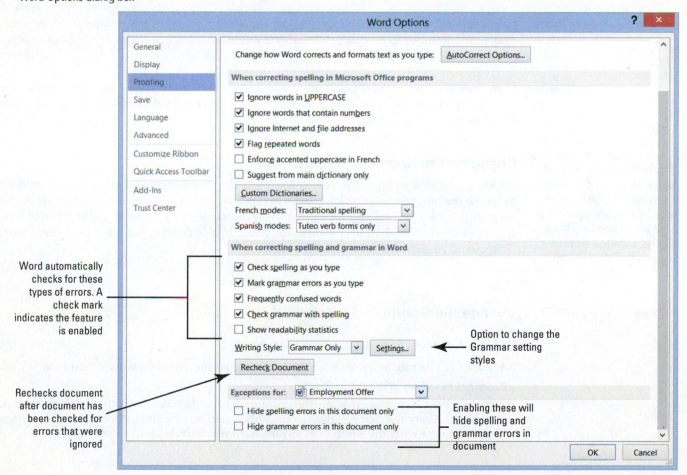

Word automatically checks for these types of errors. A check mark indicates the feature is enabled

Option to change the Grammar setting styles

Rechecks document after document has been checked for errors that were ignored

Enabling these will hide spelling and grammar errors in document

3. Click the **Recheck Document button** to check for errors that were ignored.

4. A prompt appears stating *This operation resets the spelling checker and the grammar checker so that Word will recheck words and grammar you previously checked and chose to ignore. Do you want to continue?* Click **Yes** (see Figure 9-4). The document flags misspellings.

Figure 9-4

Resets Spelling and Grammar checker

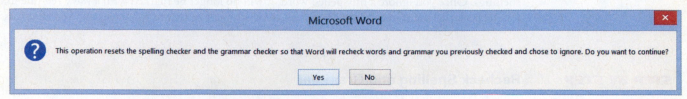

5. Click **OK** to close the *Word Options* dialog box.

6. In the Proofing group, click the **Spelling & Grammar** button. The Spelling task pane opens.

7. The Spelling and Grammar tool highlights *Süours*. This spelling is correct, so click **Ignore All**. Click **OK**.

   The tool now ignores every occurrence of this spelling in the document.

8. **SAVE** the document in the lesson folder on your flash drive.

PAUSE. LEAVE the document open to use in the next exercise.

Take Note   When Word detects a spelling error, you can choose to change one occurrence of the instance or change all instances. Click *Change* to change a single occurrence or click *Change All* to change all occurrences in the document.

Take Note   If you run the Spelling and Grammar command in the middle of the document, it will check from that point to the end of the document. A prompt will appear asking if you want to continue checking the document from the beginning.

Another Way
Click the *Proofing Error* button on the status bar (or press the keyboard shortcut, *F7*) to open the Spelling task pane. You can also right-click on a misspelled word, and Word displays a shortcut menu with suggested words at the top.

Changing the Grammar Settings

Word's grammar settings enable you to determine the punctuation and other stylistic guidelines by which the program will check for and detect errors. You can change the writing style to check for grammar only or check stylistic rules, such as contractions, hyphenated and compound words, sentence length (more than sixty words), and more. In this exercise, you learn to change the style settings and customize them to meet your needs.

STEP BY STEP   **Change the Grammar Settings**

USE the document from the previous exercise.

1. Click the **File tab**, and then click **Options** to open the *Word Options* dialog box.

2. Select **Proofing** in the left pane.

3. In the *When correcting spelling and grammar in Word* section, click the **Settings button** to open the *Grammar Settings* dialog box. This dialog box includes the writing style where you can customize the Grammar Only or Grammar & Style options (see Figure 9-5).

Figure 9-5

Grammar Settings dialog box

Change how punctuation should be detected

Adding a check mark will enable how style errors should be detected

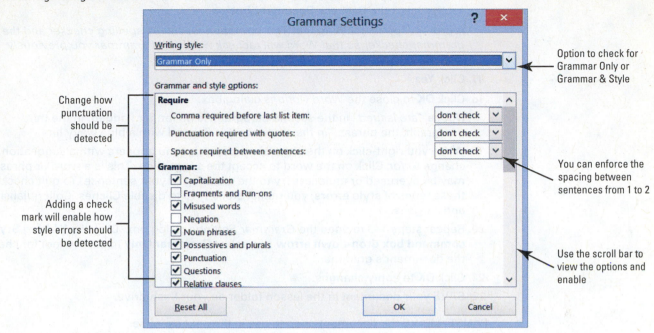

Option to check for Grammar Only or Grammar & Style

You can enforce the spacing between sentences from 1 to 2

Use the scroll bar to view the options and enable

4. Click the **drop-down arrow** in the Writing Style section and select **Grammar & Style**.

5. Under the *Require* section, the *Spaces required between sentences* setting is set to **don't check**. Click the **drop-down arrow** and select **2**. You are changing the style to reflect two spaces after the punctuation between each sentence.

Take Note The current standard is one space after a punctuation mark. However, in this example we are using two spaces to illustrate Word's error-checking abilities more clearly.

6. Click **OK**.

7. In the *Word Options* dialog box, under the *When correcting spelling and grammar in Word* section, click the **Recheck Document button**.

8. A prompt appears stating that *This operation resets the spelling checker and the grammar checker so that Words will recheck words and grammar you previously checked and chose to ignore. Do you want to continue?* Click **Yes**.

9. Click **OK** to close the *Word Options* dialog box. Word flags and marks the punctuation at the end of sentences with a blue wavy line because there is only one space, and we selected 2.

   Notice in the second paragraph, the document flags *are issued*.

10. **Right-click** on the phrase and a pop-up menu appears. It states "Passive Voice (consider revising)."

11. Press **ESC** to close the pop-up menu.

12. Repeat steps 1 and 2 to open the *Grammar Settings* dialog box.

13. Under the *Require* section, click the **drop-down arrow** to change the *Spaces required between sentences* setting to **don't check**.

14. Scroll down and disable all *Styles* with the exception of **Clichés, Colloquialisms, and Jargons**. One style is kept active.

15. Click **OK**.

16. In the *Word Options* dialog box, under *When correcting spelling and grammar in Word* section, click the **Recheck Document button**.

A prompt appears stating that *This operation resets the spelling checker and the grammar checker so that Word will recheck words and grammar you previously checked and chose to ignore. Do you want to continue?*

17. Click **Yes**.

18. Click **OK** to close the *Word Options* dialog box.

Notice *"are issued"* in the second paragraph is no longer flagged. In the third paragraph, the phrase *"in the amount of"* is flagged with a blue wavy line.

19. When you right-click on the phrase, the pop-up menu appears with a suggestion to change to *for*. Click on the word to accept the suggestion. This is a word or phrase that may be overused or unnecessary to the meaning of your sentence. To quit checking for these types of style errors, you repeat steps 7–10 to disable Clichés, Colloquialisms, and Jargons.

20. Repeat steps 1–3 to open the *Grammar Settings* dialog box. Click the **Writing Style command box drop-down arrow** and select **Grammar Only** to set the tool for checking the document's grammar.

21. Click **OK** to apply changes.

22. **SAVE** your document in the lesson folder on your flash drive.

PAUSE. LEAVE the document open to use in the next exercise.

Understanding the Meaning of a Word

Microsoft Word has added a new command to learn the meaning of a word. This is beneficial to you especially when a dictionary is not available. Before clicking on the Define button, you need to install the dictionary in your computer. In this exercise, you learn to define words in the document.

STEP BY STEP   **Understand the Meaning of a Word**

USE the document from the previous exercise.

1. Click the **Define** button.

The Dictionaries task pane opens with options of free dictionaries to install as shown in Figure 9-6. The terms and conditions, and privacy policy links are available for review and acceptance. The ratings for each dictionary is also shown.

2. Click the **Download button** under *English Dictionary* and begin downloading the dictionary application. The process for downloading is quick (refer to Figure 9-6).

Figure 9-6

Dictionaries task pane

Dictionaries   ▾ ✕

Install a dictionary from the Office Store to see definitions.

Language: English (United States)

Dictionary - Merriam-Webster

Price: Free

Rating: 2

Terms & Conditions

Privacy Policy

Download

English Dictionary

Price: Free

Rating: 3

Terms & Conditions

Privacy Policy

Download

Bing Dictionary (English)

Price: Free

Rating: 4

Terms & Conditions

Privacy Policy

Download

By downloading a dictionary, you agree to its terms and conditions and grant it permission to use the currently selected text.

3. Select *employment* in the first paragraph.

The definition of the selected text is shown in Figure 9-7. This *new* feature in Word can save you time from having to manually look up a word in a dictionary book. You must be signed into your Microsoft account before you access this feature.

Figure 9-7

English Dictionary task pane
definition of word

Figure 9-7

English Dictionary task pane
definition of word

English Dictionary   ▼ ×

employment, employ

(noun) the state of being employed or
having a job

*"they are looking for employment";
"he was in the employ of the city"*

employment, work

(noun) the occupation for which you are
paid

*"he is looking for employment"; "a lot
of people are out of work"*

employment, engagement

(noun) the act of giving someone a job

See more...

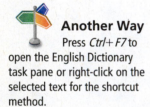

Another Way
Press *Ctrl+F7* to
open the English Dictionary
task pane or right-click on the
selected text for the shortcut
method.

4. Close the English Dictionary task pane.

5. **SAVE** the document in the lesson folder on your flash drive.

PAUSE. LEAVE the document open to use in the next exercise.

Finding Words Using the Thesaurus

A Thesaurus provides a listing of synonyms and antonyms of common words to help you expand your choice of words in your document. A **synonym** is defined as a word that has the same meaning as another word (e.g., good and great). An **antonym** is the opposite meaning of the word (such as good and bad). The Thesaurus is a great tool to use when working on research papers or other documents and will assist you in avoiding using the same words multiple times. If you have difficulty in pronouncing a word, you can hear how the word is pronounced in the Thesaurus task pane. In this exercise, you learn to use the thesaurus.

STEP BY STEP   **Find Words Using the Thesaurus**

USE the document from the previous exercise.

1. Select **pleasure** in the first paragraph and click the **Thesaurus** 📖 **button**.

The Thesaurus task pane opens, displaying many options to select as shown in Figure 9-8.

Figure 9-8

Thesaurus task pane

Selected text
appears in box

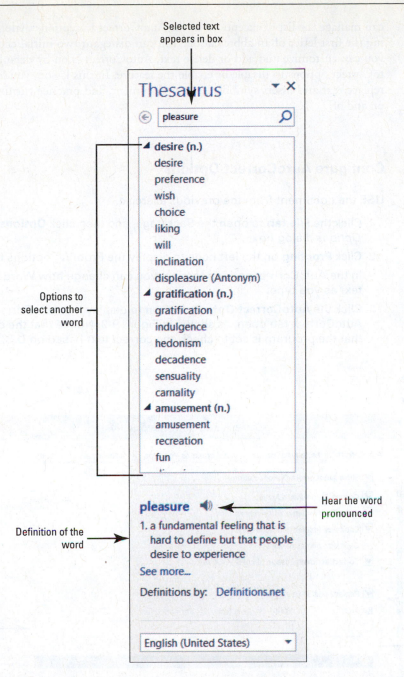

Options to
select another
word

Definition of the
word

Hear the word
pronounced

2. Click the 🔊 **icon** to hear the pronunciation of the word.

3. Replace the word with the synonym *gratification* by moving the mouse over *gratification* in the Thesaurus task pane, and then click the drop-down arrow and select **Insert**. If you click on a word in the task pane, Word displays a new listing of words to choose.

4. Close the Thesaurus task pane by clicking the **Close button**.

5. **SAVE** the document in the lesson folder on your flash drive.

PAUSE. LEAVE the document open to use in the next exercise.

Another Way

Press *Shift+ F7* to open the Thesaurus task pane or right-click on the selected text for the shortcut method.

CONFIGURING AUTOCORRECT SETTINGS

The Bottom Line

The Proofing pane of the Word Options dialog box also contains Word's AutoCorrect setting options. **AutoCorrect** is a feature that replaces symbols, commonly misspelled words, and abbreviations with specific text strings. For instance, to add the Trademark symbol, type *(tm)* and it automatically inserts the symbol ™. As you can see, AutoCorrect saves time in typing text. You can manage the list of exceptions in the AutoCorrect Exceptions dialog box, such as not capitalizing the first letter of an abbreviation. You can disregard two initial caps, such as a student ID, or you can customize and add or delete text. AutoCorrect is on by default, but you can use the AutoCorrect options to disable or enable the feature. In this lesson, you learn to use AutoCorrect to replace text and insert symbols in your document, and practice turning the AutoCorrect feature on and off.

STEP BY STEP   ## Configure AutoCorrect Options

USE the document from the previous exercise.

1. Click the **File tab** to open the Backstage, and then click **Options** to display the *Word Options* dialog box.

2. Click **Proofing** on the left pane to display the Proofing options in the right pane.

   In the AutoCorrect options section, you can change how Word corrects and formats text as you type.

3. Click the **AutoCorrect Options button** to display the AutoCorrect dialog box with the AutoCorrect tab open, as shown in Figure 9-9. Notice that the dialog box title indicates that the program is set to check and correct text based on U.S. English.

Figure 9-9

AutoCorrect dialog box

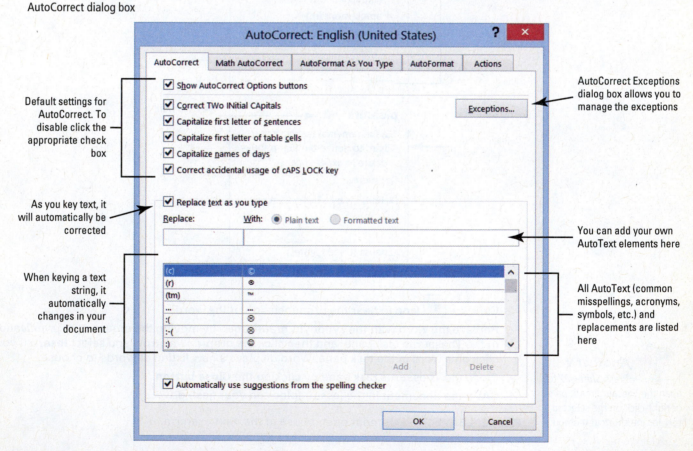

Default settings for AutoCorrect. To disable click the appropriate check box

As you key text, it will automatically be corrected

When keying a text string, it automatically changes in your document

AutoCorrect Exceptions dialog box allows you to manage the exceptions

You can add your own AutoText elements here

All AutoText (common misspellings, acronyms, symbols, etc.) and replacements are listed here

4. Type **BYA** in the Replace box.

5. Type **Blue Yonder Airlines** in the With box.

   Verify your spelling.

6. Click the **Add button**.

7. Click **OK** to close the *AutoCorrect* dialog box, and then click **OK** to close the *Word Options* dialog box.

8. In the first paragraph at the end of the first sentence, place the insertion point after *r* in *for* and press the **Spacebar** once.

9. Type **BYA** and press the **Spacebar** once. *BYA* is automatically replaced with *Blue Yonder Airlines*.

10. Delete the extra space before the punctuation.

   Adding acronyms or other text to AutoCorrect can save you time from having to type additional characters.

11. Repeat steps 1–3 to open the *AutoCorrect* dialog box.

12. In the Replace box, type **BYA**. *BYA* and *Blue Yonder Airlines* are highlighted in the list of AutoText corrections, as shown in Figure 9-10.

13. Click the **Delete button** to remove the highlighted entries. Click **OK** two times to close both dialog boxes.

Another Way

You also can use the Find and Replace command to replace words or phrases.

Figure 9-10

AutoCorrect dialog box with custom entry in the AutoCorrect list

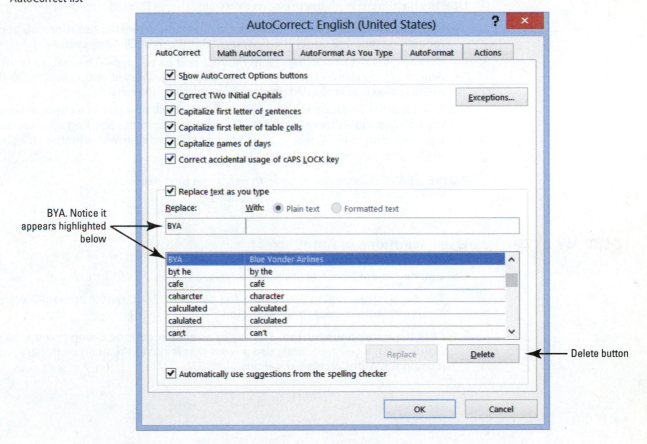

BYA. Notice it appears highlighted below

Delete button

Now, if you type **BYA** in your document and press the **Spacebar**, no action will occur.

14. **SAVE** the file as *Employment Offer1* in the lesson folder on your flash drive.

PAUSE. LEAVE the document open to use in the next exercise.

STEP BY STEP **Insert Special Characters Using AutoCorrect**

USE the document from the previous exercise.

1. Position the insertion point after the *s* in *Airlines* in the first body paragraph.
2. *Blue Yonder Airlines* is the trademark name for the company and requires the trademark symbol after the name.

 Cross Ref In Lesson 7, you learn to insert special characters using the Symbol dialog box.

3. Type **(tm)** to insert the trademark symbol after *Airlines*.

   The trademark symbol is placed in the document as a superscript element.
4. **SAVE** the file as *Employment Offer2* in the lesson folder on your flash drive.

PAUSE. LEAVE the document open to use in the next exercise.

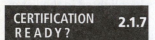

CERTIFICATION READY? 2.1.7

How do you insert a special character?

STEP BY STEP **Disable AutoCorrect**

USE the document from the previous exercise.

1. By default, the AutoCorrect Options are enabled. To disable AutoCorrect, begin by repeating steps 1–3 under the *Configure AutoCorrect Options* section.
2. Click to clear the check mark from *Replace text as you type.* The feature is off and the *Automatically Use Suggestions from the Spelling Checker* option located at the bottom of the dialog box is shaded gray to show that it is unavailable.
3. To enable the AutoCorrect function, click the **check box** again; a check mark appears in the box and the *Automatically Use Suggestions from the Spelling Checker* option again becomes available. (Check with your instructor to determine whether you should leave AutoCorrect disabled or enabled.)

PAUSE. LEAVE the document open to use in the next exercise.

STEP BY STEP **Use Exceptions in AutoCorrect**

USE the document from the previous exercise.

The AutoCorrect dialog box should still be open. If not, repeat steps 1–3 under the *Configure AutoCorrect Options* section.

1. Click the **Exceptions button**. The *AutoCorrect Exceptions* dialog box opens (see Figure 9-11). If you frequently use a word that is not in the main dictionary, you can add it using the AutoCorrect Exceptions.

Figure 9-11

AutoCorrect Exceptions
dialog box

Add and delete your
own personalized
capitalizations

Add and delete your
own abbreviations

Add other corrections
with an option to
delete

2. Click the **INitial CAps tab** and type **(EIDs)**.

3. Click the **Add button**.

4. Click **OK** to close the *AutoCorrect Exceptions* dialog box.

   When a word is added to the Exceptions list, the word is also added to the default custom dictionary.

5. Click **OK** to close the *AutoCorrect* dialog box.

6. Click **OK** to close the *Word Options* dialog box.

7. At the end of the fourth body paragraph, type **Employee IDs (EIDs) will be provided to you on location.**

   Adding IDs to the exceptions avoids flagging the word.

8. **SAVE** the document as *Employment Offer3* in the lesson folder on your flash drive.

PAUSE. LEAVE the document open to use in the next exercise.

INSERTING AND MODIFYING COMMENTS IN A DOCUMENT

The Bottom Line

Word's Comment feature enables reviewers to integrate people and communication in different settings. The new visual look catches your attention with the *new* **Person Card** shown on the right side of the document with the individual's name and picture—this identifies the user who made the comment and has an active Microsoft account. The Person Card allows you to check whether the person is available and communicate with them through IM, voice, video, or one of the latest social sites.

The new Word 2013 default view for comments is the **Simple Markup** that gives the document a more polished look, and a little balloon appears alongside of the document. If you use your tablet or computer to read your comments, you can read your document without the clutter of markups displayed on your screen—which makes for easier reading.

Figure 9-12

Comments group

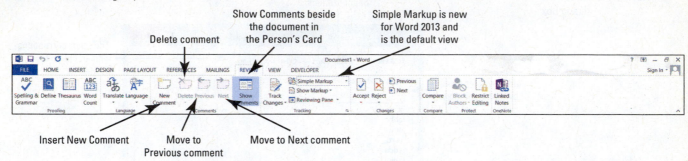

Inserting, Editing, and Deleting a Comment

The commands in the Comments group on the Review tab are used to insert comments to yourself or for others to provide feedback. When the Person Card appears, this indicates that this individual has a Microsoft Account and has signed in to one of the Office 2013 applications. When a comment is added to the document, the person's profile appears as a card when comments are displayed. Microsoft has improved the comments features by allowing you to communicate with individuals who have commented on your document by providing the options in the Person Card. Another *new* feature in Word 2013 is marking a comment as done—instead of deleting a comment.

Comments are easily added by using the New Comment button or using the shortcut menu. Comments can be deleted, marked as done, and edited. Moving through a document with comments can be accomplished using the navigation buttons on the Ribbon. In this exercise, you learn to insert, navigate, edit, delete, and mark a comment as done.

STEP BY STEP   **Insert a Comment**

USE the document from the previous exercise.

1. In the first sentence of the second paragraph, select **$55,000**.

2. On the **Review tab**, in the Comments group, click the **New Comment** button.

   A *new* comment appears in the right margin, labeled with the individual's name and photo icon. To see the Person Card, hover over or click on the photo icon. As you continue adding comments in a document, you will see when the comment was added in minutes— eventually this will change to the date the comment was added after the document is shared. For this lesson, images in the figures appear as Sign In, as shown in Figure 9-13.

Figure 9-13

Person Card

The Person Card is displayed by clicking on the photo in the Comments balloon. When signed in, you will see the person's name and profile picture

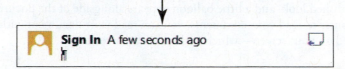

 Cross Ref   In Lesson 2, you learn about the *new* Read Mode. In the Read Mode, you can display all comments.

 Cross Ref   In Lesson 13, you learn to create a Microsoft account. In the upper-right corner of the document screen, you will see the Microsoft account Sign In. The icon displays an image of the person once he or she has signed into the account and if he or she has inserted a profile image.

3. Type into the comment balloon **Will you please confirm if the salary is correct?**

4. In the first sentence of the third paragraph, select **$2,500**.

5. **Right-click**, and then select **New Comment** from the shortcut menu; a second comment appears in the right margin.

6. In the new comment, type **The relocation amount is $5,000**.

Figure 9-14 displays both comments as balloons. If your screen is not displaying as shown in the figure, click Simple Markup in the Tracking group.

Figure 9-14

Document with comments displayed with Simple Markup

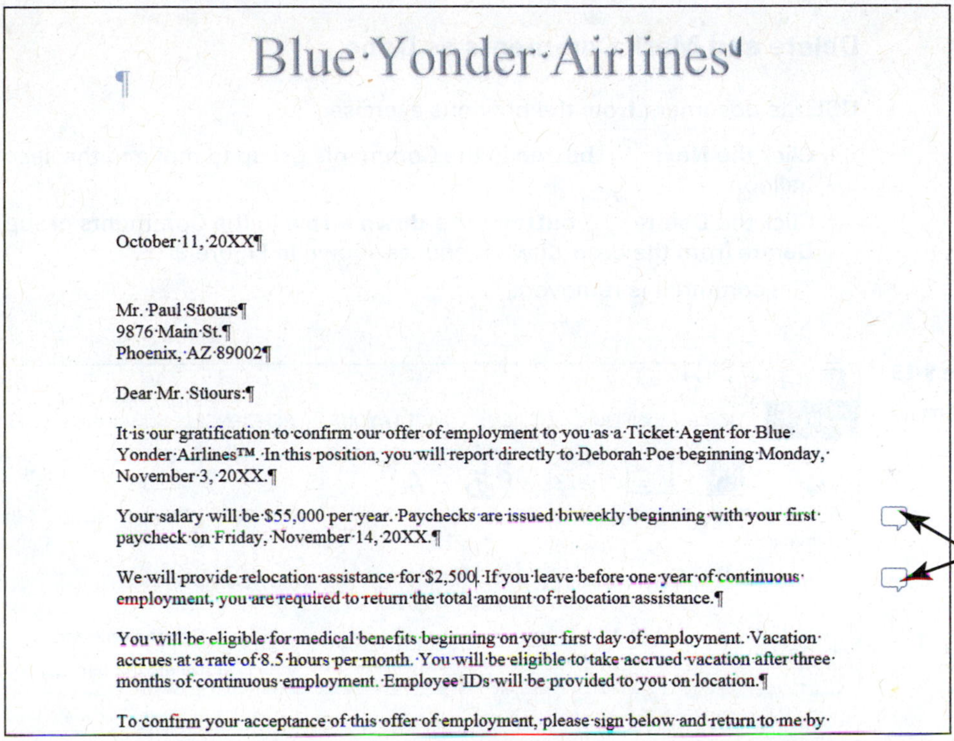

Blue·Yonder·Airlines¶

¶

October·11,·20XX¶

Mr.·Paul·Süours¶
9876·Main·St.¶
Phoenix,·AZ·89002¶

Dear·Mr.·Süours:¶

It·is·our·gratification·to·confirm·our·offer·of·employment·to·you·as·a·Ticket·Agent·for·Blue·Yonder·Airlines™.·In·this·position,·you·will·report·directly·to·Deborah·Poe·beginning·Monday,·November·3,·20XX.¶

Your·salary·will·be·$55,000·per·year.·Paychecks·are·issued·biweekly·beginning·with·your·first·paycheck·on·Friday,·November·14,·20XX.¶

We·will·provide·relocation·assistance·for·$2,500.·If·you·leave·before·one·year·of·continuous·employment,·you·are·required·to·return·the·total·amount·of·relocation·assistance.¶

You·will·be·eligible·for·medical·benefits·beginning·on·your·first·day·of·employment.·Vacation·accrues·at·a·rate·of·8.5·hours·per·month.·You·will·be·eligible·to·take·accrued·vacation·after·three·months·of·continuous·employment.·Employee·IDs·will·be·provided·to·you·on·location.¶

To·confirm·your·acceptance·of·this·offer·of·employment,·please·sign·below·and·return·to·me·by·

Comments appear alongside document displaying as a little balloon. With the Simple Markup enabled, the document has a clean look

7. **SAVE** the document as *Employment Offer Comments* in the lesson folder on your flash drive.

PAUSE. LEAVE the document open to use in the next exercise.

STEP BY STEP **Navigate and Edit a Comment**

USE the document from the previous exercise.

1. Click the **Previous** button in the Comments group to move back to the first comment. When you jump to a comment, you are ready to begin editing.

2. Place the insertion point at the end of the text in the first comment, and type **I would appreciate a response by 5 p.m. today**.

3. **SAVE** the document in the lesson folder on your flash drive.

PAUSE. LEAVE the document open to use in the next exercise.

STEP BY STEP **Show Comments**

USE the document from the previous exercise.

1. Click the **Show Comments** button to display comments in the document.

The comments are placed on the right side of the document and if you hover over them, you see how long ago the comment was added. If the person has signed into his or her Microsoft account, you also see his or her name and picture.

The Show Comments button is a toggle to show and hide comments.

PAUSE. LEAVE the document open to use in the next exercise.

STEP BY STEP   **Delete and Mark Comments as Done**

USE the document from the previous exercise.

1. Click the **Next** button in the Comments group to move to the second comment balloon.
2. Click the **Delete** button drop-down arrow in the Comments group, and then select **Delete** from the drop-down menu, as shown in Figure 9-15.

    The comment is removed.

Figure 9-15

Comment Delete menu

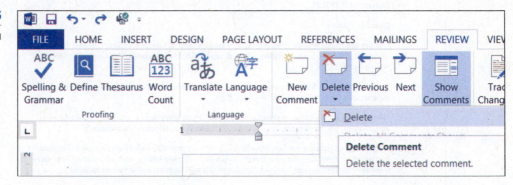

Another Way

You also can delete a comment by right-clicking on it and selecting *Delete Comment* from the shortcut menu.

3. Click **Undo** to bring the comment back.
4. **Right-click** both comments separately and click **Mark Comment Done**.

    This option shrinks and fades all comments and places them in the document background.

Take Note   You can also reverse the action by right-clicking on the comments individually and clicking *Mark Comment Done* to remove the check mark. Remove the check mark from both comments.

5. **SAVE** the document as *Employment Offer Comments1* in the lesson folder on your flash drive.

PAUSE. LEAVE the document open to use in the next exercise.

VIEWING COMMENTS

The Bottom Line

As you learned previously in this lesson, Word displays comments as little balloons in the document with the default Simple Markup enabled. Comments can also be shown inline in the document or as balloons. **Balloons** are markups and when comments are shown, the person's card displays on the right side of the document when you select that person's icon. **Inline** comments are hidden; the reviewer's initials appear in square brackets beside the selected text. ScreenTips appear when comments are inline and the mouse pointer is placed over the inline comment. Both the balloons and inline comments can be used with track changes, which is discussed later in the lesson.

The Show Markup menu allows you to change how comments appear and to determine which reviewers' comments are displayed. When in Draft view, certain elements in a document are not visible.

Viewing Comments Inline and as Balloons, and Hiding and Showing Reviewer Comments

In this exercise, you learn to change the comments display from balloons to inline. In a later lesson, you create a Microsoft Account so that when adding comments, your profile will be displayed.

STEP BY STEP   **View Comments Inline**

USE the document from the previous exercise.

1. In the Tracking group, click the **Track Changes** button to turn the feature on.

   The button is now highlighted to show it is on. Track Changes must be turned on to view comments Inline.

2. Click the **drop-down arrow** by Simple Markup and select **All Markup** to change the default setting for the markup.

3. In the Tracking group, click the **Show Markup** button to display the menu as shown in Figure 9-16.

   Options are available on how markup should display in the document.

Figure 9-16

Show Markup menu

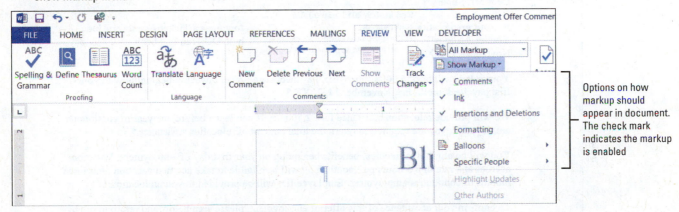

4. Select **Balloons**, and then click **Show All Revisions Inline** (see Figure 9-17).

Figure 9-17

Document with comments shown inline

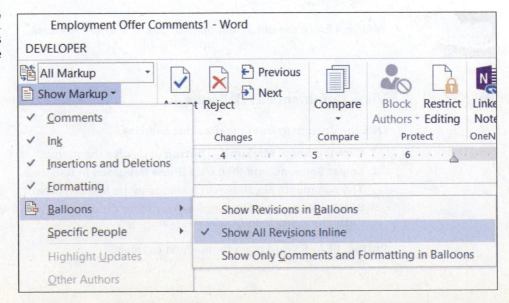

Position the mouse pointer over your initials in the second paragraph. The comment appears in a ScreenTip, as shown in Figure 9-18. Inline comments are hidden and indicated by bracketed reviewer initials beside the selected text.

Figure 9-18

Comment displayed in ScreenTip

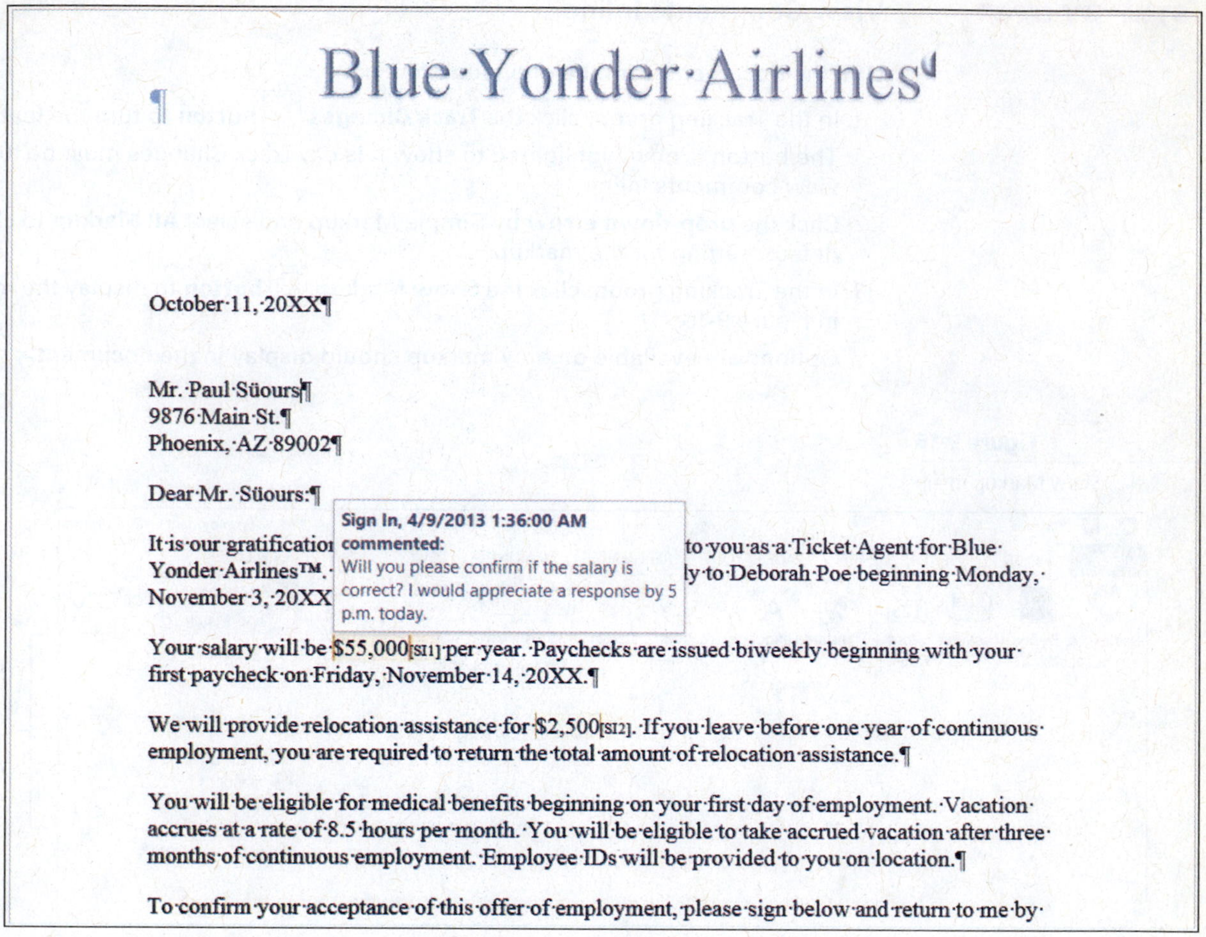

5. **SAVE** the document as *Employment Offer Comments2* in the lesson folder on your flash drive.

PAUSE. LEAVE the document open to use in the next exercise.

STEP BY STEP   **View Comments as Balloons**

USE the document from the previous exercise.

1. Click the **Show Markup** 📄 **button** to display the menu.
2. Select **Balloons**, and then click **Show Revisions in Balloons**.

   The comments are shown in balloons in the Markup area.
3. **SAVE** the document as *Employment Offer Comments3* in the lesson folder on your flash drive, and then **CLOSE** the file.

PAUSE. LEAVE Word open for the next exercise.

Hide and Show Reviewer Comments

1. **OPEN** the *Initial Employment Offer* document in the lesson folder. The document opens with the All Markup settings selected.
2. In the Tracking group, change the markup to Simple Markup.
3. In the Comments group, the **Show Comments button** should be highlighted displaying all comments by all reviewers.
4. Click the **Show Markup button** and select **Specific People** as shown in Figure 9-19.

Figure 9-19

All Reviewers

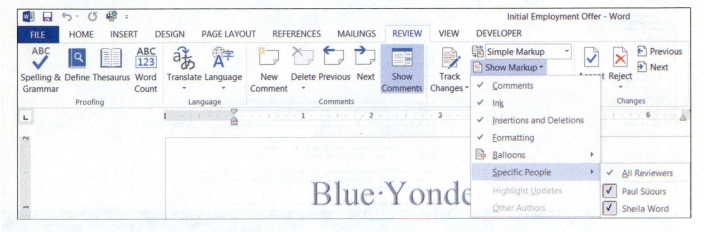

5. In the drop-down list of All Reviewers, click the check box beside *Paul Süours* to remove the check mark. Both comments no longer appear in the document because Sheila Word responded to Paul's concerns.
6. **SAVE** the document as *Initial Offer Comments* in the lesson folder on your flash drive.

PAUSE. LEAVE the document open to use in the next exercise.

Displaying the Reviewing Pane

Comments and track changes are tracked on the Reviewing Pane either vertically on the left side of the screen or horizontally across the bottom of the screen. When the Reviewing Pane opens, a summary displays the number of insertions, deletions, moves, formatting changes, and comments that have been made in the document. In this lesson, you learn to change the Reviewing Pane's display from vertical to horizontal.

Display the Reviewing Pane

USE the document that is open from the previous exercise.

1. From the **Review tab**, in the Tracking group, click the **Reviewing Pane drop-down arrow** and select **Reviewing Pane Horizontal** from the drop-down menu.

   The Reviewing Pane opens horizontally across the bottom of the Word window. It tracks and documents all changes.

2. To view the Reviewing Pane vertically, click the **Reviewing Pane drop-down arrow** and select **Reviewing Pane Vertical**.

   The Reviewing Pane displays vertically along the left side of the document as shown in Figure 9-20.

Figure 9-20

Reviewing Pane Vertical position

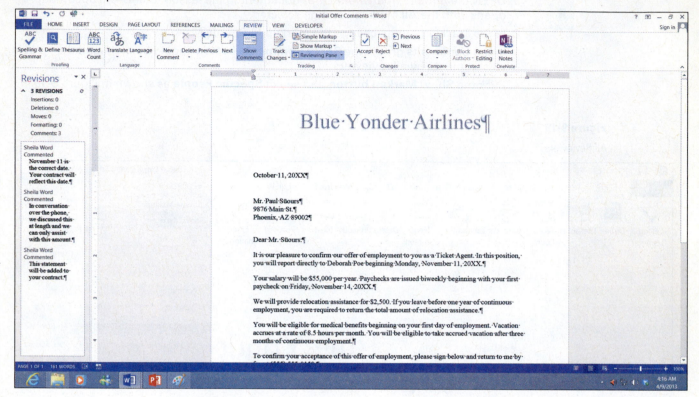

3. Click the **X** on the Vertical Reviewing Pane to close or click the **Reviewing Pane button** to close.

4. **SAVE** the document in the lesson folder on your flash drive, and then **CLOSE** the file.

PAUSE. LEAVE Word open for the next exercise.

TRACKING CHANGES IN A DOCUMENT

The Bottom Line

The Track Changes command enables reviewers to track revisions and feedback from other users. With the *new* Person Card, you can easily identify who has made changes and where the changes were made in the document. With the new Simple Markup being the default, changes made in a document display a red line near the left margin. When you click the red line or balloon, the view of the markup changes to the All Markup view. If you want to see only comments in the document and not changes, then click the *Show Comments* button.

To begin tracking changes, click the *Track Changes* button and to turn off, click again. You see the button highlighted when turned on. A *new* feature in Track Changes is **Lock Tracking**—this prevents anyone from turning Track Changes off. After reviewing all changes in the document, you accept or reject changes. For permanent changes, you need to accept or reject and stop tracking.

Additional choices are provided on how markups appear in the document. As mentioned previously, Simple Markup is the default; the other choices are **All Markup**, which displays all changes and comments; **No Markup**, which displays the document in a final copy without the markup; **Original**, which displays the original document with no markups.

As introduced previously, the Show Markup menu allows you to change how changes or comments appear in the document. The markups can appear as balloons, inline, or shown only with comments and formatting in balloons. The appearance of changes can be altered by disabling comments, ink, insertions and deletions, and formatting. By default, these are enabled. When there are several individuals who have made changes in a document and you want to see changes from only specific individuals, you can specify which individual's changes to display in your document. Previously in the lesson, you learned to display the Reviewing Pane horizontally or vertically—this works the same way for track changes.

The Track Changes Options dialog box allows you to change the user name. Additional options are available but they are not discussed in this lesson.

In this exercise, you learn to change a user's name, track changes, change how markups are displayed, print markups, lock tracking, and accept and reject changes. Figure 9-21 shows the Tracking and Changes groups.

Figure 9-21

Tracking and Changes groups

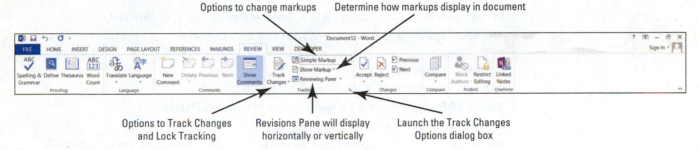

Use this figure as a reference throughout this lesson and the rest of this book.

STEP BY STEP   **Change a User's Name**

OPEN the *Handbook* document from the lesson folder.

1. **LAUNCH** the *Track Changes Options* dialog box by clicking the dialog box launcher on the Tracking group.
2. Click the **Change User Name button** (see Figure 9-22).

   The *Word Options* dialog box opens.

Figure 9-22

Tracking Changes Options dialog box

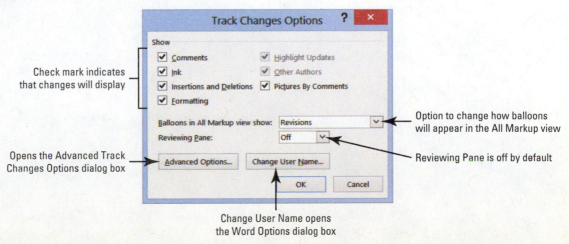

Another Way

To change the user name, click *File*, and then click *Options* to open the Word Options dialog box. Type your name and initials under *Personalize your copy of Microsoft*.

3. Under *Personalize your copy of Microsoft Office*, type **Aggie Becker** in the User name box, and then type **ab** in the Initials box.

4. Click **OK** to close the *Word Options* dialog box.

5. Click **OK** to close the *Track Changes Options* dialog box.

PAUSE. LEAVE the document open to use in the next exercise.

STEP BY STEP   **Track Changes in a Document**

USE the document from the previous exercise.

1. Display the **Review tab**, and then click the **Track Changes** button to turn it on.

2. In the first sentence of the first paragraph, select **B & B**, and then press **Delete**. The Simple Markup displays a red line on the left margin, letting you know that a change has been made.

3. In the same paragraph, select **B & B**. **Bold** and color the text **dark red**.

   The text appears in the document with changes made.

4. Position the insertion point in the second paragraph, in front of *B* in *B & B* and type **Books and Beyond**.

   The new inserted text is shown in the document.

5. Select **B&B** in the second paragraph, and then press **Delete**.

   A second markup is placed on the left margin.

6. **SAVE** the document as *Handbook Draft1* in the lesson folder on your flash drive.

PAUSE. LEAVE the document open for the next exercise.

STEP BY STEP   **Change Markups in a Document**

USE the document from the previous exercise.

Take Note   By default, the Simple Markup is enabled and the markup is displayed in the left margin where changes have been made. When text is inserted in a document, it displays in the document.

1. Click the drop-down arrow by Simple Markup and select **All Markup**.

   The markups are displayed in the right margin showing where text has been deleted with a dashed line showing the location of the deletion. The name "Author" appears in the document as shown in Figure 9-23 because the user has not signed into his or her Microsoft account. The inserted text is underlined and displays in the default track changes color.

Figure 9-23

Document displayed in All Markup view

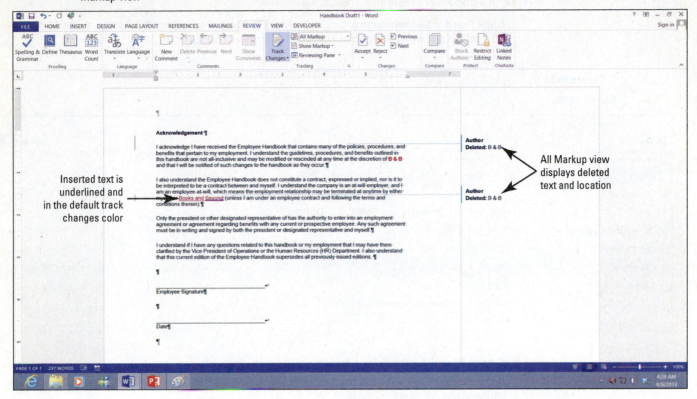

Inserted text is underlined and in the default track changes color

All Markup view displays deleted text and location

2. Click the **drop-down arrow** by All Markup and select **No Markup**.

   No markups appear in the document.

3. Change the *No Markup* to **Original**. The document is returned to its format displaying only the formatted text.

4. Return the document back to display **Simple Markup**.

5. **SAVE** the document in the lesson folder on your flash drive.

PAUSE. LEAVE Word open for the next exercise.

STEP BY STEP   **Show Markups in a Document**

USE the document from the previous exercise.

1. Click the **drop-down arrow** by Show Markup to display the menu.

   The check marks indicate that the markups for these features are enabled.

2. Click the **check mark** by Insertions and Deletions to turn it off.

   The markups no longer display in the document.

3. Turn the **Insertions and Deletions** markup back on.

4. **SAVE** the document in the lesson folder on your flash drive.

PAUSE. LEAVE Word open for the next exercise.

Display Markups in Balloons and Inline

USE the document from the previous exercise.

1. Click the **drop-down arrow** by Show Markup, and then select **Balloons**. A check mark is placed by Show Revisions in Balloons as shown in Figure 9-24.

Figure 9-24

Balloon options

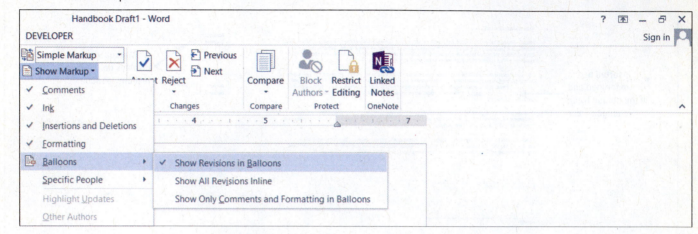

2. Select **Show All Revisions Inline**.

   Notice that no changes occurred in the document. To view changes inline, the markup must be in All Markup view.

3. Change to **All Markup** view, and then hover over the deleted text in the document to see markups inline.

4. **SAVE** the document as *Handbook Draft2* in the lesson folder on your flash drive.

PAUSE. LEAVE Word open for the next exercise.

Print Markups

USE the document from the previous exercise.

1. From the File tab, click the **Print command** to open the additional options. In Lesson 1, you learn about using some of the print settings.

2. Under Settings, click the first **drop-down arrow**, and then select **List of Markup**.

3. Click the **Print button** to produce a copy of the markups made in the document.

   The markups print comments and changes made in the document.

PAUSE. LEAVE Word open for the next exercise.

Use Lock Tracking

USE the document from the previous exercise.

Take Note   Track Changes can be locked with a password and this prevents anyone from turning track changes off. When it's locked, the Track Changes button cannot be turned off; nor can you accept or reject changes in the document.

1. Click the **drop-down arrow** by Track Changes and select **Lock Tracking**.
2. Type the password **HDBK^%**, and then reconfirm by typing the password again.
3. Click **OK** (see Figure 9-25).

Figure 9-25

Lock Tracking dialog box

The Track Changes, Accept, and Reject buttons turn gray and are not accessible.

4. Click the drop-down arrow by Track Changes and select **Lock Tracking**, and then reenter the password **HDBK^%** and click **OK** to turn the commands back on.

It is good practice to write all your passwords down and keep them in a safe place. If you cannot remember your password, you will not be able unlock Track Changes.

5. **SAVE** the document in the lesson folder on your flash drive.

PAUSE. LEAVE Word open for the next exercise.

STEP BY STEP   **Accept and Reject Changes**

USE the document from the previous exercise. Be sure to start from the beginning of the document.

1. In the Changes group, click the drop-down arrow under Accept to produce a menu as shown in Figure 9-26.

You have options on accepting the changes one at a time or all at once.

Figure 9-26

Accept menu

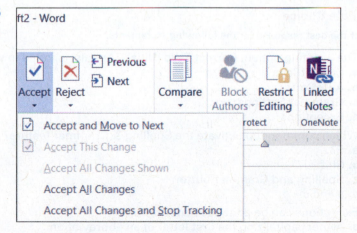

2. Click **Accept and Move to Next**.

Word accepts the changes and jumps to the next change in the document.

3. Click the **drop-down arrow** under Reject to produce a menu.
4. Click **Reject and Move to Next**.

The change made to insert text is not inserted in the document.

5. Change the view by selecting **No Mark up** to display for review.

This is what the final version of the document will look like. The changes are not deleted and will display again each time the document is opened. Note, to delete the track changes permanently, you must accept or reject changes and stop tracking.

6. Before closing the document, click the **Track Changes** **button** to turn it off.

7. **SAVE** the document as *Handbook Final* in the lesson folder on your flash drive.

CLOSE Word.

Cross Ref   In Lesson 13, you learn about inspecting your document before sharing. The Document Inspector is a tool that checks for tracked changes and comments, hidden text, and personal names in properties that you might not want to share.

SKILL SUMMARY

In This Lesson, You Learned To:	Exam Objective	Objective Number
Validate Content by Using Spelling and Grammar Checking Options		
Configure AutoCorrect Settings	Insert special characters (©, ™, £).	2.1.7
Insert and Modify Comments in a Document		
View Comments		
Track Changes in a Document		

Knowledge Assessment

Multiple Choice

Select the best response for the following statements.

1. The proofing option, Correct TWo INitial CApitals, is found in which option?
   a. CorrectCaps
   b. AutoCorrect
   c. Grammar Settings
   d. Exceptions

2. Which command(s) activate the Spelling & Grammar feature?
   a. F7
   b. Shift+F7
   c. Spelling and Grammar button
   d. a and c

3. Exceptions can be added to AutoCorrect:
   a. by not capitalizing the first letter of an abbreviation.
   b. by ignoring the INitial CAps.
   c. from the Other Corrections tab.
   d. All of the above

4. Comments are used to add _____ to Word documents.
   a. concerns
   b. questions
   c. reminders
   d. All of the above

5. The Comments ScreenTips appear in which view?
   a. Showing Revisions in Balloons
   b. Show All Revisions Inline
   c. Show Only Comments and Formatting in Balloons
   d. ScreenTips display only on the Ribbon

6. How do you display only one reviewer's comments in a Word document containing multiple reviewers' comments?
   a. Leave the check mark in the All Reviewers check box.
   b. Deselect the All Reviewers check box and place a check mark beside only that one reviewer's name.
   c. This feature displays only all reviewers' comments.
   d. This feature cannot display one reviewer's comments.

7. The Vertical Reviewing Pane displays:
   a. to the right of the document.
   b. below the Ribbon.
   c. to the left of the document.
   d. above the status bar.

8. A summary of the total number of comments and revisions in a document will appear in the:
   a. Vertical Reviewing Pane.
   b. Horizontal Reviewing Pane.
   c. status bar.
   d. a and b

9. The Personalizing your copy of Microsoft Office options:
   a. are located in the Word Options dialog box from Backstage view.
   b. are located in the Tracking group.
   c. cannot be changed.
   d. automatically change when Word is launched.

10. You can insert comments in which of the following types of documents?
    a. Research papers
    b. Resumes
    c. Marketing plans
    d. All of the above

True/False

Circle T if the statement is true or F if the statement is false.

T F **1.** The Proofing pane in the Word Options dialog box contains options to change how Word corrects and formats text.

T F **2.** You can change your name and initials from the Tracking group.

T F **3.** You should always proof documents before sharing them.

T F **4.** The AutoCorrect Settings can be found in the Word Options dialog box from the Backstage view Display screen.

T F **5.** By default, comments are shown inline.

T F **6.** AutoCorrect cannot be turned off.

T F **7.** Inline comments are placed in brackets.

T F **8.** You can right-click on a comment and use the shortcut menu to delete the comment.

T F **9.** The default Writing Style setting is Grammar & Style.

T F **10.** The status bar contains a proofing error button for quick access.

Competency Assessment

Project 9-1: Proofing a Research Paper

You have agreed to help your friend proof her reference letter.

GET READY. LAUNCH Word if it is not already running.

1. **OPEN** the *Reference Letter* document from the lesson folder.
2. **SAVE** the document as *9-1 Reference Letter* in the lesson folder on your flash drive.
3. Click the **File tab** to open Backstage, and then click **Options**.
4. Select **Proofing** and under the *When correcting spelling and grammar in Word* section. Beside the Writing Style command box select **Grammar Only.**
5. Click **OK**.
6. On the Review tab in the *Proofing* group, click the **Spelling & Grammar button**.
7. The Spelling task pane opens and will stop on the words/phrases listed in the following table; for each misspelled word, take the action indicated in the table. Also, if you are unsure of how a word is pronounced, click the Sound button.
8. When the prompt appears stating that the spelling and grammar check is complete, click **OK**.

Misspelled Word	Corrected Word	Action to Take
emplyed	employed	Change All
suprvision	supervision	Change All
demstrated	demonstrated	Change All
recomend	recommend	Change All

9. Click **Word Count** on the Proofing group to review the information on the document then close.
10. **SAVE** the document in the lesson folder on your flash drive, and then **CLOSE** the file.

LEAVE Word open for the next project.

Project 9-2: Books and Beyond Handbook

You work for Books and Beyond, and the manager needs your assistance in using the AutoCorrect Options in Word. Your task is to manually proof the document and locate the three occurrences of *B & B*. You have learned that the AutoCorrect command can save you time in typing text and adding special symbols in a document.

GET READY. LAUNCH Word if it is not already running.

1. **OPEN** the *Handbook Acknowledge* document in the lesson folder.
2. **SAVE** the document as *9-2 Handbook Acknowledge Update* in the lesson folder on your flash drive.
3. Click the **File tab** to open Backstage, and then click **Options**.
4. In the Proofing section, click the **AutoCorrect Options button**.
5. In the Replace box, type **B & B** and in the With box, type **Books and Beyond**.
6. Click the **Add button**.
7. Click **OK** to close the *AutoCorrect* dialog box.
8. Click **OK** to close the *Word Options* dialog box.
9. In the first paragraph, locate and select *B & B*, and then press **Delete**.
10. In the same location, type **B & B**, and then press the **spacebar**.

11. Locate the second occurrence, select **B & B** and press **Delete**. Then type **B & B** and press the **spacebar**.

12. Locate the third occurrence, select **B & B** and press **Delete**. Then type **B & B** and press the **spacebar**.

13. In the first paragraph, first sentence, place your insertion point after *d* in *Beyond*. Type **(c)** to insert the copyright symbol in the document.

14. In the first paragraph, second sentence, place your insertion point after *d* in *Beyond*. Type **(c)** to insert the copyright symbol in the document.

15. In the second paragraph, second sentence, place your insertion point after *d* in *Beyond*. Type **(c)** to insert the copyright symbol in the document.

16. Repeat steps 3 and 4 to open the AutoCorrect dialog box.

17. In the Replace box, type **B & B**. The text should appear in the list below.

18. Click the **Delete button**.

19. Click **OK** to close the *AutoCorrect* dialog box.

20. Click **OK** to close the *Word Options* dialog box.

21. **SAVE** the document in the lesson folder on your flash drive.

LEAVE the document open for the next project.

Proficiency Assessment

Project 9-3: Books and Beyond Handbook Review

Sonny is one of the managers at Books and Beyond and has asked you to comment on the document that you completed for the Project 9-2 Handbook Acknowledge Update.

GET READY. LAUNCH Word if it is not already running.

1. **SAVE** the document as *9-3 Handbook My Comments* in the lesson folder on your flash drive.

2. For every occurrence of Books and Beyond, add the following comments: **Format text by bolding and applying a font color.**

3. Use the Find command and locate the title, *Vice President of Operations*, and add the following comment: **The Vice President of Operations title has been changed to Vice President of Support Services.**

4. **SAVE** the document in the lesson folder on your flash drive.

LEAVE the document open for the next project.

Project 9-4: Showing Comments as Inline

Sonny is out of town and is interested in reviewing any comments you might have regarding the handbook. You will email this document to him with comments displayed as inline. You will work with the previous document from Project 9-3 to show comments as Inline.

GET READY. LAUNCH Word if it is not already running.

1. **SAVE** the document as *9-4 Handbook Inline Comments* in the lesson folder on your flash drive.

2. If necessary, change the Show Markup settings to display comments as inline only. Also, change the view to **All Markup**.

3. **SAVE** the document in the lesson folder on your flash drive, and then **CLOSE** the file.

LEAVE the document open for the next project.

Mastery Assessment

Project 9-5: Blue Yonder Airlines Stock Agreements

The job description for flight attendants has arrived and you are ready to review the comments from the flight attendants. Use the track changes command to make changes in the document.

GET READY. LAUNCH Word if it is not already running.

1. **OPEN** the *Flight Attendant Job Description* document from the lesson folder.
2. **SAVE** the document as *9-5 Job Description* in the lesson folder on your flash drive.
3. Turn on Track Changes and change the user name to **Margaret Wright** and initials to **mw**.
4. Under the *Responsibilities* heading, add a new bullet item at the end and type **Prepare for emergency landings and the evacuation of passengers**.
5. Under the *Requirements* heading, add two new bullets at the end and type **Excellent interpersonal communication skills** and **Able to work as part of a team**.
6. Under the *Responsibilities* heading, add a new bullet as the first bulleted item. Type **Safety of the passengers should be a priority**.
7. Select the bulleted item that you typed in step 6.
8. Insert a new comment from Margaret Wright and type **The order of the list should be changed.**
9. Display the markup in Simple Markup.
10. To prevent anyone from turning off Track Changes in the document, use the Lock Tracking command and use the password **JobDES**.
11. **SAVE** the document in the lesson folder on your flash drive.

LEAVE the document open for the next project.

Project 9-6: Job Description

A week has passed and you are ready to continue working on the job description for the flight attendants from Project 9-5. These changes will be the final changes made to the job descriptions.

GET READY. LAUNCH Word if it is not already running.

1. **SAVE** the document as *9-6 Job Description Final* in the lesson folder on your flash drive.
2. Unlock the tracking.
3. Delete all comments.
4. Accept all changes and stop tracking.
5. **SAVE** the document in the lesson folder on your flash drive, and then **CLOSE** the file.

CLOSE Word.

LESSON SKILL MATRIX

Skill	Exam Objective	Objective Number
Formatting a Research Paper		
Creating Citations	Insert citations.	4.1.6
	Change citation styles.	4.1.8
	Insert citations placeholders.	4.1.5
Adding Captions	Add captions.	4.2.1
	Change caption formats.	4.2.3
	Change caption labels.	4.2.4
	Set caption positions.	4.2.2
	Exclude labels from captions.	4.2.5
Creating and Modifying Headers or Footers	Insert page numbers.	1.3.6
	Insert simple headers and footers.	1.3.4
Creating a Works Cited Page	Insert bibliography.	4.1.7
Inserting Footnotes and Endnotes	Manage footnote locations.	4.1.2
	Modify footnote numbering.	4.1.4
	Insert endnotes.	4.1.1
	Configure endnote formats.	4.1.3
Creating a Table of Contents		
Adding a Title Page		
Inserting Hyperlinks	Insert hyperlinks.	1.2.2
Creating Bookmarks	Create bookmarks.	1.2.3
	Demonstrate how to use Go To	1.2.4

© Viorika/iStockphoto

KEY TERMS

- bibliography
- bookmark
- caption
- citation
- endnote
- footer
- footnote
- header
- hyperlink
- Hyper Text Transfer Protocol (HTTP)
- MLA style
- plagiarism
- source
- tab leader
- table of contents
- works cited

© Viorika/iStockphoto

You are working a full-time job at Northwind Traders and taking night courses at the local college to complete your degree. The courses you have registered for require that you submit a research paper. You will follow the Modern Language Association (MLA) style for your research paper, but it would be in your best interest to also learn about the other available styles. Your instructor will require that you learn how to insert hyperlinks and **bookmarks** and prepare the document for sharing. You have completed your paper and now you need to format your document. In this lesson, you will learn to format a research paper using the MLA style, apply a hyperlink to text and graphics, and apply bookmarks.

SOFTWARE ORIENTATION

References Tab

Commands on the References tab are used to create a table of contents, footnotes and endnotes, citations and bibliography, captions, index, and table of authorities.

Use this figure as a reference throughout this lesson as well as the rest of this book.

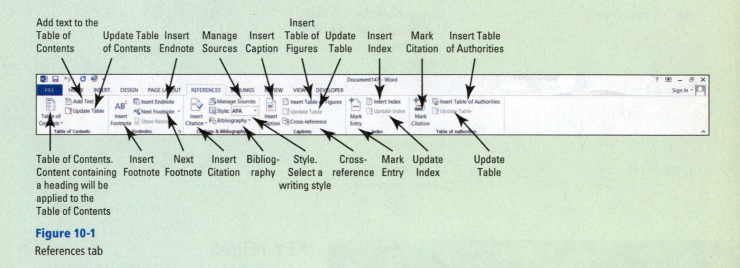

Figure 10-1

References tab

FORMATTING A RESEARCH PAPER

The Bottom Line

The Modern Language Association (MLA) style has been adopted as the style of choice by many colleges and universities. In this section we use MLA style to show how a research paper is formatted. The MLA style guidelines continue to be updated for standardization to accommodate documentation for websites, digital publications, interviews, electronic sources, and more. Later in this lesson we discuss alternative styles and show you how to format in one of those (APA style).

Formatting a Research Paper

As a college student, you most likely have to take a technical writing class for one of your humanities or liberal arts courses. As you begin working on your research paper, you will outline it to make it more manageable and help keep you organized. In a later lesson, you will learn more about outlines then you can begin putting your skills all together. Formatting a document with heading styles will make it easier to create a table of contents. Recall that in Lesson 2, you learned to enable the Navigation Pane and browse through the document by headings—inserting a table of contents will allow you to jump to that heading quickly. *Word* has made it easy for you to format your research paper, add and manage your sources, select a style, insert a bibliography, insert **captions**, create a table of contents, and add footnotes and endnotes. You will learn to cite your **sources** to avoid plagiarism. Compromising your work by copying a majority of the content and taking credit for it is **plagiarism**. In this exercise, you learn how to apply skills that have been covered in previous lessons; learn how to format a research paper using the MLA style; and how to insert citations, captions, footnotes and endnotes, a table of contents, bibliography, hyperlinks, and bookmarks.

STEP BY STEP   **Format a Research Paper**

GET READY. Before you begin these steps, be sure to launch Microsoft Word.

1. **OPEN** the *First Ladies* document from the lesson folder. The document is unformatted.

2. Position the insertion point at the beginning of the document and create a couple of blank lines.

   The MLA style requires information to be placed at the beginning of the document. On the first line, the student's name will appear, followed by the instructor, course, and date. Key the following information on the appropriate line.

First line:	**Victoria DeLeon**
Second line:	**Professor Frank Smith**
Third line:	**History 101**
Fourth line:	**March 19, 20XX**

3. Select the whole document then change the font size to **12 pt**, font to **Arial**.

4. Change the margins to **1"** top, bottom, left and right then change the line spacing to **double.**

5. Apply a **first line indent** only to paragraphs—avoid the title and headings.

6. Under the heading, *Women in Politics*, position the insertion point in the second paragraph beginning with "The nation has always . . . in the background." Adjust the left indent to 1" without a first-line indent.

   The rule of thumb for formatting quotations with less than four lines is considered a short quotation. These are enclosed with the double quotation marks, double-spaced, the author and specific page number is cited, and the punctuation mark should be placed after the parenthesis. This is also included in the bibliography page. Quotations longer than four lines should be double-spaced and one-inch from the left of the margin with no quotation marks. Do not indent the first line unless you are citing several paragraphs. The block format for short or long quotations should be used for citing two or more paragraphs that follow each other, and the first line is indented 1 ½" from the left margin.

7. Position the insertion point anywhere within the title, *The Evolving Role of the First Lady* then **center** the title.

8. Select the headings below, and apply a **Heading 1** style and make the headings **bold**.

   The Heading 1 style keeps the titles left-aligned.

   Introduction

   Women in Politics

   History of First Ladies

   Role of First Ladies

   Power of First Ladies

   Conclusion

 Cross Ref   In Lesson 3, you learned to apply and modify styles to a document.

9. **SAVE** the document as *Research on First Ladies* in the lesson folder on your flash drive.

PAUSE. LEAVE the document open to use in the next exercise.

CREATING CITATIONS

The Bottom Line

Now that you formatted your research paper, citations should be placed in the document. Citing sources should be included in documents, such as research papers, articles, or reports that analyze or describe research you have completed on a topic. When you cite a source, you do so at the relevant location within the text. *Word* enables you to insert a citation and create a source at the same time. These can be managed, modified, or deleted when necessary.

Creating Citations

A **citation** is a note mentioning the source of information. There are many rules that can be applied to a specific citation. In this lesson, you will learn to use the basic in-text citation, which places parentheses after a quote that includes the author's name and page number. Note, you can also modify citations.

A **source** includes all the information about where specific information comes from so the reader can find the original work. It could be a book, report, journal article, or website.

When you add a new citation to a document, you also create a new source that will appear in the bibliography. A **bibliography** is a list of sources and is placed at the end of a document. This is also referred to as a **works cited** page.

Each time you create a new source in any document, the information is saved on your computer in a master list, so you can find and use any source previously used in other documents. *Word* also creates a current list, which contains all sources within your current document. This list can be modified at any time.

When you have not gathered all the data for a source, you can insert a placeholder that can be filled in at a later time. To add a placeholder, click *Add New Placeholder* on the Insert Citation menu. In this exercise you learn to create a citation.

STEP BY STEP   **Create Citations**

You can choose from many different reference styles when formatting your citations, sources, and bibliography. American Psychological Association (APA) and Modern Language Association (MLA) are the most common. Additional formats are also available so make sure you check with your instructor on the style. The selected format inserts the information in the correct layout.

USE the document that is open from the previous exercise.

1. On the References tab, in the Citations & Bibliography group, click the **drop down arrow** by *Style* then change the style to *MLA Seventh Edition* (see Figure 10-2).

Figure 10-2

Style menu

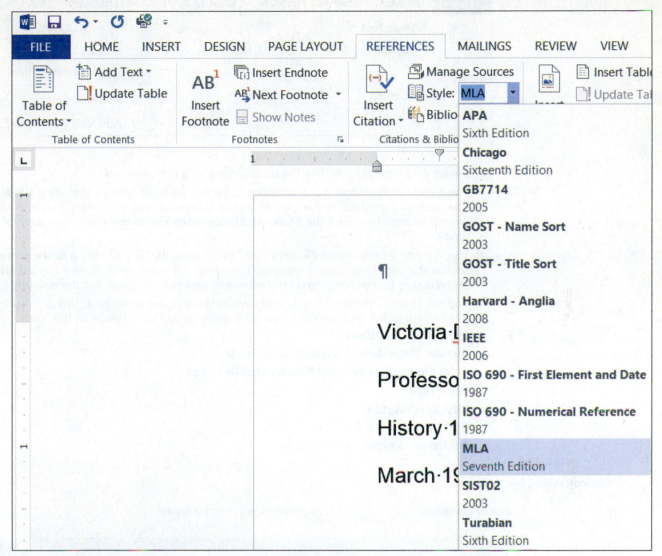

2. Under the heading, *Women in Politics*, position the insertion point at the end of the first paragraph, after *Meringolo.*

3. Click the **Insert Citation** button in the *Citations & Bibliography* group. A menu appears (see Figure 10-3).

Figure 10-3

Citation menu

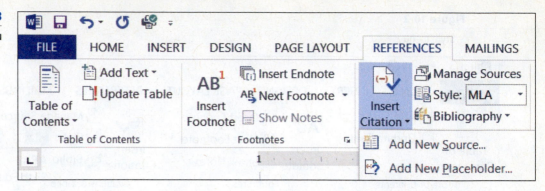

4. Select *Add New Source*. The *Create Source* dialog box appears.

   The *Create Source* dialog box contains fields for the book source, including the author, title, year of copyright, city where publisher is located, and publisher. To add additional source information, click the **Show All Bibliography Fields** box to display additional fields.

5. The *Type of Source* menu displays Book as the default. Click the **drop down arrow** to review the additional source options. The fields will automatically be adjusted for you in the dialog box depending on the source type. Keep the source at the default.

6. Key the source information that is shown below and in Figure 10-4. Notice: You will need to check the box next to Show All Bibliography Fields to see all the fields.

   Type of Source: Book

   Author: Mayo, Edith; Meringolo, Denise D.

   Title: First Ladies Political Role and Public Image

   Year: 1990

   City: Washington

   State/Province: D.C.

   Publisher: Smithsonian Institute

Figure 10-4

Create Source dialog box

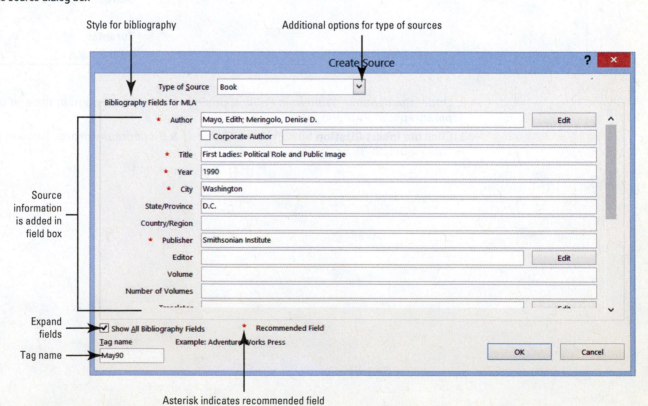

Asterisk indicates recommended field

7. Click **OK**. The citation is added to the text, and the source information is saved. The author names *(Mayo and Meringolo)* are in parentheses. When you use the MLA format, the author-page method is used and is placed in parentheses. The page number is not appearing, and later you will learn to modify the citation.

8. Under the heading, *History of First Ladies*, click to position the insertion point at the end of the second sentence following the word *speech* and before the period.

9. Click the **Insert Citation** button and select *Add New Source*.

   Did you notice that the first source appeared when you clicked the Insert Citation button?

10. In the *Type of Source* menu, select **Book**.

11. Key the source information for MLA style in the dialog box, as shown below (see also Figure 10-5).

   Type of Source: Book

   Author: Anthony, Carl Sferrazza

   Title: America's First Families: An Inside View of 200 Years of Private Life in the White House

   Year: 2000

   City: New York

   Publisher: Simon & Schuester, Inc.

Figure 10-5

Create Source dialog box

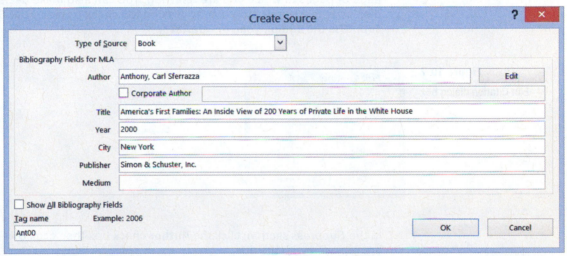

12. Click **OK**. The citation is inserted.

13. **SAVE** the document in the lesson folder on your flash drive.

PAUSE. LEAVE the document open to use in the next exercise.

CERTIFICATION READY? 4.1.6

How do you create a citation?

Modifying a Citation and a Source

Word makes editing sources easy by providing menus on the citation placeholders, allowing you easy access to dialog boxes used to modify citations and sources.

STEP BY STEP   **Modify a Citation and a Source**

When you insert a citation, *Word* inserts it into your document inside a placeholder. When you hover your mouse over the citation it appears shaded. You can easily modify the text within the placeholder or the source or citation data that goes along with it.

USE the document that is open from the previous exercise.

1. At the end of the second paragraph, click on the first citation you inserted. Click the **drop down arrow** to display a menu (see Figure 10-6).

Figure 10-6

Citation placeholder and menu

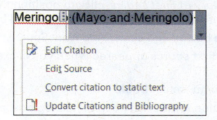

2. Select **Edit Source** from the menu. The *Edit Source* dialog box appears, filled with the information you keyed earlier about the source.

3. In the *Year* field, change the year of publication to **1994**.

4. Click **OK**. Word displays a prompt asking: *"This source exists in your master list and current document. Do you want to update both lists with these changes?"*

5. Click **Yes**.

6. The citation is still selected. Click the downward-pointing arrow on the placeholder again, and this time select *Edit Citation*. The *Edit Citation* dialog box appears (see Figure 10-7).

   The *Edit Citation* dialog box enables you to add page numbers specifying the source's page or pages to which you are referring. You can also make decisions about what to display within the citation text by clicking the check boxes under *Suppress*. You can suppress the author, year, or title.

Figure 10-7

Edit Citation dialog box

7. In the *Suppress* section, click the **Author** check box then click **OK**. The authors' names are replaced with the title.

8. Under the heading, *Women in Politics*, position the insertion point after the word *background*; located in the paragraph, *"The nation has . . . background."*

9. In the *Citations & Bibliography* group, click **Insert Citation**. The menu lists two sources that you have cited in the current document. This is your current list. Select the *Mayo, Edith, Meringolo, Denise D.* citation. The citation is inserted.

10. Click the citation. Click the **drop down arrow** to display the citation options and select **Edit Citation**.

11. In the *Add* section, key **8** in the *Pages* box, and in the *Suppress* section, click the check boxes by **Author** and **Title**. Click **OK**.

    In the above steps, you have modified the citation styles for this document by suppressing one or more of the options.

CERTIFICATION
READY?   4.1.8

How do you change
citation styles?

12. **SAVE** the document in the lesson folder on your flash drive.

13. Under the heading, *Women in Politics*, click the **drop down arrow** to display the citation option and select **Edit Citation**. You want to edit the first citation in this section.

14. Remove the check mark by Author and click **OK**.

15. Select the second citation and remove the check marks by Author and Title. Click **OK**.

16. Under the heading, *History of First Ladies*, place the insertion point at the end of the paragraph after *shakers* and before the period.

In this next step, you will insert a citation placeholder. A citation placeholder is a tag name of the source. You can also use this as a reference for yourself as you continue working on your research paper. Tag names can also be edited in the Edit Source dialog box.

17. Click the **Insert Citation** button; select **Add New Placeholder**.

The Placeholder Name dialog box appears instructing you to *"Type the tag name of the source. You can add more information to this source later by clicking Edit in the Source Manager."*

18. Key **Research_source**; then click **OK**.

In the Placeholder Name dialog box, spaces are not permitted.

19. **SAVE** the document as *Research on First Ladies Update* in the lesson folder on your flash drive.

PAUSE. LEAVE the document open to use in the next exercise.

CERTIFICATION READY? 4.1.5

How do you insert a citation placeholder?

Manage Sources

The Source Manager displays all the sources you have created and provides options for their management. The Source Manager displays two lists: the master list, which contains all the sources for all documents you have created using *Word*, and the current list, which includes all sources you have created in the current document. The Source Manager enables you to manage these sources by sorting, moving, copying, deleting, or creating sources. In this exercise, you learn to manage your sources.

STEP BY STEP | **Manage Sources**

USE the document that is open from the previous exercise.

1. Click the **Manage Sources** button in the *Citations & Bibliography* group. The *Source Manager* dialog box appears (see Figure 10-8).

Figure 10-8

Source Manager dialog box

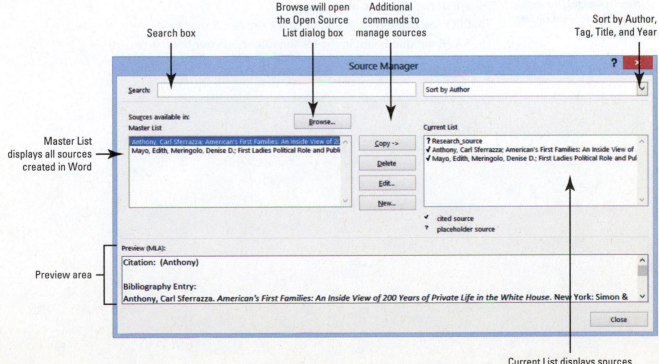

Current List displays sources from current document

2. In the *Master List* section, select the *Anthony* source.

3. Click the **Edit** button. The *Edit Source* dialog box appears. Using the *Source Manager* allows you to edit your sources.

4. Click the check box by *Show All Bibliography Fields*. The *Edit Source* dialog box expands to include additional fields.

5. Key **NY** in the *State/Province* field; and click **OK** to close the Edit Source dialog box.

6. Word displays a prompt asking: *"This source exists in your master list and current document. Do you want to update both lists with these changes?"*. Click **Yes**.

7. Click the **Close** button on the Source Manager dialog box.

8. **SAVE** the document in the lesson folder on your flash drive.

PAUSE. LEAVE Word open for the next exercise.

Removing a Citation

You can remove a citation from your document without removing the source data. The source data remains saved in the current document list and in the master list; therefore, if you decide you need to cite that source in another location, you can choose it from the Insert Citation menu. If you want to remove the citations permanently, you would complete this action by opening the Source Manager dialog box; then select the source; and then click the Delete button. In this exercise, you learn to remove a citation without removing the source.

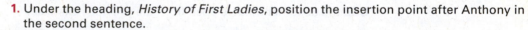

STEP BY STEP   **Remove a Citation**

USE the document that is open from the previous exercise.

Another Way
You can remove a source from the master or current list and from the bibliography by selecting the source in Source Manager and clicking the Delete button.

1. Under the heading, *History of First Ladies*, position the insertion point after Anthony in the second sentence.

2. Click the **citation placeholder** tab to select the entire citation. Hint, at the beginning of the placeholder, you will see a tab with three vertical dots—it makes it easier to select.

3. Press **Delete** to remove the citation from the document.

4. Open the Source Manager dialog box, Notice the source is still in both lists. When you are done, close the dialog box.

5. Click the **Undo** button on the *Quick Access Toolbar*.

6. **SAVE** the document in the lesson folder on your flash drive.

PAUSE. LEAVE Word open for the next exercise.

SOFTWARE ORIENTATION

Caption Dialog Box

When working with captions in a document, you will use the Caption dialog box (see Figure 10-9). From here you can select various caption options, including labels and numbering.

Use this figure as a reference throughout this lesson as well as the rest of this book.

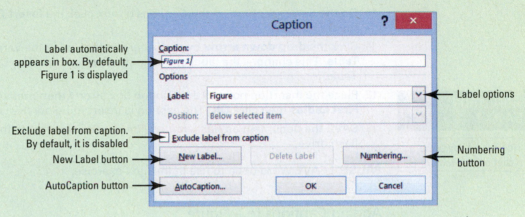

Figure 10-9
Caption dialog box

ADDING CAPTIONS

The Bottom Line

Word can automatically add captions in your document when you have tables, figures, or other objects or you can manually add captions.

Adding Captions

A **caption** is a line of text that describes an object and can appear above or below the object it describes. As you continue working on your paper, you decide to add a table and insert a picture. Adding a caption below or above the table would be informative to anyone who reads your report. As you continue working with captions, you also learn that captions can be used for figures and equations. For this exercise, you will be provided steps for creating one of these types of captions but will not actually use them in your paper. In this exercise, you learn to add a caption to a figure, table, and equation.

STEP BY STEP   **Add Captions to a Table**

USE the document that is open from the previous exercise.

1. On the View tab, enable the Navigation Pane.
2. Under the heading, *Power of First Ladies,* position the insertion point at the end of the last paragraph ending with *hurt her husband's career* and add a blank line.
3. Close the Navigation Pane.
4. Insert a **2x3 table** at the blank line. Key the following information in the table.
   First column first row: First Ladies
   Second column first row: Year in White House
   Second column second row: 1981, January 20 – 1989, January 20
   Second column third row: 1993, January 20 – 2001, January 20

Another Way
To insert a picture into the document, double-click the name of the file in the Insert Picture box.

Cross Ref

5. From the lesson folder, insert the *Nancy Reagon* image in the *first column second row* from the lesson folder.

6. From the lesson folder, insert the *Hillary Clinton* image in the *first column third row* from the lesson folder.

7. The height for both images should be adjusted to **1.27"**.

8. Apply the **AutoFit to Contents** command to the whole table.

In Lesson 8, you learned to insert pictures.

9. Position the insertion point below the table at a blank line.

10. On the *References* tab, in the *Captions* group, click the **Insert Caption** button to open the *Caption* dialog box.

11. Click the **drop down arrow** by the *Label* box to display the various labels then select **Table.** This changes the label option in the *Caption* box. The *Caption* box now displays *Table 1*.

12. Place the insertion point in the *Caption* box after *1* then press the **spacebar** once. Key **First Ladies** then click **OK**. The caption is inserted below the table.

13. **SAVE** the document as *Research on First Ladies Update1* in the lesson folder on your flash drive.

PAUSE. LEAVE Word open to use in the next exercise.

CERTIFICATION READY?   4.2.1

How would you add a caption to a table?

Adding Captions to a Figure

The same process you used to add captions to a table is used for figures and any other object. Your research paper contains two images, and you would like to insert a caption for each image. In this exercise, you will insert a caption for the images you inserted earlier.

STEP BY STEP   **Add Captions to a Figure**

USE the document that is open from the previous exercise.

1. Select the first image, **Nancy Reagan**.

2. Click the **Insert Caption** button then change the label to *Figure*.

3. Add a check mark by *Exclude label from caption*. Did you notice that *Figure 1* was replaced with a *1*?

   Adding a check by Exclude label from caption will allow you to customize your own label.

4. Click the **New Label** button then key **Nancy Reagan**. Click **OK**. A *1* appears after her name. Click **OK**. Click the **drop down arrow** by Position; then select **Above selected item**. Click **OK**. The caption appears above her image.

5. Select the second image, *Hillary Clinton*.

6. Click the **Insert Caption** button. In the Caption box, you will see *Nancy Reagan's* name. If you were to use another picture of Mrs. Reagan, then you would select her label. *Word* automatically numbers each label.

7. Change the label to **Figure**.

8. Click the **New Label** button, then key **Hillary Clinton**. Click **OK**.

   As mentioned in step 6, if you were to add another picture of Mrs. Clinton, then you would use her label. *Word* will automatically number each caption even for new labels.

9. Click the **drop down arrow** by Position; then select **Above selected item**. Click **OK**.

10. **SAVE** the document in the lesson folder on your flash drive.

PAUSE. LEAVE the document open for another exercise. You will return to this document later in the lesson.

CERTIFICATION READY?   4.2.1

How would you add a caption to a figure?

CERTIFICATION READY?   4.2.4

How would you change the label to a caption?

Adding Captions to an Equation

The same method for adding a caption to a table and figure is used for equations by simply selecting a different item in the *Label* list—or creating a new label. If you were writing a paper that contained equations, you would want to add a description for each equation. This document does not contain an equation, so a new document will be created. When you reopen the Caption dialog box, the previously selected label and numbering format will be displayed along with the next sequential number. For example, if you inserted the caption "*Figure 1*," the next time you open the Caption dialog box in that document, "*Figure 2*" will be displayed. In this exercise, you learn to add a caption, reposition, and change the numbering format.

STEP BY STEP   **Add Captions to an Equation**

OPEN a blank Word document.

1. Press **Enter** to create a blank line.
2. On the *Insert* menu, in the *Symbols* group, click the **drop down arrow** next to the *Equation* button to display the menu.

 Cross Ref   In Lesson 7, you learned to insert equations from the Ribbon and from the Building Blocks Organizer.

3. Click **Area of a Circle** to insert the equation into the document.
4. Click the shortcut **drop down arrow** by the equation, select *Justification* then click **Left**. The equation is placed at the left side of the document.
5. Move the insertion point to the blank line above the equation.
6. On the *References* tab, in the *Captions* group, click the **Insert Caption** button to display the *Caption* dialog box.
7. In the *Label* box, select **Equation** and in the *Position* box, the caption is already set to *Below selected item*.

   The equation was not selected. Selecting the equation would provide you options to change to *Above* or *Below selected item*. The insertion point is above the equation; therefore, the caption will be placed on the blank line above the equation.

8. Click the check box by *Exclude label from caption* to add a check mark. The text, *Equation*, is removed from the *Caption* box.
9. Click the **Numbering** button to display the *Caption Numbering* dialog box (see Figure 10-10).

CERTIFICATION READY?   4.2.1

How would you add a caption to an equation?

CERTIFICATION READY?   4.2.2

How would you change the position of a caption?

Figure 10-10

Caption Numbering dialog box

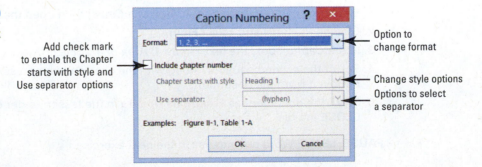

Add check mark to enable the Chapter starts with style and Use separator options

Option to change format

Change style options

Options to select a separator

CERTIFICATION READY?   4.2.3

How would you change the caption format?

10. In the *Format* box, select **A, B, C . . .** then click the box by *Include chapter number* to view the options. Your research paper must contain heading styles to use this option as well as adding a separator.
11. Remove the check mark by *Include chapter number*. Click **OK**.

CERTIFICATION READY? 4.2.5

How do you exclude labels from captions?

12. A new numbering caption appears in the *Caption* box. Click the **check box** by *Exclude label from caption* to disable this feature. Did you notice that the text, *Equation A*, appears in the *Caption* box?

   In step 10, you changed the number format to letters which will now be included in the caption.

13. In the *Caption* box, place the insertion point after *A* then key a colon, press the **Spacebar** once, and then key **Area of a Circle**.

14. Click **OK**.

15. Place the insertion point at the end of the equation and press **Enter** twice.

16. Insert the *Binomial Theorem* equation.

17. Select the equation then click the **Insert Caption** button to display the *Caption* dialog box. In the *Caption* box, *Equation B* is automatically added. Word tracks which caption you are using and renumbers for you.

CERTIFICATION READY? 4.2.4

How would you change a label in a caption?

18. Position the insertion point after *B* then key a **colon** followed by a **space**; then key **Binomial Theorem Equation**.

19. Position the caption, *Above selected item*. Click **OK**.

20. **SAVE** the document as ***Equations with Caption*** in the lesson folder on your flash drive.

PAUSE. LEAVE the document open to use in the next exercise.

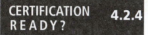 **Troubleshooting** Word inserts captions as text, but the sequential caption number is inserted as a field. If your caption looks similar to {SEQ Figure * ALPHABETIC}, Word is displaying field codes instead of field results. To see the field results, press Alt+F9.

Editing and Deleting Captions

When a new caption is inserted, *Word* automatically updates all caption numbers. However, when a caption is moved or deleted, all captions will need to be manually updated. To update all captions after making changes, press *Ctrl+A* to select the entire document, right-click on a caption, and then click *Update Field* on the shortcut menu. To make changes to a caption, you could select a different label, such as changing "Equation 1" to "Figure 1". In this exercise, you learn to edit and delete captions.

STEP BY STEP   **Edit and Delete Captions**

USE the document that is open from the previous exercise.

1. Select the caption, *Equation A: Area of a Circle*; then open the *Caption* dialog box.

2. Change the label and select **Figure**.

3. In the *Caption* box, the text *Figure 1: Area of a Circle* now appears. Click **OK**.

4. Select the second equation along with the caption, then press **Delete**. The caption is removed from the document.

5. **SAVE** the document as ***Equations Update*** in the lesson folder on your flash drive then **CLOSE** the file.

PAUSE. LEAVE Word open to use in the next exercise.

CREATING AND MODIFYING HEADERS AND FOOTERS

The Bottom Line

A **header** appears on the top of a document's page, and a **footer** appears at the bottom. The *Header & Footer* group is found on the Insert tab and contains commands for inserting built-in headers, footers, and page numbers into a *Word* document.

The *Page Number* button in the *Header & Footer* group has commands for inserting page numbers in the header, the footer, or the side margin of a page using the built-in gallery. In this exercise, you learn to insert page numbers in a document.

Adding a Header with a Page Number

You now need to add a header on every page, displaying your last name followed by a page number, according to the MLA style.

Add a Header with a Page Number

USE the *Research on First Ladies Update1* document that is open from a previous exercise.

1. Place the insertion point anywhere on the first page.
2. Click the **Insert** tab.
3. In the *Header & Footer* group, click the **Page Number** button.
4. In the menu that appears, point to *Top of Page*.
5. In the pull-down menu select *Plain Number 3* (see Figure 10-11). Page numbers are inserted on all pages.

   Notice that the *Header & Footer Tools* opens with the *Design* tab active. The page number is also positioned on the right side as stated in the MLA style guidelines.

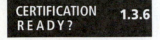

CERTIFICATION READY?   1.3.6

How would you add a page number?

Figure 10-11

Page Number menu

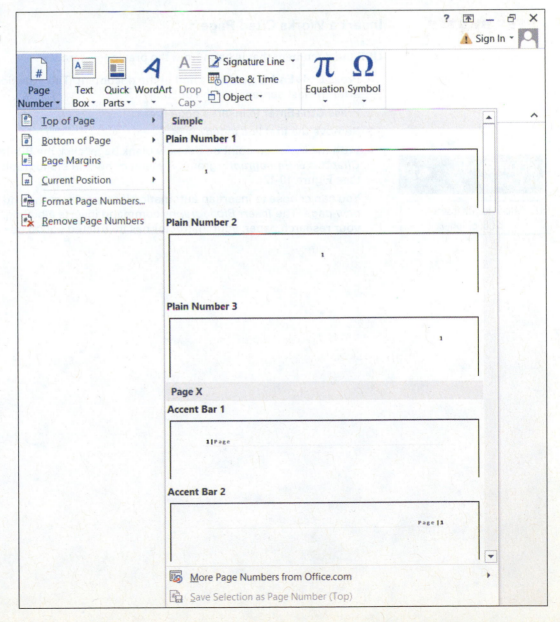

6. Make sure the insertion point is resting in front of the Page Number field. Key the last name: *DeLeon*; then press the **Spacebar** once. A page header will be inserted on every page in the document.

7. Click the **Close Header and Footer** button in the *Close* group.

8. **SAVE** the document in the lesson folder on your flash drive.

PAUSE. LEAVE the document open to use in the next exercise.

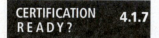

CERTIFICATION READY? 1.3.4

How would you insert a header?

CREATING A WORKS CITED PAGE

The Bottom Line

Word provides a gallery of bibliography formats from which to choose and enables you to automatically generate a bibliography from the sources in the *Current List* of the *Source Manager* dialog box. A **bibliography** is a page that lists all sources in your paper. Make sure you follow your instructor's instruction as to which format to use. You can choose to insert a bibliography at the end of the document or you can insert a page break to create a new page for the bibliography. After you insert the bibliography, Word allows you to update by adding and deleting sources or removing the bibliography. A bibliography is the same as creating a works cited page. In this exercise, you learn to insert a works cited page.

STEP BY STEP | **Insert a Works Cited Page**

USE the document that is open from the previous exercise.

1. Press **Ctrl+End** to get to the end of the document. The insertion point is positioned after the last sentence of the document.

2. Press **Ctrl+Enter** to insert a page break.

3. Remove the first line indent.

4. With the insertion point on the new blank page, click the **Bibliography** button in the *Citations & Bibliography* group. A menu of built-in bibliography styles appears (see Figure 10-12).

CERTIFICATION READY? 4.1.7

How do you insert a bibliography?

You can choose to insert an automatic bibliography at the end of the document or on a new page. The *Insert Bibliography* command inserts a bibliography without a title. For your research paper, your instructor has instructed you to use the *Works Cited* style.

Figure 10-12

Bibliography menu

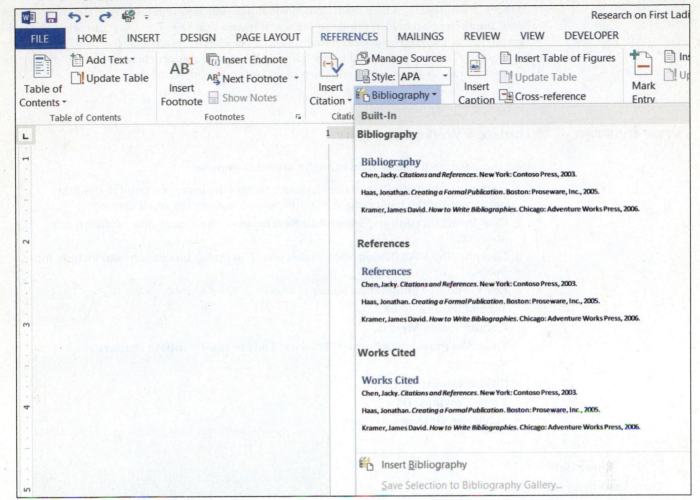

5. Select the *Works Cited* style. The works cited is inserted on the new page (see Figure 10-13). The title is also inserted for you and the header continues on the new page.

Figure 10-13

Works Cited page

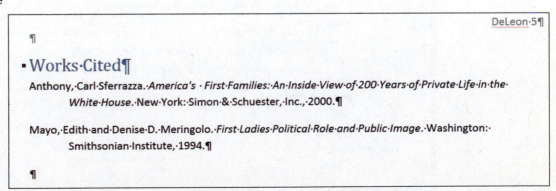

6. SAVE the document in the lesson folder on your flash drive.

PAUSE. LEAVE the document open to use in the next exercise.

Updating a Works Cited Page

After adding new sources or modifying sources, you need to update the bibliography to reflect the changes or additions you have made. When you hover your insertion point over the bibliography, Word shows the placeholder, similar to the way it inserts citations. Thus, you can select the bibliography using the placeholder tab—to display the placeholder, place your insertion point by the bibliography heading and a solid arrow pointing down will appear; click the icon to display the placeholder tab. In this exercise, you learn to update your works cited page.

STEP BY STEP   **Update a Works Cited Page**

USE the document that is open from the previous exercise.

1. Under the heading, *Role of First Ladies*, position the insertion point in the first paragraph, at the beginning of the fifth sentence, after the word *Gutin*.

2. Click **Insert Citation** and select **Add New Source**. The *Create Source* dialog box appears.

3. Click the **Show All Bibliography Fields** box. The dialog box expands to include more fields.

4. Key the source information below as shown in Figure 10-14.

   Type of Source: **Book**

   Author: **Gutin, Myra G.**

   Title: **The President's Partner: The First Lady in the Twentieth Century**

   Year: **1989**

   City: **Westport**

   State/Province: **CT**

   Publisher: **Greenwood Press**

Figure 10-14

Create Source dialog box

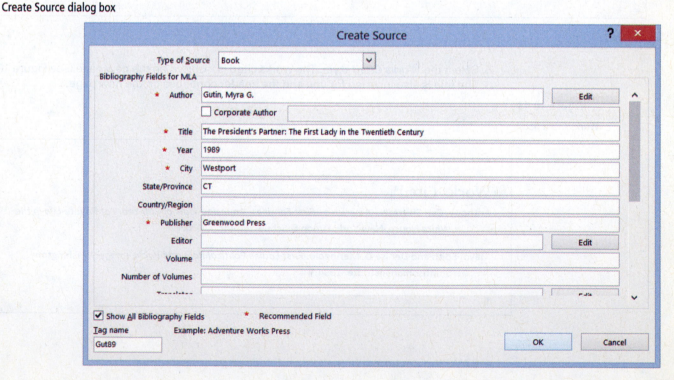

5. Click **OK**. The citation is inserted.

6. Scroll to the works cited page to update with the new source.

7. Place your insertion point by the works cited heading and solid arrow pointing downward ◢ will appear; click the icon to display the placeholder tab. The *Works Cited* heading collapses the content.

8. Click the **Update Citations and Bibliography** 📄 button. The page is automatically updated. To view the changes, click the **solid arrow** ▷ to expand the works cited page content. The new source is added to the page (see Figure 10-15).

Figure 10-15

Works Cited page updated

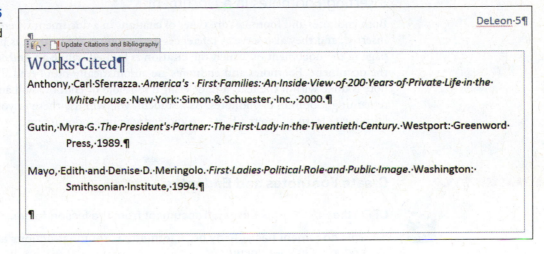

9. **SAVE** the document in the lesson folder on your flash drive.

PAUSE. LEAVE Word open for the next exercise.

Another Way
You can also update a bibliography by pressing the shortcut key **F9**.

Deleting a Works Cited Page

You can easily delete a bibliography. However, remember that the source information is still saved with the current document, as well as within *Word's* master list. When *Word* inserts a bibliography, a placeholder is inserted within another placeholder. To delete the entire bibliography, click the placeholder tab next to the title and press the *Delete* key.

STEP BY STEP   **Delete a Works Cited Page**

USE the document that is open from the previous exercise.

1. Click the placeholder tab (three vertical dots) to select the entire bibliography and source list.

2. Press the **Delete** key. The bibliography is deleted.

3. Click the **Undo** button on the *Quick Access Toolbar*.

4. **SAVE** the document in the lesson folder on your flash drive then **CLOSE** the file.

PAUSE. LEAVE Word open for the next exercise.

INSERTING FOOTNOTES AND ENDNOTES

The exercises you completed above demonstrated how to format your research paper using MLA style. You will apply the skills that you have learned in the exercises below by inserting footnotes, endnotes, a table of contents, and a title page. A title page is created and if your instructor instructed you to insert a table of contents, *Word* easily inserts this into your document. A table of contents page follows the title page and should be separated with a *next page* section break so that headers, footers, and page numbers can be formatted correctly.

Inserting Footnotes in a Document

Both endnotes and footnotes are types of citations in a document where additional information is inserted, and they also serve as references to the source. A **footnote** is placed at the bottom of the page in the document on which the **citation** is located, while an **endnote** is placed at the end of the document. Footnotes and endnotes are automatically numbered. Editing a footnote or endnote is done within the text, and deleting a footnote or endnote will automatically renumber the remaining footnotes or endnotes. As a student, you will use these in your research papers. In this lesson, you learn to insert a footnote and endnote into a document.

Create Footnotes and Endnotes

OPEN the *First Ladies Research* document from the lesson folder.

1. This document has already been formatted. Your instructions are to insert footnotes or endnotes in your document.

2. Under the heading, *Women in Politics*, position the insertion point at the end of the second paragraph.

3. Click the **Insert Footnote** button in the *Footnotes* group (see Figure 10-16). A superscript [1] is placed after the paragraph and at the end of the page. You will be citing the source in the footnote area.

Figure 10-16

Footnotes group

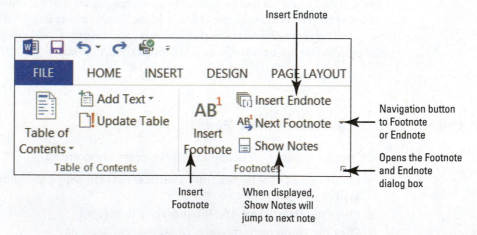

4. Key **Mayo, Edith and Denise, Meringolo. First Ladies: Political Role and Public Image. Washington: Smithsonian Institute, 1994**. You have entered the book title source for the footnote.

5. Place the insertion point by the superscript at the end of the second paragraph, and a ScreenTip appears displaying the footnote text.

6. Under the heading, *History of First Ladies*, place the insertion point at the end of the second sentence (before *Anthony*). In the *Footnotes* group, click the **Insert Footnote** button. A superscript [2] is placed at the bottom of page 2.

7. At the bottom of the document page, key **Anthony, Carl Sferrazza. America's First Families: An Inside View of 200 Years of Private Life in the White House. New York: Simon & Schuster, Inc., 2000**. The bottom of page 2 should resemble Figure 10-17.

Figure 10-17

Unformatted footnote

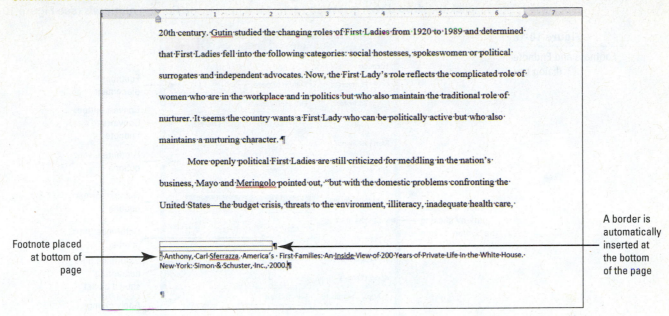

Footnote placed at bottom of page

A border is automatically inserted at the bottom of the page

8. Position the insertion point under the heading, *Role of First Ladies*, at the end of third sentence. In the *Footnotes* group, click the **Insert Footnote** button. A superscript ³ is placed after the punctuation.

9. At the bottom of the document page, key **Gutin, Myra G. The President's Partner: The First Lady in the Twentieth Century. Westport: Greenwood Press, 1989**.

10. **SAVE** the document as ***First Ladies Research Second Update*** in the lesson folder on your flash drive.

PAUSE. LEAVE the document open to use in the next exercise.

Formatting Footnotes and Endnotes

According to the **Modern Language Association (MLA),** a bottom of the page footnote in **MLA Style** is single spaced with a hanging indent and double spacing between each footnote, while an endnote is double spaced with a first line indent. In this lesson, you learn to format and delete a footnote and endnote.

STEP BY STEP   **Format Footnotes**

USE the document open from the previous exercise.

1. Press and hold the left mouse button to select the second and third footnote beginning with *Anthony . . . 1989*.

2. Change the indent to a *hanging indent*. The line spacing is already set to single space.

3. Click **OK**.

4. Place the insertion point after the second footnote (the first footnote on page 2) and increase the spacing after to **12 pt**. This action creates spacing between the footnotes.

5. Format the first footnote (on page 1) by changing the indent to a hanging indent, and set the spacing after to 12 pt.

6. Select the paragraph on page 1, beginning with *"The nation . . . background."*[1]

7. Format the paragraph with a *one-inch left indent*.

8. Change the line spacing to *single*.

9. Select the superscript [1] in the footnote at the bottom of the document on page one.

10. On the *References* tab in the *Footnotes* group, launch the *Footnote and Endnote* dialog box.

11. The *Footnote and Endnote* dialog box opens. In the *Format* section by the *Number format* click the **drop down arrow** and select the *uppercase Roman numerals* (see Figure 10-18).

Figure 10-18

Footnote and Endnote
dialog box

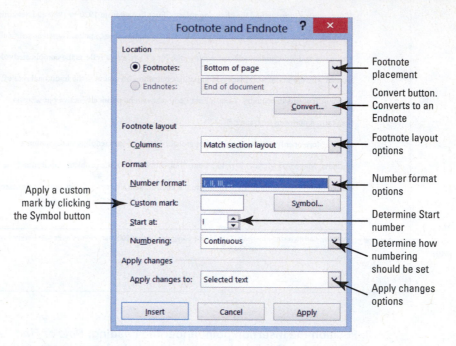

12. Click **Apply**. Notice the numbering format has changed for the footnotes in the document.

13. **SAVE** the document in the lesson folder on your flash drive.

14. Place the insertion point after the second footnote in the text under the heading, *History of First Ladies*. **Delete** the footnote.

Notice that the footnote disappeared from page two. When there are more footnotes in your document and you delete one, the rest of the footnotes are automatically renumbered.

15. Click **Undo**.

16. **SAVE** the document in the lesson folder on your flash drive.

PAUSE. LEAVE the document open to use in the next exercise.

CERTIFICATION READY? 4.1.4

How do you modify footnote numbering?

Converting Footnotes and Endnotes

It is easy to convert from a footnote to an endnote or from an endnote to a footnote. In this exercise, you learn to convert from footnotes to endnotes and to format the endnote.

STEP BY STEP   **Convert Footnotes and Endnotes**

CERTIFICATION READY? 4.1.1

How would you insert an endnote?

USE the document open from the previous exercise.

1. Place the insertion point at the beginning of the first footnote below the horizontal line.

2. In the *Footnotes* group, click the **arrow** to launch the *Footnote and Endnote* dialog box.

3. Click the **Convert** button. The *Convert Notes* dialog box opens. The first option *Convert all footnotes to endnotes* is selected (see Figure 10-19).

Figure 10-19

Convert Notes dialog box

4. Click **OK** to convert the notes and close the *Convert Notes* dialog box.

5. Click **Insert** OR **Apply** to close the *Footnote and Endnote* dialog box. Scroll through to the end of the document and notice the footnotes are no longer positioned at the end of the page. The endnotes display at the end of the document in lowercase roman numerals.

CERTIFICATION READY?   4.1.3

How would you convert a footnote to an endnote?

6. Place the insertion point after the last paragraph in the document and insert a page break to separate the Endnotes from the document and place on a new page.

7. Select the first endnote and change the format to *1, 2, 3...*—the endnotes are renumbered with the new format. Change the spacing to a *double space* and *first line indent* for the endnotes.

8. **SAVE** the document as ***First Ladies Research with Endnotes*** in the lesson folder on your flash drive.

PAUSE. LEAVE the document open to use in the next exercise.

SOFTWARE ORIENTATION

Table of Figures Dialog Box

When working with your research paper, adding a table of contents would make it easy for the reader to locate a section of your paper quickly. The table of contents makes it easy to jump from one location in your document to another. Links are automatically created for you, and should you decide to present online, the links will be in your document.

Use this figure as a reference throughout this lesson as well as the rest of this book.

Figure 10-20
Table of Contents group

CREATING A TABLE OF CONTENTS

The Bottom Line

A table of contents is usually found at the beginning of a long document to help readers quickly locate topics of interest. A **table of contents** (TOC) is an ordered list of the headings in a document, along with the page numbers on which they are found. The table of contents follows the title page.

Creating a Table of Contents

Word makes inserting a table of contents easy when using the built-in gallery of styles on the Table of Contents menu. You can use one of the styles from the built-in gallery or manually format a table of contents. Your document must contain heading styles in order for Word to automatically build your Table of Contents. *Word* will construct your Table of Contents based on any heading style that is used in the document. For example, if you use *Heading 1*, *Heading 2*, and *Heading 3* styles in your document and then generate a table of contents, Word automatically knows which heading style you are using. In this exercise, you learn to create a table of contents.

Create a Table of Contents

USE the document open from the previous exercise.

1. Position the insertion point at the beginning of the document. Add a *next page* section break and then move the insertion point to the first page.

   By inserting a section break, you separate the Table of Contents from the rest of the document because you may need to insert page numbers differently.

2. Press **Enter** twice to create a blank line above the section break.

3. Place the insertion point on line one.

 Cross Ref   In Lesson 5, you learned to insert different types of breaks in a document.

4. On the *References* tab, in the *Table of Contents* group, click the **Table of Contents** button. A gallery of built-in styles and a menu appears (see Figure 10-21).

Figure 10-21

Table of Contents menu

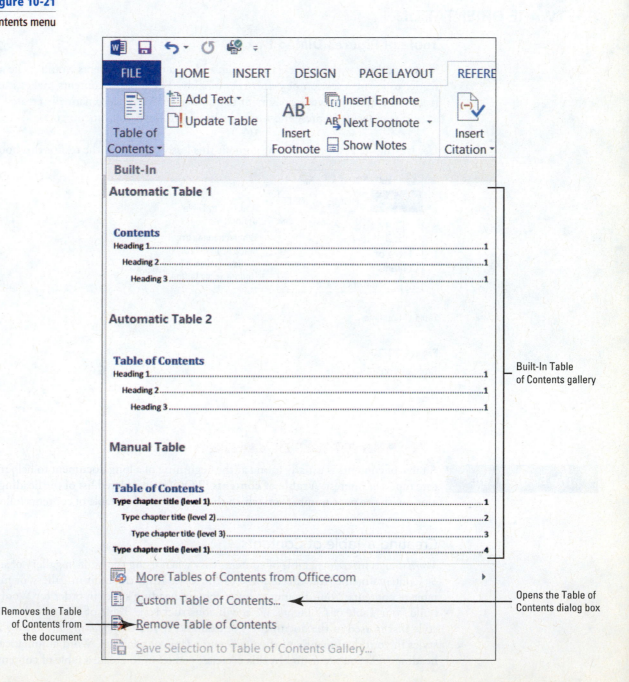

5. Select the **Automatic Table 2** style. The table of contents is inserted in the document (see Figure 10-22).

   When you click inside the table of contents, it is shaded in gray. Each entry is linked to the heading in the document and has a ScreenTip that will appear. The Table of Contents style that was selected contains a heading for this page and right tab settings with dot leaders, and the page numbers are automatically positioned by each heading. When the table is selected, the *Table of Contents* tab appears at the top of the table to allow you to select the table, change the format, and update the table quickly.

Figure 10-22

Automatic Table 2 style
applied to document

Table of Contents tab

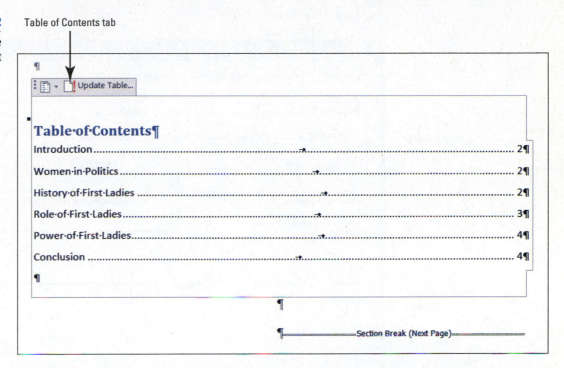

6. Press **Ctrl** then click the **mouse button** to follow the link for *Power of First Ladies. Word* jumps to that section of the document quickly. Press **Ctrl+Home** to go to the beginning of the document.

7. **SAVE** your document as *First Ladies Research with TOC* in the lesson folder on your flash drive.

PAUSE. LEAVE the document open to use in the next exercise.

Formatting a Table of Contents

The Table of Contents dialog box has other formatting options you can specify, including whether to show page numbers or right-align page numbers. You can also specify **tab leaders**, which are the symbols that appear between the table of contents topic and the corresponding page number. In this lesson, you learn to format a table of contents by changing the alignment tab leaders and levels.

STEP BY STEP   **Format a Table of Contents**

USE the document that is open from the previous exercise.

1. In the *Table of Contents* group, click the **Table of Contents** button.

2. Select **Custom Table of Contents** from the menu. The *Table of Contents* dialog box appears (see Figure 10-23).

The *Print Preview* box lists the styles used to create the table of contents while the *Web Preview* displays hyperlinks instead of page numbers. The *Table of Contents* dialog box offers options for you to specify whether to show page numbers and whether to right-align those page numbers. Tab leaders are symbols that serve as a visual guide from the headings to the page numbers. These can appear as periods, hyphens, lines, or none. The format for the *Table of Contents* can be changed to display different heading levels in the Table of Contents.

Figure 10-23

Table of Contents dialog box

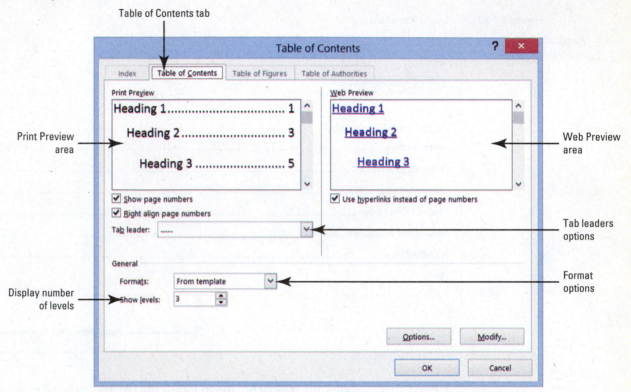

3. Scroll through the options and view the table of contents in the preview area.

4. Click the **drop down arrow** by *Formats* and select the *Simple* format. You can see the differences in the format in the preview area.

5. Click the **Options** button to open the *Table of Contents Options* dialog box (see Figure 10-24).

Figure 10-24

Table of Contents Options dialog box

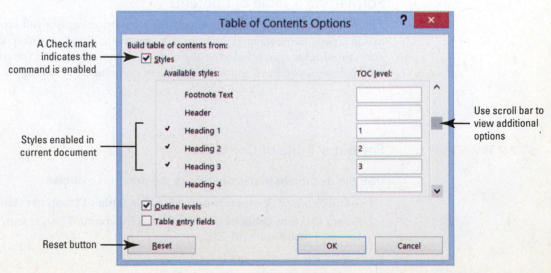

6. In the *Build table of contents from* section, scroll through the Table of Contents level list. Notice the styles and their levels marked for inclusion in the table of contents.

7. Add a *TOC level 4* by keying **4** in the box by *Heading 4*. A check mark is automatically placed by the heading.

8. Click **OK** to close the *Table of Contents Options* dialog box, and then click **OK** to close the *Table of Contents* dialog box.

9. If prompted to replace the selected table of contents, click **Yes**.

10. The table of contents contains the page number by the heading with no tab leader. If you had four levels in your document, you would see *Heading 4* in the *Styles* group of the *Home* tab.

Take Note   To remove Heading 4, open the Table of Contents dialog box and delete the 4.

11. Remove the *Heading 4* in the *Table of Contents Options* dialog box.

12. Change the format to *Distinctive*. The Table of Contents now appears with a line as a leader followed by the page number. Click **OK** and then click **Yes**.

13. **SAVE** the document as ***First Ladies Research with TOC1*** in the lesson folder on your flash drive.

PAUSE. LEAVE the document open to use in the next exercise.

Adding Selected Text to a Table of Contents

Sometimes in a table of contents you might want to include text that has not been formatted with a heading style. The *Add Text* menu enables you to choose the level at which the new text will appear. The levels available in the *Add Text* drop down menu are *Do Not Show in Table of Contents, Level 1, Level 2, and Level 3*. When working with tables of contents in other documents that have more levels, additional options may be available on the styles in the *Table of Contents Options*.

STEP BY STEP   **Add Selected Text to a Table of Contents**

USE the document that is open from the previous exercise.

1. Scroll to page 2 of the document and position the insertion point before the W in *Women in Politics*. Even though this heading contains a style, you can still apply the *Add Text* command.

2. On the *Insert* tab, in the *Pages* group, click the **Page Break** button to move that section to a new page.

3. Select the *Women in Politics* text.

4. In the *Table of Contents* group, click the **drop down arrow** by the *Add Text* button to display the menu.

5. Select *Level 2* from the menu (see Figure 10-25). This changes the existing level to the new level.

Text that is not formatted with a heading style can also be added as a level to include in a table of contents.

Figure 10-25

Add Text button and menu

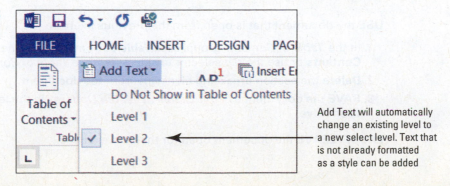

Add Text will automatically change an existing level to a new select level. Text that is not already formatted as a style can be added

6. Select the heading *"The Evolving Role of the First Lady."* Click the *Add Text* button and select *Level 1*. The heading moves to the left of the document.

7. **SAVE** the document as ***First Ladies Research with TOC2*** in the lesson folder on your flash drive.

PAUSE. LEAVE the document open to use in the next exercise.

Updating a Table of Contents

After adding new text, a new page, or modifying the table of contents; the next step is to update the table of contents. You can update the entire table or only the page numbers. In this exercise, you learn to update the table of contents.

STEP BY STEP   **Update a Table of Contents**

USE the document that is open from the previous exercise.

1. Scroll to the beginning of page 1 and click the **tab selector** in the **Table of Contents** tab to select. The *Update Table of Contents* dialog box appears. The default option button for *Update page numbers only* is selected (see Figure 10-26).

Figure 10-26

Update Table of Contents dialog box

You can update page numbers only or the entire table

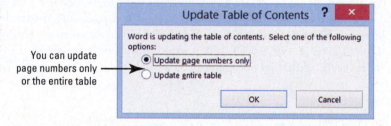

2. Select the option button to *Update entire table* then click **OK**. The table of contents is updated, and notice the *Women in Politics* heading is indented 0.15" from the left margin. You also see the differences in the levels in the table of contents. You can also click the *Update Table* button on the tab or in the *Table of Contents* group.

3. **SAVE** the document in the lesson folder on your flash drive.

Another Way
You can also use the shortcut key **F9** to open the Update Table of Contents dialog box.

PAUSE. LEAVE the document open to use in the next exercise.

Removing a Table of Contents

If you no longer need the Table of Contents in your document, you can remove it quickly from the document.

STEP BY STEP   **Remove a Table of Contents**

USE the document that is open from the previous exercise.

1. In the *Table of Contents* group, click **Table of Contents** and then click **Remove Table of Contents** or use the tab selector to select *Remove Table of Contents*.

2. **Delete** the section break and blank line from the document.

3. **SAVE** the document as ***First Ladies Research Update2*** in the lesson folder on your flash drive.

PAUSE. LEAVE the document open for the next exercise.

ADDING A TITLE PAGE

The Bottom Line

A title page appears at the beginning of the document with the title of the document, followed by your name and school name.

Adding a Title Page

A title page should be separated from the rest of the document with a section break, so you can apply formatting that will not affect the whole document. Always check with your instructor as to which style you will be using for your report and whether a title page is required. A title page is placed before the table of contents. Always separate your title page with a section breaks to avoid formatting errors. In this exercise, you learn to add a title page.

STEP BY STEP **Add a Title Page**

USE the document that is open from the previous exercise.

1. Position the insertion point at the beginning of the document, and then select the heading *The Evolving Role of the First Lady.*

2. Earlier in the lesson, you changed the heading to a Level 1 so that it would appear in the Table of Contents. In the *Table of Contents* group, select *Add Text* and then select *Do Not Show in Table of Contents.*

3. Position the insertion point at the end of the line and insert a *Next Page section break.* The heading is moved to the beginning of the document.

4. Press **Enter** three times to create blank lines after the heading and before the section break.

 Cross Ref In Lesson 5, you learned to insert different types of breaks in a document.

5. On the blank line, key **Victoria DeLeon** and then press **Enter**.

6. Key **Local College** as your school's name. Make sure that the font and font size is the same. It should be *Times New Roman, 12* pt.

7. *Center* the three lines and change the page layout to *center vertically* on the page. Change the *spacing after* the title to *162* pt.

8. **SAVE** the document as ***First Ladies Research Update3*** in the lesson folder on your flash drive.

9. Position the insertion point on the blank line above *Introduction.*

10. Insert a page break and move the insertion point to where the page break appears and insert a blank line before the page break.

11. Insert the *Automatic Table 1* table of contents.

12. **SAVE** the document in the lesson folder on your flash drive then **CLOSE** the file.

PAUSE. LEAVE Word open for the next exercise.

INSERTING HYPERLINKS

The Bottom Line

Hyperlinks can also be added to a research paper or any documents that require a link to help the reader quickly find the source you are referring to in your document. Your instructor may require you to share your document online with others; which will allow your readers to follow links in your document. In another lesson, you will learn to use the *Present Online* command which will automatically create a link to your document. A **hyperlink** is a way to jump from one location to another. It can be in the same document or to an external location. To follow the link, you would press the Ctrl key with left mouse button on the hyperlink. Hyperlinks can be applied to text or graphics. Hyperlinks can be external links to a web page on the Internet to a specific target location within the document as a bookmark or heading, to an email address, or to a different document.

Inserting a Hyperlink

A hyperlink quickly takes you to a location within the document, web page, a different document, or email address. In this exercise, you learn to insert a hyperlink in text and an image, add a ScreenTip, and remove a hyperlink and ScreenTip.

Insert a Hyperlink

OPEN the *Research on First Ladies Update1* document from a previous exercise.

1. Go to page four and select the *Nancy Reagan* picture.
2. On the *Insert* tab, in the *Links* group, click the **Hyperlink** button to open the *Insert Hyperlink* dialog box (see Figure 10-27).

Figure 10-27

Insert Hyperlink dialog box

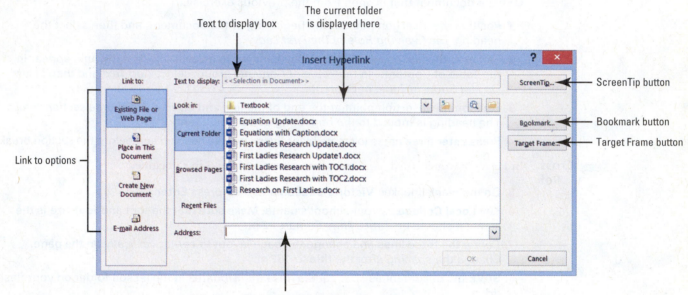

Full address link is placed in the Address box

By default, the Existing File or Web Page is selected. There are additional options on where to place the link.

3. Key **http://www.firstladies.org/biographies/** in the *Address* box; then click **OK**.

   Hypertext Transfer Protocol (HTTP) is how the data is transferred to the external site through the servers. The picture is now linked to the external site.

4. To test the link, press **Ctrl** then click the left mouse button. When you hover over the link, a ScreenTip automatically appears with instructions on what to do.

5. Select the *Hillary Clinton* picture and repeat steps 2 and 3. *Word* recalls the last address, and the full address will appear once you start typing. You have now linked two pictures to an external site.

   It is recommended that you always test your links before posting or sharing. You can add links to text or phrases and use the same process that you just completed.

6. Insert hyperlinks with the same Web address to both First Ladies names. Both names are now underlined, showing that they are linked.

7. Hover over Nancy Reagan's picture and you should see the full address that you keyed. It would be better to change the ScreenTip with the First Lady's full name. Select *Nancy Reagan's* picture.

8. Press **Ctrl+K** to open the *Edit Hyperlink* dialog box.

9. Click the **ScreenTip** button. The *Set Hyperlink ScreenTip* dialog box appears.

CERTIFICATION READY?   1.2.2

How do you insert a hyperlink?

10. Key **First Lady Nancy Reagan**.

11. Click **OK** to close the dialog box. Click **OK** to close the *Edit Hyperlink* dialog box.

12. Place your insertion point over the image and notice the ScreenTip; it now appears as *First Lady Nancy Reagan*.

13. Repeat steps 7–11 for *First Lady Hillary Clinton* and review your ScreenTip.

14. **SAVE** the document as ***Research on First Ladies with Links*** in the lesson folder on your flash drive.

PAUSE. LEAVE the document open to use in the next exercise.

Another Way

Right-click to open the Insert Hyperlink or Edit Hyperlink dialog box.

Removing a Hyperlink and ScreenTip

Once a hyperlink is removed, it will no longer be linked to a document or external web location. Hyperlinks are removed the same way for text and images. After a ScreenTip is deleted, it will no longer be displayed in the hyperlink; however, the link will remain active. In this exercise, you learn to remove a hyperlink and ScreenTip.

<table>
<tr><td>**STEP BY STEP**</td><td>**Remove a Hyperlink and ScreenTip**</td></tr>
</table>

USE the document open from the previous exercise.

1. Select the image of Hillary Clinton.

2. Use the shortcut method, **Ctrl+K**, to access the *Edit Hyperlink* dialog box.

3. Click **Remove Link** to remove the hyperlink.

4. Hover over the image and notice that the ScreenTip no longer appears and the hyperlink has been removed.

5. Select the image of Nancy Reagan, and on the *Links* group, click the **Hyperlink** button.

6. Click the **ScreenTip** button; then select and **delete** *First Lady Nancy Reagan*.

7. Click **OK** twice.

8. Hover over the image and the ScreenTip is no longer showing but the image is still linked to an external site.

9. Use the right mouse button to open the shortcut menu and remove the links on the two text hyperlinks and on the image.

10. **SAVE** the document as ***Research on First Ladies with no Links*** in the lesson folder on your flash drive.

PAUSE. LEAVE the document open to use in the next exercise.

Adding an Email as a Hyperlink

An email address link is used to provide contact information, elicit feedback, or request information. In this exercise, you learn to add an email as a hyperlink.

<table>
<tr><td>**STEP BY STEP**</td><td>**Add an Email as a Hyperlink**</td></tr>
</table>

USE the document open from the previous exercise.

1. Press **Ctrl+Home** to move to the beginning of the document.

2. Select *Victoria DeLeon*.

Take Note   Email links can be applied to text or images.

3. Click the **Hyperlink** button or press **Ctrl+K**. The *Insert Hyperlink* dialog box opens.

Victoria is the manager at Proseware and would prefer to receive her email notifications at work.

4. Under the *Link to* section, click **E-mail Address**. Notice the dialog box changes what information is to be filled in.

5. In the *E-mail address* box, key **manager@proseware.com**. The *text mailto;* automatically appears when you begin keying the email address.

6. For the *Subject* box, key **Research Paper on First Ladies** as displayed in Figure 10-28.

Figure 10-28

Insert Hyperlink dialog box
E-mail Address link

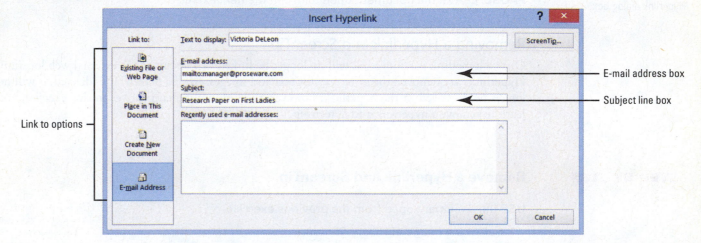

7. Click the **ScreenTip** button to open the *Set Hyperlink ScreenTip* dialog box; then in the *ScreenTip* text box, key **Manager**.

8. Click **OK** twice.

An email link can also be inserted for an image.

9. Test your email link by pressing the **Ctrl** key and clicking the left mouse button once. The *mailto* link opens the Outlook messaging box with the email address and subject line already inserted.

If Outlook is not set up on your computer, you will be unable to use this feature.

10. **SAVE** the document as *Research on First Ladies1* in your lesson folder on your flash drive.

PAUSE. LEAVE the document open to use in the next exercise.

CERTIFICATION
READY?   1.2.2

How do you create an email
hyperlink?

CREATING BOOKMARKS

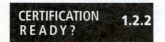
The Bottom Line

A **bookmark** is a reference point, a location, or a selection of text that you name and identify for future reference. For instance, you may like to revisit a page in a document and locate text. You could create a bookmark; then use the Bookmark dialog box to get there quickly using the name of the bookmark you created.

Adding a Bookmark

For your research paper, you will be sharing your work online and inserting bookmarks in your document that will make it easier for your readers to navigate through the document. In this exercise, you learn to add a bookmark in a document. Bookmark names can contain numbers, but they must begin with a letter. Spaces are not valid when naming a bookmark; therefore, separate text with an underscore or keep text together with no space, for example, *Trade_Secrets* or *TradeSecrets*.

STEP BY STEP　　**Add Bookmark**

USE the document open from the previous exercise.

1. Select the *The Evolving Role of the First Lady* text.

2. In the *Links* group, click the **Bookmark** button. The *Bookmark* dialog box opens (see Figure 10-29).

   Bookmark names can contain up to 40 characters and spaces are not allowed when using Bookmarks; therefore, you would use an underscore to separate words.

Figure 10-29

Bookmark dialog box

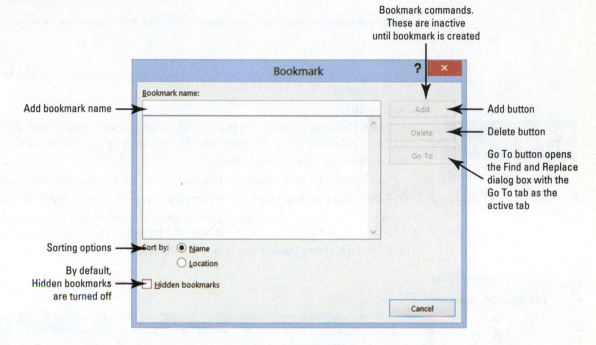

3. Key **Title** in the Bookmark name.

4. Click the **Add** button.

5. Open the *Bookmark* dialog box again to view the bookmark in the middle box; then close.

6. Select *Introduction;* then click the **Bookmark** button.

7. Key **Introduction** in the *Bookmark* name box.

8. Click **Add**.

9. Create a bookmark for each heading in the document. Remember to use underscores in place of spaces.

10. Select the caption, *Table 1 First Ladies* and create a bookmark for this table.

    Captions can also contain a bookmark.

    Now that you have finished creating the locations for the bookmark, it's time to test it. Use the *Go To* command to go directly to the bookmark.

11. On the *Home* tab, in the *Editing* group, click the **drop down arrow** next to *Find* and select **Go To**. The *Find and Replace* dialog box opens with the *Go To* tab open.

12. In the *Go to What* section, select *Bookmark* (see Figure 10-30).

    The right side of the box displays the bookmarks that you created in the previous steps.

Figure 10-30

Find and Replace dialog box

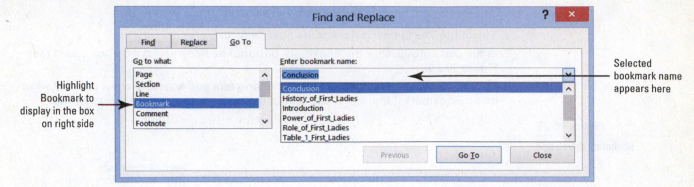

Highlight Bookmark to display in the box on right side

Selected bookmark name appears here

13. Select *Title;* then click the **Go To** button. It automatically jumps to the bookmark in the document.

14. Test all bookmarks.

CERTIFICATION READY? 1.2.4

How would you use the Go To command?

15. Press **Ctrl+End** to move to the end of the document, and create one blank line below the *Work Cited* page. It should appear below the *Works Cited* box.

16. Key **Back to Top** and right-align.

You will create one more link to move to the beginning of the document.

17. Select **Back to Top**; then press **Ctrl+K** to open the *Insert Hyperlink* dialog box.

18. In the *Link to* section, select *Place in This Document* and notice the center section changes and displays the headings and bookmarks in the document.

19. Click **Top of the Document** then click **OK** (see Figure 10-31).

Figure 10-31

Edit Hyperlink dialog box

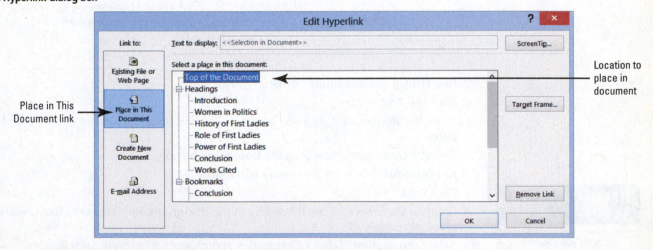

Place in This Document link

Location to place in document

20. Press **Ctrl+Click** to test the link. It jumps to the beginning of the document. This document is ready to be shared online with others.

21. **SAVE** the document as ***Research on First Ladies2*** in the lesson folder on your flash drive then **CLOSE** the file.

CLOSE Word.

 Cross Ref

You can access the *Go To* command in one of the following ways: (1) press the shortcut key **F5**; (2) in the Editing group, click the Find button arrow; (3) press Ctrl+G; or (4) open the Navigation Pane. Using any one of these commands will open the *Find and Replace* dialog box as you learned in Lesson 2.

 **Troubleshooting** If your bookmark does not run properly, delete the bookmark, select the text, the same name, and then click Add.

SKILL SUMMARY

In this lesson you learned to:	Exam Objective	Objective Number
Format a Research Paper		
Create Citations	Insert citations.	4.1.6
	Change citation styles.	4.1.8
	Insert citations placeholders.	4.1.5
Add Captions	Add captions.	4.2.1
	Change caption formats.	4.2.3
	Change caption labels.	4.2.4
	Set caption positions.	4.2.2
	Exclude labels from captions.	4.2.5
Create and Modify Headers or Footers	Insert page numbers.	1.3.6
	Insert simple headers and footers.	1.3.4
Create a Works Cited Page	Insert bibliography.	4.1.7
Insert Footnotes and Endnotes	Manage footnote locations.	4.1.2
	Modify footnote numbering.	4.1.4
	Insert endnotes.	4.1.1
	Configure endnote formats.	4.1.3
Create a Table of Contents		
Add a Title Page		
Insert Hyperlinks	Insert hyperlinks.	1.2.2
Create Bookmarks	Create bookmarks.	1.2.3
	Demonstrate how to use Go To.	1.2.4

Knowledge Assessment

Multiple Choice

Select the best response for the following statements.

1. A table of contents is located at the _____ of the document.
   a. Middle
   b. End
   c. Beginning
   d. None of the above

2. Tab leaders can be changed into what types of symbols for use in a table of contents?
   a. Periods
   b. Hyphens
   c. Lines
   d. All of the above

3. Which menu will allow you to add content to the table of contents?
   a. Update Table
   b. Add Text
   c. Add Bookmark
   d. None of the above

4. When adding a page or text to a table of contents, it is recommended that you
   a. Click the Update Table button on the Ribbon
   b. Press F9
   c. Click the Update Table button above the table of contents
   d. All of the above

5. By default, a footnote is placed
   a. At the beginning of the document
   b. At the end of the document
   c. At the end of the page
   d. Below text

6. Formatting a footnote in a document, per MLA style, should be
   a. single spaced with a hanging indent and triple spaced between each footnote
   b. single spaced with a hanging indent and doubled spaced between each footnote
   c. doubled spaced with a hanging indent and single spaced between each footnote
   d. No format is needed.

7. Hyperlinks can be linked
   a. From one page to another page
   b. To a website
   c. To an email
   d. All of the above

8. Reference points in a document are created using which command?
   a. Bookmark
   b. Hyperlink
   c. Email
   d. All of the above

9. The Footnote and Endnote dialog box contains an option to change the page number format to
   a. Uppercase Roman numerals
   b. A1, A2, A3, etc.
   c. a and b
   d. This is not an option.

10. Endnotes can be converted to which of the following?
    a. Table of contents
    b. Footnotes
    c. Hyperlinks
    d. They cannot be converted

True/False

Circle T if the statement is true or F if the statement is false.

T F 1. A table of contents is usually found at the end of a document.

T F 2. The Custom Table of Contents option allows you to create a table of contents on your own.

T F 3. You can choose a hyphen as tab leaders for a table of contents.

T F 4. Only text formatted with a heading style can be included in a table of contents.

T F 5. You can choose to update only the page numbers in a table of contents.

T F 6. Hyperlinks can be applied to text or graphics.

T F 7. When you create an email link, the Outlook application will automatically open.

T F 8. A bookmark is a reference point in a document.

T F 9. An endnote is a citation that is placed at the end of the document.

T F 10. Deleting a footnote or endnote will automatically renumber the remaining footnotes or endnotes.

Competency Assessment

Project 10-1: Mom's Favorite Recipes

You know that your mom will be sending you more recipes for her cookbook. You decide to create a table of contents using headings in the cookbook, making it easy to update as recipes are added.

GET READY. LAUNCH Word if it is not already running.

1. **OPEN** *Moms Favorites Recipes* from the data files for this lesson.
2. On the *Home* tab, turn on your *Show/Hide* command.
3. **SAVE** the document as *10-1 Moms Recipes TOC* in the lesson folder on your flash drive.
4. Use the *Go To* command to go to page 3.
5. Select the *Breads* heading and apply the *Heading 1* style.
6. Select the *Banana Nut Bread/Chocolate Chip Muffins* heading and apply the *Heading 2* style.
7. Apply the *Heading 2* style to the remaining recipe headings under the *Breads* section.
8. Position the insertion point before the *M* in *Main Dishes* on the first page.
9. On the *References* tab, in the *Table of Contents* group, click the **Table of Contents** button.
10. Select *Automatic Table 1* from the menu.
11. Center the title, *Contents,* make it bold, and apply the *Title* style.
12. Select the table tab and click the **Update Table** button.
13. Update the page numbers only.
14. **SAVE** the document in the lesson folder on your flash drive, and then **CLOSE** the file.

PAUSE. LEAVE Word open for the next project.

Project 10-2: Margie's Travel

You will be updating the Family Vacation8 flyer created in an earlier lesson. Since this flyer will be shared by email, you want to insert hyperlinks and Margie's email address.

GET READY. LAUNCH Word if it is not already running.

1. **OPEN** the *Family Vacation8* document from the lesson folder.
2. **SAVE** the document as *10-2 Vacation Flyer Update* in the lesson folder on your flash drive.
3. Select the text *Margie's Travel Agency.* On the *Insert* tab in the *Links* group, select *Hyperlink.*
4. In the Address box, key **http://www.margiestravel.com**. Click **OK**.
5. Place the insertion point at the end of the body paragraph, and press **Enter**.
6. Key **Contact: Margie** and *align right.*
7. Select *Margie* and in the *Links* group, click **Hyperlink**, then select *E-mail address.*
8. For the *E-mail address*, key **Margie@margiestravel.com**.
9. Key **More information on Travel Plans** in the Subject box.
10. Click **OK**.
11. **SAVE** the document in the lesson folder on your flash drive then **CLOSE** the file.

LEAVE Word open for the next project.

Proficiency Assessment

Project 10-3: Real Estate

You will be updating one of the marketing flyers that you created. This flyer will be posted in the newspaper, school papers, and real estate brochures. A caption is needed.

GET READY. LAUNCH Word if it is not already running.

1. **OPEN** the *Marketing Flyer* document from the lesson folder.
2. **SAVE** the document as *10-3 Marketing Flyer Update* in the lesson folder on your flash drive.
3. Apply a shadow page border and select *Green, Accent 6, Darker 50%*. Select the ninth option from the *Style* list.
4. Add a page color and select *Green, Accent 6, Lighter 80%*.
5. Insert a figure caption to the SmartArt graphic and key **Tech Terrace Real Estate helped the Loston's purchase their new home**.
6. **SAVE** the document in the lesson folder on your flash drive then **CLOSE** the file.

LEAVE Word open for the next project.

Project 10-4: British Novel – Mothers and Daughters of Bleak House

You and your friend are taking a British Literature class. Elizabeth has finished her paper, but you noticed that formatting needs to be corrected, and you have agreed to format the document for her and insert a header with a page number.

GET READY. LAUNCH Word if it is not already running.

1. **OPEN** *Mothers and Daughters of Bleak House* from the lesson folder.
2. **SAVE** the document as *10-4 Bleak House – British Novel* in the lesson folder on your flash drive.
3. Change the style to *MLA*.
4. Change the font to *Times New Roman* and font size to *12* pt for the entire document.
5. Change the line spacing to *double*.
6. *Center* the title.
7. *Indent* the first line for all paragraphs.
8. Key the following information on the appropriate line.

   First line: **Elizabeth Steele**
   Second line: **ENG 5306: British Novel**
   Third line: **Dr. P. Hartman**
   Fourth line: **May 6, 20XX**

9. Insert a *header* with her last name followed by the *page number*—apply the *Plain Number 3*.
10. Format the header to *Times New Roman* and change the font size to *12* pt.
11. **SAVE** the document in the lesson folder on your flash drive then **CLOSE** the file.

PAUSE. LEAVE Word open for the next project.

Mastery Assessment

Project 10-5: USA Proposal

You have completed a course at the local community college and learned how easy it is to add a table of contents in a document. However, this document was created without any heading styles. Use the *Add Text* command to create a table of contents.

GET READY. LAUNCH Word if it is not already running.

1. **OPEN** *USA Proposal* from the data files for this lesson.
2. **SAVE** the document as *10-5 USA Proposal Update* in your flash drive in the lesson folder.
3. Apply the **Add Text** command to create a table of contents with three levels. *Level 1 — Proposal Description, Level 2 —* the three *Options*, and *Level 3 —* the *cities* listed under each option.
4. Add a *Next Page* section break at the beginning of the document and remove the formatting.
5. Key **Table of Contents** and press **Enter** two times.
6. Change the font to *Arial*, font size *14 pt*, spacing after to *12 pt* and *center*.
7. Create a *Custom Table of Contents* using the *Formal* format.
8. Add a page break at the beginning of each option then update the entire table.
9. **SAVE** the document in the lesson folder on your flash drive then **CLOSE** the file.

PAUSE. LEAVE Word open for the next exercise.

Project 10-6: Bleak House – British Novel

You are continuing with Project 10-4. Elizabeth added her sources of references to the document manually. As you two were discussing your papers, you mentioned there was an easier way to insert footnotes. You will show her how to add a few footnotes and how easy it is to convert them to an endnotes page. Format the footnotes according to the MLA guidelines. Use the Line Numbers to assist you in finding the paragraphs.

GET READY. LAUNCH Word if it is not already running.

1. **OPEN** the *10-4 Bleak House – British Novel* document.
2. **SAVE** the document as *10-6 Bleak House – British Novel* in the lesson folder on your flash drive.
3. Follow the instruction in the table below and key the information (making sure to format the footnotes according to the MLA guidelines):

Place the insertion point at the end of the third paragraph and insert a footnote.	McCormick, Marjorie. *Mothers in the English Novel: From Stereotype to Archetype*. London: Garland, 1991. Print.
Indent the seventh paragraph one-inch from the left and right margin and remove the first line indent and quotation marks. Then at the end of the paragraph, insert a second footnote.	Stubbs, Patricia. *Women and Fiction: Feminism and the Novel 1880–1920*. Sussex: Harvester, 1979. Print.
At the end of paragraph nine, insert a footnote.	Nord, Deborah Epstein. *Walking the Victorian Streets: Women, Representations, and the City*. London: Cornell University, 1995. Print.
At the end of paragraph 14, insert a footnote.	Dever, Carolyn M. "Broken Mirror, Broken Words: Autobiography, Prosopopeia, and the Dead Mother in Bleak House." *Studies in the Novel* 17.1 (1995): 42–63. Web. 19 Apr. 2012.
At the end of paragraph 19, insert a footnote.	Vonyke. "Characters and Things in Bleak House which Seem Confusing." *Bleak House Connections*. Bleakhouseconnections.blogspot.com, 21 Oct. 2009. Web. 13 Apr. 2012.
Use the Go To command and locate line number 89 (paragraph 17); locate line number 168; then locate line number 242. (Complete these steps separately.)	
Indent the paragraphs one-inch from the left and right margin and remove the first line indent and quotation marks.	
Disable the Line Numbering feature.	

4. **SAVE** the document in the lesson folder on your flash drive.
5. Convert the footnotes to endnotes and separate with a page break. Key **Endnotes** and *center*.
6. **SAVE** the document as *10-6a Bleak House – British Novel* in the lesson folder on your flash drive.

CLOSE Word.

LESSON SKILL MATRIX

Skill	Exam Objective	Objective Number
Setting Up Mail Merge		
Executing Mail Merge		
Merging a Document with a Different File Format		
Creating Envelopes and Labels		

© kyoshino/iStockphoto

KEY TERMS

- chevrons
- data source
- database
- field names
- main document

You are employed at Graphic Design Institute as an admissions officer in the Office of Enrollment Services. Because you frequently send out letters containing the same content to different recipients, it is essential that you know how to perform mail merges. In this lesson, you learn how to create merged documents and merge data into form letters.

© kyoshino/iStockphoto

SOFTWARE ORIENTATION

Mailings Tab

Commands on the Mailings tab are used to perform mail merges, as well as to create envelopes and labels for a group mailing (see Figure 11-1).

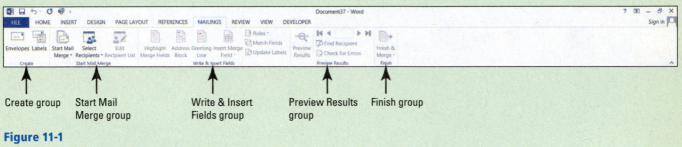

Create group   Start Mail   Write & Insert   Preview Results   Finish group
                Merge group   Fields group   group

Figure 11-1

Mailings tab

SETTING UP MAIL MERGE

The Bottom Line

Mail merges are useful for creating multiple documents that have the same basic content and personalizing them with unique information from a data source—for example, a form letter sent to multiple customers using different recipient names and addresses. In essence, mail merges are used for internal and external correspondence such as memorandums, labels, invitations, and more. The mail merge document contains the same information that everyone will receive. The individuals receiving the document are created in a data source, which is the list of recipients, and contains information for each individual with variable data, such as the person's first and last name, address, city, state, zip code, phone number, and so on. The data source can be created as a table using Word where Word provides the fields and you type the data in them. You also customize the fields to fit your document. Other programs can be used for the data source such as an Excel worksheet, an Access table or query, or your Outlook contacts list.

Setting Up a Main Document Using the Mail Merge Wizard

To begin a mail merge, the main document is set up from a new or an existing document. The **main document** contains text and graphics that are the same for each version of the merged document. The Mail Merge Wizard is a step-by-step process in setting up a main document, and then creating or using an existing list that can be a database, spreadsheet, table, or other source; and taking these two sources of information and merging it into one document. In this exercise, you learn to set up a main document using the Mail Merge Wizard, set up mail merge manually, use the Check for Errors command, and preview and print the merge document.

Set Up a Main Document Using the Mail Merge Wizard

 GET READY. Before you begin these steps, be sure to launch Microsoft Word and open a blank document.

1. On the Mailings tab, in the Start Mail Merge group, click the **Start Mail Merge menu** drop-down arrow to display the Start Mail Merge menu as shown in Figure 11-2.

Figure 11-2

Start Mail Merge menu

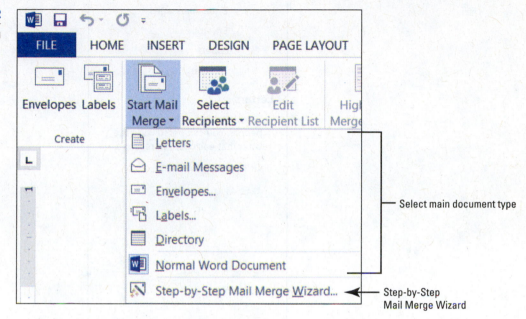

2. Click **Step-by-Step Mail Merge Wizard**.

   The Mail Merge pane opens as shown in Figure 11-3. The Mail Merge Wizard has six steps to complete.

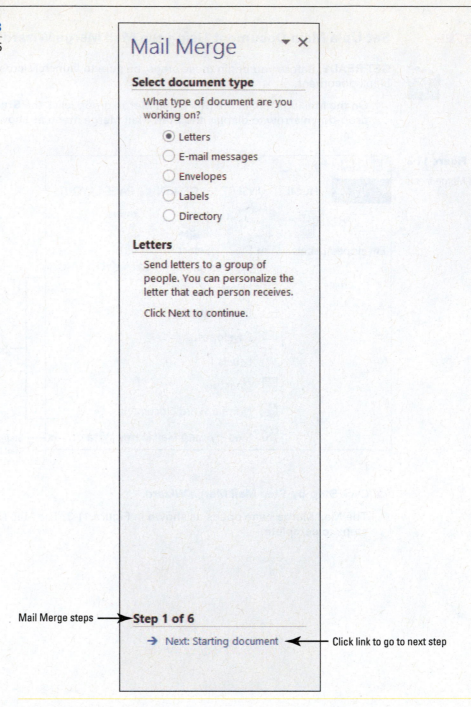

Mail Merge steps ⟶ **Step 1 of 6**

→ Next: Starting document ⟵ Click link to go to next step

STEP BY STEP   **Step 1: Select the Document Type**

In the *Select document type* section, Letters is the default. You use the default for the main document.

1. Click the link at the bottom of the Mail Merge pane, **Next: Starting document**.

Step 2: Select the Starting Document

This step contains three options on setting up the letter. You open an existing document in the lesson folder.

1. Below the *Select starting document* section, click the **Start from existing document option button**.

2. Below the section, *Start from existing*, click the **Open button** as shown in Figure 11-4. The *Open* dialog box displays.

Figure 11-4

Mail Merge pane Step 2 of 6

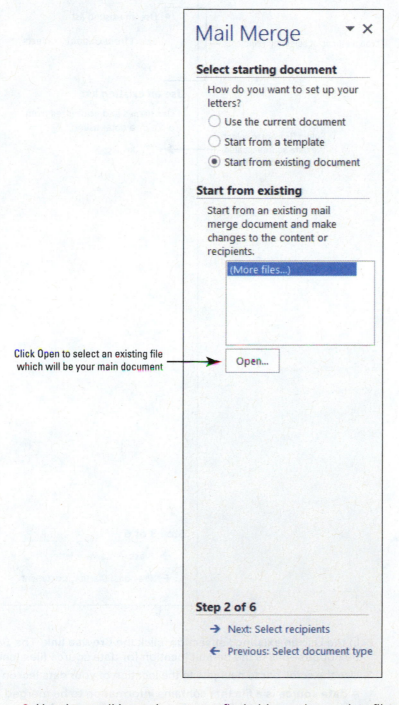

Click Open to select an existing file which will be your main document

3. Use the scroll bar to locate your flash drive and open data files from your lesson folder.

4. Select the *Scholarship* document and **double-click** to open it or click the **Open button**. The document is opened in the document screen.

5. At the bottom of the Mail Merge pane, click the **Next: Select recipients link**.

1. In the *Select recipients* section (see Figure 11-5), you use the default setting, Use an existing list. The existing list is located in the data lesson folder in your flash drive.

Figure 11-5

Mail Merge pane Step 3 of 6

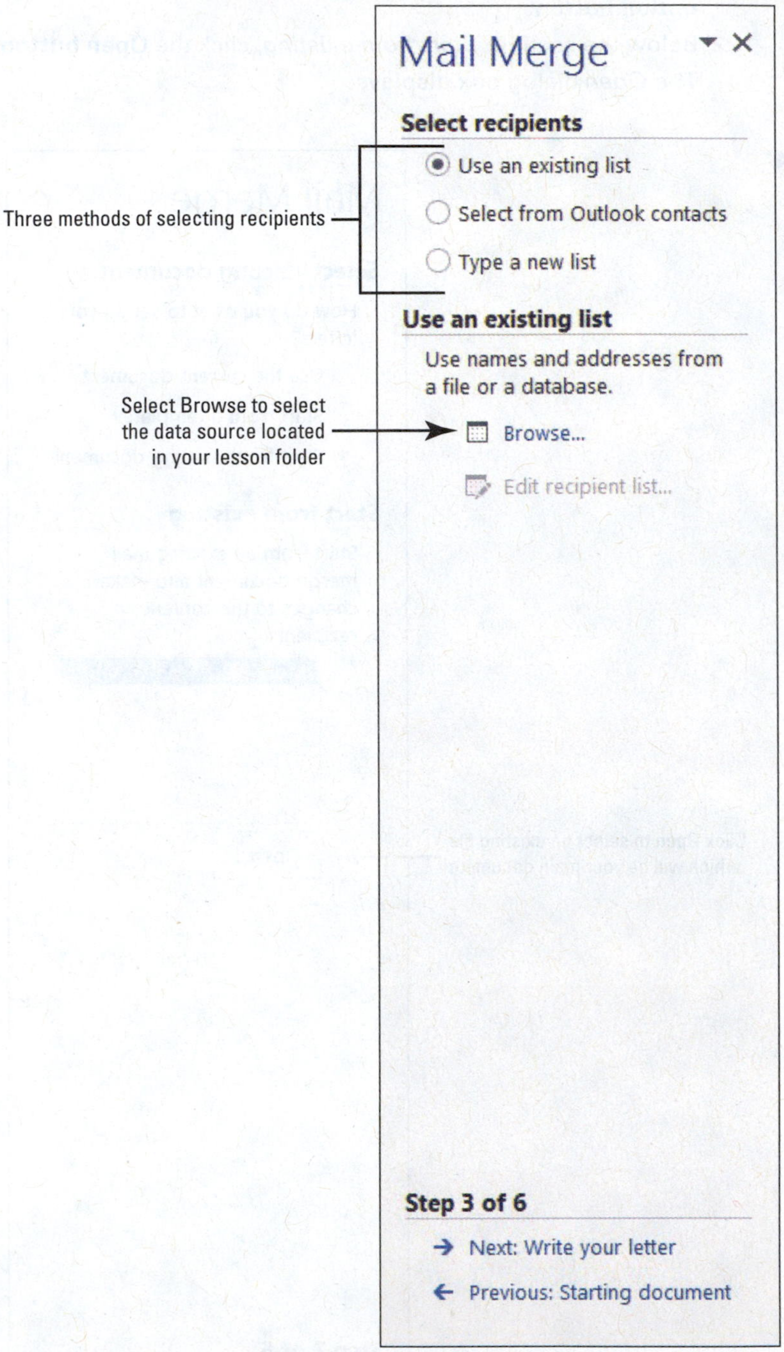

> ## Mail Merge ▾ ✕
>
> **Select recipients**
>
> ● Use an existing list
>
> ○ Select from Outlook contacts
>
> ○ Type a new list
>
> **Use an existing list**
>
> Use names and addresses from a file or a database.
>
> ▦ Browse...
>
> ▭ Edit recipient list...
>
> **Step 3 of 6**
>
> → Next: Write your letter
>
> ← Previous: Starting document

Three methods of selecting recipients —

Select Browse to select the data source located → in your lesson folder

2. In the Use an existing list section, click the **Browse link**. The *Select Data Source* dialog box opens—this is the default location for data source files (see Figure 11-6).

3. Use the scroll bar to navigate to the location of your data lesson folder in your flash drive.

   A ==data source== is a file that contains information to be merged in the main document. A data source can be from an Excel spreadsheet, an Access database, or a Word document containing a single table, an electronic address book such as Outlook, or any text that has data fields. ==Field names== provide a description for the specific data, such as a person's first name, last name, address, city, state, and zip code, to be merged from the data source. Fields usually correspond to the column headings in the data file.

Figure 11-6

Select Data Source dialog box

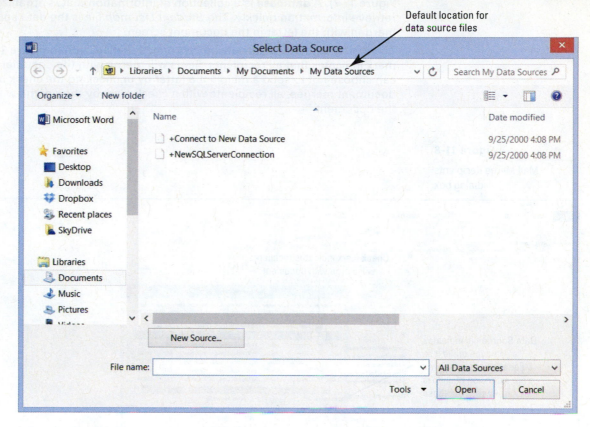

Default location for data source files

4. Select the *Student List.mdb* as shown in Figure 11-7, and double-click or click the **Open** button.

Figure 11-7

Location for data file

Select data source for folder

Location of data lesson files will appear here. Note, your location will be different

Date source file created in Access. Notice the difference in the icons

Data source file created in Word

Data source button

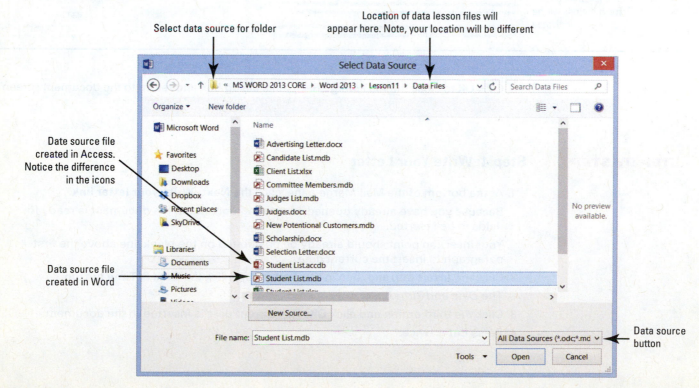

The icon listed for *Student List.mdb* is a database file created in Word—notice the difference in the icon between the database created in Word and Access (refer Figure 11-7). A **database** is a collection of information that is organized so that you can retrieve information quickly. The *Student List.mdb* file is the data source that will be merged with the letter in the document screen.

The *Mail Merge Recipients* dialog box opens as displayed in Figure 11-8. The check mark indicates that all recipients' fields will merge with the document. You can choose not to send a recipient a letter by unchecking the check box. When the document merges, all recipients with a check mark by their name will be merged with the document.

Figure 11-8

Mail Merge Recipients dialog box

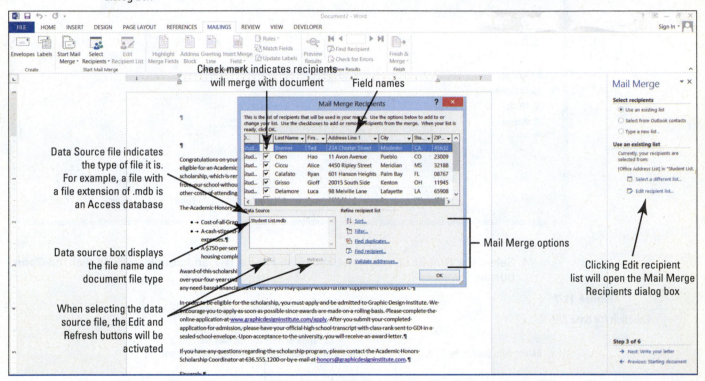

5. Click **OK** to close the *Mail Merge Recipients* dialog box and return to the document screen.

STEP BY STEP   **Step 4: Write Your Letter**

1. At the bottom of the Mail Merge pane, click the **Next: Write your letter link**.

   Because you have already opened an existing document, the document is ready for fields to be inserted.

   Your insertion point should already be positioned on the blank line above the first paragraph to insert the current date.

2. Click the **Insert** tab, and then in the Text group, click the **Date & Time button**.

   The *Date and Time* dialog box opens.

3. Click the third option and click **OK**. The current date is inserted in the document.

4. Press **Enter** twice.

In the Mail Merge pane, in the *Write your letter* section, it shows four links (see Figure 11-9). The Address block link contains the fields from the recipient's list, the Greeting line link contains the salutation, the Electronic postage link inserts the electronic postage, and the More items link opens the *Insert Merge Field* dialog box, which provides an option to insert fields individually.

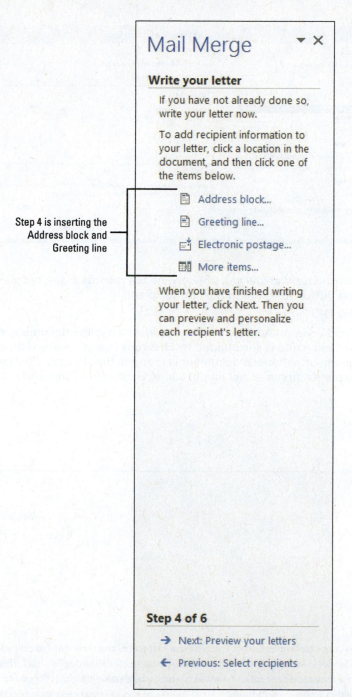

Step 4 is inserting the
Address block and
Greeting line

5. In the *Write your letter* section, click the **Address block link**.

The *Insert Address Block* dialog box opens as shown in Figure 11-10. Under *Specify address elements*, in the Insert recipient's name in this format list, the fifth option is selected with a specific format as displayed in the Preview section. On the Preview side, there are four arrows: First ⏮, Previous ◀, Next ▷, and Last ⏭. Notice that the First and Previous arrow buttons are grayed out. When these arrow buttons are shaded in gray, it indicates that these are not available because you are previewing the first record. The first recipient's name and address is displayed and when you click the Next or Last arrow, the First and Previous arrows will become available.

Figure 11-10

Insert Address Block
dialog box

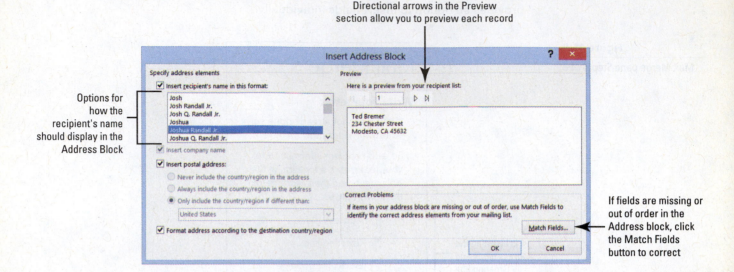

Directional arrows in the Preview
section allow you to preview each record

Options for
how the
recipient's name
should display in the
Address Block

If fields are missing or
out of order in the
Address block, click
the Match Fields
button to correct

6. Click the **Next arrow** and preview the ten records in the recipient list, and then click the **First** button to return to the first recipient.

7. Click **OK**.

   A field code <<Address Block>> is inserted in the document as shown in Figure 11-11. The field name is surrounded by **chevrons** (<< >>) which do not display in the merged document. When the document is merged, the *Address Block* will be replaced with the recipients' first and last name, address, city, state, and postal code.

Figure 11-11

Address Block inserted in
document

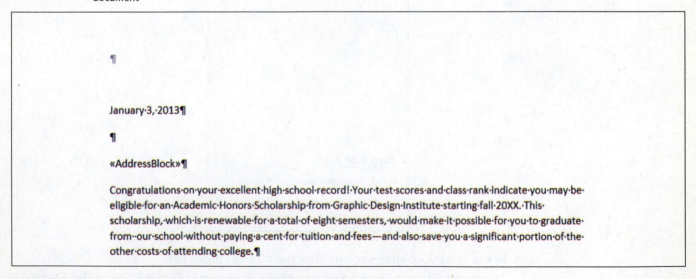

¶

January·3,·2013¶

¶

«AddressBlock»¶

Congratulations·on·your·excellent·high·school·record!·Your·test·scores·and·class·rank·indicate·you·may·be·eligible·for·an·Academic·Honors·Scholarship·from·Graphic·Design·Institute·starting·fall·20XX.·This·scholarship,·which·is·renewable·for·a·total·of·eight·semesters,·would·make·it·possible·for·you·to·graduate·from··our·school·without·paying·a·cent·for·tuition·and·fees—and·also·save·you·a·significant·portion·of·the·other·costs·of·attending·college.¶

8. Press the **Enter key** once.

9. Click the **Greeting line link** to open the *Insert Greeting Line* dialog box as shown in Figure 11-12. The drop-down arrows in the *Greeting line format* provide options to select the salutation, name, and punctuation. You use the salutation **Dear** for the letter.

Figure 11-12

Insert Greeting Line dialog box

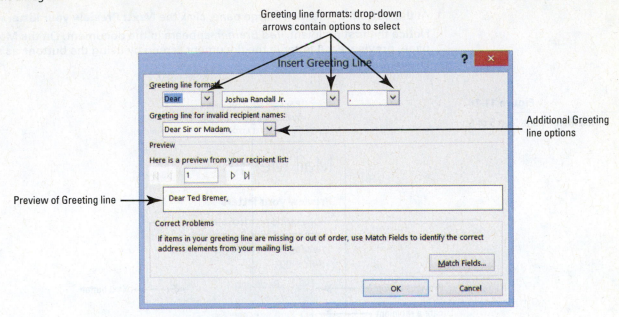

Greeting line formats: drop-down arrows contain options to select

Preview of Greeting line

Additional Greeting line options

Figure 11-12

Insert Greeting Line dialog box

10. Click the **drop-down arrow** next to *Joshua Randall Jr.* to view the options. Keep the default as the selection.

11. Click the **drop-down arrow** next to the comma and select the colon (**:**).

Take Note In the Insert Greeting Line dialog box, the comma is the default punctuation and is not used in most business letter formats.

12. Click **OK**. Your document should match Figure 11-13. You have inserted two field codes in your document.

Figure 11-13

Document with field codes

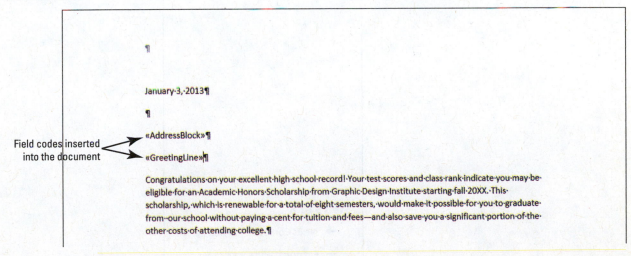

Field codes inserted into the document

Step 5: Preview Your Letter

1. At the bottom of the Mail Merge pane, click the **Next: Preview your letters link**.

   Notice the first recipient, *Ted Bremer*, appears in the document. On the Mail Merge pane, preview each letter in the document screen by using the buttons as shown in Figure 11-14.

Figure 11-14

Mail Merge pane Step 5 of 6

Preview each recipient by clicking the Previous or Next arrows

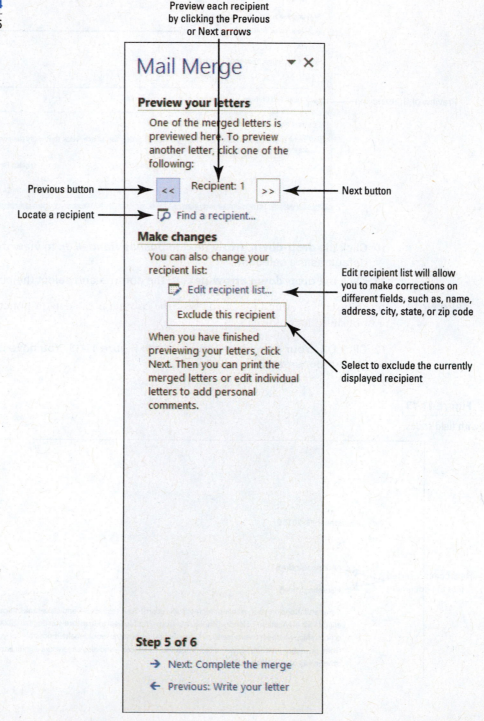

Previous button →

Locate a recipient →

Next button ←

Edit recipient list will allow you to make corrections on different fields, such as, name, address, city, state, or zip code

Select to exclude the currently displayed recipient

2. Click the **Next button**, preview each letter, and return to the first recipient.

   Before finalizing the merge, the mailing address contains extra spacing between the lines that need correction.

3. Select the text beginning with *Ted Bremer*, including the address through the zip code, *45632*.

4. Now it is time to format the main letter with the correct spacing so that when you complete the merge, all letters will be updated. On the Home tab, in the Paragraph group, click the drop-down arrow to display the Line and Paragraph Spacing menu and select **Remove Space Before Paragraph**. This separates the Address Block from the salutation.

5. The document should display as shown in Figure 11-15. Preview each letter again by using the **Next** and **Previous** buttons on the Mail Merge pane and return to the first recipient. Each recipient should be in the correct format.

Figure 11-15

Formatted document

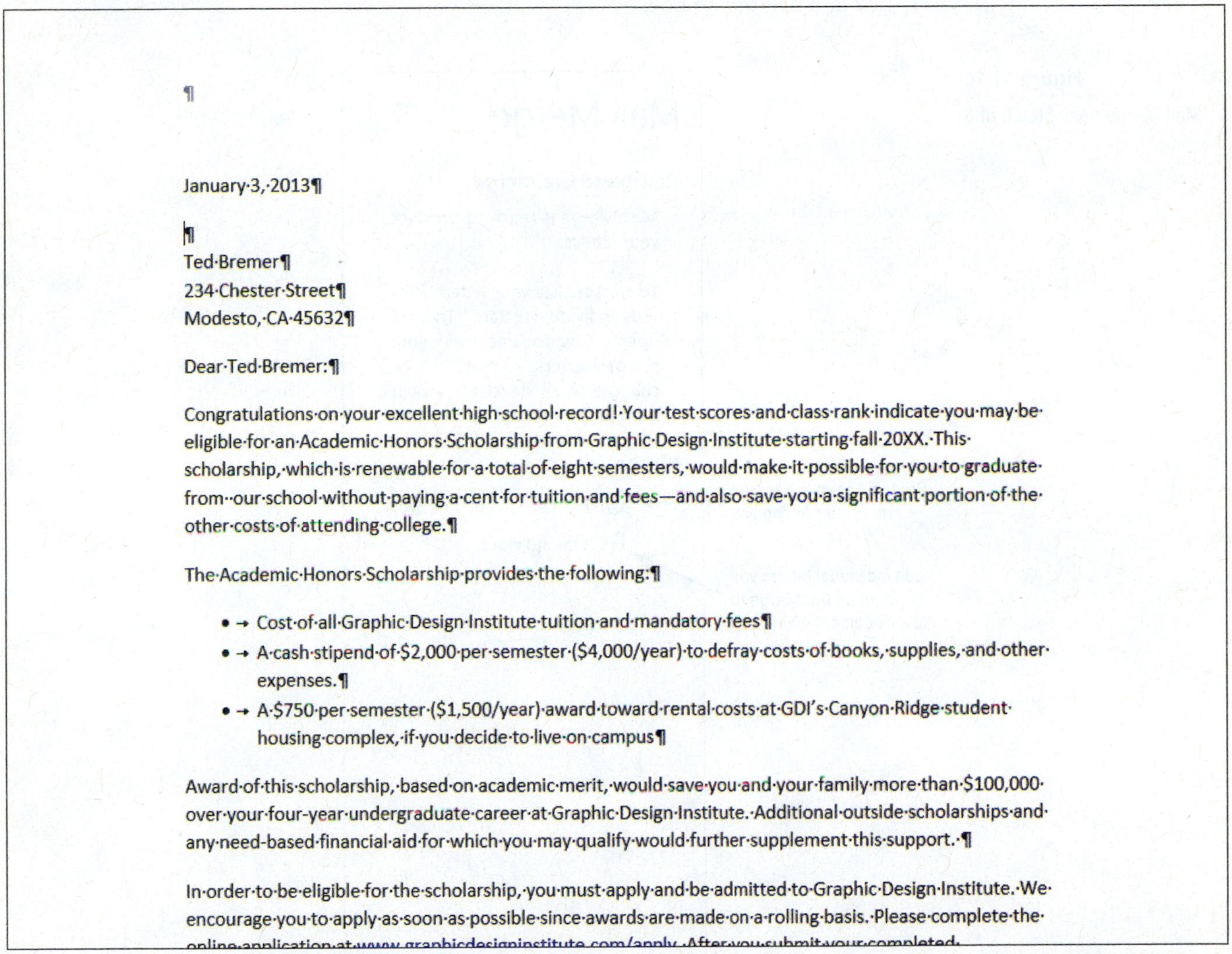

January·3,·2013¶

¶

Ted·Bremer¶
234·Chester·Street¶
Modesto,·CA·45632¶

Dear·Ted·Bremer:¶

Congratulations·on·your·excellent·high·school·record!·Your·test·scores·and·class·rank·indicate·you·may·be·eligible·for·an·Academic·Honors·Scholarship·from·Graphic·Design·Institute·starting·fall·20XX.·This·scholarship,·which·is·renewable·for·a·total·of·eight·semesters,·would·make·it·possible·for·you·to·graduate·from··our·school·without·paying·a·cent·for·tuition·and·fees—and·also·save·you·a·significant·portion·of·the·other·costs·of·attending·college.¶

The·Academic·Honors·Scholarship·provides·the·following:¶

- → Cost·of·all·Graphic·Design·Institute·tuition·and·mandatory·fees¶
- → A·cash·stipend·of·$2,000·per·semester·($4,000/year)·to·defray·costs·of·books,·supplies,·and·other·expenses.¶
- → A·$750·per·semester·($1,500/year)·award·toward·rental·costs·at·GDI's·Canyon·Ridge·student·housing·complex,·if·you·decide·to·live·on·campus¶

Award·of·this·scholarship,·based·on·academic·merit,·would·save·you·and·your·family·more·than·$100,000·over·your·four-year·undergraduate·career·at·Graphic·Design·Institute.·Additional·outside·scholarships·and·any·need-based·financial·aid·for·which·you·may·qualify·would·further·supplement·this·support.·¶

In·order·to·be·eligible·for·the·scholarship,·you·must·apply·and·be·admitted·to·Graphic·Design·Institute.·We·encourage·you·to·apply·as·soon·as·possible·since·awards·are·made·on·a·rolling·basis.·Please·complete·the·online·application·at·www.graphicdesigninstitute.com/apply.·After·you·submit·your·completed·

STEP BY STEP   **Step 6: Complete the Merge**

1. At the bottom of the Mail Merge pane, click the **Next: Complete the merge link** to advance to Step 6 as shown in Figure 11-16. The letter is already merged and ready to **Print** or you can edit each letter individually.

When you click the **Edit individual letters** link in the Merge section, the *Merge to New Document* dialog box opens. When you select the **All** option button, Word opens one new document with a copy of the main document for each record, and *Letters1* displays on the title bar. When you finish editing the letters, you are ready to save the letters—all letters will be saved as one document.

If your insertion point is on the third letter, and you click the **Edit individual letters** link in the Merge section of Step 6 and then select the option button for **Current Record**, only the third letter opens in a new screen as a new document and *Letters* followed by a number appears on the title bar. Edit the document and when you save the document, only the third letter will be saved with the changes made.

If you select the third option button **From** in the *Merge to New Document* dialog box, you type the beginning number to the ending number of the documents you want to merge. For example, if you want to merge letters 3 through 5, you type **3** in the From box and **5** in the To box.

Figure 11-16

Mail Merge pane Step 6 of 6

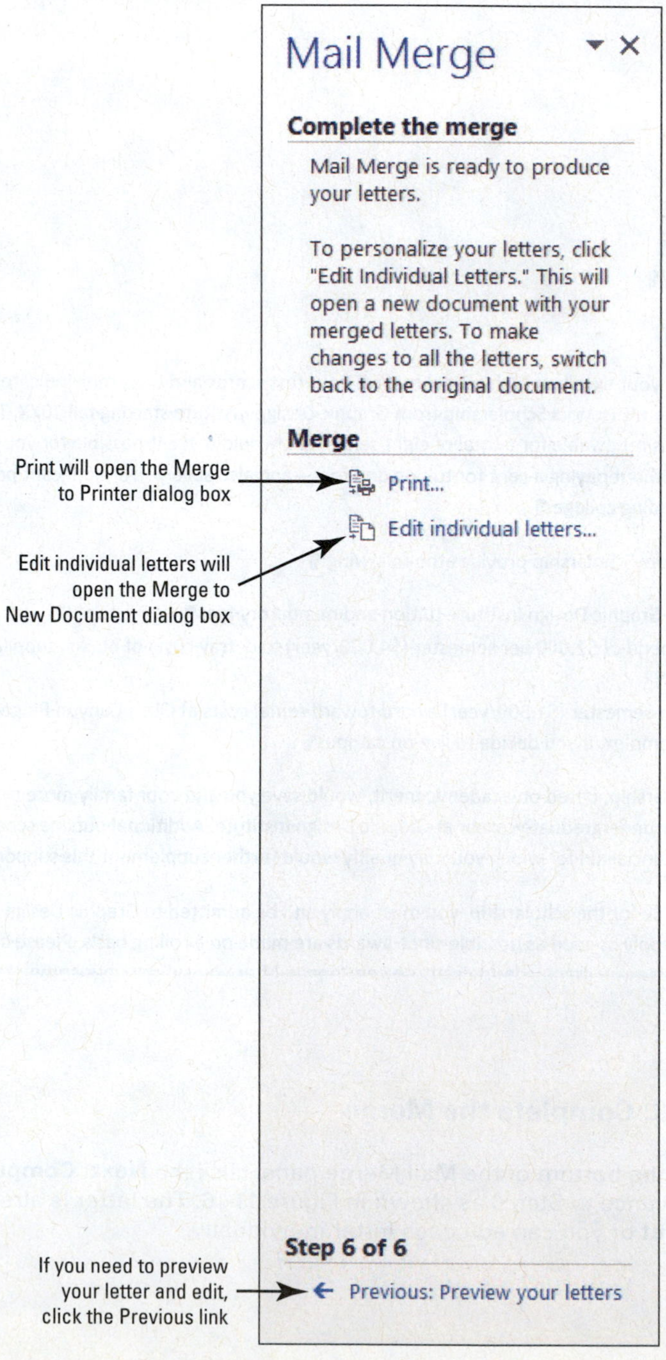

Mail Merge ▼ ✕

Complete the merge

Mail Merge is ready to produce your letters.

To personalize your letters, click "Edit Individual Letters." This will open a new document with your merged letters. To make changes to all the letters, switch back to the original document.

Merge

Print will open the Merge to Printer dialog box → 🖫 Print...

Edit individual letters will open the Merge to New Document dialog box → 🖺 Edit individual letters...

Step 6 of 6

If you need to preview your letter and edit, click the Previous link → ← Previous: Preview your letters

2. In the Mail Merge pane, in the Merge section, click **Print** to print each letter. The *Merge to Printer* dialog box opens with three options to select.

   Selecting the **All option button** prints all letters, the Current record prints the record where your insertion point is located, and From is where you specify which records to print. For example, if you specify records 2 to 4, only those three records will print. Be careful, if you select the Print option for Step 6, you will not be given the opportunity to edit the letters.

3. Make sure the **All option button** is selected and click **OK** to print.

4. Now that you printed all letters, you now need to save the merged letter. Click the **Edit individual letters link** in the Merge section.

5. Click **OK** to open a new document with a letter to all recipients.

6. **SAVE** the merge document as *Merged Congratulation Letter* in the lesson folder on your flash drive, and then **CLOSE** the file.

7. **CLOSE** the Mail Merge pane.

8. The main document appears on the screen with the first record being displayed. In the Preview Results group on the Mailings tab, click the **Preview Results** **button** to disable.

   Disabling the **Preview Results button** displays the <<Address Block>> and <<Greeting Line>> field codes.

9. **SAVE** the main document as *Congratulation Letter* in the lesson folder on your flash drive, and then **CLOSE** the file.

PAUSE. LEAVE Word open to use in the next exercise.

Setting Up a Main Document Manually

You can begin working with Mail Merge by typing your letter, and then using an existing data source, creating your own data source list and typing your recipients' information, or using Outlook to get your contacts information. You don't need to have a database program installed on your computer because Word makes it easy to create your list of recipients. It is easy to create a table in Word because the fields are already identified for you and easy to customize. After setting up your document, the address block and greeting line are inserted the same way they were in the step-by-step Mail Merge Wizard. You can preview your results and check for errors using the tools available in the Preview Results group, and then perform the merge. In this exercise, you create a document, type information, insert an existing data source, insert the address block and greeting line, check for errors in the document, preview the letters, and merge.

STEP BY STEP   **Set Up a Main Document Manually**

1. Create a new blank document by selecting the **File tab**, and then click **New**, and click **Blank document**.

2. Click the **Mailings tab**, and in the Start Mail Merge group, click the **drop-down arrow** to display the Start Mail Merge menu.

3. Choose **Letters**.

PAUSE. LEAVE Word open to use in the next exercise.

STEP BY STEP   **Select Recipients**

1. In the Start Mail Merge group, click the **Select Recipients**   **button** to display the menu as shown in Figure 11-17.

Figure 11-17

Select Recipients menu

Use the Ribbon to create
a Mail Merge manually

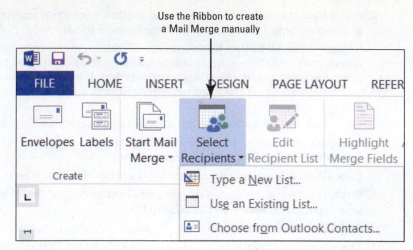

There are three options available. (You will open an existing data source file from your lesson folder. Notice some of the commands on the Ribbon are faded, therefore, not available until a data source file is opened.)

2. Select **Use an Existing List**. The *Select Data Source* dialog box opens. Use the scroll bar to locate your flash drive and navigate to your data files for the lesson folder.

3. **OPEN** the *Student List.accdb* data source file from the lesson folder. The *Student List* file is a database.

After opening the data source file, most of the commands on the Mailings tab on the Ribbon become active (see Figure 11-18). When selecting a data source file, this file can be a database, an Excel spreadsheet, a table in Word, or it can be opened from your Outlook contacts.

Figure 11-18

Mailings tab on the Ribbon

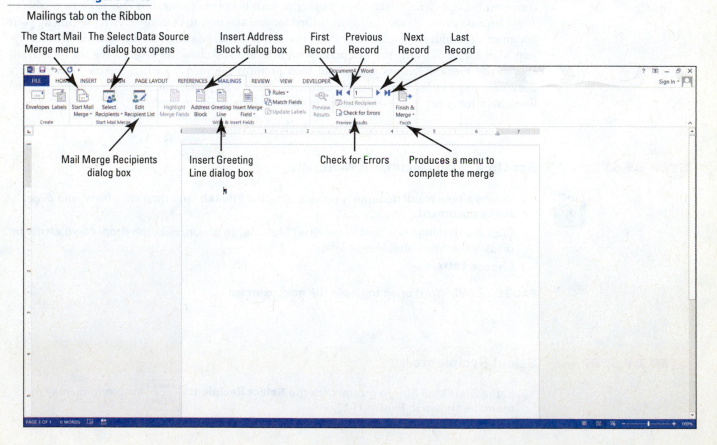

4. At the insertion point, type **March 19, 20XX**. Press the **Enter key** twice. By default, the Spacing After is set to 8 pt and later you will format the document to an appropriate business format.

Take Note   *If the formatting of the date changes, press Ctrl+Z to Undo.*

PAUSE. LEAVE the document open to use in the next exercise.

STEP BY STEP   **Prepare Merge Fields**

USE the document open from the previous exercise.

1. On the Mailings tab, in the Write & Insert Fields group, click the **Address Block button**. The *Insert Address Block* dialog box opens.

   When using the Mail Merge Wizard or completing the Mail Merge manually, the same dialog boxes are opened.

2. Notice that the street address is missing in the preview area. Click the **Match Fields** 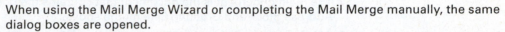 **button**. To correct the error, select the **drop-down arrow** by Address 1 and select the **Address Line** field. Click **OK** to close the *Match Fields* dialog box.

3. Click **OK** to accept the address settings with the correction (refer to Figure 11-10).

4. Press **Enter** once.

5. On the Mailings tab, in the Write & Insert Fields group, click the **Greeting Line button**. The *Insert Greeting Line* dialog box opens.

6. For the Greeting Line format, the salutation *Dear* will be used. You use the default where *Joshua Randall Jr.* is shown.

7. Change the comma to a colon.

8. Click **OK**. Press **Enter** once.

PAUSE. LEAVE the document open to use in the next exercise.

STEP BY STEP   **Write the Letter**

USE the document open from the previous exercise.

1. Type the following letter:

   The president of the college, Dr. Jose A. Torres, is extending an invitation to all students who received scholarships for the next academic semester. The Graphic Design Institute recognizes all students for their academic excellence. A reception is being held in your honor on March 29 at 12 noon in the President's Conference Room 19. [Press **Enter** once.]

   Please confirm your attendance by calling 915-999-9999. [Press **Enter** once.]

   Regards, [Press **Enter** twice.]

   Jerry Wright [Press **Shift+Enter** to insert a line break.]

   Scholarship Committee Chair

PAUSE. LEAVE the document open to use in the next exercise.

STEP BY STEP   **Preview the Document**

USE the document open from the previous exercise.

1. In the Preview Results group, click the **Preview Results button**. The first recipient appears. Click the **Next Record arrow button** to preview the letters for each recipient.

2. Disable Preview Results by clicking the **Preview Results button** again.

3. Place the insertion point in the *<<Address Block>>* field. Click the **Home tab**, and then in the Paragraph group, click the **Line and Paragraph Spacing button**, and then click **Remove Space After Paragraph**.

4. Place the insertion point in the *<<Greeting Line>>* field and click the **Page Layout tab**. In the Paragraph group, click the **Spacing Before up arrow** until you see **6 pt**. The Spacing Before is increased by 6 pts and separates the address block and greeting line.

5. On the Page Layout tab, in the Page Setup group, click the **Margins button**, and then click **Custom Margins**. Type **2** in the Top box to change the top margin. Click **OK**.

   Customized letterheads are used by organizations to print their letters. The top margin must be adjusted to avoid text printing over the organization's logo.

6. Click the **Mailings tab**, and then in the Preview Results group, click the **Preview Results button** to view the formatting changes made to the document. After you finish your review, disable **Preview Results**.

7. The main document is the document that contains the body of the letter as well as the Address Block and Greeting Line merge codes.

8. **SAVE** the main document as *Reception Letter* in the lesson folder on your flash drive.

   Saving the main document as a separate document allows you to merge with a new data source file—when you need to use the same letter again but with a different recipient list. When you open a main document that contain field codes, Word asks you for the data source file.

   PAUSE. LEAVE the document open to use in the next exercise.

Take Note   Once the main document has been set up, you can format at the beginning of the mail merge process.

EXECUTING MAIL MERGE

The Bottom Line

The final steps in a mail merge are to check for errors, preview the merge, and finalize the merge. The Check for Errors feature mimics the merge before you complete the final merge and print process. If there is an error, you can correct it in the main document. For instance, if you used the Insert Merge Field button and forgot to insert the field for city, you would see the error in the document. To correct the error, make sure you do this in the main document.

STEP BY STEP   **Check for Errors**

USE the document open from the previous exercise.

1. On the Preview Results group, click the **Check for Errors button**. The *Checking and Reporting Errors* dialog box opens as shown in Figure 11-19.

Figure 11-19

Checking and Reporting Errors dialog box

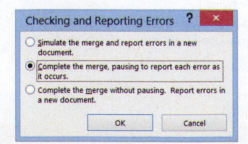

2. Select the first option, **Simulate the merge and report errors in a new document**.

3. Click **OK**.

4. A prompt appears indicating *No mail merge errors have been found* in *Reception Letter*. Click **OK**.

PAUSE. LEAVE the document open to use in the next exercise.

STEP BY STEP **Complete the Merge**

USE the document open from the previous exercise.

1. In the Finish group, click the **drop-down arrow** to display the Finish & Merge menu as shown in Figure 11-20.

Figure 11-20

Finish & Merge menu

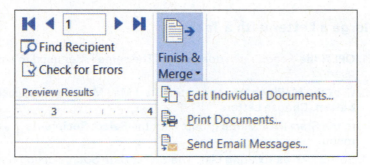

2. Select **Edit Individual Documents**. The *Merge to New Document* dialog box opens as shown in Figure 11-21.

Figure 11-21

Merge to New Document dialog box

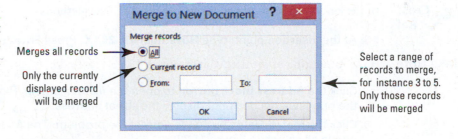

The All option merges all letters to a new document, Current record merges only that record on which your insertion point is positioned, and in the From option, you type the first record and end record to merge. For instance, to merge only records 2 and 3, you type **2** to **3**.

3. For this exercise, in the From section, type **3** in the first box and in the To box, type **5**. Click **OK**. A new document is produced that displays letters for records 3 through 5 in one document. Scroll through the document to preview that the document is ready to print.

4. **SAVE** the merged document as *Merged Reception Letter* in the lesson folder on your flash drive, and then **CLOSE** the file.

5. **CLOSE** the main document *Reception Letter* and a prompt appears asking, *Do you want to save changes made to Reception Letter?* Click **SAVE**.

When you save the main document with the field codes, you will be able to return to your document and recipient list and use the tools available in the Mailings tab. You can also edit the list of recipients and open another data source to send the same letter to another group. When saving the main document, make sure you turn off the Preview Results.

PAUSE. LEAVE Word open for the next exercise.

Troubleshooting | A document must be opened in Word for the mail merge commands to be available.

MERGING A DOCUMENT WITH A DIFFERENT FILE FORMAT

The Bottom Line

Previously in this lesson, you learn to use two different methods to merge an existing data source with a main document. One of the data sources was created in Word whereas the other data source was created using a database application; and the document was created in Word. Data sources can be used from other programs such as an Excel worksheet, an Access table or query, an Outlook contact list, or a table created in Word. Each of these different formats include fields—name, address, city, state, zip code, and so on. If the format does not match, then you can use the Match Fields button to correct any errors. In this exercise, you learn to merge an existing letter with different file formats using one of the two methods—using the Mail Merge Wizard or setting up a mail merge manually.

 STEP BY STEP   **Merge a Letter with a Table**

1. **OPEN** the *Scholarship* document. (The same letter used in a previous exercise will be used.)

2. Click the **Mailings tab**, and in the Start Mail Merge group, click the **Start Mail Merge button**. Choose **Letters**.

3. In the Start Mail Merge group, click the **Select Recipients** 🖼 **button** to display the menu.

4. Select **Use an Existing List**. The *Select Data Source* dialog box opens. Use the scroll bar to locate your flash drive and navigate to your data files for the lesson folder.

5. **OPEN** the *Student Listing.docx* data source file from the lesson folder. The Student Listing file was created as a table in Word. The data source file is a table that contains fields as headers with the records displayed within the table.

🔍 **Cross Ref**   In Lesson 6, you learn to create tables using different methods.

6. At the insertion point, type **November 28, 20XX**. Press **Enter** twice.

Take Note   If the formatting of the date changes, press *Ctrl+Z* to Undo.

7. Click the **Address Block button** to open the *Insert Address Block* dialog box. Notice that the preview area does not display the street address.

8. Click the **Match Fields** button to correct the problem. The *Match Fields* dialog box opens as shown in Figure 11-22.

   Under *Required for Address Block*, Address 1 displays *Not Matched* because the field heading in the table is listed as Address Line and does not directly match the Address Block in Word.

Figure 11-22

Match Fields dialog box

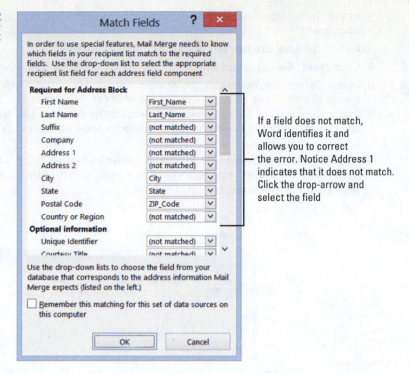

Click the **drop-down arrow** next to Address 1, select **Address_Line**, and then click **OK** to close the dialog box.

10. Review the preview area and notice that the problem has been corrected and the address is now displayed correctly.

11. Click **OK** to close the *Insert Address Block* dialog box.

12. Insert the Greeting line and change the punctuation to a colon.

13. Click the **Preview Results button** and notice the spacing in the Address Block needs to be formatted correctly. Click the **Preview Results** button again to see the field codes.

14. Select the **<<Address Block>>** and on the Page Layout tab, decrease the Spacing Before to **zero**.

15. Change the top margin to **2**″ and the left and right margins to **1**″.

16. Preview the results before finishing the merge.

17. Click the **Finish & Merge button**, and then click **Edit Individual Documents**.

18. In the *Merge to New Document* dialog box, keep the defaults and click **OK**. The document opens a new screen with the merged document displaying all records.

19. **SAVE** the document as *Merged Academic Honors Scholarship* in the lesson folder on your flash drive, and then **CLOSE** the file.

20. Make sure you turn off the Preview results so that the field codes are displayed in the main document. **SAVE** the main document as *Academic Honors Scholarship Letter* in the lesson folder on your flash drive, and then **CLOSE** the file.

PAUSE. LEAVE Word open for the next exercise.

STEP BY STEP   **Merge a Letter with Excel**

In this exercise, you learn to merge a letter with Excel using the wizard, Ribbon, and insert field codes to complete the mail merge process.

OPEN the *Scholarship* document from the lesson folder.

1. Click the **Start Mail Merge button** from the Mailings tab and select the **Step-by-Step Mail Merge Wizard** to open the Mail Merge pane.

2. In the *Select document type* section, Letters is the default. Click **Next: Starting document.**

3. Select the **Use the current document option button**.

4. Click **Next: Select recipients** from the Mail Merge pane to advance to the next step.

5. In the *Select recipients* section, the defaults will be used. Click the **Browse button** and locate the *Student List.xlsx* file. The format for this document is a Microsoft Excel file. In the *Select Data Source* dialog box, locate the Student List from the lesson folder—use the scroll bar to view the Type—it should read *Microsoft Excel Worksheet*. Click **Open.**

6. The *Select Table* dialog box opens as shown in Figure 11-23. The selected First row of data contains column headers check box indicates that Word automatically recognizes the headings in the worksheet. Click **OK**.

Figure 11-23

Select Table dialog box

The worksheet name appears here

It automatically reads the worksheets with column headers

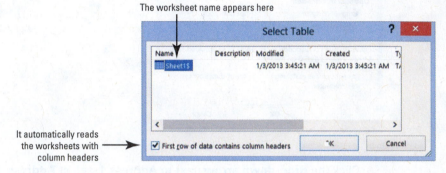

The *Mail Merge Recipients* dialog box opens. Notice that under the Data Source heading, it shows the file data source as *Student List.xlsx.*

7. Click **OK** to close the dialog box.

8. Close the Mail Merge pane.

9. Position the insertion point at the beginning of the document and insert the current date.

10. Press **Enter** twice.

11. Click the **Insert Merge Field button** to open the *Insert Merge Field* dialog box (see Figure 11-24).

Figure 11-24

Insert Merge Field dialog box

Insert field options

Match Fields dialog box opens

Insert field into document

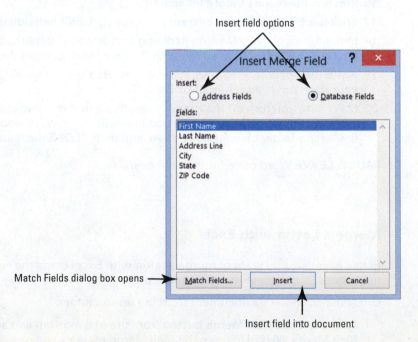

12. With the *First Name* selected, click the **Insert button** to insert the <<First_Name>> field code in the document.

13. Click the **Close button** to close the *Insert Merge Field* dialog box. Press the **spacebar** once.

14. Click the **Insert Merge Field drop-down arrow** to display the fields. This is another way to also insert field codes in a document.

15. Select *Last_Name* to insert the <<Last_Name>> field code in the document.

16. Press **Enter** to create a blank line.

17. Click the **Insert Merge Field drop-down arrow** and select *Address_Line* to insert the <<Address_Line>> field code in the document.

18. Press **Enter** to create a blank line.

19. Click the **Insert Merge Field drop-down arrow** and select **City** to insert the <<City>> field code in the document.

20. Type a comma after <<City>> and press the **spacebar** once.

21. Click the **Insert Merge Field drop-down arrow** and select **State** to insert the <<State>> field code in the document; press the **spacebar** once.

22. Click the **Insert Merge Field drop-down arrow** and select **ZIP_Code** to insert the <<ZIP_Code>> field code in the document.

23. Press **Enter** once to create a blank line.

24. Type **Dear** and press the **spacebar** once.

25. Click the **Insert Merge Field drop-down arrow** and select *First_Name* to insert in the document.

26. Press the **spacebar** once.

27. Click the **Insert Merge Field drop-down arrow** and select *Last_Name* to insert in the document.

28. Type a colon after <<Last_Name>>.

    Notice the spacing between the lines of the field codes.

29. Select <<**First_Name**>> through <<**ZIP_Code**>>.

30. On the Page Layout tab, decrease the Spacing Before to **zero** and change the top margin to **2″** and the left and right margins to **1″**. Preview the results before finishing the merge.

31. Click the **Finish & Merge button**, and then click **Edit Individual Documents.**

32. In the *Merge to New Document* dialog box, keep the defaults and click **OK**. A new document appears, with the merged document displaying all records.

33. **SAVE** the document as *Merged Academic Scholarship* in the lesson folder on your flash drive, and then **CLOSE** the file.

    Make sure you turn off the Preview Results so that the field codes are displayed in the main document and close the Mail Merge pane.

34. **SAVE** the main document as *Academic Scholarship Letter* in the lesson folder on your flash drive, and then **CLOSE** the file.

    PAUSE. LEAVE Word open for the next exercise.

STEP BY STEP　　**Merge a Letter with Access**

In this exercise, you reinforce what you learned in merging a document with a different file type.

OPEN the *Scholarship* document from the lesson folder.

1. Click the **Start Mail Merge button** from the Mailings tab and select the **Step-by-Step Mail Merge Wizard** to open the Mail Merge pane.

2. In the *Select document type* section, Letters is the default. Click **Next: Starting document**.

3. Select the **Use the current document option button**.

4. Click **Next: Select recipients** from the Mail Merge pane to advance to the next step.

5. In the *Select recipients* section, the defaults will be used. Click the **Browse button** and locate the ***Student List.accdb*** file. The format for this document is a Microsoft Access database (refer to Figure 11-7 to review the database icon). In the *Select Data Source* dialog box, locate the Student List.accdb file from the lesson folder—use the scroll bar to view the Type—it should read *Microsoft Access Database*.

6. Click **Open.**

   The *Mail Merge Recipients* dialog box opens. Notice that under the *Data Source* heading and preview area, the file data source displays as *Student List.accdb*.

7. Click **OK** to close the *Mail Merge Recipients* dialog box.

8. Click **Next: Write your letter**.

9. Position the insertion point at the beginning of the document and insert the current date.

10. Press **Enter** twice.

11. Insert the Address Block and notice that the street address is missing in the preview area.

12. Click the **Match Fields** | Match Fields... | **button** (refer to Figure 11-22). To correct the error, select the drop-down arrow and select the **Address Line** field. Click **OK**.

13. Click **OK** again.

14. Press **Enter** once.

15. Insert the Greeting line, accept the default settings, and click **OK**.

16. Click the **Preview Results button** and notice the spacing in the Address Block needs to be formatted correctly. Select the **<<Address Block>>** and in the Page Layout tab, decrease the Spacing Before to **zero** and change the top margin to **2″** and the left and right margins to **1″**. Preview the results before finishing the merge.

17. Click the **Finish & Merge button**, and then click **Edit Individual Documents**.

18. In the *Merge to New Document* dialog box, keep the defaults and click **OK**. A new document appears, with the merged document displaying all records.

19. **SAVE** the document as ***Merged Academic Scholarship Letter*** in the lesson folder on your flash drive, and then **CLOSE** the file.

20. Make sure you turn off the Preview Results so that the field codes are displayed in the main document and close the Mail Merge pane. **SAVE** the main document as ***Academic Scholarship Main Letter*** in the lesson folder on your flash drive, and then **CLOSE** the file.

PAUSE. LEAVE Word open for the next exercise.

CREATING ENVELOPES AND LABELS

The Bottom Line

After a document has been merged, the next step is to create envelopes using the same data source. The process is similar; the difference is selecting the type of document to be merged. Businesses usually have their own preprinted envelopes that have their company address on it. Check with your instructor for your school address so that you can type your school address in the return address area. In this exercise, you create envelopes and labels.

STEP BY STEP   **Create an Envelope**

OPEN a blank document.

1. Click the Mailings tab, and in the Start Mail Merge group, click the **Start Mail Merge button**.

2. Choose **Envelopes**.

   The *Envelope Options* dialog box opens as displayed in Figure 11-25.

3. Use the default settings, and click **OK**.

   In this dialog box you have the option to change the size of the envelope and font for the delivery and return address.

Figure 11-25

Envelope Options dialog box

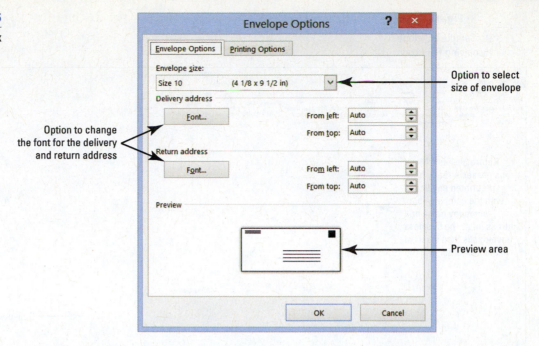

4. Click the **Select Recipients button** and select **Use an Existing List**. The *Select Data Source* dialog box opens. Navigate to your data files for the lesson folder.

5. **OPEN** the *Student List.accdb* (database) data source file from the lesson folder. Each time you open a data source file, the commands on the Ribbon become active.

6. Place the insertion point in the delivery address location in the envelope, and then click the **Address Block button**.

   As shown in the preview area, the fields do not match and the address needs to be corrected.

7. Click the **Match Fields button**.

8. To correct the Address 1 field, click the **drop-down arrow** and select *Address Line*. Click **OK.** The address has been corrected and is ready to be merged.

9. Click **OK** again to close the Insert *Address Block* dialog box.

10. Preview the envelopes by clicking the **Preview Results button**, and then review each record in the envelope and return to the first record. Turn off the Preview Results. The envelope should match Figure 11-26.

Figure 11-26

Sample envelope
displaying field code

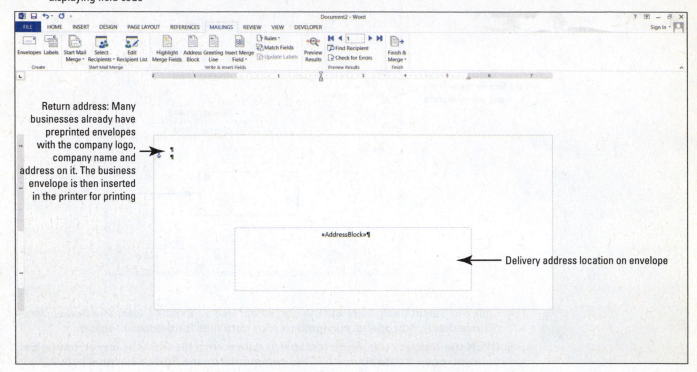

Return address: Many
businesses already have
preprinted envelopes
with the company logo,
company name and
address on it. The business
envelope is then inserted
in the printer for printing

«AddressBlock»¶

Delivery address location on envelope

11. Complete the merge by clicking the **Finish & Merge button**.

12. Select **Edit Individual Documents**, and then click **OK**.

   Each record has its own envelope and you are ready to print. Check with your instructor before printing.

13. **SAVE** the merged envelopes document as *Merged Scholarship Envelope* in the lesson folder on your flash drive, and then **CLOSE** the file.

   Make sure you turn off the Preview Results so that the field codes are displayed in the main document.

14. **SAVE** the main document as *Scholarship Main Envelope* in the lesson folder on your flash drive, and then **CLOSE** the file.

   PAUSE. LEAVE Word open for the next exercise.

STEP BY STEP **Create Labels**

OPEN a blank document.

1. From the Mailings tab, in the Start Mail Merge group, click the **Start Mail Merge button**. Choose **Labels**.

   The *Label Options* dialog box opens as displayed in Figure 11-27. You have options to change vendors and product number.

2. Change the Label vendors option to **Microsoft**. Change the Product number to **30 Per Page** with the dimensions of Type: **Address Label,** Height: **1**"; Width: **2.63**"; Paper size: **8.5" x 11"** as shown in Figure 11-27. Click **OK**.

3. Click the **Select Recipients button** and select **Use an Existing List**. The *Select Data Source* dialog box opens. Navigate to your data files for the lesson folder.

4. **OPEN** the *Student List.accdb* (database) data source file from the lesson folder.

   As discussed, each time you open a data source file the commands on the Ribbon become active. The first label appears blank whereas the remaining labels display *<<Next Record>>*.

Figure 11-27

Label Options dialog box

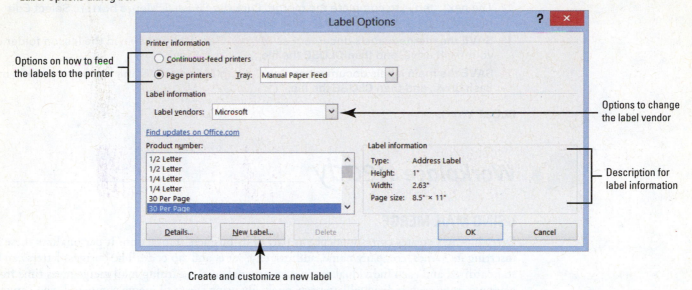

Options on how to feed the labels to the printer

Options to change the label vendor

Description for label information

Create and customize a new label

5. Click the **Address Block button** to begin inserting the Address Block. Notice that the fields do not match.

6. Correct the address by clicking the **Match Fields button**.

7. To correct the Address 1 field, click the **drop-down arrow** and select *Address Line*.

8. Click **OK**.

The address line has been corrected as shown in the preview area.

9. Click **OK** again to close the *Insert Address Block* dialog box.

10. Click the **Update Labels** button in the Write & Insert Fields group. The Address Block field appears on each label as shown in Figure 11-28.

Labels are created using the table format and when opened, the Table Tools opens. The skills that you learn in Lesson 6 can be applied to format labels.

Figure 11-28

Sample label document displaying field codes

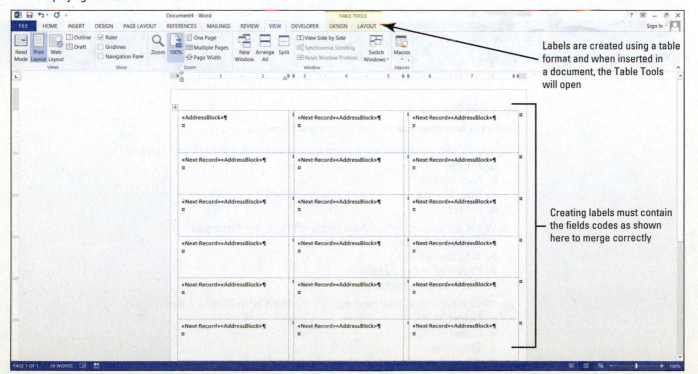

Labels are created using a table format and when inserted in a document, the Table Tools will open

Creating labels must contain the fields codes as shown here to merge correctly

11. Preview the labels by clicking the **Preview Results button**. Each record appears on the label. Turn off the Preview Results.

12. The next step is to complete the merge. Click the **Finish & Merge button**. Select **Edit Individual Documents**, and then click **OK**.

13. **SAVE** the merged labels document as *Merged Scholarship Label* in the lesson folder on your flash drive, and then **CLOSE** the file.

14. **SAVE** the main labels document as *Scholarship Main Label* in the lesson folder on your flash drive, and then **CLOSE** the file.

CLOSE Word.

Workplace *Ready*

USING MAIL MERGE

Every business creates correspondence as part of its business transaction. It personalizes these by inserting its names, company name, address, city, state, and zip code. The business letters can be standardized and each individual receives an original copy. Learning mail merge saves time from having to type each individual letter separately. By using the mail merge command, you can save time and money from having to sort manually or typing the information manually.

SKILL SUMMARY

In this lesson you learned to:	Exam Objective	Objective Number
Set Up Mail Merge		
Execute Mail Merge		
Merge a Document with a Different File Format		
Create Envelopes and Labels		

Knowledge Assessment

Multiple Choice

Select the best response for the following statements.

1. Which tab contains the commands used to perform mail merges?
   a. Merge
   b. Mailings
   c. Mail Merge
   d. Insert

2. What do you do first when performing a mail merge?
   a. Set up the main document.
   b. Add merge fields.
   c. Preview the results.
   d. Choose the recipients.

3. Which type of document can be merged with a data source file?
   a. Letter
   b. Label
   c. Envelope
   d. All of the above

4. Which is NOT an option for selecting a list of recipients for the mail merge?
   a. Download from an online directory
   b. Type a new list
   c. Use an existing list
   d. Use your Outlook contacts

5. To merge information into your main document, you must first connect the document to a(n):
   a. address validator.
   b. form letter.
   c. data source.
   d. website.

6. When mail merge fields have been inserted into a document, Word will automatically replace them with information from a data source when the:
   a. main document is saved.
   b. recipients are selected.
   c. merge fields are inserted.
   d. mail merge is performed.

7. Mail merge fields are enclosed by:
   a. quotation marks (" ")
   b. chevrons (<< >>)
   c. apostrophes (' ')
   d. brackets ([ ])

8. When previewing the mail merge document, Word replaces the merge fields with:
   a. sample data.
   b. blank spaces.
   c. actual data.
   d. highlighted headings.

9. When a user selects Current Record using the Finish & Merge menu, which document appears in a new document window?
   a. All documents
   b. Only the document where the insertion point is placed while previewing
   c. Records 1 and 3
   d. It will not appear in a new document window

10. When you save the main document, you also save:
   a. all the data in an Excel spreadsheet.
   b. any other open file.
   c. the default return address for Word.
   d. its connection to the data source.

True/False

Circle T if the statement is true or F if the statement is false.

T F 1. In a merge, the main document does not contain the same text or graphics for each merged document.

T F 2. The data source is a file that contains the information to be merged into the main document (for example, names and addresses).

T F 3. Mail merge fields are inserted in a document using a data source file.

T F 4. It is a good practice to check for errors before completing the merge process.

T F 5. Word makes the process easy to use an existing list of recipients in a new mail merge document.

T F 6. The Address Block also includes the Greeting Line.

T F 7. The edit recipient's list allows you to make changes to the list of recipients and decide which one will receive your letter.

T F 8. Fields correspond to the column heading in the data source.

T F 9. Word generates a copy of the main document for reach record when you perform a mail merge.

T F 10. You cannot preview a document before merging.

Competency Assessment

Project 11-1: Creating a Mail Merge Letter for the Contest Judges

As the director of business and marketing education at the School of Fine Arts, you have recruited professional members of the local business community to serve as volunteers to judge a state contest for high school business students. You are sending a mail merge letter that contains necessary information to the judges and want to set up the main document.

GET READY. LAUNCH Word if it is not already running.

1. **Open** the *Judges* document from the lesson folder.

2. Click the **Mailings tab**, and then the Start Mail Merge group, click the **Start Mail Merge drop down arrow** and select the **Step-by-Step Mail Merge Wizard**.

3. Accept the default document type of Letters. At the bottom of the Mail Merge pane, click the **Next: Starting document link**.

4. In the *Select starting document* section, *Use the current document* is already selected. At the bottom of the pane, click the **Next: Select recipients link**.

5. In the *Select recipients* section, you will use the default settings, *Use an existing list*. Click the **Browse link** in the *Use an existing list* section.

6. Navigate to the data files in the lesson folder. Select *Judges List*, and click **Open**.

7. The *Mail Merge Recipients* dialog box opens. Click the check box for **Houston, Peter** to remove the check from the check box and click **OK**. Turning off the check mark for Peter Houston removes him as a recipient; therefore, he will not receive a letter. His name will still remain in the data source file.

8. Advance to the next step, by clicking the **Next: Write your letter link** at the bottom of the Mail Merge pane. The letter is the current document.

9. The insertion point should be resting in front of the *T* in *Thank* in the first line of text in the letter. Press **Enter** twice, and move your insertion point to the first blank line.

10. Type **March 29, 20XX**. Press the **Enter key** twice.

11. On the Mail Merge pane, click the **Address block link**.

12. Keep the default settings and click **OK**.

13. Move the insertion point to the blank line below Address Block.

14. On the Mail Merge pane, click the **Greeting line link**.

15. In the Greeting line format, keep the first options the same and change the comma to a **colon**. Click **OK**.

16. At the bottom of the Mail Merge pane, click the **Next: Preview your letters link**.

17. Beginning with the first recipient, select **Ms. Karen Archer** through the zip code, **44501**. The whole address is now selected; on the Home tab, in the Paragraph group, click the **Line and Paragraph Spacing button** and select **Remove Space After Paragraph**.

18. Place your insertion point in the salutation, *Dear Ms. Archer*. In the Paragraph group, click the **Line and Paragraph Spacing button** and select **Add Space Before Paragraph**.

19. At the bottom of the Mail Merge pane, click the **Next: Complete the merge link**. The Mail Merge is ready to produce your letter.

20. Change the top margin to **2"**.

21. **SAVE** the main document as *11-1 Judges Main Letter* in the lesson folder on your flash drive.

LEAVE the document open for the next project.

Project 11-2: Judges for Business Student's Contest

You are ready to complete the mail merge to the list of professional members of the local business community volunteering to judge a state contest for high school business students.

GET READY. USE the document that is open from the previous exercise.

1. In the Merge section of the Mail Merge pane, click **Edit individual letters**. The default option *All* is selected.
2. Click **OK**.
3. A new document (Letters1) opens; it is comprised of all four merged letters opens.
4. **SAVE** the merged document as ***11-2 Judges Merged*** in the lesson folder on your flash drive, and then **CLOSE** the file.
5. **SAVE** the main document as ***11-1 Judges Main Letter*** in the lesson folder on your flash drive, and then **CLOSE** the file.

LEAVE Word open for the next project.

Proficiency Assessment

Project 11-3: Advertising Letter

The marketing representative, Isabel Diaz, has asked you to prepare a short letter to the committee reminding it of a deadline. Use the Step-by-Step Mail Merge Wizard to create the merge document.

GET READY. OPEN the ***Advertising Letter*** document from the lesson folder.

1. Set up the letter as the main document for a mail merge.
2. Select the ***Committee Members*** file as the recipient's list from the lesson folder.
3. Type **May 29, 20XX** under the image and then press **Enter**.
4. Insert the **Address Block** and **Greeting Line**. Use the **colon** in place of the comma.
5. Place your insertion point in the Address Block, and click the **Home tab**. In the Paragraph group, click the **Line and Paragraph Spacing button** and select **Remove Space After Paragraph**.
6. Place your insertion point in the Greeting Line. In the Paragraph group, click the **Line and Paragraph Spacing button** and select **Add Space Before Paragraph**.
7. Click **Check for Errors** and select the first option.
8. Click the **Preview Results button**.
9. Click **Finish & Merge** and **Edit Individual Documents**, and then click **OK**.
10. **SAVE** the merged document as ***11-3 Advertising Merged Letter*** in the lesson folder on your flash drive, and then **CLOSE** the file.
11. **SAVE** the main document as ***11-3 Advertising Main Letter*** in the lesson folder on your flash drive, and then **CLOSE** the file.

LEAVE Word open for the next project.

Project 11-4: Welcome Letter

You are the marketing manager at one of the local home improvement stores. Every month a selected group of customers are invited to receive special promotions and offers. Open an existing letter and data source and merge.

GET READY. LAUNCH Word if it is not already running.

1. **OPEN** the *Welcome Letter* file located in your lesson folder and set it up as the main document in a mail merge.

2. **OPEN** the *New Potential Customers* file as the recipient list.

3. Press **Enter** to create two blank lines after the date.

4. Insert the **Greeting Line** to display only the first name. Use the default salutation and comma in the Greeting Line format.

5. Check and correct any errors, and then preview the document before printing.

6. **SAVE** the merged document as *11-4 Potential Customers Merged Letter* in the lesson folder on your flash drive, and then **CLOSE** the file.

7. **SAVE** the main document as *11-4 Welcome Customers MainItr* in the lesson folder on your flash drive, and then **CLOSE** the file. Make sure the field codes are displayed before saving.

LEAVE Word open for the next project.

Mastery Assessment

Project 11-5: Office Manager Position

As the assistant to the office manager at Tech Terrace Real Estate, you have been asked to set up a main document. There were many candidates who applied for the office manager's position.

GET READY. LAUNCH Word if it is not already running.

1. **OPEN** the *Selection Letter* and set it up as the main document in a mail merge.

2. **OPEN** the *Candidate List* file as the recipient list.

3. Insert the **Address Block** and **Greeting Line**. Use the colon in the Greeting Line format.

4. Change the top margin to **2″** and the left and right margins to **1″** to accommodate the logo on the company's letterhead. Correct any formatting errors if necessary.

5. **SAVE** the main document as *11-5 Selection MainItr* in the lesson folder on your flash drive.

LEAVE the document open for the next project.

Project 11-6: Merging the Office Manager Position Letters

You are continuing with the previous project and are ready to complete the merge process.

GET READY. USE the document that is open from the previous exercise.

1. Edit the recipient's list and remove the check mark from **Ted Bremer** and **Eric Rothenberg**. Removing the check mark by the recipient's name excludes them from the merge document. Their names remain in the recipient's data source file.

2. Check and correct any errors then preview the document before printing.

3. **SAVE** the merged document as *11-6 Selection Merged Letter* in the lesson folder on your flash drive, and then **CLOSE** the file.

4. **SAVE** the main document in the lesson folder on your flash drive.

CLOSE Word.

Circling Back 3

As a fourth-grade writing teacher at a private elementary school, you have been asked to present a research paper at a national conference. You use Word to write and edit the research paper.

Project 1: Adding Bookmarks

While working on the research paper, you often refer to the same places in the document. Insert bookmarks to help you jump to specific text more quickly. You will also apply styles to the headings to view when using the Navigation Pane or Bookmark commands.

GET READY. LAUNCH Word if it is not already running.

1. **OPEN** *Research* from the data files for this lesson.
2. Format the document according to the *MLA* style guidelines. Your instructor's name is **Jerry Wright**, the date for submission is **May 2, 20XX**; and the class is **IT 1301: Computer-Mediated Literature Circles**; the title of the paper is **Getting On-board with Being Online**.
3. **SAVE** the document as *Research Paper MLA* in the lesson folder on your flash drive.
4. Select **Introduction** and apply the **Heading 1** style.
5. Apply the **Heading 1** style to the remaining headings in the document: **Community in the Classroom**, **Technology within Literature Circles**, **Computer-Mediated Discussion Groups**, and **Conclusion**.
6. Modify the *Heading 1* style and change the spacing before from *30* pt to **12** *pt*. Apply only to this document—make sure you remove the check mark by *Add to the Styles gallery*.
7. Open the Navigation Pane and click **Introduction** to take you back to the beginning of the document. Then close the Navigation Pane.
8. Select the **Introduction** heading again.
9. Insert a Bookmark, and then type the same name for the bookmark.
10. Create a bookmark for each of the remaining headings in the document. Use the following abbreviated headings as bookmark names: **Community**, **Technology**, **Discussion**, and **Conclusion**.
11. Insert a comment by *Conclusion* and type **Test each bookmark**.
12. Select any word in the document and use the **Define** command.
13. **SAVE** the document in the lesson folder on your flash drive.

PAUSE. LEAVE Word and the document open for the next project.

Project 2: Table of Contents

A table of contents helps readers quickly locate topics of interest quickly as well as enabling the Navigation Pane. Because your research paper is a long document, both of these are helpful. Insert a table of contents in your document. Change the style of the paper to APA.

GET READY. LAUNCH Word if it is not already running.

USE the document that is open from the previous project.

1. **SAVE** the document as *Research Paper APA* in the lesson folder on your flash drive.
2. Format the document using the *APA* style.
3. Remove the comment by *Conclusion*.
4. Insert a blank page at the beginning of the document.
5. Select the **Automatic Table 2** style to insert a table of contents on its own page.
6. **SAVE** the document in the lesson folder on your flash drive, and then **CLOSE** the file.

PAUSE. LEAVE Word open for the next project.

Project 3: Main Document

Insert merge fields to create a main document.

GET READY. LAUNCH Word if it is not already running.

1. **OPEN** *Speaker Thank You Letter* from the lesson folder.
2. Select recipients from an existing list—the *Speaker List* document is located in the lesson folder on your flash drive.

3. Delete text beginning with **Jo Berry** through **64163**.
4. Insert the **Address Block** in the appropriate location on the letter. Use the default settings.
5. Insert the **Greeting Line** and apply the format of *Dear Mr. Randall* and change the punctuation to a colon.
6. Position the insertion point at the end of the first sentence, after the blank space following the word *on* and type **September 30**.
7. **SAVE** the main document as *Speaker Thank You LTR-Main*.
8. Click the **Check for Errors** button. Preview each letter for errors then close.
9. Preview each letter, and then click the **Finish & Merge** button.
10. Click **Edit Individual Documents**.
11. In the *Merge to New Document* dialog box, select **All** and click **OK**.
12. **SAVE** the merged document as *Thank You Merged LTR*, and then **CLOSE** the file.
13. **CLOSE** the main document without saving.

PAUSE. CLOSE Word.

LESSON SKILL MATRIX

Skill	Exam Objective	Objective Number
Arranging Document Views		
Recording Macros	Assign shortcut keys.	1.4.9
	Record simple macros.	1.4.8
Monitoring Macro Security	Manage macro security.	1.4.10

KEY TERMS

- digital signature
- hacker
- macro
- master document
- subdocuments

© Photomorphic/iStockphoto

You are the president of the Lakeville.NET User's Group, which is a group of students, faculty, and professionals in the community whose purpose is to educate, help build development skills, and provide a forum for networking. This group meets monthly and schedules regular workshops and speakers on relevant topics. In this role, you discover that you use many of the same types of documents on a regular basis, and you would like to streamline the process of creating similar documents. In this lesson, you learn to work with outlines, arrange master documents and subdocuments, and record and manage macros.

© Photomorphic/iStockphoto

SOFTWARE ORIENTATION

Outline View

When you open the Outline view from the View tab, the Outlining tab contains buttons for working with long documents and arranging the document into smaller sections. The Outlining tab is shown in Figure 12-1.

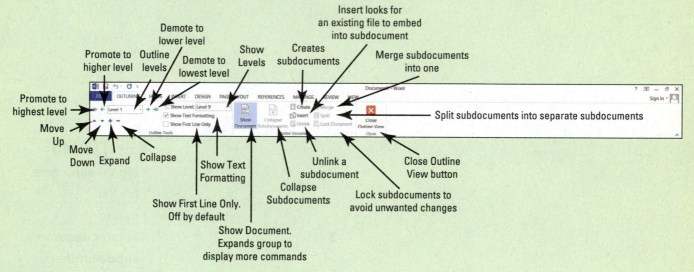

Figure 12-1

Outlining tab

Use this figure as a reference throughout this lesson as well as the rest of this book.

ARRANGING DOCUMENT VIEWS

Creating master documents enables you to work efficiently with large reports such as your research paper or other long reports. These long documents are broken down into subdocuments making it more manageable and easy to edit.

Working with a Master and Subdocuments

A **master document** is the main document created in Word, such as your research paper. A research paper or another long report contains information such as a title, thesis, introduction, techniques, results, and works cited to name a few. This document can be a 60-page document, and scanning through the whole document could be cumbersome. Working with a master document can organize the heading sections into smaller sections called **subdocuments**, which are sections within the master document that have been separated into subsections. When a subdocument is created, it becomes a separate file from the master although it still remains linked to the master document. This allows you to open a small 2- or 3-page document rather than a 20-page document.

For example, you create a master document for long reports and research papers. When you finish formatting your master document with heading styles, you can separate it into a subdocument for each heading and its content. Subdocuments are created based on their heading styles; the subdocument is saved with the heading as the filename.

As a student, you will most likely have to take a technical writing class for one of your core courses and prepare a research paper. As you begin working on your research paper, you will outline it to make it more manageable and to keep yourself organized. Working with the master and subdocuments is similar to how you work on sections of your paper. You can edit from your whole master document or work in the subdocument as a separate document. When you edit and save subdocuments independently, the master document automatically gets updated because the subdocument is linked to the master document. When you need to review the master document, all editing changes will appear in the document.

Saving the Master Document

To help you manage the master document, it is best to save the master document and all the subdocuments in the same folder. Creating a folder makes locating subdocuments quick. The document that you will work on is already formatted with heading styles. In this exercise, you learn to create a folder, and then save the master document.

STEP BY STEP   **Save the Master Document**

OPEN the *Hosting* document from lesson folder.

1. To save the document in a specific folder, click the File tab, and then click **Save As**. Click **Computer** and then click **Browse**.

   The *Save As* dialog box opens for you to locate your flash drive.

2. Click the **New folder button** located under the address bar and type **Master Hosting** and press **Enter** to accept the new folder name.

3. With the folder selected, click the **Open button** or **double-click** to place the master folder in the address bar.

   Creating a folder is easy and makes your job easier to locate the master document and subdocuments. When naming a folder, choose a name closely related to the document.

4. In the File name box, type **Master Proposal**.

   Figure 12-2 displays the file in the folder.

Figure 12-2

Save As dialog box

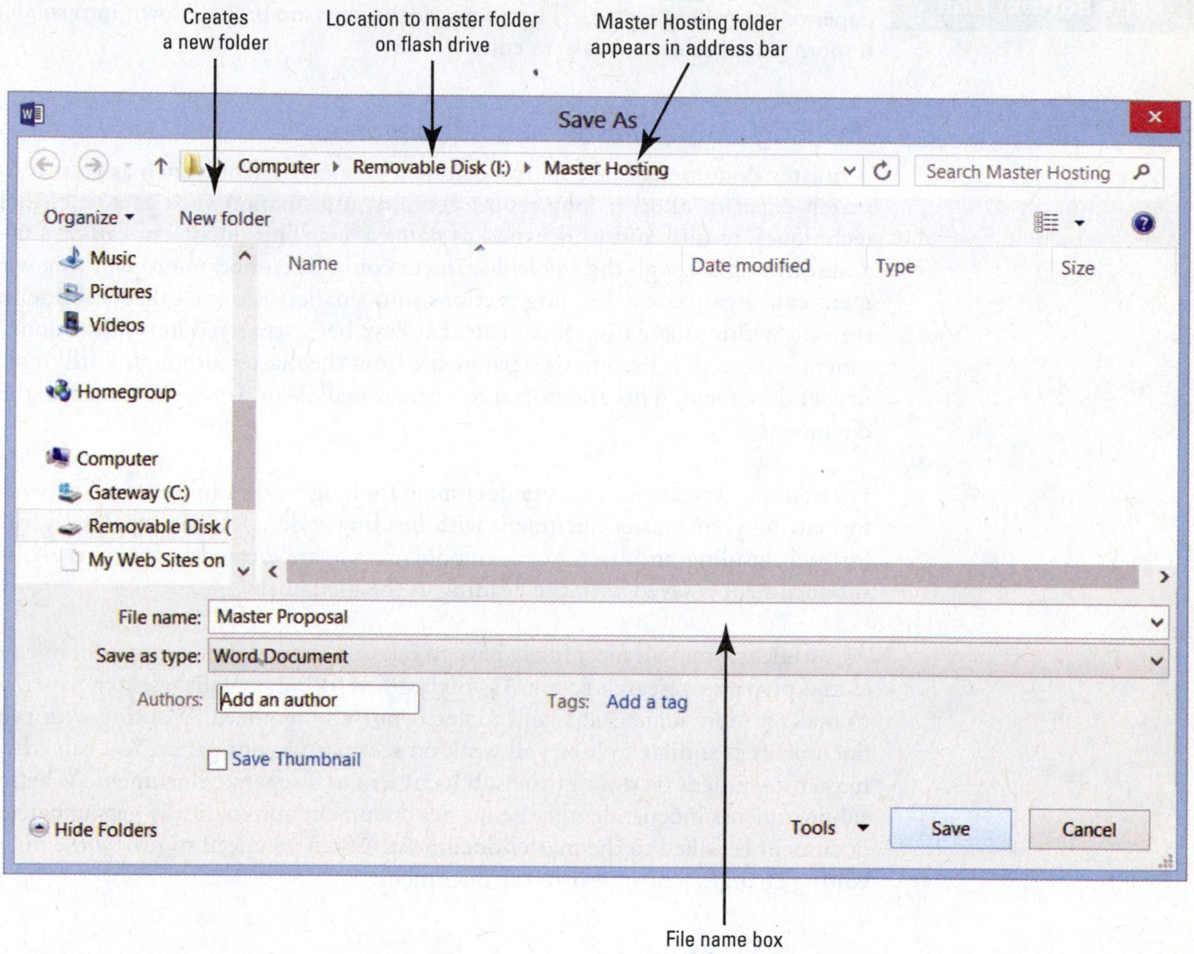

Creates a new folder

Location to master folder on flash drive

Master Hosting folder appears in address bar

Save As

← → ↑ Computer ▸ Removable Disk (I:) ▸ Master Hosting ⌄ C Search Master Hosting 🔍

Organize ▾   New folder

🎵 Music
🖼 Pictures
🎬 Videos

| Name | Date modified | Type | Size |

🏠 Homegroup

💻 Computer
💿 Gateway (C:)
💾 Removable Disk (
📄 My Web Sites on

File name: Master Proposal

Save as type: Word Document

Authors: Add an author   Tags: Add a tag

☐ Save Thumbnail

⊙ Hide Folders   Tools ▾   Save   Cancel

File name box

5. Click the **Save button** to save the document in the Master Hosting folder.

PAUSE. LEAVE the document open for the next exercise.

Cross Ref Creating and saving documents is covered in Lesson 1.

Creating Subdocuments

A subdocument is part of the master document and is separated into small sections. Each subdocument has a unique filename based on the heading style that was applied to the document when it was created. As a student, this feature is useful for a large research paper—you work on one subdocument section at a time rather than having the whole document open. The first step is identifying the levels within the subdocuments just like you would in creating an outline. For example, Level 1, Level 2, and Level 3 is similar to creating an outline and identifying headings with Roman numerals I, II, and II.

When formatting your research paper, you apply a heading style to each new section in your paper (styles are covered in Lesson 3). When you are editing subdocuments separately, the master document is automatically updated. The Outlining tab contains the Collapse and Expand subdocument buttons that correlate with the master document. In this exercise, you create subdocuments that are saved separately.

Create Subdocuments

USE the document open from the previous exercise.

1. Click the **View tab**. In the Views group, click the **Outline button**. The Outlining tab opens and is placed by the Home tab.

2. In the Outline Tools group, click the drop-down arrow by *Show Level* and select **Level 1** to make the document more manageable.

   This document has already been formatted with heading styles; when the levels are changed, the document collapses and only Level 1 displays on the screen as shown in Figure 12-3.

Figure 12-3

Document displayed by Level 1

Click the Expand (+) button to display content within heading

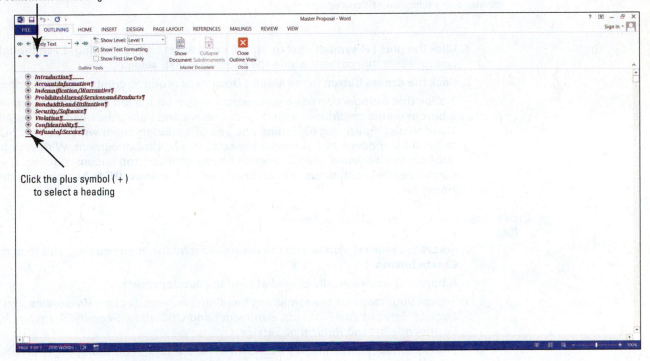

Click the plus symbol (+) to select a heading

3. In the Master Document group, click the **Show Document button** to display additional commands as shown in Figure 12-4.

Figure 12-4

Show Document displaying
additional commands

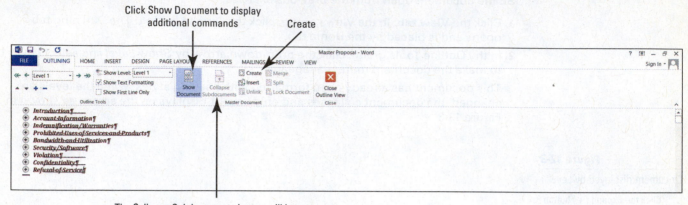

The Collapse Subdocuments button will become
activated after a subdocument is created

4. Click the **plus (+) symbol** next to *Introduction* to select the heading. Even though you cannot see it, the content within the heading is also selected.

5. Click the **Create button** in the Master Document group to create a subdocument.

   Notice that *Introduction* has a subdocument icon on the left side and is surrounded by a border with a *continuous section break* above and below the heading. This allows Word to distinguish the beginning and end of a subdocument with a continuous flow to the master document. A border indicates this is a subdocument. With your first subdocument created, the Collapse Subdocuments button becomes active. If you cannot see the continuous section break, select the **Show/Hide button** from the Home tab.

 Cross Ref   Section breaks are covered in Lesson 5.

6. Select the **plus (+) symbol** next to the *Account Information* heading, and then click the **Create button**.

   A border is automatically placed around the subdocument.

7. Repeat your steps for the remaining headings: *Indemnification/Warranties, Prohibited Uses of Services and Products, Bandwidth and Utilization, Security/Software, Violation, Confidentiality,* and *Refusal of Service*.

   The document should display as shown in Figure 12-5. A border appears around each subdocument along with continuous section breaks.

Figure 12-5

Document with subdocuments

Subdocument icon. When you click the icon, the subdocument heading and contents are selected

A border is placed around the subdocument after it is created

Collapse Subdocuments button becomes active after a subdocument is created

Continuous section breaks are automatically inserted to separate subdocuments

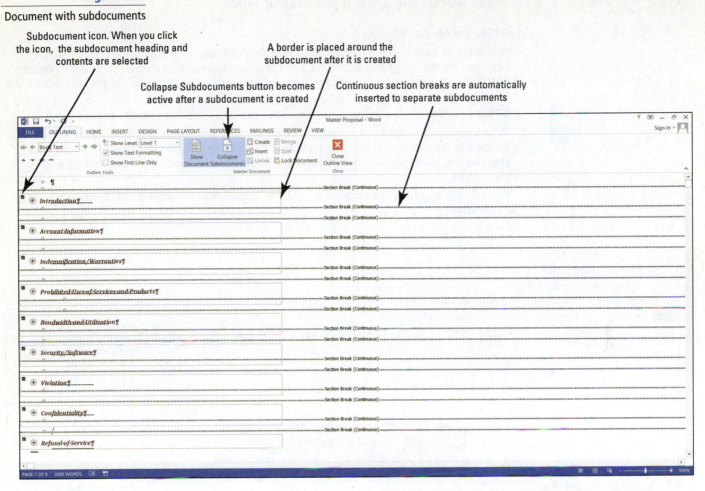

PAUSE. LEAVE the document open to use in the next exercise.

Saving Subdocuments

The next step is to save the master document with the subdocuments. Word automatically creates a filename for each of the subdocuments based on the text formatted with the heading styles. It saves them as a separate file, but in the same folder. For example, the document that you are working on contains many headings with a Heading 1 style applied to them. Figure 12-4 shows each of the headings in the document. When the master document is saved, each of the headings and the text under the heading is saved into a separate file automatically. In this exercise, you learn to save the master document with the subdocuments.

STEP BY STEP   **Save Subdocuments**

USE the document that is open from the previous exercise.

1. Click the **SAVE** 🖫 **button** on the Quick Access Toolbar to save the *Master Proposal* document and the created subdocuments.

   Word saves each subdocument as a separate file based on the heading style (Heading 1) that was applied to the document. Each of the subdocuments are linked to the master document.

2. **CLOSE** the master document.

PAUSE. LEAVE Word open.

View the Subdocuments in the Master Folder

1. **OPEN** the *Master Hosting* folder.

   You started with one file in your *Master Hosting* folder and now you have several subdocuments in the folder. When subdocuments are created and then saved, Word automatically saves each subdocument as a separate file. Word uses the text within the heading as the filename.

2. **OPEN** the *Master Proposal* document. The document opens in Print Layout view.

   When opening a master document, the subdocuments show the location in a hyperlink to the file. You see your flash drive letter followed by the *Master Hosting* folder and then by the subdocument filename. By default the subdocuments are locked and collapsed.

   Figure 12-6 displays the document with the location of the saved subdocuments with hyperlinks.

Figure 12-6

Master document with subdocuments

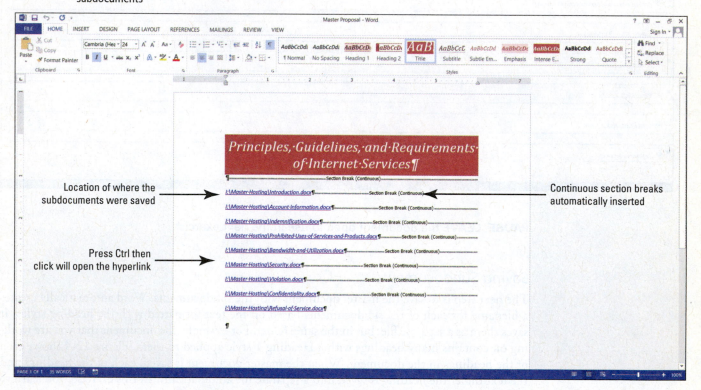

3. When you are ready to follow a link in Word, press **Ctrl**, and then click one of the links.

   Each hyperlink goes directly to the subdocument when you click on the link. Later in this lesson, you open a subdocument.

PAUSE. LEAVE the document open to use in the next exercise.

Expanding and Collapsing Subdocuments

To view the master document with its contents, click the Expand Subdocuments button on the Outlining tab. Once the Expand Subdocuments button is clicked, you can switch views and the document remains expanded. The Collapse Subdocuments button closes the subdocuments. In this exercise, you expand and collapse subdocuments.

STEP BY STEP	**Expand and Collapse Subdocuments**

USE the document that is open from the previous exercise.

1. Change the view of the document to **Outline**.

   With the Outlining tab open, you can now work with the buttons in the Master Document group.

2. Click the **Expand Subdocuments**  **button** and notice that all subdocuments are shown along with their contents (see Figure 12-7).

   Each heading and its contents now appear. Now that the subdocuments are expanded the Expand Subdocuments button is replaced with the Collapse Subdocuments button.

⚠ **Troubleshooting**   If you do not see the headings and contents in a border, click the Show Document button in the Master Documents group.

Figure 12-7

Subdocuments expanded

When subdocuments are expanded,
the Collapse Subdocuments button appears on the Ribbon

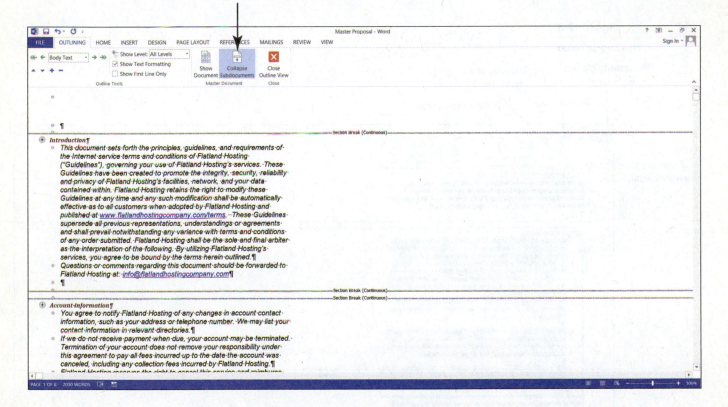

3. Click the **Collapse Subdocuments** **button** to collapse each of the subdocuments.

   The Expand Subdocuments button appears again.

PAUSE. LEAVE the document open to use in the next exercise.

Promoting and Demoting Subdocuments

When you rearrange levels in a master document, you move the subdocument heading to another level by using the commands in the Outlining tab by either promoting or demoting the level. For instance, to move a topic in the paper under another heading, you demote that heading. As you continue working on your research paper, you come to realize that the Heading 1 style applied to one of the headings should be a Heading 2. In the Outlining tab, you have options to change the levels of the headings by using the promote or demote buttons. It is easy to demote a Level 1 to a Level 2 or vice versa. So in this case, you demote the Level 1 to a Level 2. In this exercise, you learn to use promote and demote buttons.

<table>
<tr><td>**STEP BY STEP**</td><td>**Promote and Demote Subdocuments**</td></tr>
</table>

USE the document that is open from the previous exercise.

1. Click the **Expand Subdocuments** button to expand all subdocuments.

   Point at the **plus (+) symbol** next to the *Account Information* heading—notice that the mouse pointer changes to four arrows.

2. Click the **plus (+) symbol** once to select the heading and all the contents within the subdocument.

3. In the Outline Tools group, click the **Demote** button once.

   Did you see the Outline Level box change from a Level 1 to a Level 2? The *Account Information* has been demoted to a Level 2 as shown in Figure 12-8.

Figure 12-8

Heading demoted

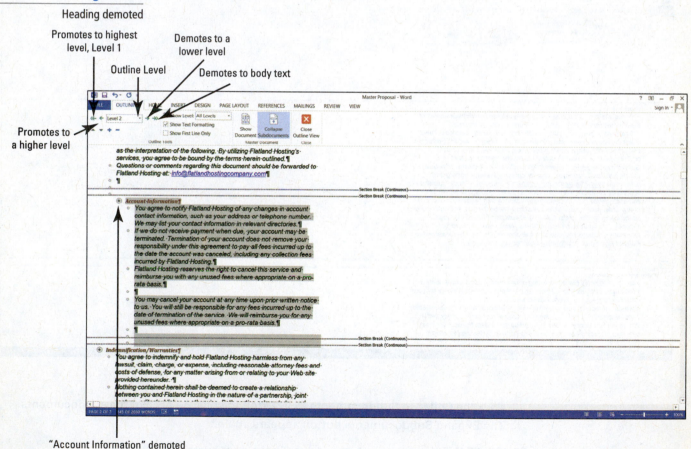

Promotes to highest level, Level 1

Outline Level

Demotes to a lower level

Demotes to body text

Promotes to a higher level

"Account Information" demoted to the next lower level

4. With the Account Information subdocument still selected, click the **Promote** arrow once.

   The *Account Information* has been promoted back to a Level 1. Demote back to a Level 2.

Another Way
You can click the drop-down arrow by the Outline Level box to select the level.

5. Click the **SAVE button** on the Quick Access Toolbar. The master document is saved with the updated changes.

PAUSE. LEAVE the document open to use in the next exercise.

Reorganizing Subdocuments

Subdocuments can be rearranged within the master document. The order of subdocuments can be changed by moving the subdocuments from one location to another using the command buttons on the Outlining tab or by dragging and dropping. Once you move a subdocument, you need to unlink it and recreate it. You can also merge two or more subdocuments into one subdocument. In this exercise, you reorganize subdocuments.

STEP BY STEP   **Reorganize Subdocuments**

USE the document that is open from the previous exercise.

1. Deselect *Account Information* by clicking in a blank area of the document screen.
2. Add a check mark next to **Show. First Line Only**.

   This displays a few lines for each of the subdocuments and hides the remaining content—making the subdocuments more manageable.
3. Scroll down and click to select the **plus (+) symbol** by the *Security/Software* heading and its contents.
4. Click the **Show Document button** to display the additional commands in the Master Document group.
5. On the Outline Tools group, click the **Move Down ▾ button** (four times) until the heading is positioned below the continuous section break below *Violation*.

   Hint, two continuous section breaks should appear above *Security/Software*.

   The *Security/Software* subdocument is surrounded by a border, which extends to the *Confidentiality* subdocument.
6. **Delete** the two continuous section breaks under *Security/Software* and *Confidentiality*.

   Deleting these continuous section breaks makes it easy to unlink the subdocuments.

PAUSE. LEAVE the document open to use in the next exercise.

Another Way
Click the subdocument icon to select the heading and contents, and drag and drop to the new location.

STEP BY STEP   **Unlink Subdocuments**

USE the document that is open from the previous exercise.

Currently, there is only one subdocument 🔳 icon for both levels as shown in Figure 12-9. Both of these subdocuments are linked to the master document and must be unlinked to create separate subdocuments.

Figure 12-9

Repositioned subdocuments

Repositioning subdocuments places a border
around two subdocuments and displays one subdocument icon

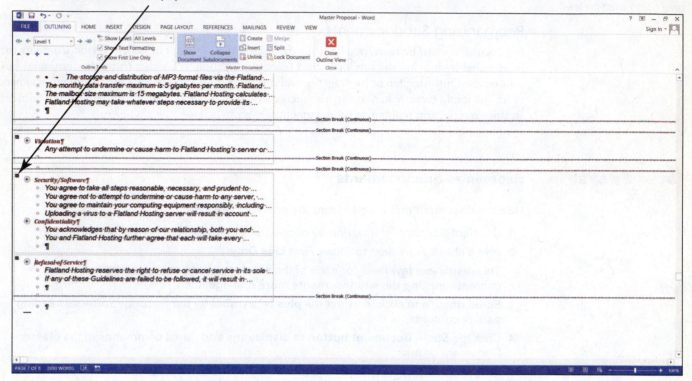

1. Click the **plus (+) symbol** by *Security/Software* to select it, and then click the **Unlink button**.

   The subdocument icon disappears.

2. Click the **Create button** to create a subdocument.

   This places a border around this level and the subdocument icon appears.

3. Click the **plus (+) symbol** by *Confidentiality*.

4. Check whether the Unlink button is showing. If it is, then click **Unlink**, and then click **Create**. If the Unlink button is not displayed, click just the **Create button**.

5. Click the **check box** to turn off *Show First Line Only*. Change the Level to display only **Level 1**.

   Changing the display of the level makes it more manageable to create a subdocument and see the borders around each of the subdocuments.

6. Click the **Collapse Subdocuments button** and a prompt appears asking *Do you want to save changes to the master document "Master Proposal."* Click **OK**.

   Your screen should match Figure 12-10. Word automatically saves the subdocument with a new filename and drops the last character of the filename and adds a *1* at the end. The two additional files that you see in your flash drive are *Securit1* and *Confidentialit1*. Each time you create a subdocument, it is automatically linked to the master document and the original subdocuments are no longer linked to the master document.

Figure 12-10

Master document with hyperlinks with repositioned subdocuments

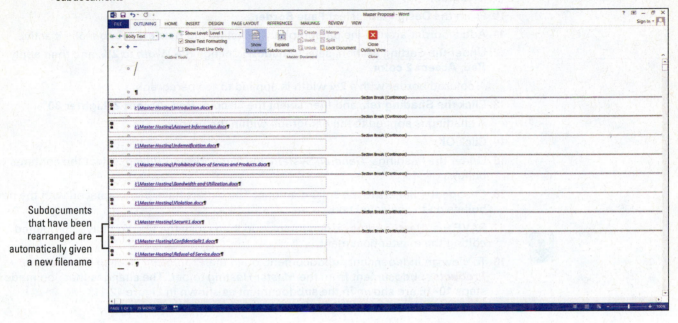

Subdocuments that have been rearranged are automatically given a new filename

PAUSE. LEAVE the document open to use in the next exercise.

Editing an Individual Subdocument

Subdocuments can be edited directly in the master document, or you can open the subdocument as a separate file in its own window. In this exercise, you edit a subdocument separately and within the master document.

STEP BY STEP   **Edit an Individual Subdocument**

USE the document that is open from the previous exercise.

1. Point to the *Master Hosting/Introduction* subdocument hyperlink, press **Ctrl** and **Click** to follow the hyperlink and open the subdocument in a separate window. It is now ready for editing and formatting.

2. You will edit text in the first and second sentences. Select *principles*, *guidelines*, and *requirements* from the first sentence. In the second sentence, select *integrity, security, reliability*, and *privacy*. All seven words should be selected.

🔍 **Cross Ref**   In Lesson 2, you learn to select text using different methods. To select multiple areas of text, press CTRL and select the text.

3. **Bold** the selected text, and then change the font color to **dark red**.

4. Click **SAVE** on the Quick Access Toolbar; then close the *Introduction* subdocument file. If prompted to save changes, click **SAVE**.

5. Click the *Outlining* tab to make it available with its commands.

6. In the Master Document group, click the **Expand Subdocuments** **button**.

   Notice the bolded dark red text under the *Introduction* heading. Changes made in the *Introduction* subdocument automatically update the master document.

7. Click the **Close Outline View button** to take you to the Print Layout view.

8. Scroll down to page **3**.

9. Under the heading, *Prohibited Uses of Services and Products*, select the second paragraph.

10. From the Design tab, select **Page Borders**.

11. Add a border around the paragraph by selecting the **Borders tab** to make it active.

12. Under the Setting section, select **Shadow**. Change the *Width* to **2¼**, and then apply **Red**, **Accent 2 color**.

    A colored border with a 2¼ width is applied to the paragraph.

13. Click the **Shading tab**, and then select the fill color **Red**, **Accent 2**, **Lighter 80%**.

    A shading is applied to the paragraph within the border.

14. Click **OK**.

15. Under the headings, *General, System and Network*, and *Billing*, select the contents with bullets.

16. Change the bullets to the solid diamond. The bullets have been replaced with the new bullets on the selected text.

17. **SAVE** the *Master Proposal* document, and then close the file. You have completed editing the master document.

18. To view an independent subdocument, open the *Prohibited Uses of Services and Products* subdocument from the *Master Hosting* folder. The changes that you made in steps 10–16 are shown in the subdocument as shown in Figure 12-11.

Figure 12-11

Subdocument with changes

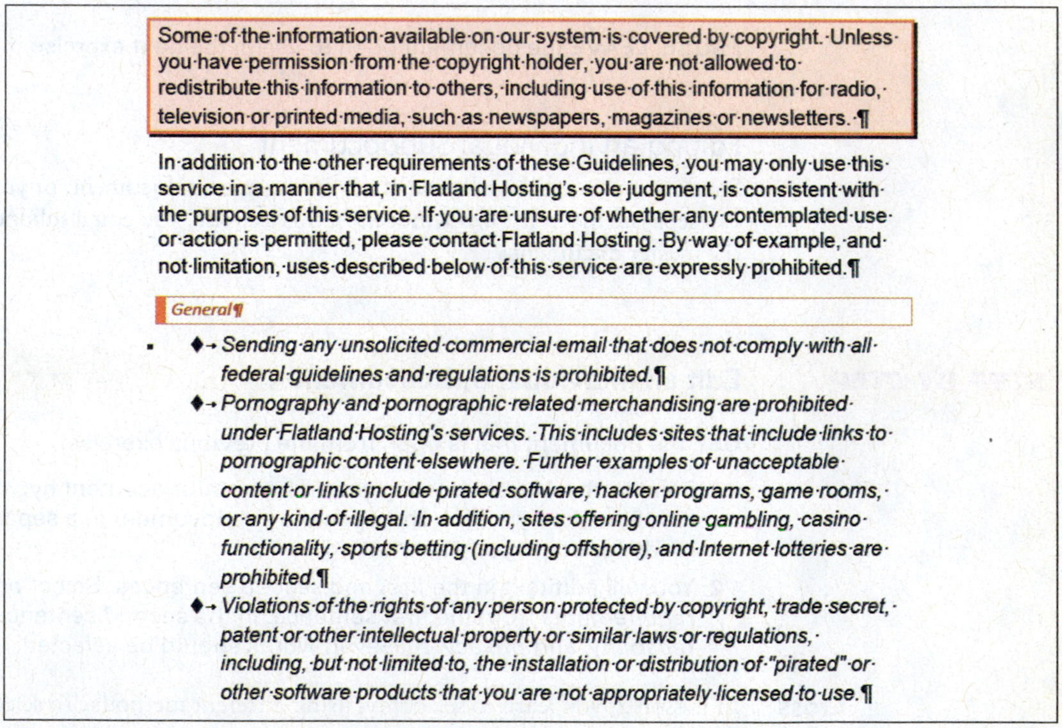

> Some·of·the·information·available·on·our·system·is·covered·by·copyright.·Unless· you·have·permission·from·the·copyright·holder,·you·are·not·allowed·to· redistribute·this·information·to·others,·including·use·of·this·information·for·radio,· television·or·printed·media,·such·as·newspapers,·magazines·or·newsletters.·¶

In·addition·to·the·other·requirements·of·these·Guidelines,·you·may·only·use·this· service·in·a·manner·that,·in·Flatland·Hosting's·sole·judgment,·is·consistent·with· the·purposes·of·this·service.·If·you·are·unsure·of·whether·any·contemplated·use· or·action·is·permitted,·please·contact·Flatland·Hosting.·By·way·of·example,·and· not·limitation,·uses·described·below·of·this·service·are·expressly·prohibited.¶

General¶

- ♦→ *Sending·any·unsolicited·commercial·email·that·does·not·comply·with·all· federal·guidelines·and·regulations·is·prohibited.¶*
- ♦→ *Pornography·and·pornographic·related·merchandising·are·prohibited· under·Flatland·Hosting's·services.·This·includes·sites·that·include·links·to· pornographic·content·elsewhere.·Further·examples·of·unacceptable· content·or·links·include·pirated·software,·hacker·programs,·game·rooms,· or·any·kind·of·illegal.·In·addition,·sites·offering·online·gambling,·casino· functionality,·sports·betting·(including·offshore),·and·Internet·lotteries·are· prohibited.¶*
- ♦→ *Violations·of·the·rights·of·any·person·protected·by·copyright,·trade·secret,· patent·or·other·intellectual·property·or·similar·laws·or·regulations,· including,·but·not·limited·to,·the·installation·or·distribution·of·"pirated"·or· other·software·products·that·you·are·not·appropriately·licensed·to·use.¶*

19. **CLOSE** the document.

LEAVE Word open.

SOFTWARE ORIENTATION

Recording Macros

Do you find yourself performing the same task in Word over and over again? If so, recording macros simplifies your task. You belong to the Lakeville.NET User's Group, and you are responsible for providing everyone with copies of upcoming workshops. You bring together the skills that you have learned from other lessons to record a macro. For instance, in Lesson 6, you learn to create and format tables, and use formulas within the tables. You're always on the go and now you find yourself in a situation where you are not accomplishing much because of repetitive tasks. It is essential that you learn about macros to help you manage your time more wisely, increase productivity, and still have time for yourself. In this exercise, you learn to record and run a macro.

RECORDING MACROS

The Bottom Line

A **macro** is a recorded sequence of commands to automate a task. It is a series of commands and actions that can be recorded and run whenever you need to perform the task. When a macro is created, you can run it manually or assign it to run whenever a specific key or series of keystrokes are pressed.

STEP BY STEP   **Assign Shortcut Keys**

A keyboard shortcut is a combination of two or more keys to perform a specific action. In the lessons that you have already covered, you applied a keyboard shortcut to open a new document by pressing **Ctrl+N** or to bold text by pressing **Ctrl+B**. Word contains many different shortcuts and these shortcuts are assigned to a specific action to perform, therefore, cannot be used.

GET READY. If necessary, before you begin these steps, **LAUNCH** Word.

1. **OPEN** a blank document.
2. In the View tab, click the drop-down arrow by *Macros* to produce a menu (see Figure 12-12).

Figure 12-12

Macros menu

After macros are recorded, you can view them here

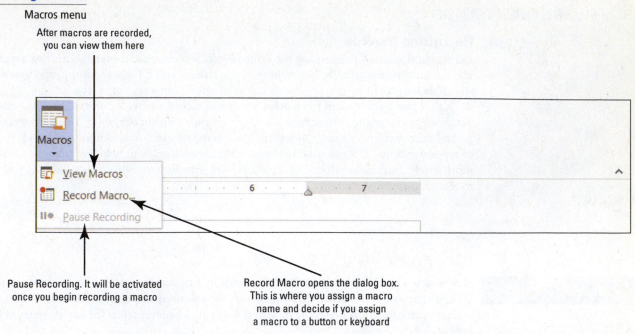

Pause Recording. It will be activated once you begin recording a macro

Record Macro opens the dialog box. This is where you assign a macro name and decide if you assign a macro to a button or keyboard

3. Click **Record Macro** to open the *Record Macro* dialog box. In the dialog box, you need to assign a name to the macro and decide which option to use to assign a macro. You have two choices as shown in Figure 12-13. You can assign a macro by button or by keyboard.

Figure 12-13

Record Macro dialog box

Macro name cannot contain spaces

Choose how you want to assign the macro

Option on where to store macro

Add a description to describe macro

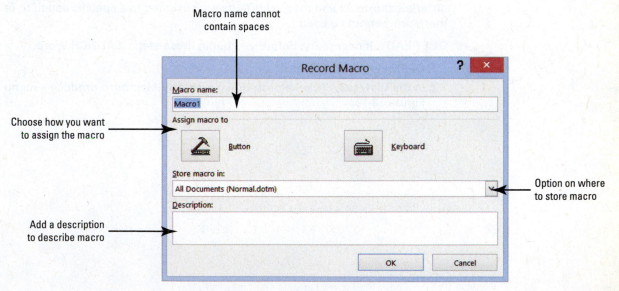

4. In the Macro name box, type **Upcoming_Workshops**.

Spaces are not allowed; you need to add an underscore. Adding a number at the end of the macro name is also valid.

5. Keep the default setting for *Store macro in*.

It will be stored in *All Documents (Normal.dotm)*.

You want it stored there because you will access this macro on a monthly basis. If someone else is working on your computer and you've provided this person with the keyboard shortcut, he or she too can access the macro. (Hint: You can add the shortcut key in the description, in case you forget it or want to share it.)

The first macro will be assigned to a keyboard command. This means whenever you press the keyboard commands, the macro will run.

Before you click the Keyboard button, you want to add a description to the macro.

6. In the Description box, type **Use this table for all upcoming workshops.**

7. Click the **Keyboard button** to open the *Customize Keyboard* dialog box as shown in Figure 12-14.

In the Commands box, the macro is stored in *Normal.NewMacros.Upcoming_Workshops.* This shows the location of where the macro will be stored.

Figure 12-14

Customize Keyboard dialog box

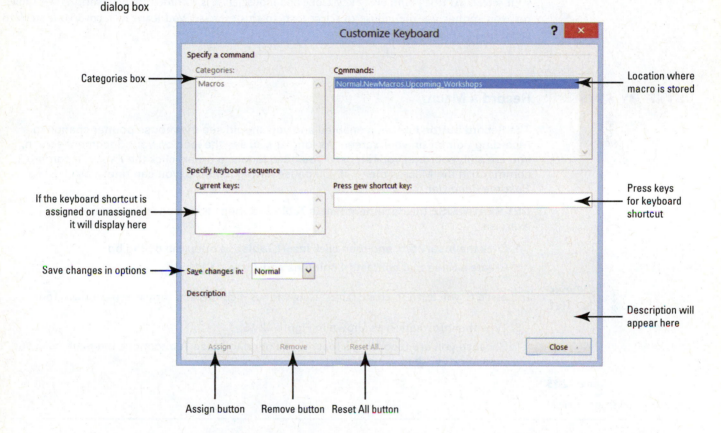

Categories box

Location where macro is stored

If the keyboard shortcut is assigned or unassigned it will display here

Press keys for keyboard shortcut

Save changes in options

Description will appear here

Assign button   Remove button   Reset All button

8. It's time to see whether a keystroke has been assigned to another command. In the *Press new shortcut key* box, press **Ctrl+T** (do not type the plus symbol).

This shortcut key is already assigned to the HangingIndent command as shown in the dialog box.

9. Press **Backspace** to remove *Ctrl+T*.

Let's try another shortcut key.

10. Press **Ctrl+Alt+T**.

And again, this shortcut key is already taken by the ™ Trademark command. It may take you several attempts to find an unassigned shortcut key.

11. Press **Backspace** to remove *Ctrl+Alt+T*.

12. Press **Alt+T**.

Notice that this keystroke is not assigned.

13. Click the **Assign button** to assign this shortcut key to the new macro. The *Alt+T* command is moved to the *Current keys* box for this macro.

The changes will be assigned in the Normal template instead of Document1. This macro will be saved on the computer that you are recording the macro and can be accessed by anyone who is working on your computer.

Take Note Word allows you to override assigned keyboard keys, but you don't want to do that. Find one that is unassigned.

How do you assign a keyboard shortcut to a macro?

14. Click **CLOSE**.

PAUSE. LEAVE Word open for the next exercise.

Recording a Macro

Once you determine which method to assign the macro, the next step is recoding your steps. While Word is recording a macro, you see the mouse pointer change to a recording pointer on your screen. At this point, every keystroke and mouse click is recorded. When working with macros, you cannot use the mouse to select text. In this exercise, you learn to record your steps to create and format a table.

STEP BY STEP **Record a Macro**

The Record button has been enabled and you should see the mouse pointer change to a recording pointer on your screen. As long as you see the icon on your document screen, you are still recording your steps. If you need to take a break, click the *Pause Recording* command in the Macros menu. If you pause during a macro, you can return by clicking *Resume Recorder*.

GET READY. USE the document that is **Table** and then click open from the previous exercise.

1. Click the **Insert tab**, and then click **Insert Tables** to open the dialog box.

2. Create a table that contains **4** columns and **7** rows. Click **OK**.

Cross Ref In Lesson 6, you learn to create tables using various methods and format using Tables Tools.

3. Type the information as shown in Figure 12-15.

Because you are recording a macro, you need to press **Tab** to move between cells and press **Shift+Tab** to move back.

Figure 12-15

Upcoming Workshop document

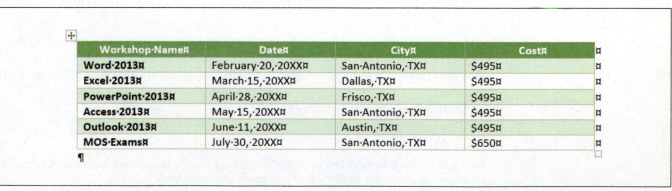

Workshop·Name¤	Date¤	City¤	Cost¤	¤
Word·2013¤	February·20,·20XX¤	San·Antonio,·TX¤	$495¤	¤
Excel·2013¤	March·15,·20XX¤	Dallas,·TX¤	$495¤	¤
PowerPoint·2013¤	April·28,·20XX¤	Frisco,·TX¤	$495¤	¤
Access·2013¤	May·15,·20XX¤	San·Antonio,·TX¤	$495¤	¤
Outlook·2013¤	June·11,·20XX¤	Austin,·TX¤	$495¤	¤
MOS·Exams¤	July·30,·20XX¤	San·Antonio,·TX¤	$650¤	¤

¶

4. After you type the data, click the **Layout tab** from the Tables Tools and Select Tables.

While you are recording a macro, you cannot use your mouse to select text or tables. The whole table is now selected.

5. In the Table Styles group of the Design tab, click the **More button** to display the gallery.

6. In the Grid Tables group, select **Grid Table 4 – Accent 6** to apply a style to the table.

7. Use the arrow keys on the keyboard to move up to the first row that contains the headings.

8. On the Layout tab, click **Select** in the Table group and choose **Select Row**, and then select **Align Center**. For now, these are the only changes you will record for this macro.

9. The next step is to stop recording. Click the View tab, click **Macros**, and then click **Stop Recording**.

   You recorded your first macro and will be able to access it quickly. If you share your computer with another individual, this person too can use the keyboard shortcut to apply the macro as long as you provide him or her with the shortcut key. This table can be used for all upcoming workshops—all you have to do is change the data.

10. **CLOSE** the document without saving. (Hint: When a warning prompt appears, click **Don't Save**.)

PAUSE. LEAVE Word open for the next exercise.

CERTIFICATION READY? **1.4.8**

How do you record a macro?

Running a Macro

Once a macro is recorded, you can press the keyboard shortcut to run it in a blank or existing document. In this exercise, you learn to run your macro in a blank document.

STEP BY STEP	**Run a Macro**

OPEN a blank document.

1. Press **Alt+T**. The table automatically appears on your document screen.

   When you need to work on this table, you can now access it quickly, edit the data, and then save with a new filename.

2. **SAVE** the document as *Upcoming Workshops* in the lesson folder on your flash drive, and then **CLOSE** the file.

3. **OPEN** a blank document.

   Now, let's run the macro again another way.

4. On the View tab, click **Macros**, and then click **View Macros** to open the *Macros* dialog box as shown in Figure 12-16.

Figure 12-16

Macros dialog box

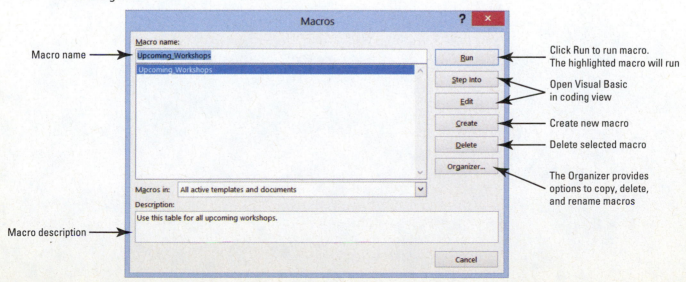

5. Click **Run**. The table appears on the document screen.

Additional commands are available in the dialog box and will not be discussed in this lesson. Some of these commands open the Visual Basic Application—this is where you can create or edit a macro. If you accidently open it, just close the application.

6. CLOSE the document without saving.

PAUSE. LEAVE Word open for the next exercise.

 **Troubleshooting**   Creating and running a macro takes practice. If your macro does not run correctly, delete the macro and repeat your steps from the beginning.

Deleting a Macro

You determine you no longer need this macro and want to delete it. In this exercise, you learn to delete a macro.

STEP BY STEP   **Delete a Macro**

OPEN a blank document.

1. On the View tab, click **Macros**, and then click **View Macros** to open the *Macros* dialog box (refer to Figure 12-16).

2. Select the macro, and then click the **Delete button**.

3. A warning prompt appears asking *Do you want to delete macro Upcoming_Workshops?*

4. Click **No**. You can return later to delete. Click **Cancel**.

PAUSE. LEAVE Word open for the next exercise.

SOFTWARE ORIENTATION

Controlling Macro Security

You learned to streamline your work using macros. Now, you are concerned about how security works with macros. Macro security involves active content in files that might come from a site that has no digital signature or from someone who has written code with a virus. If someone sends you a document and it contains macros with active content, it might pose a security risk and harm your computer. A **hacker** is a person who writes malicious programs such as viruses intended to harm your computer or access your data illegally. Every day we hear about hackers breaking into large companies and accessing confidential information. Organizations have security in place to identify and stop anyone from accessing data from their network; so, it's important to know, when working with macros, who your trusted sources are. Word has a macro virus security that comes from trusted sources and locations. This macro security determines whether the macro is safe to run on your computer. You want reassurance that macros coming from other sources are from a trusted publisher. A **digital signature** is a code digitally signed by a company or person. You can create your own digital signature but it wouldn't be issued from a trusted certificate authority. In this exercise, you learn to review the securities on your system.

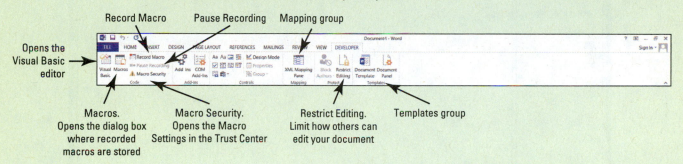

Figure 12-17
Developer tab

Use this figure as a reference throughout this lesson as well as the rest of this book.

MONITORING MACRO SECURITY

The Bottom Line

Macro security has preventive measures in place to determine whether a macro source is safe to run.

STEP BY STEP   **Review Macro Security Settings**

GET READY. If necessary, before you begin these steps, **LAUNCH** Word.

1. From the File tab, select **Options** on the Backstage page.
2. Select **Trust Center** from the *Word Options* dialog box.

   In the *Trust Center* screen, Microsoft has provided links to articles on protecting your privacy, computer, and security. At your leisure, take time to read these articles.

CERTIFICATION READY?   **1.4.10**

How would you change the macro settings?

3. Click the **Trust Center Settings button** to open the *Trust Center* screen. In the left pane, *Macro Settings* is highlighted.

   This is where you manage how macros run. You can choose to disable all macros with or without notification, disable all macros with the exception of those that are digitally signed, or enable all macros that could harm your computer.

Adding a check mark by *Trust access to the VBA project object model* allows access to the Visual Basic for Applications object model. Leave the settings at the default settings (see Figure 12-18).

4. Click the **Cancel button** to exit the *Trust Center* dialog box.

Figure 12-18

Trust Center

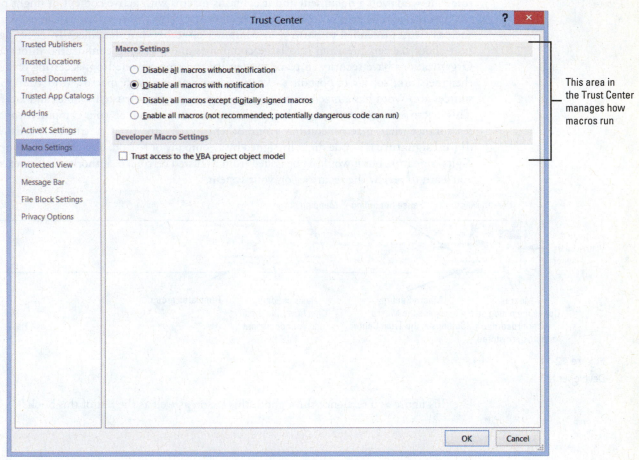

PAUSE. LEAVE the Word Options dialog box open to use in the next exercise.

Now you will learn to add the Developer Tab to the ribbon.

Review the Developer Tab

GET READY. USE the document that is open from the previous exercise.

1. Click **Customize Ribbon** on the left pane.

   This screen is where you customize the Ribbon or, in this case, turn on a Ribbon tab that is off by default.

 Cross Ref   In Lesson 14, you learn to customize the Ribbon with your favorite commands.

2. Under *Customize the Ribbon*, select the check box by *Developer* (refer to Figure 12-19).

3. Click **OK**.

Figure 12-19

Customize Ribbon

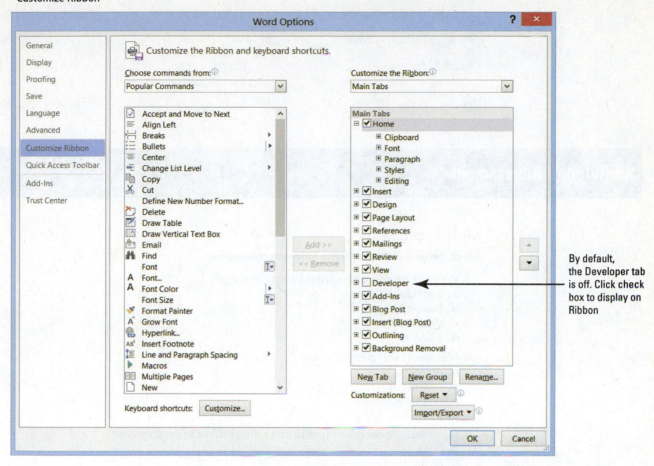

By default, the Developer tab is off. Click check box to display on Ribbon

4. Click the **Developer tab** to display the groups and commands.

The Developer tab contains commands that are used with macros, which includes codes, templates, controls used in forms, add-ins, and more (refer to Figure 12-17 for details on the Developer tab).

Previously, you opened the *Macros* dialog box to run a macro that you created. From the Developer tab, the *Macros* dialog box can be accessed in the Code group by clicking the **Macros button**. In the same group, you can record a macro and pause a recording—these are the same commands from the Macros group in the View tab.

Clearly the Developer tab contains more commands. The Macro Security button opens the Trust Center. This displays the macro settings for your computer. If you have a programming background or feel comfortable writing code, you can write your own macro using the Visual Basic editor.

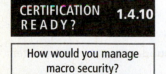

CERTIFICATION READY?   1.4.10

How would you manage macro security?

CLOSE Word.

Take Note   To find additional information on macros, use the Help feature by pressing the *F1* button or click the *Help* icon.

SKILL SUMMARY

In this lesson you learned to:	Exam Objective	Objective Number
Arrange Document Views		
Record Macros	Assign shortcut keys. Record simple macros	1.4.9 1.4.9
Monitor Macro Security	Manage macro security.	1.4.10

Knowledge Assessment

Multiple Choice

Select the best response for the following statements.

1. Where can you open Trust Center settings?
   a. Backstage
   b. Developer tab
   c. View tab
   d. a and b

2. Microsoft will protect your:
   a. privacy.
   b. computer.
   c. unsafe sources.
   d. a and b

3. By default, how many levels does the Outline View contain?
   a. Nine
   b. Eight
   c. Seven
   d. Five

4. Clicking the Show Document button in the Outlining tab displays:
   a. Backstage view.
   b. more commands.
   c. Create.
   d. None of the above

5. Clicking the Expand button will:
   a. show all the text in the subdocument.
   b. close the subdocument.
   c. open only the selected content.
   d. a and c

6. To view the hyperlinks in the subdocuments, you must:
   a. open the master document after creating and saving the subdocument in the master document.
   b. open the original document.
   c. open the individual subdocuments separately.
   d. None of the above

7. Macros are used for:
   a. boring work.
   b. research papers.
   c. repetitive work.
   d. work that is not performed daily.

8. A macro that has been assigned a keyboard shortcut can be run in:
   a. a blank document.
   b. an existing document.
   c. a template.
   d. All of the above

9. When assigning a keyboard shortcut, it is recommended that you use one that is:
   a. assigned to a command.
   b. designated to a command.
   c. already used.
   d. unassigned.

10. Which one of these keyboard shortcuts are not assigned?
    a. Ctrl+B
    b. Ctrl+I
    c. Ctrl+H
    d. Alt+Q

True/False

Circle T if the statement is true or F if the statement is false.

T F   1. A subdocument contains the whole document.

T F   2. Macros will not automate tasks.

T F   3. When you create subdocuments, they are saved with the master document.

T F   4. When recording a macro, you can format a document with many features to enhance the document.

T F   5. When assigning a name to a macro, spaces can be used.

T F   6. A master document can be reorganized.

T F   7. Moving a subdocument to another location in the master document still retains it as a subdocument.

T F   8. Short essays should be separated into subdocuments.

T F   9. If you plan to create subdocuments, identifying the heading should be the first step especially if the document does not already contain heading styles.

T F 10. Macros can be accessed in both the View and Developer tabs.

Competency Assessment

Project 12-1: Creating a Simple Macro

In your job at Books and Beyond, you continue to work on documents that will be part of the employee handbook. You create a simple macro to be used for this employee handbook. In this project, you apply skills that you have learned from previous lessons.

GET READY. LAUNCH Word if not already running.

1. **OPEN** a blank document.

2. On the View tab, click **Macros** and then click **Record Macro** in the Macros group.

3. Type the information in the appropriate box:

   Macro name: **Books_and_Beyond**

   Description: **Formatted report for B&B handbook**.

4. Click **Keyboard** and in the *Press new shortcut key* box, type **Alt+L**. This is an unassigned shortcut key.

5. Click **Assign**, then click **Close**.

6. In the Design tab, select the **Basic (Stylish) Style Set** from the Document Formatting group.

7. Type **BOOKS AND BEYOND**. Apply **Heading 1** from the Styles group on the Home tab.

8. Press **Enter** once.

9. Type **Second section heading**.

10. Select **Heading 2**.

11. Press **Enter** twice.

12. Type **Third section heading**.

13. Select **Heading 3**.

14. Press **Enter** twice.

15. Click **Stop Recording** from the Macros group on the View tab.

CLOSE the document without saving. **LEAVE** Word open for the next project.

Project 12-2: Creating Separate Files for the Books and Beyond Master Document

You work at Books and Beyond and your manager has asked you to work with this document and create separate files from the master document. In your computer class, you learned about master documents and how Word automatically saves subdocuments.

GET READY. LAUNCH Word if not already running.

1. OPEN *Books Beyond* from the lesson folder.

2. From the File tab, click **Save As**.

3. Click Browse and use the scroll bar to locate your flash drive. In the *Save As* dialog box, click **New folder** and name it **BOOKS BEYOND**.

4. In the File name box, type **Master Books** and save it in the *BOOKS BEYOND* folder.

5. Select the heading, *Acknowledgement,* and format with the **Heading 1** style.

6. Select the *Introduction* heading and format with the **Heading 1** style.

7. Select the *General Performance Expectation Guidelines* heading and format with the **Heading 1 style**.

8. On the View tab, click the **Outline button**.

9. In the Outline Tools group, click the **drop-down arrow** by *Show Level* to display *Level 1*.

10. Click the **plus (+) symbol** next to *General Performance Expectation Guidelines*.

11. Click the **Demote button** to change the level for *the General Performance Expectation Guidelines* heading.

The heading is now a Level 2.

12. Click the **Show Document button**.

13. Select the **plus (+) symbol** next to *Acknowledgement* to select the heading and contents under that header.

14. Click the **Create button** in the Master Document group.

15. Click the **plus (+) symbol** by *Introduction* to select the heading and contents under that heading.

16. Click the **Create button** in the Master Document group.

17. Click the **Save button** on the Quick Access Toolbar, and then **CLOSE** the file.

18. **OPEN** the *Master Books* document and preview your document in Print Layout view. You should see two hyperlinks **CLOSE** the file.

LEAVE Word open for the next project.

Proficiency Assessment

Project 12-3: Running the Books and Beyond Macro

You are ready to run the macro created from Project 12-1.

GET READY. LAUNCH Word if not already running.

1. **OPEN** a blank document.
2. Press **Alt+L**.
3. **SAVE** the document as *12-3 B&B Report* in the lesson folder on your flash drive, and then **CLOSE** the file.

LEAVE Word open for the next project.

Project 12-4: Books and Beyond

In this project, you continue working with the files from Project 12-2.

GET READY. LAUNCH Word if not already running.

1. **OPEN** the *Introduction* document from the *BOOKS BEYOND* folder.
2. Use the Find and Replace command to find all occurrences of *Books and Beyond* and replace with **B&B**. Change the formatting and apply the **bold italic** style, font size **12** pt, underline style **Words only**, and **dark blue** font color. (There are 13 occurrences to find.)
3. Change all bullets to the number format and select **1)**.
4. Change the number format listed under the *Set Alarm* and *Deactivate Alarm* headings to a solid circle bullet.

5. **SAVE** the document in the *BOOKS BEYOND* folder on your flash drive.
6. **OPEN** the *Master Books* document and change the view to **Outline**.
7. Press **CTRL+Click** to open the *Acknowledgement* link and select **I acknowledge** from the first paragraph and **I understand** from the fourth paragraph. **Bold** and change to uppercase.
8. **SAVE** the document in the *BOOKS BEYOND* folder on your flash drive, and then **CLOSE** both documents.

LEAVE Word open for the next project.

Mastery Assessment

Project 12-5: Creating a Macro with Formulas

Create a macro with formulas and format the table. Take a screenshot of the Macros dialog box to validate that you completed this project and provide a copy to your instructor.

GET READY. LAUNCH Word if not already running.

1. **OPEN** a blank document.
2. Create a macro, named **Expenses**, and in the Description box, type **Expense Report for trips**. Look for an unassigned shortcut key and assign it to this macro.
3. Create a table as shown in Figure 12-20, and then enter the data and apply the formatting.

Figure 12-20

Table document

Apply the Grid Table 5 Dark style →

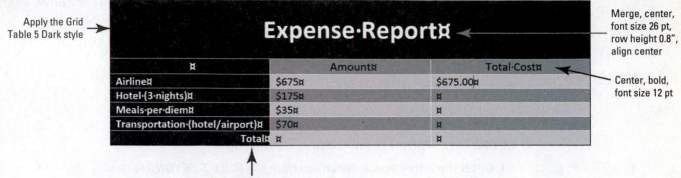

Merge, center, font size 26 pt, row height 0.8", align center

Center, bold, font size 12 pt

Key Total and align right

4. In the first blank cell in the last column, use the Formula dialog box to calculate the hotel total cost. Delete the formula leaving the equal sign.

5. Type **B4*3**. Click **OK**.

6. Calculate the total cost for meals. Type **B5*3**.

7. Calculate the total cost for transportation. Type **B6*2**.

8. Calculate the grand total cost summing the previous values. Use the third option to format the number.

9. Click **Stop Recording**.

10. **CLOSE** the document without saving.

LEAVE Word open for the next project.

Project 12-6: Running Macros and Showing Field Codes

In Project 12-5, you created a macro to prepare a table in a table format that contains formulas. In this project, your job is to run the macro and display the fields. Print a copy of both tables and submit to your instructor. Before closing your computer, change the display back to its default setting.

GET READY. LAUNCH Word if not already running.

1. **OPEN** a blank document.

2. Run the macro.

3. Change the display to show the field codes.

4. **SAVE** the document as *12-6 Expense Report* in the lesson folder on your flash drive.

CLOSE Word.

LESSON SKILL MATRIX

Skill	Exam Objective	Objective Number
Protecting and Sharing Documents	Protect documents with passwords.	1.5.5
Managing Document Versions		
Sharing Documents	Save files to remote locations.	1.5.4

© youngvet/iStockphoto

© youngvet/iStockphoto

Blue Yonder Airlines is a large company with hundreds of employees. In your job as a human resources specialist, you are involved in hiring new employees, employee benefit programs, and employee communications. Because many of the documents you work with relate to employee issues, you have to be careful about keeping documents confidential and available only to those who are authorized to have access. In this lesson, you learn different ways to guard the security of documents. You prepare an employee evaluation for sharing with a supervisor and work together with a colleague to create a job offer letter.

SOFTWARE ORIENTATION

The Bottom Line

In Word 2013, Backstage provides commands to allow you to sign in to your Microsoft account; protect, inspect, and share documents; and manage versions of your documents as shown in Figure 13-1.

Backstage provides commands to protect, inspect, and manage your documents The drop down arrow contains additional commands

Access to properties

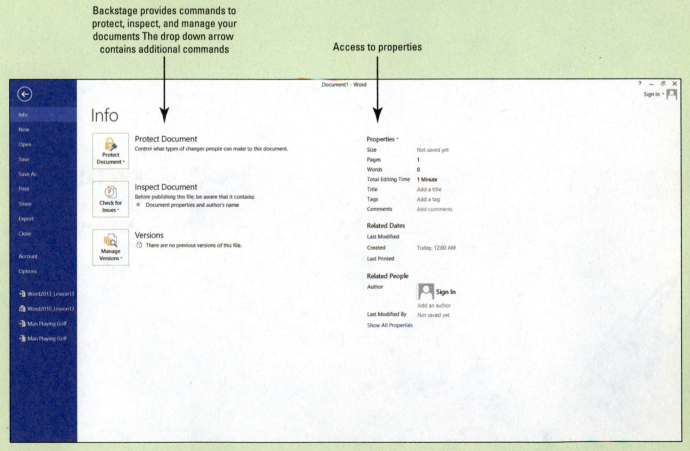

Figure 13-1
Backstage

Use Figure 13-1 as a reference for this lesson.

PROTECTING AND SHARING DOCUMENTS

Protecting a Document

There might be a time when you need to set a password for sensitive documents. These documents can include payroll, budgets, employee evaluations, or hiring agreements. There are two different types of options to protecting a document: Save as Tools and Restrict Editing. Documents such as these are meant for certain individuals who have been granted permission; all others are denied access. Those granted access to confidential documents are provided a password to open and modify the document. When you save a document, you can save with a password to open the document as read only. Individuals who receive this document are able to read only the document. If you want certain individuals to edit, then a password is given to them to allow them to edit. Managing documents with passwords help you oversee sensitive tasks while maintaining security for these type of documents. You can even restrict the type of editing that can be done in a document by using the Restrict Editing command.

Setting an Access Password for a Document

Protecting a document with a password to open as read only and to allow modifications is one way to secure confidential material. In this exercise, you learn to set and remove encrypted passwords in an evaluation form.

STEP BY STEP   **Set an Access Password for a Document**

OPEN the *Peer Review* document from the lesson folder.

1. **SAVE** the document as *Peer Review Draft* in the lesson folder on your flash drive.
2. In the *Save As* dialog box, click the **Tools button** as shown in Figure 13-2.

Figure 13-2

Tools menu

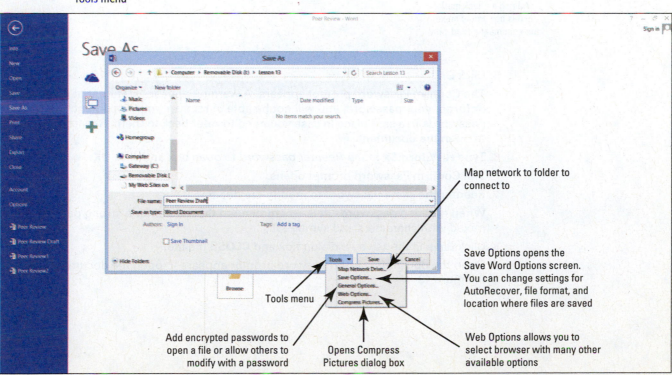

Map network to folder to connect to

Save Options opens the Save Word Options screen. You can change settings for AutoRecover, file format, and location where files are saved

Web Options allows you to select browser with many other available options

Tools menu

Add encrypted passwords to open a file or allow others to modify with a password

Opens Compress Pictures dialog box

3. Select **General Options** from the menu. The *General Options* dialog box appears.

Once a password is entered to open and modify the document, the file will be encrypted. When a file is encrypted, the data is converted to a code.

4. Type **HR%form$#** in the *Password to open* box (see Figure 13-3).

Word enables you to specify two different passwords—one to open a document and one to modify a document—and both are optional. You can specify passwords for both actions—or just specify a different password for each action. Passwords are case-sensitive, which means you can specify upper and/or lowercase letters. For this exercise, use the same password to open and modify. In the *Password to modify* box, type **HR%form$#**.

Figure 13-3

General Options dialog box

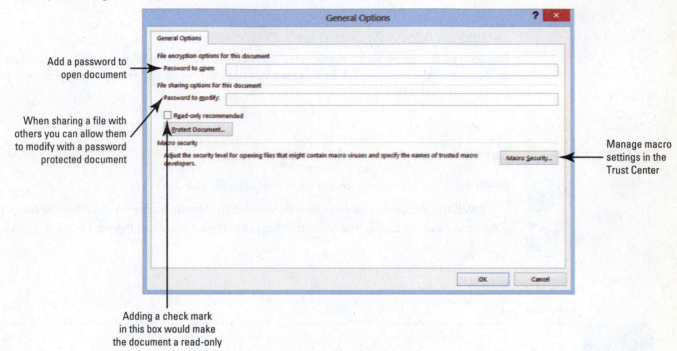

Add a password to open document

When sharing a file with others you can allow them to modify with a password protected document

Adding a check mark in this box would make the document a read-only

Manage macro settings in the Trust Center

5. Click **OK**.

The Confirm Password prompt appears. A warning appears stating that if you lose or forget your password, you will not be able to recover your document. Keep all passwords in a safe place in case you need to refer back to them. Reenter the password to open the document.

6. Type **HR%form$#** in the *Reenter password to open* box and click **OK**.

The Confirm Password prompt opens.

7. Reenter the same password to modify the document.

When entering passwords, it is recommended that you enter a strong password that is mixed with characters and symbols.

8. Click **Save** in the *Save As* dialog box and **CLOSE** the file.

9. Open the document and a Password prompt appears to open the document, as shown in Figure 13-4.

Figure 13-4

Password prompt to open file

10. Type **HR%form$#** in the box and click **OK**.

11. The Password prompt opens again, but this time you reenter the same password to allow for modifications.

    Only those individuals who are provided this password will be allowed to edit the document (see Figure 13-5).

Figure 13-5

Password prompt to modify or open read only

CERTIFICATION
READY?   1.5.5

How would you add a password to a document?

PAUSE. LEAVE the document open to use in the next exercise.

STEP BY STEP   **Remove a Password**

GET READY.

1. Click the **File tab** and notice the Protect Document button is highlighted in a light yellow color.

   Under *Protect Document* it states, "A password is required to open this document."

2. Select **Save As** and select the **Browse button** to open the *Save As* dialog box.

3. Click the **Tools button**, and then select **General Options** from the menu.

4. Remove the password protection by selecting the hidden passwords and press **Delete**.

5. Click **OK**.

6. **SAVE** the document as *Peer Review1* in your flash drive in the lesson folder.

   You now have two copies of the same document: one with a password and one without.

PAUSE. LEAVE the document open to use in the next exercise.

Take Note   It is important for you to remember your password. If you forget your password, Microsoft cannot retrieve it for you. Record and store your password in a safe location, such as, placing it in your security safe or a secure place at home. Use strong passwords that combine uppercase and lower-case letters, numbers, and symbols. Weak passwords do not mix these elements. An example of a strong password is *W5!dk8aG*; a weak password is *CAR381*. Passwords should be 8 or more characters in length. A password phrase that uses 14 or more characters is better.

Protecting a Document as Read Only

Safeguarding your documents is one way to protect them from having other individuals changing the content and format. As you learned, a document can have an encrypted password so it is read only, or you can allow modifications to be made to the document. Another way to protect your document is to restrict editing. This allows the document to be opened without a password, but the types of changes that can be made to the document are limited. For instance, you might want to limit formatting changes to specific styles, or you might want them to be able to add only comments or fill in forms or make changes that are tracked. It's your choice as to whom you share the document with and what type of restrictions you put in place. In this exercise, you learn to set a document as read only, limit the document to comments only, and restrict formatting in the document.

STEP BY STEP   **Protect a Document as Read Only**

USE the document open from previous exercise.

1. **OPEN Backstage**, and then click **Protect Document** to display the menu.
2. Click **Restrict Editing** as displayed in Figure 13-6.

Figure 13-6

Protect Document menu

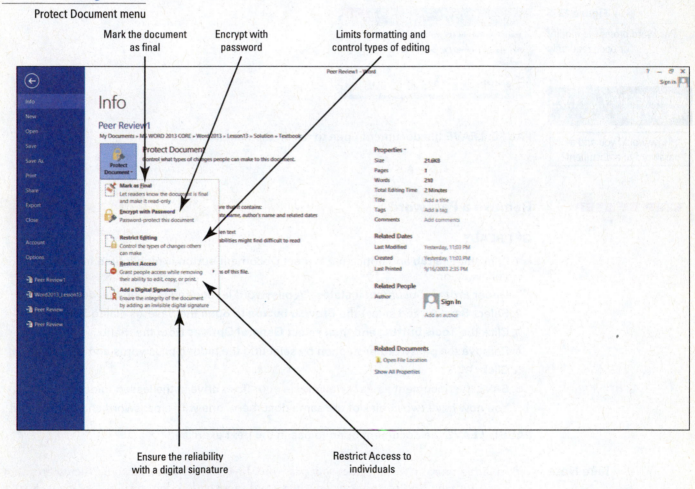

Mark the document as final

Encrypt with password

Limits formatting and control types of editing

Ensure the reliability with a digital signature

Restrict Access to individuals

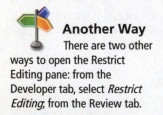

Another Way

There are two other ways to open the Restrict Editing pane: from the Developer tab, select *Restrict Editing*; from the Review tab.

The Restrict Editing pane displays on the right pane on your screen as shown in Figure 13-7. Item one is the *Formatting restrictions*, which is where you determine what type of formatting changes are allowed.

The second item is *Editing restrictions, No changes (Read only)*. You control the limitations on editing.

Figure 13-7

Restrict Editing pane

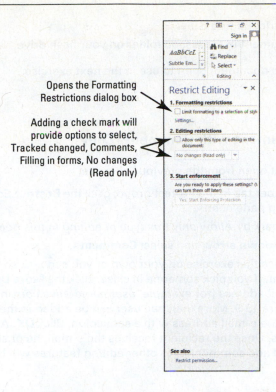

Opens the Formatting
Restrictions dialog box

Adding a check mark will
provide options to select,
Tracked changed, Comments,
Filling in forms, No changes
(Read only)

3. Add a check mark by *Allow only this type of editing in the document.* By default, *No changes (Read only)* is selected as the first option.

4. In the third item, *Start Enforcement,* click **Yes, Start Enforcing Protection**.

   The *Start Enforcing Protection* dialog box opens as shown in Figure 13-8. The *Start Enforcing Protection* turns on the set restriction to begin restricting the document as a Read only type of document. The first option shows that by adding a password, the document will not be encrypted. *User authentication* adds an encryption to the document with the restricted access enabled preventing sensitive documents from being printed, forwarded, or copied. Before you can use *User authentication*, your computer must be set up for the Information Rights Management (IRM).

Figure 13-8

Start Enforcing Protection
dialog box

5. Type **BYA$%HRDept** in the *Enter new password* box and *Reenter password to confirm* box, and then click **OK**.

   The document is now protected from any editing, and only you may view this region. A <mark>region</mark> is the location in the document that you are allowed to edit. The Restrict Editing pane displays two available options: *Find Next Region I Can Edit* and *Show All Regions I Can Edit*. This displays the areas in your document that you have been granted permission to edit. Click the first button and notice that Word states that it has finished searching the document—there were no regions highlighted. Click the second button and no regions are highlighted. This is a read only document, so no editing is allowed.

6. Click the **Stop Protection button** at the bottom of the pane.

7. To unprotect the document, in the *Unprotect Document* dialog box, enter the password **BYA$%HRDept** and click **OK**.

8. Click **Allow only this type of editing** in the document box to remove the check mark.

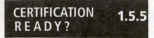

CERTIFICATION READY?   1.5.5

How would you protect a document with a password?

9. Close the Restrict Editing pane.

10. **SAVE** the document in the lesson folder on your flash drive.

PAUSE. LEAVE the document open to use in the next exercise.

STEP BY STEP   **Restrict a Document with Comments Only**

USE the document open from the previous exercise.

1. On the Developer tab in the Protect group, click the **Restrict Editing button**. The Restrict Editing pane opens.

2. Add a check mark by *Allow only this type of editing in this document*.

3. Click the **drop-down arrow** and select **Comments**.

   You can practice this exercise on your own or you can pick someone in class to edit your document. If you pick someone in class, click the **More Users...** link and enter the person's e-mail address (for example, *user name@live.com* in the *Add Users* dialog box). See Figure 13-9. More than one user can be added in the dialog box as long as you separate the e-mail address with a semicolon. Click **OK**. Add a check mark by the e-mail address. Once the recipient receives the e-mail, he or she will be able to edit the document and add comments. No other editing features will be enabled.

Figure 13-9

Add Users dialog box

Add users in email separate each user with a semicolon

4. In the *Start Enforcement* section, click the **Yes, Start Enforcing Protection button**. The *Start Enforcing Protection* dialog box opens, which turns on the set restriction for comments only.

5. Type **BYA$%HRDept** in the *Enter new password (optional)* box and in the *Reenter password to confirm* box, and click **OK**.

   Only comments can be added to the region. As mentioned previously, a region is the area in the document where you are allowed to make changes.

6. Click **Show All Regions I Can Edit**; the insertion point moves to the heading. Then select **Jill A. Williams**, insert a comment, and type **Jill's middle initial is E**. The comment appears alongside of the document.

7. Click the **Stop Protection button** at the bottom of the Restrict Editing pane.

   The *Unprotect Document* dialog box is displayed.

8. Type **BYA$%HRDept** and click **OK**.

CERTIFICATION READY?   1.5.5

How would you protect a document with a password?

9. Click the **Allow only this type of editing in the document** box to remove the check mark.

10. **SAVE** the document as *Peer Review2* in the lesson folder on your flash drive.

PAUSE. LEAVE the document open to use in the next exercise.

 Cross Ref   In Lesson 9, you learn about inserting, editing, and deleting comments.

STEP BY STEP   **Limit Formatting Styles in a Document**

USE the document open from the previous exercise.

1. In the *Formatting restrictions* section, click the **Limit formatting to a selection of styles check box**.

   Selecting this option enables you to set formatting restrictions for this document.

2. Click the **Settings** link.

The *Formatting restrictions* dialog box opens, as shown in Figure 13-10. The check mark indicates that styles are allowed.

Figure 13-10

Formatting Restrictions dialog box

By default, formatting is limited to selection of styles

All turns on all check marks

To allow or block, click to add check mark

Selecting None will turn off all check marks

Recommended Minimum will disable some styles

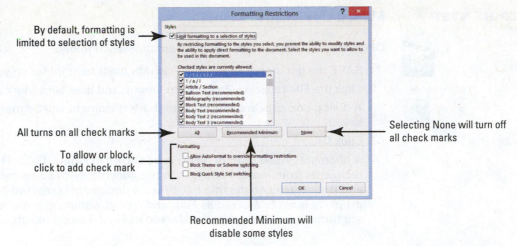

3. Under the Formatting section, click the **Block Theme or Scheme switching check box** and then click **OK**.

Selecting this option blocks the user from making any changes to the structure, pattern, or theme of the document.

A prompt appears on your screen stating that *This document may contain formatting or styles that aren't allowed. Do you want to remove them?*

4. Click **Yes**.

On the Design tab, in the Document Formatting group, notice that *Themes* is shaded gray making it unavailable.

5. In the Restrict Editing pane, click **Settings** again to open the *Formatting Restrictions* dialog box.

6. Remove the check mark by **Block Theme or Scheme switching**.

7. Click **OK**.

8. Click **Yes** to the prompt to remove.

Notice the Themes group is now available. You can now use the Themes commands in the group.

9. In the *Formatting restrictions* section of the Restrict Editing pane, click the **Limit formatting to a selection of styles** check box to remove the check mark.

10. Close the Restrict Editing pane.

11. **SAVE** the document with the filename *Peer Review3* in the lesson folder on your flash drive.

12. In the Document Formatting group, of the Design tab, change the Style Set to **Lines (Simple)**.

The headings, *Employee Information, Review Guidelines,* and *Evaluation* are not displaying correctly in the table.

13. Change the cell height to **0.3"** to accommodate the content in those cells.

14. Change the font color to the heading and select **White, Background 1** and **bold**.

15. Keep the document open for ten minutes.

Later in this lesson, you learn about managing versions.

16. Minimize the document to place it on the taskbar. You will use this document later in this lesson.

PAUSE. LEAVE the program open for the next exercise.

Take Note Restricting comments can be made to the whole document or you can select portions of the document where editing changes are allowed.

Mark a Document as Final

OPEN the *Review Form* document from the lesson folder.

1. **SAVE** the document as *Review Form1* in the lesson folder on your flash drive.
2. Click the **File tab**, click **Protect Document**, and then click **Mark as Final**.

    A dialog box appears indicating that this document will be marked as final and then saved.

3. Click **OK**.

    A Microsoft Word prompt displays as shown in Figure 13-11. The mark as final prevents recipients from making changes to the document—the document becomes read only and is displayed on the title bar. When a document is marked as final, the status property is set to *Marked as Final* and typing, editing commands, and proofing marks are turned off. Notice that the Marked as Final icon on the status bar.

Figure 13-11

Microsoft Word Marked as Final

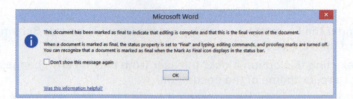

4. Click **OK**.

    The document is *Marked as Final* and displays in the *Protect Document* section highlighted in a light yellow color to discourage editing.

5. Return to the document and notice the yellow bar below the Ribbon indicating that *An author has marked this document as final to discourage editing.*

    If you need to edit the document, click the **Edit Anyway button**.

6. Click any of the tabs on the Ribbon and notice these are shaded in gray indicating the commands are not available.

7. Continue to click the other tabs to view how the commands are not activated.

8. Select the title of the document and try to delete it.

    When a document is marked as final, typing, editing commands, and proofing marks are disabled, because the document becomes a read-only document.

    Notice the title bar also shows the document as a (Read-Only) document.

Another Way
On the document screen, click *Edit Anyway* to return document to its original status.

9. On the File tab, click the **Protect Document button**, select **Mark as Final** to return the document to its original status, and then return to the document.

10. Select the **B** in *Blue Yonder Airlines* and press the **Delete key**. You can now make changes to the document.

11. Click the **Undo button** on the Quick Access Toolbar.

12. **SAVE** the document with the same filename in the lesson folder on your flash drive.

PAUSE. LEAVE the document open to use in the next exercise.

Take Note Documents that have been marked as final in a 2013 Microsoft Office program will not be read only if they are opened in earlier versions of Microsoft Office programs. It is important to recognize that the Mark as Final command is not a security feature—anyone who receives an electronic copy of a document that has been marked as final can edit that document by removing the Mark as Final status from the document.

Applying Protection Using the Ribbon

==Encryption== protects a document so that it cannot be opened without a password.

STEP BY STEP	**Encrypt a Document**

USE the document open from the previous exercise.

1. Go to **Backstage**, click the **Protect Document button**, and then select **Encrypt with Password**.

   The *Encrypt Document* dialog box opens as shown in Figure 13-12.

   Encrypting protects the document by making it unreadable because it encrypts the information into a code.

2. In the *Encrypt the contents of this file* box, type **HRDept&%3**.

3. Retype the password and click **OK**.

   Notice that *Protect Document* is highlighted and indicates that a password is required to open this document.

4. **CLOSE** the document.

5. Click **Save** when prompted with *Do you want to save the changes you made to Review Form1?*

6. Reopen the document and type **HRDept&%3** to open the document.

Take Note To unprotect the document, you must already be inside the document (with the correct password). From within the document, select the *Backstage* tab, click the *Protect Document* button, select *Encrypt with Password*, delete the password from the dialog box, and select *Save*.

   Do not delete the password at this time.

7. **SAVE** the document as *Review Form2* in the lesson folder on your flash drive, and then **CLOSE** the file.

PAUSE. LEAVE Word open to use in the next exercise.

CERTIFICATION READY? 1.5.5

How would you protect a document with a password?

Opening Documents in Protected View

Protecting your document from an unsafe location is necessary to avoid viruses, worms, or other kinds of malware that might harm your computer. Documents received by e-mail as attachments can harm your computer; therefore, it is important to know whether the source is reliable. Files that open in Protected View can be opened from the Internet or you might have received it in your Outlook 2013 e-mail as an attachment, the sender of the e-mail was marked as unsafe, the document was opened from the Temporary Internet Files on your computer, your Information Technology Department might have blocked certain file types, or the Office program might have detected a problem with the file—Microsoft might have not identified it as a trusted publisher or site location. In this exercise, you open a document in protected view and enable editing.

STEP BY STEP   **Open a Document in Protected View**

GET READY. OPEN Word if it is not already running.

1. **OPEN** the *Proposal* document from the lesson folder.

   The document opens in Protected View. The yellow prompt states *This file originated from an Internet location and might be unsafe* as shown in Figure 13-13.

Take Note   This document opens in Protected View on the author's machine because Word is able to detect that she downloaded the file from an FTP site and saved it on her machine. However, if someone else receives the file from a trusted source (such as from a CD or a secure e-mail), Word is able to detect this and open the file in normal view. Therefore, when you open this file, depending upon how you received the file, Word might actually not open it in Protected View. Unfortunately, we cannot create a file that will always open in Protected View.

Figure 13-13

Document in Protected View

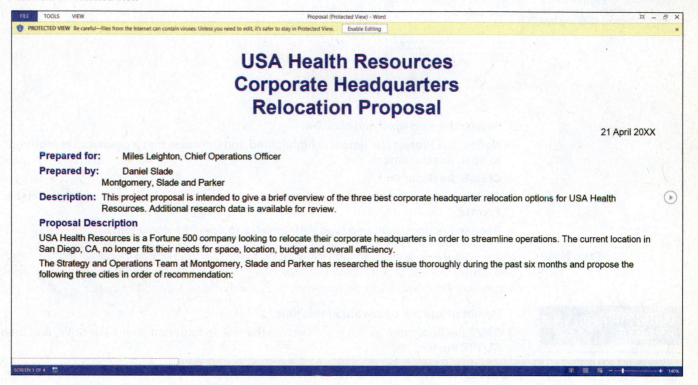

2. Click the **File tab**.

   Notice that the Enable Editing button is highlighted in a light yellow color informing you that *This file originated from an Internet location and might be unsafe* as shown in Figure 13-14.

Figure 13-14

Protected View in Backstage

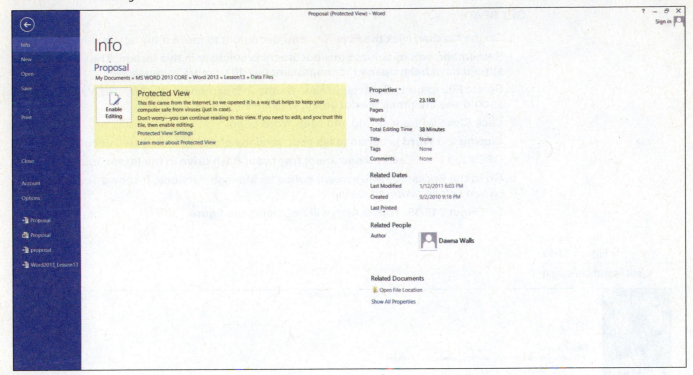

Another Way

Click the *Protected View* button in Backstage.

3. When you are ready to edit the document, click the **Enable Editing button** on the yellow prompt.
4. **CLOSE** the document without saving.

PAUSE. LEAVE Word open for the next exercise.

MANAGING DOCUMENT VERSIONS

The Bottom Line

Retrieving a document by versions or recovering an unsaved file has been made easier by Microsoft. Have you accidently deleted your whole document or turned off your computer before saving? Word can help you retrieve your document by using the manage versions. Document versions can be managed in Backstage using the Info command and selecting which version to save. Word provides an option to Recover Unsaved Document by saving every ten minutes by default. You will be able to recover versions of your document as long as you haven't closed your document or program. Also, if the Word program stops working for some reason, then you will be able to recover your document; but you will not see your previous versions until the document is saved. Under Manage Versions, you can also browse for unsaved files. In this exercise, you manage a document's version with an existing file and a new file, and recover an unsaved version.

Managing Document Versions

The AutoRecovery command allows you flexibility in saving your Word documents, including making more frequent backups. In this exercise, you will learn how to change the default Save settings from 10 minutes to 3 minutes.

Manage Document Versions

GET READY.

1. On the taskbar, click the *Peer Review3* document to make it the active document.

   Remember, you minimized this document previously in this lesson. The document should have been opened for approximately 10 or more minutes.

2. Select **File** to go to Backstage view. On the *Info* screen, under *Manage Versions*, you should see the times the document was saved.

3. Click **Close** without saving and keep Word open.

   Closing the Word program loses your versions of the *Peer Review3* document.

4. **OPEN** the *Peer Review3* document from your flash drive in the lesson folder.

5. Go to the Backstage *Info* screen; notice by Manage Versions, it shows *Today, time (when I closed without saving)*.

   See Figure 13-15. Your screen will not match the figure.

Figure 13-15

Versions without saving

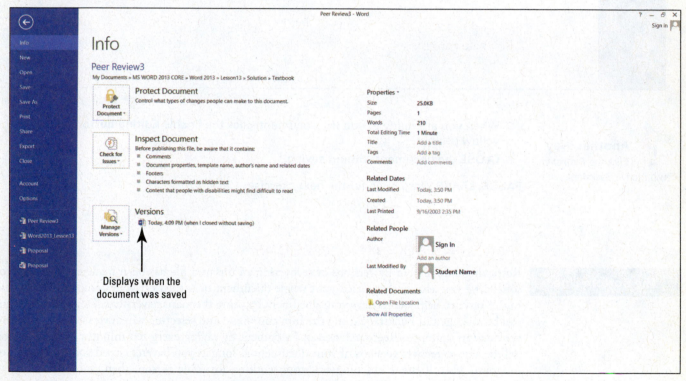

6. In the Backstage view, select **Options** to open the *Word Options* dialog box.

7. From the list in the left pane, select **Save**.

   By default, the *Save AutoRecover* information is set every *10* minutes. Also *Keep the last autosaved version if I close without saving* is enabled. In step 3, you closed the document without saving and when you reopened and reviewed the *Managed Versions*, it showed when the document was last saved in Autosave.

   The default time for *Save AutoRecover* can be changed in the *Word Options* Dialog box.

8. Under the *Save documents* section, select the default **10** and type **3** minutes or click the down arrow by *Save AutoRecover information* as shown in Figure 13-16.

Figure 13-16

Word Options Save screen

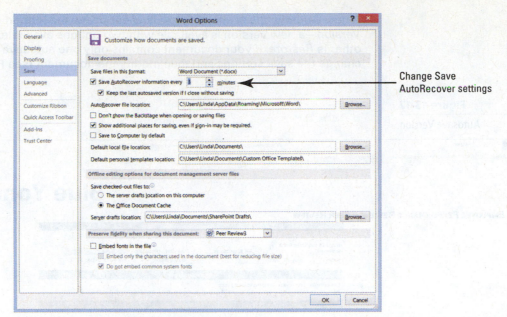

Change Save
AutoRecover settings

9. Click **OK**.

10. Create a new blank document and type **Working with unsaved documents can be found in Backstage in the Info screen**.

Keep this document open, until you are instructed to work on the next step.

11. On the View tab, click **Switch Windows** and select the *Peer Review3* document.

12. Return to Backstage and under *Versions,* you should see at least one or two versions of the document saved.

13. **SAVE** the document in the lesson folder on your flash drive.

PAUSE. LEAVE the document open for the next exercise.

Take Note   Clicking the down arrow key in Manage Versions allows you to Recover Unsaved Documents; the Open dialog box opens files specifically from the location where unsaved files are saved.

Restoring an Earlier Version of Your Document

The Save AutoRecover saves documents automatically by time and displays as *Today (current date)*. In the previous exercise, you changed the Save setting from the default of 10 minutes to 3 minutes. As you modify your document, AutoRecover autosaves changes. The updates are saved to different versions and can be located in Backstage under Manage Versions. In this exercise, you restore an earlier version of your document.

STEP BY STEP   **Restore an Earlier Version of Your Document**

USE the document open from the previous exercise.

1. Select the **Blue Yonder Airlines heading**.

2. Change the font color to **Dark Blue**, **Text 2**.

3. Increase the font size to **28** pt.

4. Where *Jill A. Williams'* name appears, replace *A.* with **E.**

5. Change the review period from *Dec 20XX* to **April 20XX**.

You need to modify the document in order for Autosave to save the updated changes.

6. Go to Backstage and under *Versions*, click the version where it indicates *(autosave)*.

A new window opens showing a yellow bar below the Ribbon displaying, *Autosave Version*—a new version is available with two options available. One is *Compare* and the other is *Restore*. If your document contains only one autosave version, make sure you change the save settings and then modify the document (see Figure 13-17).

Figure 13-17

Autosave Version

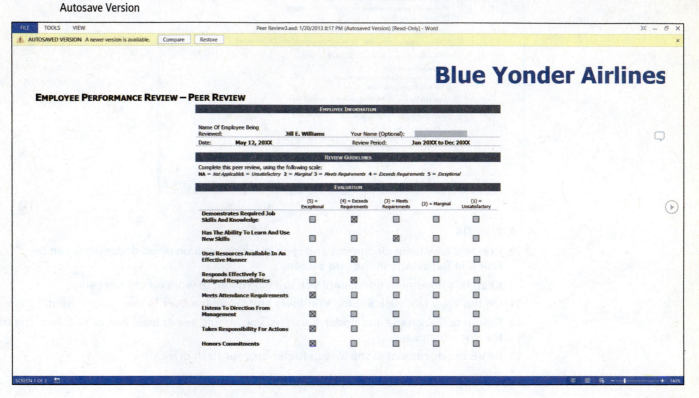

When you click on *Compare,* a summary that compares the original document and the revised document displays on one screen. The *Restore* button prompts you to overwrite your previous document.

7. Click **Restore** to overwrite your previous document.

   Compare versions is one of Word's advanced features; for more information, use Help.

8. You will be prompted to overwrite the last saved version with the selected version. Click **OK**.

9. **CLOSE** the document.

PAUSE. LEAVE Word open for the next exercise.

Recovering Unsaved Documents

Overall, as you continue working on documents, you can browse or recover unsaved files through Manage Versions in Backstage. You can also open a document based on the time or the last version within that session. In this exercise, you recover an unsaved document.

STEP BY STEP   **Recover Unsaved Documents**

Previously you typed, *Working with unsaved documents can be found in Backstage in the Info screen.* And in a previous step, you changed the *Save AutoRecover information* from the default to three minutes.

GET READY.

1. **CLOSE** the document that you typed.

   A prompt appears on your screen to save changes. The prompt states, *If you click "Don't Save," a recent copy of this file will be temporarily available.* It also indicates that a temporary file will be saved. If you do not see this, review the information in the Troubleshooting sidebar next.

2. Click **Don't Save**.

Troubleshooting   If a prompt did not appear on your screen to save your document, you can change the Auto-Recovery preferences from the default. The default for AutoRecovery is to save every ten minutes; it can be found in Backstage, Options command, in the Save settings category. For instructional purposes, you might need to change the settings to three or five minutes. Close the document without saving, and the prompt will indicate that the file will be temporarily saved.

3. Click the **File tab**, and then click **Open**.

4. On the bottom right side of the screen, click **Recover Unsaved Documents** as shown in Figure 13-18.

   Your screen will not match this figure.

Figure 13-18

Recovering Unsaved Document

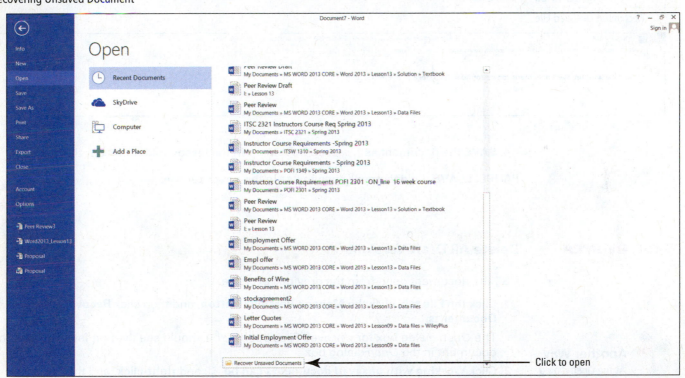

5. On the *Open* dialog box, locate your file based on the date and time you closed the document or program or locate *Working with unsaved documents can be...* (see Figure 13-19).

   The document was closed without saving it with a filename; therefore, the name will show the first part of the text that you typed. Unsaved documents are in a temporary location on your hard drive and identified by the .ASD file extension.

Figure 13-19

Open dialog box for unsaved files

Location of unsaved files

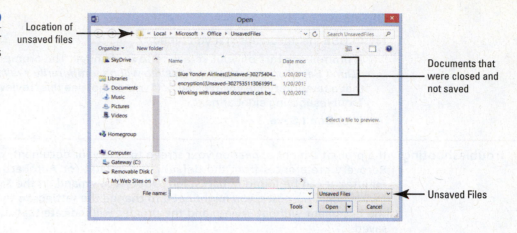

Documents that were closed and not saved

Unsaved Files

6. Select the unsaved document and click **Open**.

   The document opens with the *Recovered Unsaved File* yellow prompt appearing above the document stating, *This is a recovered file that is temporarily stored on your computer.*

7. Click **Save As** (see Figure 13-20).

Figure 13-20

Recovered Unsaved File

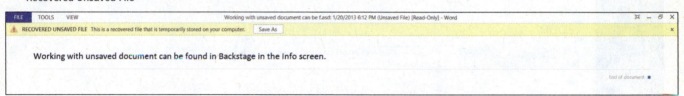

8. **SAVE** the document as *Unsaved Document* in the lesson folder on your flash drive.

   PAUSE. LEAVE the document open to use in the next exercise.

STEP BY STEP   **Delete All Draft Versions**

USE the document open from the previous exercise.

1. Click the **File tab**, click the **Manage Versions button**, and then click **Recover Unsaved Documents**.

   The *Open* dialog box for Unsaved Files opens. You should see the first few words of the document in the *Open* dialog box.

Another Way

At the Open dialog box for Unsaved Files, click the *Organize* button and then click *Delete*. At the prompt, *Are you sure you want to move this file to the Recycle Bin?*, click *Yes*.

2. Click **Working with unsaved documents can be . . .** and **right-click**, and then select **Delete**.

3. Click **Yes** to the prompt, *Are you sure you want to move this file to the Recycle Bin?*

4. Select **Cancel** to close the *Open* dialog box.

5. **CLOSE** the *Unsaved Document*.

   PAUSE. LEAVE Word open to use in the next exercise.

Take Note   Unsaved Documents are found in a specific location on your hard drive. A file extension of ASD has been assigned to unsaved documents. The files located in Recovering Unsaved Files are temporary files until saved.

SHARING DOCUMENTS

The Bottom Line

Many of the documents created in a business environment will need to be shared with others. Before you share a document, it is important to ensure the document has a professional appearance. Microsoft Word 2013 has three tools to help you with this: Document Inspector, Accessibility Checker, and Compatibility Checker. In addition, Microsoft Word 2013 makes it easy for you to share your documents with colleagues, clients, and others using several formats, including e-mail attachments, PDF documents, social networking sites, and blog posts.

Using the Document Inspector

Word contains a feature that removes unwanted information from your document. This unwanted information can be in the document properties. The Document Inspector is used to find and remove hidden data and personal information in Word 2013 documents as well as earlier versions. It is a good idea to practice inspecting the document before sharing an electronic copy such as an e-mail attachment. In this exercise, you inspect the document and remove personal information.

STEP BY STEP **Use the Document Inspector**

GET READY. OPEN Word if it is not already running.

1. **OPEN** the *Employment Offer Letter* document from your lesson folder.

   Notice that the document opened in Compatibility Mode? Keep this in mind for later.

2. Open **Backstage**, click the **Check for Issues button**, then click **Inspect Document**.

   The *Document Inspector* dialog box appears.

   This command checks for hidden properties and personal information.

3. Click the **Inspect button** (see Figure 13-21).

   Word inspects the document and displays the results in the Document Inspector window. Three warnings appear in the Document Inspector.

Figure 13-21

Document Inspector dialog box

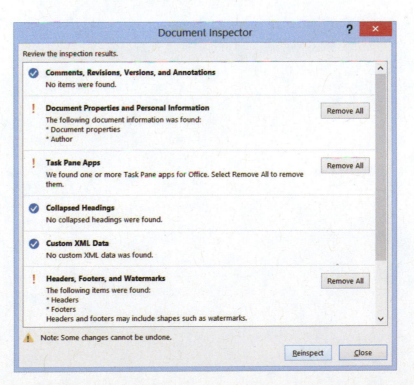

4. In the *Document Properties and Personal Information* section, click **Remove All**.

   Personal information from the properties is removed and the document is ready to be shared. The dialog box is updated.

5. Make no changes to *Task Pane Apps* and *Headers, Footers, and Watermarks*.

6. Click **Close**.

7. In the *Inspect Document* section, click the **Allow this information to be saved in your file link**.

8. **SAVE** the document as ***Employment Offer Letter1*** in the lesson folder on your flash drive. You are prompted by Microsoft Word stating *"Your document will be upgraded to the newest file format."* Click **OK**.

PAUSE. LEAVE the document open to use in the next exercise.

Checking Accessibility

The Accessibility Checker determines whether there are potential errors in your document and alerts you that the content might be difficult for an individual with a disability to read. Accessibility is defined as being accessible to those with disabilities. Before sharing your document, it is important to inspect your document in case someone with a disability opens the document. In this exercise, you learn to check whether there are errors in your document.

STEP BY STEP	Use the Accessibility Checker

USE the document that is open from the previous exercise.

1. Open **Backstage**, click the **Check for Issues button**, and then click **Check Accessibility**.

   The Accessibility Checker pane appears on the right pane, as shown in Figure 13-22. If there are errors in your document, the *Accessibility Check* shows issues, warnings, or tips. In this case, a warning appears displaying *Objects Not Inline*.

Figure 13-22

Accessibility Checker pane

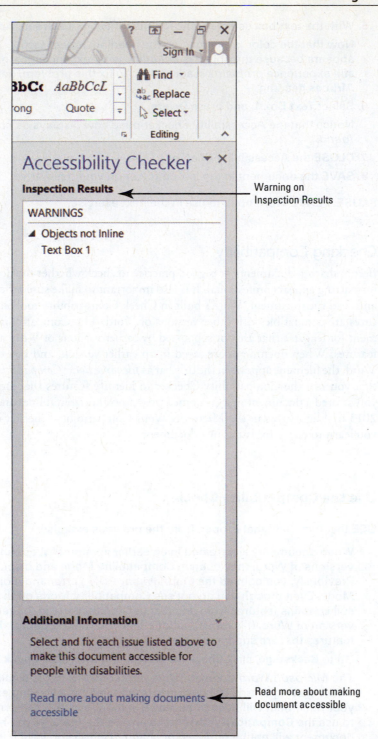

Warning on Inspection Results

Read more about making document accessible

2. Return to Backstage and below *Inspect Document* indicates that *Content that people with disabilities find difficult to read*.

   Word flags the document letting you know that there are potential problems in the document that not everyone will be able to read.

3. Return to the document.

4. In the Accessibility Checker pane, click **Text Box 1** to select.

   Notice that a text box appears in your document screen with *Blue Yonder Airlines* appearing very light in the background. Individuals with a disability would find this difficult to read.

5. With the text box selected, change the font color to **Green**, **Accent 1**, **Darker 50%**.

   Now that the color is changed on the heading, repeat step 2. The same warning appears because the object is *not inline with text* and a person with a disability might still experience problems reading this. To fix this problem, delete the **Blue Yonder Airlines** heading.

6. Select **Text Box 1**, and press **Delete**.

   Notice that the Accessibility Checker pane now displays as *no accessibility issues found*.

7. **CLOSE** the Accessibility Checker.

8. **SAVE** the document in the lesson folder on your flash drive.

PAUSE. LEAVE Word open to use in the next exercise.

Checking Compatibility

Before sharing documents, it is good practice to check whether the document is error free and the formatting appears professional. It is also important to make sure other people will be able to open and read the document. Word's built-in Check Compatibility tool ensures that a document's features are compatible with other versions of Word. The Compatibility Checker searches a document for features that are not supported by earlier versions of Word and lists a summary of these features. When documents are saved in an earlier version, and you open in the latest version of Word, the filename appears in the title bar as *filename.docx (Compatibility Mode)*. It is recommended that you run the Compatibility Checker to identify features that are supported. For example, if you created a document that contained predefined horizontal lines and saved it Word 2007, Word 2013 highlights this in the Microsoft Word Compatibility Checker dialog box. In this exercise, you learn to check for issues in a document.

| STEP BY STEP | Use the Compatibility Checker |

USE the document that is open from the previous exercise.

When documents are created in an earlier version of Word and opened in newer versions of Word, they open in Compatibility Mode and display in the title bar. Previously, you opened the ***Employment Offer Letter*** and it opened in Compatibility Mode. Even though you do not see Compatibility Mode on the title bar, this document still contains features from an older version that are no longer supported by the latest version of Word. It is recommended that you run the **Compatibility Checker** to identify features that are supported in older versions.

1. Go to **Backstage**, click **Check for Issues**, and then click **Check Compatibility**.

   The *Microsoft Word Compatibility Checker* dialog box is displayed as in Figure 13-23. When sharing Word 2013 documents with individuals using earlier versions of Word, your document will need to be saved in the Word 97-2003 format. It is good practice to use the **Compatibility Checker** to ensure the features you have included in your document will not be removed or changed when you save it in the Word 97-2003 format.

   The Compatibility Checker displays the message, *The following features in this document are not supported by earlier versions of Word. These features may be lost or degraded when opening this document in an earlier version of Word or if you save this document in an earlier file format.*

Figure 13-23

Compatibility Checker
dialog box

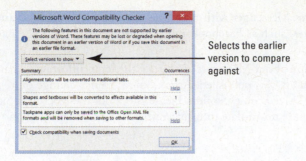

Selects the earlier
version to compare
against

2. Click **OK**.

3. **SAVE** the document as *Employment Offer 20XX* (replace *XX* with the current year) and make sure the file type displays as *Word Document*.

PAUSE. LEAVE the document open to use in the next exercise.

Sending Documents

Electronic documents are sent via e-mail, web, and Internet fax. In Backstage, you can save the document in a PDF and XPS format, or attach it to e-mail. You can also change and create a document in different file formats. In this exercise, you send a document by e-mail and SkyDrive, discuss how installation of drivers is used for the Internet fax, send PDF/XPS documents, discuss posting to social networks, use the online presentation, and register and publish a blog.

STEP BY STEP **Send Documents via Email Using Outlook**

USE the document open from the previous exercise.

Take Note For this exercise, you must use Microsoft Outlook 2013. If you are unsure, check with your instructor to determine whether you have access to Microsoft Outlook 2013 on your computer.

1. Open **Backstage**, and click **Share** to display the options on how the document will be shared with others.

2. Click **Email** and the right pane displays various options on how you can send the document.

   The document can be e-mailed as an attachment, you can send it as a PDF or XPS file, or as an Internet fax. You also have a *new* option to send the document as a link, but it must be saved in a shared location first.

3. Select the first option to **Send as Attachment**.

   The open document is automatically attached to the e-mail message and is ready to be sent.

4. Type the [**email address**] of a friend, classmate, or coworker in the *To* box and type a short message, and then click the **Send button**.

PAUSE. LEAVE the document open to use in the next exercise.

Windows Live SkyDrive is an online service provided by Microsoft. **SkyDrive** is an online file storage location where you can store documents and pictures. At the time of this publication, Microsoft provides SkyDrive members with 7 GB of free online storage space for personal use. SkyDrive is password protected—so you control who has access to your files. You can access your files on SkyDrive anywhere and anytime from your computer, tablet, or smartphone.

SkyDrive stores any document, but it is best for sharing documents in Word, Excel, PowerPoint, and OneNote. Also, you can create a personal album to share pictures with your contacts or on your social networking site; create and send e-mails; manage your contacts; add events to your calendar; access Messenger with real-time chat; and stay updated and connected to your social networking sites, such as Facebook and LinkedIn.

Take Note   The information about Microsoft SkyDrive, the login information, and images are all current at the time this book was published. As you know, things change quite frequently on the web, and Microsoft SkyDrive is no exception. Please check out the Microsoft SkyDrive website or use Bing to search for more up-to-date information.

STEP BY STEP   **Send Documents via SkyDrive**

USE the document open from the previous exercise.

1. For this exercise, you need a Microsoft account. If you have a SkyDrive, Outlook, Hotmail, Xbox Live account, or other Microsoft service account, then you already have a Microsoft account and can skip steps 2 and 3.

2. If you need a Microsoft account, launch the **Internet Explorer** browser and complete the steps as listed in the website. At the address bar, enter the **https://signup.live.com/** site (see Figure 13-24).

Figure 13-24

Microsoft Signup account

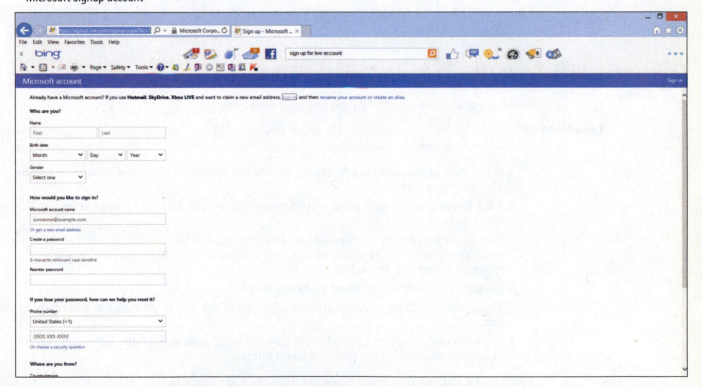

3. Follow the prompts on your screen to complete the registration for a Microsoft account. Once you complete the process, close Internet Explorer. You will sign in to your account in the *Account* screen in Word.

4. Go to **Backstage**, and then click **Account**.

5. Under *Sign in to Office*, click the **Sign In button**.

6. Click **Microsoft Account** and in the next screen enter your e-mail account and password you just set up for this account.

7. Once you are connected, the *Account* screen changes and your personal profile appears. You will be able to upload, create, edit, and share documents (see Figure 13-25).

Figure 13-25

Account screen

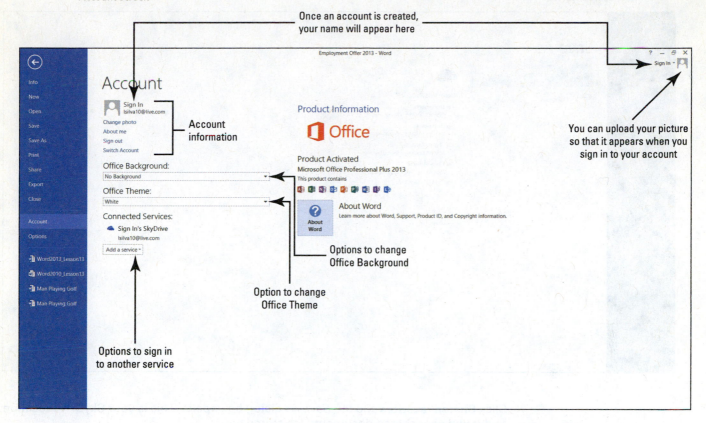

Once an account is created, your name will appear here

Account information

You can upload your picture so that it appears when you sign in to your account

Options to change Office Background

Option to change Office Theme

Options to sign in to another service

8. Select the **drop-down arrow** by *Office Background* and scroll through each option. Look at the upper-right corner as the screen background changes.

9. Select any option.

10. Select the **drop-down arrow** by *Office Themes* and select the **Dark Gray** and watch how the background color darkens.

   Under *Add a service*, you have additional options to add Images & Videos and videos from your favorite sites. Click **YouTube** and watch how YouTube is automatically added.

11. Click **Remove** to remove, and then click **Yes**. It's that easy to add and remove a service. The second option allows you to store documents to *Office 365 SharePoint* or *SkyDrive*. The third option allows you to connect Microsoft Word to *Facebook, LinkedIn,* or *Twitter*.

   Now that you have signed in, you're ready to share your document via SkyDrive.

12. Click **Share** on the left pane, then under *Invite People*, click **Save to Cloud**. When the screen changes to the *Save As* screen, select your SkyDrive.

   On the right side of the screen, the SkyDrive's folders appear. (Note that your screen will not match Figure 13-26.)

Figure 13-26

Microsoft SkyDrive

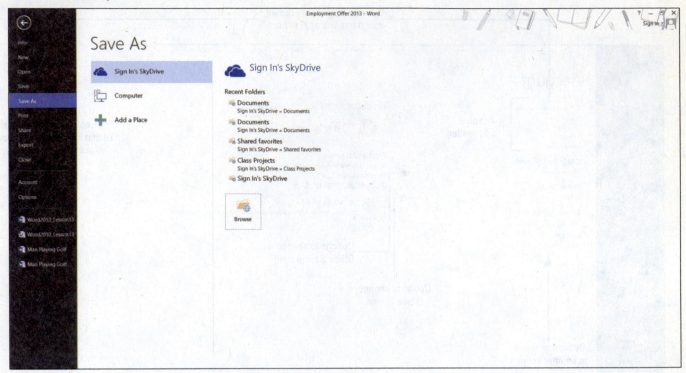

13. Click **Shared favorites** and the *Save As* dialog box opens. This is your SkyDrive location folder and your shared documents are stored here.

14. Click **Save**.

    The *Share* screen changes and now you can share the *Employment Offer 20XX* letter with anyone by sending them an invite to edit or view the document (see Figure 13-27).

15. Select someone in class and type his or her **[email address]** along with a short message.

    You can also practice on your own by creating another account for yourself.

Figure 13-27

Share screen Invite People

Opens the Address Book: Global Address List

Option to "Can edit" or "Can view"

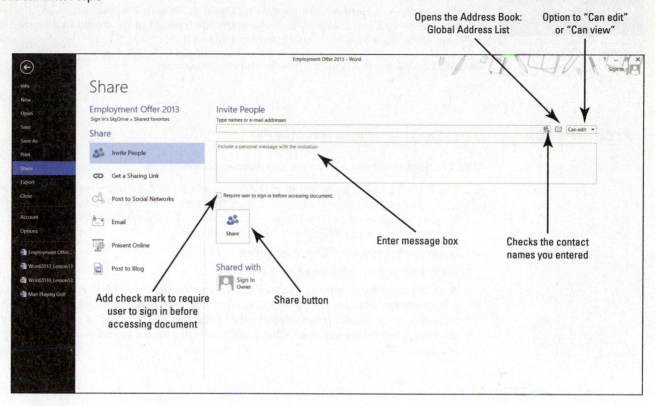

Add check mark to require user to sign in before accessing document

Share button

Enter message box

Checks the contact names you entered

16. Click the **Share button** and an e-mail is automatically sent to him or her.

When he or she opens the e-mail, a link to the document appears. The document opens in the Microsoft Word Web App and should resemble Figure 13-28. The individual receiving the e-mail should be signed in to the Microsoft account before editing the document.

Figure 13-28

Document opens in the Microsoft Web App

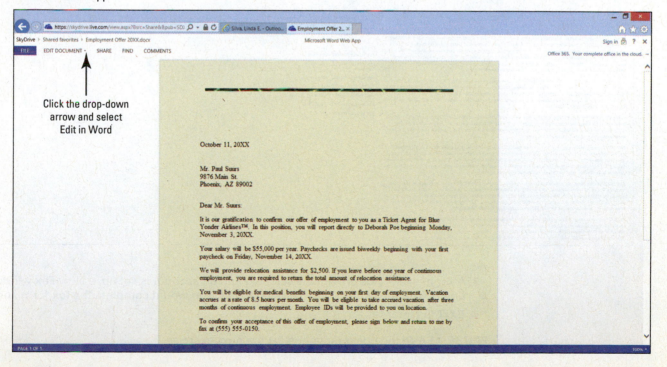

Click the drop-down arrow and select Edit in Word

CERTIFICATION
READY?   1.5.4

How would save files
to SkyDrive?

On the left pane is the *Get a Sharing Link.* This is good for large groups of people or when you don't know an e-mail address, you can create a link for viewing or editing.

Previously, you sent a document using Outlook. In step 2 of that exercise, a reference was made to *Send a Link* by e-mail but the file needed to be stored in a shared location. This is the step you would complete to share a link.

PAUSE. LEAVE the document open for the next exercise.

STEP BY STEP   **Send Documents via Internet Fax**

USE the document open from the previous exercise.

The Internet Fax is an alternative to having a fax machine because you use your computer to send files via the web. By default the Windows Fax feature is disabled and it must be installed before sending documents via Internet fax. A utility is built into Windows to use the Windows Fax and Scan utility.

1. Open **Backstage**, click **Share**, and then click **Email**.
2. On the right side, click **Send as Internet Fax**.

   A prompt appears stating, *To use Fax Services to send your fax, you must sign up with a fax service provider.* If you click **OK**, your web browser opens and you choose a provider. Your screen resembles Figure 13-29. Typically, each fax service provider charges a fee for its services. Check with your instructor to see whether the services are available.

Figure 13-29

Available Fax Services

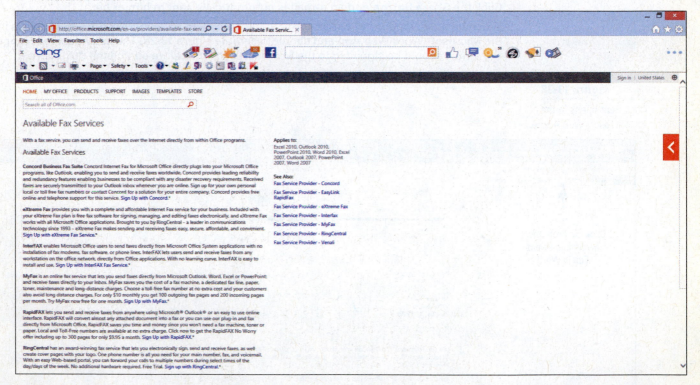

3. After a fax service provider is selected and an account is set up, a New Fax window opens with the current document attached. You would complete the fax form and send.
4. **EXIT** the Internet.

PAUSE. LEAVE the document open for the next exercise.

STEP BY STEP **Send Documents as PDF or XPS**

USE the document open from the previous exercise.

1. Open **Backstage**, click **Share**, and then click **Email**.

2. Under *Email*, click **Send as PDF**. The Word document automatically saves as a PDF file and the e-mail message screen opens. Type an **[email address]** and short message, and then click the **Send button**. The PDF document is shown in the e-mail message as an attachment.

   You can also send the document as an XPS by following the steps and selecting **Send as XPS**.

 Cross Ref In Lesson 1, you learn about file extensions and saving files in different file formats.

PAUSE. LEAVE the document open for the next exercise.

STEP BY STEP **Post to Social Networks**

USE the document open from the previous exercise.

   You should already be signed in to your Microsoft account.

1. In the *Account* screen, select **add a service** and select **Facebook**.

2. When you click **Connect**, the Facebook login screen opens.

   Once you are connected, you are ready to share documents and photos. There will be additional steps to follow to upload your documents and photos to your Facebook profile.

PAUSE. LEAVE the document open for the next exercise.

STEP BY STEP **Present Online**

USE the document open from the previous exercise.

   Sharing a Word document by using the Present Online feature is easy because there is no setup. The Present Online feature allows you to create a link to your document and present to others even if they do not have Word installed on their computer. The link that you create will open in a browser. In this exercise, a link will be created to share with others to view your document in a web browser.

   To use this feature, you must have a Microsoft account to start the online presentation.

1. In Backstage, select the **Share** group.

2. Clicking the **Present Online button** means you agree to the terms. Read the *Service Agreement*.

3. Add a check mark by **Enable remote viewers to download the document**.

4. After agreeing to the agreement, click **Present Online** to begin connecting to *Office Presentation Services* (see Figure 13-30.)

   You have two options available on how to present. You can select *Copy Link* or *Send in Email*—send an invitation that links to your presentation.

Figure 13-30

Present Online

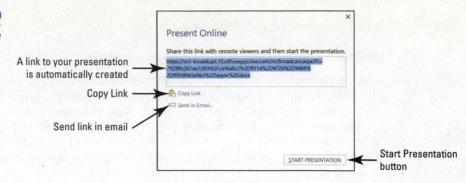

A link to your presentation
is automatically created

Copy Link

Send link in email

Start Presentation
button

5. Click **Start Presentation**. Your screen should match Figure 13-31.

You can send invitations and invite others to view your presentation and if you need to edit the document, you can do so in the same screen.

Figure 13-31

Present Online screen

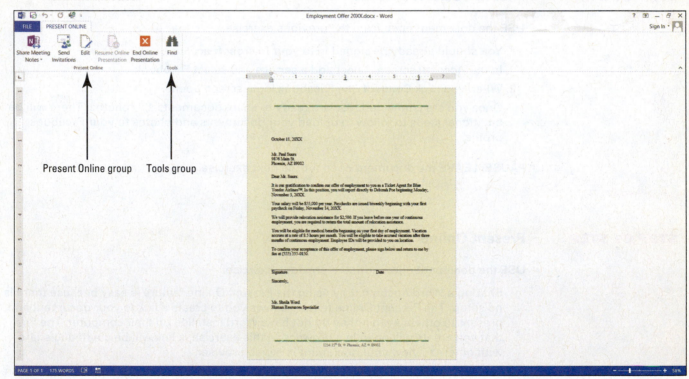

Present Online group   Tools group

6. Click **End Online Presentation**. A warning prompt appears and states, *All people will be disconnected if you continue. Do you want to end this online presentation?*

7. Click **End Online Presentation**.

8. **CLOSE** the file. When you close the file, you will be prompted to save, and then the file will be saved to your SkyDrive account.

PAUSE. LEAVE the document open for the next exercise.

CERTIFICATION
READY?   1.5.4

How would save to a
remote location for viewing
or editing?

Registering and Publishing a Blog Post

A **blog** is an online interactive location where anyone can leave comments. Blogs are maintained by companies, instructors, and individuals who post information, events, news, and more. Word provides a feature where you can register your blog's URL, add a post, and publish it. You can use an existing document and post to a blog or use a template. Before you can post a blog, you must register for a blog account.

<table>
<tr><td>**STEP BY STEP**</td><td>**Register and Publish a Blog Post**</td></tr>
</table>

OPEN a blank document screen.

You can publish a Word document as a blog post, use a blog template, or create a new blog. Before you can publish, you need to register for your own blog space. You will use WordPress as your blog service provider. Create your own space at *wordpress.com.* The service is free. Follow the instructions on its home page and use your live account for your e-mail address. You identify a blog address, your user name and a strong password.

1. In Backstage, click **Share**, and then click **Post to Blog**. Because this is your first blog, you have to go through the registration process (see Figure 13-32).

Figure 13-32

Post to Blog screen

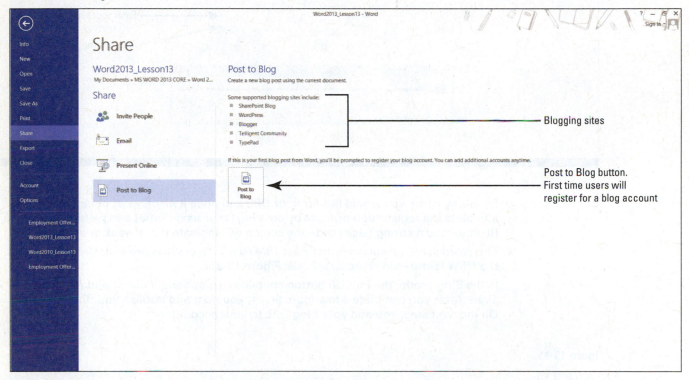

2. Click the **Post to Blog button**. The *Register a Blog Account* dialog box opens as shown in Figure 13-33.

Figure 13-33

Register a Blog Account dialog box

3. Click the **Register Now button**, click the **drop-down arrow**, select **WordPress**, and then click the **Next button**.

At the time this book was published, WordPress services were free.

4. In the New Press Account, enter a Blog Post URL. For example, *http://wordwise2013. wordpress.com/xmlrpc.php* is shown in Figure 13-34 along with the confirmation that the account registration is successful (the user name and password is hidden). Avoid entering this URL because the domain name is already taken.

Figure 13-34

New WordPress Account
and Account registration
successful

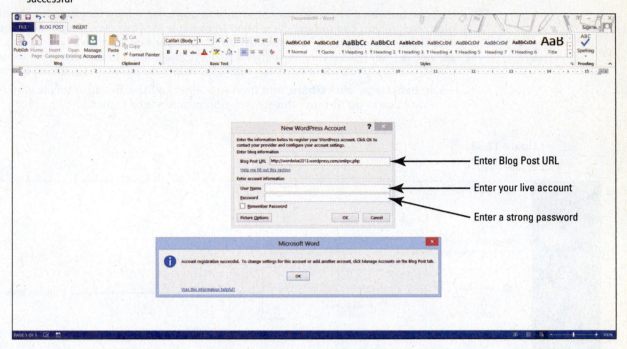

5. Enter any name you would like for your URL and once it displays as being available complete the registration process by creating **[your user name]** and **[your password]**. (It should be a strong password—the screen will indicate if it is weak or strong.)

6. The Word screen displays *[Enter Post Title Here]*. Type **What are your thoughts about the NEW features in Word 2013?** (see Figure 13-35).

   In the Blog group, the Publish button contains two options: *Publish* and *Publish as Draft*. After you complete a few more steps, you post and publish your first blog. On the next step, you add your blog URL to your account.

Figure 13-35

New post entered

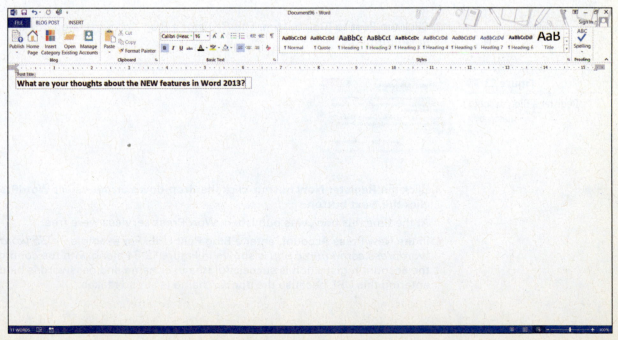

7. On the Blog group, click the **Manage Accounts button** to display the *Blog Accounts* dialog box as shown in Figure 13-36. Under *Manage Accounts,* you should see your Blog URL.

Figure 13-36

Blog Accounts

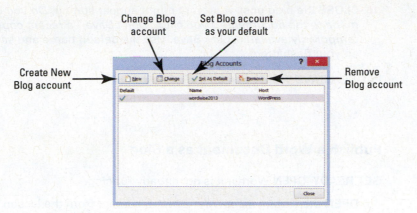

8. If you do not see your URL, click the **New button**.

The *New Blog Account* dialog box opens.

9. Click the **drop-down arrow** to display the menu, select **WordPress**, and click **Next**. The *New WordPress Account* dialog box opens. Enter your Blog Post URL, *<Enter your blog URL here>*; for example, *wordwise2013.wordpress.com*, and then enter **[your user name]** and **[your password]**.

If you would like Word to remember your password, click the **Remember Password box** to add a check mark. Another option is *Picture Options*. When you publish your blog post, your picture needs to be uploaded to a picture provider on its storage location. Options to consider if you decide to upload a picture include: You can upload to *My blog provider, My own server,* and *None*—don't upload pictures. For this exercise, do not use the *Picture Options*.

10. After entering **[your blog post URL]**, **[your user name]**, and **[your password]**, a prompt appears stating, *When Word sends information to the blog service provider, it may be possible for other people to see that information. This includes your user name and password. Do you want to continue?* Click **Yes**.

11. Click the **Manage Accounts button** again in the Blog group to see your account shown in Figure 13-36. Click **Close**.

12. Click the **Publish button** on Blog group to display the *Connect to [your Blog URL]* dialog box. Figure 13-37 displays *Connect to wordwise2013*. Type **[your user name]** and **[your password]** to post and publish.

13. A prompt appears stating, *When Word sends information to the blog service provider, it may be possible for other people to see that information. This includes your user name and password. Do you want to continue?* Click **Yes**.

Figure 13-37

Connect to wordwise2013

A gray prompt appears in your Word blog document screen stating, *This post was published to <your blog URL site>* followed by the time and date; for example, *This post was published to wordwise2013 at 7:13:49 PM 1/21/2013.*

14. When you click the **Home Page** 🏠 **button** on the Blog group, it automatically connects the Internet directly to your Blog URL website after you have logged in.

Take Note   You can blog and publish from your blog URL site.

15. The Insert Category button allows you to categorize postings on your blog. When you click on this button, you are prompted to log in again. When you categorize your blog post, you can select from the drop-down menu. In the meantime, you do not see any category. If you clicked on the Insert Category button, click the **Undo button** on the Quick Access Toolbar to remove. The Open Existing button opens a published blog.

16. **CLOSE** the blog post. A prompt might appear stating, *Do you want to save changes made to the document? If you click "Don't Save," a recent copy of this file will be temporarily available.* Click **Save**. Use the default name and save to your lesson folder on your flash drive.

PAUSE. LEAVE Word open for the next exercise.

STEP BY STEP   **Publish a Word Document as a Blog**

GET READY. OPEN Word if it is not already running.

1. **OPEN** the *Employment Offer 20XX* document from the lesson folder. You are now ready to publish an existing Word document as a blog.

2. Go to **Backstage**, and click **Share**. Click **Post to Blog**, and then click the **Post to Blog button**. The *Employment Offer 20XX* document is inserted in the *Word Blog* layout and appears below the horizontal line.

3. Click the **Publish button** in the Blog group to display *Connect to <your Blog URL site>, Connect to wordwise2013*. Enter your user name and password, and then click **OK**.

4. A prompt appears stating, *When Word sends information to the blog service provider, it may be possible for other people to see that information. This includes your user name and password. Do you want to continue?* Click **Yes**.

5. A gray prompt appears on the screen stating, *This post was published to your <Blog URL site> at time is displayed and date.*

6. **SAVE** the blog post with the default name in the lesson folder on your flash drive.

7. **CLOSE** the *Employment Offer 20XX* document.

PAUSE. CLOSE Word.

STEP BY STEP   **Remove a Blog on Your Blog Site**

GET READY. OPEN Word if it is not already running.

1. **LAUNCH** your Internet browser and log in to your WordPress 2013 blog. On the left side of the screen, click **Post**, and then click **All Posts**.

2. Add a check mark in the check box, and then select **Trash**.

3. Log out of your blog URL site.

   Have fun blogging!

CLOSE the Internet.

SKILL SUMMARY

In this lesson you learned to:	Exam Objective	Objective Number
Protecting and Sharing Documents	Protect documents with passwords.	1.5.5
Managing Document Versions		
Sharing Documents	Save files to remote locations.	1.5.4

Knowledge Assessment

True/False

Circle T if the statement is true or F if the statement is false.

T F   **1.** You can specify two different passwords, one to open a document and one to modify it.

T F   **2.** You should run the Compatibility Checker on all document files.

T F   **3.** The Compatibility Checker ensures that the document's features are compatible with other versions of Word.

T F   **4.** When you restore an earlier version of your document, the AutoSave Version prompt will appear in as yellow bar, alerting you that a newer version is available. As a user, you have the option to compare and restore.

T F   **5.** The Compatibility Checker lists a summary of features not supported by earlier versions.

T F   **6.** Using SkyDrive is another way to share documents.

T F   **7.** Formatting restrictions allow users to limit the formatting styles in a document.

T F   **8.** Read only prevents changes to a document.

T F   **9.** Inspect Document does not provide options on removing features that might have been used in the document.

T F   **10.** The Restrict Formatting and Editing pane cannot be accessed on the Ribbon.

Multiple Choice

Select the best response for the following statements.

1. Requiring a password to open a document is accomplished by using:
   a. Encrypt with Password.
   b. Restrict Editing.
   c. Restrict Formatting.
   d. Word does not support this feature.

2. A document that is protected from editing, but allows comments is protected using which feature?
   a. Restrict Formatting
   b. Protected from using comments
   c. Comments features was turned off
   d. Editing Restrictions

3. Unsaved documents can be recovered using:
   a. multiple users.
   b. Manage Versions.
   c. SkyDrive.
   d. Save As.

4. Internet faxing is available to users:
   a. at no charge.
   b. for a fee by service providers.
   c. only if you have access to a fax machine.
   d. It is not available.

5. Word provides blogging as an option, but as a user you must:
   a. register a blog URL.
   b. post and publish.
   c. maintain your blog URL site.
   d. All of the above

6. You must register a Blog space before:
   a. blogging.
   b. posting a blog.
   c. sharing.
   d. publishing.

7. If your document contains potential problems where the content is difficult to read by an individual with a disability, you would be alerted under which command?
   a. Check Accessibility
   b. Check Compatibility
   c. Inspect Document
   d. All of the above

8. Before sharing a document, it is good practice to remove personal information using which command?
   a. Check Accessibility
   b. Check Compatibility
   c. Inspect Document
   d. No command is available.

9. Draft versions of documents can be deleted by:
   a. right-clicking, and then selecting Delete.
   b. using Manage Versions.
   c. pressing the Delete key.
   d. a and b

10. Recovering unsaved documents is located under which command?
   a. Info
   b. Recent
   c. Open
   d. Save & Send

Proficiency Assessment

Project 13-1: Formatting the Coffee Menu

Your manager has asked you to format the coffee menu document appropriately and have it ready for a meeting in an hour.

GET READY. LAUNCH Word if not already running.

1. **OPEN** *Coffee Menu document* from the lesson folder.

2. Go to **Backstage**, click **Options**, and then **Save**.

3. Under the Save section, by *Save AutoRecover information every,* change to **3** minutes.

4. Select the heading **Grand Street Coffee Shop**.

5. Change the font color and select **Purple**, **Accent 4**, **Lighter 80%**.

6. Change the page border with a **shadow** style with the border color of **Purple**, **4 ½″** wide.

7. Select **Menu**, **italicize**, **bold**, and change the font size to **26** pts.

8. Change the font to **Cambria** and color to **Purple**, **Accent 4**, **Darker 50%**.

9. Select **Menu** and use the **Format Painter** and apply to *Nutritional Information*.

10. Apply a page color, and select **Purple**, **Accent 4**, **Lighter 80%**.

11. **CLOSE** the document without saving. A prompt should appear on your screen: *If you don't save, a recent copy of the document will be temporarily available.* If the prompt did not appear, check step 2. Click **Don't Save**. In the next exercise, you recover your unsaved document.

LEAVE Word open for the next project.

Project 13-2: Managing Versions

You are continuing with the previous project and realized that you inadvertently didn't save the document. Your task is to retrieve the unsaved document.

GET READY. LAUNCH Word if not already running.

1. Go to **Backstage**, click the **Manage Versions button**.
2. Select **Recover Unsaved Documents**.
3. Locate the file and click **Open** and click **Restore**.
4. **SAVE** the document as *13-2 Coffee Menu* in the lesson folder on your flash drive, and then **CLOSE** the file.

LEAVE Word open for the next project.

Competency Assessment

Project 13-3: Posting the Coffee Menu for Review

You are ready to post your new menu to your class for review. Inspect the document and mark it as final.

GET READY. LAUNCH Word if not already running.

1. **OPEN** *13-2 Coffee Menu* from the lesson folder.
2. **SAVE** the document as *13-3 Coffee Menu for Review* in the lesson folder on your flash drive.
3. Open **Backstage**, select **Check for Issues**, and then select **Inspect Document**.
4. Click **Inspect** the document and click **Remove All** by the *Document Properties and Personal Information* section.
5. Click **Close**.
6. Click **Allow this information to be saved in your file**.
7. **SAVE** the document in the lesson folder on your flash drive, and then **CLOSE** the file.

LEAVE Word open for the next project.

Project 13-4: Encrypting Relocation Proposal with a Password

Your task is to remove all document properties in the stock agreement document before sharing with eligible employees.

GET READY. LAUNCH Word if not already running.

1. **OPEN** *Relocation Proposal* document from the lesson folder.
2. **SAVE** the document as *13-4 Relocation Proposal* in the lesson folder on your flash drive.
3. Inspect the document.
4. Click **Remove All** on the *Document Properties and Personal Information setting* and *Headers, Footers, and Watermarks* setting.
5. Click **Close**.
6. Encrypt the document with a password and enter **BYA%$#agree**.
7. **SAVE** the document in the lesson folder on your flash drive.

LEAVE the document open for the next project.

Mastery Assessment

Project 13-5: Saving Relocation Proposal to SkyDrive

You have finalized the relocation proposal document and are ready to share it with employees from around the region. Your task is to save the document and create a shared link for everyone to view.

GET READY. LAUNCH Word if not already running.

1. **OPEN** the *Relocation Proposal* document from the lesson folder.
2. **SAVE** the document as *13-5 Relocation Proposal* in the lesson folder on your flash drive.
3. Invite five students from class and include your instructor.
4. Type in the message box, **This is the first draft for the relocation proposal**. Sign with your name, and then **Share**.
5. **CLOSE** the file.

LEAVE Word open for the next project.

Project 13-6: Creating a Document with a Password

Create a document that only you can access.

GET READY. LAUNCH Word if not already running.

1. **SAVE** the document as *Password* in the lesson folder on your flash drive.
2. Type the following:
   Name: **Giovanni**
   E-mail address: **someone@live.com**
   The importance of using a password:
   Unauthorized access to your document
   A password added to documents prevents unwanted changes
   The document can only be opened by those who know the password
3. Apply the default numbering format to the previous three items.
4. Protect the document by securing it with the following password, and type **dap&27#%**. Use the same password to open and modify the document.
5. **SAVE** the document in the lesson folder on your flash drive, and then **CLOSE** the file.

CLOSE Word.

LESSON SKILL MATRIX

Skill	Exam Objective	Objective Number
Customizing Word		

KEY TERMS
- **metadata**

You are employed as a researcher at A Datum Corporation, a company that provides custom consulting services to information technology companies. Many of the default options for Word are suitable, but there are times you need to make changes to settings for features such as compatibility, editing, printing, and saving. In this lesson, you learn how to access options that enable you to customize Word to best fit the tasks that you perform such as changing display options, setting save options, using advanced options, customizing the Quick Access Toolbar, and customizing the Ribbon.

© GlobalStock/iStockphoto

SOFTWARE ORIENTATION

Word Options

The Word Options dialog box provides a wide variety of methods to customize how Word is used. Ten different option categories are provided. To access these options, click the File tab and then click Options as shown in Figure 14-1.

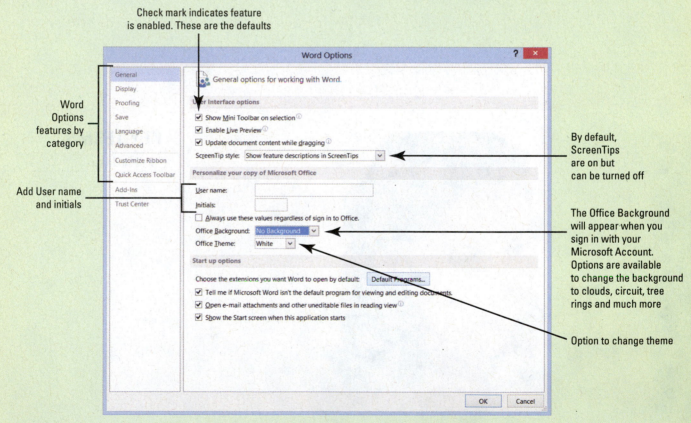

Figure 14-1
Word Options dialog box with General settings displayed

Use this figure as a reference throughout this lesson as well as the rest of this book.

CUSTOMIZING WORD

The Bottom Line

Word can be customized through the different options available in the Word Options dialog box.

Personalizing Word

In previous lessons, you open the Word Options dialog box in Backstage and change the default settings. The General settings contain some of the most frequently used options that can be customized in Word, including options to personalize Word, such as changing the user name and initials. Take time to explore the contents of each screen. The more familiar you become with the options available, the better able you will be to customize Word to suit your needs. In this exercise, you learn to personalize Word and add information in Properties.

STEP BY STEP **Personalize Word**

GET READY. Before you begin these steps, be sure to **LAUNCH** Microsoft Word.

1. **OPEN** the *A Datum* document from the lesson folder.

2. Click the **File tab**, and then click **Options** to display the *Word Options* dialog box. The General settings are already displayed (refer to Figure 14-1).

3. In the *Personalize your copy of Microsoft Office* section, type **[your name]** in the User name box and **[your initials]** in the Initials box. Your name and initials appear only here.

 Cross Ref

In Lesson 9, you learn to change a user's name in the Track Changes Options dialog box.

4. Click **OK**.

5. Open **Backstage** and notice the Properties pane on the right side.

This pane displays the properties of the document size, pages, words, editing time, date the document was created or modified, and author and any other person who might have reviewed the document.

6. Display the Advanced Properties by clicking the drop-down arrow under Properties, and then select **Advanced Properties**. The *Advanced Properties* dialog box opens as shown in Figure 14-2.

Figure 14-2

Properties dialog box

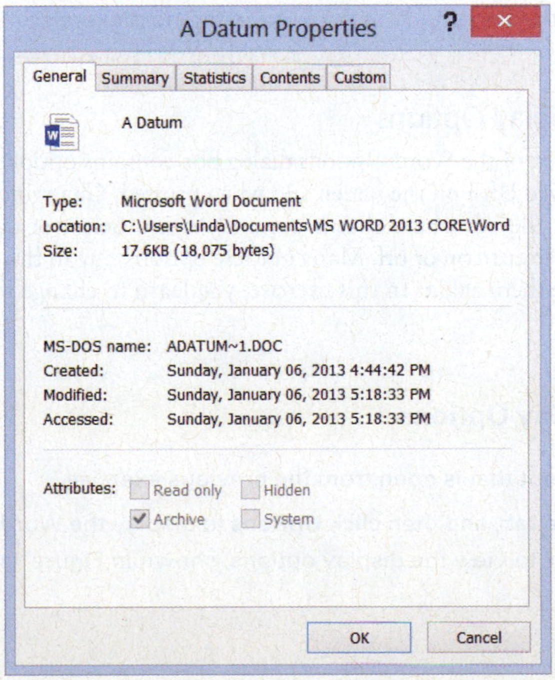

| A Datum Properties | ? | ✕ |

| General | Summary | Statistics | Contents | Custom |

A Datum

Type: Microsoft Word Document
Location: C:\Users\Linda\Documents\MS WORD 2013 CORE\Word
Size: 17.6KB (18,075 bytes)

MS-DOS name: ADATUM~1.DOC
Created: Sunday, January 06, 2013 4:44:42 PM
Modified: Sunday, January 06, 2013 5:18:33 PM
Accessed: Sunday, January 06, 2013 5:18:33 PM

Attributes: ☐ Read only ☐ Hidden
            ☑ Archive   ☐ System

OK   Cancel

Cross Ref In Lesson 2, you learn to display the Document Panel to show above the document and open the Advanced Properties. You can also display the Advanced Properties from Backstage.

7. Click the **Summary tab** to add information that describes your document.

   Data that describes other data is called **metadata**. Information in the properties is also known as metadata, which includes details about the document.

8. Type the information as shown in Figure 14-3, and then click **OK**.

Figure 14-3

A Datum Properties
Summary tab

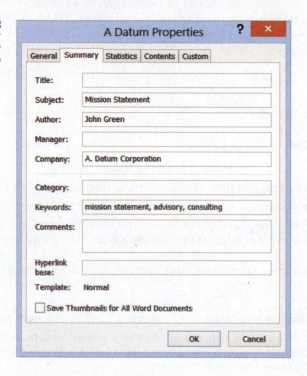

9. Select **Show All Properties** at the bottom of the Properties pane.

   Review the updated properties in Backstage to see the author's name and tags.

10. Return to the document.

PAUSE. LEAVE the document open to use in the next exercise.

Changing Display Options

The Display screen of the Word Options dialog box contains options for changing how document content is displayed both on the screen and when printed. Changing these options affects all documents, not just the document that is currently open. Select or deselect the check box for any option you want to turn on or off. Many of these options stay in this state for all Word documents until you change them again. In this exercise, you learn to change the display options.

STEP BY STEP **Change Display Options**

USE the document that is open from the previous exercise.

1. Click the **File tab**, and then click **Options** to display the Word Options dialog box.

2. Click **Display** to view the display options, shown in Figure 14-4.

Figure 14-4

Display options screen

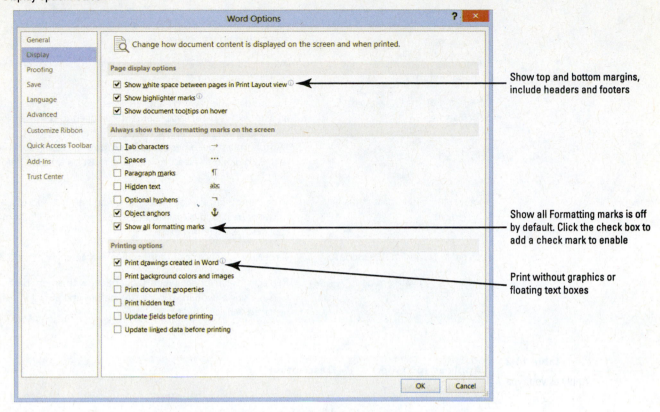

In the *Always show these formatting marks on the screen* section, the check box is empty beside the *Show all formatting marks.*

3. Click to add a check mark next to **Show all formatting marks.**

4. Click **OK.**

   Notice that the paragraph marks appear in the document.

5. Open the **Display screen** and click to remove the check mark by **Show all formatting marks.** By default, this feature is disabled.

6. Click **OK.**

7. **CLOSE** the document without saving.

PAUSE. LEAVE Word open to use in the next exercise.

Turning AutoFormat Off or On

When *AutoFormat As You Type* options are turned on, Word allows you to apply formatting quickly as you type bullets and number lists, fractions, numbers, borders, ordinals, and hyphenate text. Other options that you have available are *Apply as you type* and *Automatically as you type*. When the automatic formatting has been applied, you can undo the changes by using the AutoCorrect Options button in the AutoCorrect dialog box. In this exercise, you learn how to turn off certain features using the AutoCorrect Options button.

You can access *AutoFormat As You Type* by opening the Word Options dialog box and selecting *Proofing*. Then open the *AutoCorrect* dialog box. Tables 14-1, 14-2, and 14-3 provide a description of what will occur after each specified action has been performed.

Table 14-1

AutoFormat As You Type

Replace as you type	Description
"Straight quotes" with "smart quotes"	Straight quotations marks (" ") and straight apostrophes (') are replaced with curved, open, and closed quotations marks (" ") and curved apostrophes.
Fractions (1/2) with fraction character (½)	When you type "1/2", it is replaced with ½. This option only replaces ¼, ½, and ¾.
Bold and _italic_ with real formatting	The bold element will be applied when text begins and ends with an asterisk (*). The italic element is applied to text beginning and ending with an underscore (_). For example, *AutoFormat* becomes **AutoFormat** and _text_ becomes *text*. By default, this feature is off and must be enabled before using.
Internet and networks paths with hyperlinks	Word automatically recognizes when an Internet address, network path, and e-mail address are typed and will automatically replace these with hyperlinks.
Ordinals (1st) with superscript	Order set of sequence numbers. For example, 1st, 2nd, and 3rd.
Hyphens (--) with em dash (—)	Replaces two hyphens typed sequentially with an em dash (—); a single hyphen with a space before and after (-) will be replaced with an en dash (–).

Table 14-2

Apply as you type

Apply as you type	Description
Automatic bulleted lists	When typing one of these characters *, -, > followed by a space or tab, a bulleted list will be created.
Border lines	When you type three consecutive characters (~, #, *, -, _, or =) on a new line and then press Enter, a line with that character will appear across the page.
Built-in Heading styles	When fewer than five words are used in headings and the Enter key is pressed twice, the built-in heading style will be applied. For each new heading that you type, a new line is followed by the Tab. For example, Heading 1, type a line; for Heading 2, press Tab; Heading 3 press Tab twice.
Automatic numbered lists	When you begin a numbered list and type the number 1 followed by a period or tab, a numbered list is created.
Tables	A single row of a table is created when you type +-----+-----+----+-----+ and then press the Enter key. Four columns and one row are created. The number of hyphens between the plus symbols is the column width.

Table 14-3

Automatically as you type

Automatically as you type	Description
Format beginning of list item like the one before it	Formats the beginning text of a list item like the previous list.
Set left- and first-indent with tabs and backspaces	Indent the first line of a paragraph by putting the cursor before the first line, and then press the Tab key. Indent the whole paragraph by putting the cursor before any line in the paragraph with the exception of the first line and then press Tab. Place insertion point before the first line, and then press the Backspace key to remove.
Define styles based on your formatting	When text has been formatted manually, the same style will be applied when the Enter key is pressed.

STEP BY STEP	Turn AutoFormat Off or On

OPEN the *A Datum Security Alarm* document from the lesson folder.

1. Click the **File tab**, and then click **Options**.

2. Click **Proofing** to display the options.

3. Click the **AutoCorrect Options button**, and then click the **AutoFormat As You Type tab**.

4. Under the *Apply as you type* section, select the check box by **Automatic bulleted lists** to clear it (an empty check mark indicates the feature is off).

5. Click again to place a check mark in the box to turn **Automatic bulleted lists** back on (see Figure 14-5).

Figure 14-5

AutoCorrect dialog box displaying the AutoFormat As You Type tab

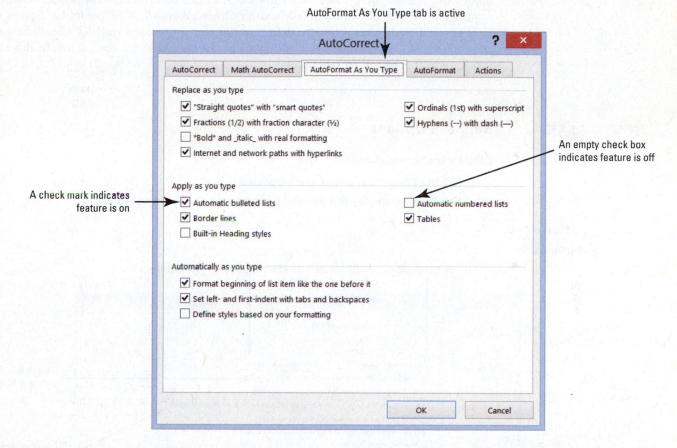

6. Click **OK** to close the *AutoCorrect* dialog box, and then click **OK** to close the *Word Options* dialog box.

7. Position the insertion point after the last bulleted item and press **Enter** twice to move to the next line and clear the added bullet.

8. On the Page Layout tab, in the Page Setup group, select **Continuous** from the Line Numbers command, and then place the insertion point on line 14.

9. Type ~ ~ ~ three times and press **Enter**.

   A wavy border line is placed across the page.

10. Access the *Proofing* settings in the Word Options dialog box and click the **AutoCorrect Options button**.

11. Add a check mark by *Bold* and *_italic_ with real formatting* to enable this feature.

12. Click **OK** two times to close both dialog boxes.

13. On line 26, select **Ready** and type ***Ready***. The text is automatically bolded.

14. In the AutoCorrect Options, remove the check mark by ***Bold* and _italic_ with real formatting**.

15. **SAVE** the document as ***Security Alarm Update*** in the lesson folder on your flash drive, and then **CLOSE** the file.

PAUSE. LEAVE Word open to use in the next exercise.

 Cross Ref   In Lesson 9, you learn about accessing the AutoCorrect Options.

Setting Save Options

The Save screen of the Word Options dialog box contains options for customizing how documents are saved, including preserving information in backup files for your documents, sharing files using a document management server, and embedding fonts in a file. For example, you can change the default format used to save documents, or you can change how often your documents are backed up by using AutoRecover. The Documents folder, located on drive C, is the default working folder for all the documents created in Microsoft Office programs. A yellow folder appears on the taskbar and directly takes you to the default settings for your folders and files. On the Save screen, you can choose a different default working folder (for example, your flash drive). In this exercise, you learn to change and set save options.

STEP BY STEP   **Set Save Options**

OPEN a blank document.

1. Click the **File tab**, and then click **Options**.

2. Click **Save** to display the *Save* options screen as shown in Figure 14-6.

Figure 14-6

Save options screen

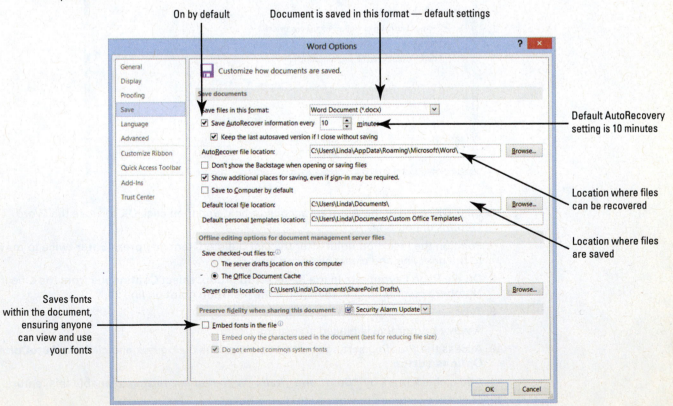

3. In the *Save documents* section, click the drop-down arrow in the *Save files in this format* box.

   The menu displays the options available for changing the default file format used when saving backup files. The default setting to save your work is set to every 10 minutes.

4. In the *Save AutoRecover information every* box, change the setting to **3**.

   Your documents will be saved every three minutes. Check with your instructor before changing the settings. If you change the settings, don't forget to return the setting back to its default.

5. **LEAVE** the *Word Options* dialog box open for the next exercise.

PAUSE. LEAVE Word open to use in the next exercise.

Take Note   Any change made to the default working folder applies only to the application that you are currently using. For example, if a different default working folder is selected for Word, the default working folder for Excel remains Documents if you are using Windows 8 or Windows 7.

Using Advanced Options

The Advanced screen in the Word Options dialog box contains many complex choices for working with Word documents, including options for editing, displaying, printing, and saving. There are many options available but the Advanced screen contains the majority of options. Some are selected by default and some are not. Browse through them to see how you might use some of the options to work more efficiently in Word. In addition to the multitude of options found on this screen, several dialog boxes can be accessed for additional customization. In this exercise, you learn to use the advanced options.

STEP BY STEP   **Use Advanced Options**

USE the document open from the previous exercise.

1. From the *Word Options* dialog box, click **Advanced** to display the *Advanced* options.

   There are several advanced options, many of which are shown in Figures 14-7 through 14-10.

Figure 14-7

Advanced options screen;
Editing options

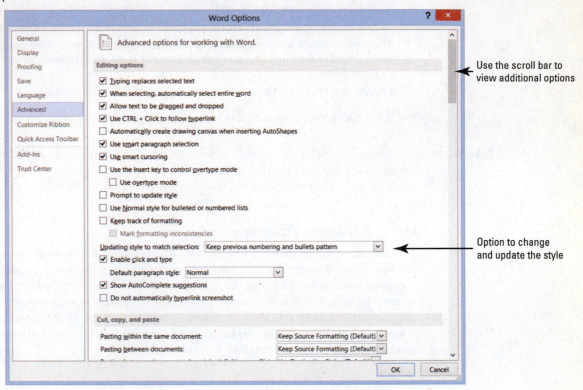

2. Scroll down and locate the *Display* section (shown in Figure 14-8); click the down arrow next to the number in the *Show this number of Recent Documents* list box to change it from *25* to **10**.

Figure 14-8

Advanced options screen;
Display and Print options

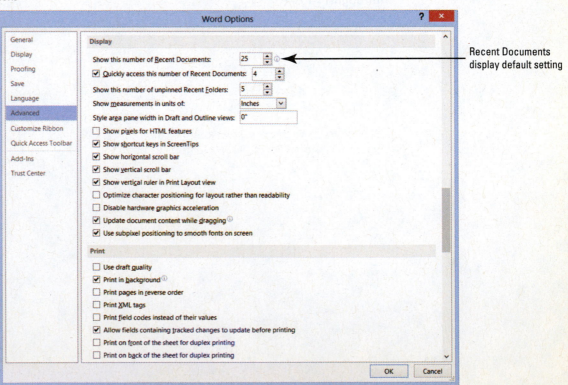

3. Click **OK**.

4. Click the **File tab**, and then click **Open**. Ten documents display under *Recent Documents*.

5. Return the settings back to default, and leave the *Word Options* dialog box open.

6. Scroll down to the *Save* section (shown in Figure 14-9) and click the check box to enable **Prompt before saving Normal template**. Now if you change the default template, Word will prompt you if you want to save the changes to that template.

Figure 14-9

Advanced options screen;
Print and Save options

If the default
template is changed,
Word will ask if
you want to
save changes

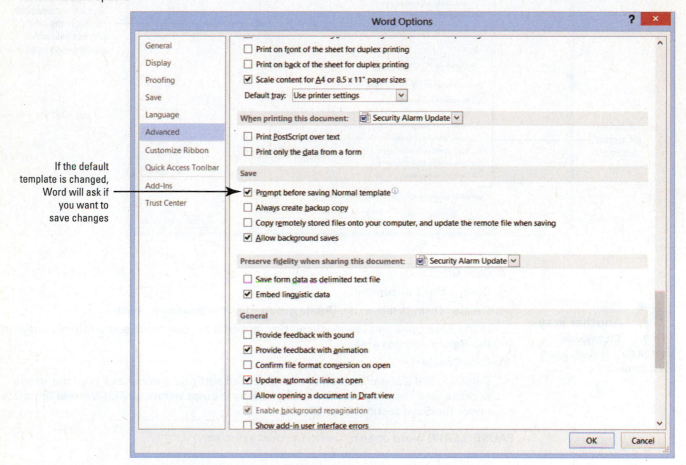

7. Scroll down to the *General* section (shown in Figure 14-10) and type **[your name and address]** in the Mailing address box.

Figure 14-10

Advanced options screen;
General options

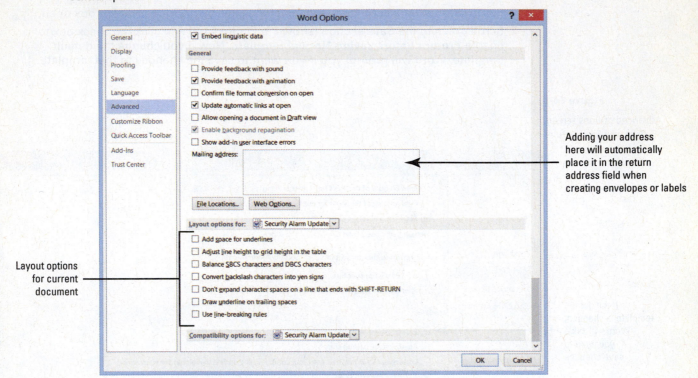

Adding your address
here will automatically
place it in the return
address field when
creating envelopes or labels

Layout options
for current
document

8. Click **OK**.

9. Open a blank document.

10. On the Mailings tab, in the Create group, click the **Envelopes button**.

    In the *Envelopes and Labels* dialog box, notice that your name and address appear in the *Return address* area.

11. Click **Cancel**.

12. Return to the *General* section of the Advanced settings and remove your name and address, and then remove the check mark by **Prompt before saving Normal template** under the *Save* section. Click **OK**.

PAUSE. LEAVE Word open to use in the next exercise.

Customizing the Quick Access Toolbar and Ribbon

The Customize Ribbon and Quick Access Toolbar screens enable you to customize the Quick Access Toolbar, the Ribbon, and keyboard shortcuts. Adding frequently used commands to the Quick Access Toolbar ensures that those commands are always just a single click away. Only commands can be added to the Quick Access Toolbar. The contents of most lists, such as indent and spacing values and individual styles, which also appear on the Ribbon, cannot be added to the Quick Access Toolbar. In this exercise, you add commands to the Quick Access Toolbar, customize a keyboard shortcut, and customize the Ribbon.

Another Way
The keyboard shortcut Ctrl+N opens a new blank document.

STEP BY STEP   **Customize the Quick Access Toolbar**

USE the document open from the previous exercise.

1. Click the **File tab**, and then click **Options**.

2. Click **Quick Access Toolbar** in the left pane to display the customization options, shown in Figure 14-11.

Figure 14-11

Word Options; Custom the
Quick Access Toolbar settings

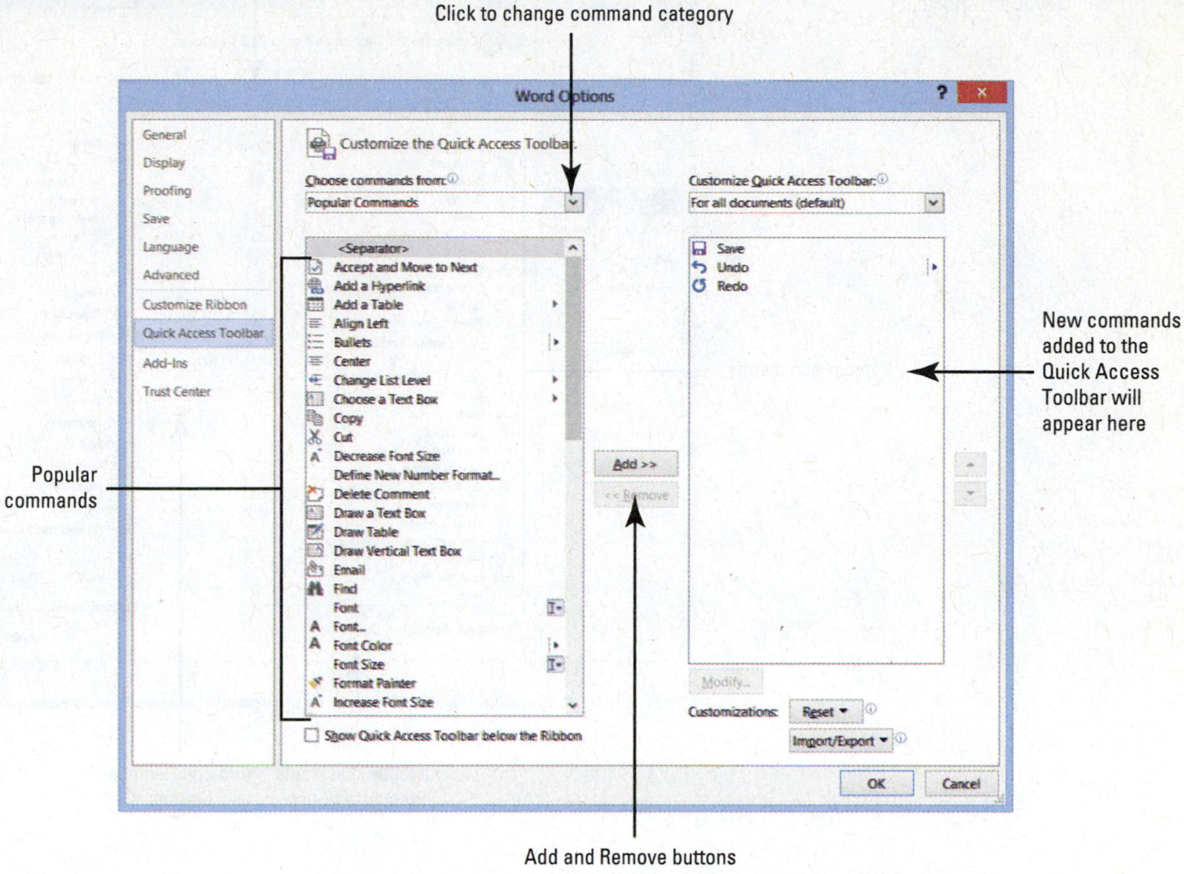

Click to change command category

Popular
commands

New commands
added to the
Quick Access
Toolbar will
appear here

Add and Remove buttons

**Cross
Ref**

You first learn about the Quick Access Toolbar in Lesson 1.

In the *Choose commands from* list, *Popular Commands* is already selected.

3. Scroll down the list of commands, select **Page Setup**, and then click the
   Add button.

4. Select **Page Width**, and then double-click to quickly add to the Customize Quick Access
   Toolbar list. Repeat the step for the Numbering command.

5. Click **OK**. The Quick Access Toolbar is now customized with new commands that are
   easily accessible. Check with your instructor to see if these commands should remain
   on the toolbar.

Another Way
You can open the
customization screen using the
*Customize Quick Access
Toolbar, More Commands* menu
option.

PAUSE. LEAVE Word open to use in the next exercise.

Take Note
To remove a command from the Quick Access Toolbar, place the mouse pointer on the com-
mand in the Quick Access Toolbar, right-click the command, and then click *Remove from Quick
Access Toolbar.*

STEP BY STEP   **Customize the Keyboard**

USE the document open from the previous exercise.

1. Open the **Word Options dialog box**, and click **Customize Ribbon** to open the
   customization screen (see Figure 14-12).

Figure 14-12

Word Options dialog box; Customize the Ribbon and keyboard shortcuts

Click to change command category

Customize the Ribbon

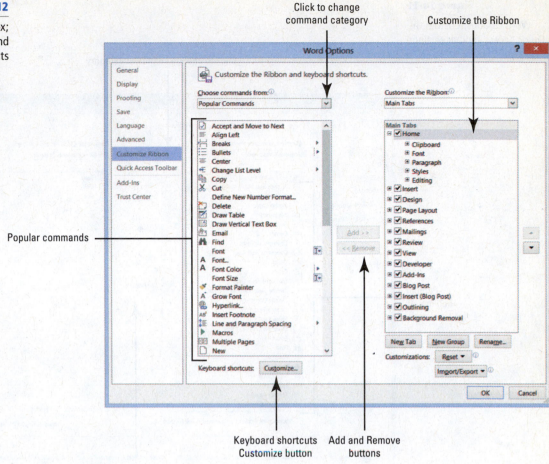

Popular commands

Keyboard shortcuts Customize button

Add and Remove buttons

2. On the bottom left, click the **Customize button** next to *Keyboard shortcuts*. The *Customize Keyboard* dialog box appears, as shown in Figure 14-13.

Figure 14-13

Customize Keyboard dialog box

Category listing

Existing keyboard shortcut (if any exists)

Commands

New keyboard shortcut

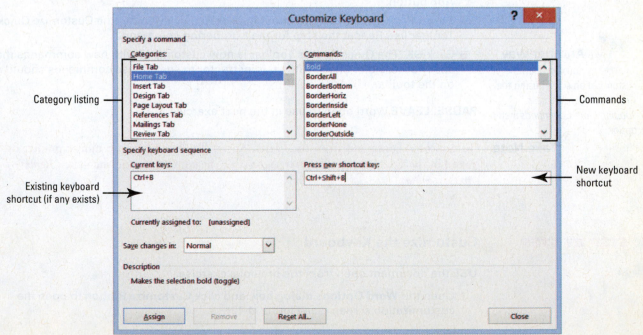

3. In the Categories box, click **Home Tab**.

You should see *Bold* highlighted under the Commands box.

Two shortcut key command appears in the Current keys box. The Ctrl+B shortcut is a reserved key and assigned to the Bold command. The Ctrl+Shift+B shortcut is also assigned to the Bold command.

4. In the Current Keys box, select **Ctrl+Shift+B** and then click **Remove**.

5. In the *Press new shortcut key* box, type **Ctrl+Shift+U** as shown in Figure 14-14. Under the Current keys box, it shows that this command is *[unassigned]*.

Figure 14-14

Customize Keyboard dialog box showing shortcut keys are unassigned

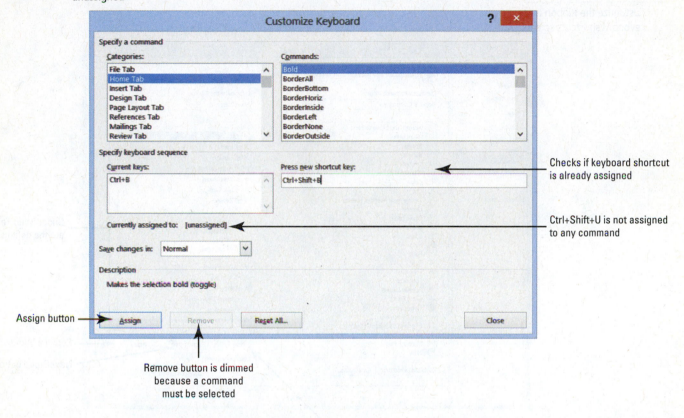

6. Click the **Assign** button.

7. Return to the Word document and type any word, and then select the word and press **Ctrl+Shift+U**. The text should be underlined.

8. Open the **Customize Keyboard dialog box**, and then select **Home Tab**. The two shortcut key commands appear in the Current keys box.

9. Select **Ctrl+Shift+U**, and then click the **Remove** button to remove the shortcut key.

Removing Ctrl+Shift+U now makes it available to be used for another shortcut keyboard command.

10. Click **Close** to close the *Customize Keyboard* dialog box.

11. Leave the *Word Options* dialog box open for the next exercise.

PAUSE. LEAVE Word open to use in the next exercise.

Another Way
You can also add an item to the Quick Access Toolbar by clicking the *Customize Quick Access Toolbar* button or by right-clicking anywhere on the Quick Access Toolbar.

STEP BY STEP   **Customize the Ribbon**

In this exercise, you create a customized Ribbon tab and place your favorite commands in one group on a new tab. You can add commands already found on other tabs, and you also have the option to place commands not found in any of the tabs.

USE the document open from the previous exercise.

1. Access **Word Options**, and then click **Customize Ribbon** to open the customization screen (see Figure 14-15).

Figure 14-15

Customize the Ribbon and keyboard shortcuts screen

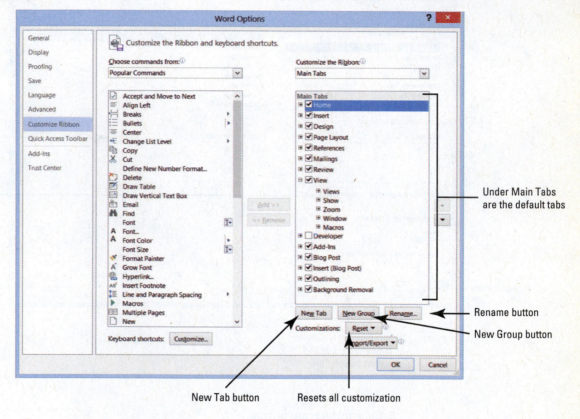

Under Main Tabs are the default tabs

Rename button

New Group button

New Tab button   Resets all customization

2. Under *Main Tabs*, click the **minus (−) sign** to collapse the groups listed under *Home*, if necessary. The *Home tab* should appear selected.

3. Click the **New Tab button**. Two objects appear: one is identified for the new tab whereas the other is for the group as shown in Figure 14-16.

Figure 14-16

New Tab and New Group

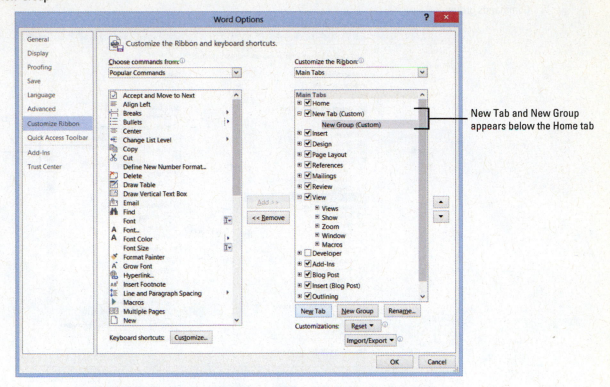

New Tab and New Group appears below the Home tab

4. Select **New Tab (Custom)**, and then click the **Rename** button.

   The *Rename* dialog box appears.

5. Type **My Favorites** in the Display name box (see Figure 14-17).

Figure 14-17

Rename dialog box

6. Click **OK**.

7. Select **New Group (Custom)**, and then click the **Rename** button.

   The *Rename* dialog box appears with icons to identify your command group.

8. Type **My Commands** in the Display name box.

9. Select the smiley face.

10. Click **OK**.

    With *My Commands* selected under *Main Tabs*, you are ready to add commands to this group.

11. Under the *Popular Commands*, select then click the **Add button** to place in *My Commands*.

12. Select **Accept and Move to Next**, and then click the **Add button**.

    This command is placed under *My Commands*.

13. Select **Breaks** and **Draw Table** separately, and then click the **Add button**. Your screen should match Figure 14-18.

Figure 14-18

Commands added to My
Commands group

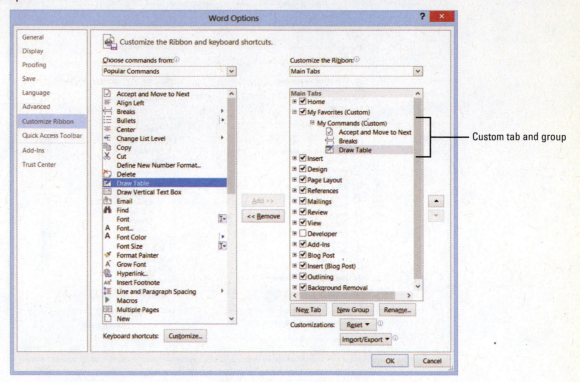

Custom tab and group

14. Click **OK**.

15. Click the **My Favorites tab** and review your customized tab and group of commands
(see Figure 14-19).

Figure 14-19

My Favorites tab on Ribbon

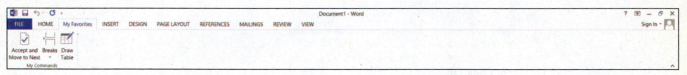

16. To remove the customized tab, return to the customization screen, and then click the
Reset All Customizations button. Select **Yes** to confirm, and click **OK**.

STOP. CLOSE Word.

SKILL SUMMARY

In this lesson you learned to:	Exam Objective	Objective Number
Customize Word		

Knowledge Assessment

Multiple Choice

Select the best response for the following statements.

1. To assign a new keyboard shortcut, you would access Backstage, Word Options, and then:
   a. Customize Quick Access Toolbar.
   b. Customize Backstage button.
   c. Customize Ribbon, New Keyboard commands.
   d. Customize Ribbon, Keyboard shortcuts, and the Customize button.

2. Which tab would you click to display the Options command?
   a. Insert
   b. Advanced
   c. File
   d. Display

3. The shortcut key, Ctrl+C, is:
   a. unassigned.
   b. accessible.
   c. assigned.
   d. not a shortcut key.

4. The Display screen in the Word Options dialog box displays which hidden formatting marks?
   a. Spaces
   b. Tab characters
   c. Paragraph marks
   d. All of the above

5. The Quick Access Toolbar is for:
   a. frequently used commands.
   b. commands from the File menu.
   c. contents of lists on the Ribbon.
   d. recently used documents.

6. A check mark displayed in the Word Options dialog box, indicates the feature is:
   a. off.
   b. not available.
   c. disabled.
   d. on.

7. As a user of Word, you can change the AutoRecover minutes to set how Word protects you from losing your work in which screen of the Word Options dialog box?
   a. Save
   b. Options, Save
   c. Save As
   d. None of the above

8. Where would you place a customized command?
   a. Ribbon
   b. Quick Access Toolbar
   c. Does not appear
   d. A new Ribbon

9. Changes made in the Word Options dialog box will affect:
   a. only new documents.
   b. all documents.
   c. only documents opened as a template.
   d. a and c

10. To locate where files are automatically saved, you would find this setting on which screen of the Word Options dialog box:
    a. General
    b. Save
    c. Proofing
    d. Advanced

True/False

Circle T if the statement is true or F if the statement is false.

T F 1. The Advanced screen contains the largest number of options available in the Word Options dialog box.

T F 2. The Quick Access Toolbar and keyboard shortcuts cannot be customized.

T F 3. When creating keyboard shortcuts, Word informs you when shortcut keys have been assigned.

T F 4. In the Word Options dialog box, you can add your name and initials under the Personalize your copy of Microsoft Office section.

T F 5. The default settings in the Word Options dialog box cannot be changed.

T F 6. When customizing the Ribbon, you cannot add the same commands to a new tab if they are listed on another Ribbon tab.

T F 7. Changing the Display options affects how content appears on your computer.

T F 8. When you personalize Word by adding your name to the User Name box, the Document Properties panel will display your name in the Author box.

T F 9. The formatting marks can be turned off in the Display screen of the Word Options dialog box.

T F 10. When customizing the Ribbon, you have the option to group commands within a tab.

Competency Assessment

Project 14-1: Creating a Default Return Address for Lost Art Photos

In your position as a marketing assistant at LostArt Photos, you frequently mail promotional letters. You prepare envelopes for these mailings in Word, and making the company's return address your default option would save time. Change your Word options to set this up.

GET READY. LAUNCH Word if it is not already running.

1. **OPEN** a blank new document.
2. **SAVE** the document as *14-1 Mailing Address* in the lesson folder on your flash drive.
3. Click the **File tab**, and then select **Options** to display the *Word Options* dialog box.
4. Click **Advanced** in the left pane to display the advanced options.
5. Scroll down to the *General* section, and in the Mailing address box, type:

   LostArtPhotos

   5500 Bissell Street

   Grand Junction, CO 98445
6. Press the **Print Scrn** button on the keyboard.
7. Click **OK** to close the *Word Options* dialog box.
8. **Right-click** in the document screen, and then click **Paste**.
9. **SAVE** the document in the lesson folder on your flash drive, and then **CLOSE** the file.

LEAVE Word open for the next project.

Project 14-2: Setting Research Options

A Datum Corporation has an overseas branch in the United Kingdom. In your position as a researcher, you need content to stand out in your document. You will change the settings to turn on the feature that will allow real formatting as you type.

GET READY. LAUNCH Word if it is not already running.

1. **OPEN** a blank document.
2. **SAVE** your document as *14-2 Changing Settings* in the lesson folder on your flash drive.
3. Click the **File tab**, and then click **Options**.
4. Click **Proofing**, and then click the **AutoCorrect Options button**.
5. Select the **AutoFormat As You Type tab**, and add a check mark by ***Bold* and _italic_ with real formatting**.
6. Click **OK** to close the dialog box.
7. Click **OK** again.
8. Type ***United Kingdom***. Press **Enter**.
9. Type the underscore three times, and then press **Enter**.
10. Remove the check mark by ***Bold* and _italic_ with real formatting**.
11. Click **OK** twice to close the dialog boxes.
12. **SAVE** the document in the lesson folder on your flash drive, and then **CLOSE** the file.

LEAVE Word open for the next project.

Proficiency Assessment

Project 14-3: Customizing the Quick Access Toolbar

As a paralegal in a busy legal practice, you are always looking for ways to streamline your work. As you learn more about Word, you want to use the available options to help customize the program for your daily tasks.

GET READY. LAUNCH Word if it is not already running.

1. Press **Ctrl+N** to open a new blank document.
2. **SAVE** the document as *14-3 Customizing QAT* in the lesson folder on your flash drive.
3. **OPEN** the *Word Options* dialog box.
4. Display the customization screen for the Quick Access Toolbar.
5. Choose five commands that you use frequently, but that are not currently located on the Quick Access Toolbar. Add the commands to the Quick Access Toolbar.
6. Click **OK** to close the *Word Options* dialog box.
7. Press the **Print Scrn** button on the keyboard.
8. **Right-click** in the document, and then click **Paste**.
9. Crop and enlarge the image to show the Quick Access Toolbar.
10. **SAVE** the document in the lesson folder on your flash drive, and then **CLOSE** the file.

LEAVE Word open for the next project.

Project 14-4: Removing Commands from the Quick Access Toolbar

You are continuing to work with customized Quick Access Toolbar from Project 14-3. Now that you have added five additional commands to your Quick Access Toolbar, you realize you no longer need these commands. You remember seeing the Remove button below the Add button in the customization screen.

GET READY. LAUNCH Word if it is not already running.

1. **SAVE** a new blank document as *14-4 Removing Commands* in the lesson folder on your flash drive.

2. Display the customization screen for the Quick Access Toolbar.

3. Remove all commands that you added to the Quick Access Toolbar and close all open dialog boxes.

4. Press the **Print Scrn** button on the keyboard.

5. **Right-click** in the document and then click **Paste**.

6. Crop and enlarge the image to show the Quick Access Toolbar.

7. **SAVE** the document in the lesson folder on your flash drive, and then **CLOSE** the file.

LEAVE Word open for the next project.

Mastery Assessment

Project 14-5: Saving Settings

Your instructor has asked you to change the Save AutoRecover setting to five minutes and provide a copy of your screen shot.

GET READY. LAUNCH Word if it is not already running.

1. **SAVE** a new blank document as *14-5 Save Settings* in your flash drive in the lesson folder.

2. Open the Word Options dialog box and change the *Save AutoRecover* setting to **5** minutes.

3. Press the **Print Scrn** button on the keyboard, click **OK**, and then right-click in the document and click **Paste**. This will capture your screen as an image.

4. **SAVE** the document in the lesson folder on your flash drive, and then **CLOSE** the file.

LEAVE Word open for the next project.

Project 14-6: Word Options

Your task is to remove the LostArt Photos mailing address that you added in Project 14-1. To show your instructor that you completed this project, provide a copy of your screen shot and save as a Word document.

GET READY. LAUNCH Word if it is not already running.

1. **SAVE** a new blank document as *14-6 Address Removed* in your lesson folder on your flash drive.

2. Remove the mailing address.

3. Press the **Print Scrn** button on the keyboard, click **OK**, and then right-click in the document and click **Paste**. This will capture your screen as an image.

4. **SAVE** the document in the lesson folder on your flash drive, and then **CLOSE** the file.

CLOSE Word.

Circling Back 4

Project 1: Preparing the Speaker Letter

Now that you incorporated the changes suggested, prepare the document for distribution.

GET READY. LAUNCH Word if it is not already running.

1. **OPEN** *Speaker Thank You* from the data files for this lesson.
2. Inspect the document and remove all document properties and personal information and Headers, Footers, and Watermarks.
3. **SAVE** the document as *Inspected Document with Password* in the lesson folder on you flash.
4. **SAVE** the document with an encrypted password and type **nap#5^%**.
5. **SAVE** the document in the lesson folder in your flash drive, and then **CLOSE** the file.

PAUSE. LEAVE Word open for the next project.

Project 2: Master and Subdocument for Research Paper

You are taking a computer class this semester and have been assigned a group project. The research project needs to be divided into sections so that you and your group members can work separately on the document.

GET READY. LAUNCH Word if it is not already running.

1. **OPEN** the *Research* document from the lesson folder.
2. Create a new folder named **Master Research** in your lesson folder on your flash drive.
3. **SAVE** the document as *Master Research* in the *Master Research* folder.
4. Select each heading in the document beginning with *Introduction* and apply the **Heading 1** style.
5. Modify the *Heading 1* style and change the spacing before to **12** pt and apply only to the document.
6. Change the view to **Outline**.
7. In the Outline Tools, click the drop-down arrow at **Show Level** and select **Level 1**.
8. In the Master Document group, click **Show Document**.
9. Select the **plus (+) symbol** by *Introduction* to select.
10. In the Master Document group, click the **Create** button. *Introduction* is surrounded by a border.
11. Repeat your steps for the remaining headings in the document, *Community in the Classroom*, *Technology within Literature Circles*, *Computer-Mediated Discussion Groups*, and *Conclusion*.
12. **SAVE** the document and **CLOSE**.
13. **OPEN** the *Master Research* document—the subdocuments are linked.

14. Press the **Ctrl** key and click to open the *Computer* subdocument.
15. In the first paragraph, locate and select **Students that are physically handicapped and even speech impeded students are afforded a safer place**.
16. Select **Intense Emphasis**, and then **Bold**.
17. **SAVE** the subdocument and **CLOSE**.
18. Click the **Show Document** button to display the controls. You may need to switch back to Outline view before performing this step.
19. Click the **Expand Subdocuments** button, and then select the **plus (+) symbol** for *Computer-Mediated Discussion Groups*. Then place a check mark by **Show First Line Only**.
20. Click the **Move Up** button until it is positioned below the continuous section break below *Community in the Classroom*.

21. Click the **Show Document** button.
22. Unlink the two subdocuments, and then create two separate subdocuments.
23. Click the **Collapse Subdocuments** button.
24. **SAVE** the document in the folder on your flash drive, and then **CLOSE** the file.

PAUSE. LEAVE Word open for the next project.

Project 3: Sharing Documents

You have prepared the *Master Research* document for sharing. You are now ready to share a section of the document with one member of your group, and then you will share the whole document to the group using the Present Online command.

GET READY. LAUNCH Word if it is not already running.

1. **OPEN** the *Introduction* document from the *Master Research* folder.
2. Click the **File** tab, and then click **Account** and **sign-in**.
3. Click **Share**, and then click **Save To Cloud**.
4. Click **Save As** and then click **Sign In's SkyDrive**, and then click the **Shared favorites** folder. Click **Save**.
5. Identify someone from your class and send this person an e-mail.
6. **CLOSE** the file.

7. **OPEN** the *Master Research* document.
8. Go to **Backstage**, click **Share**, and then select **Present Online**.
9. Send an invitation by e-mail to three individuals in class.

PAUSE. LEAVE Word open for the next project.

Project 4: Creating a Simple Macro

You work with Tech Terrace Real Estate Agency and you are responsible for sending a follow-up e-mail or letter to potential clients. Create a simple macro that can be used to follow up with clients. Prepare the letter in a block format so that it can be used in Outlook or mailing. Test your macro before sharing.

GET READY. LAUNCH Word if it is not already running.

1. Create a blank document.
2. Change the top margin to **2"**.
3. Assign **Alt+F** as the keyboard command and save changes in the document.
4. Type the following information:

   Good afternoon <<first name>>:

   On a daily basis you receive emails from Tech Terrace Real Estate Agency listing the available home sites. I just wanted to check in and see if anything looked appealing and if you were interested in seeing any of the sites? Are the listings you receive still meeting your search criteria?

   Please let me know if there are any changes I should make on the site locations.

   Best Regards,

   Veronica

5. **SAVE** the document as *Follow-up Letter* in the lesson folder on your flash drive, and then **CLOSE** the file.

CLOSE Word.

Microsoft Office Specialist (MOS) Skills for Word 2013: Exam 77-418

Matrix Skill	Objective Number	Lesson Number
Create and Manage Documents	**1**	
Create a Document.	1.1	
Create new blank documents.	1.1.1	1
Create new documents and apply templates.	1.1.2	1
Import files.	1.1.3	3, 11
Open non-native files directly in word.	1.1.4	3
Open a PDF in Word for editing.	1.1.5	3
Navigate through a Document.	1.2	
Search for text within a document.	1.2.1	2
Insert hyperlinks.	1.2.2	10
Create bookmarks.	1.2.3	10
Demonstrate how to use Go To.	1.2.4	2, 10
Format a Document.	1.3	
Modify page setup.	1.3.1	5
Change document themes.	1.3.2	7
Change document style sets.	1.3.3	7
Insert simple headers and footers.	1.3.4	10
Insert watermarks.	1.3.5	7
Insert page numbers.	1.3.6	10
Customize Options and View for Document.	1.4	
Change document views.	1.4.1	2
Demonstrate how to use zoom.	1.4.2	2
Customize the Quick Access toolbar.	1.4.3	1
Customize the Ribbon.	1.4.4	2
Split the window.	1.4.5	2
Add values to document properties.	1.4.6	2
Demonstrate how to use Show/Hide.	1.4.7	1
Record simple macros.	1.4.8	12

Matrix Skill	Objective Number	Lesson Number
Assign shortcut keys.	1.4.9	12
Manage macro security.	1.4.10	12
Configure Documents to Print or Save.	1.5	
Configure documents to print.	1.5.1	1
Save documents in alternate file formats.	1.5.2	1
Print document sections.	1.5.3	1
Save files to remote locations.	1.5.4	13
Protect documents with passwords.	1.5.5	13
Set print scaling.	1.5.6	1
Maintain backward compatibility.	1.5.7	1
Format text, Paragraphs, and Sections.	**2**	
Insert Text and Paragraphs.	2.1	
Append text to documents.	2.1.1	7
Find and replace text.	2.1.2	2
Copy and paste text.	2.1.3	2
Insert text via AutoCorrect.	2.1.4	9
Remove blank paragraphs.	2.1.5	2
Insert built-in fields.	2.1.6	7
Insert special characters (©, ™, €).	2.1.7	9, 7
Format Text and Paragraphs.	2.2	
Change font attributes.	2.2.1	3
Demonstrate how to use Find and Replace to format text.	2.2.2	2
Demonstrate how to use Format Painter.	2.2.3	3
Set paragraph spacing.	2.2.4	4
Set line spacing.	2.2.5	4
Clear existing formatting.	2.2.6	3
Set indentation.	2.2.7	4
Highlight text selections.	2.2.8	3
Add styles to text.	2.2.9	3
Change text to WordArt.	2.2.10	3, 8
Modify existing style attributes.	2.2.11	3
Order and Group Text and Paragraphs.	2.3	
Prevent paragraph orphans.	2.3.1	5
Insert breaks to create sections.	2.3.2	5

Matrix Skill	Objective Number	Lesson Number
Create multiple columns within sections.	2.3.3	5
Add titles to sections.	2.3.4	5
Force page breaks.	2.3.5	5
Create Tables and Lists	**3**	
Create a table	3.1	
Convert text to tables.	3.1.1	6
Convert tables to text.	3.1.2	6
Define table dimensions.	3.1.3	6
Set AutoFit options.	3.1.4	6
Demonstrate how to use Quick Tables.	3.1.5	6
Set a table title.	3.1.6	6
Modify a table.	3.2	
Apply styles to tables.	3.2.1	6
Modify fonts within tables.	3.2.2	6
Sort table data.	3.2.3	6
Configure cell margins	3.2.4	6
Demonstrate how to apply formulas to a table.	3.2.5	6
Modify table dimensions.	3.2.6	6
Merge cells.	3.2.7	6
Create and Modify a List.	3.3	
Add numbering or bullets.	3.3.1	4
Create custom bullets.	3.3.2	4
Modify list indentation.	3.3.3	4
Modify line spacing.	3.3.4	4
Increase and decrease list levels.	3.3.5	4
Modify numbering.	3.3.6	4
Apply References	**4**	
Create Endnotes, Footnotes, and Citations.	4.1	
Insert endnotes.	4.1.1	10
Manage footnote locations.	4.1.2	10
Configure endnote formats.	4.1.3	10
Modify footnote numbering.	4.1.4	10
Insert citation placeholders.	4.1.5	10
Insert citations.	4.1.6	10

Matrix Skill	Objective Number	Lesson Number
Insert bibliography.	4.1.7	10
Change citation styles.	4.1.8	10
Create Captions.	4.2	
Add captions.	4.2.1	10
Set caption positions.	4.2.2	10
Change caption formats.	4.2.3	10
Change caption labels.	4.2.4	10
Exclude labels from captions.	4.2.5	10
Insert and Format Objects	5	
Insert and Format Building Blocks	5.1	
Insert Quick Parts.	5.1.1	7
Insert textboxes.	5.1.2	7
Demonstrate how to use Building Blocks Organizer.	5.1.3	7
Customize Building Blocks.	5.1.4	7
Insert and Format Shapes and SmartArt.	5.2	
Insert simple shapes.	5.2.1	8
Insert SmartArt.	5.2.2	8
Modify SmartArt properties (color, size, shape).	5.2.3	8
Wrap text around shapes.	5.2.4	8
Position shapes.	5.2.5	8
Insert and Format Images.	5.3	
Insert and Format images.	5.3.1	8
Apply artistic effects.	5.3.2	8
Apply picture effects.	5.3.3	8
Modify image properties (color, size, shape).	5.3.4	8
Add Quick Styles to images.	5.3.5	8
Wrap text around images.	5.3.6	8
Position images.	5.3.7	8

A

Access keys   A tool that enhances the keyboard shortcuts and appears as small letters on the Ribbon. Also known as key tips.

Alignment   A setting that refers to how text is positioned between the margins.

All Markup   A setting that allows a user to see all changes and comments that have been made to a document.

antonym   The opposite meaning of a given word.

ascending   An arrangement of text from the beginning to the end, such as from A to Z, 1 to 10, and January to December.

AutoComplete   A command that automatically completes the text of the current date, day of the week, and month.

AutoCorrect   A feature that replaces commonly misspelled words with the correct spelling or replaces symbols and abbreviations with specific text strings.

AutoText   Text entries that are inserted automatically when you type a specific set of characters.

B

Backstage view   A tool that offers quick access to commands for performing many file management tasks—such as opening, closing, saving, printing, and sharing Word documents.

balloons   Shaded blocks of text used for comments

bibliography   A list of sources placed at the end of a document.

bookmark   A location or a selection of text that you name and identify for future reference.

Block Style   a format style which aligns text along the left margin

blog   An online interactive location maintained by companies, instructors, and individuals who post information, events, news, and more, where anyone can leave comments.

building blocks   Built-in reusable content such as text, graphics, and objects that can be easily managed and inserted in a document for a quick format.

C

caption   A few descriptive words providing readers with information regarding a figure, table, or equation.

cell range   Two or more cells within a table.

cells   The rectangles that are formed when rows and columns intersect.

character   Any single letter, number, symbol, or punctuation mark.

character styles   A style that is applied to individual characters or words that users have selected.

chevrons   In a mail merge, the symbols (<< and >>) that surround the field name in the merged document.

citation   A note mentioning the source of information.

clip art   A collection of media files available to insert in Microsoft Office documents that can include illustrations, photographs, video, or audio content.

Clipboard   A feature that allows a user to copy and paste text and graphics from multiple sources into a document.

Clip Organizer   A tool supplied within Microsoft office that collects and stores clip art, photos, animations, videos, and other types of media to use in your documents.

columns   Vertical blocks of text in which text flows from the bottom of one column to the top of the next.

Command   An instruction users give Word by clicking a button or entering information into a command box.

compress   Reduce the size of an object.

content controls   Individual programs within Word that allows you to add information in a document, such as a header or footer.

Copy   A command in Word that places a duplicate copy of selected text in the Clipboard.

crop   The process of trimming the horizontal or vertical edges of a picture to get rid of unwanted areas.

Cut   A command in Word that removes selected text from the original location and places the deleted text in the Clipboard collection.

D

database   A collection of information that is organized so that you can retrieve information quickly.

data source   A file that contains information to be merged in the main document during a mail merge.

descending   An arrangement of text from the end to the beginning, such as from A to Z, 10 to 1, and December to January.

dialog box   A box that displays additional options or information you can use to execute a command.

dialog box launcher   A small arrow in the lower-right corner of the group.

digital signature   is a code digitally signed by a company or person.

document properties   Information that identifies the creator of the document, date the document was created, subject, category, and keywords that can be used to search for the document.

document theme   A set of predefined formatting options that includes theme colors, fonts, and effects.

drawing canvas   A frame-like boundary that keeps multiple drawing objects together.

drop cap   A large initial letter that drops down two or more lines at the beginning of a paragraph to indicate that a new block of information is beginning and to give interest to newsletters or magazine articles.

E

embedded object   A picture or other object inserted into a document that becomes part of the document. Compare to *linked object*.

encryption   A feature that protects a document so that it cannot be opened without a password.

endnote   A citation in a document placed at the end of the document in which the citation is located.

F

field   A placeholder where Word inserts content in a document. Word automatically uses fields when specific commands are activated, such as those for inserting dates, page numbers, and a table of contents.

field code   placeholders for data that might change in a document

field names   In a mail merge, the description for the specific data, such as a person's first name, last name, address, city, state, and zip code, to be merged from the data source.

first-line indent   A setting that inserts a one-half inch of blank space between the left margin and the first line of the paragraph; one-half inch is the default setting for this indent.

floating object   An image or other object positioned precisely on the page, allowing the text to wrap around it in one of several available formats. Compare to *inline object*.

font   A set of characters that have the same design.

footer   Text that appears on the bottom of a page.

footnote   A citation in a document placed at the bottom of the page in the document on which the citation is located.

formulas   A type of field code.

G

Go To   A command in the scroll box that enables users to browse by field, endnote, footnote, comment, section, page, edits, headings, graphics, or tables.

Gridlines   A tool that provides a grid of vertical and horizontal lines that help you align graphics and other objects in a document.

groups   Collections of related word commands.

H

hacker   is a person who writes malicious programs such as viruses intended to harm your computer or access your data illegally.

hanging indent   A setting that begins the first full line of text in a paragraph at the left margin; all the remaining lines in the paragraph are indented one-half inch from the left margin.

header   Text that appears on the top of a page.

header row   The first row of the table that is formatted differently and should be repeated for tables that continue beyond one page.

horizontal alignment   A setting that refers to how text is positioned between the left and right margins.

hyperlink   A block of text or a graphic that when mouse-clicked takes the user to a new location to an internal or external page.

Hyper Text Transfer Protocol (HTTP)   The way data is transferred to an external site through a server.

hyphenation   A dash that is used to join words and separate syllables of a single word; by default hyphenation is turned off in Word so that words appear on a single line.

I

I-beam   The large "I" created when users place the cursor near the insertion point.

indent   A blank space inserted between text and the left or right margin.

Inline   Another way of displaying comments, instead of using balloons on the right, is to display them within the paragraphs of text itself.

inline object   An image or other object that moves along with the text that surrounds it. Compare to *floating object*.

insertion point   The blinking point at the upper-left side of the document where you will begin creating your text.

K

KeyTips   A tool that replaces some keyboard shortcuts from earlier versions of Microsoft.

L

label   A descriptive name that can be easily identified when inputting data into the worksheet

landscape orientation   A format commonly used for brochures, graphics, tables, and so on that orients text across the longer dimensions of the page.

leaders   A tool identified with symbols such as dotted, dashed, or solid lines that fill the space before tabs.

line break   A feature that keeps text together when changing the alignment of a document.

line spacing   The amount of space between lines of text in a paragraph.

linked object   A picture or other object inserted into a document by creating a connection between the document and picture file but not combining them in the same file. Compare to *embedded object*.

live preview   A feature that allows a user to view how changes, such as font style or size, will look in a document.

Lock Tracking   A feature that prevents anyone without a password from turning track changes off.

M

macro   A feature that allows a user to automate repetitive tasks.

main document   In a mail merge, the document that contains the text and graphics that are for each version of the merged document.

margins   The blank borders that occupy the top, bottom, and sides of a document.

markup   A markup is a version of a document with comments and revision marks displayed for easy viewing.

master document   The main document from a Word file; it is organized into smaller sections.

menu   A list of options.

merge cells   To combine two or more cells into one.

Mini toolbar   A small toolbar with popular commands that appears when you point to selected text.

mixed punctuation   A style that requires a colon after the salutation and a comma after the closing.

MLA style   Modern language Association Style guidelines.

monospaced   A font in which all of its characters take up the same amount of horizontal space.

multi-selection   A word feature that enables users to select multiple items of the text that are not adjacent.

N

Navigation Pane   A tool that appears in the left side of the window when you select its command in the Show command group.

negative indent   A setting that extends paragraph text into the left margin.

No Markup   A version of the document that displays without the markup

non-breaking spaces   A tool used to keep selected text on a single line.

nonprinting characters   Symbols for certain formatting commands that can help users create and edit documents.

O

Object Zoom   A feature that allows you to zoom in and make tables, charts and images in your document fill the screen.

open punctuation   A style that requires no punctuation after the salutation or the closing.

Original   The first version of the document before any revisions were made.

orphan   The first line of a paragraph that appears alone at the bottom of a page.

P

page break   The location in a document where one page ends and a new page begins.

paragraph styles   A style in which the formats are applied instantly to all text in the paragraph where the insertion point is located, whether or not text is selected.

paste   A command that pastes text from the Clipboard to a new location in the original document or new document.

Person Card   A feature that allows you to check whether the person is available and communicate with them through IM, voice, video, or one of the latest social sites.

plagiarism   Copying information and taking credit for it.

point size   A measurement that refers to the height of characters with one point equaling approximately 1/12 of an inch.

portrait orientation   A format commonly used for business documents in which text extends across the shorter length of the documents.

Preview   A tool that enables users to visually check your document for errors before printing.

Print   To send a document to a printer.

proportional space   A font in which the horizontal spacing varies.

pull quote   A sentence or other text displayed within a box on the page for emphasis and for ease of movement; often used along with drop caps in newsletters, advertisements, and magazines.

Q

Quick Access Toolbar   A toolbar that contains commands that users use most often, such as Save, Undo, and Redo.

Quick Tables   Built-in preformatted tables.

R

Read Mode   changes the page layout of the document with a larger font for easier reading.

Redo   A command that repeats a user's last action.

region   is the location in the document that you are allowed to edit.

Replace   A command that enables users to replace one word or phrase with another.

resetting   Discards all formatting changes you made to a picture, including changes to contrast, color, brightness, and style.

Ribbon   A tool that is divided into eight tabs that contain groups.

rulers   Measuring tools to align text, graphics, and other elements used within a document.

S

sans serif   A font that does not have the small line extensions on its characters.

Save   A button in the Quick Access Toolbar that saves an existing document.

Save As   A dialog box that will save a document in a specific format.

scale   The process of increasing or decreasing an original picture's height and width by the same percentage.

Screen Clippings   An image capture of only a part of your computer screen that you have selected.

screenshot   An image capture of the entire current display on your computer screen.

ScreenTip   A tool that provides more information about commands.

scroll bars   A tool that allows the user to move up or down within the document.

scroll box   A tool that allows users to move horizontally and vertically through a document more quickly than the scroll buttons, or to see a ScreenTip displaying a user's position in the document.

scroll buttons   Buttons that allow a user to move up or down one line at a time.

section break   A tool used to create layout or formatting changes in a portion of the document.

Serif   A font that has small lines at the beginning and end of characters and that is usually used with large amounts of text.

Settings   An option that enables users to set document properties.

shapes   Figures such as lines, rectangles block arrows, equation shapes, flowcharts, stars and banners, and callouts that you can add to your document or drawing campus.

shortcut menu   A menu that contains a list of useful commands.

Simple Markup   A clean view of the document, with indicators to show where tracked changes have been made.

SkyDrive   An online file storage service provided by Microsoft where you can store up to 25GB of documents and pictures for free.

SmartArt graphics   Graphical illustrations available within Word from a list of various categories, including List diagrams, process diagrams, Cycle diagrams, Hierarchy diagrams, Relationship diagrams, Matrix diagrams, and Pyramid diagrams.

sort   To arrange data alphabetically, numerically, and chronologically.

source   Includes all the information about where specific information comes from so the reader can find the original work. It could be a book, report, journal article, or website.

split cells   To divide one cell into two or more cells.

Style Set   A feature that allows a user to set a specific font and font size.

subdocuments   The sections within the master document that have been separated into smaller sections.

synonym   A word that has the same meaning as another word.

T

tab leader   The symbols that appear in a table of contents between a topic and the corresponding page number.

table   An arrangement of data made up of horizontal rows and vertical columns.

table of contents   An ordered list of the topics in a document, along with the page numbers on which they are found. Usually located at the beginning of a long document.

tabs   Eight areas of activity on the Ribbon that contain groups or collections of related Word commands.

template   A master document with predefined page layout, fonts, margins, and styles that is used to create new documents.

text box   An invisible, formatted box in which you can insert and position text and/or graphic objects.

Text Effects   A new font command group that adds a distinctive appearance, such as outlines, shadows, glows, or reflections, to selected text.

thumbnails   Tiny images of your document pages

U

undo A command that allows users to cancel or undo their last command or action.

Unicode A symbol that enables most of the languages in the world to be symbolized with a special character identification.

V

vertical alignment A setting that refers to how text is positioned between the top and bottom margins of the page.

W

watermarks Built-in text that display lightly behind the document's main text conveying the sensitivity of the document, such as, *confidential, draft,* or *urgent*

widow The last line of a paragraph that appears at the top of a page.

Wildcard Characters that find words or phrases that contain specific letters, or combinations of letters.

WordArt A feature within Word that creates decorative effects with a string of text.

works cited A bibliography.